The depth, detail, and thoroughness of this book easily surpasses any other VXLAN/EVPN book on the market. And it is the only book available that covers the topic from a Juniper Junos and an Apstra perspective. Whether you want a VXLAN/EVPN technical deep-dive, want to learn how to configure it on Junos, want to learn Apstra's Intent-Based Networking platform, or are studying for your JNCIE-DC lab, this book is essential for data center engineers and architects.

—*Jeff Doyle, Director of Solutions Architecture*
Juniper Networks/Apstra

Aninda has written the new definitive guide for learning, building and operating EVPN networks. This book should be on the shelves of any network engineer, from NOC technicians to senior architects.

—*Pete Lumbis, CCIE No. 28677, CCDE 2012:3*

Today's data centers require modern technologies that simplify operations and assure reliability at the tremendous scale demanded by AI training and digital applications. Juniper innovation is in the forefront with Apstra Intent-Based Networking automation for EVPN VXLAN multivendor networks. *Deploying Juniper Data Centers with EVPN VXLAN* is a comprehensive guide that includes all these technologies in one place to understand how they work together for robust, automated DC operations. Architects and operators responsible for the integrity of the data center will want this go-to book to advise step by step how to set up and run their network following Juniper recommended, best practice designs, tools, and workflow.

—*Mansour Karam, GVP*
Juniper Networks

Juniper's data center fabric solutions are world-renowned for their completeness and quality. This book begins right at the beginning, with basic data center fabric design, BGP in the data center, and VXLAN. After covering these topics, Aninda moves into an explanation of Apstra, one of the most complete multi-vendor intent-based data center fabric systems.

The many graphics and screen shots, combined with the detailed configuration and sample outputs, provide designers and operators alike with deeply researched and well-explained information about building and operating a data center fabric using Juniper hardware and software.

I even learned a few things about Apstra reading through this book—although I have built and operated networks using Apstra's technology.

I highly recommend this book for engineers looking for a good explanation of Juniper data center solutions.

—*Russ White*

Aninda is an outstanding engineer with an insatiable thirst for knowledge and discovery. His drive is endless and a wonderful opportunity for himself and many others to learn and explore subjects and technologies, as he is able to simplify them in a way that allows others to learn seamlessly. I have enjoyed Aninda's content for several years now. He has contributed [to] the community through webinars, articles, white papers, and blogs, which makes his book a logical step to consolidate his contributions and knowledge.

Aninda's work will always have my support and endorsement.

—*David Penaloza, Principal Engineer*

Deploying Juniper Data Centers with EVPN VXLAN

Deploying Juniper Data Centers with EVPN VXLAN

Aninda Chatterjee

Addison-Wesley

For information about buying this title in bulk quantities, or for special sales opportunities (which may include electronic versions; custom cover designs; and content particular to your business, training goals, marketing focus, or branding interests), please contact our corporate sales department at corpsales@pearsoned.com or (800) 382-3419.

For government sales inquiries, please contact governmentsales@pearsoned.com.

For questions about sales outside the U.S., please contact intlcs@pearson.com.

Visit us on the Web: informit.com/aw

Library of Congress Control Number: 2024934201

Published by:

Addison-Wesley

Hoboken, New Jersey

ISBN-13: 978-0-13-822539-1

ISBN-10: 0-13-822539-7

3 2024

GM K12, Early Career and Professional Learning: Soo Kang

Executive Editor: Brett Bartow

Development Editor: Ellie C. Bru

Managing Editor: Sandra Schroeder

Senior Project Editor: Tonya Simpson

Copy Editor: Bill McManus

Indexer: Erika Millen

Proofreader: Donna E. Mulder

Compositor: codeMantra

Technical Reviewers: Jeff Doyle, Vivek Venugopal, and Ridha Hamidi

Editorial Assistant: Cindy Teeters

Cover Designer: Chuti Prasertsith

Figure Credits

Figures 3.11–3.15, 5.7, 5.8, 5.12, 5.13, 5.21, 5.22, 5.28, 5.30, 5.32, 5.33, 5.35, 5.47, 5.52–5.54, 6.7, 6.12, 6.13, 6.17, 7.8, 7.13, 7.14, 7.19, 7.22, 7.24, 7.26, 8.11, 8.13, 8.16, 8.21, 8.22, 8.26, 8.28, 9.5, 9.10, 10.4, 10.6, 10.8, 10.9, 10.12–10.14, 10.18, 10.19, 11.10, 11.17, 11.18, 11.21, 11.27–11.30, 11.34, 11.38–11.40, 12.15–12.18, 13.9, 13.40, 13.41: Wireshark Foundation

Figures 12.1–12.4, 12.6, 12.8, 12.10, 12.13, 12.14, 12.19–12.28, 12.30–12.40, 12.42–12.65, 12.67–12.75, 13.2–13.8, 13.12–13.26, 13.28–13.39, 13.42, 13.43, 13.45–13.59, 14.2–14.10, 15.3–15.7, 15.11–15.16, 15.18, 15.19, 15.24–15.33: Juniper Networks, Inc

Dedications

This book is dedicated to the family I was born into, and the family I married into.

Foreword

The titans of the networking industry stand tall not because they have proven themselves masters of theory. Nor is it because they have waxed poetic about all manners of enabling our connected world. Those whose heads and shoulders rise above achieve their place because they are practitioners.

And so, as we evaluate technical works for their transformative potential, we should come to know our authors by their hands-on skills more than their willingness to pontificate. Their experience is the bedrock on which truly great works are built.

But let's be honest. Our industry is one where most of the really important work is done behind closed doors, in places where peering eyes might never reach. So how do you assess skills when the work they deliver is hidden by design?

I have had the great pleasure of building multiple organizations over the years. I have led data center businesses at multiple large vendors, which has given me the opportunity to assemble all kinds of teams. Early in my career, I would seek out experience. But as I matured and became a better leader, I learned to hunt for potential.

In my not terribly humble opinion, the highest potential exists at the intersection of capability, drive, and humility. Capability is table stakes of course, and drive is an obvious prerequisite for progress. But humility might be the secret ingredient that brings everything together.

You see, it's easy to be humble when you are starting out because you lack the experience to know how good you are. All too often, there is an inverse relationship between experience and humility—indeed, many of us become louder as we develop a stronger command over our domains! But you cannot become a true master without true humility because it is the constant awareness of what you do not know that provides the impetus to continue learning.

Naturally, our industry's strongest spokespeople will then be brimming over with humility. When Aninda and I first crossed paths, he spoke fluently about technology and experience—the kinds of things you lead with during an interview, of course. But what I heard was different. As accomplished as Aninda is, I could see that he has a real learner's mind.

That learner's mind might make for some restless nights as Aninda never seems quite comfortable with where he is in his journey. But I can't help but think of the great Theodor Seuss Geisel book *Oh, the Places You'll Go!*, because oh, what a journey it will be.

This book represents a checkpoint of sorts in Aninda's journey so far. It's meant to be an approachable guide to data center networking, explaining how EVPN VXLAN data centers are architected and operated, but importantly, using the hands-on experience that Aninda has earned through the years to make it tangible.

And if you read this book with the same learner's mind with which it has been written, oh, the places you will go.

—Michael Bushong
VP, Data Center
Nokia

Acknowledgments

As the author, it is easy to say that I wrote this book, but that is hardly the complete truth. Technically, yes, I put these words on paper, but there were so many people who helped me get to the point in my journey where I felt confident and capable enough to do this.

There are many excellent engineers who helped keep this book technically accurate, provided support when I was lost, and validated what I wrote. This also includes individuals who probably have no idea how much I have learned from them by reading their books, learning from content created by them, or have supported me in my professional and personal growth. In no particular order, they are Ridha Hamidi, Vivek Venugopal, Soumyodeep Joarder, Anupam Singh, Selvakumar Sivaraj, Wen Lin, Mehdi Abdelouahab, JP Senior, Jeff Doyle, Russ White, Jeff Tantsura, Ivan Pepelnjak, Dinesh Dutt, Pete Lumbis, Richard Michael, Peter Paluch, David Peñaloza, Daniel Dib, Naveen Bansal, Manasi Jain, and Astha Goyal.

To Brett Bartow, Eleanor Bru, Tonya Simpson, Bill McManus, Donna E. Mulder, and everyone from Pearson who helped bring this book to life: Thank you for giving me the opportunity to write this and taking a chance on a nobody. Your support through the writing, production, and composition process has been nothing short of exceptional.

To my technical reviewers, Ridha Hamidi, Vivek Venugopal, and Jeff Doyle: Thank you for reading my manuscript with gentle hands. You made it better in every way, giving constructive but honest feedback. I'd have never imagined there would come a day when I would be collaborating with Jeff Doyle, whose books I learned my networking skills from. Professional dreams do come true.

To Souvik Ghosh and Reghu Rajendran: Back in late 2011, sitting in a meeting room in the offices of Cisco Systems, Bangalore, you both interviewed me and gave me the opportunity of a lifetime. My days in Cisco TAC were some of my best. I followed you into heavy-hitting escalation roles, working together on some of the most challenging technical escalations. Thank you for guiding and mentoring me.

To Dale Miller: You are, undoubtedly, the best mentor I could have asked for. You saw potential in me when I saw none. You pushed me to new heights, to try things out of my comfort zone, and taught me what true customer advocacy means. Cisco Live conferences, bringing up new TAC centers, and solving some of the hardest escalations—we've been through it all together. You are one of the brightest spots in my career and I am glad I can call you my friend. And to Matt Esau: Like Dale, you mentored me through tough times, and even now I can reach out to you for guidance and support. I am lucky to know you and to have worked with you.

To Pete Lumbis: I can't believe we haven't worked together yet, despite literally being one "yes" away from it. You are one of the most talented engineers I have the privilege of knowing and learning from. And with all that brain power, you continue to be humble and down to earth, and you constantly reach out with helping hands. Most importantly, you genuinely look out for your peers, and you nurture those just starting this journey. You read the entire manuscript for this book, even when you had no reason to, just to give feedback and show your support.

To my dearest friends, Vivek and Gino: It's funny how long our bond has lasted because I was quite certain I was intolerable on the TAC floor, with all my cursing. But I guess like minds do think alike. We've looked out for each other since 2012. It has truly been a blessing to have both of you by my side in this journey.

To Cathy Gadecki and Mike Bushong: I have been a network engineer for over 12 years now, spanning five different roles across several companies. Your leadership, unequivocally, is the best I have experienced. For me, it wasn't about technical growth—I know how to get that for myself. You both provided personal growth and helped me nurture skills I considered irrelevant. Mike, there's no leader like you, and I don't think there ever will be. There's a reason people follow you—sure, part of it is loyalty, but there's so much more to it. You genuinely care about people and you do everything in your control to make their lives better.

To my parents, Aloke and Sujata Chatterjee, my brother, Arnab Chatterjee, and his wife, Radhika Arora: You have shaped me, as an individual, throughout my life. My interaction with the world is modeled after you and the values you taught me. Everything I have and I am stems from your kindness and love.

To my wife, Deepti: There is no measure of success without you. This last year has been grueling trying to balance work and writing this book. You were supportive every step of the way, giving me the time and space to write while managing your own work, taking care of our home, and being the best mother to our little girl. You make me a better person and a better father every day. I love you dearly and I am glad I get to walk this winding road of life with you by my side.

And to my little one, Raya: You're too young to read this, but maybe some day you will. You are the light of our lives. Now and forever.

About the Author

Aninda Chatterjee holds a Bachelor of Engineering degree in Information Science. His networking career started at AT&T, troubleshooting Layer 1 circuit issues, eventually transitioning to customer support at Cisco TAC, specializing in Layer 2. After his stint at Cisco TAC, he has held several roles across different organizations, with functions including escalation support for enterprise and data center engineering, designing, implementing, and troubleshooting enterprise and data center networks, and technical marketing for Cisco Software Defined Access (SDA).

In his current role as a senior technical marketing engineer at Juniper Networks, Aninda specializes in data center networks with EVPN VXLAN, while also focusing on the high demand of networking infrastructure for high-performance computing and AI/ML clusters.

Aninda actively writes on his personal blog, www.theasciiconstruct.com.

About the Technical Reviewers

Jeff Doyle is a director of solutions architecture at Juniper Networks. Specializing in IP routing protocols, complex BGP policy, SDN/NFV, data center fabrics, IBN, EVPN, MPLS, and IPv6, Jeff has designed or assisted in the design of large-scale IP and IPv6 service provider networks in 26 countries over 6 continents.

Jeff is the author of *CCIE Professional Development: Routing TCP/IP*, Volumes I and II; *OSPF and IS-IS: Choosing an IGP for Large-Scale Networks*; *Intent-Based Networking for Dummies*; was a co-author of *Network Programmability and Automation Fundamentals*; *Software Defined Networking: Anatomy of OpenFlow*; and is an editor and contributing author of *Juniper Networks Routers: The Complete Reference*. Jeff is currently writing *CCIE Professional Development: Switching TCP/IP*. He has also written for *Forbes*, has blogged for both *Network World* and *Network Computing*, and is co-host of the livestream show *Between 0x2 Nerds*. Jeff is one of the founders of the Rocky Mountain IPv6 Task Force, is an IPv6 Forum Fellow and a 2019 inductee into the IPv6 Internet Hall of Fame, and serves on the executive board of the Colorado chapter of the Internet Society (ISOC) and the advisory board of the Network Automaton Forum (NAF).

Vivek Venugopal has been in the computer network industry for more than 15 years. His experience spans multiple domains such as enterprise, data center, service provider networking, and network security. He has worked with a variety of networking giants such as Cisco Systems, Juniper Networks, and VMware in various capacities, and has founded a startup in the networking education space as well.

Ridha Hamidi, PhD, has decades-long experience in the telecommunications and Internet industries and has worked with both service providers and equipment vendors. He holds multiple industry-recognized certifications, such as JNCIE-SP, Emeritus. In his current role as a senior technical marketing engineer at Juniper Networks, Ridha has multiple responsibilities in projects involving data center technologies such as EVPN-VXLAN and, more recently, AI/ML Workloads.

Contents at a Glance

Contents

Introduction

My professional growth is built on the shoulders of tech and educational giants such as Jeff Doyle, Russ White, and Dinesh Dutt and their work. They have inspired generations, and just as their work inspired me, I hope this book inspires many others.

This book is a culmination of over a decade of technical learning and writing, working through customer escalations and designing, implementing, and troubleshooting small to large-scale enterprise and data center networks. And thus, this book is rooted in servant leadership and experiential learning. The goal of this book is not only to *show* but also to help you *learn* the finer details, the foundational knowledge that largely does not change as data center networks continue to evolve over time. More generally, the goal is to help you develop a mindset and a sound methodology behind building and troubleshooting data center networks.

To that end, each chapter is written with an unwavering focus on the "why." My approach to learning new technologies has always been to understand the history behind how they evolved and what were the driving factors. In this book, I have adapted that approach to *teaching* you new technologies. Outside of focusing on the configuration that is necessary to build data centers with Junos, each chapter aims to unpack what happens behind the scenes to give you a deeper understanding of this infrastructure, while also providing historical context, wherever necessary.

By the end of this book, you will have gained expert-level knowledge about the following topics:

- The Junos CLI and how to navigate it
- The history and evolution of data centers, moving from three-tier designs to a Clos architecture, necessitated by the predominance of east-west traffic resulting from the rise of server virtualization and a shift to a microservices architecture
- The history and evolution of VXLAN, moving from a flood-and-learn model to coupling it with BGP EVPN for control plane dissemination of MAC addresses, while also providing Layer 3 reachability
- EVPN route types 1 through 5
- Building small to large-scale data centers using VXLAN with BGP EVPN and different overlay models, based on customer need, such as bridged overlay, edge-routed bridging, routed overlay, or host-routed bridging
- Connecting multiple data centers using different interconnect options such as over-the-top DCI or Integrated Interconnect with IP and MPLS transports
- Using Juniper Apstra to orchestrate data centers built using user intent with continuous validation of intent
- Using a network emulation tool such as Containerlab to build and deploy virtual lab infrastructure

While this book is not written with the intent of helping you to pass a specific certification exam, it does act as an excellent supplemental source for studying to obtain the JNCIA-DC, JNCIS-DC, JNCIP-DC, and JNCIE-DC certifications.

How This Book Is Organized

Although this book is intended to be read cover to cover, each chapter stands on its own and can be read individually, depending on your need. The first four chapters are introductory chapters, providing the proper historical context behind data center design and evolution, while also introducing the Junos CLI and how to navigate and use it. These chapters cover the following topics:

- **Chapter 1, "Introducing the Juniper Ecosystem":** This chapter introduces the Juniper ecosystem with a focus on gaining familiarity with the Junos CLI by implementing common Layer 2 and Layer 3 features in a collapsed core design and using various **show** commands to validate user intent, including how to read and understand the MAC address table and various routing tables.
- **Chapter 2, "Overview of Data Center Architecture":** This chapter dives into the history and evolution of data centers, focused on the driving factors that influenced and led to these changes, moving from a traditional three-tier architecture to a Clos design.

- **Chapter 3, "BGP for the Data Center"**: This chapter introduces how BGP is used for modern data centers built with a scale-out strategy using the Clos architecture.

- **Chapter 4, "VXLAN as a Network Virtualization Overlay"**: This chapter introduces VXLAN as a network overlay, elevating network services into a logical layer on top of the physical infrastructure. It also provides historical context on how VXLAN evolved from using a flood-and-learn mechanism to using BGP EVPN as a control plane to disseminate MAC address information.

Chapters 5 through 11 form the core of the book. These provide the basic building blocks of designing and operating small to large-scale data centers. Chapter 5, especially, is the main building block of this book, introducing, and diving deeper into, core VXLAN with BGP EVPN functionality; it is foundational to every chapter that comes after it. These seven chapters cover the following topics:

- **Chapter 5, "Bridged Overlay in an EVPN VXLAN Fabric"**: This chapter focuses on understanding, configuring, and validating a bridged overlay in an EVPN VXLAN fabric. It also provides a foundational understanding of how MAC addresses are learned in EVPN VXLAN fabrics and dives deeper into important aspects of such networks, such as how BUM traffic is replicated, EVPN multihoming, Route Targets, MAC mobility, loop detection, and Bidirectional Forwarding Detection.

- **Chapter 6, "MAC-VRFs"**: This chapter introduces MAC-VRFs, a construct that provides Layer 2 multitenancy in EVPN VXLAN fabrics. This chapter also explores different EVPN service types such as VLAN-Based and VLAN-Aware.

- **Chapter 7, "Centrally Routed Bridging"**: This chapter introduces the concept of integrated routed bridging and explores routing in EVPN VXLAN fabrics using a centrally routed bridging model.

- **Chapter 8, "Edge-Routed Bridging"**: This chapter builds on the previous chapter, introducing the edge-routed bridging design, while exploring the asymmetric and symmetric routing models.

- **Chapter 9, "Routed Overlay and Host-Routed Bridging"**: This chapter introduces the routed overlay and host-routed bridging designs, commonly used in infrastructures with cloud-native applications, with no requirement of Layer 2 overlays.

- **Chapter 10, "DHCP in EVPN VXLAN Fabrics"**: This chapter introduces the challenges with DHCP in such routed fabrics, diving deeper into DHCP functionality in both bridged overlay and edge-routed bridging designs, while also exploring EVPN VXLAN network designs with a dedicated services VRF where the DHCP server is located.

- **Chapter 11, "Data Center Interconnect"**: This chapter introduces how two or more data centers can be connected using the over-the-top DCI or Integrated Interconnect DCI options with IP or MPLS transports.

Chapters 12 through 15 introduce Juniper Apstra, an intent-based networking system, and dive deeper into how data centers can be deployed using Apstra. These chapters cover the following topics:

- **Chapter 12, "Building Data Centers with Juniper Apstra, Part I—Apstra Foundation"**: This chapter provides a first look at Juniper Apstra and introduces the building blocks used in designing data centers with Apstra, demonstrating how these building blocks are used to build and deploy a bridged overlay EVPN VXLAN fabric.

- **Chapter 13, "Building Data Centers with Juniper Apstra, Part II—Advanced Apstra Deployments"**: This chapter builds on the previous chapter, demonstrating how an edge-routed bridging design is built using Juniper Apstra. Various DCI options such as over-the-top DCI and Integrated Interconnect are also explored in detail in this chapter.

- **Chapter 14, "Building Virtual Fabrics with vJunos, Containerlab, and Juniper Apstra"**: This chapter introduces the need for virtual network infrastructure and how to build it using Containerlab, enabling organizations to build digital twins for network validation and pre-change and post-change testing, usually integrated in a CI/CD pipeline.

- **Chapter 15, "Large-Scale Fabrics, Inter-VRF Routing, and Security Policies in Apstra"**: The closing chapter of this book introduces and demonstrates how to build 5-stage Clos networks and the use of policies in Apstra to secure communication in EVPN VXLAN fabrics. This chapter also explores inter-VRF design options in Apstra.

## Chapter 1

Introducing the Juniper Ecosystem

Data centers are a cornerstone of today's digital age and a critical part of modern IT infrastructure. With the advent of cloud computing, artificial intelligence, and machine learning, it has become imperative for network engineers to gain an understanding of how data centers are designed, deployed, and operationally managed.

Embarking on learning a new technology or domain in the networking space can be hard. What makes it harder is the need to learn a new networking operating system as well, with all its features and quirks. While this book is written with the aim of building transferrable and vendor-agnostic skills in the data center domain, the implementation is specific to the Junos network operating system and the Juniper ecosystem.

This chapter introduces the Juniper ecosystem, with a focus on helping you to gain familiarity with the *Junos OS* and *Junos OS Evolved* (commonly shortened to *Junos Evolved* or *Junos Evo*) network operating systems. These separate operating systems are often referred to generically as *Junos*. Architecturally, these operating systems are different (as briefly described in the following section); however, for an operator using the command line interface (CLI) to configure and interact with either operating system, functionally, there are minimal to no differences. Thus, this chapter, and the remainder of this book, uses the terms Junos, Junos OS, and Junos OS Evolved interchangeably, calling out any differences when necessary.

To help you get up and running with Junos, this chapter demonstrates how to configure simple Layer 2 and Layer 3 features using the CLI, such as access and trunk interfaces, routing protocols like Open Shortest Path First (OSPF), and various other management features. Validating what you have configured is equally important, so this chapter introduces various **show** commands in Junos that enable you to confirm your intent and the state of the network built; this coverage will also help you to understand the MAC address table and different routing tables. This chapter wraps up by presenting some miscellaneous features of the operating system that showcase its strengths and versatility.

This chapter serves as the first step to designing, building, and deploying complex EVPN VXLAN–based data centers with Junos.

Junos Architecture

Junos OS is a network operating system with a modular software architecture, developed on top of FreeBSD, which is an open-source operating system. Services run as daemons in their own protected memory space. Thus, for example, even if one daemon were to have a memory leak and eventually crash, other daemons would be unaffected by it, unlike monolithic architectures, where one service can crash the entire system. A high-level, simplified architectural view of Junos OS is shown in Figure 1-1.

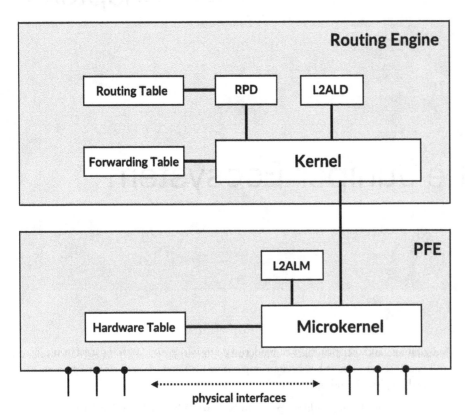

Figure 1-1 *Junos OS high-level architecture*

The overall Junos architecture includes a control plane and a data plane, a separation that Juniper pioneered by building routers with physically separate hardware for the data plane. The control plane is where Junos runs, along with other daemons such as the routing protocol daemon called *RPD*, the management daemon called *MGD*, the interface daemon called *DCD*, the Layer 2 learning daemon called *L2ALD*, and many others. The software routing table is programmed by RPD in the Routing Engine, with each routing protocol configured in the system running as a separate task within RPD. The *Packet Forwarding Engine (PFE)* is the data plane, which also houses application-specific integrated circuits (ASICs) for hardware traffic forwarding. The best routes are moved to a forwarding table, in the Routing Engine, which pushes its state to the PFE. The hardware is eventually programmed by the PFE microkernel via a hardware abstraction layer. In addition to this, the PFE has daemons such as the Layer 2 Address Learning Manager (L2ALM), which provides an abstracted hardware view of MAC address learning.

Junos OS Evolved or Junos Evolved, unlike Junos OS, runs natively on Linux, providing several additional advantages:

- Multiple software releases can be installed on a device, with the ability to roll back to any previously installed release as needed.

- With a native Linux base, support for third-party tools and applications on Linux can be easily integrated into Junos Evolved.

- A Distributed Data Store (DDS) stores data of different constructs in the system, including both operational and configuration state. Applications talk to each other through their DDS interface, which uses a publish-subscribe messaging model. This means that each application does not talk directly to other applications via inter-process communication (IPC), thus eliminating the typical IPC mesh that usually exists in such architectures.

- Using a DDS, applications can also fail independently and recover quickly by pulling last-known state from the data store, requiring no intervention by the system to bring the application back to its correct state.

Every process in Junos Evolved runs as an application managed by a special process called *systemd*. Like Junos OS, each application runs as its own separate service, with complete fault isolation, interacting with the DDS through a single interface. A high-level visual representation of the Junos Evolved architecture is shown in Figure 1-2.

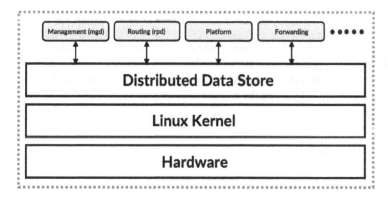

Figure 1-2 *Junos Evolved high-level architecture*

Building Layer 2 and Layer 3 Networks with Junos

Building a complete, albeit small, network is the best way to learn a new operating system. This provides the opportunity to understand how several pieces fit together, how multiple aspects of the network can be configured using a new CLI to reach an end network state, and how to validate the configured network using different tools available in the operating system.

Thus, to help you gain familiarity with Junos, this section demonstrates how to configure the collapsed core network depicted in Figure 1-3. This network does not necessarily follow design best practices. The configuration includes

- Configuring Layer 2 trunk interfaces between the cores and the access switches

- Configuring a Layer 2 trunk interface between the cores

- Configuring VLAN 10 and VLAN 20 for hosts h1 and h2, respectively

- Configuring an integrated routing and bridging (IRB) interface for both VLANs on core1

- Configuring Spanning Tree Protocol (STP) for the entire network, with core1 as the root bridge with a priority of 4096

- Configuring OSPF between the two core devices and the WAN edge device

Following these steps, this section introduces the Junos CLI and how to navigate and use it.

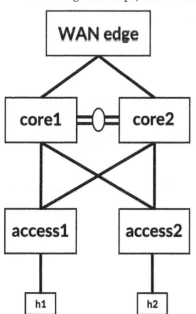

Figure 1-3 *Reference topology to gain familiarity with Junos CLI*

Introducing the Junos CLI

The Junos CLI has two main CLI modes: operational mode and configuration mode. Operational mode enables you to monitor and view the status of different features, protocols, and interfaces configured on the system by using various **show** commands. Configuration mode enables you to configure various aspects of the system. Operational mode is signified by the > prompt. Configuration mode is entered from operational mode by using the command **configure** and is signified by the # prompt, as shown in Example 1-1.

Example 1-1 *Operational mode and configuration mode in Junos CLI*

```
admin@access1> configure
Entering configuration mode


[edit]
admin@access1#
```

The Junos CLI and configuration are structured and hierarchical, with related functions all grouped together into a top-level tree. This hierarchy also lends to the output of structured data, built from the ground up from a programmability point of view. This structure can be used to navigate and find pieces of configuration very quickly.

Junos offers two ways to configure a system: by using **set** commands from the top-level hierarchy (and specifying the exact hierarchical path) or by using the **edit** command to navigate to a specific configuration hierarchy, and then using **set** commands. Some basic initial configuration of a system running Junos is shown in Example 1-2 using **set** commands. This includes enabling SSH, enabling NETCONF using SSH for the system, and configuring a new user called *anindac*, assigned to the *super-user* class, with a plain-text password.

Example 1-2 *Basic system configuration in Junos CLI*

```
admin@access1# set system services ssh

[edit]
admin@access1# set system services netconf ssh

[edit]
admin@access1# set system login user anindac class super-user authentication plain-text-password
New password:
Retype new password:
```

While in configuration mode, the current hierarchy is displayed within square brackets. In Example 1-2, [edit] confirms that the current hierarchy is the top-level hierarchy in configuration mode, where all configuration options are available via **set** commands, as shown in Example 1-3. Using the **?** option shows all available hierarchies at that level, providing you easy access to determine where to go next. This is applicable in operational mode as well for **show** commands, as an example.

Example 1-3 *All available set commands in top-level hierarchy of configuration mode in Junos CLI*

```
admin@access1# set ?
Possible completions:
> access              Network access configuration
> accounting-options  Accounting data configuration
> applications        Define applications by protocol characteristics
+ apply-groups        Groups from which to inherit configuration data
> chassis             Chassis configuration
> class-of-service    Class-of-service configuration
```

```
> dynamic-profiles     Dynamic profiles configuration
> event-options        Event processing configuration
> firewall             Define a firewall configuration
> forwarding-options   Configure options to control packet forwarding
> groups               Configuration groups
> interfaces           Interface configuration
```

snip

To navigate to a specific hierarchy, you can use the **edit** command, as shown in Example 1-4. In this instance, instead of configuring a user from the top-level hierarchy, it is configured by navigating to the *system login* hierarchy. Notice how the hierarchy now reflects the current location as *[edit system login]*, highlighted in Example 1-4. From here, you can use **set** commands, specific to this hierarchy, for configuration.

Example 1-4   *Navigating to a specific configuration hierarchy using the **edit** command in Junos CLI*

```
admin@access1# edit system login


[edit system login]
admin@access1# set ?
Possible completions:
  announcement          System announcement message (displayed after login)
+ apply-groups          Groups from which to inherit configuration data
+ apply-groups-except   Don't inherit configuration data from these groups
> class                 Login class
> deny-sources          Sources from which logins are denied
  idle-timeout          Maximum idle time before logout (1..60 minutes)
  message               System login message
> password             Password configuration
> retry-options        Configure password retry options
> user                 Username


admin@access1# set user aninda class super user authentication plain-text-password
New password:
Retype new password:
```

When in a specific hierarchy in configuration mode, you can use the **top** and **up** command options to navigate upward from the current configuration hierarchy, where **top** takes you back to the top-level hierarchy and **up** takes you only one level up from the current hierarchy, by default (with an optional parameter that can be used to specify how many levels up you want to go). This enables you to quickly navigate to specific hierarchies by combining some of these options, as shown in Example 1-5, where **top** is used to go to the top-level hierarchy and is combined with **edit system services** to move to the *system services* hierarchy, which is where you can configure services like NETCONF and SSH.

Example 1-5   *Using **top** and **edit** together in Junos CLI*

```
admin@access1# top edit system services


[edit system services]
admin@access1#
```

Junos has a multistep configuration process and includes several features to confirm the changes being made in the system. This is a Git-like functionality (for those familiar with Git's commit process and revision control), with Junos providing the user the ability to view a diff of what is being committed, confirm the validity of the changes being committed, and roll back to a previous version of the configuration if needed. This is shown in Figure 1-4.

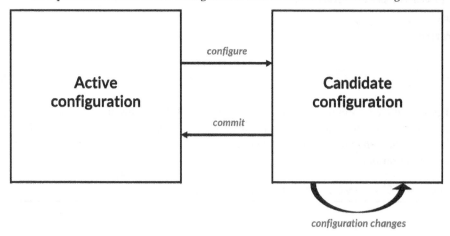

Figure 1-4   *Active and candidate configuration in Junos*

The active configuration is the current configuration of the system and is the configuration that is being actively used. When you enter the command **configure** while in operational mode, the active configuration is copied as the candidate configuration, and any changes you make while in configuration mode apply to the candidate configuration only and are considered staged. To move these changes to the active configuration and have them take effect, you must commit them using the **commit** command.

Staged configuration, which is basically uncommitted configuration, can be compared with the active configuration by using the **show** | **compare** command. This produces a diff between the candidate configuration and the active configuration, showing all modified configuration changes that are uncommitted. These could be changes that were newly added or existing configuration that was modified or deleted. Going back to the basic system configuration shown in Example 1-2, Example 1-6 shows the diff output from running **show** | **compare**.

Example 1-6   *Viewing a diff between the active configuration and the candidate configuration*

```
admin@access1# show | compare
[edit system login]
+    user anindac {
+        class super-user;
+        authentication {
+            encrypted-password "$6$iw2C7uIC$SSDs2w8vN42zaa1NJkh9zw6edZOQerHKTVJ9jvZKcS94ZRGKs5ssjaOyoFiEGvcH1vg5w5Ps/msx-
UBPxbE31yO"; ## SECRET-DATA
+        }
+    }
```

Any configuration line that starts with the + symbol is present in the candidate configuration and is not present in the active configuration. In Example 1-6, only the new user and its corresponding password and class are shown, which implies that any other configuration in Example 1-2 was already present in the active configuration. While in configuration mode, you can roll back any uncommitted (staged) configuration by using the **rollback** command.

To commit changes and move the candidate configuration to the active configuration, you have several options:

- Use the command **commit** to commit changes present in the candidate configuration.

- Use the command **commit confirmed** to commit changes present in the candidate configuration temporarily while you decide whether to confirm the commit. After a default timer of 10 minutes, the configuration will be automatically rolled back unless you enter **commit** again in configuration mode. This is very useful when committing questionable changes, which, for example, may lock you out of the system. You can also input an optional timer to the command instead of relying on the default timer, using **commit confirmed** [*timer in minutes*].

- Use the command **commit check** to run a sanity check of the staged changes, which then prints any warnings or errors as needed. This command does not commit any changes; instead, it simply validates them. You still need to explicitly commit any staged changes.

- Use the command **commit comment** to add a commit message as part of the commit process. This is useful when viewing commit history using the command **show system commit** in operational mode.

- Use the command **commit at** to schedule the commit for a future date and time.

- Uses the command **commit and-quit** to commit the staged changes and exit automatically back into operational mode of the Junos CLI.

The changes in Example 1-6 can now be committed using the **commit** command. Example 1-7 shows the commit process and how the configuration can be viewed again, specific to the **system login** hierarchy. Any **show** command in configuration mode shows the configuration of the system (either specific to the hierarchy in which you are currently located or all system configuration if you are in the top-level hierarchy), while **show** commands in operational mode show the state of the system.

Example 1-7 *Committing and viewing configuration in configuration mode*

```
admin@access1# commit
commit complete


[edit]
admin@access1# show system login
user admin {
    uid 2000;
    class super-user;
    authentication {
        encrypted-password "$6$GK8jGjx5$QIo831ewbnayBIoYPxUZ5NzU3hqSFUYmOqPL/kSn585LynpzfxVLT5QFnAdmmEG1RbV1S/PldHOxLqN-
ziljBTO"; ## SECRET-DATA
    }
}
user anindac {
    uid 2001;
    class super-user;
    authentication {
        encrypted-password "$6$iw2C7uIC$SSDs2w8vN42zaa1NJkh9zw6edZOQerHKTVJ9jvZKcS94ZRGKs5ssjaOyoFiEGvcH1vg5w5Ps/msxUBPx-
bE31yO"; ## SECRET-DATA
    }
}
```

The active configuration, as well as previous revisions of the configuration (up to 50), is stored in the file system of the device. The first three configuration revisions, along with the active configuration, are stored under the **/config** path, while all others are stored in the **/var/db/config/** path. This is shown in Example 1-8, from a Junos device on which many configuration revisions have occurred. The FreeBSD or Linux shell is accessed by using the command **start shell** in operational mode.

Example 1-8 *Configuration files in Junos*

```
root@access1> start shell
root@access1:RE:0% ls -l /config/ | grep juniper.conf
-rw-r-----  1 root  wheel   5150 Dec  1 13:15 juniper.conf.1.gz
-rw-r-----  1 root  wheel   5125 Dec  1 12:49 juniper.conf.2.gz
-rw-r-----  1 root  wheel   5154 Dec  1 12:39 juniper.conf.3.gz
```

```
-rw-r-----  1 root  wheel    5180 Dec  1 13:54 juniper.conf.gz
----------  1 root  wheel      32 Dec  1 13:54 juniper.conf.md5


root@access1:RE:0% ls -l /var/db/config/
total 456
-rw-r-----  1 root  wheel  4109 Nov 14 12:43 juniper.conf.10.gz
-rw-r-----  1 root  wheel  4106 Nov 13 15:01 juniper.conf.11.gz
-rw-r-----  1 root  wheel  3115 Nov 11 07:03 juniper.conf.12.gz
-rw-r-----  1 root  wheel  4780 Nov 11 07:00 juniper.conf.13.gz
-rw-r-----  1 root  wheel  4597 Nov 11 05:38 juniper.conf.14.gz
-rw-r-----  1 root  wheel  4109 Nov 11 05:32 juniper.conf.15.gz
-rw-r-----  1 root  wheel  3180 Nov 10 15:51 juniper.conf.16.gz
-rw-r-----  1 root  wheel  3115 Nov 10 12:46 juniper.conf.17.gz
-rw-r-----  1 root  wheel  3186 Nov  9 12:45 juniper.conf.18.gz
-rw-r-----  1 root  wheel  3115 Nov  7 10:31 juniper.conf.19.gz
-rw-r-----  1 root  wheel  2784 Nov  7 05:44 juniper.conf.20.gz
-rw-r-----  1 root  wheel  2774 Nov  7 04:06 juniper.conf.21.gz
-rw-r-----  1 root  wheel  2764 Nov  6 09:31 juniper.conf.22.gz
-rw-r-----  1 root  wheel  2704 Nov  4 12:18 juniper.conf.23.gz
-rw-r-----  1 root  wheel   525 Nov  4 12:13 juniper.conf.24.gz
-rw-r-----  1 root  wheel   526 Nov  4 12:13 juniper.conf.25.gz
-rw-r-----  1 root  wheel  1036 Nov  4 12:13 juniper.conf.26.gz
-rw-r-----  1 root  wheel   994 Nov  4 12:13 juniper.conf.27.gz
-rw-r-----  1 root  wheel   996 Nov  4 05:34 juniper.conf.28.gz
-rw-r-----  1 root  wheel  1005 Nov  4 05:34 juniper.conf.29.gz
-rw-r-----  1 root  wheel  1001 Oct 18 05:37 juniper.conf.30.gz
-rw-r-----  1 root  wheel   879 Oct 17 07:08 juniper.conf.31.gz
-rw-r-----  1 root  wheel   936 Oct  7 10:56 juniper.conf.32.gz
```

snip

The active configuration, highlighted in Example 1-8, is named **juniper.conf.gz** and is considered revision 0 of the configuration. The previous revision is revision 1 and is appropriately named **juniper.conf.1.gz**. In the same way, all other revisions are numbered and stored, all the way up to revision 49, thus storing 50 configuration files in total. At any point in time, you can execute the **compare rollback** command to view the difference between the active configuration and any previous revision of the configuration. Example 1-9 demonstrates how this command is used.

Example 1-9   *Using compare rollback to compare active configuration with a previous configuration revision*

```
admin@access1> show configuration | compare rollback 1
[edit system login]
-   user test {
-       uid 2002;
-       class super-user;
-       authentication {
-           encrypted-password "$6$6PZOin4S$XjZDWSVxxsyY2DJ.64bZsER63J6reW64xJljclcNv6nkxszFJ8n4ORFlARMhZERjNNUGFHlFo.
cPImoMa6O3z."; ## SECRET-DATA
-       }
-   }
```

The diff is based on what is additional, missing, or modified from the perspective of the active configuration when compared to the revision specified in the command. In Example 1-9, the output can be interpreted as follows: a user named *test* is not present in the active configuration, and thus it can be safely assumed that this user was deleted as part of the previous commit, leading to the creation of revision 1 of the configuration, which is being compared here. An alternate way of comparing configurations is by using the **show system rollback compare** [*first revision number*] [*second revision number*] operational mode command, which displays similar information as Example 1-9.

In both operational and configuration modes, you have the option to display the output of a **show** command in a programmatically friendly way. Junos was written, from the ground up, to be automation friendly, and this option exemplifies it. Example 1-10 shows how an output can be redirected to be displayed in XML and JSON formats for easier consumption by automation tools and infrastructure.

Example 1-10   *Displaying output in Junos in XML or JSON format*

```
admin@access1# show system login | display json
{
    "configuration" : {
        "@" : {
            "junos:changed-seconds" : "1703653636",
            "junos:changed-localtime" : "2023-12-27 05:07:16 UTC"
        },
        "system" : {
            "login" : {
                "user" : [
                {
                    "name" : "admin",
                    "uid" : 2000,
                    "class" : "super-user",
                    "authentication" : {
                        "encrypted-password" : "$6$GK8jGjx5$QIo831ewbnayBIoYPxUZ5NzU3hqSFUYmOqPL/kSn585LynpzfxVLT5QFnAdm-
mEG1RbV1S/PldHOxLqNziljBTO"
                    }
                },
                {
                    "name" : "anindac",
                    "uid" : 2001,
                    "class" : "super-user",
                    "authentication" : {
                        "encrypted-password" : "$6$iw2C7uIC$SSDs2w8vN42zaa1NJkh9zw6edZOQerHKTVJ9jvZKcS94ZRGKs5ssjaOyoFiEGv
cH1vg5w5Ps/msxUBPxbE31yO"
                    }
                }
                ]
            }
        }
    }
}

admin@access1# show system login | display xml
<rpc-reply xmlns:junos="http://xml.juniper.net/junos/23.2R1.14/junos">
    <configuration junos:changed-seconds="1703653636" junos:changed-localtime="2023-12-27 05:07:16 UTC">
```

```
            <system>
                <login>
                    <user>
                        <name>admin</name>
                        <uid>2000</uid>
                        <class>super-user</class>
                        <authentication>
                            <encrypted-password>$6$GK8jGjx5$QIo831ewbnayBIoYPxUZ5NzU3hqSFUYmOqPL/kSn585LynpzfxVLT5QFnAdm-
mEG1RbV1S/PldHOxLqNziljBTO</encrypted-password>
                        </authentication>
                    </user>
                    <user>
                        <name>anindac</name>
                        <uid>2001</uid>
                        <class>super-user</class>
                        <authentication>
                            <encrypted-password>$6$iw2C7uIC$SSDs2w8vN42zaa1NJkh9zw6edZOQerHKTVJ9jvZKcS94ZRGKs5ssja0yo-
FiEGvcH1vg5w5Ps/msxUBPxbE31y0</encrypted-password>
                        </authentication>
                    </user>
                </login>
            </system>
        </configuration>
        <cli>
            <banner>[edit]</banner>
        </cli>
    </rpc-reply>
```

If you need to view the configuration in the format of set commands instead of a more structured output, you can do so by using the **display set** option after the | symbol, as shown in Example 1-11.

Example 1-11   *Displaying configuration in Junos set command format*

```
admin@access1# show system login | display set
set system login user admin uid 2000
set system login user admin class super-user
set system login user admin authentication encrypted-password
"$6$GK8jGjx5$QIo831ewbnayBIoYPxUZ5NzU3hqSFUYmOqPL/kSn585LynpzfxVLT5QFnAdmmEG1RbV1S/PldHOxLqNziljBTO"
set system login user anindac uid 2001
set system login user anindac class super-user
set system login user anindac authentication encrypted-password
"$6$iw2C7uIC$SSDs2w8vN42zaa1NJkh9zw6edZOQerHKTVJ9jvZKcS94ZRGKs5ssja0yoFiEGvcH1vg5w5Ps/msxUBPxbE31y0"
```

In addition to this, using the | symbol provides you with several utilities for filtering, searching, and matching specific data from the expected output. These include options such as **find**, **match**, and **except**, among many others, as shown in Example 1-12.

You may find that Junos takes some time to get used to due to its inherent differences from how other network operating systems look and feel, but the flexibility it offers makes it much easier to navigate and harder to make mistakes, providing word-by-word syntax checking, automatic tab completion of commands, and a commit process that enables you to stage a configuration and make it active only when you are ready for it.

Example 1-12 *Utilities provided to act on the data from the output of a show command*

```
admin@access1> show interfaces terse | ?
Possible completions:
  append          Append output text to file
  count           Count occurrences
  display         Show additional kinds of information
  except          Show only text that does not match a pattern
  find            Search for first occurrence of pattern
  hold            Hold text without exiting the --More-- prompt
  last            Display end of output only
  match           Show only text that matches a pattern
  no-more         Don't paginate output
  refresh         Refresh a continuous display of the command
  request         Make system-level requests
  resolve         Resolve IP addresses
  save            Save output text to file
  tee             Write to standard output and file
  trim            Trim specified number of columns from start of line
```

Building a Network with Junos

Armed with the basic knowledge of navigating the Junos CLI, it is time to build the simple network previously shown in Figure 1-3. All interfaces between the core and the access switches need to be configured as Layer 2 trunk interfaces. In general, in Junos, an interface has the configuration structure shown in Example 1-13.

Example 1-13 *General interface configuration structure in Junos*

```
interfaces {
    interface-name {
        physical-properties;
        [...]
        unit <logical-unit-number> {
        logical-properties;
        [...]
        }
    }
}
```

Each physical interface must have at least one logical interface to function. These logical interfaces are created by specifying a unit number under the physical interface using the **unit** [*logical-unit-number*] option. This structure also divides the interface into a set of physical properties and logical properties; maximum transmission unit (MTU) is an example of a physical property, while the family, such as IPv4 (using the **family inet** option) or IPv6 (using the **family inet6** option), is an example of a logical property, which is specific to a logical unit.

In Junos, an interface is written in the format *interface-type-[fpc-number]/[pic-number]/[port-number]*. The *interface-type* naming convention is as follows:

- **ge** for 1G interfaces
- **xe** for 10G interfaces
- **et** for 25G and above interfaces

The syntax FPC stands for *Flexible PIC Concentrator*, and PIC stands for *Physical Interface Card*. An FPC is inserted into a device, housing one or more PICs, which host the actual physical interfaces. As an example, for a Juniper QFX5130-32CD, which natively has 32×400G ports, the naming convention is et-0/0/0 through et-0/0/31, since it has only one FPC and one PIC, housing all ports. Example 1-14 shows how the number of FPCs and PICs can be validated, in a QFX5130-32CD, using the **show chassis hardware** operational mode command. This command also shows all SFPs inserted into the corresponding PIC, along with their part numbers and serial numbers (omitted here).

Example 1-14   *FPC and PIC details on a Juniper QFX5130-32CD*

```
root@qfx5130> show chassis hardware
Hardware inventory:
Item             Version  Part number  Serial number   Description
Chassis                                <omitted>       QFX5130-32CD
PSM 0            REV 05   740-085431   <omitted>       JPSU-1600W-AC-AFO
PSM 1            REV 05   740-085431   <omitted>       JPSU-1600W-AC-AFO
Routing Engine 0          BUILTIN      <omitted>       RE-QFX5130-32CD
CB 0            REV 06   650-109783   <omitted>       QFX5130-32CD
FPC 0                     BUILTIN      <omitted>       QFX5130-32CD
  PIC 0                   BUILTIN      <omitted>       32X400G-QSFP-DD
    Xcvr 0      REV 01   740-032986   <omitted>       QSFP+-40G-SR4
    Xcvr 1      REV 01   740-032986   <omitted>       QSFP+-40G-SR4
    Xcvr 2      REV 01   740-054053   <omitted>       QSFP+-4X10G-SR
    Xcvr 3      REV 01   740-032986   <omitted>       QSFP+-40G-SR4
    Xcvr 4      REV 01   740-067442   <omitted>       QSFP+-40G-SR4
    Xcvr 6      REV 01   740-046565   <omitted>       QSFP+-40G-SR4
    Xcvr 8      REV 01   740-032986   <omitted>       QSFP+-40G-SR4
Fan Tray 0                                             QFX5130-32CD Fan Tray, Front to Back Airflow - AFO
Fan Tray 1                                             QFX5130-32CD Fan Tray, Front to Back Airflow - AFO
Fan Tray 2                                             QFX5130-32CD Fan Tray, Front to Back Airflow - AFO
Fan Tray 3                                             QFX5130-32CD Fan Tray, Front to Back Airflow - AFO
Fan Tray 4                                             QFX5130-32CD Fan Tray, Front to Back Airflow - AFO
Fan Tray 5                                             QFX5130-32CD Fan Tray, Front to Back Airflow - AFO
```

A Layer 2 interface in Junos also requires a unit, configured with the family **ethernet-switching**. This family is mutually exclusive to other families such as **inet** or **inet6**, meaning that it cannot be configured alongside any of these other families. Example 1-15 shows how a Layer 2 trunk interface is configured on access1 in Figure 1-3, allowing two VLANs 10 and 20 over this interface. The example also shows how a Layer 2 access interface is configured on access1 for the host-facing interface.

Example 1-15   *Configuring a Layer 2 trunk and access interface using Junos CLI*

```
root@access1# show vlans
v10 {
    vlan-id 10;
}
v20 {
    vlan-id 20;
}

root@access1# show interfaces ge-0/0/0
```

```
unit 0 [
    family ethernet-switching {
        interface-mode trunk;
        vlan {
            members [ v10 v20 ];
        }
    }
}


root@access1# show interfaces ge-0/0/2
unit 0 {
    family ethernet-switching {
        interface-mode access;
        vlan {
            members v10;
        }
    }
}
```

All access and core switches are configured in the same way. Once this is done, Spanning Tree is enabled on each switch, with core1 being configured with a priority of 4096 to make it the primary root bridge, and core2 configured with a priority of 8192 to make it a backup root bridge. Junos offers three flavors of Spanning Tree as follows (support may also depend on the Juniper hardware platform and Junos version):

- **Rapid Spanning Tree Protocol (RSTP):** Creates one instance of STP on the device, using RSTP mechanisms for forwarding and convergence.

- **Virtual Spanning Tree Protocol (VSTP):** Creates one instance of STP per enabled VLAN, like PVST+ functionality offered by Cisco Systems.

- **Multiple Spanning Tree Protocol (MSTP):** Allows multiple instances of STP to be configured on the system, with user-defined grouping of VLANs to STP instance.

Example 1-16 demonstrates how VSTP is enabled on a Junos device, using access1 as a reference. The bridge priority for core1 and core2 is set to 4096 and 8192, respectively.

Example 1-16   *VSTP configuration on Junos*

```
admin@access1# show protocols vstp
interface ge-0/0/0 {
    mode point-to-point;
}
interface ge-0/0/1 {
    mode point-to-point;
}
interface ge-0/0/2 {
    edge;
}
vlan all;


admin@core1# show protocols vstp
interface ge-0/0/0 {
    mode point-to-point;
```

```
}
interface ge-0/0/1 {
    mode point-to-point;
}
vlan all {
    bridge-priority 4k;
}


admin@core2# show protocols vstp
interface ge-0/0/0 {
    mode point-to-point;
}
interface ge-0/0/1 {
    mode point-to-point;
}
vlan all {
    bridge-priority 8k;
}
```

You can use the commands **show spanning-tree bridge** and **show spanning-tree interface** to validate VSTP state on Junos devices. Example 1-17 confirms that core1 is the root bridge, as the bridge ID matches the root ID for both VLANs 10 and 20, with all its interfaces in a forwarding, designated state. The example also takes access1 as a reference, to show that its direct interface connecting to core1 is selected as the root port and is in a forwarding state.

Example 1-17 *VSTP bridge and interface validation*

```
admin@core1> show spanning-tree bridge
STP bridge parameters
Routing instance name            : GLOBAL
Enabled protocol                 : RSTP


STP bridge parameters for VLAN 10
  Root ID                        : 4106.2c:6b:f5:91:fd:d0
  Hello time                     : 2 seconds
  Maximum age                    : 20 seconds
  Forward delay                  : 15 seconds
  Message age                    : 0
  Number of topology changes     : 2
  Time since last topology change : 711 seconds
  Local parameters
    Bridge ID                    : 4106.2c:6b:f5:91:fd:d0
    Extended system ID           : 10


STP bridge parameters for VLAN 20
  Root ID                        : 4116.2c:6b:f5:91:fd:d0
  Hello time                     : 2 seconds
  Maximum age                    : 20 seconds
  Forward delay                  : 15 seconds
  Message age                    : 0
  Number of topology changes     : 2
```

```
  Time since last topology change   : 710 seconds
  Local parameters
    Bridge ID                       : 4116.2c:6b:f5:91:fd:d0
    Extended system ID              : 20
```

admin@core1> **show spanning-tree interface**

Spanning tree interface parameters for VLAN 10

Interface	Port ID	Designated port ID	Designated bridge ID	Port Cost	State	Role
ge-0/0/0	128:1	128:1	4106.2c6bf591fdd0	20000	FWD	DESG
ge-0/0/1	128:2	128:2	4106.2c6bf591fdd0	20000	FWD	DESG

Spanning tree interface parameters for VLAN 20

Interface	Port ID	Designated port ID	Designated bridge ID	Port Cost	State	Role
ge-0/0/0	128:1	128:1	4116.2c6bf591fdd0	20000	FWD	DESG
ge-0/0/1	128:2	128:2	4116.2c6bf591fdd0	20000	FWD	DESG

admin@access1> **show spanning-tree interface**

Spanning tree interface parameters for VLAN 10

Interface	Port ID	Designated port ID	Designated bridge ID	Port Cost	State	Role
ge-0/0/0	128:1	128:1	4106.2c6bf591fdd0	20000	FWD	ROOT
ge-0/0/1	128:2	128:1	8202.2c6bf5a52dd0	20000	BLK	ALT
ge-0/0/2	128:3	128:3	32778.2c6bf524cfd0	20000	FWD	DESG

Spanning tree interface parameters for VLAN 20

Interface	Port ID	Designated port ID	Designated bridge ID	Port Cost	State	Role
ge-0/0/0	128:1	128:1	4116.2c6bf591fdd0	20000	FWD	ROOT
ge-0/0/1	128:2	128:1	8212.2c6bf5a52dd0	20000	BLK	ALT

The next step is to create an aggregated interface between core1 and core2. In Junos, these are called *Aggregated Ethernet (AE) interfaces*, which is the link aggregation implementation defined in the IEEE 802.3ad standard. Example 1-18 demonstrates how interfaces *ge-0/0/2* and *ge-0/0/3* are assigned to an AE interface. The AE interface is then enabled for Link Aggregation Control Protocol (LACP), in an active mode with a user-defined system identifier, and configured as a trunk interface, allowing VLANs 10 and 20. The AE interface is also added to the VSTP configuration.

It is important to note that the device must be explicitly configured to support AE interfaces by using the **chassis aggregated-devices ethernet device-count** configuration option. This enables the operator to set a limit on the number of expected AE interfaces on the device, with a minimum value of 1 for one AE interface to come up.

Example 1-18   *Configuring link aggregation using Junos CLI*

```
admin@core1# show chassis
aggregated-devices {
    ethernet {
        device-count 1;
    }
}


admin@core1# show interfaces ge-0/0/2
ether-options {
    802.3ad ae1;
}


admin@core1# show interfaces ge-0/0/3
ether-options {
    802.3ad ae1;
}


admin@core1# show interfaces ae1
aggregated-ether-options {
    lacp {
        active;
        system-id 00:00:00:00:00:11;
    }
}
unit 0 {
    family ethernet-switching {
        interface-mode trunk;
        vlan {
            members [ v10 v20 ];
        }
    }
}


admin@core1# show protocols vstp
interface ge-0/0/0 {
    mode point-to-point;
}
interface ge-0/0/1 {
    mode point-to-point;
}
interface ae1 {
    mode point-to-point;
}
vlan all {
    bridge-priority 4k;
}
```

Once core2 is also configured in the same way, link aggregation can be validated using the **show lacp interface** [*ae-interface*] **extensive** operational mode command. This shows all the LACP flags and their state, along with the actor and partner system IDs. Example 1-19 shows this validation, from the perspective of core1, confirming that the link aggregation was successful between core1 and core2 for interfaces *ge-0/0/2* and *ge-0/0/3*.

Example 1-19   *Validation of link aggregation using Junos CLI*

```
admin@core1> show lacp interfaces ae1 extensive
Aggregated interface: ae1
    LACP state:       Role   Exp  Def  Dist  Col  Syn  Aggr  Timeout  Activity
      ge-0/0/2        Actor  No   No   Yes   Yes  Yes  Yes   Fast     Active
      ge-0/0/2        Partner No  No   Yes   Yes  Yes  Yes   Fast     Active
      ge-0/0/3        Actor  No   No   Yes   Yes  Yes  Yes   Fast     Active
      ge-0/0/3        Partner No  No   Yes   Yes  Yes  Yes   Fast     Active
    LACP protocol:        Receive State  Transmit State       Mux State
      ge-0/0/2                 Current   Fast periodic Collecting distributing
      ge-0/0/3                 Current   Fast periodic Collecting distributing
    LACP info:        Role   System            System       Port    Port    Port
                             priority          identifier   priority number  key
      ge-0/0/2        Actor     127   00:00:00:00:00:11      127      1      2
      ge-0/0/2        Partner   127   00:00:00:00:00:22      127      1      2
      ge-0/0/3        Actor     127   00:00:00:00:00:11      127      2      2
      ge-0/0/3        Partner   127   00:00:00:00:00:22      127      2      2
```

The end goal of the network is to provide reachability between VLANs 10 and 20. For this, *integrated routing and bridging (IRB)* is used by creating logical IRB interfaces for each Layer 2 VLAN and associating them to their respective VLANs on the cores. With IRB, you can both route and bridge on the same device, without the need to connect a dedicated external device for Layer 3 routing. The concept of IRB interfaces is explored in more detail in Chapter 7, "Centrally Routed Bridging."

Additionally, *Virtual Router Redundancy Protocol (VRRP)* is configured for each IRB interface, enabling redundant gateways in a primary and backup model, with core1 as the primary and core2 as the backup in this case. The configuration for the IRB interfaces and VRRP is shown in Example 1-20 on both core1 and core2, where the **l3-interface** [*irb-interface*] configuration option is used to associate a Layer 2 VLAN with an IRB interface.

Example 1-20   *Creating IRB interfaces and configuring VRRP using Junos CLI on core1 and core2*

```
admin@core1# show vlans
v10 {
    vlan-id 10;
    l3-interface irb.10;
}
v20 {
    vlan-id 20;
    l3-interface irb.20;
}

admin@core1# show interfaces irb
unit 10 {
    family inet {
        address 172.16.10.252/24 {
```

```
                        vrrp-group 10 {
                            virtual-address 172.16.10.254;
                            priority 120;
                            preempt;
                            accept-data;
                            track {
                                route 0.0.0.0/0 routing-instance default priority-cost 30;
                            }
                        }
                    }
                }
            }
        }
    unit 20 {
        family inet {
            address 172.16.20.252/24 {
                vrrp-group 20 {
                    virtual-address 172.16.20.254;
                    priority 120;
                    preempt;
                    accept-data;
                    track {
                        route 0.0.0.0/0 routing-instance default priority-cost 30;
                    }
                }
            }
        }
    }
}


admin@core2# show vlans
v10 {
    vlan-id 10;
    l3-interface irb.10;
}
v20 {
    vlan-id 20;
    l3-interface irb.20;
}


admin@core2# show interfaces irb
unit 10 {
    family inet {
        address 172.16.10.253/24 {
            vrrp-group 10 {
                virtual-address 172.16.10.254;
                preempt;
                accept-data;
                track {
                    route 0.0.0.0/0 routing-instance default priority-cost 30;
                }
```

```
            }
        }
    }
}
unit 20 {
    family inet {
        address 172.16.20.253/24 {
            vrrp-group 20 {
                virtual-address 172.16.20.254;
                preempt;
                accept-data;
                track {
                    route 0.0.0.0/0 routing-instance default priority-cost 30;
                }
            }
        }
    }
}
```

The VRRP configuration includes creating a unique VRRP group specific to each IRB interface, assigning a virtual address that is shared between the two cores participating in VRRP, and tracking a default route that is expected to be received from the WAN edge device. If the default route is missing, a penalty is applied to the VRRP priority of the device, reducing it by a value of 30, as per the configuration shown in Example 1-20. The **accept-data** configuration option allows a virtual address to accept data destined to it, enabling operators to perform basic connectivity tests such as using the **ping** tool to validate if the gateway is reachable or not.

Example 1-21 shows the VRRP state of both core1 and core2, confirming that core1 is the primary and core2 is the backup. The **show vrrp detail** operational mode command confirms that, since no default route is seen in the default routing table, the priority has been reduced by 30.

Example 1-21   *Validating VRRP state on core1 and core2*

```
admin@core1> show vrrp brief
Interface    State    Group    VR state VR Mode    Timer    Type    Address
irb.10       up          10    master   Active    A  0.198  lcl     172.16.10.252
                                                             vip     172.16.10.254
irb.20       up          20    master   Active    A  0.768  lcl     172.16.20.252
                                                             vip     172.16.20.254

admin@core2> show vrrp brief
Interface    State    Group    VR state VR Mode    Timer    Type    Address
irb.10       up          10    backup   Active    D  3.310  lcl     172.16.10.253
                                                             vip     172.16.10.254
                                                             mas     172.16.10.252
irb.20       up          20    backup   Active    D  3.099  lcl     172.16.20.253
                                                             vip     172.16.20.254
                                                             mas     172.16.20.252


admin@core1> show vrrp detail
Physical interface: irb, Unit: 10, Address: 172.16.10.252/24
  Index: 348, SNMP ifIndex: 546, VRRP-Traps: disabled, VRRP-Version: 2
  Interface state: up, Group: 10, State: master, VRRP Mode: Active
```

```
  Priority: 90, Advertisement interval: 1, Authentication type: none
  Advertisement threshold: 3, Computed send rate: 0
  Preempt: yes, Accept-data mode: yes, VIP count: 1, VIP: 172.16.10.254
  Advertisement Timer: 0.162s, Master router: 172.16.10.252
  Virtual router uptime: 14:12:59, Master router uptime: 00:09:16
  Virtual Mac: 00:00:5e:00:01:0a
  Preferred: yes
  Tracking: enabled
    Current priority: 90, Configured priority: 120
    Priority hold time: disabled
    Interface tracking: disabled
    Route tracking: enabled, Route count: 1
      Route            VRF name      Route state     Priority cost
      0.0.0.0/0        default       down                       30


Physical interface: irb, Unit: 20, Address: 172.16.20.252/24
  Index: 349, SNMP ifIndex: 547, VRRP-Traps: disabled, VRRP-Version: 2
  Interface state: up, Group: 20, State: master, VRRP Mode: Active
  Priority: 90, Advertisement interval: 1, Authentication type: none
  Advertisement threshold: 3, Computed send rate: 0
  Preempt: yes, Accept-data mode: yes, VIP count: 1, VIP: 172.16.20.254
  Advertisement Timer: 0.009s, Master router: 172.16.20.252
  Virtual router uptime: 14:12:59, Master router uptime: 00:09:16
  Virtual Mac: 00:00:5e:00:01:14
  Preferred: yes
  Tracking: enabled
    Current priority: 90, Configured priority: 120
    Priority hold time: disabled
    Interface tracking: disabled
    Route tracking: enabled, Route count: 1
      Route            VRF name      Route state     Priority cost
      0.0.0.0/0        default       down                       30
```

At this point, the two hosts, h1 and h2, can communicate with each other. On each host, the respective VLAN's VRRP virtual address is configured as the default gateway. Example 1-22 confirms that host h1 has a default gateway of 172.16.10.254 and h2 has a default gateway of 172.16.20.254.

Example 1-22   *Default routes on hosts h1 and h2*

```
root@h1:~# ip route
default via 172.16.10.254 dev eth1
172.16.10.0/24 dev eth1 proto kernel scope link src 172.16.10.1


root@h2:~# ip route
default via 172.16.20.254 dev eth1
172.16.20.0/24 dev eth1 proto kernel scope link src 172.16.20.2
```

Thus, when host h1 wants to communicate with h2 using the **ping** tool, it must first resolve its default gateway's MAC address using the Address Resolution Protocol (ARP) process, since the two hosts are in different subnets. Host h1 generates an ARP request for 172.16.10.254, which, when received on access1, causes h1's MAC address to be learned locally. This is shown in Figure 1-5.

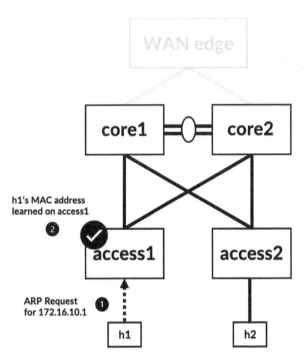

Figure 1-5 *Host h1 resolving default gateway using ARP*

Only the primary VRRP device responds to this ARP request. In this case, core1 sends an ARP reply back, using the virtual MAC address that is automatically generated for VRRP. Thus, access1 now has both host h1's MAC address, mapped to the host-facing interface, and the MAC address for the default gateway, associated with the VRRP virtual address, mapped to the interface toward core1. This is confirmed by using the **show ethernet-switching table** operational mode command, as shown in Example 1-23, which also provides the first look at how to view the MAC address table using the Junos CLI.

Example 1-23 *MAC address table on Junos*

```
admin@access1> show ethernet-switching table vlan-id 10

MAC flags (S - static MAC, D - dynamic MAC, L - locally learned, P - Persistent static, C - Control MAC
          SE - statistics enabled, NM - non configured MAC, R - remote PE MAC, O - ovsdb MAC
          GBP - group based policy, B - Blocked MAC)


Ethernet switching table : 3 entries, 3 learned
Routing instance : default-switch
    Vlan            MAC                 MAC       Age   GBP   Logical            NH      RTR
    name            address             flags           Tag   interface          Index   ID
    v10             00:00:5e:00:01:0a   D         -           ge-0/0/0.0         0       0
    v10             2c:6b:f5:91:fd:f0   D         -           ge-0/0/0.0         0       0
    v10             aa:c1:ab:75:97:0e   D         -           ge-0/0/2.0         0       0
```

The MAC address table provides a view of all MAC addresses learned by the system, displayed line by line, with the VLAN each MAC address was learned on, along with the interface it was learned over. For example, in Example 1-23, MAC address *00:00:5e:00:01:0a* was learned on the VLAN named *v10* over interface *ge-0/0/0.0*. The flag *D*, against the MAC address, confirms that this was learned dynamically.

With the IP-to-MAC address resolution complete, and populated on host h1, h1 can build an IP packet with an Internet Control Message Protocol (ICMP) payload destined to the gateway's resolved MAC address in the Ethernet header, and host h2's IP address in the IP header. This is received on access1, switched out toward core1 using the MAC address table, and eventually received by core1.

Since core1 has both IRB interfaces, it routes the packet from the received VLAN (VLAN 10) to the destination VLAN (VLAN 20), essentially performing inter-VLAN routing. This can be confirmed by using the **show route** operational mode command, as shown in Example 1-24, which also provides the first look at how to view the routing table using the Junos CLI. You can also be specific about which table to view by adding the **table** [*table-name*] option to the **show route** command.

Example 1-24   *Routing table on Junos*

```
admin@core1> show route table inet.0

inet.0: 8 destinations, 8 routes (8 active, 0 holddown, 0 hidden)
Limit/Threshold: 1048576/1048576 destinations
+ = Active Route, - = Last Active, * = Both

172.16.10.0/24      *[Direct/0] 15:07:51
                     > via irb.10
172.16.10.252/32    *[Local/0] 15:07:51
                         Local via irb.10
172.16.10.254/32    *[Local/0] 01:04:06
                         Local via irb.10
172.16.20.0/24      *[Direct/0] 15:07:51
                     > via irb.20
172.16.20.252/32    *[Local/0] 15:07:51
                         Local via irb.20
172.16.20.254/32    *[Local/0] 01:04:06
                         Local via irb.20

admin@core1> show route table inet.0 172.16.20.2

inet.0: 8 destinations, 8 routes (8 active, 0 holddown, 0 hidden)
Limit/Threshold: 1048576/1048576 destinations
+ = Active Route, - = Last Active, * = Both

172.16.20.0/24      *[Direct/0] 15:11:31
                     > via irb.20
```

While most vendors implement a routing information base (RIB) for Border Gateway Protocol (BGP), Junos implements a similar logic for all tables. The Routing Engine, and more specifically, the RPD daemon, controls how routes are installed in the routing table, which determines active routes to a destination.

By default, Junos has a routing table called *inet.0*, which is the default IPv4 unicast routing table. All routing protocols, such as BGP, OSPF, and IS-IS, insert their routes in this table, along with direct routes and any configured static routes. From here, the active route is selected and copied to the forwarding table on the Routing Engine, and eventually to the Packet Forwarding Engine by the kernel. The following list provides a high-level overview of some of the different routing tables on Junos:

- **inet.0:** This table holds IPv4 unicast routes.
- **inet6.0:** This table holds IPv6 unicast routes.
- **inet.1:** This table holds multicast (S,G) routes.
- **inet.2:** This table holds IPv4 routes used for multicast reverse path forwarding (RPF) checks.

- inet.3: This table is used for resolving BGP next-hop addresses for a label-switched path (LSP) in a Multiprotocol Label Switching (MPLS) infrastructure.

- bgp.evpn.0: This table holds BGP EVPN routes.

- mpls.0: This table is used for label switching in MPLS networks. Transit routers use this table to determine how to forward a packet in a label-switched path.

Some of these tables can also be created by the Routing Engine to be specific to routing instances of type VRF. For example, a virtual routing and forwarding (VRF) instance named Tenant1 will have an IPv4 unicast table called *Tenant1.inet.0*. To understand how to read the IPv4 unicast routing table and how routes are pushed into the forwarding table, Example 1-25 demonstrates how to configure Layer 3 interfaces on the cores, toward the WAN-edge device, and enable a routing protocol (OSPF, in this case).

Example 1-25   *Layer 3 interface and OSPF configuration on core1 and core2*

```
admin@core1# show interfaces ge-0/0/4
unit 0 {
    family inet {
        address 198.51.100.0/31;
    }
}


admin@core2# show interfaces ge-0/0/4
unit 0 {
    family inet {
        address 198.51.100.2/31;
    }
}


admin@core1# show protocols ospf
area 0.0.0.0 {
    interface ge-0/0/4.0 {
        interface-type p2p;
    }
}


admin@core2# show protocols ospf
area 0.0.0.0 {
    interface ge-0/0/4.0 {
        interface-type p2p;
    }
}
```

With the WAN edge device configured in the same way, OSPF peering should be established between the devices and in a *FULL* state, as shown in Example 1-26. The WAN edge device is also originating a default route into OSPF, which can be seen in the IPv4 unicast routing table of the cores. The *[OSPF/150]* parameter against the route indicates that the route was learned from the protocol OSPF, with a route preference (also known as *administrate distance*) of 150. This is the default preference assigned to external OSPF routes. Additionally, the *to 198.51.100.1 via ge-0/0/4.0* parameter indicates that the next-hop address is *198.51.100.1* via exit interface *ge-0/0/4.0*.

Example 1-26   *OSPF peering and default route from WAN edge received on core1 and core2*

```
admin@wan-edge> show ospf neighbor
Address         Interface       State       ID              Pri  Dead
198.51.100.0    ge-0/0/0.0      Full        172.16.10.252   128  36
198.51.100.2    ge-0/0/1.0      Full        172.16.10.253   128  32


admin@core1> show route table inet.0

inet.0: 11 destinations, 11 routes (11 active, 0 holddown, 0 hidden)
Limit/Threshold: 1048576/1048576 destinations
+ = Active Route, - = Last Active, * = Both


0.0.0.0/0          *[OSPF/150] 00:04:42, metric 0, tag 0
                   >  to 198.51.100.1 via ge-0/0/4.0
172.16.10.0/24     *[Direct/0] 17:32:59
                   >  via irb.10
172.16.10.252/32   *[Local/0] 17:32:59
                      Local via irb.10
172.16.10.254/32   *[Local/0] 03:29:14
                      Local via irb.10
172.16.20.0/24     *[Direct/0] 17:32:59
                   >  via irb.20


*snip*


admin@core2> show route table inet.0

inet.0: 9 destinations, 9 routes (9 active, 0 holddown, 0 hidden)
Limit/Threshold: 1048576/1048576 destinations
+ = Active Route, - = Last Active, * = Both


0.0.0.0/0          *[OSPF/150] 00:06:26, metric 0, tag 0
                   >  to 198.51.100.3 via ge-0/0/4.0
172.16.10.0/24     *[Direct/0] 17:35:01
                   >  via irb.10
172.16.10.253/32   *[Local/0] 17:35:01
                      Local via irb.10
172.16.20.0/24     *[Direct/0] 17:35:01
                   >  via irb.20


*snip*
```

The default route learned via OSPF is copied into the Routing Engine's forwarding table since it is the active route, indicated by the * against the OSPF route. This can be confirmed as shown in Example 1-27.

Example 1-27   *Forwarding table on core1 and core2*

```
admin@core1> show route forwarding-table table default
Routing table: default.inet
Internet:
```

```
Destination        Type RtRef Next hop         Type Index    NhRef Netif
default            user    0 c:0:2a:3:4f:1      ucst    605     4 ge-0/0/4.0
172.16.10.0/24     intf    0                    rslv    587     1 irb.10
172.16.10.0/32     dest    0 172.16.10.0        recv    585     1 irb.10
172.16.10.1/32     dest    0 aa:c1:ab:75:97:e   ucst    601     1 ge-0/0/0.0
172.16.10.252/32   intf    0 172.16.10.252      locl    586     2
172.16.10.252/32   dest    0 172.16.10.252      locl    586     2
172.16.10.254/32   intf    0 172.16.10.254      locl    599     2
172.16.10.254/32   dest    0 172.16.10.254      locl    599     2
```

snip


```
admin@core2> show route forwarding-table table default
Routing table: default.inet
Internet:
Destination        Type RtRef Next hop         Type Index    NhRef Netif
default            user    0 c:0:69:50:67:2     ucst    601     4 ge-0/0/4.0
default            perm    0                    rjct     36     1
0.0.0.0/32         perm    0                    dscd     34     1
172.16.10.0/24     intf    0                    rslv    587     1 irb.10
172.16.10.0/32     dest    0 172.16.10.0        recv    585     1 irb.10
172.16.10.253/32   intf    0 172.16.10.253      locl    586     2
172.16.10.253/32   dest    0 172.16.10.253      locl    586     2
172.16.10.255/32   dest    0 172.16.10.255      bcst    584     1 irb.10
172.16.20.0/24     intf    0                    rslv    591     1 irb.20
```

snip

Features such as equal-cost multipath (ECMP) are explored in more detail in Chapter 3, "BGP for the Data Center," with a focus on BGP and how to enable the forwarding table and the hardware to install equal-cost routes.

Miscellaneous Junos Features

Junos has some exceptional features that make it one of the most flexible and versatile network operating systems in the market. This introductory chapter would be incomplete without a demonstration of a few of these features.

Rescue Configuration

Starting with a straightforward feature, Junos allows the operator to save the last known good configuration as a *rescue* configuration. Even though Junos uses a stage and commit process for configuration and stores up to 50 revisions of the previous configuration of the device, it can be hard for the operator of the system to remember which revision is the last known good revision. A rescue configuration solves this problem by providing an easy to track, and find, revision of the device configuration that can be used to restore state to a known working state, if needed.

You can create a rescue configuration by using the command **request system configuration rescue save** in operational mode. You can then stage this rescue configuration, to be committed, using the **rollback rescue** configuration mode command. Once the rescue configuration is created, it is stored in the **/config** path, as shown in Example 1-28.

Example 1-28   *Rescue configuration file*

```
root@access1> request system configuration rescue save
root@access1> start shell
root@access1:RE:0% ls -l /config/ | grep juniper.conf
-rw-r-----  1 root  wheel    5150 Dec  1 13:15 juniper.conf.1.gz
-rw-r-----  1 root  wheel    5125 Dec  1 12:49 juniper.conf.2.gz
-rw-r-----  1 root  wheel    5154 Dec  1 12:39 juniper.conf.3.gz
-rw-r-----  1 root  wheel    5180 Dec  1 13:54 juniper.conf.gz
-rw-r-----  1 root  wheel    1012 Dec 29 09:41 rescue.conf.gz
```

Junos Copy Utility

Next up is a very handy tool called **copy**, which enables you to copy configuration within a hierarchy. For example, if additional host-facing interfaces were added to the reference topology in Figure 1-3 after interface *ge-0/0/2* was already configured, you can use this utility to quickly configure those interfaces. Example 1-29 shows how this feature can be leveraged to configure interface *ge-0/0/3* in the same way as *ge-0/0/2* with the **copy** command.

Example 1-29   *The copy utility in Junos*

```
admin@access1# copy interfaces ge-0/0/2 to ge-0/0/3

[edit]
admin@access1# show interfaces ge-0/0/3
unit 0 {
    family ethernet-switching {
        interface-mode access;
        vlan {
            members v10;
        }
    }
}
```

Junos Groups

Naturally, the **copy** utility cannot scale well when many interfaces must be configured with common parameters. This could be the same MTU or same Layer 2 configuration, as an example. In this case, Junos offers a feature called *groups*, which enables you to define a specific grouping of configurations that can be applied as needed. In conjunction with interface ranges and wildcards, this feature can be used to configure several interfaces with the same configuration using the simple property of inheritance. This is shown in Example 1-30, where an interface range is created for interfaces *ge-0/0/4* to *ge-0/0/11*. A group called *v10-access* is then created with a wildcard matching on all interfaces, configured to be a Layer 2 access interface in VLAN *v10* and applied using the configuration option **apply-groups** under the interface range.

Example 1-30   *Junos groups and inheritance using apply-groups*

```
admin@access1# show groups v10-access
interfaces {
    <*> {
        unit 0 {
            family ethernet-switching {
                vlan {
                    members v10;
```

```
        ]
      }
    }
  }
}
```

```
admin@access1# show interfaces interface-range v10-interfaces
member-range ge-0/0/4 to ge-0/0/11;
apply-groups v10-access;
```

By default, an inherited configuration is not shown in Junos CLI. To view any inherited configuration from a Junos group, use the option **display inheritance**, as shown in Example 1-31. When displaying inherited configuration, Junos CLI includes comments by default, providing details about which group a specific configuration was inherited from. However, when dealing with large portions of inherited configuration and a large configuration in general, it is useful to exclude such comments. Example 1-31 also demonstrates how the **no-comments** option can be used with inherited configuration for such a use case.

Example 1-31 *Displaying inherited configuration in Junos*

```
admin@access1# show interfaces ge-0/0/4

<no output>


admin@access1# show interfaces ge-0/0/4 | display inheritance
##
## '0' was inherited from group 'v10-access'
##
unit 0 {
    ##
    ## 'ethernet-switching' was inherited from group 'v10-access'
    ##
    family ethernet-switching {
        ##
        ## 'vlan' was inherited from group 'v10-access'
        ##
        vlan {
            ##
            ## 'v10' was inherited from group 'v10-access'
            ##
            members v10;
        }
    }
}


admin@access1# show interfaces ge-0/0/4 | display inheritance no-comments
unit 0 {
    family ethernet-switching {
        vlan {
            members v10;
        }
    }
}
```

Junos Insert Utility

The last feature to discuss in this section is the **insert** utility. As the name suggests, this utility can be used to insert or move pieces of configuration higher or lower in a configuration hierarchy. This is especially useful when working with firewall filters or routing policies and their terms. A firewall filter, in Junos, is the same as a network access control list (ACL) and is used to control traffic transiting the device or traffic destined for the Routing Engine (CPU). Firewall filters, with the flexibility they offer, can be much more powerful and easier to interpret with an understanding of the syntax used for configuration.

For example, consider the firewall filter in Example 1-32, preconfigured in a system running Junos.

Example 1-32   *Sample firewall filter in Junos*

```
admin@access1# show firewall
family inet {
    filter PROTECT_RE {
        term bgp {
            from {
                protocol tcp;
                port bgp;
            }
            then accept;
        }
        term deny-all {
            then {
                count discard-re;
                reject;
            }
        }
    }
}
```

Any new term created now falls below the term *deny-all*, which is discarding all packets. Example 1-33 shows a new term called *ssh* added, which is placed below the term *deny-all*.

Example 1-33   *Adding a new term in a firewall filter in Junos*

```
admin@access1# set firewall family inet filter PROTECT_RE term ssh from protocol tcp
admin@access1# set firewall family inet filter PROTECT_RE term ssh from destination-port ssh
admin@access1# set firewall family inet filter PROTECT_RE term ssh then accept

admin@access1# show firewall
family inet {
    filter PROTECT_RE {
        term bgp {
            from {
                protocol tcp;
                port bgp;
            }
            then accept;
        }
        term deny-all {
```

```
        then {
            count discard-re;
            reject;
        }
    }
    term ssh {
        from {
            protocol tcp;
            destination-port ssh;
        }
        then accept;
    }
  }
}
```

This order can now be rearranged using the **insert** utility, as shown in Example 1-34, with the command moving the *ssh* term before the *deny-all* term. This is just a simple example to demonstrate how you can use this command.

Example 1-34 *Moving firewall filter terms higher (or lower) in the configuration hierarchy using the **insert** utility*

```
admin@access1# insert firewall family inet filter PROTECT_RE term ssh before term deny-all

admin@access1# show firewall
family inet {
    filter PROTECT_RE {
        term bgp {
            from {
                protocol tcp;
                port bgp;
            }
            then accept;
        }
        term ssh {
            from {
                protocol tcp;
                destination-port ssh;
            }
            then accept;
        }
        term deny-all {
            then {
                count discard-re;
                reject;
            }
        }
    }
}
```

Summary

This chapter introduced how to build and configure basic Layer 2 and Layer 3 constructs such as Layer 2 access and trunk interfaces, Layer 3 interfaces, integrated routing and bridging, inter-VLAN routing, and link aggregation using the Junos CLI. This chapter also provided a first look at viewing and interpreting the MAC address table and the routing table, including a summary of the different routing tables available in Junos, and what kind of routes are installed in each of them.

While this chapter may seem trivial within the larger scope of the book, it provided the foundation for working with the Junos CLI, which you will use throughout the book as you move toward building complex data centers with EVPN VXLAN and Junos.

## Chapter 2

Overview of Data Center Architecture

Understanding modern data center designs requires a foundational understanding of the history and evolution of data centers, so this chapter first provides that historical context and describes the driving factors that influenced and eventually led to data center design changes. The first section dives deeper into the impact of server-side, scale-up designs versus scale-out designs on the network infrastructure and why traditional architectures with Layer 2 protocols, such as Spanning Tree Protocol (STP), were no longer feasible, paving the way for the Clos architecture.

This chapter also covers common data center designs, such as the 3-stage Clos fabric, the 5-stage fabric, and the collapsed spine design, while also providing a clear differentiation between the underlay and the overlay (further explored in Chapter 4, "VXLAN as a Network Virtualization Overlay").

History and Evolution of Data Centers

Traditional data centers typically are designed using a three-tier architecture, with core, distribution, and access layers. Alternatively, a collapsed core architecture is used for small to medium-sized data centers, with the core and distribution layers collapsed into a single core layer. These three layers have the following functions:

- The core layer is typically composed of chassis-based, high-radix (high port density and speeds) switches focused on advanced routing capabilities and high throughput, connected to the WAN exit node. The goal of these switches is to route traffic in and out of the local network as fast as possible. The core utilizes only Layer 3 links, connecting to the WAN node and the distribution switches.

- The distribution layer is an aggregation point for access layer switches and logically connects the users from the access switches into the core, while also providing a point of interconnection between all access switches. Typically, the default gateways (in the form of integrated routing and bridging [IRB] interfaces or switch virtual interfaces [SVIs]) for all VLANs deployed in the network exist on the distribution layer, with features such as Hot Standby Router Protocol (HSRP) or Virtual Router Redundancy Protocol (VRRP) providing high availability for these Layer 3 gateways. The Spanning Tree root bridge is configured to be at this layer, aligning with the active gateway.

- The access layer is where users are physically connected and authenticated to access the network and its services. Various loop prevention and security guards are configured at this layer, ensuring no rogue devices are connected to hijack the network. The access switches connect to the distribution switches using Layer 2 links, with Spanning Tree blocking redundant links to prevent a Layer 2 bridging loop.

This three-tier network design is driven by monolithic server architecture, where all functions of an application, such as a database component and a browser engine (catering to inbound requests from clients), exist within the same physical server. This architecture generates traffic patterns that are mostly north-south, where hosts from the Internet initiate TCP sessions to this application to access a service hosted by it.

The three-tier architecture is shown in Figure 2-1.

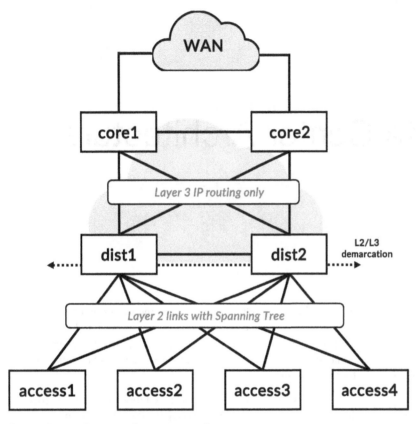

Figure 2-1   *Three-tier data center architecture*

Such an architecture has several drawbacks:

■ Inefficient usage of all available links, since Spanning Tree blocks redundant links, making them largely unusable. This also makes capacity planning less predictable.

■ Inefficient path selection due to blocked redundant links.

■ Susceptibility to Layer 2 bridging loops due to failures in STP, which can have network-wide impact, depending on how far the Layer 2 domain extends. Layer 2 loops have far-reaching consequences since Layer 2 packets such as a broadcast ARP frame do not have a Time to Live (TTL) field, causing them to loop endlessly until action is taken to break the loop.

■ The potential impact of failures is very high, depending on how far the Layer 2 domain extends.

■ To support more clients and sessions, the server requirements must be *scaled up* in such a design. Scaling up essentially implies increasing the memory, storage, CPU footprint, and network capabilities (such as additional network interface cards) on that single server. This has a direct impact on the network, since the expected traffic rate from a scaled-up server will be higher, which means that the network must be scaled up as well. This is why the core and distribution switches are typically chassis-based switches, enabling more line cards (supporting different link speeds as well) to be added to allow the network to scale up.

■ Business needs and investment into network infrastructure usually are not proportional to the usage of services provided. At times, the network capacity may be more than needed, while at other times, the network capacity may be less than needed, constraining the business with such an architecture.

Several network design and technological advancements have been made to overcome some of these limitations, which was a natural evolution influencing both enterprise and data center design. To reduce the impact of Spanning Tree and the blocking of redundant links, the concept of link aggregation was enhanced to logically bundle two switches together, known as *Multichassis Link Aggregation* (*MC-LAG* or *MLAG*). Other vendors have different names for it, but functionally, the technology is mostly the same. For example, for the Cisco Nexus portfolio, this technology is called *virtual Port-Channel* (*vPC*), and for the Catalyst portfolio, it is called StackWise Virtual (formerly Virtual Switching System [VSS]).

With such a design, shown in Figure 2-2, two switches bound together as one logical system connect to downstream hosts (or access switches) using a link aggregation group, which by its nature can forward traffic over all bundled ports using a hashing mechanism, thus eliminating one of the biggest drawbacks of Spanning Tree.

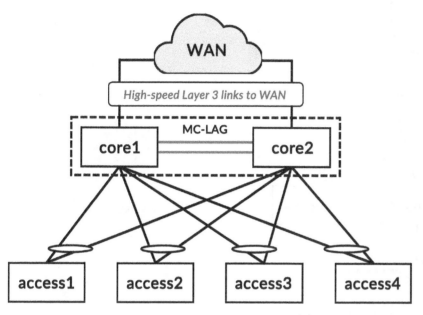

Figure 2-2 *MC-LAG design in enterprise and data centers*

However, this MC-LAG (or vPC/StackWise Virtual) architecture presents its own set of problems, as described here:

- For such an architecture to work, the two switches bundled together must constantly be in sync, since traffic from downstream switches can hash to one switch and return traffic can hash to the other. For this reason, a dedicated physical link is required between the switches to sync state between them (with minimal latency), while another physical link (typically an aggregated group of two or more interfaces) is used as backup for data traffic, in case of downstream/ upstream link failures or for single-homed hosts. In certain cases (such as Cisco vPC), this technology has been advanced further to eliminate the need for a dedicated physical link to sync state, instead using the network fabric itself for this.

- This syncing of state between the switches is vendor-proprietary, following no specific standard. This also implies some form of vendor lock-in, and incompatibility with other vendors.

- Only two devices can be logically bundled in such a state.

- Syncing and tracking state in such a way is hard from a software engineering perspective, often leading to catastrophic bugs and causing high-impact network outages.

Additionally, over time and with the advent of network virtualization, applications also have evolved from traditional client/server architecture to a highly distributed microservices architecture comprised of cloud-native workloads and services. Instead of having all components in the same physical server, they are now spread out, connected to different access switches using a *scale-out* approach, as shown in Figure 2-3. In this figure, two common components of a web application, the database and the browser engine, are now separated into their own servers, connected to different access switches.

To increase server capacity for more users, these components can be scaled out. Another database server can be spun up, connected to a different access switch, with database *sharding* (that is, breaking data into multiple logical datasets, distributed across different database servers). In the same way, a new browser engine can be connected to another access switch, with a load-balancer redirecting requests to each engine.

With this architecture, incoming requests require exponentially higher server-to-server communication since the applications' components are distributed in the network. Thus, this scale-out design has led to increased server-to-server communication and introduced an exponential rise in east-west traffic in data centers. Traditional data centers, with a three-tier architecture, are not designed to handle such a shift in traffic pattern, since they include suboptimal traffic paths, traffic tromboning, and inconsistent latency. This east-west traffic pattern puts considerable burden on the network infrastructure and requires more efficient routing and predictable latency.

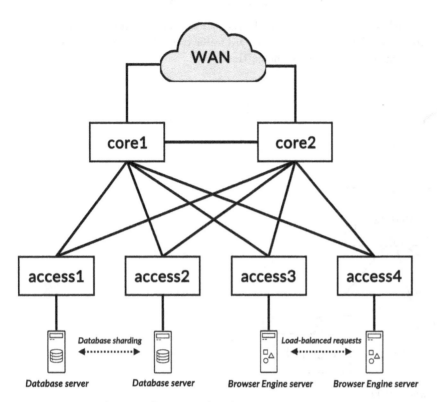

Figure 2-3   *Scale-out architecture of applications*

In 1952, Charles Clos (pronounced *Klo*) wrote a paper, published in the *Bell System Technical Journal* in 1953, describing his formalization of Edson Erwin's concept of building large-scale switching fabrics for telephony systems, popularly known as the *Clos network*. The original paper, titled "A Study of Non-Blocking Switching Networks," is available on the IEEE website and is cited in hundreds of subsequent papers. A Clos network, for telephony systems, was composed of three stages, with each stage having several crossbar switches. The intention behind introducing stages (instead of using just a single large crossbar) was to reduce the number of crosspoint interconnections needed to build large-scale crossbar-like functionality, and thus reduce complexity and cost.

Imagine a strictly non-blocking crossbar switch (often abbreviated to *crossbar*), with *n* inputs and *n* outputs, as shown in Figure 2-4, and with interconnecting lines connecting an input and an output. *Non-blocking* implies that for an idle input line and an idle output line, a connection can be made without interrupting any other connected lines. This is a fundamental property of a crossbar. The complexity of such a crossbar switch is $O(n^2)$.

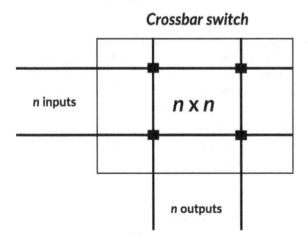

Figure 2-4   *Non-blocking crossbar switch with n input lines and n output lines*

To service more calls, the size of a single crossbar can be increased with respect to the number of input and output lines (and the number of crosspoints). However, such increase in crossbar size implies that the number of crosspoints grows at a rate of

n^2 as well. In addition to this, crossbars have a controller programmed with selection logic, which determines how these connections are made. Exponentially increasing a single crossbar puts a heavy load on this controller, which cannot scale indefinitely.

Thus, instead of looking to scale a single crossbar switch, Clos' idea was to scale by connecting multiple crossbars together, in stages. The three stages in a Clos network are not an arbitrary number of stages, and it is important to understand why. Consider the depiction in Figure 2-5 of crossbars connected in two stages.

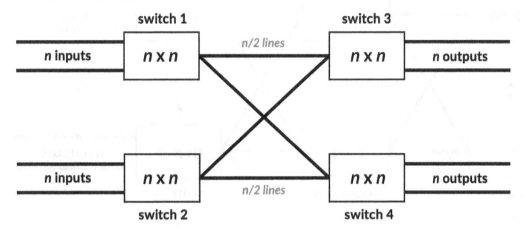

Figure 2-5 *2-stage crossbar interconnection*

In Figure 2-5, four $n \times n$ crossbars are connected in such a way that each crossbar in the first stage has $n/2$ lines going to every crossbar in the second stage. If $n/2$ inputs on switch1 need to connect to output lines in switch3, then all the lines between switch1 and switch3 will be occupied, while still having free input and output lines per switch. Thus, if a new input arrives on switch1 that needs to exit via an output line on switch3, the input is blocked since there are no free lines between the two crossbars. With this 2-stage design, the network is no longer non-blocking.

There are methods to make this 2-stage interconnection non-blocking. This can be achieved using $n \times m$ crossbars, where m is n times the number of crossbars per stage. Considering the same 2-stage interconnection from Figure 2-5, a new variation of this is shown in Figure 2-6, which is now non-blocking because the connection between each crossbar (across stages) is with n lines, and thus n inputs can be sent in a non-blocking fashion to egress any crossbar in the second stage.

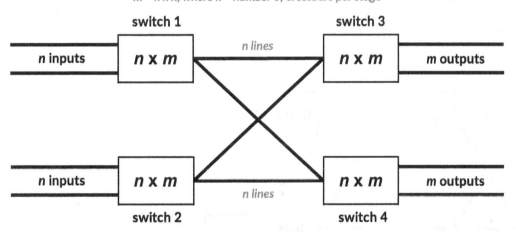

Figure 2-6 *A non-blocking $n \times m$ 2-stage crossbar interconnection*

Thus, while a 2-stage interconnection, as per the design in Figure 2-6, makes the network non-blocking, it does little to reduce the crosspoint complexity. In general, mathematically, this problem is associated with an even number of stages, which is why a 3-stage (odd-numbered stage) network was eventually formalized.

The three stages in the Clos network, for telephony systems, were the input (or ingress) stage, the middle stage, and the output (or egress) stage. The middle stage acts as a fan-out, connecting the ingress and the egress stages, facilitating multiple available paths between them. A call enters the input stage, uses one of the available paths via the middle stage (identified by some form of control logic), and exits the egress stage. This 3-stage Clos network is depicted in Figure 2-7.

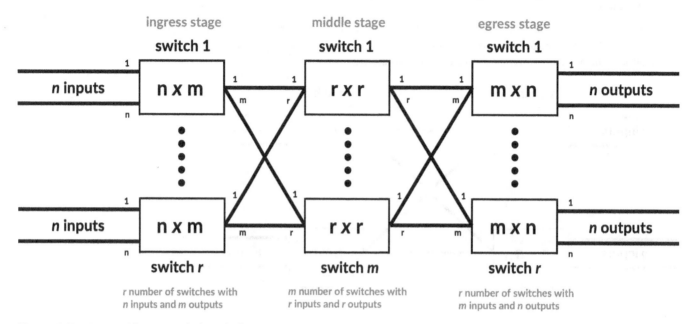

Figure 2-7 *3-stage Clos network for telephony systems*

The 3-stage Clos network, under certain mathematical conditions, is strictly non-blocking, implying that an unused input can be connected to an unused output without impacting any existing connections or calls, which was the basis of the paper published by Charles Clos in 1953. If there is no available path through the network for a new call, then admission into the network is denied via a busy signal. Additionally, it can be proven mathematically (not shown here for the sake of simplicity) that the 3-stage network shown in Figure 2-7 has lower crosspoint complexity than $O(n^2)$.

For packet-switched networks (or data center networks), the 3-stage Clos fabric was adopted as a *folded* fabric, implying that there is no separate ingress or egress stage, since each switch can do both functions. The network is folded at the spines, with the ingress and egress switches on top of one another. Such networks are *non-contending* rather than non-blocking. This means that every host in the network can send traffic to every other host simultaneously, and the network is built with the intelligence to optimize and prioritize traffic flows as needed, to minimize contention. When translating this to packet-switched networks, the crossbars are replaced with network switches. The crossbars in the input and output stages are called the *leafs*, and the crossbars in the middle stage are called the *spines*, as shown in Figure 2-8.

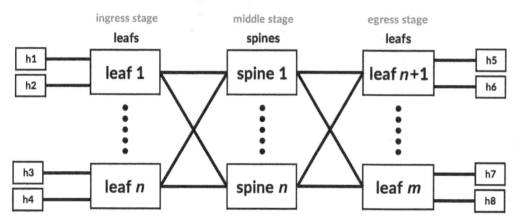

Figure 2-8 *3-stage Clos network for packet-switched networks*

Since there are no fixed ingress or egress stages and the network is a folded fabric (any leaf can be an ingress as well as egress point in the network), this 3-stage Clos network is often redrawn as depicted in Figure 2-9.

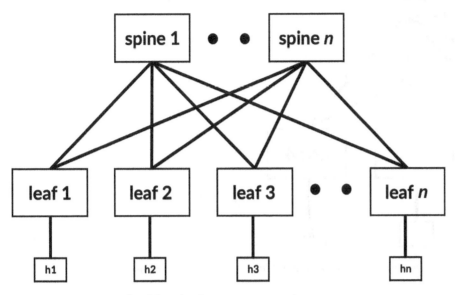

Figure 2-9 *3-stage Clos fabric for data center networks*

While a 3-stage Clos network provides guidance on physical connectivity for the fabric, to deal with the growing server scale with virtualization and the rise of large hyperscalers, other solutions to overcome Layer 2 limitations imposed by Spanning Tree were proposed, the most popular of which was Transparent Interconnections of Lots of Links (TRILL). TRILL was eventually adopted by vendors as their own versions of the protocol, such as FabricPath, implemented by Cisco Systems.

FabricPath was a proprietary adaptation of TRILL, with its own proprietary FabricPath header, understood only by Cisco switches (a subset of Cisco switches only, to be precise). This meant that every hop in the FabricPath network had to be compatible with this protocol, because otherwise it could not be positioned to be a part of the network. Naturally, this was not an industry-wide scalable solution, and eventually the industry converged to adopt standards-based VXLAN instead, initially with a flood-and-learn mechanism and then, with maturity, a BGP EVPN–based control plane. Within this context, VXLAN is the data plane of the network, with BGP EVPN used as the control plane, and the Clos architecture dictating the physical connectivity of the infrastructure.

Data Center Designs and Overlay Architectures

This section provides a high-level overview of the common designs and overlay architectures used in data center fabrics. The following data center designs are covered:

- 3-stage Clos fabric
- 5-stage fabric, also known as a Beneš fabric or a butterfly fabric (or a combination of both)
- Collapsed spine

3-Stage Clos Fabric

A 3-stage Clos fabric, as discussed earlier, is an adaptation for modern data center architecture of the design formalized by Charles Clos for telephony systems. In such a design, the Clos architecture uses point-to-point routed links between the leafs and the spines of the network, moving away from a traditional Layer 2 design. This allows for equal cost distribution of traffic over these paths using an ECMP hash (which is typically a five-tuple hash). Visually, this can be represented as shown in Figure 2-10.

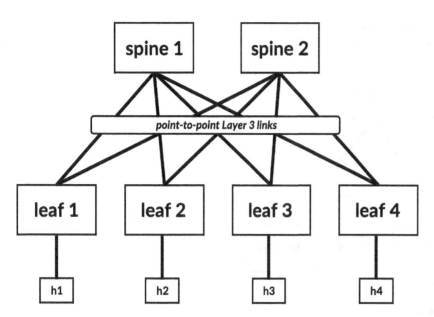

Figure 2-10   *3-stage Clos fabric for data center networks with point-to-point links between leafs and spines*

Such a design is built with the following characteristics:

■ Layer 3 links between leafs and spines, eliminating Layer 2 links and the need for Spanning Tree Protocol.

■ High fan-out via spines, with equal cost paths across multiple spines. This enables load-balancing through the fabric.

■ Scale-out architecture to accommodate increase in data center sizing needs.

■ Modularity in architecture, since leaf to spine connectivity is the same, and these building blocks can be replicated as needed.

■ Every host is the same number of hops away from every other host in the fabric, enabling predictable latency between them.

A 3-stage Clos fabric is an architecture that dictates the physical connectivity between the switches in the fabric, facilitating the actual goal of the network—to provide connectivity between the workloads and the servers in the fabric (and the external world). To provide connectivity between these endpoints, a routing protocol is used. Based on RFC 7938, BGP is the recommended routing protocol, with the spines and leafs establishing an external BGP (eBGP) peering with each other. Such a fabric is called an *IP fabric* and forms the underlay for a VXLAN-based fabric.

Note   Other routing protocols such as OSPF or IS-IS can be used for an IP fabric as well. However, this book is written from the point of view of eBGP as the chosen protocol, based on RFC 7938, section 5.1 of which provides additional detail on why eBGP is more suitable.

A VXLAN fabric, on the other hand, introduces a level of abstraction in the network that elevates the workloads and the services it provides into another layer, called the *overlay*, while using the same physically connected 3-stage Clos network. This is achieved by using a method of data plane encapsulation such as Generic Routing Encapsulation (GRE) or MPLS (which adds an MPLS label). These are tunneling mechanisms, leveraging the underlying network to tunnel packets from one point to another. In the case of VXLAN, a VXLAN header is added, which comprises an IP header, a UDP header, and a VXLAN header. A network device configured for such encapsulation is called a *VXLAN Tunnel Endpoint (VTEP)*. This is explored in more detail in Chapter 4. However, it is important to briefly differentiate here between the underlay and the overlay in a VXLAN fabric.

The *underlay* comprises the Layer 3 point-to-point interfaces between the leafs and the spines, with a routing protocol (eBGP, in this case) used to exchange routing information between the nodes of the fabric. The goal of the underlay is to provide connectivity between the loopbacks of VTEPs in the fabric (typically the leafs) by using eBGP to advertise these addresses. This is shown in Figure 2-11.

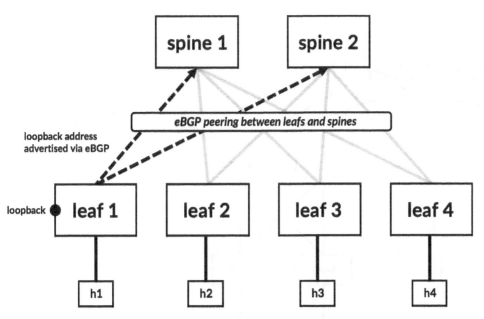

Figure 2-11 *Underlay in a VXLAN 3-stage Clos fabric*

The overlay, as stated earlier, is the data plane encapsulation layer, used to transport packets from one VTEP to another by using an outer IP header added to the original packet, where the source IP address is the loopback of the originating VTEP and the destination IP address is the loopback of the terminating VTEP, as shown in Figure 2-12.

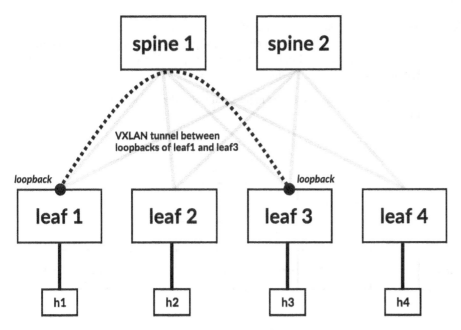

Figure 2-12 *Overlay in a VXLAN 3-stage Clos fabric*

5-Stage Fabric

The 3-stage Clos fabric also forms the basis of building massively scalable data center fabrics. Often called a 5-stage fabric, in this data center design, multiple 3-stage fabrics, referred to as *pods*, are connected using another layer of spines, called *superspines*. A 5-stage fabric is depicted in Figure 2-13, with two 3-stage Clos fabrics (pod1 and po2) connected via a set of superspines.

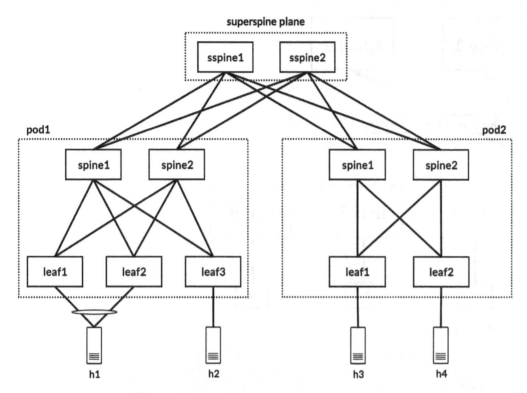

Figure 2-13 *5-stage fabric with two pods*

With a 5-stage fabric, intra-pod traffic stays within the pod while inter-pod traffic traverses the superspine layer. In such a design, different strategies can be used to incorporate scaling per pod and scaling across pods. This includes using unique subnets per pod and exchanging only EVPN Type-5 routes (explored in more detail in Chapter 9, "Routed Overlay and Host-Routed Bridging") between pods for IP connectivity, with no Layer 2 extension across pods.

Like a 3-stage Clos network, the five stages in a 5-stage fabric consider the ingress path and the egress path for a packet that traverses the network, as shown in Figure 2-14.

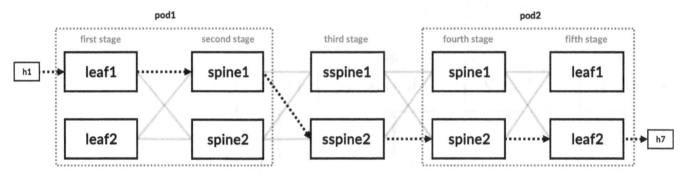

Figure 2-14 *Five stages of 5-stage fabric*

Collapsed Spine Design

As the name suggests, in a collapsed spine design, the leaf and spine function is collapsed into a common spine layer that incorporates the VTEP functionality. This design is typically used for small-scale data centers with predominantly north-south traffic or in migrations where legacy top-of-rack (ToR) switches, generally referred to as *access switches* in this design, do not support EVPN VXLAN and therefore a collapsed spine design is used to connect to these ToR switches, as depicted in Figure 2-15. The spine switches are connected to each other in this design to provide connectivity for single-homed devices or in case of downlink failures from one spine.

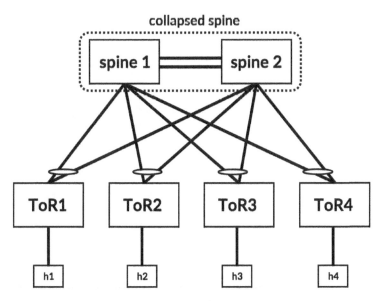

Figure 2-15 *Collapsed spine design for EVPN VXLAN*

With the three types of data center designs discussed in this section, different overlay architectures can be deployed over the physical infrastructure. The most common architectures are bridged overlay, centrally routed bridging overlay (covered in Chapter 7, "Centrally Routed Bridging"), and edge-routed bridging overlay (covered in Chapter 8, "Edge-Routed Bridging").

Summary

This chapter provided an architectural overview of data center networks, with historical context behind the evolution of such an infrastructure and how the advent of server virtualization had direct impact on how data centers are built, moving away from a three-tier design to a 3-stage Clos network to support the increasing needs of server-to-server east-west traffic.

In addition, this chapter provided an overview of common data center designs, such as a 3-stage Clos fabric, a 5-stage Clos fabric, and a collapsed spine.

## Chapter 3

BGP for the Data Center

As described in Chapter 2, "Overview of Data Center Architecture," modern data centers are built with a *scale-out* strategy (rather than a *scale-up* strategy), with predominantly east-west traffic as opposed to the north-south traffic in the traditional three-tier architecture. This shift in strategy was prompted by many factors, including the rise of server virtualization, deployment of high-density server clusters (requiring inter-server communication), new technologies facilitating virtual machine migrations, a shift toward cloud-native applications and workloads, and, more recently, deployment of GPU clusters for artificial intelligence.

In line with this shift in strategy, data center topologies have evolved from a three-tier architecture to a 3-stage Clos architecture (and 5-stage Clos fabrics for large-scale data centers), with the need to eliminate protocols such as Spanning Tree, which made the infrastructure difficult (and more expensive) to operate and maintain due to its inherent nature of blocking redundant paths. Thus, a routing protocol was needed to convert the network natively into Layer 3, with ECMP for traffic forwarding across all available equal cost links. Operational expenditure (OPEX) considerations are equally important as well, since OPEX greatly exceeds capital expenditure (CAPEX) in most IT budgets—the goal should be using a simpler control plane, attempting to reduce control plane interaction as much as possible, and minimizing network downtime due to complex protocols.

In the past, BGP has been used primarily in service provider networks, to provide reachability between autonomous systems globally. BGP was (and still is) the protocol of the Internet, for inter-domain routing. BGP, being a path vector protocol, relies on routing based on policy (with the autonomous system number [ASN] usually acting as a tie-breaker), compared to interior gateway protocols such as Open Shortest Path First (OSPF) and Intermediate System-to-Intermediate System (IS-IS), which use path selection based on a shortest path first logic.

RFC 7938, "Use of BGP for Routing in Large-Scale Data Centers," provides merit to using BGP with a routed design for modern data centers with a 3-stage or 5-stage Clos architecture. For VXLAN fabrics, external BGP (eBGP) can be used for both the underlay and the overlay. This chapter provides a design and implementation perspective of how BGP is adapted for the data center, specifically with eBGP for the underlay, offering the following features for large-scale deployments:

- It enables a simpler implementation, relying on TCP for underlying transport and to establish adjacency between BGP speakers.

- Although BGP is assumed to be slower to converge, with minimal design changes and well-known ASN schemes, such problems are nonexistent.

- Implementing eBGP for the underlay (for the IPv4 or IPv6 address family) and eBGP for the overlay (for the EVPN address family) using BGP groups in Junos provides a clear, vertical separation of the underlay and the overlay.

- Using BGP for both the underlay and overlay provides a simpler operational and maintenance experience. Additionally, eBGP is generally considered easier to deploy and troubleshoot, with internal BGP (iBGP) considered to be more complicated with its need for route reflectors (or confederations) and its best path selection.

■ Implementing auto-discovery of BGP neighbors using link-local IPv6 addressing and leveraging RFC 8950 (which obsoletes RFC 5549) to transport IPv4 Network Layer Reachability Information (NLRI) over an IPv6 peering for the underlay enables plug-and-play behavior for any new leafs and spines.

BGP Path Hunting and ASN Scheme for Data Centers

Every BGP-speaking system requires an ASN to be assigned to exchange network reachability information with other BGP-speaking systems. An iBGP peering is defined as two BGP speakers with the same ASN peering to each other; an eBGP peering is defined as two BGP speakers with different ASNs peering to each other. For the Internet, publicly owned and assigned ASNs are used (allocated by the *Internet Assigned Numbers Authority*, or *IANA*), but this is dangerous for private data centers. One of the most common outages on the Internet is caused by ASN hijacking, in which an organization advertises routes from an ASN that is publicly owned by a different organization or service provider.

For this reason, IANA provides a list of 16-bit and 32-bit private ASNs that organizations can use. The 16-bit private ASNs range from 65412 to 65534, giving only 1023 available ASNs for use. To overcome this limitation, IANA offers 32-bit private ASNs for use as well, providing a much larger range, from 4200000000 to 4294967294. It is imperative that organizations building their own private data centers use ASNs from these private ranges for internal peering.

BGP is designed to route between autonomous systems, where the destination IP prefix is chosen based on the shortest number of AS hops (assuming no policy modification). These AS hops are tracked as part of a BGP attribute called AS_PATH.

In a densely interconnected topology such as a 3-stage Clos network, BGP can suffer from a problem known as *path hunting*. Path hunting occurs when BGP, on losing a route, *hunts* for reachability to the destination via all other available paths, not knowing whether the route still exists in the network or not.

Consider the 3-stage Clos network shown in Figure 3-1, with every node assigned a unique ASN from the 16-bit private ASN range.

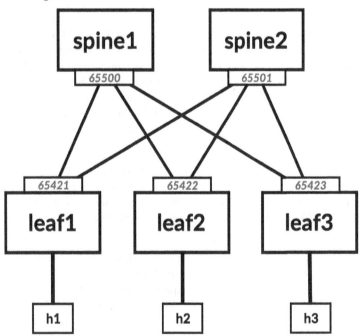

Figure 3-1   *Three-stage Clos network with unique ASNs per fabric node*

In this topology, leaf1 advertises a subnet x/y to spine1, as shown in Figure 3-2. This route is learned on spine1 with an AS_PATH attribute of [65421]. At the same time, the route is also advertised to spine2, and both spines advertise the route to leaf2 and leaf3.

BGP, by default, only advertises the best route to its neighbors. When leaf2 and leaf3 receive this route from both spine1 and spine2, they must elect one path as the best path. With no policy modification, the best path is chosen based on the shortest AS_PATH attribute, but in this case, the AS_PATH length is the same because the route received from spine1 will have an AS_PATH of [65500 65421] and the route received from spine2 will have an AS_PATH of [65501 65421]. Eventually, this tie-breaker is broken by selecting the oldest path. Assuming the elected best path is via spine2 (since it is the oldest path), leaf2 and leaf3 advertise this route to their eBGP peer list, which, in this case, consists only of spine1 (the route cannot be advertised back to spine2 because it originally sent the route that was elected as the best route).

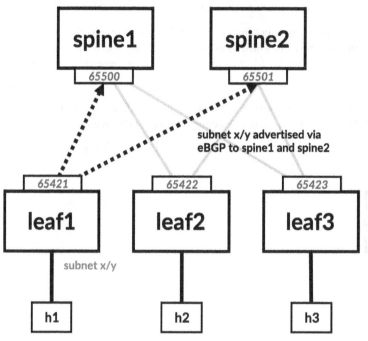

Figure 3-2   *Subnet x/y advertised to spine1 and spine2 by leaf1*

Thus, spine1 receives this route back from leaf2 and leaf3. At this point, spine1 has multiple paths available to reach subnet x/y advertised by leaf1; however, only the direct path (via leaf1) is selected as the best path, since it has the shortest AS_PATH length (again, assuming there are no policy modifications), as shown in Figure 3-3.

Route table on spine1

```
x/y -> leaf1 via [65421] *
    -> leaf2 via [65422 65501 65421]
    -> leaf3 via [65423 65501 65421]
```

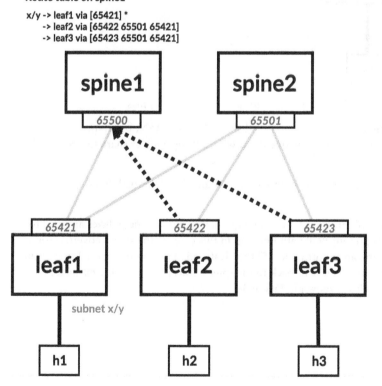

Figure 3-3   *Routing table on spine1 showing all available paths for subnet x/y*

When spine1 loses its best path to subnet x/y, which is via leaf1 (leaf1 goes down or withdraws the route), it hunts for an alternate best path from all available paths. At the same time, spine1 also sends a BGP withdraw to its neighbors, informing them of the lost route via leaf1 for subnet x/y. Eventually, once all withdraws have converged and the subnet has been fully purged from the network, spine1 has no available paths for it, and the route is removed from its routing table.

While this path-hunting behavior might appear to be a minor problem, it becomes increasingly problematic as the fabric size increases with more leafs, creating many alternate paths to hunt through. Thus, to avoid this problem, and to speed up BGP convergence, either of the following two methodologies can be followed, with the same end goal of ensuring that the spines do not learn alternate, suboptimal routes reflected from other leafs:

■ Use an ASN scheme, leveraging eBGP's built-in loop-prevention mechanism of dropping updates that include its own ASN in its AS_PATH list. This is the default BGP behavior, and you do need to configure any additional policies for this.

■ Use routing policies to prevent spines from accepting routes that were originally advertised by any other spine.

This ASN scheme is represented in Figure 3-4.

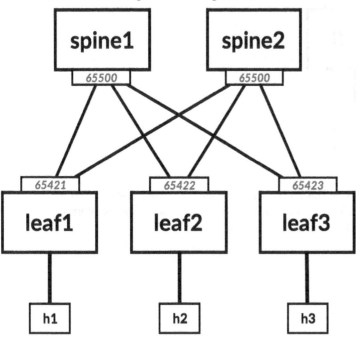

Figure 3-4 *BGP ASN scheme for a 3-stage Clos fabric to avoid path hunting with same ASN on all spines*

For a 5-stage Clos fabric, the ASN scheme mandates that all spines within a pod share the same ASN, but spines across pods have unique ASNs. Additionally, all leafs in each pod are assigned a unique ASN, while all superspines share the same ASN. This ASN scheme is represented in Figure 3-5.

Thus, for a 3-stage or 5-stage Clos fabric, with the ASN schemes shown in Figures 3-4 and 3-5, BGP path hunting is natively prevented.

The second methodology uses an ASN scheme in which all fabric nodes use a unique ASN, and routing policies are used to control how routes are advertised back to the spines to prevent BGP path hunting. In this case, as the spines advertise routes to the leafs, they are tagged with a BGP community using an export policy. On the leafs, an export policy is used to prevent the advertisement of routes with this BGP community from being sent back to the spines, thus preventing the existence of route state on the spines that can lead to path hunting. This is shown in Figure 3-6.

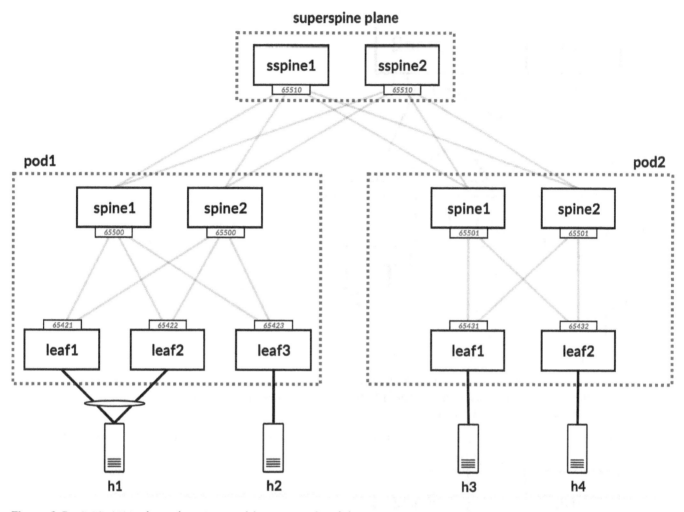

Figure 3-5 *BGP ASN scheme for a 5-stage fabric to avoid path hunting*

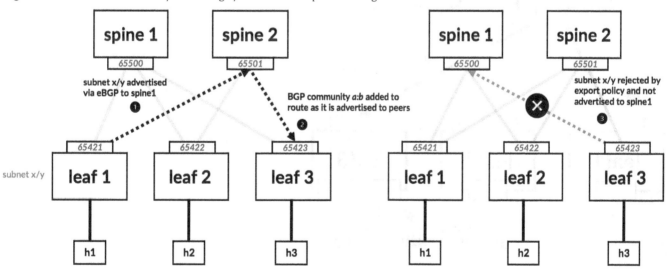

Figure 3-6 *Routing policy logic to prevent path hunting*

This implementation, while more complex and requiring additional operational overhead in the form of policy configuration, is necessary in certain designs where external devices are connected to the fabric for inter-VRF routing. Consider the topology shown in Figure 3-7, where the same ASN is used for both spines and a firewall is connected to leaf3 for inter-VRF routing.

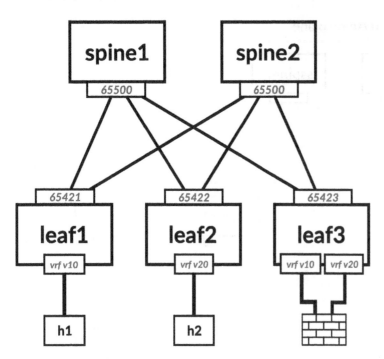

Figure 3-7   *Firewall connected to fabric leaf for inter-VRF routing*

In Figure 3-7, leaf1 is configured with an IP VRF *v10*, which includes an IPv4 subnet 172.16.10.0/24, and leaf2 is configured with an IP VRF *v20*, which includes an IPv4 subnet 172.16.20.0/24. The firewall has a BGP peering to leaf3 over both these IP VRFs to leak routes from one VRF to another.

The IPv4 subnet 172.16.10.0/24 is advertised by leaf1 toward leaf3, and eventually to the firewall, with an AS_PATH list of [65423 65500 65421], as shown in Figure 3-8.

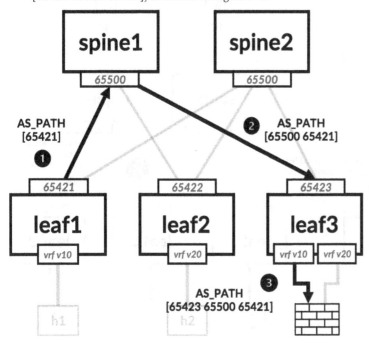

Figure 3-8   *AS_PATH attribute as a prefix, originated by leaf1, is advertised toward firewall*

The firewall "leaks" this route into IP VRF *v20* by advertising it to the VRF-specific BGP neighbor on leaf3. Thus, leaf3 receives this in IP VRF *v20* and advertises it to the rest of the fabric via the spines. However, when the spines receive this BGP update, they drop it because their local ASN is present in the AS_PATH list and BGP loop prevention rules indicate that such an update must be dropped. This is shown in Example 3-1, with BGP debugs on spine1.

Example 3-1 *Spines dropping BGP update due to AS loop prevention rules*

```
Jan 14 17:34:26.497233 BGP RECV 192.0.2.13+179 -> 192.0.2.101+61507

Jan 14 17:34:26.497273 BGP RECV message type 2 (Update) length 128

Jan 14 17:34:26.497369 BGP RECV Update PDU length 128

Jan 14 17:34:26.497452 BGP RECV flags 0x40 code Origin(1): IGP

Jan 14 17:34:26.497517 BGP RECV flags 0x40 code ASPath(2) length 22: 65423 65510 65423 65500 65421

Jan 14 17:34:26.497550 BGP RECV flags 0xc0 code Extended Communities(16): 2:502:502 encapsulation:vxlan(0x8) router-
mac:2c:6b:f5:75:70:f0

Jan 14 17:34:26.497561 BGP RECV flags 0x90 code MP_reach(14): AFI/SAFI 25/70

Jan 14 17:34:26.497577 BGP RECV nhop 192.0.2.13 len 4

Jan 14 17:34:26.497650 BGP RECV 5:192.0.2.14:502::0::172.16.10.0::24/248 (label field value 0x2906 [label 656, VNID
10502]) (esi 00:00:00:00:00:00:00:00:00:00)

Jan 14 17:34:26.497661 End-of-Attributes

Jan 14 17:34:26.497910 As loop detected. Rejecting update
```

snip

Figure 3-9 shows a visual representation of the same behavior.

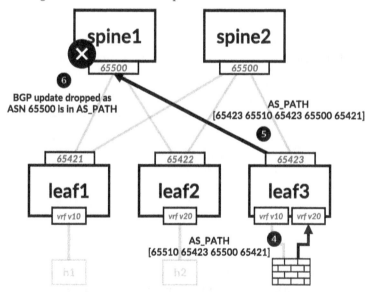

Figure 3-9 *BGP update dropped on spine1 due to local ASN 65500 in AS_PATH*

These problems can be circumvented by allowing the same ASN to be present in the AS_PATH attribute using several con-figuration options in Junos or by using an ASN scheme where each spine is assigned a unique ASN. Intent-based networking systems such as Juniper Apstra take away the complexity of implementing such an ASN scheme by automating and orches-trating the configuration of necessary policies to prevent path hunting (since that is the prevailing problem when each spine is assigned a unique ASN), with no requirement of operator intervention, while also facilitating designs as shown in Figure 3-7.

Implementing BGP for the Underlay

This section provides implementation specifics for building an eBGP underlay for an IP fabric or a VXLAN fabric using net-work devices running Junos. A unique ASN per fabric node design is used to demonstrate how spines can have suboptimal paths that can lead to path hunting, since the implementation of using the same ASNs on all spines in a 3-stage Clos network is straightforward and requires no demonstration. Then, routing policies are implemented to prevent path hunting. The implementation is based on the topology shown earlier in Figure 3-1.

In this network, for the underlay, each fabric-facing interface is configured as a point-to-point Layer 3 interface, as shown in Example 3-2 from the perspective of leaf1.

Example 3-2   *Point-to-point Layer 3 interface configuration on leaf1 for fabric-facing interfaces*

```
admin@leaf1# show interfaces ge-0/0/0
description "To spine1";
mtu 9100;
unit 0 {
    family inet {
        address 198.51.100.0/31;
    }
}

admin@leaf1# show interfaces ge-0/0/1
description "To spine2";
mtu 9100;
unit 0 {
    family inet {
        address 198.51.100.2/31;
    }
}
```

The goal of the underlay is to advertise the loopbacks of the *VXLAN Tunnel Endpoints (VTEPs)*, since these loopbacks are used to build end-to-end VXLAN tunnels. Thus, on each VTEP, which are the fabric leafs in this case, a loopback interface is configured, as shown on leaf1 in Example 3-3.

Example 3-3   *Loopback interface on leaf1*

```
admin@leaf1# show interfaces lo0
unit 0 {
    family inet {
        address 192.0.2.11/32;
    }
}
```

The underlay eBGP peering is between these point-to-point interfaces. Since a leaf's loopback address is sent toward other leafs via multiple spines, each leaf is expected to install multiple, equal cost paths to every other leaf's loopback address. In Junos, to enable ECMP routing, both the protocol (software) and the hardware need to be explicitly enabled to support it. In the case of BGP, this is enabled using the **multipath** knob (with the **multiple-as** configuration option if the routes received have the same AS_PATH length but different ASNs in the list). A subset of the eBGP configuration, for the underlay, is shown from the perspective of both spines and leaf1 in Example 3-4.

Example 3-4   *BGP configuration on spine1, spine2, and leaf1*

```
admin@spine1# show protocols bgp
group underlay {
    type external;
    family inet {
        unicast;
    }
    neighbor 198.51.100.0 {
        peer-as 65421;
    }
```

```
    neighbor 198.51.100.4 {
        peer-as 65422;
    }
    neighbor 198.51.100.8 {
        peer-as 65423;
    }
}

admin@spine2# show protocols bgp
group underlay {
    type external;
    family inet {
        unicast;
    }
    neighbor 198.51.100.2 {
        peer-as 65421;
    }
    neighbor 198.51.100.6 {
        peer-as 65422;
    }
    neighbor 198.51.100.10 {
        peer-as 65423;
    }
}

admin@leaf1# show protocols bgp
group underlay {
    type external;
    family inet {
        unicast;
    }
    export allow-loopback;
    multipath {
        multiple-as;
    }
    neighbor 198.51.100.1 {
        peer-as 65500;
    }
    neighbor 198.51.100.3 {
        peer-as 65501;
    }
}
```

Every leaf is advertising its loopback address via an export policy attached to the BGP group for the underlay, as shown in Example 3-4. The configuration of this policy is shown in Example 3-5, which enables the advertisement of direct routes in the 192.0.2.0/24 range to its eBGP peers.

Example 3-5 *Policy to advertise loopbacks shown on leaf1*

```
admin@leaf1# show policy-options policy-statement allow-loopback
term loopback {
    from {
        protocol direct;
        route-filter 192.0.2.0/24 orlonger;
    }
    then accept;
}
term discard {
    then reject;
}
```

> **Note** It is important to note that each routing protocol is associated with a default routing policy in Junos. For BGP, active BGP routes are readvertised to BGP speakers without the need of an export policy, while following protocol-specific rules, such as those for iBGP neighbors, which is why there is no need for an explicit export policy on the spines to advertise received routes from a leaf to all other leafs.

With the other leafs configured in the same way, the spines can successfully form an eBGP peering with each leaf, as shown in Example 3-6.

Example 3-6 *eBGP peering on spine1 and spine2 with all leafs*

```
admin@spine1> show bgp summary

Threading mode: BGP I/O
Default eBGP mode: advertise - accept, receive - accept
Groups: 1 Peers: 3 Down peers: 0
Table          Tot Paths  Act Paths Suppressed    History Damp State    Pending
inet.0
                     3          3         0           0       0            0
Peer                 AS    InPkt   OutPkt    OutQ   Flaps Last Up/Dwn State|#Active/Received/Accepted/Damped...
198.51.100.0      65421     191      189       0       0    1:24:41 Establ
  inet.0: 1/1/1/0
198.51.100.4      65422     184      182       0       0    1:21:12 Establ
  inet.0: 1/1/1/0
198.51.100.8      65423     180      179       0       0    1:19:35 Establ
  inet.0: 1/1/1/0


admin@spine2> show bgp summary

Threading mode: BGP I/O
Default eBGP mode: advertise - accept, receive - accept
Groups: 1 Peers: 3 Down peers: 0
Table          Tot Paths  Act Paths Suppressed    History Damp State    Pending
inet.0
                     3          3         0           0       0            0
Peer                 AS    InPkt   OutPkt    OutQ   Flaps Last Up/Dwn State|#Active/Received/Accepted/Damped...
```

```
198.51.100.2        65421     194      191      0     0     1:25:52 Establ
  inet.0: 1/1/1/0
198.51.100.6        65422     183      181      0     0     1:20:57 Establ
  inet.0: 1/1/1/0
198.51.100.10       65423     180      179      0     0     1:19:21 Establ
  inet.0: 1/1/1/0
```

With the policy configured as shown in Example 3-5, and the BGP peering between the leafs and the spines in an *Established* state, the loopback address of each leaf should be learned on every other leaf in the fabric.

Consider leaf1 now, to understand how equal cost paths for another leaf's loopback address are installed. For the loopback address of leaf2, advertised by both spine1 and spine2 to leaf1, two routes are received on leaf1. Since BGP is configured with **multipath**, both routes are installed as equal cost routes in software, as shown in Example 3-7.

Example 3-7 *Equal cost routes to leaf2's loopback on leaf1*

```
admin@leaf1> show route table inet.0 192.0.2.12

inet.0: 7 destinations, 9 routes (7 active, 0 holddown, 0 hidden)
Limit/Threshold: 1048576/1048576 destinations
+ = Active Route, - = Last Active, * = Both

192.0.2.12/32       *[BGP/170] 02:10:44, localpref 100, from 198.51.100.1
                       AS path: 65500 65422 I, validation-state: unverified
                       to 198.51.100.1 via ge-0/0/0.0
                    >  to 198.51.100.3 via ge-0/0/1.0
                    [BGP/170] 02:10:44, localpref 100
                       AS path: 65501 65422 I, validation-state: unverified
                    >  to 198.51.100.3 via ge-0/0/1.0
```

A validation-state of *unverified*, as shown in Example 3-7, implies that the BGP route validation feature has not been configured (this is a feature to validate the origin and the path of a BGP route, to ensure that it is legitimate), and the route has been accepted but it was not validated.

These equal cost routes must also be installed in hardware. This is achieved by configuring the Packet Forwarding Engine (PFE) to install equal cost routes, and in turn, program the hardware, by applying an export policy under the **routing-options** hierarchy, as shown in Example 3-8. The policy itself simply enables per-flow load balancing. This example also demonstrates how the forwarding table, on the Routing Engine, can be viewed for a specific destination IP prefix, using the **show route forwarding-table destination** [*ip-address*] **table** [*table-name*] operational mode command.

Example 3-8 *Equal cost routes in PFE of leaf1 with a policy for load-balancing per flow*

```
admin@leaf1# show routing-options forwarding-table
export ecmp;

admin@leaf1# show policy-options policy-statement ecmp
then {
    load-balance per-flow;
}

admin@leaf1> show route forwarding-table destination 192.0.2.12/32 table default
Routing table: default.inet
Internet:
Destination        Type RtRef Next hop           Type Index    NhRef Netif
```

```
192.0.2.12/32     user    0                        ulst  1048574    3
                            198.51.100.1    ucst     583      4 ge-0/0/0.0
                            198.51.100.3    ucst     582      4 ge-0/0/1.0
```

While the control plane and the route installation in both software and hardware are as expected on the leafs, the spines paint a different picture. If the loopback address of the leafs, advertised by spine1 to other leafs, is chosen as the best route, spine2 will receive and store all suboptimal paths in its routing table. Again, considering leaf1's loopback address as an example here, spine2 has three paths for this route, as shown in Example 3-9.

Example 3-9   *Multiple paths for leaf1's loopback address on spine2*

```
admin@spine2> show route table inet.0 192.0.2.11/32


inet.0: 10 destinations, 16 routes (10 active, 0 holddown, 0 hidden)
Limit/Threshold: 1048576/1048576 destinations
+ = Active Route, - = Last Active, * = Both


192.0.2.11/32     *[BGP/170] 15:05:38, localpref 100
                     AS path: 65421 I, validation-state: unverified
                  >  to 198.51.100.2 via ge-0/0/0.0
                   [BGP/170] 00:02:39, localpref 100
                     AS path: 65422 65500 65421 I, validation-state: unverified
                  >  to 198.51.100.6 via ge-0/0/1.0
                   [BGP/170] 00:01:02, localpref 100
                     AS path: 65423 65500 65421 I, validation-state: unverified
                  >  to 198.51.100.10 via ge-0/0/2.0
```

This includes the direct path via leaf1, an indirect path via leaf2, and another indirect path via leaf3. Thus, in this case, if spine2 loses the direct path via leaf1, it will start path hunting through the other suboptimal paths, until the network fully converges with all withdraws processed on all fabric nodes. This problem can be addressed by applying an export policy on the spines that adds a BGP community to all advertised routes, and then using this community on the leafs to match and reject such routes from being advertised back to the spines.

In Junos, a routing policy controls the import of routes into the routing table and the export of routes from the routing table, to be advertised to neighbors. In general, a routing policy consists of terms, which include match conditions and associated actions. The routing policy on the spines is shown in Example 3-10 and includes the following two policy terms:

- **all-bgp:** Matches all BGP learned routes, accepts them, and adds a community value from the community name spine-to-leaf.

- **loopback:** Matches all direct routes in the IPv4 subnet 192.0.2.0/24. The **orlonger** configuration option matches any IPv4 address that is equal to or longer than the defined prefix length.

Example 3-10   *Policy to add a BGP community on the spines as they advertise routes to leafs*

```
admin@spine2# show policy-options policy-statement spine-to-leaf
term all-bgp {
    from protocol bgp;
    then {
        community add spine-to-leaf;
        accept;
    }
}
```

```
term loopback {
    from {
        protocol direct;
        route-filter 192.0.2.0/24 orlonger;
    }
    then {
        community add spine-to-leaf;
        accept;
    }
}
```

```
admin@spine2# show policy-options community spine-to-leaf
members 0:15;
```

Once the policy in Example 3-10 is applied as an export policy on the spines for the underlay BGP group, the leafs receive all BGP routes attached with a BGP community of value 0:15. This can be confirmed on leaf2, taking leaf1's loopback address into consideration, as shown in Example 3-11.

Example 3-11 *Leaf1's loopback address received with a BGP community of 0:15 on leaf2*

```
admin@leaf2> show route table inet.0 192.0.2.11/32 extensive

inet.0: 9 destinations, 12 routes (9 active, 0 holddown, 0 hidden)
Limit/Threshold: 1048576/1048576 destinations
192.0.2.11/32 (2 entries, 1 announced)
TSI:
KRT in-kernel 192.0.2.11/32 -> {list:198.51.100.5, 198.51.100.7}
Page 0 idx 0, (group underlay type External) Type 1 val 0x85194a0 (adv_entry)
   Advertised metrics:
     Nexthop: 198.51.100.5
     AS path: [65422] 65500 65421 I
     Communities: 0:15
   Advertise: 00000002
Path 192.0.2.11
from 198.51.100.5
Vector len 4.  Val: 0
        *BGP    Preference: 170/-101
                Next hop type: Router, Next hop index: 0
                Address: 0x7a46fac
                Next-hop reference count: 3, Next-hop session id: 0
                Kernel Table Id: 0
                Source: 198.51.100.5
                Next hop: 198.51.100.5 via ge-0/0/0.0
                Session Id: 0
                Next hop: 198.51.100.7 via ge-0/0/1.0, selected
                Session Id: 0
                State: <Active Ext>
                Local AS: 65422 Peer AS: 65500
                Age: 3:35
```

```
                Validation State: unverified
                Task: BGP_65500.198.51.100.5
                Announcement bits (3): 0-KRT 1-BGP_Multi_Path 2-BGP_RT_Background
                AS path: 65500 65421 I
                Communities: 0:15
                Accepted Multipath
                Localpref: 100
                Router ID: 192.0.2.101
                Thread: junos-main
        BGP     Preference: 170/-101
                Next hop type: Router, Next hop index: 577
                Address: 0x77c63f4
                Next-hop reference count: 5, Next-hop session id: 321
                Kernel Table Id: 0
                Source: 198.51.100.7
                Next hop: 198.51.100.7 via ge-0/0/1.0, selected
                Session Id: 321
                State: <Ext>
                Inactive reason: Active preferred
                Local AS: 65422 Peer AS: 65501
                Age: 5:30
                Validation State: unverified
                Task: BGP_65501.198.51.100.7
                AS path: 65501 65421 I
                Communities: 0:15
                Accepted MultipathContrib
                Localpref: 100
                Router ID: 192.0.2.102
                Thread: junos-main
```

On the leafs, it is now a simple matter of rejecting any route that has this community to stop it from being readvertised back to the spines. A new policy is created for this, and it is applied using an *and* operation to the existing policy that advertises the loopback address, as shown in Example 3-12 from the perspective of leaf1.

Example 3-12   *Policy on leaf1 to reject BGP routes with a community of 0:15*

```
admin@leaf1# show policy-options policy-statement leaf-to-spine
term reject-to-spine {
    from {
        protocol bgp;
        community spine-to-leaf;
    }
    then reject;
}
term accept-all {
    then accept;
}

admin@leaf1# show policy-options community spine-to-leaf
members 0:15;
```

```
admin@leaf1# show protocols bgp
group underlay {
    type external;
    family inet {
        unicast;
    }
    export ( leaf-to-spine && allow-loopback );
    multipath {
        multiple-as;
    }
    neighbor 198.51.100.1 {
        peer-as 65500;
    }
    neighbor 198.51.100.3 {
        peer-as 65501;
    }
}
```

With this policy applied on all the leafs, the spines will not learn any suboptimal paths to each of the leaf loopbacks. This is confirmed in Example 3-13, with each spine learning every leaf's loopback address via the direct path to the respective leaf.

Example 3-13   *Route to each leaf's loopback address on spine1 and spine2*

```
admin@spine1> show route table inet.0 192.0.2.11/32

inet.0: 10 destinations, 10 routes (10 active, 0 holddown, 0 hidden)
Limit/Threshold: 1048576/1048576 destinations
+ = Active Route, - = Last Active, * = Both

192.0.2.11/32      *[BGP/170] 15:45:36, localpref 100
                      AS path: 65421 I, validation-state: unverified
                   >  to 198.51.100.0 via ge-0/0/0.0

admin@spine1> show route table inet.0 192.0.2.12/32

inet.0: 10 destinations, 10 routes (10 active, 0 holddown, 0 hidden)
Limit/Threshold: 1048576/1048576 destinations
+ = Active Route, - = Last Active, * = Both

192.0.2.12/32      *[BGP/170] 15:42:09, localpref 100
                      AS path: 65422 I, validation-state: unverified
                   >  to 198.51.100.4 via ge-0/0/1.0

admin@spine1> show route table inet.0 192.0.2.13/32

inet.0: 10 destinations, 10 routes (10 active, 0 holddown, 0 hidden)
Limit/Threshold: 1048576/1048576 destinations
+ = Active Route, - = Last Active, * = Both
```

```
192.0.2.13/32       *[BGP/170] 15:40:35, localpref 100
                       AS path: 65423 I, validation-state: unverified
                    >  to 198.51.100.8 via ge-0/0/2.0


admin@spine2> show route table inet.0 192.0.2.11/32


inet.0: 10 destinations, 10 routes (10 active, 0 holddown, 0 hidden)
Limit/Threshold: 1048576/1048576 destinations
+ = Active Route, - = Last Active, * = Both


192.0.2.11/32       *[BGP/170] 15:47:10, localpref 100
                       AS path: 65421 I, validation-state: unverified
                    >  to 198.51.100.2 via ge-0/0/0.0


admin@spine2> show route table inet.0 192.0.2.12/32


inet.0: 10 destinations, 10 routes (10 active, 0 holddown, 0 hidden)
Limit/Threshold: 1048576/1048576 destinations
+ = Active Route, - = Last Active, * = Both


192.0.2.12/32       *[BGP/170] 15:42:18, localpref 100
                       AS path: 65422 I, validation-state: unverified
                    >  to 198.51.100.6 via ge-0/0/1.0


admin@spine2> show route table inet.0 192.0.2.13/32


inet.0: 10 destinations, 10 routes (10 active, 0 holddown, 0 hidden)
Limit/Threshold: 1048576/1048576 destinations
+ = Active Route, - = Last Active, * = Both


192.0.2.13/32       *[BGP/170] 15:40:45, localpref 100
                       AS path: 65423 I, validation-state: unverified
                    >  to 198.51.100.10 via ge-0/0/2.0
```

Junos also offers the operator a direct way to test the policy, which can be used to confirm that a leaf's locally owned loopback address is being advertised to the spines, and other loopback addresses learned via BGP are rejected. This uses the **test policy** operational mode command, as shown in Example 3-14, where only leaf1's loopback address (192.0.2.11/32) is accepted by the policy, while leaf2's and leaf3's loopback addresses, 192.0.2.12/32 and 192.0.2.13/32 respectively, are rejected by the policy.

Example 3-14   *Policy rejecting leaf2's and leaf3's loopback addresses from being advertised to the spines on leaf1*

```
admin@leaf1> test policy leaf-to-spine 192.0.2.11/32


inet.0: 9 destinations, 11 routes (9 active, 0 holddown, 0 hidden)
Limit/Threshold: 1048576/1048576 destinations
+ = Active Route, - = Last Active, * = Both


192.0.2.11/32       *[Direct/0] 1d 04:38:27
                    >  via lo0.0
```

```
Policy leaf-to-spine: 1 prefix accepted, 0 prefix rejected

admin@leaf1> test policy leaf-to-spine 192.0.2.12/32

Policy leaf-to-spine: 0 prefix accepted, 1 prefix rejected

admin@leaf1> test policy leaf-to-spine 192.0.2.13/32

Policy leaf-to-spine: 0 prefix accepted, 1 prefix rejected
```

With this configuration in place, the fabric underlay is successfully built, with each leaf's loopback address reachable from every other leaf, as shown in Example 3-15, while also preventing any path-hunting issues on the spines by using appropriate routing policies.

Example 3-15 *Loopback reachability from leaf1*

```
admin@leaf1> ping 192.0.2.12 source 192.0.2.11
PING 192.0.2.12 (192.0.2.12): 56 data bytes
64 bytes from 192.0.2.12: icmp_seq=0 ttl=63 time=3.018 ms
64 bytes from 192.0.2.12: icmp_seq=1 ttl=63 time=2.697 ms
64 bytes from 192.0.2.12: icmp_seq=2 ttl=63 time=4.773 ms
64 bytes from 192.0.2.12: icmp_seq=3 ttl=63 time=3.470 ms
^C
--- 192.0.2.12 ping statistics ---
4 packets transmitted, 4 packets received, 0% packet loss
round-trip min/avg/max/stddev = 2.697/3.490/4.773/0.790 ms


admin@leaf1> ping 192.0.2.13 source 192.0.2.11
PING 192.0.2.13 (192.0.2.13): 56 data bytes
64 bytes from 192.0.2.13: icmp_seq=0 ttl=63 time=2.979 ms
64 bytes from 192.0.2.13: icmp_seq=1 ttl=63 time=2.814 ms
64 bytes from 192.0.2.13: icmp_seq=2 ttl=63 time=2.672 ms
64 bytes from 192.0.2.13: icmp_seq=3 ttl=63 time=2.379 ms
^C
--- 192.0.2.13 ping statistics ---
4 packets transmitted, 4 packets received, 0% packet loss
round-trip min/avg/max/stddev = 2.379/2.711/2.979/0.220 ms
```

Auto-Discovered BGP Neighbors

The previous section demonstrated how to build an eBGP-based fabric underlay using point-to-point Layer 3 interfaces. This requires extensive IP management and operational maintenance as the fabric grows. An alternate, more efficient approach is to use a BGP feature called *BGP auto-discovery* (also referred to as *BGP unnumbered*), which uses link-local IPv6 addressing to automatically peer with its discovered neighbor by leveraging IPv6 Neighbor Discovery (ND). This is very beneficial for several reasons:

- It eliminates the need for IP address management of the underlay and enables plug-and-play insertion of new fabric nodes.

- It allows for easier automation of the underlay of the fabric since every fabric interface is configured the same way, with no IP addressing required. BGP, unlike IGPs, is designed to peer with untrusted neighbors, and thus the default need to specify a peer address, assign an ASN, and configure authentication for BGP peering. In a data center, which is largely a trusted environment, BGP is utilized more like an IGP, which makes automating it much easier, reducing any configuration complexity.

This section provides an implementation example of how to configure and deploy BGP auto-discovery, using packet captures for a deeper understanding of the same. The topology shown in Figure 3-10 is used to demonstrate this feature.

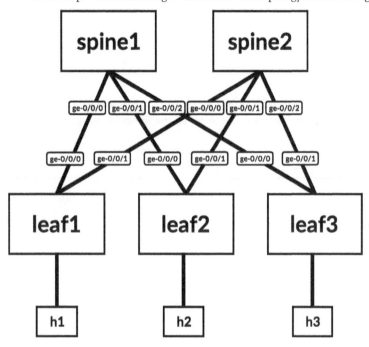

Figure 3-10   *Topology to implement BGP auto-discovered neighbors*

BGP auto-discovery relies on IPv6 Neighbor Discovery Protocol (NDP), which uses ICMPv6 messages to announce its link-local IPv6 address to its directly attached neighbors and learn the neighbors' link-local IPv6 addresses from inbound ICMPv6 messages, replacing the traditional IPv4 ARP process. More specifically, this is achieved using an ICMPv6 message type called *Router Advertisement (RA)*, which has an opcode of 134.

To enable BGP auto-discovery, the following steps must be done:

■ Enable IPv6 on the fabric-facing point-to-point interfaces. The IPv4 family must be enabled as well if IPv4 traffic is expected on the interface. Even though the peering between neighbors uses IPv6, the interface can carry traffic for any address family. No IPv6 or IPv4 address is required to be configured on these interfaces.

■ Enable **protocol router-advertisements** on the fabric-facing interfaces (the default RA interval is 15 seconds).

■ Configure BGP to automatically discover peers using IPv6 ND by enabling the underlay group for the IPv6 unicast address family and using the **dynamic-neighbor** hierarchy to define neighbor discovery using IPv6 ND for the fabric-facing interfaces.

■ Configure BGP for the IPv4 unicast address family, with the **extended-nexthop** configuration option. This allows IPv4 routes to be advertised via BGP with an IPv6 next-hop using a new BGP capability defined in RFC 8950 (which obsoletes RFC 5549) called the Extended Next Hop Encoding capability. This capability is exchanged in the BGP OPEN message.

The configuration of spine1 is shown in Example 3-16 as a reference. For the spines, since each leaf is in a different ASN, the **peer-as-list** configuration option is used to specify a list of allowed peer ASNs to which a BGP peering can be established. It is important that this peer ASN list be carefully curated, since a peering request from any other ASN (outside of this list) will be rejected.

Example 3-16 *BGP auto-discovery configuration on spine1*

```
admin@spine1# show interfaces
ge-0/0/0 {
    unit 0 {
        family inet;
        family inet6;
    }
}
ge-0/0/1 {
    unit 0 {
        family inet;
        family inet6;
    }
}
ge-0/0/2 {
    unit 0 {
        family inet;
        family inet6;
    }
}

admin@spine1# show protocols router-advertisement
interface ge-0/0/0.0;
interface ge-0/0/1.0;
interface ge-0/0/2.0;

admin@spine1# show protocols bgp
group auto-underlay {
    family inet {
        unicast {
            extended-nexthop;
        }
    }
    family inet6 {
        unicast;
    }
    dynamic-neighbor underlay {
        peer-auto-discovery {
            family inet6 {
                ipv6-nd;
            }
            interface ge-0/0/0.0;
            interface ge-0/0/1.0;
            interface ge-0/0/2.0;
        }
    }
    peer-as-list leafs;
}
```

Once the respective fabric interfaces are enabled with IPv6 RA, the fabric nodes discover each other's link-local IPv6 addresses. For example, leaf1 has discovered spine1's and spine2's link-local IPv6 addresses (as well as the corresponding MAC addresses) over its directly attached interfaces, as shown in Example 3-17, using the **show ipv6 neighbors** operational mode command.

Example 3-17 *IPv6 neighbors discovered using RA on leaf1*

```
admin@leaf1> show ipv6 neighbors
IPv6 Address                    Linklayer Address State      Exp  Rtr  Secure  Interface
fe80::e00:b3ff:fe09:1001        0c:00:b3:09:10:01  reachable  9    yes  no      ge-0/0/1.0
fe80::e00:ffff:fee3:3201        0c:00:ff:e3:32:01  reachable  14   yes  no      ge-0/0/0.0
Total entries: 2
```

This process of sending Router Advertisements can be seen in the packet capture shown in Figure 3-11, from the perspective of the link between leaf1 and spine1.

```
No.   Time     Source                  Destination             Protocol  Length  Info
  4 2023-1…  fe80::e00:ffff:fee3:3201  ff02::1                 ICMP…     78   Router Advertisement from 0c:00:ff:e3:32:01
  6 2023-1…  fe80::e00:ecff:fe11:c601  ff02::1                 ICMP…     78   Router Advertisement from 0c:00:ec:11:c6:01
 10 2023-1…  fe80::e00:ecff:fe11:c601  fe80::e00:ffff:fee3:3201  BGP     167  OPEN Message
 11 2023-1…  fe80::e00:ffff:fee3:3201  fe80::e00:ecff:fe11:c601  BGP     167  OPEN Message
 13 2023-1…  fe80::e00:ffff:fee3:3201  fe80::e00:ecff:fe11:c601  BGP     105  KEEPALIVE Message
 14 2023-1…  fe80::e00:ecff:fe11:c601  fe80::e00:ffff:fee3:3201  BGP     105  KEEPALIVE Message
 16 2023-1…  fe80::e00:ffff:fee3:3201  fe80::e00:ecff:fe11:c601  BGP     146  UPDATE Message, UPDATE Message
 17 2023-1…  fe80::e00:ecff:fe11:c601  fe80::e00:ffff:fee3:3201  BGP     146  UPDATE Message, UPDATE Message
```

```
> Frame 4: 78 bytes on wire (624 bits), 78 bytes captured (624 bits)           0000  33 33 00 00
> Ethernet II, Src: 0c:00:ff:e3:32:01 (0c:00:ff:e3:32:01), Dst: IPv6mcast_01 (33:33:00:00:00:01)   0010  00 00 00 18
> Internet Protocol Version 6, Src: fe80::e00:ffff:fee3:3201, Dst: ff02::1      0020  ff ff fe e3
v Internet Control Message Protocol v6                                          0030  00 00 00 00
    Type: Router Advertisement (134)                                            0040  00 00 00 00
    Code: 0
    Checksum: 0xb754 [correct]
    [Checksum Status: Good]
    Cur hop limit: 64
  > Flags: 0x00, Prf (Default Router Preference): Medium
    Router lifetime (s): 1800
    Reachable time (ms): 0
    Retrans timer (ms): 0
  v ICMPv6 Option (Source link-layer address : 0c:00:ff:e3:32:01)
      Type: Source link-layer address (1)
      Length: 1 (8 bytes)
      Link-layer address: 0c:00:ff:e3:32:01 (0c:00:ff:e3:32:01)
```

Figure 3-11 *Packet capture of ICMPv6 Router Advertisement*

Packet #4, highlighted in Figure 3-11, is an ICMPv6 Router Advertisement sent by spine1, while packet #5 is an ICMPv6 Router Advertisement sent by leaf1. Such packets are sent using the link-local IPv6 address as the source, destined to the well-known IPv6 multicast group of FF02::1. The link-local IPv6 address of leaf1's interface can be confirmed as shown in Example 3-18.

Example 3-18 *IPv6 link-local address assigned to ge-0/0/0.0 on leaf1*

```
admin@leaf1> show interfaces ge-0/0/0.0
  Logical interface ge-0/0/0.0 (Index 349) (SNMP ifIndex 540)
    Flags: Up SNMP-Traps 0x4004000 Encapsulation: ENET2
    Input packets : 847
    Output packets: 857
    Protocol inet, MTU: 1500
    Max nh cache: 100000, New hold nh limit: 100000, Curr nh cnt: 0, Curr new hold cnt: 0,
    NH drop cnt: 0
      Flags: Sendbcast-pkt-to-re, Is-Primary, 0x0
```

```
Protocol inet6, MTU: 1500
Max nh cache: 100000, New hold nh limit: 100000, Curr nh cnt: 1, Curr new hold cnt: 0,
NH drop cnt: 0
  Flags: Is-Primary, 0x0
  Addresses, Flags: Is-Preferred 0x800
    Destination: fe80::/64, Local: fe80::e00:ecff:fe11:c601
Protocol multiservice, MTU: Unlimited
  Flags: Is-Primary, 0x0
```

With the link-local IPv6 addresses discovered for a given link, a TCP session can be initiated to establish BGP peering between the fabric nodes. The entire communication is IPv6 only, including the initial TCP three-way handshake and all the BGP messages exchanged between the prospective neighbors, such as the BGP OPEN and the BGP UPDATE messages shown in Figure 3-11.

The entire handshake, as well as the instantiation of the BGP session, is shown in Figure 3-12 as a reference.

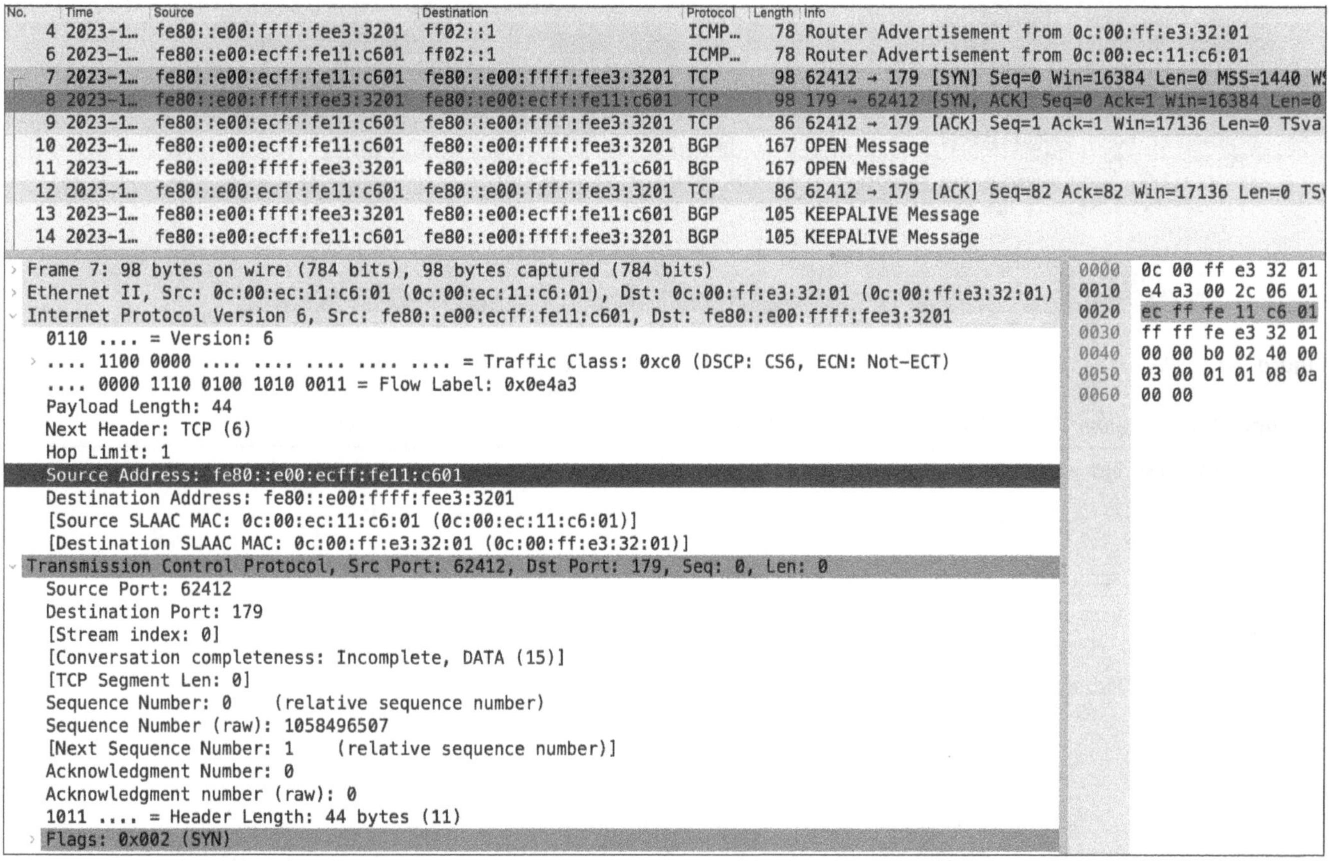

Figure 3-12 *Packet capture of TCP three-way handshake using IPv6 link-local addresses*

In the BGP OPEN message exchanged between spine1 and leaf1, the extended next-hop capability is advertised, confirming that both devices support IPv4 NLRI encoded with an IPv6 next-hop address, as shown in Figure 3-13.

Once all leafs and spines are configured in the same way, an eBGP peering is established between the fabric nodes, as shown in Example 3-19 from the perspective of spine1 and spine2.

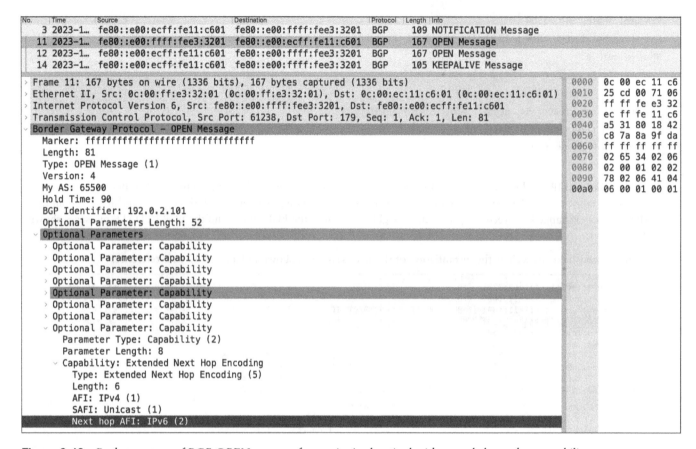

Figure 3-13   *Packet capture of BGP OPEN message from spine1 advertised with extended next-hop capability*

Example 3-19   *Summary of BGP peers on spine1 and spine2*

```
admin@spine1> show bgp summary

Threading mode: BGP I/O

Default eBGP mode: advertise - accept, receive - accept

Groups: 1 Peers: 3 Down peers: 0

Auto-discovered peers: 3

Table          Tot Paths  Act Paths Suppressed   History Damp State    Pending
inet.0
                       0          0          0         0         0           0
inet6.0
                       0          0          0         0         0           0
Peer                    AS     InPkt    OutPkt    OutQ    Flaps Last Up/Dwn State|#Active/Received/Accepted/Damped...
fe80::e00:36ff:fe96:af01%ge-0/0/1.0    65422    207    205    0    0    1:31:38 Establ
  inet.0: 0/0/0/0
  inet6.0: 0/0/0/0
fe80::e00:bdff:fed8:c901%ge-0/0/2.0    65423    206    204    0    0    1:31:00 Establ
  inet.0: 0/0/0/0
  inet6.0: 0/0/0/0
fe80::e00:ecff:fe11:c601%ge-0/0/0.0    65421    275    273    0    0    2:02:23 Establ
  inet.0: 0/0/0/0
  inet6.0: 0/0/0/0
```

```
admin@spine2> show bgp summary


Threading mode: BGP I/O

Default eBGP mode: advertise - accept, receive - accept

Groups: 1 Peers: 3 Down peers: 0

Auto-discovered peers: 3

Table           Tot Paths  Act Paths Suppressed   History Damp State   Pending
inet.0
                     0          0          0          0        0          0
inet6.0
                     0          0          0          0        0          0
Peer                   AS     InPkt    OutPkt    OutQ   Flaps Last Up/Dwn State|#Active/Received/Accepted/Damped...
fe80::e00:11ff:fe86:9602%ge-0/0/1.0      65422      207       206       0      0   1:31:54 Establ
  inet.0: 0/0/0/0
  inet6.0: 0/0/0/0
fe80::e00:7dff:fe45:5902%ge-0/0/0.0      65421      211       209       0      0   1:33:18 Establ
  inet.0: 0/0/0/0
  inet6.0: 0/0/0/0
fe80::e00:95ff:feec:8502%ge-0/0/2.0      65423      206       205       0      0   1:31:16 Establ
  inet.0: 0/0/0/0
  inet6.0: 0/0/0/0
```

The last piece of the puzzle is how IPv4 routes are advertised over this IPv6 BGP peering. Since the BGP group is configured to use an extended next-hop for the IPv4 address family, IPv4 routes can be advertised with an IPv6 next-hop address, as shown in Figure 3-14. In this packet capture, leaf1's loopback address, 192.0.2.11/32, is advertised with an IPv6 next-hop address that matches leaf1's respective link-local IPv6 address.

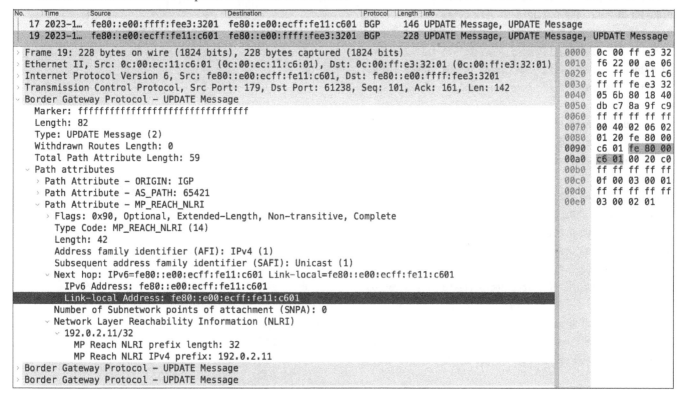

Figure 3-14 *Packet capture of leaf1's IPv4 loopback address advertised with an IPv6 next-hop*

Taking leaf1 as an example again, all remote leaf loopback addresses are now learned with IPv6 next-hop addresses, as shown in Example 3-20, which also confirms loopback to loopback reachability between the leafs.

Example 3-20   *IPv4 loopback addresses learned with an IPv6 next-hop*

```
admin@leaf1> show route table inet.0

inet.0: 3 destinations, 5 routes (3 active, 0 holddown, 0 hidden)
Limit/Threshold: 1048576/1048576 destinations
+ = Active Route, - = Last Active, * = Both


192.0.2.11/32      *[Direct/0] 1d 11:41:30
                    > via lo0.0
192.0.2.12/32      *[BGP/170] 00:00:27, localpref 100
                      AS path: 65500 65422 I, validation-state: unverified
                    > to fe80::e00:ffff:fee3:3201 via ge-0/0/0.0
                    [BGP/170] 00:00:27, localpref 100
                      AS path: 65500 65422 I, validation-state: unverified
                    > to fe80::e00:b3ff:fe09:1001 via ge-0/0/1.0
192.0.2.13/32      *[BGP/170] 00:00:07, localpref 100
                      AS path: 65500 65423 I, validation-state: unverified
                    > to fe80::e00:b3ff:fe09:1001 via ge-0/0/1.0
                    [BGP/170] 00:00:07, localpref 100
                      AS path: 65500 65423 I, validation-state: unverified
                    > to fe80::e00:ffff:fee3:3201 via ge-0/0/0.0


admin@leaf1> ping 192.0.2.12 source 192.0.2.11
PING 192.0.2.12 (192.0.2.12): 56 data bytes
64 bytes from 192.0.2.12: icmp_seq=0 ttl=63 time=3.290 ms
64 bytes from 192.0.2.12: icmp_seq=1 ttl=63 time=2.319 ms
64 bytes from 192.0.2.12: icmp_seq=2 ttl=63 time=2.914 ms
64 bytes from 192.0.2.12: icmp_seq=3 ttl=63 time=2.259 ms
^C
--- 192.0.2.12 ping statistics ---
4 packets transmitted, 4 packets received, 0% packet loss
round-trip min/avg/max/stddev = 2.259/2.696/3.290/0.428 ms


admin@leaf1> ping 192.0.2.13 source 192.0.2.11
PING 192.0.2.13 (192.0.2.13): 56 data bytes
64 bytes from 192.0.2.13: icmp_seq=0 ttl=63 time=2.849 ms
64 bytes from 192.0.2.13: icmp_seq=1 ttl=63 time=2.453 ms
64 bytes from 192.0.2.13: icmp_seq=2 ttl=63 time=2.734 ms
64 bytes from 192.0.2.13: icmp_seq=3 ttl=63 time=2.936 ms
^C
--- 192.0.2.13 ping statistics ---
4 packets transmitted, 4 packets received, 0% packet loss
round-trip min/avg/max/stddev = 2.453/2.743/2.936/0.182 ms
```

From the perspective of the data plane, there is no change—the underlay is purely hop-by-hop routing, with a resolution of the Layer 2 address (MAC address) required for every hop. This is already resolved using the IPv6 Router Advertisement messages exchanged between the leafs and the spines, as shown in Example 3-17. Thus, the packet is still an IPv4 packet as shown in Figure 3-15, which is a packet capture of leaf1's reachability to leaf2's loopback address using the **ping** tool, while sourcing its own loopback address.

```
No.   Time        Source        Destination   Protocol  Length Info
   1 2023-1…  192.0.2.11    192.0.2.12    ICMP      98 Echo (ping) request    id=0x4d46, seq=63/16128, ttl=64 (reply in 2)
   2 2023-1…  192.0.2.12    192.0.2.11    ICMP      98 Echo (ping) reply      id=0x4d46, seq=63/16128, ttl=63 (request in 1)
   3 2023-1…  192.0.2.11    192.0.2.12    ICMP      98 Echo (ping) request    id=0x4d46, seq=64/16384, ttl=64 (reply in 4)
   4 2023-1…  192.0.2.12    192.0.2.11    ICMP      98 Echo (ping) reply      id=0x4d46, seq=64/16384, ttl=63 (request in 3)

> Frame 1: 98 bytes on wire (784 bits), 98 bytes captured (784 bits)        0000  0c 00 ff e3 32
v Ethernet II, Src: 0c:00:ec:11:c6:01 (0c:00:ec:11:c6:01), Dst: 0c:00:ff:e3:32:01 (0c:00:ff:e3:32:01)  0010  00 54 a1 be 00
  > Destination: 0c:00:ff:e3:32:01 (0c:00:ff:e3:32:01)                      0020  02 0c 08 00 23
  > Source: 0c:00:ec:11:c6:01 (0c:00:ec:11:c6:01)                           0030  8e 59 08 09 0a
    Type: IPv4 (0x0800)                                                     0040  16 17 18 19 1a
v Internet Protocol Version 4, Src: 192.0.2.11, Dst: 192.0.2.12            0050  26 27 28 29 2a
    0100 .... = Version: 4                                                  0060  36 37
    .... 0101 = Header Length: 20 bytes (5)
  > Differentiated Services Field: 0x00 (DSCP: CS0, ECN: Not-ECT)
    Total Length: 84
    Identification: 0xa1be (41406)
  > 000. .... = Flags: 0x0
    ...0 0000 0000 0000 = Fragment Offset: 0
    Time to Live: 64
    Protocol: ICMP (1)
    Header Checksum: 0x54d3 [validation disabled]
    [Header checksum status: Unverified]
    Source Address: 192.0.2.11
    Destination Address: 192.0.2.12
> Internet Control Message Protocol
```

Figure 3-15 *Packet capture of leaf1's reachability test to leaf2's loopback, using the* **ping** *tool*

Summary

This chapter introduced how BGP can be adapted for a data center, with the benefits it brings, especially for larger-scale data centers. Problems such as BGP path hunting can easily be avoided by using ASN schemes for 3-stage and 5-stage Clos fabrics, or as an alternative, by using routing policies to ensure that sub-optimal paths, which can lead to path hunting, do not exist in the network.

Using eBGP as the underlay and the overlay provides a consolidated and simpler operational and maintenance experience, while continuing to provide vertical separation between the underlay and the overlay by leveraging Junos BGP groups. However, IP addressing for the underlay is operationally challenging and can get complex, very quickly, as the network grows.

With the BGP auto-discovery feature, which uses IPv6 Neighbor Discovery behind the scenes, underlay IP addressing complexity can be eliminated. This also provides an underlay framework that enables easier plug-and-play of fabric nodes, and the capability to automate the underlay without tracking any IP addressing schemes, since all fabric-facing interfaces are configured the same way.

## Chapter 4

VXLAN as a Network Virtualization Overlay

Chapter 2, "Overview of Data Center Architecture," and Chapter 3, "BGP for the Data Center," explored the shift in data center design from a traditional three-tier architecture to a more densely interconnected 3-stage Clos network (or a 5-stage Clos network for large-scale data centers), with a scale-out strategy designed to handle the predominantly east-west traffic in the network. In these designs, the need for Layer 2 protocols such as Spanning Tree is eliminated by moving to a fully routed architecture for network-facing ports, using point-to-point Layer 3 links between the leafs and the spines of the fabric and using a routing protocol such as BGP to propagate endpoint reachability information through the network.

With all the benefits of a routed architecture in modern data centers, the need for Layer 2 connectivity between endpoints still existed, which presented a challenge since the Layer 2 boundary in a Clos design terminates at the leafs. Most of these requirements were from older storage clusters, which needed Layer 2 connectivity between the individual nodes in the cluster, across different racks in a data center, typically for heartbeats and to determine cluster membership. There were instances where legacy applications were built with such requirements as well, and thus, moving to a routed, modern data center architecture was problematic. Therefore, operationally, there was a need to support Layer 2 connectivity over a Layer 3 network.

Note Relatively newer storage frameworks such as Hadoop, used for data processing and data storage, do not require a flat Layer 2 network and can fully function over modular, Layer 3 environments.

Having said this, the need for connecting two or more data centers, and not just racks in a data center, is not new. This need has existed for a long time, with several technological solutions solving this "problem," including technologies such as *Virtual Private Wire Service (VPWS)* and *Virtual Private LAN Service (VPLS)* in the service provider world. VPWS offered point-to-point Layer 2 connectivity over an MPLS core, using a pseudowire that would essentially emulate a Layer 2 circuit between two sites. However, this was limited to point-to-point connectivity, meaning a full mesh of pseudowires needed to be created if connectivity was required between more than two sites or customer edge (CE) devices. This was eventually advanced with VPLS, which provided point-to-multipoint connectivity, replacing the need for a full mesh of pseudowires. The service provider cloud, offering VPLS to a customer, can be reimagined as a virtual switch that all CEs are plugged into.

VPLS, however, had its drawbacks:

- It relied on data plane learning, by way of flooding, to disseminate MAC address information across sites. The VPLS cloud is like a virtual switch, and frames are flooded to connected CEs. MAC addresses are learned as a frame is received and associated with the pseudowire it was received over. This flooding behavior resulted in poor scalability of such designs.

- VPLS designs lacked active/active multihoming support. Customer edge devices required dual connectivity for redundancy to the provider edge (PE) devices, and in such cases, the redundant link would be blocked to prevent Layer 2 loops, thus making such architectures susceptible to traditional Layer 2 problems. There were tricks and hacks to achieve multihoming as desired, but this made the infrastructure unnecessarily complex, adding high cost to operational support and maintenance while also making the infrastructure extremely difficult to debug.

■ VPLS could only extend Layer 2 across sites and did not cater to IP connectivity and Layer 3 requirements.

■ VPLS relied on MPLS transport.

At the same time, Cisco Systems also brought to market its own proprietary technology called *Overlay Transport Virtualization (OTV)*. OTV was a transport-agnostic, MAC-in-IP encapsulation method, using a control plane (IS-IS, in this case) to distribute MAC address information across sites, to provide Layer 2 extension between data centers. In addition to this, OTV enabled native multihoming support by electing one CE as the *authoritative edge device* (OTV lingo), which became the active forwarder for the multihomed segment.

Eventually, the industry moved toward standards-based *BGP Ethernet VPN (EVPN)*. This is described in RFC 7432, which was written from the perspective of MPLS transport. This was then adopted in RFC 8365 for a *Network Virtualization Overlay (NVO)* in data centers, using Virtual Extensible LAN (VXLAN) as an encapsulation method over IP. RFC 8365 also defines other encapsulation types, such as Network Virtualization using Generic Routing Encapsulation (NVGRE) and Generic Network Virtualization Encapsulation (GENEVE), but the focus of this chapter, and the book, is VXLAN.

This chapter introduces both VXLAN as a data plane encapsulation type and BGP EVPN as a control plane, distributing MAC and IP information in modern, VXLAN-based data center fabrics. EVPN uses several route types for this purpose, facilitating both Layer 2 and Layer 3 communication, each with its own specific use cases. These use cases are explored in detail, with packet formats for each of these route types.

Introducing VXLAN

Most modern data centers are designed as 3-stage or 5-stage Clos fabrics, with the physical infrastructure and the point-to-point Layer 3 interfaces between the spines and leafs forming the underlay. This common physical infrastructure can be logically carved to provide different services on top of it, by elevating the endpoints and the applications connected to the network into the overlay, thus creating a form of *network virtualization*.

Network virtualization, in such an architecture, has become necessary for several reasons:

■ Host virtualization and multitenancy requirements have become commonplace in today's data centers. Building and maintaining unique physical infrastructure for every tenant is, naturally, a costly affair. Additionally, maintaining state for 100,000 hosts or more might not be feasible in most environments. Network virtualization enables the core of the network (the spines of the fabric, in this case) to be pure IP forwarding devices, requiring no knowledge of the endpoints.

■ Multitenant environments were often limited by the 4K VLAN range, especially in environments such as cloud computing.

■ Host mobility forces the network to retain constructs such as the same network gateway across leaf boundaries to ensure the mobility function does not break.

■ Layer 2 requirements of legacy applications, host mobility, and storage clusters drive the need for a flat, Layer 2 network over a routed infrastructure.

Network virtualization is achieved by adding a layer of encapsulation on a packet as it enters the network, essentially building a network *overlay*. Thus, the overlay is simply a logical network that sits on top of the physical infrastructure. This concept of an overlay allows for multiple logically separated and isolated networks to be built and connected on top of the same physical network.

Virtual Extensible LAN (VXLAN), defined in RFC 7348, is a data plane encapsulation type that can be used to build a network overlay, allowing for both Layer 2 and Layer 3 payloads. This is analogous to a *virtual LAN (VLAN)*, which provides logical separation of a broadcast or bridging domain in the network but is limited in its scalability to 4K VLANs only. VXLAN, on the other hand, provides a 24-bit identifier called a *VXLAN Network Identifier (VNI)* in the VXLAN header, supporting up to 16 million network segments, giving the network administrator more flexibility to logically partition the network.

Because of its encapsulating trait, VXLAN is essentially a stateless tunnel that originates at one endpoint and terminates on another. These endpoints, participating in the encapsulation and decapsulation of a VXLAN tunnel, are called *VXLAN Tunnel Endpoints (VTEPs)*. Before diving deeper into VXLAN itself, it is important to understand that these tunnels can originate and terminate on a network device or a server, using a virtual switch such as Open vSwitch, with a VXLAN module in the kernel, typically with some hardware acceleration so that these packets are not processed in software by the CPU. This gives rise to network-to-network overlays, host-to-network overlays, or host-to-host overlays, as shown in Figure 4-1.

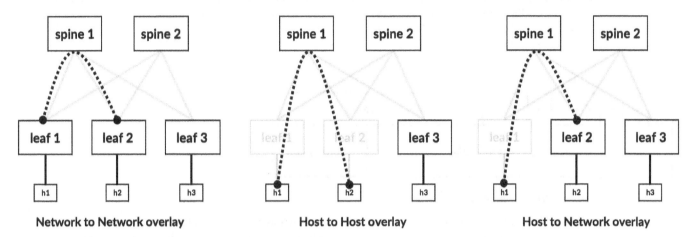

Figure 4-1 *VXLAN overlay origination and termination options*

Predominantly, network-to-network overlays are deployed, with native support for VXLAN encapsulation and decapsulation in hardware on data center switches such as the Juniper QFX5120-48Y. Host-based overlays typically require additional hardware capable of VXLAN acceleration (essentially offloading VXLAN packet processing to hardware), since processing of such packets (which requires encapsulation and decapsulation of packets) can cause considerable CPU overhead and performance impact to the application.

VXLAN is a MAC-in-IP/UDP encapsulation type, adding a total of 50 bytes to the original packet post-encapsulation. This is not just a single header, but multiple headers added to the original packet—this includes a VXLAN header, a UDP header, an IP header, and an Ethernet header, as shown in Figure 4-2.

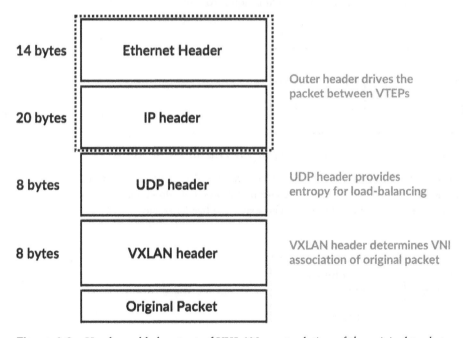

Figure 4-2 *Headers added as part of VXLAN encapsulation of the original packet*

Each header has a specific purpose, and it is crucial to break these down. The original packet, received by a VTEP on its host-facing port, is stripped of any 802.1Q headers, which include the VLAN tags for the packet, prior to encapsulating the packet, as defined in Section 6 of RFC 7348. There are configuration options that enable Q-in-Q–style behavior over VXLAN fabrics, but that topic is outside the scope of this introduction.

The VXLAN header is an 8-byte header, which identifies the network segment for the host, using a 24-bit VNI field, through the fabric. The VLAN association of the packet, as it is received inbound on a VTEP from its host-facing port, is used to determine the corresponding VNI to be added in the VXLAN header. In its initial implementation, as per RFC 7348, the header was mostly reserved fields, with one flag bit (the *Instance* bit) being set to 1 to indicate a valid VNI. This original header format is shown in Figure 4-3.

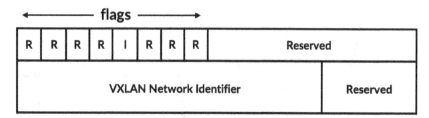

Figure 4-3   *Original VXLAN header, defined in RFC 7348*

The reserved bits in the header are all set to zero on transmission and ignored on receipt. However, over time, there have been extensions to this VXLAN header. Two extensions discussed here are the group-based policy extension (currently an expired IETF draft) and the Generic Protocol Extension (GPE) for VXLAN (VXLAN-GPE, an active IETF draft). These extensions add important functionalities to the header.

The group-based policy extension defines new flags and a new 2-byte field in the header called the *Group Policy ID*. This field can be used to assign a group-based identifier, enabling policy enforcement for packets based on this identifier instead of more granular constructs such as IP addresses (which consume more resources and can get very complicated). This extension is very commonly used in enterprise solutions such as Cisco Software-Defined Access, in which Cisco Identity Services Engine (ISE) assigns a Security Group Tag (SGT) to an authenticated and authorized endpoint. This SGT is added as the Group Policy ID in the VXLAN header, enabling policy enforcement, in the form of Security Group ACL policies, that determine whether the source can communicate with the destination. The new VXLAN header, as part of this extension, is shown in Figure 4-4. The G bit in the flags field is set when the Group Policy ID field is non-zero.

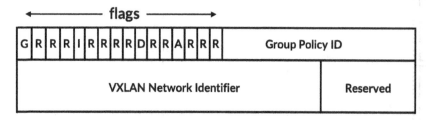

Figure 4-4   *VXLAN header extension, as defined in expired VXLAN group policy IETF draft*

The second extension, VXLAN-GPE, is an active IETF draft, as of 2023. This extension was written to provide more visibility and diagnostic capabilities for the overlay (with VXLAN as the encapsulation type), along with versioning functionality, enabling VXLAN to have payloads beyond just Ethernet. This extension header is shown in Figure 4-5.

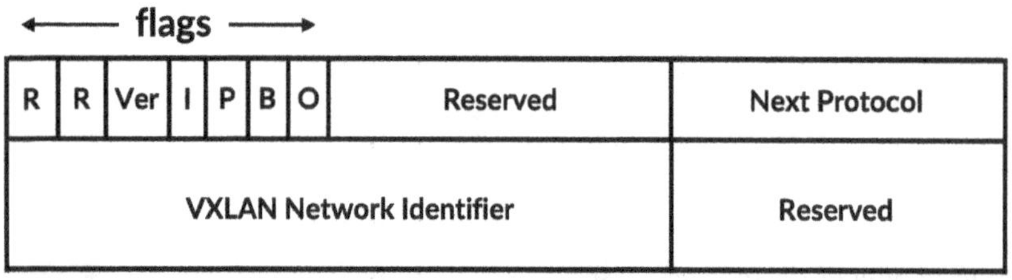

Figure 4-5   *VXLAN-GPE header, as defined in VXLAN-GPE IETF draft*

More specifically, this extension provides the following added functionality:

■ The P bit, called the Next Protocol bit, is set to indicate that the *Next Protocol* field is present, which contains the protocol number of the encapsulated payload, providing support for more than just Ethernet payloads.

■ The B bit, called the BUM traffic bit (BUM being short for broadcast, unknown unicast, and multicast), is set when a packet is ingress-replicated in a VXLAN fabric. This helps the egress VTEP differentiate between a known unicast packet and an unknown unicast packet and enables it to subject an unknown unicast flooded packet to designated forwarding rules over a shared Ethernet Segment.

■ The O bit provides support for OAM (Operations, Administration, and Maintenance). When this bit is set, the packet is considered an OAM packet, and appropriate OAM processing must occur.

Note   Both these extensions are backward compatible with the original VXLAN header, defined in RFC 7348.

After the VXLAN header, a UDP header is added as part of the encapsulation process. This UDP header solves an important problem with overlays. Encapsulation mechanisms like VXLAN abstract away details of the original packet/payload, which also means losing all the variability that the original payload provides for ECMP. And one of the biggest benefits of routed designs, like a 3-stage Clos network, is equal cost paths across the fabric. Thus, building an overlay just to lose this benefit feels counterintuitive, since the outer IP header information will always be the same when tunneling traffic between two VTEPs, meaning that the same hash will be generated every time, regardless of varying traffic flows that comprise the inner payload.

This is where the UDP header helps—it provides entropy for load-balancing across the fabric. Typically, a 5-tuple hash will generate the UDP source port by using the source IP address, destination IP address, protocol number, source port, and destination port fields of the original IP packet. Alternatively, for a Layer 2 packet, the source MAC address and the destination MAC address are used in the hashing algorithm. In this way, as different traffic flows require VXLAN encapsulation, the UDP source port generated for each flow is unique, enabling better load-balancing across available equal paths, since the UDP header can now be used in generating a hash for the post-encapsulated packet.

Note   The destination port, in the UDP header, is 4789, which is the well-known port for VXLAN.

Before moving on from UDP, there's another important question to consider here: Why use UDP in the first place? Why not TCP? TCP over TCP (since the payload can also be TCP) is known to be problematic. Stacking TCP over TCP can often lead to a TCP meltdown, where loss in one layer causes the other layer to overcompensate, which increases exponentially.

After the UDP header, outer IP and Ethernet headers are added to complete the encapsulation. These headers are meant to drive the packet, hop by hop, from the source VTEP to the destination VTEP. The source IP address is the source VTEP's loopback address (which essentially forms the source address for the VXLAN tunnel) and the destination IP address is the terminating VTEP's loopback address. These loopback addresses, as discussed in Chapter 3, are advertised in the fabric underlay so that all participating VTEPs are aware of all loopback addresses. The source MAC address and the destination MAC address change per hop, like any routed packet traveling from one point to another.

Since VXLAN encapsulation adds a 50-byte overhead to the original packet, increased MTU in the fabric infrastructure is a minimum requirement for such deployments.

VXLAN, in its initial conception in RFC 7348, used a flood-and-learn mechanism, suffering from the same scalability limitations as VPLS. This was a data-driven learning mechanism, requiring a multicast-enabled underlay infrastructure for distribution of multi-destination traffic (also referred to as BUM traffic) such as an ARP packet, facilitating the learning of MAC addresses in the fabric. Consider the topology in Figure 4-6, where hosts h1 and h3 are in VLAN 10.

This is a simple 3-stage Clos fabric, demonstrating how a multicast-enabled underlay is used for this flood-and-learn mechanism of VXLAN. In this topology, spine1 acts as the rendezvous point (RP) with Protocol Independent Multicast (PIM) in the underlay. Each leaf or VTEP is configured with a multicast group-to-VNI mapping, prompting them to generate PIM (*,G) joins toward the RP to build a shared multicast tree.

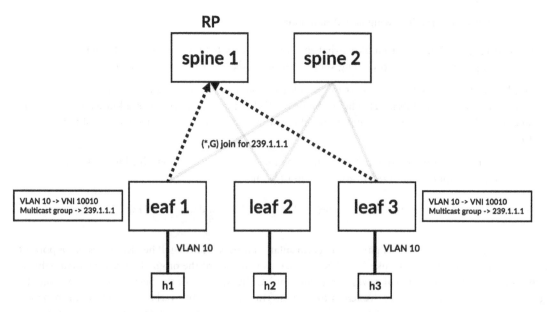

Figure 4-6   *3-stage Clos fabric with multicast in the underlay for VXLAN flood-and-learn*

When host h1 wants to communicate with h3, it generates an ARP request to resolve h3's IP address into a MAC address. This ARP request is VXLAN encapsulated by leaf1 and flooded into the fabric using the multicast tree, with leaf1 becoming a multicast source for this group. This multicast tree will eventually carry the ARP packet to leaf3 (and any other VTEPs configured with the same multicast group), where the source MAC address of the inner packet is mapped to leaf1's VTEP address and stored in the MAC address table, as shown in Figure 4-7.

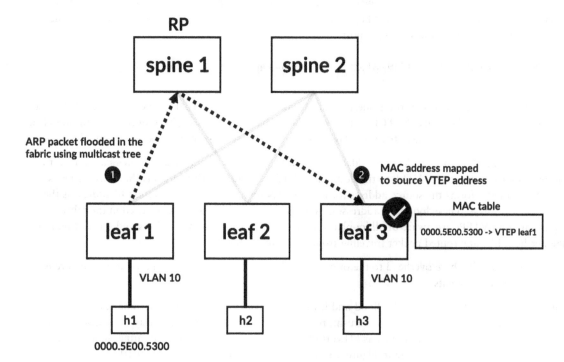

Figure 4-7   *ARP packet flooded using a multicast tree in VXLAN flood-and-learn deployments*

Host h3, upon receiving the ARP request, responds with an ARP reply destined to h1's MAC address. This is now sent as a unicast VXLAN-encapsulated packet by leaf3, since it knows h1's MAC address resides behind VTEP leaf1. When this encapsulated packet arrives at leaf1, it learns host h3's MAC address from the source MAC address of the inner packet and maps it to VTEP leaf3. Thus, this flood-and-learn process achieves two things: it facilitates the discovery of remote VTEPs in the fabric and learns endpoint addresses.

However, flood-and-learn has major drawbacks, and it became necessary to couple a control plane with VXLAN. Some of these drawbacks are as follows:

■ With flood-and-learn, there is an indeterministic amount of unknown unicast and broadcast flooding in the fabric.

■ It is not scalable for large data centers because of pure data-driven learning. This also leads to slower convergence for mobility events.

■ It forces additional complexity in the core with a multicast requirement in the underlay.

■ It only supports bridging, and not routing, in the fabric. To route between VNIs, a central gateway is necessary.

RFC 7432 introduced BGP EVPN for MPLS data plane networks. However, this was eventually adapted for VXLAN, as a network virtualization overlay, using RFC 8365. The next section explores the advantages of using BGP EVPN as a control plane, with an introductory look at the different types of EVPN routes, facilitating both Layer 2 and Layer 3 functionality in a VXLAN fabric.

EVPN for Data Center VXLAN Fabrics

EVPN is a Multiprotocol BGP (MP-BGP) control plane mechanism, defined with an Address Family Indicator (AFI) value of 25 (L2VPN) and Subsequent Address Family Indicator value of 70 (EVPN). While EVPN was originally defined for an MPLS data plane, this was coupled with the VXLAN data plane for data center fabrics to overcome the shortcomings of VXLAN flood-and-learn, which, as discussed in the previous section, relied purely on data-driven learning of endpoint addresses.

EVPN provides the following advantages:

■ Local data plane learning, combined with remote control plane learning across the fabric via BGP EVPN updates.

■ Support for both Layer 2 and Layer 3 overlays.

■ Reduces flooding in the fabric by building ARP entries from EVPN Type-2 routes and leveraging functionalities such as ARP suppression and proxy ARP to limit flooding.

■ Active/active multihoming using Ethernet Segments and Ethernet Segment Identifier Link Aggregation Groups (ESI LAG).

■ Mass withdrawal using EVPN Type-1 routes, to achieve faster convergence in case of failures.

BGP EVPN has several route types, each serving a different purpose, providing different functionality in an EVPN-based VXLAN fabric. These route types are as follows:

■ **Route Type 1:** Also known as the Ethernet Auto-Discovery (EAD) route, this route type is used for EVPN multihoming (also known as ESI LAG). It is generated per Ethernet Segment (and per EVPN Instance), and is leveraged for aliasing, mass withdrawal, and split horizon. This route type is explored in detail in Chapter 5, "Bridged Overlay in an EVPN VXLAN Fabric."

■ **Route Type 2:** Also known as the MAC/IP advertisement route, this route type is used to advertise a MAC address and an optional IP address via BGP EVPN. This route type is explored in detail in Chapter 5.

■ **Route Type 3:** Also known as the Inclusive Multicast Ethernet Tag (IMET) route, this route type is used to advertise a VTEP's association to a VNI, enabling automatic VTEP discovery, facilitating the population of a flood list for flooding of BUM traffic in the fabric. This route type is explored in detail in Chapter 5.

■ **Route Type 4:** Also known as the Ethernet Segment route, this route type is used for the Designated Forwarder election between ESI LAG peers to determine which peer is allowed to forward multi-destination traffic, received over the fabric, into an Ethernet Segment. This route type is explored in detail in Chapter 5.

■ **Route Type 5:** Also known as the IP Prefix route, this route type decouples the MAC address from an IP address, and only advertises an IP prefix. This route type is explored in detail in Chapter 9, "Routed Overlay and Host-Routed Bridging."

In addition to the preceding route types, RFC 9251 defines three more BGP EVPN routes that are specific to multicast operation. These routes are not explored in detail in this book, but they are presented here for the sake of completeness:

- **Route Type 6:** Also known as the Selective Multicast Ethernet Tag (SMET) route, this route is used to carry IGMP multicast group membership information when a host indicates interest to receive traffic for a specific group using IGMP reports.

- **Route Type 7:** Also known as the Multicast Membership Report Synch route, this route is used to synchronize multicast state between ESI LAG peers for a given Ethernet Segment when an IGMP join is received from a host.

- **Route Type 8:** Also known as the Multicast Leave Synch route, this route is used to synchronize multicast state between ESI LAG peers for a given Ethernet Segment when an IGMP Leave message is received from a host.

Chapter 3 explored BGP design for the data center, specifically for the underlay. BGP, with its EVPN address family, is the routing protocol of choice for the overlay, with the same eBGP design and ASN scheme. Instead of carrying IPv4 or IPv6 loopback addresses for underlay reachability, BGP EVPN advertises the route types described earlier for overlay functionality. It is imperative that in such designs the VTEPs advertise the BGP EVPN routes with their respective loopback addresses as the next-hop addresses. This enables VTEPs to build a VXLAN tunnel between each other, with the appropriate encapsulation and decapsulation data programmed in software and hardware. Consider the topology shown in Figure 4-8, where the spines are configured to not change the NEXT_HOP BGP attribute for the EVPN address family.

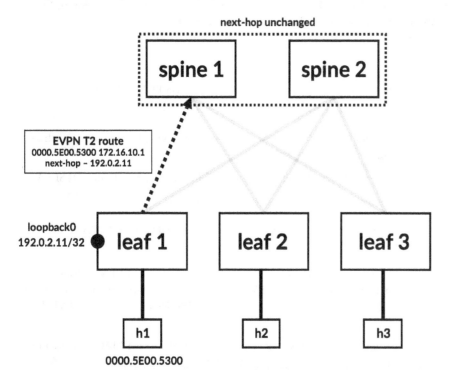

Figure 4-8 *The spines, in a 3-stage Clos fabric, configured to not change the next-hop for BGP EVPN routes*

Thus, when leaf1 (which is a VTEP in this topology) advertises an EVPN Type-2 route with host h1's MAC address and IP address, it sets its own loopback address, 192.0.2.11, as the next-hop address in the BGP update. The spines, configured to not change the next-hop address, advertise this route to other VTEPs, including leaf2, as shown in Figure 4-9. When this is processed on leaf2, the next-hop address in the BGP update is used to build a VXLAN tunnel to the VTEP (leaf1, in this case). In this way, the default eBGP behavior must be explicitly changed—network operating systems such as *Free Range Routing* (often abbreviated to *FRRouting* or *FRR*) have changed the default eBGP behavior for the EVPN address family to not modify the NEXT_HOP BGP attribute, while other network operating systems like Junos require explicit configuration for the same.

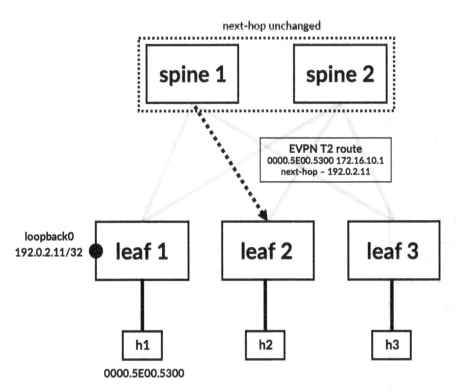

Figure 4-9 *EVPN Type-2 route advertised by the spines to leaf2 without changing next-hop*

Since BGP EVPN is used as the routing protocol for the network virtualization overlay (VXLAN, in this case), another key property of such an infrastructure is the ability to differentiate between multiple logical tenants using the same physical infrastructure while also providing granular control over how routes are imported into tenant-specific tables. This is like MPLS L3VPNs, and the same BGP parameters are used here, as follows:

- A Route Distinguisher is added to every BGP EVPN route to uniquely identify the route globally, across different VPN/tenant tables.

- Route Targets are added to control how routes are imported from the global BGP EVPN table into tenant-specific VPN tables.

While subsequent chapters dive deeper into different EVPN route types, their functionality in an EVPN VXLAN fabric, with packet captures and packet walks, a summary of the packet format of EVPN Route Types 1 through 5 is provided in this chapter as a reference. Each route type is encoded as Network Layer Reachability Information (NLRI) in the BGP update. Since Route Targets are added as BGP communities, and not a part of the NLRI data itself, they are not shown in the packet formats.

EVPN Type-1 routes have the format shown in Figure 4-10. This includes a Route Distinguisher, an Ethernet Segment Identifier that uniquely identifies the Ethernet Segment this Type-1 route is generated for, an Ethernet Tag ID, which is either set to its maximum value of 4294967295 or set to 0 (based on whether this is an EAD route per Ethernet Segment or per EVPN Instance), and, finally, the VXLAN Network Identifier. Since these routes are not specific to any VNI, this field is set to 0.

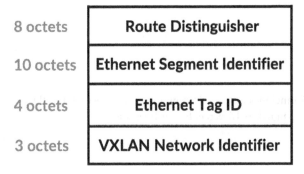

Figure 4-10 *EVPN Type-1 route NLRI packet format*

EVPN Type-2 routes have the format shown in Figure 4-11. This NLRI includes a Route Distinguisher, a MAC address length field, a MAC address, an optional IP address (shown as 4 octets, but for an IPv6 address, this would expand to 16 octets), an Ethernet Segment Identifier, an Ethernet Tag ID, the Layer-2 VNI, and, optionally, the Layer-3 VNI. The concept of a Layer 2 VNI (L2VNI) is explored in Chapter 5, while the concept of a Layer 3 VNI (L3VNI) is explored in Chapter 8, "Edge-Routed Bridging."

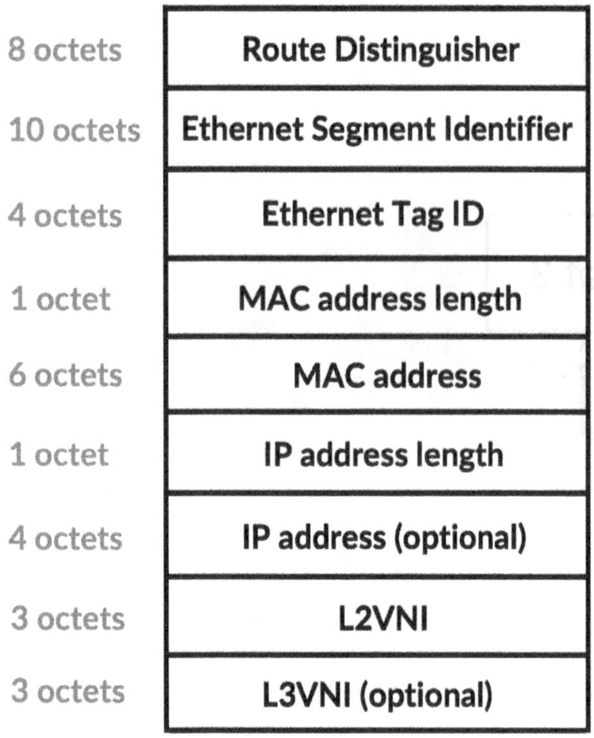

8 octets	**Route Distinguisher**
10 octets	**Ethernet Segment Identifier**
4 octets	**Ethernet Tag ID**
1 octet	**MAC address length**
6 octets	**MAC address**
1 octet	**IP address length**
4 octets	**IP address (optional)**
3 octets	**L2VNI**
3 octets	**L3VNI (optional)**

Figure 4-11 *EVPN Type-2 route NLRI packet format*

EVPN Type-3 routes have the format shown in Figure 4-12. This NLRI includes a Route Distinguisher, an Ethernet Tag ID, an IP address length field, and an IP address (shown as 4 octets, but expanded to 16 octets for an IPv6 address). The value in the IP address field identifies the VTEP originating the Type-3 route. For EVPN Type-3 routes, it is mandatory that the BGP update carry a path attribute called the Provider Multicast Service Interface (PMSI) Tunnel attribute. This attribute, along with EVPN Type-3 routes and its usage, is explored in Chapter 5.

8 octets	**Route Distinguisher**
4 octets	**Ethernet Tag ID**
1 octet	**IP address length**
4 octets	**IP address**

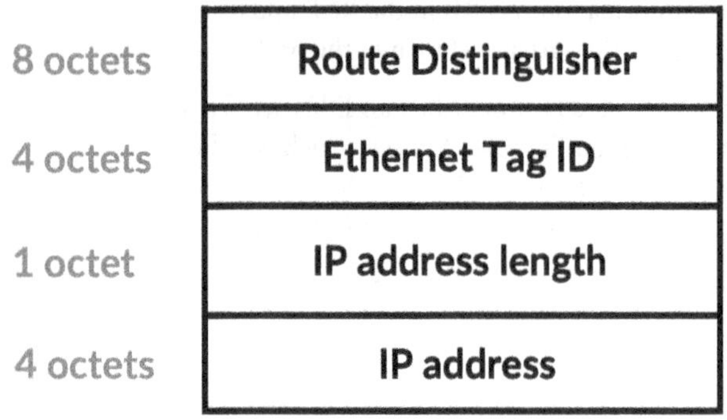

Figure 4-12 *EVPN Type-3 route NLRI packet format*

EVPN Type-4 routes have the format shown in Figure 4-13. This NLRI includes a Route Distinguisher, an Ethernet Tag ID, an IP address length field, and an IP address (shown as 4 octets, but expanded to 16 octets for an IPv6 address).

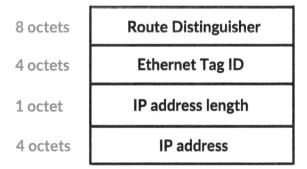

8 octets	Route Distinguisher
4 octets	Ethernet Tag ID
1 octet	IP address length
4 octets	IP address

Figure 4-13 *EVPN Type-4 route NLRI packet format*

Finally, EVPN Type-5 routes have the format shown in Figure 4-14. This NLRI includes a Route Distinguisher, an Ethernet Segment Identifier, an Ethernet Tag ID, an IP Prefix length field, an IP Prefix, a gateway IP address, and the Layer-3 VNI.

8 octets	Route Distinguisher
10 octets	Ethernet Segment Identifier
4 octets	Ethernet Tag ID
1 octet	IP Prefix length
4 octets	IP Prefix
4 octets	Gateway IP address
3 octets	L3VNI

Figure 4-14 *EVPN Type-5 route NLRI packet format*

Summary

This chapter introduced VXLAN as a network virtualization overlay, with the need to couple a control plane protocol for remote learning of MAC addresses. BGP Ethernet VPN (EVPN) was adapted for such VXLAN-based data center fabrics, providing numerous advantages over traditional Layer 2 extension mechanisms such as VPLS. This includes the ability to build both Layer 2 and Layer 3 overlays, providing IP reachability information as well, while also moving away from data-driven learning, which did not scale well and required additional complexity in the underlay to disseminate MAC address information.

EVPN uses several route types for the functioning of a VXLAN-based data center fabric, and this chapter introduced Route Types 1 through 8, with brief descriptions of each route type, along with their corresponding packet formats.

## Chapter 5

Bridged Overlay in an EVPN VXLAN Fabric

The focus of this chapter is understanding, configuring, and validating a bridged overlay in an EVPN VXLAN fabric, but it also serves as a foundation for several other features that are fundamental to know both for this book and for data center design and deployment in general. This chapter includes the following topics:

- Understanding how local and remote MAC addresses are learned
- Replicating broadcast, unknown unicast, and multicast (BUM) traffic
- Multihoming with ESI LAG and Core Isolation
- Route Targets and auto-generation of Route Targets
- MAC mobility
- Loop detection in an EVPN VXLAN fabric
- Bidirectional Forwarding Detection (BFD) for the underlay and overlay

Through the course of this chapter, EVPN Type-1, Type-2, Type-3, and Type-4 routes are examined in detail as well, through packet captures and via the CLI, to understand various aspects of these route types and their implications. A clear understanding of these route types is fundamental for designing, maintaining, and troubleshooting EVPN VXLAN–based data centers.

At its core, a bridged overlay constitutes extending the traditional Layer 2 VLAN (or bridge domain) over a routed fabric underlay, such as the 3-stage Clos fabric, and providing hosts in the same subnet, but on different leafs, a means to communicate with each other via a Layer 2 overlay. For example, consider the topology shown in Figure 5-1, wherein the subnet 213.0.113.0/24 is stretched across the routed underlay, and hosts behind different leafs belong to this subnet.

If moving the L2/L3 demarcation down to the leafs brings all the benefits of a fully routed architecture, then why design for a bridged overlay? This is rooted in how applications have evolved over time (and, ironically, in some ways, not evolved) and what modern applications look like.

Traditionally, an application would be hosted on a single server, with all its software components contained within a single package, which was typical of monolithic applications. With time and a transition to client/server architecture, and eventually a distributed microservices architecture, an application could have its software components spread across the network, with the requirement of these components communicating with each other over the network infrastructure. The general market has also slowly shifted to cloud-native applications, which implies many different things—these could be container- or Kubernetes-based applications, designed to exist over a routed infrastructure, with no requirements of host mobility and virtual machines, thus communicating purely over Layer 3.

However, despite this shift to a leaf-spine Clos and a distributed microservices architecture, numerous older generations of applications remain—these applications require communication over Layer 2. Unfortunately, even some modern applications continue to be built poorly, requiring this Layer 2 connectivity (storage applications are notorious for this). Thus, as someone who is responsible for the network infrastructure, to facilitate communication for such applications, you must design a bridged overlay on top of a fully routed underlay.

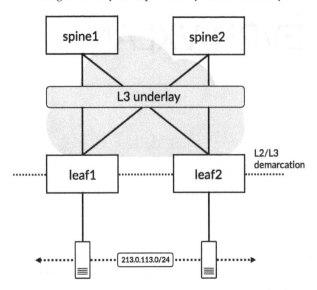

Figure 5-1 *Layer 2 extended across a routed underlay*

Configuring and Validating a Bridged Overlay EVPN VXLAN Fabric

This section focuses on configuring and validating a bridged overlay EVPN VXLAN fabric. This acts as a quick reference to get the fabric up and running and provides a packet walk of how traffic flows through the fabric, enabling you to gain a high-level understanding of this design. The following sections dive deeper into what happens behind the scenes, details of different EVPN route types, and everything that comes together to make it all work. But for now, as a baseline, you'll see how to configure this fabric and ensure that all hosts can reach each other.

As a reference, the topology in Figure 5-2 will be used for the entirety of this chapter. The network infrastructure comprises two spines, five leafs, and four hosts, connected in a 3-stage Clos design. One of these hosts (h2) is multihomed to leaf2 and leaf3. Details of how multihoming works within the context of EVPN VXLAN fabrics are explored later in this chapter in the section "EVPN Multihoming with ESI LAG and EVPN Type-1/Type-4 Routes."

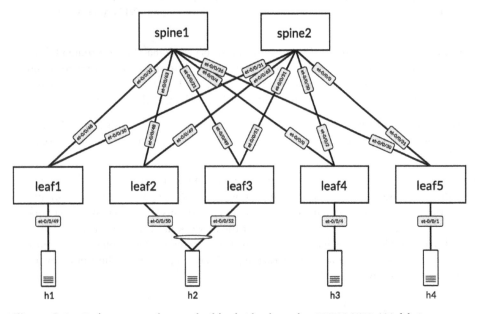

Figure 5-2 *Reference topology to build a bridged overlay EVPN VXLAN fabric*

Configuring the Underlay

Interfaces between the leafs and the spines are Layer 3, point-to-point interfaces, making this a fully routed underlay, designed as a 3-stage Clos fabric. The IPv4 subnet 198.51.100.0/24 is used for this. This is one of the available IPv4 subnet ranges that can be used for network documentation purposes, as defined in RFC 5737.

Each interface is configured with a /31 mask to ensure there is no wastage of the address space. The MTU is also increased to 9200 to accommodate larger-sized packets (VXLAN encapsulation adds a 50-byte overhead to the original frame). Examples 5-1 and 5-2 show the interface configuration between leaf1 and the spines, as an example.

Example 5-1 *Point-to-point interfaces on spine1 and spine2 to leaf1*

```
root@spine1# show interfaces et-0/0/32
description "p2p interface to leaf1";
mtu 9200;
unit 0 {
    family inet {
        address 198.51.100.1/31;
    }
}

root@spine2# show interfaces et-0/0/31
description "p2p interface to leaf1";
mtu 9200;
unit 0 {
    family inet {
        address 198.51.100.3/31;
    }
}
```

Example 5-2 *Point-to-point interfaces on leaf1 to spine1 and spine2*

```
root@leaf1# show interfaces et-0/0/48
description "p2p interface to spine1";
mtu 9200;
unit 0 {
    family inet {
        address 198.51.100.0/31;
    }
}

root@leaf1# show interfaces et-0/0/50
description "p2p interface to spine2";
mtu 9200;
unit 0 {
    family inet {
        address 198.51.100.2/31;
    }
}
```

All remaining interfaces between the other leafs and the spines are configured in a similar way. The goal of the underlay is to provide reachability between the loopbacks of each VXLAN Tunnel Endpoint (VTEP), with the leafs being the VTEPs here, since the loopback addresses are used to form end-to-end VXLAN tunnels. Thus, once all interfaces are configured with IP addresses, BGP is deployed to distribute loopback reachability.

From a BGP design perspective, private autonomous system numbers (ASNs) are used, as shown in Figure 5-3. All spines share the same BGP ASN, while each leaf is assigned a unique BGP ASN. This ASN scheme is explored in detail in Chapter 3, "BGP for the Data Center," and is used to prevent BGP path hunting natively (since the spines share the same BGP ASN).

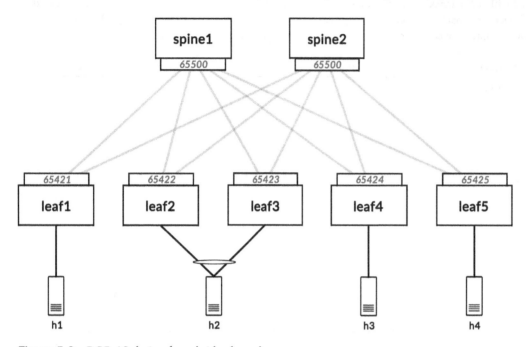

Figure 5-3 *BGP AS design for a bridged overlay*

BGP is configured to peer over the point-to-point interfaces, and the loopback address of each device is injected into BGP using an export policy. Every device also has a policy attached to the forwarding table to enable per-flow ECMP, along with multipath enabled for BGP, as explored in Chapter 3. This enables equal cost paths to be installed in the forwarding table, and the hardware, for a remote VTEP's loopback address. Examples 5-3, 5-4, and 5-5 show the BGP configuration on leaf1, spine1, and spine2, respectively.

Example 5-3 *BGP configuration on leaf1*

```
root@leaf1# show routing-options
router-id 192.0.2.11;
autonomous-system 65421;
forwarding-table {
    export ECMP;
}

root@leaf1# show policy-options
policy-statement ECMP {
    then {
        load-balance per-flow;
    }
}
policy-statement allow-loopback {
    term 1 {
        from interface lo0.0;
        then accept;
```

```
    }
    term 10 {
        then reject;
    }
}


root@leaf1# show protocols bgp group underlay
type external;
family inet {
    unicast;
}
export allow-loopback;
peer-as 65500;
multipath;
neighbor 198.51.100.1 {
    description "p2p address for spine1";
};
neighbor 198.51.100.3 {
    description "p2p address for spine2";
};
```

Example 5-4 *BGP configuration on spine1*

```
root@spine1# show routing-options
router-id 192.0.2.101;
autonomous-system 65500;
forwarding-table {
    export ECMP;
}


root@spine1# show policy-options
policy-statement ECMP {
    then {
        load-balance per-flow;
    }
}
policy-statement allow-loopback {
    term 1 {
        from {
            route-filter 192.0.2.0/24 orlonger;
        }
        then accept;
    }
    term 2 {
        then reject;
    }
}
```

```
root@spine1# show protocols bgp group underlay
type external;
family inet {
    unicast;
}
export allow-loopback;
neighbor 198.51.100.0 {
    description "p2p address for leaf1";
    peer-as 65421;
}
neighbor 198.51.100.4 {
    description "p2p address for leaf2";
    peer-as 65422;
}
neighbor 198.51.100.8 {
    description "p2p address for leaf3";
    peer-as 65423;
}
neighbor 198.51.100.12 {
    description "p2p address for leaf4";
    peer-as 65424;
}
neighbor 198.51.100.16 {
    description "p2p address for leaf5";
    peer-as 65425;
}
```

Example 5-5 *BGP configuration on spine2*

```
root@spine2# show routing-options
router-id 192.0.2.102;
autonomous-system 65500;
forwarding-table {
    export ECMP;
}

root@spine2# show policy-options
policy-statement ECMP {
    then {
        load-balance per-flow;
    }
}
policy-statement allow-loopback {
    term 1 {
        from {
            route-filter 192.0.2.0/24 orlonger;
        }
        then accept;
    }
```

```
    torm 2 {
        then reject;
    }
}
```

```
root@spine2# show protocols bgp group underlay
type external;
family inet {
    unicast;
}
export allow-loopback;
neighbor 198.51.100.2 {
    description "p2p address for leaf1";
    peer-as 65421;
}
neighbor 198.51.100.6 {
    description "p2p address for leaf2";
    peer-as 65422;
}
neighbor 198.51.100.10 {
    description "p2p address for leaf3";
    peer-as 65423;
}
neighbor 198.51.100.14 {
    description "p2p address for leaf4";
    peer-as 65424;
}
neighbor 198.51.100.18 {
    description "p2p address for leaf5";
    peer-as 65425;
}
```

The remaining leafs are configured in the same way, and once completed, BGP peering for the IPv4 family should be in an Established state between all leafs and spines. This is shown in Example 5-6, using the **show bgp summary** operational mode command. The presence of the inet.0 table statistics under each neighbor's address signifies that the peering for the IPv4 family is up.

Example 5-6 *BGP state on spine1 and spine2*

```
root@spine1> show bgp summary
Threading mode: BGP I/O
Default eBGP mode: advertise - accept, receive - accept
Groups: 1 Peers: 5 Down peers: 0
Table          Tot Paths  Act Paths Suppressed    History Damp State    Pending
inet.0
                    5          5          0          0       0           0
Peer                  AS      InPkt     OutPkt    OutQ   Flaps Last Up/Dwn State|#Active/Received/Accepted/Damped...
198.51.100.0        65421        6          4       0       7      1:05 Establ
  inet.0: 1/1/1/0
198.51.100.4        65422        6          4       0       1      1:05 Establ
  inet.0: 1/1/1/0
```

```
198.51.100.8        65423       6       5       0       1       1:05 Establ
  inet.0: 1/1/1/0
198.51.100.12       65424       6       4       0       1       1:05 Establ
  inet.0: 1/1/1/0
198.51.100.16       65425       6       4       0       1       1:05 Establ
  inet.0: 1/1/1/0
```

```
root@spine2> show bgp summary
Threading mode: BGP I/O
Default eBGP mode: advertise - accept, receive - accept
Groups: 1 Peers: 5 Down peers: 0
Table           Tot Paths  Act Paths Suppressed    History Damp State    Pending
inet.0
                    5          5          0          0        0            0
Peer                 AS      InPkt     OutPkt     OutQ     Flaps Last Up/Dwn State|#Active/Received/Accepted/Damped...
198.51.100.2       65421       6          4         0        5       1:14 Establ
  inet.0: 1/1/1/0
198.51.100.6       65422       6          4         0        1       1:14 Establ
  inet.0: 1/1/1/0
198.51.100.10      65423       6          4         0        1       1:14 Establ
  inet.0: 1/1/1/0
198.51.100.14      65424       6          5         0        1       1:14 Establ
  inet.0: 1/1/1/0
198.51.100.18      65425       6          4         0        1       1:14 Establ
  inet.0: 1/1/1/0
```

Through the BGP export policy, the loopback of each leaf is advertised to every other leaf via both spine1 and spine2. To take advantage of this fully routed underlay, and the fact that equal cost paths are available, BGP is configured with the **multipath** configuration knob as well. However, from Chapter 3, you know that this is not enough—you also need to have an export policy applied to the forwarding table to enable per-flow ECMP for the forwarding table in the Routing Engine and, eventually, the hardware table. Thus, as an example, leaf2's loopback should be reachable via both spine1 and spine2 when viewed from the perspective of leaf1, visually represented in Figure 5-4.

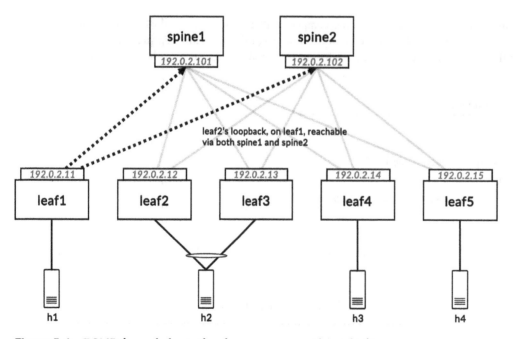

Figure 5-4 *ECMP for underlay paths, shown as an example, on leaf1*

This is confirmed in the CLI, as shown in Example 5-7, which shows both the entry in the routing table, using the **show route table inet.0** [*ip-address*] operational mode command, and the entry in the forwarding table, using the **show route forwarding-table destination** [*ip-address*] **table** [*table-name*] operational mode command.

Example 5-7 *ECMP path on leaf1 for leaf2's loopback in RIB/FIB*

```
root@leaf1> show route table inet.0 192.0.2.12/32

inet.0: 27 destinations, 31 routes (27 active, 0 holddown, 0 hidden)
+ = Active Route, - = Last Active, * = Both

192.0.2.12/32        *[BGP/170] 00:01:07, localpref 100, from 198.51.100.1
                        AS path: 65500 65422 I, validation-state: unverified
                        to 198.51.100.1 via et-0/0/48.0
                     >  to 198.51.100.3 via et-0/0/50.0
                      [BGP/170] 00:01:07, localpref 100
                        AS path: 65500 65422 I, validation-state: unverified
                     >  to 198.51.100.3 via et-0/0/50.0


root@leaf1> show route forwarding-table destination 192.0.2.12/32 table default
Routing table: default.inet
Internet:
Destination        Type RtRef Next hop        Type Index   NhRef Netif
192.0.2.12/32      user   0                   ulst 524286  5
                               198.51.100.1   ucst 1740    5 et-0/0/48.0
                               198.51.100.3   ucst 1743    5 et-0/0/50.0
```

The forwarding table in Example 5-7 confirms that the destination 192.0.2.12/32 is reachable via a unilist next-hop ID of 524286, which resolves to two unicast next-hop IDs, one for each of the spine-facing interfaces. Once BGP configuration for the underlay is complete, leaf1 should be able to reach the loopback of all leafs (and spines), while sourcing its own. This should be true for every leaf, and as an example, this reachability test is shown from the perspective of leaf1 in Example 5-8. This validates VTEP-to-VTEP reachability using loopback addresses, which is the main goal of the underlay.

Example 5-8 *Reachability of leaf1's loopback to the loopback of all other leafs*

```
root@leaf1> ping 192.0.2.12 source 192.0.2.11
PING 192.0.2.12 (192.0.2.12): 56 data bytes
64 bytes from 192.0.2.12: icmp_seq=0 ttl=63 time=7.655 ms
64 bytes from 192.0.2.12: icmp_seq=1 ttl=63 time=8.187 ms
64 bytes from 192.0.2.12: icmp_seq=2 ttl=63 time=8.891 ms
64 bytes from 192.0.2.12: icmp_seq=3 ttl=63 time=5.119 ms
^C
--- 192.0.2.12 ping statistics ---
4 packets transmitted, 4 packets received, 0% packet loss
round-trip min/avg/max/stddev = 5.119/7.463/8.891/1.423 ms


root@leaf1> ping 192.0.2.13 source 192.0.2.11
PING 192.0.2.13 (192.0.2.13): 56 data bytes
64 bytes from 192.0.2.13: icmp_seq=0 ttl=63 time=9.706 ms
64 bytes from 192.0.2.13: icmp_seq=1 ttl=63 time=8.858 ms
64 bytes from 192.0.2.13: icmp_seq=2 ttl=63 time=8.668 ms
64 bytes from 192.0.2.13: icmp_seq=3 ttl=63 time=8.276 ms
^C
```

```
--- 192.0.2.13 ping statistics ---
4 packets transmitted, 4 packets received, 0% packet loss
round-trip min/avg/max/stddev = 8.276/8.877/9.706/0.523 ms


root@leaf1> ping 192.0.2.14 source 192.0.2.11
PING 192.0.2.14 (192.0.2.14): 56 data bytes
64 bytes from 192.0.2.14: icmp_seq=0 ttl=63 time=1.941 ms
64 bytes from 192.0.2.14: icmp_seq=1 ttl=63 time=4.616 ms
64 bytes from 192.0.2.14: icmp_seq=2 ttl=63 time=10.898 ms
64 bytes from 192.0.2.14: icmp_seq=3 ttl=63 time=2.063 ms
^C
--- 192.0.2.14 ping statistics ---
4 packets transmitted, 4 packets received, 0% packet loss
round-trip min/avg/max/stddev = 1.941/4.879/10.898/3.635 ms


root@leaf1> ping 192.0.2.15 source 192.0.2.11
PING 192.0.2.15 (192.0.2.15): 56 data bytes
64 bytes from 192.0.2.15: icmp_seq=0 ttl=63 time=1.201 ms
64 bytes from 192.0.2.15: icmp_seq=1 ttl=63 time=8.067 ms
64 bytes from 192.0.2.15: icmp_seq=2 ttl=63 time=6.898 ms
64 bytes from 192.0.2.15: icmp_seq=3 ttl=63 time=46.418 ms
^C
--- 192.0.2.15 ping statistics ---
4 packets transmitted, 4 packets received, 0% packet loss
round-trip min/avg/max/stddev = 1.201/15.646/46.418/17.955 ms


root@leaf1> ping 192.0.2.101 source 192.0.2.11
PING 192.0.2.101 (192.0.2.101): 56 data bytes
64 bytes from 192.0.2.101: icmp_seq=0 ttl=64 time=5.531 ms
64 bytes from 192.0.2.101: icmp_seq=1 ttl=64 time=6.064 ms
64 bytes from 192.0.2.101: icmp_seq=2 ttl=64 time=12.507 ms
64 bytes from 192.0.2.101: icmp_seq=3 ttl=64 time=9.404 ms
^C
--- 192.0.2.101 ping statistics ---
4 packets transmitted, 4 packets received, 0% packet loss
round-trip min/avg/max/stddev = 5.531/8.377/12.507/2.809 ms


root@leaf1> ping 192.0.2.102 source 192.0.2.11
PING 192.0.2.102 (192.0.2.102): 56 data bytes
64 bytes from 192.0.2.102: icmp_seq=0 ttl=64 time=8.872 ms
64 bytes from 192.0.2.102: icmp_seq=1 ttl=64 time=6.807 ms
64 bytes from 192.0.2.102: icmp_seq=2 ttl=64 time=9.488 ms
64 bytes from 192.0.2.102: icmp_seq=3 ttl=64 time=6.915 ms
^C
--- 192.0.2.102 ping statistics ---
4 packets transmitted, 4 packets received, 0% packet loss
round-trip min/avg/max/stddev = 6.807/8.021/9.488/1.180 ms
```

Now that the underlay reachability is confirmed, you can configure and deploy BGP for the overlay.

Configuring the Overlay

For the overlay, BGP EVPN (address family L2VPN, subaddress family EVPN) is used between the leafs and the spines. The spines simply pass along BGP EVPN updates between the leafs, and do not terminate any VXLAN tunnels themselves, and thus are commonly referred to as *lean spines*. It is important that the spines do not modify the next-hop address as they send these updates. In Junos, the default behavior of eBGP, configured for the EVPN family, is to change the next-hop address to itself. For this reason, each spine is configured to not modify the next-hop address, overriding the default eBGP behavior, using the **multihop no-nexthop-change** configuration knob.

> **Note** Routing suites such as Free Range Routing (FRR) have changed default eBGP for the EVPN family to automatically not modify the next-hop address to itself, without the need for any explicit configuration for the same. Thus, it is important to read publicly available documentation to be aware of a network operating system's default behavior for such use cases.

For the overlay, the eBGP peering is between loopback addresses, which makes this a multi-hop eBGP peering. Examples 5-9 and 5-10 demonstrate how BGP is configured for the overlay, using leaf1 and the spines as an example.

Example 5-9 *BGP configuration for the overlay on leaf1*

```
root@leaf1# show protocols bgp group overlay
type external;
multihop;
local-address 192.0.2.11;
family evpn {
    signaling;
}
peer-as 65500;
multipath;
neighbor 192.0.2.101 {
    description "spine1 loopback";
};
neighbor 192.0.2.102 {
    description "spine2 loopback";
};
```

Example 5-10 *BGP configuration for the overlay on spine1 and spine2*

```
root@spine1# show protocols bgp group overlay
type external;
multihop {
    no-nexthop-change;
}
local-address 192.0.2.101;
family evpn {
    signaling;
}
multipath;
neighbor 192.0.2.11 {
    description "leaf1 loopback";
    peer-as 65421;
}
```

```
neighbor 192.0.2.12 {
    description "leaf2 loopback";
    peer-as 65422;
}
neighbor 192.0.2.13 {
    description "leaf3 loopback";
    peer-as 65423;
}
neighbor 192.0.2.14 {
    description "leaf4 loopback";
    peer-as 65424;
}
neighbor 192.0.2.15 {
    description "leaf5 loopback";
    peer-as 65425;
}


root@spine2# show protocols bgp group overlay
type external;
multihop {
    no-nexthop-change;
}
local-address 192.0.2.102;
family evpn {
    signaling;
}
multipath;
neighbor 192.0.2.11 {
    description "leaf1 loopback";
    peer-as 65421;
}
neighbor 192.0.2.12 {
    description "leaf2 loopback";
    peer-as 65422;
}
neighbor 192.0.2.13 {
    description "leaf3 loopback";
    peer-as 65423;
}
neighbor 192.0.2.14 {
    description "leaf4 loopback";
    peer-as 65424;
}
neighbor 192.0.2.15 {
    description "leaf5 loopback";
    peer-as 65425;
}
```

Once configured, both spines should be in a BGP Established state for the BGP EVPN overlay peering with all leafs, which is confirmed in Example 5-11. The presence of the bgp.evpn.0 table statistics under each neighbor's address signifies that the peering for the EVPN family is up and associated to this routing table.

Example 5-11 *BGP overlay state on spine1 and spine2*

```
root@spine1> show bgp summary group overlay
Threading mode: BGP I/O
Default eBGP mode: advertise - accept, receive - accept
Groups: 2 Peers: 10 Down peers: 0
Table          Tot Paths  Act Paths Suppressed    History Damp State    Pending
inet.0
                     5          5          0          0          0          0
bgp.evpn.0
                     0          0          0          0          0          0
Peer                   AS      InPkt     OutPkt     OutQ   Flaps Last Up/Dwn State|#Active/Received/Accepted/Damped...
192.0.2.11          65421         25         23        0       0   10:23 Establ
  bgp.evpn.0: 0/0/0/0
192.0.2.12          65422         22         20        0       0    9:05 Establ
  bgp.evpn.0: 0/0/0/0
192.0.2.13          65423         19         17        0       0    7:40 Establ
  bgp.evpn.0: 0/0/0/0
192.0.2.14          65424         19         17        0       0    7:40 Establ
  bgp.evpn.0: 0/0/0/0
192.0.2.15          65425         19         17        0       0    7:39 Establ
  bgp.evpn.0: 0/0/0/0

root@spine2> show bgp summary group overlay
Threading mode: BGP I/O
Default eBGP mode: advertise - accept, receive - accept
Groups: 2 Peers: 10 Down peers: 0
Table          Tot Paths  Act Paths Suppressed    History Damp State    Pending
inet.0
                     5          5          0          0          0          0
bgp.evpn.0
                     0          0          0          0          0          0
Peer                   AS      InPkt     OutPkt     OutQ   Flaps Last Up/Dwn State|#Active/Received/Accepted/Damped...
192.0.2.11          65421         26         24        0       0   10:36 Establ
  bgp.evpn.0: 0/0/0/0
192.0.2.12          65422         23         21        0       0    9:19 Establ
  bgp.evpn.0: 0/0/0/0
192.0.2.13          65423         19         17        0       0    7:38 Establ
  bgp.evpn.0: 0/0/0/0
192.0.2.14          65424         19         18        0       0    7:38 Establ
  bgp.evpn.0: 0/0/0/0
192.0.2.15          65425         19         17        0       0    7:38 Establ
  bgp.evpn.0: 0/0/0/0
```

This BGP EVPN peering for the overlay merely establishes a path to share EVPN updates between the leafs and the spines, but there's more to do to get the actual fabric deployed. The following list details the additional steps needed:

- Configure each VTEP to use its loopback as a source for VXLAN tunnels, and define a Route Distinguisher, under the **switch-options** configuration hierarchy.

- Configure a Route Target under the **switch-options** configuration hierarchy, added as a BGP extended community to the BGP EVPN updates. Like MPLS L3VPNs, Route Targets determine which VTEPs import EVPN routes via matching import Route Targets.

- Create appropriate VLANs and map them to VXLAN VNIs (and assign the VLANs to corresponding host-facing interfaces).

- Enable the VNIs for EVPN learning under the **protocols evpn** configuration hierarchy, using the **extended-vni-list** configuration option, which controls which VNIs are enabled for EVPN. This also allows the appropriate EVPN routes to be generated for the VNI.

Since the spines are lean spines, used purely for forwarding IP traffic between the leafs (they do not have any hosts behind them and thus are not VTEPs, in this case), only the leafs need to be configured for this.

Taking leaf1 as an example again, Example 5-12 demonstrates the required configuration.

Example 5-12 *Configuration on leaf1 to finish EVPN VXLAN deployment*

```
root@leaf1# show switch-options
vtep-source-interface lo0.0;
route-distinguisher 192.0.2.11:1;
vrf-target target:1:1;

root@leaf1# show protocols evpn
encapsulation vxlan;
extended-vni-list all;

root@leaf1# show vlans v100
vlan-id 100;
vxlan {
    vni 10100;
}

root@leaf1# show interfaces et-0/0/49
mtu 9200;
unit 0 {
    family ethernet-switching {
        interface-mode access;
        vlan {
            members v100;
        }
    }
}
```

All remaining leafs are configured in the same way, except leaf2 and leaf3, where additional configuration is needed for the multihomed host, h2. For this, an Aggregate Ethernet (AE) interface is created on both leafs, and LACP (in active mode) is used for port bundling. The AE interface is assigned an Ethernet Segment, essentially making this an ESI LAG (link aggregation group). Examples 5-13 and 5-14 demonstrate how this is configured on leaf2 and leaf3, respectively. While this information may seem overwhelming at this point, details of exactly how this works are discussed in the later section "EVPN Multihoming with ESI LAG and EVPN Type-1/Type-4 Routes," including a discussion of Multi-chassis Link Aggregation (MC-LAG or MLAG), its drawbacks, and how EVPN multihoming (ESI LAG) is more advantageous.

Example 5-13 *ESI LAG configuration on leaf2 for multihomed host h2*

```
root@leaf2# show chassis
aggregated-devices {
    ethernet {
        device-count 1;
    }
}


root@leaf2# show interfaces et-0/0/50
ether-options {
    802.3ad ae1;
}


root@leaf2# show interfaces ae1
mtu 9200;
esi {
    00:00:00:00:11:11:00:00:00:00;
    all-active;
}
aggregated-ether-options {
    lacp {
        active;
        system-id 00:00:00:00:00:11;
    }
}
unit 0 {
    family ethernet-switching {
        interface-mode access;
        vlan {
            members v100;
        }
    }
}
```

Example 5-14 *ESI LAG configuration on leaf3 for multihomed host h2*

```
root@leaf3# show chassis
aggregated-devices {
    ethernet {
        device-count 1;
    }
}


root@leaf3# show interfaces et-0/0/52
ether-options {
    802.3ad ae1;
}
```

```
root@leaf3# show interfaces ae1
mtu 9200;
esi {
    00:00:00:00:11:11:00:00:00:00;
    all-active;
}
aggregated-ether-options {
    lacp {
        active;
        system-id 00:00:00:00:00:11;
    }
}
unit 0 {
    family ethernet-switching {
        interface-mode access;
        vlan {
            members v100;
        }
    }
}
```

The host h2 has an LACP system ID of 00:00:00:00:00:22, and the state of port bundling can be confirmed, as shown in Example 5-15, using the **show lacp interface** [*intf-name*] **extensive** operational mode command. The output of this command shows the partner ID, which matches host h2's LACP system ID, and more importantly, that the LACP Collecting, Distributing, and Synchronization flags are set.

Example 5-15 *LACP state on leaf2 and leaf3 for multihomed host h2*

```
root@leaf2> show lacp interfaces ae1 extensive
Aggregated interface: ae1
    LACP state:       Role   Exp  Def  Dist Col  Syn  Aggr  Timeout  Activity
      et-0/0/50       Actor   No   No   Yes  Yes  Yes  Yes    Fast    Active
      et-0/0/50       Partner No   No   Yes  Yes  Yes  Yes    Fast    Active
    LACP protocol:        Receive State  Transmit State       Mux State
      et-0/0/50             Current    Fast periodic Collecting distributing
    LACP info:        Role   System            System         Port    Port    Port
                             priority          identifier     priority number  key
      et-0/0/50       Actor     127  00:00:00:00:00:11           127      1      2
      et-0/0/50       Partner   127  00:00:00:00:00:22           127      1      2


root@leaf3> show lacp interfaces ae1 extensive
Aggregated interface: ae1
    LACP state:       Role   Exp  Def  Dist Col  Syn  Aggr  Timeout  Activity
      et-0/0/52       Actor   No   No   Yes  Yes  Yes  Yes    Fast    Active
      et-0/0/52       Partner No   No   Yes  Yes  Yes  Yes    Fast    Active
    LACP protocol:        Receive State  Transmit State       Mux State
      et-0/0/52             Current    Fast periodic Collecting distributing
    LACP info:        Role   System            System         Port    Port    Port
                             priority          identifier     priority number  key
      et-0/0/52       Actor     127  00:00:00:00:00:11           127      1      2
      et-0/0/52       Partner   127  00:00:00:00:00:22           127      2      2
```

At this point, the configuration for the bridged overlay fabric is complete. All hosts can communicate with each other, which is confirmed in the following section with a high-level packet walk.

Packet Flow in a Bridged Overlay Fabric

To demonstrate a high-level packet flow in a bridged overlay fabric, consider communication between host h1 and h3. Both hosts are in the 10.100.100.0/24 IPv4 subnet range, with h1 having an IP address of 10.100.100.1/24 and h3 having an IP address of 10.100.100.3/24, as shown in Figure 5-5.

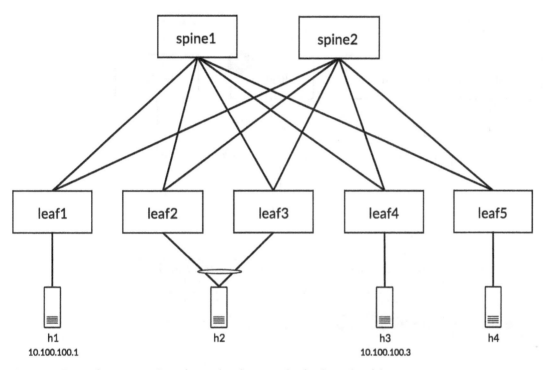

Figure 5-5 *Reference topology for packet flow in a bridged overlay fabric*

Since both hosts are in the same subnet, when h1 wants to communicate with h3, it can simply ARP for h3's IP address directly. This ARP request is received on leaf1—if leaf1 has a MAC-to-IP binding in its table for h3, and proxy ARP (and ARP suppression) is enabled, it can respond to h1, acting as a proxy for the destination. This process is discussed in detail later in this chapter in the section titled "Proxy ARP and ARP Suppression."

Assuming that leaf1 is unaware of host h3, the ARP request is flooded in the fabric via ingress replication by packaging the broadcast ARP packet into a unicast VXLAN packet, destined for each leaf that has shown interest in this virtual network. Additionally, h1's MAC address is locally learned on leaf1 and distributed in the fabric via BGP EVPN. This allows leaf4 to learn h1's MAC address and install it as a remote entry, pointing to a VXLAN tunnel to leaf1 as the egress interface.

When leaf4 receives the encapsulated ARP request, it decapsulates the packet and sends it to h3. This entire process is visualized in Figure 5-6.

The ARP reply from host h3 is a unicast packet and does not need to be flooded since leaf4 is aware of h1 now—it is simply sent over the VXLAN tunnel to leaf1, where it is decapsulated and sent to h1. During this process, leaf4 learns h3's MAC address locally and distributes it to other leafs in the fabric via BGP EVPN, which allows leaf1 to install this as a remote entry pointing to a VXLAN tunnel to leaf4 as the egress interface.

At this point, both h1 and h3 have resolved each other's IP addresses to MAC addresses and h1 can now send an IP packet destined for h3, which is an ICMP request in this case, generated using the **ping** utility, as shown in Figure 5-7.

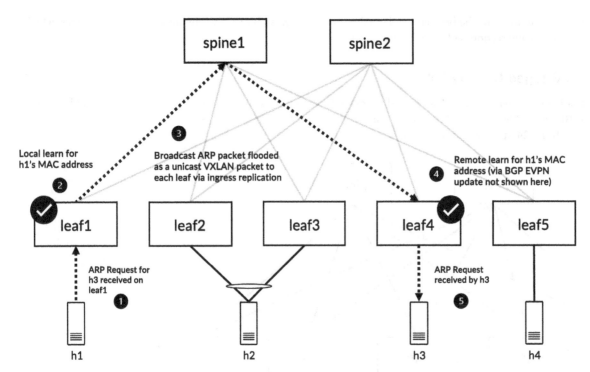

Figure 5-6   *High-level packet flow for an ARP request from h1 for h3*

```
No.   Time       Source        Destination   Protocol Length Info
  1 0.000000  10.100.100…  10.100.100…  ICMP   102 Echo (ping) request  id=0x3093, seq=222/56832, ttl=64 (reply in 2)
  2 0.000413  10.100.100…  10.100.100…  ICMP   102 Echo (ping) reply    id=0x3093, seq=222/56832, ttl=64 (request in 1)
  3 1.000987  10.100.100…  10.100.100…  ICMP   102 Echo (ping) request  id=0x3093, seq=223/57088, ttl=64 (reply in 4)
  4 1.001385  10.100.100…  10.100.100…  ICMP   102 Echo (ping) reply    id=0x3093, seq=223/57088, ttl=64 (request in 3)
```

```
Ethernet II, Src: JuniperN_b9:80:a7 (f0:4b:3a:b9:80:a7), Dst: JuniperN_b9:80:ab (f0:4b:3a:b9:80:ab)   0000  f0 4b 3a b9 80 ab f0 4b
  Destination: JuniperN_b9:80:ab (f0:4b:3a:b9:80:ab)                                                  0010  00 54 2f 6a 00 00 40 01
  Source: JuniperN_b9:80:a7 (f0:4b:3a:b9:80:a7)                                                       0020  64 03 08 00 bf a0 30 93
  Type: IPv4 (0x0800)                                                                                 0030  0f f2 08 09 0a 0b 0c 0d
  Frame check sequence: 0x5b222746 [unverified]                                                       0040  16 17 18 19 1a 1b 1c 1d
  [FCS Status: Unverified]                                                                            0050  26 27 28 29 2a 2b 2c 2d
Internet Protocol Version 4, Src: 10.100.100.1, Dst: 10.100.100.3                                     0060  36 37 5b 22 27 46
  0100 .... = Version: 4
  .... 0101 = Header Length: 20 bytes (5)
  Differentiated Services Field: 0x00 (DSCP: CS0, ECN: Not-ECT)
  Total Length: 84
  Identification: 0x2f6a (12138)
  000. .... = Flags: 0x0
  ...0 0000 0000 0000 = Fragment Offset: 0
  Time to Live: 64
  Protocol: ICMP (1)
  Header Checksum: 0x6e73 [validation disabled]
  [Header checksum status: Unverified]
  Source Address: 10.100.100.1
  Destination Address: 10.100.100.3
Internet Control Message Protocol
  Type: 8 (Echo (ping) request)
  Code: 0
  Checksum: 0xbfa0 [correct]
  [Checksum Status: Good]
  Identifier (BE): 12435 (0x3093)
  Identifier (LE): 37680 (0x9330)
  Sequence Number (BE): 222 (0x00de)
  Sequence Number (LE): 56832 (0xde00)
  [Response frame: 2]
  Timestamp from icmp data: Jun  1, 2023 19:43:15.331762000 IST
  [Timestamp from icmp data (relative): 45382.499626000 seconds]
  Data (48 bytes)
```

Figure 5-7   *ICMP request from h1 destined for h3*

When leaf1 receives the IP packet, its MAC address table points to the VXLAN tunnel to leaf4 as the egress interface for the destination MAC address (which is h3's MAC address). This is shown in Example 5-16, using the **show ethernet-switching table** [*mac-address*] operational mode command.

Example 5-16 *MAC address table for host h3's MAC address*

```
root@leaf1> show ethernet-switching table f0:4b:3a:b9:00:ab

MAC flags (S - static MAC, D - dynamic MAC, L - locally learned, P - Persistent static
           SE - statistics enabled, NM - non configured MAC, R - remote PE MAC, O - ovsdb MAC,
           B - Blocked MAC)


Ethernet switching table : 3 entries, 3 learned
Routing instance : default-switch
   Vlan           MAC               MAC     GBP  Logical          SVLBNH/     Active
   name           address           flags   tag  interface        VENH Index  source
   v100           f0:4b:3a:b9:80:ab  DR          vtep.32772                   192.0.2.14
```

The original packet is now encapsulated with VXLAN headers—this includes a VXLAN header (8 bytes), a UDP header (8 bytes), an outer IP header (20 bytes), and an outer Ethernet header (14 bytes), totaling an overhead of 50 bytes. The VXLAN header includes the VNI for this VLAN, which is 10100 in this case. This encapsulated packet is shown in Figure 5-8.

> **Note** Because of this 50-byte overhead added as part of VXLAN encapsulation, MTU becomes an important consideration in such fabrics. Thus, the MTU should be increased fabric-wide to accommodate larger-sized packets.

```
No.   Time      Source       Destination     Protocol Length Info
    1 0.000000  10.100.100…  10.100.100…     ICMP     148    Echo (ping) request  id=0xc857, seq=24/6144, ttl=64 (reply in 2)
    2 0.000130  10.100.100…  10.100.100…     ICMP     152    Echo (ping) reply    id=0xc857, seq=24/6144, ttl=64 (request in 1)

> Frame 1: 148 bytes on wire (1184 bits), 148 bytes captured (1184 bits)    0000  d8 b1 22 8a 40 2f 40 de
  Ethernet II, Src: JuniperN_7b:70:7d (40:de:ad:7b:70:7d), Dst: JuniperN_8a:40:2f (d8:b1:22:8a:40:2f)   0010  00 86 52 73 00 00 40 11
  > Destination: JuniperN_8a:40:2f (d8:b1:22:8a:40:2f)                       0020  02 0e 6d f2 12 b5 00 72
  > Source: JuniperN_7b:70:7d (40:de:ad:7b:70:7d)                            0030  74 00 f0 4b 3a b9 80 ab
    Type: IPv4 (0x0800)                                                      0040  45 00 00 54 b2 ed 00 00
  Internet Protocol Version 4, Src: 192.0.2.11, Dst: 192.0.2.14             0050  0a 64 64 03 08 00 66 a4
    0100 .... = Version: 4                                                   0060  00 0a 98 46 08 09 0a 0b
    .... 0101 = Header Length: 20 bytes (5)                                  0070  14 15 16 17 18 19 1a 1b
  > Differentiated Services Field: 0x00 (DSCP: CS0, ECN: Not-ECT)            0080  24 25 26 27 28 29 2a 2b
    Total Length: 134                                                        0090  34 35 36 37
    Identification: 0x5273 (21107)
  > 000. .... = Flags: 0x0
    ...0 0000 0000 0000 = Fragment Offset: 0
    Time to Live: 64
    Protocol: UDP (17)
    Header Checksum: 0xa3da [validation disabled]
    [Header checksum status: Unverified]
    Source Address: 192.0.2.11
    Destination Address: 192.0.2.14
  User Datagram Protocol, Src Port: 28146, Dst Port: 4789
    Source Port: 28146
    Destination Port: 4789
    Length: 114
  > Checksum: 0x0000 [zero-value ignored]
    [Stream index: 0]
  > [Timestamps]
    UDP payload (106 bytes)
  Virtual eXtensible Local Area Network
  > Flags: 0x0800, VXLAN Network ID (VNI)
    Group Policy ID: 0
    VXLAN Network Identifier (VNI): 10100
    Reserved: 0
> Ethernet II, Src: JuniperN_b9:80:a7 (f0:4b:3a:b9:80:a7), Dst: JuniperN_b9:80:ab (f0:4b:3a:b9:80:ab)
> Internet Protocol Version 4, Src: 10.100.100.1, Dst: 10.100.100.3
> Internet Control Message Protocol
```

Figure 5-8 *Encapsulated VXLAN packet*

The destination IP address, in the outer IP header, carries the packet to leaf4, where it is decapsulated and sent to h3, as shown in Figure 5-9. A similar process happens in reverse when host h3 responds with an ICMP reply.

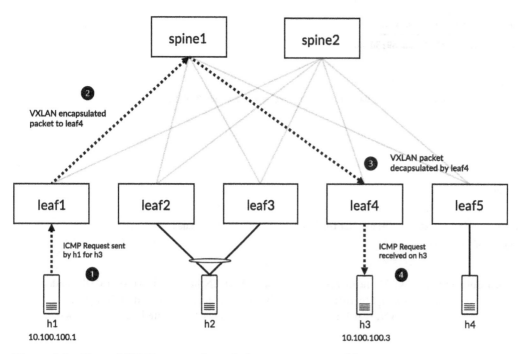

Figure 5-9   *Flow of ICMP request through the EVPN VXLAN fabric*

Example 5-17 shows that all hosts in the fabric can communicate with each other over this bridged overlay fabric, with BGP EVPN distributing MAC address information between VTEPs.

Example 5-17   *Host h1 reachability to hosts h2, h3, and h4*

```
root@h1# ping 10.100.100.2
PING 10.100.100.2 (10.100.100.2): 56 data bytes
64 bytes from 10.100.100.2: icmp_seq=0 ttl=64 time=73.059 ms
64 bytes from 10.100.100.2: icmp_seq=1 ttl=64 time=0.898 ms
64 bytes from 10.100.100.2: icmp_seq=2 ttl=64 time=0.938 ms
64 bytes from 10.100.100.2: icmp_seq=3 ttl=64 time=77.450 ms
^C
--- 10.100.100.2 ping statistics ---
4 packets transmitted, 4 packets received, 0% packet loss
round-trip min/avg/max/stddev = 0.898/38.086/77.450/37.201 ms


root@h1# ping 10.100.100.3
PING 10.100.100.3 (10.100.100.3): 56 data bytes
64 bytes from 10.100.100.3: icmp_seq=0 ttl=64 time=5.037 ms
64 bytes from 10.100.100.3: icmp_seq=1 ttl=64 time=0.867 ms
64 bytes from 10.100.100.3: icmp_seq=2 ttl=64 time=3.995 ms
64 bytes from 10.100.100.3: icmp_seq=3 ttl=64 time=29.971 ms
^C
--- 10.100.100.3 ping statistics ---
4 packets transmitted, 4 packets received, 0% packet loss
round-trip min/avg/max/stddev = 0.867/9.968/29.971/11.651 ms


root@h1# ping 10.100.100.4
PING 10.100.100.4 (10.100.100.4): 56 data bytes
64 bytes from 10.100.100.4: icmp_seq=0 ttl=64 time=0.951 ms
```

```
64 bytes from 10.100.100.4: icmp_seq-1 ttl-64 time-0.853 ms
64 bytes from 10.100.100.4: icmp_seq=2 ttl=64 time=0.901 ms
64 bytes from 10.100.100.4: icmp_seq=3 ttl=64 time=87.978 ms
^C
--- 10.100.100.4 ping statistics ---
4 packets transmitted, 4 packets received, 0% packet loss
round-trip min/avg/max/stddev = 0.853/22.671/87.978/37.705 ms
```

It is important to pay attention to how BGP, for the underlay and overlay, was configured as separate groups, essentially implying two separate sessions. This is confirmed with the output of **show system connections**, which, in this case, shows different sessions for the underlay and overlay.

In the example from leaf1, shown in Example 5-18, two TCP sessions for the underlay (one for spine1 and another for spine2) are established between the point-to-point interfaces and then two more TCP sessions for the overlay (again, one for spine1 and another for spine2) are established between the loopback addresses.

Example 5-18   *TCP sessions established for underlay and overlay*

```
root@leaf1> show system connections inet | grep "198.51.100"
tcp4    0    0  198.51.100.2.53633              198.51.100.3.179              ESTABLISHED
tcp4    0    0  198.51.100.0.49548              198.51.100.1.179              ESTABLISHED

root@leaf1> show system connections inet | grep "192.0.2"
tcp4    0    0  192.0.2.11.50932                192.0.2.102.179               ESTABLISHED
tcp4    0    0  192.0.2.11.179                  192.0.2.101.60640             ESTABLISHED
```

Note   The design of having two separate sessions differs from many other vendors who suggest using a single session to transport both the underlay and the overlay BGP families. While this method of using a single session may appear to be operationally easier at first glance, two separate sessions provide a clean separation of the underlay and the overlay, allow for easier administration of policies specific to the underlay and overlay, and are operationally easier to monitor and troubleshoot.

Learning MAC Addresses and EVPN Type-2 Routes

EVPN Type-2 routes, briefly explained in Chapter 4, "VXLAN as a Network Virtualization Overlay," carry MAC addresses and, optionally, IPv4/IPv6 addresses, facilitating remote leafs to learn these addresses via the BGP EVPN control plane. More specifically, EVPN Type-2 MAC routes are used to install MAC addresses for the corresponding VNI and bridge domain in the MAC address table associated to the originating VTEP as the egress/exit point for the address. EVPN Type-2 MAC+IP routes enable a remote leaf to build its ARP cache (using the MAC address and IP address in the route), while also installing host-specific routes in its routing table based on the kind of routing model deployed for the fabric, which is explored in detail in Chapter 8, "Edge-Routed Bridging."

This section unravels how local and remote MAC addresses are learned in a bridged overlay EVPN VXLAN fabric, and how BGP EVPN facilitates this using EVPN Type-2 routes.

High-Level Software Architecture for MAC Address Learning

To understand how local and remote MAC addresses are learned, it is important to first understand the general software architecture and the components involved. In no way is this architecture meant to be a completely accurate representation of the software architecture across different platforms—instead, it is simply used to provide some context about different components involved in this process and how they communicate with each other. To that end, Figure 5-10 depicts a high-level overview of the software architecture from a common Juniper Data Center leaf, the QFX5120. This was previously shown in Chapter 1 as well. The focus is solely on components relevant to MAC learning.

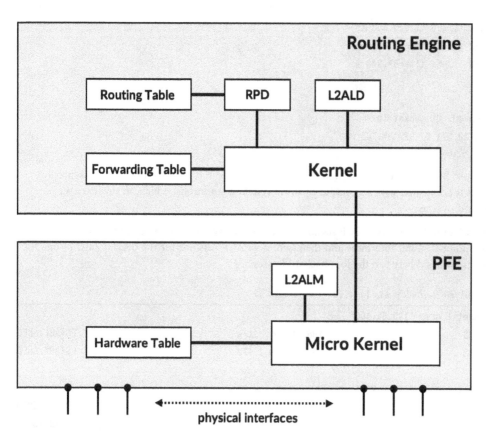

Figure 5-10   *A high-level software architectural view of components involved in MAC learning*

The Packet Forwarding Engine (PFE) includes the ASIC and the Flexible PIC Concentrator (FPC), which houses the Physical Interface Card (PIC) that provides the physical interfaces for the device. The Routing Engine is the brains of the device, and there is a clear separation of the control plane and the forwarding plane, which is pioneered by Juniper.

A locally learned MAC address, on a VTEP, is learned in the data plane via an ARP/GARP packet received on a physical interface when a host comes online for the first time. Since this is learned in hardware (over a physical interface), the Layer 2 Address Learning Manager (L2ALM) in the PFE is informed of this MAC address via the hardware layer. L2ALM sends a notification to the Layer 2 Address Learning Daemon (L2ALD) in the Routing Engine to inform it of this newly learned MAC address as well. The address is installed in the MAC address table, with the interface and VLAN/BD (bridge domain) the packet was received on, and L2ALD, in turn, sends a notification to the routing process (RPD) to inform EVPN.

EVPN installs this entry into its database and notifies BGP to generate the appropriate EVPN Type-2 routes for this and send it to its neighbors. A MAC address learned from a remote VTEP, on the other hand, undergoes the same process but in reverse. An EVPN Type-2 route is received and processed by BGP, which hands it to RPD/EVPN. RPD notifies L2ALD, which sends it to L2ALM to install the MAC address in the PFE complex and the hardware layer.

Learning Local MAC Addresses

Visually, the process of locally learning a MAC address, within the context of BGP EVPN, and the sequence of events for this, are depicted in Figure 5-11, including commands and traceoptions that can be used to get deeper insight into what happens at each step.

These commands and traceoptions will be used to gather details of what happens when host h1, in the reference topology shown in Figure 5-5, comes online for the first time and its MAC address is learned on leaf1 (as a reference, h1's MAC address is f0:4b:3a:b9:80:a7). These commands and their outputs will also allow you to gain an understanding of what the expected outputs are and what to focus on when viewing these in steady state, thus being able to spot potential deviations easily.

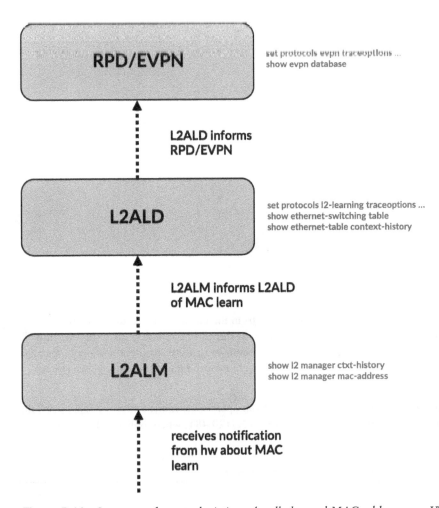

Figure 5-11 *Sequence of events depicting a locally learned MAC address on a VTEP*

Along with these traceoptions, a port analyzer is configured (sometimes called a port mirror) on spine1 to capture BGP EVPN updates sent by leaf1 when the MAC address for host h1 is learned. The output interface of the port analyzer connects to a server that captures these packets. All these are important tools in the troubleshooting toolkit for Junos. The configuration to set up traceoptions on leaf1 is shown in Example 5-19, while the configuration for the port analyzer on spine1 is shown in Example 5-20.

Example 5-19 *Traceoptions enabled on leaf1*

```
root@leaf1# show protocols l2-learning traceoptions
file h1-l2ald.log size 50m;
level all;
flag all;

root@leaf1# show protocols evpn traceoptions
file h1-evpn.log size 50m;
flag all;

root@leaf1# show protocols bgp group overlay traceoptions
file h1-bgp.log size 50m;
flag all;
```

Example 5-20   *Port analyzer configured on spine1*

```
root@spine1# show forwarding-options analyzer
mirror {
    input {
        ingress {
            interface et-0/0/32.0;
        }
        egress {
            interface et-0/0/32.0;
        }
    }
    output {
        interface xe-0/0/65.0;
    }
}
```

When a MAC address is learned in the data plane, L2ALM receives an update from the hardware layer and sends this to L2ALD. At the same time, an entry is created in L2ALM for this MAC address, as shown in Example 5-21, using the **show l2 manager mac-address** [*mac-address*] and **show l2 manager mac-table** PFE-level commands. Additionally, the **show l2 manager ctxt-history mac-address** [*mac-address*] PFE-level command can be used to dump historical data of how this MAC address was learned by L2ALM.

The PFE can be accessed by entering the shell using the **start shell** command from operational mode and then logging into the PFE using the **vty fpc0** command. FPC0 is used here because this is a Juniper QFX5120-48Y, where only one FPC is present, numbered as 0.

Example 5-21   *L2ALM context history when host h1's MAC address is learned on leaf1*

```
root@leaf1> start shell
root@leaf1:RE:0% vty fpc0


Switching platform (2200 Mhz Pentium processor, 644MB memory, 0KB flash)


FPC0(leaf1 vty)# show l2 manager ctxt-history mac-address f0:4b:3a:b9:80:a7


*snip*


ctx:2302

----------------------------------

(354:06:41.330)(1) op:1,status:0, last_status:0, error:0 (NONE), error-reason:0(NONE), bd:3, mac:f0:4b:3a:b9:80:a7,
hw_wr:0x1(HW Add Pass, )

ctx_sync:1, fwd_sync:0, ctx-flag:40000000005(Msg from RE,Mac local src,Local Origin,), ctx-reason:0(REASON_NONE),
i-op:1(INTRNL_OP_FWD_ENTRY_ALLOCATED), act:0x0(-), extf:0x0

GET_RTT, GET_MAC, ALLOCATE_MAC, GET_IFL, GET_IFF, GET_IFBD, GET_BD, ADD_TO_IFL_LIST, ADD_TO_BD_LIST, UPDATE_HARDWARE_INFO,
STOP,

le:828(0x33c), le_type:0, rtt-id:8, p_le:0(0x0), p_le_type:0, fwd_nh:0, svlbnh:0 ev:-, fwd_entry_ptr 0xb14a01aa

fwd_ifl:0, pseudo_ifl:0, fnh:0 hw_underlay_ifl:0, hw-notif-ifl:828, programmed-ifl:828 pseudo-vtep underlay-ifl-idx 0
gbp_tag_value: 0 prev_gbp_tag_val: 0 static pseudo-vtep underlay-ifl 0


 ctx:2303

----------------------------------

(354:06:41.511)(2) op:1,status:0, last_status:0, error:0 (NONE), error-reason:0(NONE), bd:3, mac:f0:4b:3a:b9:80:a7,
hw_wr:0x0(-)
```

ctx_sync:0, fwd_sync:1, ctx-flag:0(Msg from HAL,Mac local src,), ctx-reason:0(REASON_NONE), i-op:4(INTRNL_OP_FWD_ENTRY_
EXISTS), act:0x800000(Timer Start,), extf:0x0

GET_MAC, GET_IFL, GET_IFF, GET_IFBD, GET_BD, UPDATE_HARDWARE_INFO, SEND_TO_L2ALD, STOP,

le:828(0x33c), le_type:0, rtt-id:8, p_le:0(0x0), p_le_type:0, fwd_nh:0, svlbnh:0 ev:-, fwd_entry_ptr 0xb14a01aa

fwd_ifl:0, pseudo_ifl:0, fnh:0 hw_underlay_ifl:0, hw-notif-ifl:828, programmed-ifl:828 pseudo-vtep underlay-ifl-idx 0
gbp_tag_value: 0 prev_gbp_tag_val: 0 static pseudo-vtep underlay-ifl 0

snip

FPC0(leaf1 vty)# **show l2 manager mac-table**

route table name   : default-switch.8

  mac counters

    maximum   count

    0   4

  mac table information

mac address	BD Index	learn vlan	Entry Flags	GBP Tag	entry ifl	hal ifl	hardware info		
							pfe	mask	ifl
f0:4b:3a:b9:80:a7	3	0	0x0814	0	et-0/0/49.0	et-0/0/49.0	0	0x1	0
f0:4b:3a:b9:80:ab	3	0	0x0014	0	vtep.32772	vtep.32772	0	0x1	0
f0:4b:3a:b9:80:bb	3	0	0x0014	0	vtep.32771	vtep.32771	0	0x1	0
f0:4b:3a:b9:81:60	3	0	0x0014	0	esi.8388616	esi.1753	0	0x1	1753

  Displayed 4 entries for routing instance default-switch.8

FPC0(leaf1 vty)# **show l2 manager mac-address f0:4b:3a:b9:80:a7 bridge-domain 3 learn-vlan 0**

mac address	f0:4b:3a:b9:80:a7
bd_index	3
learn vlan	0
FwdEntry Addr	0xb14a01aa
entry flags	0x814
entry ext flags	0x0
entry ext flags_2	0x0
need sync flag	False
fwd_nhidx	0
esi_nhidx	0
esi_svlbnhidx	0
retry count	0
bgp sequence number	0

GBP tag value   0
In ifl list, In RTT Table, Update entry in HW

entry ifl	et-0/0/49.0
entry hw ifl	et-0/0/49.0
entry seq number	1
entry epoch	1
stp_index	13
Flush Object Addr	0xba39e090

```
Underlay ifl        0
hardware information
-------------------
install count       1
    pfe id  0    install information    S/-    src et-0/0/49.0 dest unknown
    mac=f0:4b:3a:b9:80:a7 vlan=28673 GPORT=0xb0000002   SrcHit DstHit
```

The output shown in Example 5-21 confirms that L2ALM learned this MAC address on interface *et-0/0/49.0*. It was informed of this MAC address via the *hardware abstraction layer (HAL)*. As the name signifies, HAL is an abstraction layer that sits in the PFE complex and interfaces with the hardware layer.

L2ALD receives this update from L2ALM and creates an entry for this MAC address. In the context history for L2ALM, every historical line item is associated with an action. As shown in Example 5-22, using the **show ethernet-switching context-history mac-addr** [*mac-address*] operational mode command, once L2ALD receives this update, the context history confirms that it notifies RPD as one of the actions. The acronym *NL* in the output stands for *New Learn*.

Example 5-22   *L2ALD context history when host h1's MAC address is learned on leaf1*

```
root@leaf1> show ethernet-switching context-history mac-addr f0:4b:3a:b9:80:a7

*snip*

 ctxt:6855 Type:MAC_IP reason:FROM_L2ALM NL   T:2023-05-02 22:38:18 PDT OP:add IP:10.100.100.1 MAC:f0:4b:3a:b9:80:a7 BD:3
IFL:828 NL   Mask L:0x0000000000000001 R:0x0000000000000000 Rp:0x0000000000000000 NL  D1:input mask: 0x1 ctx ifl 828
rpdf:[ctx 0x0000000000000000 ent 0x0000000000000000]  local:[ctx 0x0 ent 0xc00]  flags:[ctx 0x10000002 ent 0x10000082]
l2d_flags:[LOCAL, ENQ_TO_RPD, ] vni:0 gbp_tag_value:0 D2:actions: 0x800206200 [MACIP_ENTRY_MISSING, MACIP_ENTRY_ADDED,
IP_ENTRY_ADDED, MACIP_ENQ, SENT_TO_RPD, ] entry: 0x2e7bed0 esi: NULL ESI peer_ip:  NL  Error:MAC_NOT_IN_KERNEL
----------------------------------------------- END ctxt:6855 ----

 ctxt:6856 Type:MAC_IP reason:MAC->ADD_ENTRIES NL   T:2023-05-02 22:38:19 PDT OP:nop IP:10.100.100.1 MAC:f0:4b:3a:b9:80:a7
BD:3 IFL:828 NL   Mask L:0x0000000000000001 R:0x0000000000000000 Rp:0x0000000000000000 NL  D1:input mask: 0x0 ctx ifl 828
rpdf:[ctx 0x0000000000000000 ent 0x0000000000000000]  local:[ctx 0xc00 ent 0xc00]  flags:[ctx 0x10000082 ent 0x10000082]
l2d_flags:[LOCAL, ENQ_TO_RPD, ] vni:0 gbp_tag_value:0 D2:actions: 0x8000010010040 [FROM_MAC, EVENT_POSTED, EVENT_GENCFG_
POSTED, ] entry: 0x2e7bed0 esi: NULL ESI peer_ip:  NL  Error:None
----------------------------------------------- END ctxt:6856 ----

 ctxt:6857 Type:MAC_IP reason:MAC->ENQ_ENTRIES NL   T:2023-05-02 22:38:19 PDT OP:nop IP:10.100.100.1 MAC:f0:4b:3a:b9:80:a7
BD:3 IFL:0 NL   Mask L:0x0000000000000000 R:0x0000000000000000 Rp:0x0000000000000000 NL  D1:input mask: 0x0 ctx ifl 828
rpdf:[ctx 0x0000000000000000 ent 0x0000000000000000]  local:[ctx 0xc00 ent 0x0]  flags:[ctx 0x10000082 ent 0x0] l2d_
flags:[] vni:0 gbp_tag_value:0 D2:actions: 0x800000040 [FROM_MAC, SENT_TO_RPD, ] entry: 0x0 esi: NULL ESI peer_ip:  NL
Error:None
----------------------------------------------- END ctxt:6857 ----

 ctxt:6858 Type:MAC NL   T:2023-05-02 22:38:19 PDT OP:add MAC:f0:4b:3a:b9:80:a7 RTT:8 BD:3 VLAN:0 VNI:0 IFL:et-0/0/49.0
IflId:828 NH:0 NL   Reason:None IntrlRsn:None Mask: L:0x1, R:0x0 RVTEP: ESI:NULL ESI Error:No error: 0 NL  EntFlags:in_
hash,in_ifd,in_ifl,in_vlan,in_rtt,in_kernel,in_ifbd,adv_remote NL  SM: NL  CtxFlags:None  NL  Actions:EVENT_HANDLE,
PUSHED_KERNEL, SENT_TO_RPD,  NL    :actions:0x300080, entry_addr:0x2f43510, ctxt_flags:0x0, ent_flags:0x2101f, ent_ext_
flags:0x8000, seq:1 gbp_tag_value:0
----------------------------------------------- END ctxt:6858 ----

*snip*
```

With the l2-learning traceoptions enabled, similar but more detailed information can be gathered from L2ALD. From the snippet of the traceoptions log file, shown in Example 5-23 using the **show log** [*file-name*] operational mode command, the following can be confirmed:

1. L2ALD receives an update from L2ALM for MAC address f0:4b:3a:b9:80:a7 and IP address 10.100.100.1.

2. It creates an entry for this and notifies RPD to create an EVPN MAC route and a MAC+IP route.

3. This notification is enqueued and then successfully sent to RPD.

Example 5-23 *L2ALD traceoptions log when host h1's MAC address is learned on leaf1*

```
root@leaf1> show log h1-l2ald.log | grep f0:4b:3a:b9:80:a7

*snip*

May  2 22:38:18.940716 l2ald_mac_ip_msg_handler:3620 rcvd mac+ip entry from pfe: msgin op 1 bd 3 ip_addr 10.100.100.1
mac_addr f0:4b:3a:b9:80:a7 l2 ifl idx 828 ident 0 flags 10000002
May  2 22:38:18.940729 l2ald_mac_ip_msg_handler:3685 mac f0:4b:3a:b9:80:a7 is not available l2 ifl (828:et-0/0/49.0). add
mac for mac+ip 10.100.100.1
May  2 22:38:18.940737 l2ald_generate_mac_from_mac_ip:3359 [ifl 828 bd 3 vlan 0 mac-address f0:4b:3a:b9:80:a7]
May  2 22:38:18.940761 l2ald_mac_msg_handler:1629 From L2ALM [(1) ADD] msgin BD: 3 MAC Address: f0:4b:3a:b9:80:a7
May  2 22:38:18.940770 do_mac_process:6299 Processing [mac f0:4b:3a:b9:80:a7(epoch 1 stp 13) bd 3 vlan 0]
May  2 22:38:18.940870 l2ald_add_mac_to_global_db:417 Added MAC f0:4b:3a:b9:80:a7 from ifl 0 in global hash table
May  2 22:38:18.940900 libl2_add_mac_to_ifd_list:129 Added MAC f0:4b:3a:b9:80:a7 in ifd list for et-0/0/49
May  2 22:38:18.940939 libl2_ifl_access_add_mac_to_bd_info:432 mac f0:4b:3a:b9:80:a7 ADDED to bd_info 0x2eea6a0, bd vlan
is 100
May  2 22:38:18.941802 libl2_add_mac_to_ifl_list:285 Added MAC f0:4b:3a:b9:80:a7 in ifl list for le ifl:
(et-0/0/49.0:0x3c12010)
May  2 22:38:18.942539 libl2_add_mac_to_learn_vlan:240 Added MAC f0:4b:3a:b9:80:a7 in learn vlan list for bd v100+100.0


May  2 22:38:19.004046 l2ald_rpdf_init_dpcpmac:3964 Preparing cmd:MAC ROUTE ADD[1] sub_cmd:1 for MAC:f0:4b:3a:b9:80:a7
ip address: NHID:0 RTRID:0 ifln:et-0/0/49.0 ifld:828 rtt:8 flags:0x0000000100000002 ts:0x6451f34a
bdidgen:0x0000000300000004 vni:10100 rvtep:0.0.0.0 ESI:00:00:00:00:00:00:00:00:00:00 gbp tag value:0
May  2 22:38:19.004055 l2ald_rpdf_send_msg_to_peer:4189 MSG sent to RPD msgout op 0 opcode 1 (MAC ROUTE ADD) MAC
f0:4b:3a:b9:80:a7 ipaddr  vlan id 100 rtt id 8 ifl index 828 vni 10100 nh id 0 vtep ipaddr 0.0.0.0  bd id 3 isid 0 flags
0x0000000100000002 ifl name et-0/0/49.0, ts 0x6451f34a esi 00:00:00:00:00:00:00:00:00:00 gbp tag value 0
May  2 22:38:19.004070 l2ald_rpdf_msg_mac_enqueue:6800 Prepare MAC msg to RPD - MAC f0:4b:3a:b9:80:a7 ipaddr 0 encap type
0  vtep ipaddr 0  bd id 3 MAC_OP:1
May  2 22:38:19.004090 l2ald_ctrl_mac_post_add_rts_op:3170 ADD enqueued to RPD DPMAC:f0:4b:3a:b9:80:a7 bd_id:3
eflags:0x2101f


May  2 22:38:19.004143 l2ald_rpdf_init_dpcpmac:3964 Preparing cmd:MAC IP ROUTE ADD[7] sub_cmd:1 for MAC:f0:4b:3a:b9:80:a7
ip address:10.100.100.1 NHID:0 RTRID:0 ifln:et-0/0/49.0 ifld:828 rtt:8 flags:0x0000000100000082 ts:0x6451f34b
bdidgen:0x0000000300000004 vni:10100 rvtep:0.0.0.0 ESI:00:00:00:00:00:00:00:00:00:00 gbp tag value:0
May  2 22:38:19.004152 l2ald_rpdf_send_msg_to_peer:4189 MSG sent to RPD msgout op 0 opcode 7 (MAC IP ROUTE ADD) MAC
f0:4b:3a:b9:80:a7 ipaddr 10.100.100.1 vlan id 100 rtt id 8 ifl index 828 vni 10100 nh id 0 vtep ipaddr 0.0.0.0  bd id 3
isid 0 flags 0x0000000100000082 ifl name et-0/0/49.0, ts 0x6451f34b esi 00:00:00:00:00:00:00:00:00:00 gbp tag value 0
May  2 22:38:19.004162 l2ald_rpdf_msg_mac_enqueue:6800 Prepare MAC msg to RPD - MAC f0:4b:3a:b9:80:a7 ipaddr 164640a encap
type 0  vtep ipaddr 0  bd id 3 MAC_OP:7
May  2 22:38:19.004182 l2ald_mac_ip_enqueue:6448 Enqueue done for mac_ip_cmd 7, bd v100+100, mac_addr f0:4b:3a:b9:80:a7,
ip_addr 10.100.100.1
May  2 22:38:19.004188 l2ald_mac_ip_enqueue_entries:6523 Sucess MAC+IP enqueue: status 0 bd 3 mac f0:4b:3a:b9:80:a7 ip
10.100.100.1


*snip*
```

The MAC address table on leaf1 now has an entry for this MAC address. This is essentially the L2ALD view of the address, as shown in Example 5-24 using the **show ethernet-switching table** [*mac-address*] operational mode command.

Example 5-24   *Host h1's MAC address in the switching table on leaf1*

```
root@leaf1> show ethernet-switching table f0:4b:3a:b9:80:a7


MAC flags (S - static MAC, D - dynamic MAC, L - locally learned, P - Persistent static
           SE - statistics enabled, NM - non configured MAC, R - remote PE MAC, O - ovsdb MAC)



Ethernet switching table : 4 entries, 4 learned
Routing instance : default-switch
    Vlan            MAC             MAC    GBP  Logical             SVLBNH/    Active
    name            address         flags  tag  interface           VENH Index source
    v100            f0:4b:3a:b9:80:a7  D          et-0/0/49.0


root@leaf1> show ethernet-switching table f0:4b:3a:b9:80:a7 detail


MAC address: f0:4b:3a:b9:80:a7
  Routing instance: default-switch
  VLAN name: v100, VLAN ID: 100
  Learning interface: et-0/0/49.0
  ELP-NH: 0
  Layer 2 flags: in_hash,in_ifd,in_ifl,in_vlan,in_rtt,kernel,in_ifbd,advt_to_remote
  Epoch: 1                         Sequence number: 1
  Learning mask: 0x00000001        BGP sequence number: 0
  Time: 2023-05-02 22:38:18 PDT
```

RPD receives this notification from L2ALD, and EVPN adds this MAC address (and its corresponding IP address) in its database. It also creates an EVPN Type-2 MAC route and a MAC+IP route (if the IP address was also populated in the EVPN database) and passes it to BGP to send as an update to appropriate neighbors. In Example 5-25, the traceoptions log from EVPN shows this notification, and the command **show evpn database** displays the entry from the EVPN database.

Example 5-25   *Traceoptions for RPD and the EVPN database when host h1's MAC address is learned on leaf1*

```
root@leaf1> show log h1-evpn.log | grep f0:4b:3a:b9:80:a7


*snip*


May  2 22:38:19.046437 evpn_mac_msg_receive_from_l2ald:2639 EVPN instance default-switch [VS, Refcount: 7, Intfs: 2
(2 up), IRBs: 0 (0 up), Peers: 4,core-isolation-status-changed 0 Flags: 0x1814800] Received MAC+IP add for local MAC
f0:4b:3a:b9:80:a7 with L2 domain 10100, timestamp May 02 22:38:19.046414, interface et-0/0/49.0, ESI 0, IPv4 address
10.100.100.1

May  2 22:38:19.046454 evpn_mirror_mac_update:1310 EVPN instance default-switch [VS, Refcount: 7, Intfs: 2 (2 up),
IRBs: 0 (0 up), Peers: 4,core-isolation-status-changed 0 Flags: 0x1814800] Active RE MAC MAC+IP add for local MAC
f0:4b:3a:b9:80:a7 with rtt-index 8, VLAN 10100, interface et-0/0/49.0, flags 0x82, timestamp 0x6451f34a, seq num 0,
ESI 00:00:00:00:00:00:00:00:00:00 IPv4 address: 10.100.100.1 gbp-tag 0


May  2 22:38:19.046521 evpn_macdb_ip_addr_create:2499 EVPN MAC IP default-switch::10100::f0:4b:3a:b9:80:a7:
:et-0/0/49.0::10.100.100.1 [ESI flags: 0x40 <Local-To-Remote-Adv-Allowed>, IP flags: 0x2 <Local-Adv>] Created num_peers 0
num_mhapb 0 change_flags 0x1

May  2 22:38:19.046538 evpn_macdb_ip_move_tracking_start:850 EVPN MACDB IP tracker default-switch::10100::10.100.100.1
Added MACDB IP with source f0:4b:3a:b9:80:a7::et-0/0/49.0

May  2 22:38:19.046546 evpn_macdb_entry_add_macdb_esi:759 EVPN MAC ESI default-switch::10100::f0:4b:3a:b9:80:a7:
:et-0/0/49.0 [Active: no, Timestamp: May 02 22:38:19.046414, Flags: 0x40 <Local-To-Remote-Adv-Allowed>] Added to MAC ESI
list
```

```
May  2 22:38:19.046554 evpn_macdb_esi_create:1859 EVPN MAC ESI default-switch::10100::f0:4b:3a:b9:80:a7::et-0/0/49.0
[Active: yes, Timestamp: May 02 22:38:19.046414, Flags: 0x40 <Local-To-Remote-Adv-Allowed>] Created

May  2 22:38:19.046771 evpn_irb_intf_find_by_trans_l2domain:2192 EVPN MAC IP default-switch::10100::f0:4b:3a:b9:80:a7:
:et-0/0/49.0::10.100.100.1 [ESI flags: 0x40 <Local-To-Remote-Adv-Allowed>, IP flags: 0x2 <Local-Adv>] No bd and IRB
interface found by vni 10100

May  2 22:38:19.046785 evpn_macdb_ip_addr_adv_rt_create:1789 EVPN MAC IP default-switch::10100::f0:4b:3a:b9:80:a7:
:et-0/0/49.0::10.100.100.1 [ESI flags: 0x40 <Local-To-Remote-Adv-Allowed>, IP flags: 0x2 <Local-Adv>] Creating MAC+IP
advertisement route for locally learnt

May  2 22:38:19.046806 evpn_adv_MAC_rt:2194 EVPN route (local) [Instance: default-switch, Type: MAC advertisement (2),
ESI: 00:00:00:00:00:00:00:00:00:00, L2domain: 10100 Label 10100] Advertising MAC f0:4b:3a:b9:80:a7 with IP 10.100.100.1 ND
ext com 0x0 mhapb_val 0x4 per instance default-switch

May  2 22:38:19.046855 evpn_adv_rt_add:1586 EVPN instance default-switch [VS, Refcount: 7, Intfs: 2 (2 up), IRBs:
0 (0 up), Peers: 4,core-isolation-status-changed 0 Flags: 0x1814800] Added MAC advertisement route (type 2) for
2:192.0.2.11:1::10100::f0:4b:3a:b9:80:a7::10.100.100.1


*snip*


root@leaf1> show evpn database mac-address f0:4b:3a:b9:80:a7 extensive
Instance: default-switch


VN Identifier: 10100, MAC address: f0:4b:3a:b9:80:a7
  State: 0x0
  Source: et-0/0/49.0, Rank: 1, Status: Active
    Mobility sequence number: 0 (minimum origin address 192.0.2.11)
    Timestamp: May 02 22:38:19.047135 (0x6451f34b)
    State: <Local-MAC-Only Local-To-Remote-Adv-Allowed>
    MAC advertisement route status: Created
    IP address: 10.100.100.1
    Flags: <Local-Adv>
    History db:
      Time                      Event
      May  2 22:38:19.046 2023  et-0/0/49.0 : Created
      May  2 22:38:19.046 2023  Updating output state (change flags 0x1 <ESI-Added>)
      May  2 22:38:19.046 2023  Active ESI changing (not assigned -> et-0/0/49.0)
      May  2 22:38:19.047 2023  et-0/0/49.0 : Updating output state (change flags 0x20 <ESI-Local-State>)
```

It is important to gain familiarity with the EVPN database. For a particular MAC address, the EVPN database provides the following important parameters:

■ The EVPN Instance where this MAC address is learned. This can be the default instance, called *default-switch*, or a MAC-VRF instance, which is discussed in detail in Chapter 6, "MAC-VRFs."

■ The associated VNI for this MAC address.

■ The source of the MAC address, indicating how the MAC address was learned. For a locally learned MAC address, this is the physical interface over which it was learned. For a MAC address learned via BGP EVPN (remotely learned MAC address), this is the VTEP address of the remote VTEP, or an Ethernet Segment Identifier (ESI) value if the received EVPN Type-2 route has an ESI attached to it. The concept of an ESI is explored in the "EVPN Multihoming with ESI LAG and EVPN Type-1/Type-4 Routes" section later in this chapter.

■ The corresponding IP address. If the IP address could not be learned, then this field is left blank.

An entry in the EVPN database can be associated with multiple sources. Each source is ranked, using selection criteria, and the source with Rank 1 is marked as the *Active* source. Only the active source is processed further, which, in the case of Example 5-25, means creating corresponding EVPN Type-2 MAC and MAC+IP routes. Eventually, BGP is informed of this and it sends these routes out as BGP EVPN updates, shown in Example 5-26.

Example 5-26   *Traceoptions for BGP when host h1's MAC address is learned on leaf1*

```
root@leaf1> show log h1-bgp.log | grep f0:4b:3a:b9:80:a7
May  2 22:38:19.047420 bgp_rt_policy_rt, 7722: flash update group overlay type External nlri:evpn rth(0x9223de0
2:192.0.2.11:1::10100::f0:4b:3a:b9:80:a7 state:12002)rtt(0x7050800 bgp state:240), rti(0x988ec00 master) new_rt 0x73d1788,
processed, reach-rto enqueued

May  2 22:38:19.047609 bgp_rt_policy_rt, 7722: flash update group overlay type External nlri:evpn rth(0xaeb5330
2:192.0.2.11:1::10100::f0:4b:3a:b9:80:a7::10.100.100.1 state:12002)rtt(0x7050800 bgp state:240), rti(0x988ec00 master)
new_rt 0x73d17dc, processed, reach-rto enqueued

May  2 22:38:19.048252 BGP SEND        2:192.0.2.11:1::10100::f0:4b:3a:b9:80:a7/304 (label field value 0x2774 [label 631,
VNID 10100]) (esi 00:00:00:00:00:00:00:00:00:00) , 2:192.0.2.11:1::10100::f0:4b:3a:b9:80:a7::10.100.100.1/304 (label field
value 0x2774 [label 631, VNID 10100]) (esi 00:00:00:00:00:00:00:00:00:00)

May  2 22:38:19.048399 BGP SEND        2:192.0.2.11:1::10100::f0:4b:3a:b9:80:a7/304 (label field value 0x2774 [label 631,
VNID 10100]) (esi 00:00:00:00:00:00:00:00:00:00) , 2:192.0.2.11:1::10100::f0:4b:3a:b9:80:a7::10.100.100.1/304 (label field
value 0x2774 [label 631, VNID 10100]) (esi 00:00:00:00:00:00:00:00:00:00)
```

Figure 5-12 shows a packet capture of this BGP EVPN update generated by leaf1. This is a BGP Update packet, captured on the ingress of spine1, advertising a MAC address as the NLRI. As shown in Figure 5-12, a VNI is also included as part of the NLRI, and it is the L2VNI mapped to the VLAN that the host belongs to.

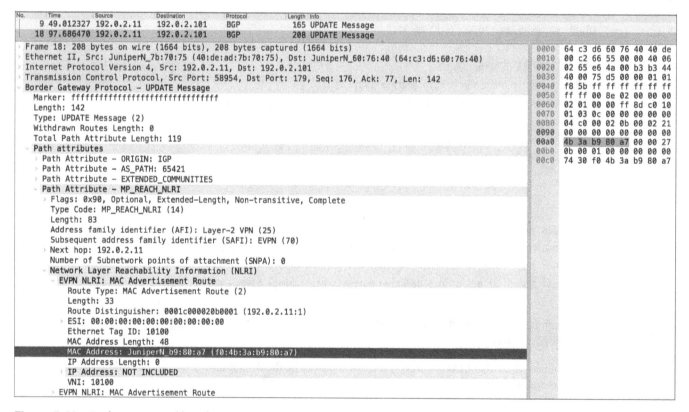

Figure 5-12   *Packet capture of host h1's MAC address being advertised via BGP EVPN*

Typically, to generate an EVPN Type-2 MAC+IP route, a VTEP must have a MAC-IP binding in its ARP cache. However, depending on the platform and whether ARP snooping and ARP suppression are supported (and if they are enabled), a VTEP can snoop the IP address as well, and generate MAC+IP routes, even if the VTEP has no corresponding IRB interface for the VLAN (and thus no ARP entry to resolve the MAC-to-IP binding). Thus, on leaf1, even though no corresponding IRB interfaces are created for VLAN *v100* (since this is a bridged overlay design), it can generate an EVPN MAC+IP route. This binding can be viewed in the MAC-IP table, as well as the EVPN ARP table, as shown in Example 5-27, using the **show ethernet-switching evpn arp-table** and **show ethernet-switching mac-ip-table** operational mode commands.

Example 5-27 *EVPN ARP cache on leaf1*

```
root@leaf1> show ethernet-switching evpn arp-table
INET            MAC              Logical       Routing        Bridging
address         address          interface     instance       domain
10.100.100.1    f0:4b:3a:b9:80:a7  et-0/0/49.0   default-switch v100
10.100.100.3    f0:4b:3a:b9:80:ab  vtep.32772    default-switch v100
10.100.100.4    f0:4b:3a:b9:80:bb  vtep.32771    default-switch v100
10.100.100.2    f0:4b:3a:b9:81:60  esi.1752      default-switch v100


root@leaf1> show ethernet-switching mac-ip-table


MAC IP flags  (S - Static, D - Dynamic, L - Local , R - Remote, Lp - Local Proxy,
              Rp - Remote Proxy, K - Kernel, RT - Dest Route, (N)AD - (Not) Advt to remote,
              RE - Re-ARP/ND, RO - Router, OV - Override, Ur - Unresolved,
              RTS - Dest Route Skipped, RGw - Remote Gateway, GBP - Group Based Policy,
              RTF - Dest Route Forced)
Routing instance : default-switch
Bridging domain : v100
  IP                MAC              Flags    GBP   Logical       Active
  address           address                   Tag   Interface     source
  10.100.100.1      f0:4b:3a:b9:80:a7  DL,K,AD        et-0/0/49.0
  10.100.100.3      f0:4b:3a:b9:80:ab  DR,K           vtep.32772    192.0.2.14
  10.100.100.4      f0:4b:3a:b9:80:bb  DR,K           vtep.32771    192.0.2.15
  10.100.100.2      f0:4b:3a:b9:81:60  DR,K           esi.1752      00:00:00:00:00:00:00:00:00:11
```

The generation of this EVPN Type-2 MAC+IP route, without an IRB interface configured, is confirmed with a packet capture, as shown in Figure 5-13. This BGP Update packet, advertised by leaf1, was captured inbound, on spine1, and confirms that an IPv4 address of 10.100.100.1 is associated to the MAC address in the EVPN NLRI.

```
No.     Time          Source        Destination    Protocol   Length  Info
   9 49.012327  192.0.2.11    192.0.2.101    BGP        165     UPDATE Message
  18 97.686470  192.0.2.11    192.0.2.101    BGP        208     UPDATE Message

> Frame 18: 208 bytes on wire (1664 bits), 208 bytes captured (1664 bits)          0000  64 c3 d6 60 76 40 40 de
> Ethernet II, Src: JuniperN_7b:70:75 (40:de:ad:7b:70:75), Dst: JuniperN_60:76:40 (64:c3:d6:60:76:40)  0010  00 c2 66 55 00 00 40 06
> Internet Protocol Version 4, Src: 192.0.2.11, Dst: 192.0.2.101                    0020  02 65 e6 4a 00 b3 b3 44
> Transmission Control Protocol, Src Port: 58954, Dst Port: 179, Seq: 176, Ack: 77, Len: 142  0030  40 00 75 d5 00 00 01 01
v Border Gateway Protocol - UPDATE Message                                          0040  f8 5b ff ff ff ff ff ff
    Marker: ffffffffffffffffffffffffffffffff                                        0050  ff ff ff 00 8e 02 00 00
    Length: 142                                                                     0060  02 01 00 00 ff 8d c0 10
    Type: UPDATE Message (2)                                                        0070  01 03 0c 00 00 00 00 00
    Withdrawn Routes Length: 0                                                      0080  04 c0 00 02 0b 00 02 21
    Total Path Attribute Length: 119                                                0090  00 00 00 00 00 00 00 00
  v Path attributes                                                                 00a0  4b 3a b9 80 a7 00 00 27
    > Path Attribute — ORIGIN: IGP                                                  00b0  0b 00 01 00 00 00 00 00
    > Path Attribute — AS_PATH: 65421                                               00c0  74 30 f0 4b 3a b9 80 a7
    > Path Attribute — EXTENDED_COMMUNITIES
    v Path Attribute — MP_REACH_NLRI
      > Flags: 0x90, Optional, Extended-Length, Non-transitive, Complete
        Type Code: MP_REACH_NLRI (14)
        Length: 83
        Address family identifier (AFI): Layer-2 VPN (25)
        Subsequent address family identifier (SAFI): EVPN (70)
      > Next hop: 192.0.2.11
        Number of Subnetwork points of attachment (SNPA): 0
      v Network Layer Reachability Information (NLRI)
        > EVPN NLRI: MAC Advertisement Route
        v EVPN NLRI: MAC Advertisement Route
            Route Type: MAC Advertisement Route (2)
            Length: 37
            Route Distinguisher: 0001c000020b0001 (192.0.2.11:1)
          > ESI: 00:00:00:00:00:00:00:00:00:00
            Ethernet Tag ID: 10100
            MAC Address Length: 48
            MAC Address: JuniperN_b9:80:a7 (f0:4b:3a:b9:80:a7)
            IP Address Length: 32
            IPv4 address: 10.100.100.1
            VNI: 10100
```

Figure 5-13 *Packet capture of a MAC+IP route being advertised via BGP EVPN for host h1*

Learning Remote MAC Addresses

With an understanding of what happens on a VTEP when a MAC address is learned locally, it is time to move on to how remote VTEPs receive and process a BGP EVPN update. The software components involved are the same, but the direction of learning is reversed.

Because a remote VTEP learns a MAC address (and associated IP address) via a BGP EVPN update, this is picked up by BGP first and then handed over to RPD/EVPN. RPD processes both the MAC route and the MAC+IP route (if received) and sends a notification to L2ALD for further processing. An overview of this flow is shown in Figure 5-14.

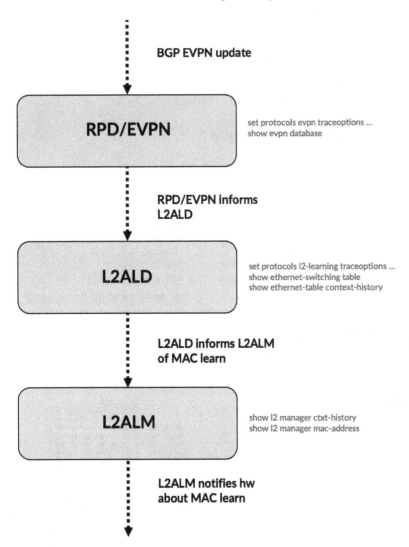

Figure 5-14 *Sequence of events on a remote leaf when a BGP EVPN update is received*

Example 5-28 shows the output of traceoptions, enabled for EVPN, when this BGP EVPN update is received on remote leaf, leaf3.

Example 5-28 *Traceoptions for EVPN on leaf3*

```
root@leaf3> show log h1-evpn.log | grep f0:4b:3a:b9:80:a7

*snip*

May  2 22:38:19.466067 evpn_process_mac_rt:305 EVPN instance default-switch [VS, Refcount: 8, Intfs: 2 (2 up), IRBs: 0
(0 up), Peers: 4,core-isolation-status-changed 0 Flags: 0x1814802] Processing ADD for remote MAC f0:4b:3a:b9:80:a7 with
```

```
L2 domain 10100, timestamp May 02 22:38:19.466032, remote PE 192.0.2.11, RD 192.0.2.11:1, ESI 0, label 10100, gbp-tag 0,
mobility sequence number 0

May  2 22:38:19.466149 evpn_macdb_entry_create:596 EVPN MAC default-switch::10100::f0:4b:3a:b9:80:a7 [Flags: 0x0] Created

May  2 22:38:19.466185 evpn_macdb_esi_peer_apply_remote_state:272 EVPN MAC ESI default-switch::10100::f0:4b:3a:b9:8
0:a7::192.0.2.11 [Active: no, Timestamp: Dec 31 16:00:00.000000, Flags: 0x0] Applying remote state to peer 192.0.2.11

May  2 22:38:19.466219 evpn_macdb_esi_peer_create:507 EVPN MAC ESI default-switch::10100::f0:4b:3a:b9:80:a7::192.0.2.11
[Active: no, Timestamp: Dec 31 16:00:00.000000, Flags: 0x0] Remote peer 192.0.2.11 created

May  2 22:38:19.466349 evpn_process_mac_rt:305 EVPN instance default-switch [VS, Refcount: 8, Intfs: 2 (2 up), IRBs: 0
(0 up), Peers: 4,core-isolation-status-changed 0 Flags: 0x1814802] Processing ADD for remote MAC f0:4b:3a:b9:80:a7 with
L2 domain 10100, timestamp May 02 22:38:19.466316, remote PE 192.0.2.11, RD 192.0.2.11:1, ESI 0, label 10100, gbp-tag 0,
mobility sequence number 0, IPv4 address 10.100.100.1

May  2 22:38:19.466428 evpn_macdb_esi_peer_apply_remote_state:272 EVPN MAC ESI default-switch::10100::f0:4b:3a:b9:8
0:a7::192.0.2.11 [Active: yes, Timestamp: May 02 22:38:19.466032, Flags: 0x0] Applying remote state to peer 192.0.2.11

May  2 22:38:19.466455 evpn_macdb_esi_peer_update:530 EVPN MAC ESI default-switch::10100::f0:4b:3a:b9:80:a7::192.0.2.11
[Active: yes, Timestamp: May 02 22:38:19.466032, Flags: 0x0] Remote peer 192.0.2.11 updated


May  2 22:38:19.466784 evpn_mac_msg_send_to_l2ald:1780 EVPN MAC default-switch::10100::f0:4b:3a:b9:80:a7 [Flags: 0x0]
Sent MAC add with NH 0, interface <none> (index 0), RTT 8, remote addr 192.0.2.11, ESI 0, VLAN 0, VNI 10100, flags
0x0000000000000000, timestamp 0x6451f34b seq num 0 gbp-tag 0  to L2ALD

May  2 22:38:19.466804 evpn_macdb_esi_sent_peer_create:820 EVPN MAC ESI default-switch::10100::f0:4b:3a:b9:8
0:a7::192.0.2.11 [Active: yes, Timestamp: May 02 22:38:19.466316, Flags: 0x0] Sent peer 192.0.2.11 record created

May  2 22:38:19.466847 evpn_mac_ip_msg_send_to_l2ald:1456 EVPN MAC default-switch::10100::f0:4b:3a:b9:80:a7 [Flags: 0x0]
Sent MAC+IP add with NH 0, interface <none>, RTT 8, IP 10.100.100.1 remote peer 192.0.2.11, ESI 0, VLAN 0, VNI 10100,
flags 0x0000000008000080, timestamp 0x6451f34b seq num 0 gbp-tag 0  to L2ALD


*snip*
```

As highlighted in Example 5-28, RPD notifies L2ALD next. L2ALD receives this update, processes it, and creates an entry in the MAC-IP table as well as the MAC address table. It then notifies L2ALM of this update to correctly program the hardware. Example 5-29 confirms the receipt of this notification from RPD to L2ALD.

Example 5-29 *Traceoptions for L2ALD on leaf3*

```
root@leaf3> show log h1-l2ald.log | grep f0:4b:3a:b9:80:a7


*snip*


May  2 22:38:19.728103 l2ald_rpdf_handle_single_mac:6992 MSG Received from RPD - op 1 opcode 1 (MAC ROUTE ADD) MAC
f0:4b:3a:b9:80:a7 ipaddr  vlan id 0 rtt id 8 ifl index 0 vni 10100 nh id 0 vtep ipaddr 192.0.2.11  bd id 3 isid 0 flags
0x0000000000000001 ifl name , ts 0x6451f34b esi 00:00:00:00:00:00:00:00:00:00 ar mode RNVE DCI DF role 0 gbp tag val 0

May  2 22:38:19.728116 l2ald_rpdf_process_mac_route:2267 Processing msgin cmd:MAC ROUTE ADD[1] for MAC:f0:4b:3a:b9:80:a7
NHID:0 RTRID:0 ifln: ifld:0 rtt:8 flags:0x0000000000000001 ts:0x6451f34b bdidgen:0x0000000300000003 vni:10100
rvtep:192.0.2.11 rtr-id:0x0 rtt: ESI:00:00:00:00:00:00:00:00:00:00 isid 0 bgp_seq_no: 0 fast-update: 0 gbp tag value 0

May  2 22:38:19.728141 build_mac_add_msg:179 [mac-add ifl 821 bd 3 vlan 0 mac-address f0:4b:3a:b9:80:a7]
flags=0x0000000000001020 bgp_seq_no: 0 gbp tag value: 0

May  2 22:38:19.728202 l2ald_mac_msg_handler:1160 installing ESI:00:00:00:00:00:00:00:00:00:00 MAC:f0:4b:3a:b9:80:a7 on
ifl:vtep.32769 bgp_seq_no: 0

May  2 22:38:19.728214 do_mac_process:6299 Processing [mac f0:4b:3a:b9:80:a7(epoch 0 stp 0) bd 3 vlan 0]

May  2 22:38:19.728323 l2ald_add_mac_to_global_db:417 Added MAC f0:4b:3a:b9:80:a7 from ifl 0 in global hash table

May  2 22:38:19.728350 libl2_add_mac_to_ifd_list:129 Added MAC f0:4b:3a:b9:80:a7 in ifd list for vtep

May  2 22:38:19.729171 libl2_add_mac_to_ifl_list:285 Added MAC f0:4b:3a:b9:80:a7 in ifl list for le
ifl:(vtep.32769:0x387d010)

May  2 22:38:19.729889 libl2_add_mac_to_learn_vlan:240 Added MAC f0:4b:3a:b9:80:a7 in learn vlan list for bd v100+100.0
```

```
May  2 22:38:19.730000 l2ald_rpdf_handle_single_mac:6992 MSG Received from RPD - op 1 opcode 7 (MAC IP ROUTE ADD) MAC
f0:4b:3a:b9:80:a7 ipaddr 10.100.100.1 vlan id 0 rtt id 8 ifl index 0 vni 10100 nh id 0 vtep ipaddr 192.0.2.11  bd id 3
isid 0 flags 0x0000000008000081 ifl name , ts 0x6451f34b esi 00:00:00:00:00:00:00:00:00:00 ar mode RNVE DCI DF role 0 gbp
tag val 0

May  2 22:38:19.730019 l2ald_rpdf_process_mac_ip_route:1955 From RPD msgin cmd:MAC IP ROUTE ADD[7] for
MAC:f0:4b:3a:b9:80:a7 ip address:10.100.100.1 NHID:0 RTRID:0 ifln: iflid:0 rtt:8 flags:0x0000000008000081 - ts:0x6451f34b
bdidgen:0x0000000300000003 vni:10100 rvtep:192.0.2.11 rtt: ESI:00:00:00:00:00:00:00:00:00:00gbp tag value 0
```

snip

The context history for L2ALD, shown in Example 5-30 using the **show ethernet-switching context-history mac-addr**
[*mac-address*] operational mode command, confirms this as well.

Example 5-30   *Context history for L2ALD on leaf3*

```
root@leaf3> show ethernet-switching context-history mac-addr f0:4b:3a:b9:80:a7

*snip*

 ctxt:6769 Type:MAC NL  T:2023-05-02 22:38:19 PDT OP:add MAC:f0:4b:3a:b9:80:a7 RTT:8 BD:3 VLAN:100 VNI:10100
IFL:vtep.32769 IflId:821 NH:0 NL  Reason:CONFIG IntrlRsn:Fwd Entry allocated Mask: L:0x0, R:0x40000000 RVTEP:192.0.2.11
ESI:NULL ESI Error:No error: 0 NL  EntFlags:in_hash,in_ifd,in_ifl,in_vlan,in_rtt,in_ifbd,ctrl_dyn,rcvd_remote NL  SM:GET_
MAC, ALLOCATE_MAC, GET_IFD, GET_IFL, GET_IFBD, GET_RTT, GET_BD, ADD_TO_GLOBAL_DB, ADD_TO_IFD_LIST, ADD_TO_IFL_LIST,
ADD_TO_IFBD_LIST, ADD_TO_RTT_LIST, ADD_TO_BD_LIST, ADD_TO_KERNEL, STOP, NL  CtxFlags:ageless mac,rcvd from remote,
NL  Actions:SRC_RPD, EVENT_POST, IN_SM, NL   :actions:0x1000042, entry_addr:0x2f433d0, ctxt_flags:0x420000, ent_
flags:0x2001f, ent_ext_flags:0x10010, seq:0 gbp_tag_value:0
-------------------------------------------------- END ctxt:6769 ----
 ctxt:6770 Type:MAC_IP reason:FROM_RPD_REMOTE NL  T:2023-05-02 22:38:19 PDT OP:add IP:10.100.100.1 MAC:f0:4b:3a:b9:80:a7
BD:3 IFL:821 NL  Mask L:0x0000000000000000 R:0x0000000000000000 Rp:0x0000000000000000 NL  D1:input mask: 0x0 ctx ifl
821 rpdf:[ctx 0x0000000008000081 ent 0x0000000008000081] local:[ctx 0x0 ent 0xc00]  flags:[ctx 0x4 ent 0x4] l2d_
flags:[REMOTE, ] vni:10100 gbp_tag_value:0 D2:actions: 0x6200 [MACIP_ENTRY_MISSING, MACIP_ENTRY_ADDED, IP_ENTRY_ADDED, ]
entry: 0x2e7bd90 esi: NULL ESI peer_ip: 192.0.2.11 NL  Error:MAC_NOT_IN_KERNEL
-------------------------------------------------- END ctxt:6770 ----
 ctxt:6771 Type:MAC_IP reason:MAC->ADD_ENTRIES NL  T:2023-05-02 22:38:19 PDT OP:nop IP:10.100.100.1 MAC:f0:4b:3a:b9:80:a7
BD:3 IFL:821 NL  Mask L:0x0000000000000000 R:0x0000000000000000 Rp:0x0000000000000000 NL  D1:input mask: 0x0 ctx ifl
821 rpdf:[ctx 0x0000000008000081 ent 0x0000000008000081] local:[ctx 0xc00 ent 0xc00]  flags:[ctx 0x4 ent 0x4] l2d_
flags:[REMOTE, ] vni:0 gbp_tag_value:0 D2:actions: 0x8000010010040 [FROM_MAC, EVENT_POSTED, EVENT_GENCFG_POSTED, ] entry:
0x2e7bd90 esi: NULL ESI peer_ip:  NL  Error:None
-------------------------------------------------- END ctxt:6771 ----
 ctxt:6772 Type:MAC NL  T:2023-05-02 22:38:19 PDT OP:add MAC:f0:4b:3a:b9:80:a7 RTT:8 BD:3 VLAN:0 VNI:0 IFL:vtep.32769
IflId:821 NH:0 NL  Reason:None IntrlRsn:None Mask: L:0x0, R:0x40000000 RVTEP: ESI:NULL ESI Error:No error: 0 NL
EntFlags:in_hash,in_ifd,in_ifl,in_vlan,in_rtt,in_kernel,in_ifbd,ctrl_dyn,rcvd_remote NL  SM: NL  CtxFlags:None  NL
Actions:EVENT_HANDLE, PUSHED_KERNEL, NL   :actions:0x100080, entry_addr:0x2f433d0, ctxt_flags:0x0, ent_flags:0x2101f,
ent_ext_flags:0x10010, seq:0 gbp_tag_value:0
-------------------------------------------------- END ctxt:6772 ----
 ctxt:6773 Type:MAC_IP reason:GENCFG->FROM_EVENT NL  T:2023-05-02 22:38:19 PDT OP:nop IP:10.100.100.1
MAC:f0:4b:3a:b9:80:a7 BD:3 IFL:821 NL  Mask L:0x0000000000000000 R:0x0000000000000000 Rp:0x0000000000000000 NL  D1:input
mask: 0x0 ctx ifl 821 rpdf:[ctx 0x0000000008000081 ent 0x0000000008000081]  local:[ctx 0xc00 ent 0xc00]  flags:[ctx 0xc
ent 0xc] l2d_flags:[REMOTE, GENCFG, ] vni:0 gbp_tag_value:0 D2:actions: 0x140000000 [IN_EVENT_GENCFG_HANDLER, GENCFG_
PUSHED, ] entry: 0x2e7bd90 esi: NULL ESI peer_ip:  NL  Error:None
-------------------------------------------------- END ctxt:6773 ----

*snip*
```

L2ALM will process the update and notify the hardware layer to install this MAC address. At this point, leaf3, which is a remote leaf, has this address programmed in its software and hardware tables, pointing to leaf1's VTEP address as the egress/exit interface for this MAC address. This is confirmed by viewing the MAC address table and the L2ALM MAC table, as shown in Example 5-31.

Example 5-31 *Switching table and L2ALM entry for host h1's MAC address on leaf3*

```
root@leaf3> show ethernet-switching table

MAC flags (S - static MAC, D - dynamic MAC, L - locally learned, P - Persistent static
          SE - statistics enabled, NM - non configured MAC, R - remote PE MAC, O - ovsdb MAC)


Ethernet switching table : 4 entries, 4 learned
Routing instance : default-switch
    Vlan          MAC                MAC      GBP    Logical         SVLBNH/      Active
    name          address            flags    tag    interface       VENH Index   source
    v100          f0:4b:3a:b9:80:a7  DR              vtep.32769                   192.0.2.11
    v100          f0:4b:3a:b9:80:ab  DR              vtep.32771                   192.0.2.14
    v100          f0:4b:3a:b9:80:bb  DR              vtep.32772                   192.0.2.15
    v100          f0:4b:3a:b9:81:60  DLR             ae1.0


FPC0(leaf3 vty)# show l2 manager mac-address f0:4b:3a:b9:80:a7 bridge-domain 3 learn-vlan 0


mac address            f0:4b:3a:b9:80:a7
bd_index               3
learn vlan             0
FwdEntry Addr          0xb123aa92
entry flags            0x14
entry ext flags        0x10
entry ext flags_2      0x0
need sync flag         False
fwd_nhidx              0
esi_nhidx              0
esi_svlbnhidx          0
retry count            0
bgp sequence number    0

GBP tag value          0
In ifl list, In RTT Table
entry ifl              vtep.32769
entry hw ifl           vtep.32769
entry seq number       0
entry epoch            0
stp_index              0
Flush Object Addr      0xb14ab030
Underlay ifl           0
```

```
hardware information
--------------------
install count        1
   pfe id  0   install information    -/D    src unknown dest vtep.32769
   mac=f0:4b:3a:b9:80:a7 vlan=28673 GPORT=0xb0000002  DstHit
```

Proxy ARP and ARP Suppression

As discussed in the previous section, a VTEP can snoop inbound ARP packets (as an example) and generate EVPN Type-2 MAC+IP routes, despite no IRB interface configured for the corresponding VLAN (and thus no ARP resolution to create an entry in the ARP cache for the MAC-IP binding). This paves the way for features like proxy ARP and ARP suppression to come into play. These are enabled by default, and this has been the case for many years now. In fact, the command to disable ARP suppression has been deprecated. It can still be configured and committed, but it is a hidden command, as there is little to no value from disabling ARP suppression and it may be required only in very special cases.

While proxy ARP and ARP suppression are two different features, they work closely together. *Proxy ARP* is the capability of a VTEP to respond to an inbound ARP request, on behalf of the target IP address, if the target IP address of the request is known and present in the local MAC-to-IP binding table. *ARP suppression* is the capability of a VTEP to suppress ARPs from being flooded in the fabric when proxy ARP is enabled and used to respond to an inbound ARP request. EVPN Type-2 MAC+IP routes are used to build the EVPN ARP cache on a VTEP, and this cache can then be used to *proxy* reply to ARP requests, while at the same time suppressing the ARP request from being injected into the fabric.

This is best explained with a packet walk. Consider the reference topology again, shown in Figure 5-15.

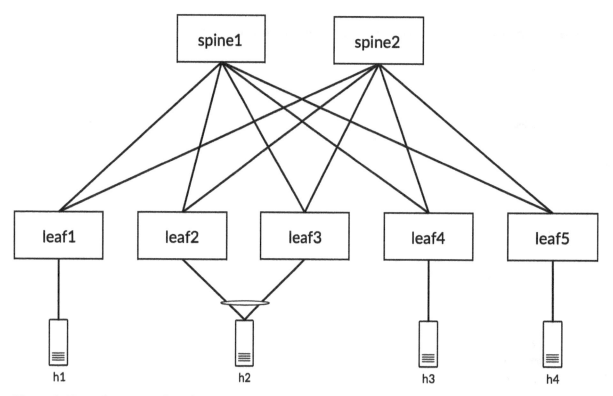

Figure 5-15   *Reference topology for proxy ARP and ARP suppression*

To confirm that ARP suppression is enabled for a particular VLAN, use the operational mode command **show ethernet-switching instance** [*instance-name*] **vlan** [*vlan-name*] **detail**, as shown in Example 5-32. The ARP/ND flood suppression flag must be set.

Example 5-32 *ARP suppression enabled for VLAN v100*

```
root@leaf1> show ethernet-switching instance default-switch vlan v100 detail

*snip*

Information for routing instance and VLAN:
Routing instance : default-switch
 VLAN Name : v100
   RTB index: 8              VLAN index: 3
   MAC limit: 294912         MACs learned: 4         Local Macs learned: 1
   MAC+IP limit: 294912      MAC+IP bindings learned: 4
   Sequence number: 0        Handle: 0x2f6c810
   VLAN id: 100
   Flags: ,BD defined,VxLAN,Ageless CPMAC,Recd MAC SYNC,Sent MAC SYNC,ARP/NDP flood suppression
   Config VLAN Id       : 100          Config operation: none
   Config params: mac tbl sz: 294912, mac age: 300000, intf mac limit: 294912,
   Config MAC+IP params: mac+ip tbl sz: 294912, intf mac+ip limit: 0,
   Config flags: vlan,VxLAN,Ageless CPMAC,no st mac cfg
   Config static MAC count : 0
   Config ownership flags: config
   Config RG Id: 0                     Active RG Id: 0
   Config service id: 0       Active service id: 0
   Config VXLAN   Id: 10100            Active VXLAN   Id: 10100
   Config VXLAN MCIP: 0.0.0.0          Active VXLAN MCIP: 0.0.0.0
   Config VXLAN Decapsulate accept inner vlan: 0
   Config VXLAN Encapsulate inner vlan    : 0
   Config VXLAN Unreachable RVTEP age timer  : 300
   Config VXLAN OVSDB Enabled: No
   SVTEP L3-RTT ID:   0                Source-VTEP IP: 192.0.2.11
   Kernel ownership flags: config
   MVRP ref count: 0
 Counters:
   Kernel write errors       : 0

*snip*
```

Even before hosts start sending data traffic in the network, an EVPN fabric can have the control plane and the forwarding plane ready. As shown in previous sections, this is because initial packets like ARP/GARP are used by a VTEP to learn addresses, and these are advertised out via BGP EVPN through the fabric, allowing remote leafs to learn them as well and program the hardware.

In the reference topology, consider a scenario where host h1 and host h3 are brought online. Through the initial DHCP process, and eventually a GARP, their directly connected leafs (leaf1 and leaf4, respectively) create a local entry for the respective MAC addresses along with a MAC-to-IP binding. These are sent as BGP EVPN updates (EVPN Type-2 MAC and MAC+IP routes) through the fabric, and other leafs, on receiving these, create a MAC entry and a MAC-to-IP binding and mark them as remote addresses.

Visually, this process is shown in Figure 5-16 from the perspective of host h1 coming online in the fabric.

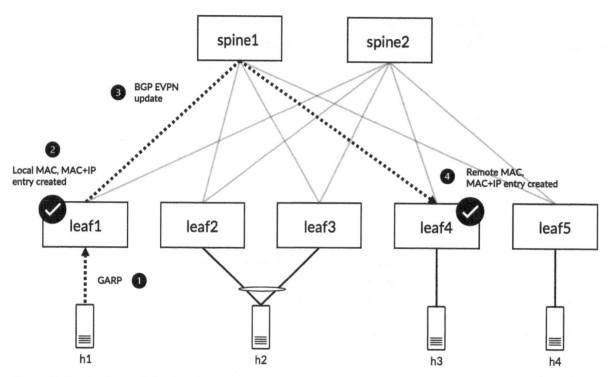

Figure 5-16 *Packet walk for host h1 coming online and how its address is learned both locally and remotely*

The MAC-to-IP binding is used to populate the EVPN ARP cache. On leaf1, a binding exists for remote host h3, and on leaf4, a binding exists for remote host h1. This is confirmed as shown in Example 5-33.

Example 5-33 *EVPN ARP cache on leaf1 and leaf4*

```
root@leaf1> show ethernet-switching evpn arp-table
INET            MAC             Logical         Routing       Bridging
address         address         interface       instance      domain
10.100.100.1    f0:4b:3a:b9:80:a7   et-0/0/49.0     default-switch v100
10.100.100.3    f0:4b:3a:b9:80:ab   vtep.32772      default-switch v100
10.100.100.4    f0:4b:3a:b9:80:bb   vtep.32771      default-switch v100
10.100.100.2    f0:4b:3a:b9:81:60   esi.1752        default-switch v100


root@leaf4> show ethernet-switching evpn arp-table
INET            MAC             Logical         Routing       Bridging
address         address         interface       instance      domain
10.100.100.1    f0:4b:3a:b9:80:a7   vtep-50.32772   default-switch v100
10.100.100.3    f0:4b:3a:b9:80:ab   et-0/0/4.0      default-switch v100
10.100.100.4    f0:4b:3a:b9:80:bb   vtep-50.32773   default-switch v100
10.100.100.2    f0:4b:3a:b9:81:60   esi.83023       default-switch v100
```

With this state built, consider a situation where host h1 wants to communicate with host h3 (to test, the **ping** utility is used on host h1, by pinging h3's IP address). Since they are in the same subnet, h1 will send an ARP request for h3's IP address. This ARP request is received on leaf1. It does a lookup in its MAC-to-IP binding table to determine if an entry exists for the target IP address (of the ARP request) and, if found, uses the MAC address mapped to that entry to send an ARP reply to the source, instead of flooding the ARP request in the fabric. If there is no match found, then the ARP request is flooded in the fabric (and a copy sent to the Routing Engine for processing). Visually, this can be represented as shown in Figure 5-17.

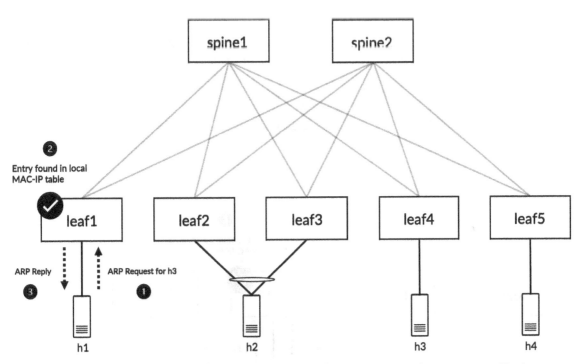

Figure 5-17 *Visual representation of proxy ARP and ARP suppression from the perspective of leaf1*

Note It is important to note that enabling traceoptions for different processes in the Routing Engine will not yield any details regarding this exchange because proxy ARP is a feature that is handled by the PFE complex. This means that the ARP request is never injected to the Routing Engine, and instead, the PFE itself responds to the request if a matching entry is found (or floods it into the fabric if not found, while sending a copy to the Routing Engine).

Once host h1 has successfully resolved h3's MAC address, it can send the IP packet destined for h3. This IP packet is encapsulated with VXLAN headers by leaf1, sent through the fabric, and eventually received on h3, as shown in Figure 5-18.

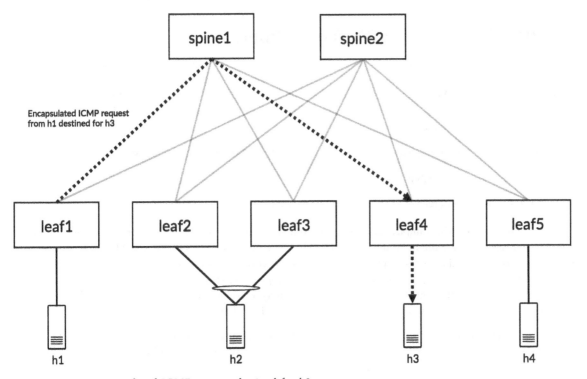

Figure 5-18 *Encapsulated ICMP request destined for h3*

When host h3 receives this, to respond, it must resolve h1's IP address. This was not resolved on h3 because the ARP request (that h1 originated for h3) was suppressed by leaf1 and thus never received by h3. The same process of proxy ARP and ARP suppression happens on leaf4 now, only this time it is for h1's address, as shown in Figure 5-19.

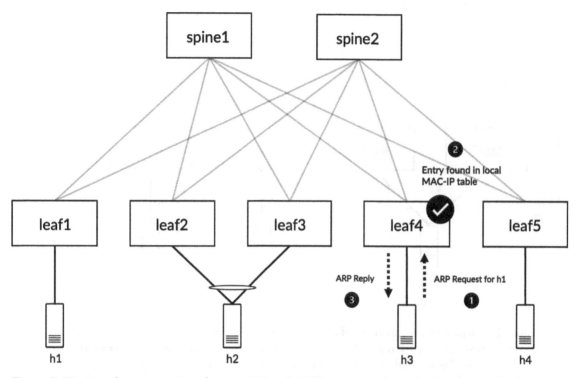

Figure 5-19 *Visual representation of proxy ARP and ARP suppression from the perspective of leaf4*

With h1's address resolved on h3, it can now respond with an IP packet. In this way, proxy ARP and ARP suppression work together to prevent unnecessary flooding in an EVPN fabric for known hosts by using EVPN Type-2 MAC+IP routes to create entries in their ARP caches and leveraging these entries to suppress ARPs from being flooded in the fabric.

Replication of BUM Traffic and EVPN Type-3 Routes

Certain types of traffic must be flooded in the fabric because it needs to reach multiple destinations (since we are, after all, working with Ethernet and essentially extending Layer 2 over Layer 3). Collectively, they are commonly known as BUM (broadcast, unknown unicast, multicast) traffic, sometimes also referred to as multi-destination traffic. What is discussed here is mostly relevant to broadcast and unknown unicast traffic—for multicast traffic, some additional EVPN route types are used by Junos, and those are not explored in this book.

There are two major trains of thought, or implementations, on how this replication should be achieved:

■ Using multicast in the underlay to distribute BUM traffic

■ Using ingress replication (sometimes referred to as headend replication)

This section is not an examination of which implementation or approach is better (or worse). Like many situations (and for questions like these), the answer is, quite often, "it depends." Each has its own pros and cons that must be carefully evaluated. Multicast in the underlay adds additional complexity and state in the core, but can scale better (or rather, more efficiently) in certain scenarios, while ingress replication puts the burden of replicating multi-destination traffic on the ingress VTEP and increases the amount of traffic sent into the core. The choice may also come down to which approach a vendor has chosen and implemented. In the case of Junos, ingress replication is used, so that is going to be the focus of this section.

Before we move on to the details of how ingress replication works behind the scenes, it is important to understand why this type of traffic needs to be flooded in the fabric. Consider the reference topology again, shown in Figure 5-20, with a broadcast packet, such as an ARP request, received from a host.

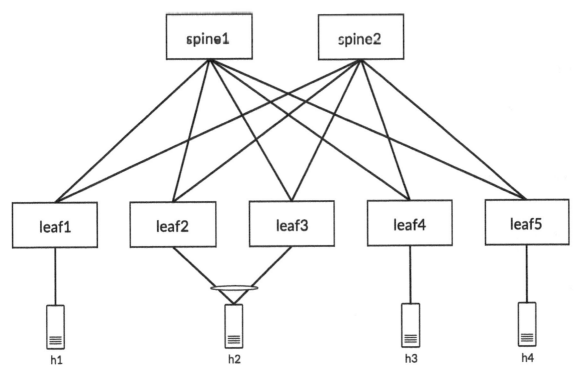

Figure 5-20 *Reference topology for replication of BUM traffic*

While ARP suppression (together with proxy ARP) is useful in suppressing ARPs for known hosts, what happens if there is no MAC-to-IP binding found for the target IP address? The broadcast ARP packet must be flooded through the fabric, in the same VLAN (bridge domain), so that the intended destination can receive it, which is typical behavior for Ethernet networks. Such hosts that do not send any traffic in the network even after booting up, and thus the network remains unaware of them, are commonly referred to as *silent hosts*.

Since the network has no knowledge of these hosts, the flooded packet must reach all VTEPs that are configured with the same VLAN/VNI as that of the source. There are two ways to do this:

■ Define a static list of remote VTEPs (on each VTEP)

■ Dynamically identify remote VTEPs that are interested in BUM traffic for this VLAN/VNI

A statically defined VTEP list does not scale very well as the number of VTEPs in the fabric grows. It is quite an administrative overhead and is often susceptible to mistakes. So, how is this achieved dynamically? This is where EVPN Type-3 routes come in.

EVPN Type-3 routes, also called as Inclusive Multicast Ethernet Tag (IMET) routes, are advertised by a VTEP to indicate their participation for a particular virtual network (identified by a VNI) for BUM traffic. When a VTEP receives this Type-3 route from another VTEP, it does two things: it allows the local VTEP to discover the remote VTEP and, at the same time, add the remote VTEP to a list of VTEPs interested in receiving BUM traffic for the virtual network, identified by the VNI in the EVPN Type-3 route.

With Junos, once an interface is configured with a VLAN mapped to a VNI, and that VNI is configured for EVPN learning, the local VTEP generates an EVPN Type-3 route for the virtual network. At least one interface must exist in that VLAN for an EVPN Type-3 route to be generated. Example 5-34 shows the relevant configuration for this, considering leaf1 as a reference.

Example 5-34 *Relevant configuration on leaf1 to generate EVPN Type-3 route for VNI 10100*

```
root@leaf1# show vlans v100
vlan-id 100,
vxlan {
    vni 10100;
}
```

```
root@leaf1# show switch-options
vtep-source-interface lo0.0;
route-distinguisher 192.0.2.11:1;
vrf-target target:1:1;

root@leaf1# show protocols evpn
encapsulation vxlan;
extended-vni-list all;

root@leaf1# show interfaces et-0/0/49
mtu 9200;
unit 0 {
    family ethernet-switching {
        interface-mode access;
        vlan {
            members v100;
        }
    }
}
```

Again, taking leaf1 as an example, the EVPN Type-3 route locally originated for VNI 10100 is shown in Example 5-35, using the **show route table bgp.evpn.0** operational mode command, and matching on EVPN Type-3 routes generated by the VTEP address 192.0.2.11 (which corresponds to leaf1) only.

Example 5-35   *EVPN Type-3 route originated by leaf1*

```
root@leaf1> show route table bgp.evpn.0 match-prefix 3:*192.0.2.11*

bgp.evpn.0: 19 destinations, 35 routes (19 active, 0 holddown, 0 hidden)
+ = Active Route, - = Last Active, * = Both

3:192.0.2.11:1::10100::192.0.2.11/248 IM
                    *[EVPN/170] 5d 10:23:32
                        Indirect

root@leaf1> show route table bgp.evpn.0 match-prefix 3:*192.0.2.11* extensive

bgp.evpn.0: 19 destinations, 35 routes (19 active, 0 holddown, 0 hidden)
3:192.0.2.11:1::10100::192.0.2.11/248 IM (1 entry, 1 announced)
TSI:
Page 0 idx 0, (group overlay type External) Type 1 val 0xacc7358 (adv_entry)
  Advertised metrics:
    Flags: Nexthop Change
    Nexthop: Self
    AS path: [65421] I
    Communities: target:1:1 encapsulation:vxlan(0x8)
    PMSI: Flags 0x0: Label 631: Type INGRESS-REPLICATION 192.0.2.11
    Advertise: 00000003
Path 3:192.0.2.11:1::10100::192.0.2.11
Vector len 4.  Val: 0
```

```
*EVPN    Preference: 170
         Next hop type: Indirect, Next hop index: 0
         Address: 0x8c067f4
         Next-hop reference count: 8, key opaque handle: 0x0, non-key opaque handle: 0x0
         Protocol next hop: 192.0.2.11
         Indirect next hop: 0x0 - INH Session ID: 0
         State: <Secondary Active Int Ext>
         Age: 5d 10:23:36
         Validation State: unverified
         Task: default-switch-evpn
         Announcement bits (1): 1-BGP_RT_Background
         AS path: I
         Communities: target:1:1 encapsulation:vxlan(0x8)
         Route Label: 10100
         PMSI: Flags 0x0: Label 10100: Type INGRESS-REPLICATION 192.0.2.11
         Primary Routing Table: default-switch.evpn.0
         Thread: junos-main
```

In the reference topology in Figure 5-20, since each VTEP is configured with at least one interface in VLAN 100, all of them advertise an EVPN Type-3 route to indicate interest for VNI 10100. Considering leaf1 as an example again, the output in Example 5-36 shows that remote leafs have been discovered using these EVPN Type-3 routes for VNI 10100. This is viewed using the **show ethernet-switching vxlan-tunnel-end-point remote** operational mode command, which displays discovered remote VTEPs per VNI and the logical VTEP interface associated to each of them.

Example 5-36 *Remote leafs discovered on leaf1 using EVPN Type-3 routes*

```
root@leaf1> show ethernet-switching vxlan-tunnel-end-point remote
Logical System Name     Id  SVTEP-IP      IFL   L3-Idx   SVTEP-Mode   ELP-SVTEP-IP
<default>               0   192.0.2.11    lo0.0  0
  RVTEP-IP      L2-RTT           IFL-Idx  Interface   NH-Id  RVTEP-Mode  ELP-IP      Flags
  192.0.2.12    default-switch   830      vtep.32769  1739   RNVE
    VNID         MC-Group-IP
    10100        0.0.0.0
  RVTEP-IP      L2-RTT           IFL-Idx  Interface   NH-Id  RVTEP-Mode  ELP-IP      Flags
  192.0.2.13    default-switch   832      vtep.32770  1745   RNVE
    VNID         MC-Group-IP
    10100        0.0.0.0
  RVTEP-IP      L2-RTT           IFL-Idx  Interface   NH-Id  RVTEP-Mode  ELP-IP      Flags
  192.0.2.14    default-switch   836      vtep.32771  1750   RNVE
    VNID         MC-Group-IP
    10100        0.0.0.0
  RVTEP-IP      L2-RTT           IFL-Idx  Interface   NH-Id  RVTEP-Mode  ELP-IP      Flags
  192.0.2.15    default-switch   831      vtep.32772  1743   RNVE
    VNID         MC-Group-IP
    10100        0.0.0.0
```

It is important to capture and analyze this EVPN Type-3 route because it carries many crucial fields for its functionality. An EVPN Type-3 route originated by leaf5 is shown in Figure 5-21. It is mandatory for such a route to carry a Provider Multicast Service Interface (PMSI) Tunnel attribute. This attribute identifies the replication mode as ingress replication and the replication endpoint is set to leaf5's VTEP address. It also sets the VNI to 10100 in this case, identifying the virtual network.

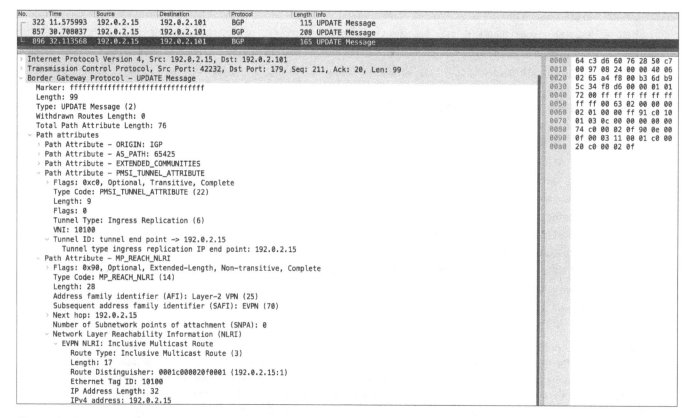

Figure 5-21 *EVPN Type-3 IMET route originated by leaf5*

The actual flood list, which determines which VTEPs a multi-destination packet is ingress replicated to, can be viewed using the **show ethernet-switching flood [extensive]** operational mode command, as shown in Example 5-37. There are several flood groups created, as shown in the example, with each being used for a different purpose.

Example 5-37 *Flood list on leaf1*

```
root@leaf1> show ethernet-switching flood
Name: default-switch
CEs: 1
VEs: 4
VLAN Name: default
VLAN Name: v100
Flood Routes:
  Prefix    Type          Owner         NhType    NhIndex
  0x30004/51 FLOOD_GRP_COMP_NH __ves__     comp      1757
  0x30005/51 FLOOD_GRP_COMP_NH __all_ces__ comp      1708
  0x30001/51 FLOOD_GRP_COMP_NH __re_flood__ comp     1742

root@leaf1> show ethernet-switching flood extensive
Name: default-switch
CEs: 1
VEs: 4
VLAN Name: default
VLAN Name: v100
  Flood route prefix: 0x30004/51
  Flood route type: FLOOD_GRP_COMP_NH
  Flood route owner: __ves__
```

```
Flood group name: __ves__
Flood group index: 0
Nexthop type: comp
Nexthop index: 1757
  Flooding to:
  Name            Type          NhType        Index
  __all_ces__     Group         comp          1707
      Composition: split-horizon
      Flooding to:
      Name            Type          NhType        Index
      et-0/0/49.0     CE            ucst          1738
Flood route prefix: 0x30005/51
Flood route type: FLOOD_GRP_COMP_NH
Flood route owner: __all_ces__
Flood group name: __all_ces__
Flood group index: 1
Nexthop type: comp
Nexthop index: 1708
  Flooding to:
  Name            Type          NhType        Index
  __all_ces__     Group         comp          1707
      Composition: split-horizon
      Flooding to:
      Name            Type          NhType        Index
      et-0/0/49.0     CE            ucst          1738
  Flooding to:
  Name            Type          NhType        Index
  __ves__         Group         comp          1756
      Composition: flood-to-all
      Flooding to:
      Name            Type          NhType        Index         RVTEP-IP
      vtep.32769      CORE_FACING   venh          1739          192.0.2.12
      vtep.32772      CORE_FACING   venh          1743          192.0.2.15
      vtep.32770      CORE_FACING   venh          1745          192.0.2.13
      vtep.32771      CORE_FACING   venh          1750          192.0.2.14
Flood route prefix: 0x30001/51
Flood route type: FLOOD_GRP_COMP_NH
Flood route owner: __re_flood__
Flood group name: __re_flood__
Flood group index: 65534
Nexthop type: comp
Nexthop index: 1742
  Flooding to:
  Name            Type          NhType        Index
  __all_ces__     Group         comp          1707
      Composition: split-horizon
      Flooding to:
      Name            Type          NhType        Index
      et-0/0/49.0     CE            ucst          1738
```

```
Flooding to:
Name            Type        NhType      Index
__ves__         Group       comp        1756
   Composition: flood-to-all
   Flooding to:
   Name          Type        NhType      Index       RVTEP-IP
   vtep.32769    CORE_FACING venh        1739        192.0.2.12
   vtep.32772    CORE_FACING venh        1743        192.0.2.15
   vtep.32770    CORE_FACING venh        1745        192.0.2.13
   vtep.32771    CORE_FACING venh        1750        192.0.2.14
```

Each flood group/route has a specific owner and function. With the **extensive** keyword for the same command, you can view detailed information for each group and route owner. This output can be a little confusing to understand, so let's break it down by focusing on the snippet shown in Example 5-38 (excerpted Example 5-37), considering the owner __all_ces__, which implies that this group is used for multi-destination traffic coming from a customer edge (CE) or host device.

Example 5-38   *__all_ces__ flood list on leaf1*

```
root@leaf1> show ethernet-switching flood extensive

*snip*

Flood route prefix: 0x30005/51
Flood route type: FLOOD_GRP_COMP_NH
Flood route owner: __all_ces__
Flood group name: __all_ces__
Flood group index: 1
Nexthop type: comp
Nexthop index: 1708
   Flooding to:
   Name          Type        NhType      Index
   __all_ces__   Group       comp        1707
      Composition: split-horizon
      Flooding to:
      Name        Type        NhType      Index
      et-0/0/49.0 CE          ucst        1738
   Flooding to:
   Name          Type        NhType      Index
   __ves__       Group       comp        1756
      Composition: flood-to-all
      Flooding to:
      Name        Type        NhType      Index       RVTEP-IP
      vtep.32769  CORE_FACING venh        1739        192.0.2.12
      vtep.32772  CORE_FACING venh        1743        192.0.2.15
      vtep.32770  CORE_FACING venh        1745        192.0.2.13
      vtep.32771  CORE_FACING venh        1750        192.0.2.14

*snip*
```

This flood list has two flooding groups that it uses to flood traffic. It uses the flooding group __ves__ to flood traffic into the EVPN VXLAN fabric, which contains a list of all the VTEPs (the logical interface and corresponding VTEP address) that sent an EVPN Type-3 route for this VNI, which in this case are leaf2, leaf3, leaf4, and leaf5. The flood list uses the flooding group __all_ces__ to flood traffic to any other CE or host on the VTEP that is a part of that VLAN, with a split-horizon rule applied to this.

As part of ingress replication, traffic is replicated to every single VTEP that has shown interest in this virtual network, by packaging the original broadcast ARP request in a unicast VXLAN packet. Thus, the burden of replication falls squarely on the shoulders of the ingress leaf, where BUM traffic is received. This also means that the traffic rate gets multiplied by the number of VTEPs that it needs to be replicated to. For example, considering the reference topology in Figure 5-20 again, if host h1 sends one ARP request to leaf1 and this needs to be flooded via ingress replication, then leaf1 creates four copies of this packet—one for leaf2, one for leaf3, one for leaf4, and the last one for leaf5.

This is confirmed by having host h1 ping a nonexistent host in the network, thereby forcing leaf1 to flood the ARP request using ingress replication, since there is no matching entry in the MAC-to-IP binding table as the host does not exist. A packet capture for this test, captured on spine1, is shown in Figure 5-22.

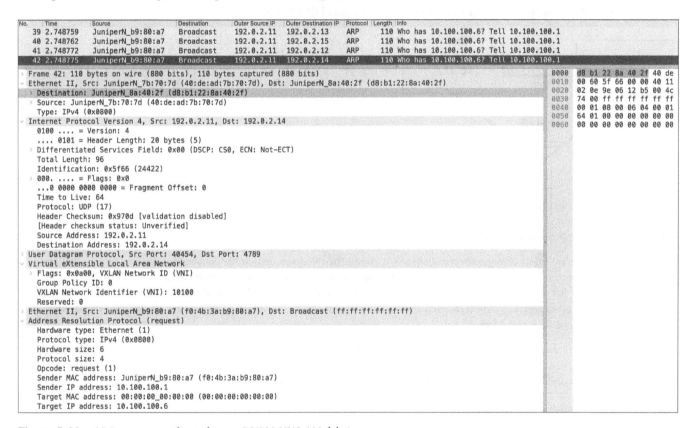

Figure 5-22 *ARP request replicated in an EVPN VXLAN fabric*

This packet capture confirms that leaf1 is sending the ARP request to all other leafs in the fabric as unicast VXLAN packets (the outer Ethernet header destination and outer IP header destination are unicast addresses). One copy is sent to each leaf—the outer IP header destination addresses, as shown in the packet capture, are 192.0.2.12 (leaf2), 192.0.2.13 (leaf3), 192.0.2.14 (leaf4), and 192.0.2.15 (leaf5).

Thus, EVPN Type-3 routes have two major functions: allow for the discovery of remote VTEPs, and facilitate building of a flood list for a virtual network so that BUM traffic can be replicated and sent to all VTEPs that are participating in that virtual network.

EVPN Multihoming with ESI LAG and EVPN Type-1/Type-4 Routes

Multihoming, within the context of network infrastructure, means that a customer edge (CE) is connected to multiple provider edges (PEs) or VTEPs, typically via some form of link aggregation. The need for multihoming has existed for a long time— it allows for redundancy and, in a way, removes the need for Spanning Tree (STP) because multiple links are coupled together to form one logical link. Multihoming also increases the overall available network bandwidth for the CE.

Note   The terms *customer edge* and *provider edge* are specific to MPLS VPNs, but within the context of EVPN VXLAN data center fabrics, a CE is a server or a host and a PE is a VTEP, and thus these are used interchangeably.

Traditionally, multihoming designs were achieved via multichassis link aggregation groups (MC-LAG), where a CE (or a host/server) could connect to at most two PEs. MC-LAG has also gone by many different names, across different vendors and platforms. For example, Cisco Systems alone refers to it as Virtual Switching System (VSS) on the Cisco Catalyst 6000 Series, StackWise Virtual on the Cisco Catalyst 9000 Series, and Virtual Port Channel (vPC) on the Cisco Nexus portfolio.

This technology involves a pair of devices that a host or server can be multihomed to, meaning that one link of the host is connected to each device that is a part of the MC-LAG pair.

With MC-LAG, as depicted in Figure 5-23, the VTEPs (usually leafs, in a data center) must be connected to each other, which is atypical of a data center Clos architecture. There are two important links that exist between the MC-LAG pair: the Inter-Chassis Link (ICL) and the Inter-Chassis Communication Protocol (ICCP) link.

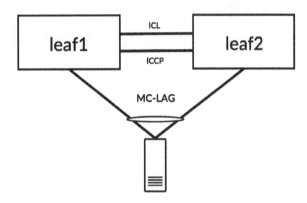

Figure 5-23   *Example topology for MC-LAG*

ICCP is used to check that configuration parameters between the two peers match for consistency. It also ensures that state is synced between the MC-LAG peers and confirms the operational state of the MC-LAG members (the links that go down to the host). The ICCP messages exchanged between the peers are typically over TCP, making them reliable. The ICL, on the other hand, is used to forward data traffic if a link fails on one of the MC-LAG peers and traffic needs to be sent across to the other peer to be forwarded out.

In general, a technology like MC-LAG introduces administrative and operational overhead. Often, there are vendor-specific nuances to implement this, thus making this technology nonstandard. Failure scenarios are important considerations to determine the efficacy and complexity of a solution, and with MC-LAG, some of these are

- What happens if the ICCP link goes down?

- How do you prevent and/or deal with split-brain situations, where the MC-LAG peers are up but isolated from each other?

- How do you deal with inconsistent state between the MC-LAG peers?

- How do you ensure traffic can get load-balanced to the peers over an EVPN VXLAN fabric?

And, most importantly, with all the considerations from the preceding list, including the nonstandard characteristic of the technology, how do you provide a stable code base, for day-to-day operations, with a solution like MC-LAG?

EVPN multihoming, sometimes simply referred to as *ESI LAG*, offers a solution that is rooted in EVPN as a protocol itself. This has existed from when EVPN was conceived and was a core requirement for MPLS networks. It has been adapted for the data center networks of today by many vendors, including Juniper Networks, and that will be the focus of the rest of this section. The same reference topology shown in Figure 5-2, with host h2 multihomed to leaf2 and leaf3, is used.

Note Because MC-LAG is a nonstandard technology, typically implemented in a vendor-proprietary manner, the factor of incompatibility needs to be considered when attempting to build a data center fabric in a multivendor environment where one vendor's devices support MC-LAG while another vendor's devices support ESI LAG.

With EVPN multihoming, the limitation of only two peers goes away—if needed, a CE can connect to more than two PEs (VTEPs). As shown earlier in Figure 5-2, the leaf-to-leaf connections are not required either, which aligns with the data center Clos architecture. The connection down to the CE is configured as a *segment* on each leaf, often referred to as an *Ethernet Segment*. This is assigned a unique 10-byte identifier, thus giving it the name *Ethernet Segment Identifier (ESI)*. This is typically enabled with LACP (defined in IEEE 802.3ad), which negotiates the bundling of the interfaces with the CE (host/server) multihomed to the leafs. Thus, it is important that all leafs (that the host is multihomed to) share the same LACP system ID, since, from the perspective of the host, it is logically connected to one device, represented by one system ID.

An Ethernet Segment can be in one of two modes: *Single-Active* or *All-Active*. For EVPN VXLAN deployments, the only supported mode is All-Active. In this mode, all ESI LAG VTEPs, sharing a common Ethernet Segment, can be used to forward traffic (received over the EVPN VXLAN fabric) to that segment, essentially meaning that traffic can be load-balanced among all the VTEPs.

To represent an Ethernet Segment, the ESI is encoded as a 10-byte non-zero integer, as shown in Figure 5-24.

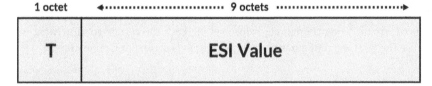

Figure 5-24 *ESI encoding*

The first octet (the most significant octet) is reserved for the ESI Type field. There are six possible ESI Types:

- **0x00:** Indicates the ESI value is manually configured by the operator, encoded as any arbitrary value.

- **0x01:** Indicates the ESI value is auto-generated and derived from the CE LACP system MAC address (high-order 6 octets) and port key (next 2 octets), with the last octet being set to 0x00 when LACP is used between the PE and CE.

- **0x02:** Indicates the ESI value is auto-generated by listening to STP BPDUs on the Ethernet Segment and using the root bridge MAC address to encode the high-order 6 octets and the root priority to encode the next 2 octets, with the last octet being set to 0x00.

- **0x03:** Indicates the ESI value is auto-generated or manually configured and uses the MAC address of the system to encode the high-order 6 octets, with a local discriminator being used for the remaining 3 octets.

- **0x04:** Indicates the ESI value is auto-generated and uses the router ID of the system to encode the high-order 4 octets, with a local discriminator being used for the next 4 octets. The last octet is set to 0x00.

- **0x05:** Indicates the ESI value is auto-generated and uses the autonomous system (AS) of the system for the high-order 4 octets. If a 2-octet AS is used, then the high-order 2 octets are set to 0x0000. A local discriminator is used for the next 4 octets, with the last octet being set to 0x00.

Configuring ESI LAG and EVPN Multihoming

From the reference topology in Figure 5-2, Figure 5-25 shows a simple, zoomed-in visualization of an Ethernet Segment on leaf2 and leaf3, connecting to host h2. Since this is a manually configured ESI with an arbitrary value, an ESI Type of 0x00 (which means the first octet is set to 0x00) is used here.

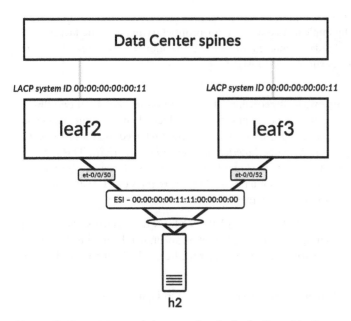

Figure 5-25   *EVPN multihoming details for leaf2 and leaf3*

Let's configure leaf2 and leaf3 first and understand what is being configured, before pulling back the curtain to show what is happening behind the scenes and how this works. The relevant configuration from both leafs is shown in Examples 5-39 and 5-40, respectively.

Example 5-39   *ESI-LAG configuration on leaf2*

```
root@leaf2# show chassis aggregated-devices
ethernet {
    device-count 1;
}


root@leaf2# show interfaces et-0/0/50
ether-options {
    802.3ad ae1;
}


root@leaf2# show interfaces ae1
mtu 9200;
esi {
    00:00:00:00:11:11:00:00:00:00;
    all-active;
}
aggregated-ether-options {
    lacp {
        active;
        system-id 00:00:00:00:00:11;
    }
}
unit 0 {
    family ethernet-switching {
        interface-mode access;
        vlan {
```

```
        members v100;
    }
  }
}
```

Example 5-40 *ESI LAG configuration on leaf3*

```
root@leaf3# show chassis aggregated-devices
ethernet {
    device-count 1;
}


root@leaf3# show interfaces et-0/0/52
ether-options {
    802.3ad ae1;
}


root@leaf3# show interfaces ae1
mtu 9200;
esi {
    00:00:00:00:11:11:00:00:00:00;
    all-active;
}
aggregated-ether-options {
    lacp {
        active;
        system-id 00:00:00:00:00:11;
    }
}
unit 0 {
    family ethernet-switching {
        interface-mode access;
        vlan {
            members v100;
        }
    }
}
```

In Junos, an Ethernet Segment is simply an Aggregated Ethernet (AE) interface, configured with an ESI. Junos devices must be explicitly configured to enable AE interfaces. This is configured under the **chassis aggregated-devices ethernet device-count** hierarchy, with both leaf2 and leaf3 configured for a count of one as shown in Examples 5-39 and 5-40, meaning only one AE interface is enabled per device.

Each physical interface, meant to be bundled in an AE interface, is configured for the same using the **ether-options 802.3ad** [*ae-number*] configuration option. The AE interface can then be configured with the expected LACP parameters, as well as different Layer 2 or Layer 3 properties. In this case, it is a Layer 2 access interface, allowing only a VLAN named *v100*. The association between these objects and their configuration can be visualized as shown in Figure 5-26.

The status of an LACP-enabled bundle can be viewed using the **show lacp interface** [*ae-number*] **extensive** operational mode command, as shown in Example 5-41, which confirms that the leaf2 and leaf3 interfaces (et-0/0/50 and et-0/0/52, respectively) are LACP Actors, while the host interfaces are LACP Partners, with each side identified with the correct LACP system IDs. In addition to this, the Distributing, Collecting, and Synchronization flags are set, confirming that the interfaces were successfully bundled.

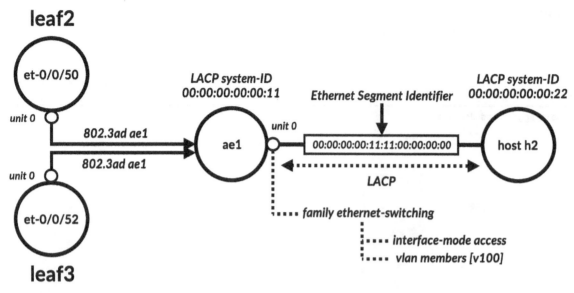

Figure 5-26   *Object association for an Ethernet Segment–enabled AE interface using LACP*

Example 5-41   *LACP status on leaf2 and leaf3*

```
root@leaf2> show lacp interfaces ae1 extensive
Aggregated interface: ae1
    LACP state:       Role   Exp  Def  Dist Col  Syn  Aggr  Timeout  Activity
      et-0/0/50       Actor   No   No   Yes  Yes  Yes  Yes    Fast     Active
      et-0/0/50       Partner No   No   Yes  Yes  Yes  Yes    Fast     Active
    LACP protocol:        Receive State  Transmit State        Mux State
      et-0/0/50               Current    Fast periodic Collecting distributing
    LACP info:        Role   System              System        Port    Port   Port
                             priority            identifier    priority number key
      et-0/0/50       Actor      127  00:00:00:00:00:11         127      1     2
      et-0/0/50       Partner    127  00:00:00:00:00:22         127     10     2


root@leaf3> show lacp interfaces ae1 extensive
Aggregated interface: ae1
    LACP state:       Role   Exp  Def  Dist Col  Syn  Aggr  Timeout  Activity
      et-0/0/52       Actor   No   No   Yes  Yes  Yes  Yes    Fast     Active
      et-0/0/52       Partner No   No   Yes  Yes  Yes  Yes    Fast     Active
    LACP protocol:        Receive State  Transmit State        Mux State
      et-0/0/52               Current    Fast periodic Collecting distributing
    LACP info:        Role   System              System        Port    Port   Port
                             priority            identifier    priority number key
      et-0/0/52       Actor      127  00:00:00:00:00:11         127      1     2
      et-0/0/52       Partner    127  00:00:00:00:00:22         127     11     2
```

MAC Address Synchronization Across ESI LAG VTEPs

At the core of EVPN multihoming lies two EVPN routes: the EVPN Type-1 route, called the Ethernet Auto-Discovery (EAD) route, and the EVPN Type-4 route, called the Ethernet Segment route. EVPN Type-1 routes are generated per Ethernet Segment (and per EVPN Instance, often abbreviated to *EVI*) and are used for aliasing, mass withdrawal, and split horizon, all of which are discussed in detail shortly.

EVPN Type-4 routes are used for the *Designated Forwarder (DF)* election between ESI LAG peers—one, out of all the peer VTEPs, is chosen as the Designated Forwarder, and only this device is allowed to forward BUM traffic, received over the EVPN VXLAN fabric, into the Ethernet Segment, while the other VTEPs must discard it. Additionally, any MAC address that is learned over an Ethernet Segment is advertised as an EVPN Type-2 route by including the ESI—this is used to synchronize state between ESI LAG peers.

In the reference topology, consider a situation in which traffic generated by host h2 gets hashed only toward leaf2. This means that leaf2 learns h2's address locally and can generate EVPN Type-2 MAC and MAC+IP routes for this, as shown in Figure 5-27.

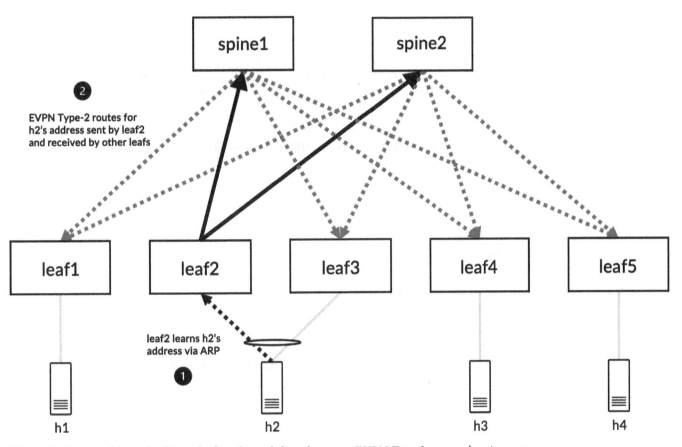

Figure 5-27 *Local learn for h2 on leaf2 only, and the subsequent EVPN Type-2 route advertisement*

Because h2 is also multihomed to leaf3, there needs to be a mechanism for leaf3 to be able to signal this to the rest of the fabric, despite, potentially, not receiving any traffic directly from h2 (and thus no locally learned MAC address). This is done via a mechanism called *aliasing*. The ESI LAG peers also need to be able to synchronize MAC address state (since only one peer may actively receive traffic and locally learn the address), and this is achieved by attaching the ESI to EVPN Type-2 routes. Its addition does two things:

- It provides a level of indirection and allows remote VTEPs to learn an endpoint's address with a next-hop that points to an ESI instead of a next-hop VTEP address. The ESI is then recursively resolved into a list of VTEPs (that are connected to that Ethernet Segment) through EVPN Type-1 routes (advertised by those VTEPs), and traffic can be load-balanced to these VTEPs in the overlay.

- It synchronizes the address with all ESI LAG peers via the BGP EVPN control plane by using the ESI attached to the route and resolving it into a local Aggregated Ethernet interface configured with the same ESI. This allows other ESI LAG VTEPs to install the address as well (against their local interface, which is mapped to the ESI), even though they do not receive traffic directly from the host.

The output from leaf2, shown in Example 5-42, displays the EVPN Type-2 routes, with the attached ESI, originated when h2's address is learned locally.

Example 5-42   *EVPN Type-2 route, advertised by leaf2, with an attached ESI for host h2*

```
root@leaf2> show ethernet-switching table interface ae1.0


MAC database for interface ae1.0


MAC flags (S - static MAC, D - dynamic MAC, L - locally learned, P - Persistent static
          SE - statistics enabled, NM - non configured MAC, R - remote PE MAC, O - ovsdb MAC)



Ethernet switching table : 1 entries, 1 learned
Routing instance : default-switch
   Vlan            MAC              MAC    GBP   Logical           SVLBNH/     Active
   name            address          flags  tag   interface         VENH Index  source
   v100            f0:4b:3a:b9:81:60   DLR         ae1.0


root@leaf2> show route table bgp.evpn.0 match-prefix 2:*192.0.2.12*f0:4b:3a:b9:81:60*


bgp.evpn.0: 19 destinations, 32 routes (19 active, 0 holddown, 0 hidden)
+ = Active Route, - = Last Active, * = Both


2:192.0.2.12:1::10100::f0:4b:3a:b9:81:60/304 MAC/IP
                    *[EVPN/170] 00:33:35
                        Indirect
2:192.0.2.12:1::10100::f0:4b:3a:b9:81:60::10.100.100.2/304 MAC/IP
                    *[EVPN/170] 00:31:48
                        Indirect


root@leaf2> show route table bgp.evpn.0 match-prefix 2:*192.0.2.12*f0:4b:3a:b9:81:60* extensive


bgp.evpn.0: 19 destinations, 32 routes (19 active, 0 holddown, 0 hidden)
2:192.0.2.12:1::10100::f0:4b:3a:b9:81:60/304 MAC/IP (1 entry, 1 announced)
TSI:
Page 0 idx 0, (group overlay type External) Type 1 val 0x9fb863c (adv_entry)
   Advertised metrics:
      Flags: Nexthop Change
      Nexthop: Self
      AS path: [65422] I
      Communities: target:1:1 encapsulation:vxlan(0x8)
   Advertise: 00000003
Path 2:192.0.2.12:1::10100::f0:4b:3a:b9:81:60
Vector len 4.  Val: 0
        *EVPN   Preference: 170
                Next hop type: Indirect, Next hop index: 0
                Address: 0x8c06f64
                Next-hop reference count: 14, key opaque handle: 0x0, non-key opaque handle: 0x0
                Protocol next hop: 192.0.2.12
                Indirect next hop: 0x0 - INH Session ID: 0
                State: <Secondary Active Int Ext>
                Age: 33:56
```

```
            Validation State: unverified
            Task: default-switch-evpn
            Announcement bits (1): 1-BGP_RT_Background
            AS path: I
            Communities: target:1:1 encapsulation:vxlan(0x8)
            Route Label: 10100
            ESI: 00:00:00:00:11:11:00:00:00:00
            Primary Routing Table: default-switch.evpn.0
            Thread: junos-main
```

```
2:192.0.2.12:1::10100::f0:4b:3a:b9:81:60::10.100.100.2/304 MAC/IP (1 entry, 1 announced)
TSI:
Page 0 idx 0, (group overlay type External) Type 1 val 0x9fb8524 (adv_entry)
   Advertised metrics:
      Flags: Nexthop Change
      Nexthop: Self
      AS path: [65422] I
      Communities: target:1:1 encapsulation:vxlan(0x8)
      Advertise: 00000003
Path 2:192.0.2.12:1::10100::f0:4b:3a:b9:81:60::10.100.100.2
Vector len 4.   Val: 0
         *EVPN    Preference: 170
                  Next hop type: Indirect, Next hop index: 0
                  Address: 0x8c06f64
                  Next-hop reference count: 14, key opaque handle: 0x0, non-key opaque handle: 0x0
                  Protocol next hop: 192.0.2.12
                  Indirect next hop: 0x0 - INH Session ID: 0
                  State: <Secondary Active Int Ext>
                  Age: 32:09
                  Validation State: unverified
                  Task: default-switch-evpn
                  Announcement bits (1): 1-BGP_RT_Background
                  AS path: I
                  Communities: target:1:1 encapsulation:vxlan(0x8)
                  Route Label: 10100
                  ESI: 00:00:00:00:11:11:00:00:00:00
                  Primary Routing Table: default-switch.evpn.0
                  Thread: junos-main
```

Example 5-43, taken from leaf1 (a remote VTEP, in this case), confirms that host h2's MAC address is installed with an egress/exit interface pointing to a logical ESI interface instead of a VTEP address, using the **show ethernet-switching table** [*mac-address*] operational mode command.

Example 5-43 *MAC address for h2 installed with a next-hop of a logical ESI interface*

```
root@leaf1> show ethernet-switching table f0:4b:3a:b9:81:60

MAC flags (S - static MAC, D - dynamic MAC, L - locally learned, P - Persistent static
          SE - statistics enabled, NM - non configured MAC, R - remote PE MAC, O - ovsdb MAC)
```

```
Ethernet switching table : 4 entries, 4 learned
Routing instance : default-switch
   Vlan          MAC              MAC     GBP   Logical        SVLBNH/       Active
   name          address          flags   tag   interface      VENH Index    source
   v100          f0:4b:3a:b9:81:60   DR           esi.1750       1751          00:00:00:00:11:11:00:00:00:00
```

In the packet capture shown in Figure 5-28, taken on spine1 as it receives a BGP EVPN update from leaf2, the ESI (for this Ethernet Segment) is attached to the EVPN Type-2 MAC and MAC+IP routes.

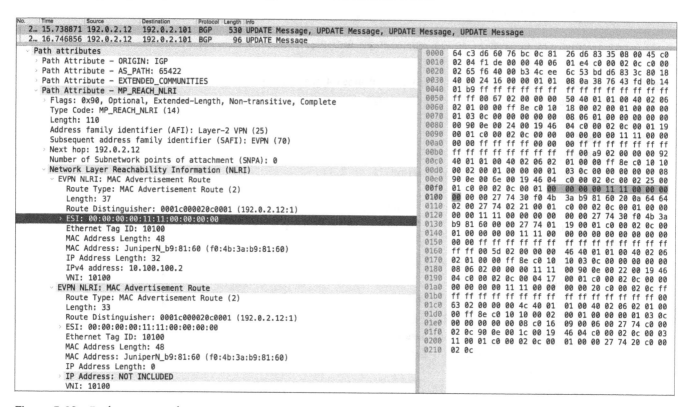

Figure 5-28 *Packet capture of an EVPN Type-2 route, advertised by leaf2, with an attached ESI for host h2*

By using the **extensive** keyword for the command shown in Example 5-43, additional information can be gleaned regarding a MAC address (from the perspective of L2ALD), including the time when the MAC address was installed and different flags associated with it, one of which indicates that the MAC address was dynamically learned via a remote VTEP. This is shown in Example 5-44.

In this case, the time associated with h2's MAC address confirms that it was first learned on leaf2, at 2023-05-13 02:19:27 PDT, and then on leaf3, at 2023-05-13 02:19:28 PDT, thus confirming that leaf3 synchronized its state via the BGP EVPN control plane. The rcvd_from_remote flag, on leaf3, also confirms the same, indicating that this was received from a peer VTEP.

Example 5-44 *Extensive output for switching table showing various flags associated with a MAC address and the time when it was learned*

```
root@leaf2> show ethernet-switching table f0:4b:3a:b9:81:60 extensive

MAC address: f0:4b:3a:b9:81:60
  Routing instance: default-switch
  VLAN name: v100, VLAN ID: 100
   Learning interface: ae1.0
   ELP-NH: 0
```

```
Layer 2 flags: in_hash,in_ifd,in_ifl,in_vlan,in_rtt,kernel,in_ifbd,advt_to_remote
Epoch: 0                         Sequence number: 5
Learning mask: 0x00000001        BGP sequence number: 0
Time: 2023-05-13 02:19:27 PDT
```

```
root@leaf3> show ethernet-switching table f0:4b:3a:b9:81:60 extensive
```

```
MAC address: f0:4b:3a:b9:81:60
  Routing instance: default-switch
  VLAN name: v100, VLAN ID: 100
    Learning interface: ae1.0
    ELP-NH: 0
    Layer 2 flags: in_hash,in_ifd,in_ifl,in_vlan,in_rtt,kernel,in_ifbd,ctrl_dyn,rcvd_from_remote
    Epoch: 0                         Sequence number: 4
    Learning mask: 0x40000000000000001000000000000000000000 BGP sequence number: 0
    Time: 2023-05-13 02:19:28 PDT
```

Both leaf2 and leaf3 are generating (and receiving) EVPN Type-1 and Type-4 routes as well, as shown in Examples 5-45 and 5-46, using the **show route table bgp.evpn.0** operational mode command, and matching on all Type-1 and Type-4 routes.

Example 5-45 *EVPN Type-1 routes on leaf2 and leaf3*

```
root@leaf2> show route table bgp.evpn.0 match-prefix 1:*

bgp.evpn.0: 21 destinations, 36 routes (21 active, 0 holddown, 0 hidden)
+ = Active Route, - = Last Active, * = Both

1:192.0.2.12:0::11::FFFF:FFFF/192 AD/ESI
                   *[EVPN/170] 2d 06:48:07
                       Indirect
1:192.0.2.12:1::11::0/192 AD/EVI
                   *[EVPN/170] 2d 06:48:08
                       Indirect
1:192.0.2.13:0::11::FFFF:FFFF/192 AD/ESI
                   *[BGP/170] 02:36:10, localpref 100, from 192.0.2.102
                      AS path: 65500 65423 I, validation-state: unverified
                    >  to 198.51.100.5 via et-0/0/48.0
                       to 198.51.100.7 via et-0/0/49.0
                    [BGP/170] 02:36:10, localpref 100, from 192.0.2.101
                      AS path: 65500 65423 I, validation-state: unverified
                    >  to 198.51.100.5 via et-0/0/48.0
                       to 198.51.100.7 via et-0/0/49.0
1:192.0.2.13:1::11::0/192 AD/EVI
                   *[BGP/170] 02:36:11, localpref 100, from 192.0.2.101
                      AS path: 65500 65423 I, validation-state: unverified
                    >  to 190.51.100.5 via et-0/0/48.0
                       to 198.51.100.7 via et-0/0/49.0
                    [BGP/170] 02:36:11, localpref 100, from 192.0.2.102
                      AS path: 65500 65423 I, validation-state: unverified
                    >  to 198.51.100.5 via et-0/0/48.0
                       to 198.51.100.7 via et-0/0/49.0
```

```
root@leaf3> show route table bgp.evpn.0 match-prefix 1:*

bgp.evpn.0: 19 destinations, 32 routes (19 active, 0 holddown, 0 hidden)
+ = Active Route, - = Last Active, * = Both


1:192.0.2.12:0::11::FFFF:FFFF/192 AD/ESI
                    *[BGP/170] 2d 06:51:29, localpref 100, from 192.0.2.102
                       AS path: 65500 65422 I, validation-state: unverified
                    >  to 198.51.100.9 via et-0/0/49.0
                       to 198.51.100.11 via et-0/0/51.0
                     [BGP/170] 2d 06:51:26, localpref 100, from 192.0.2.101
                       AS path: 65500 65422 I, validation-state: unverified
                    >  to 198.51.100.9 via et-0/0/49.0
                       to 198.51.100.11 via et-0/0/51.0
1:192.0.2.12:1::11::0/192 AD/EVI
                    *[BGP/170] 2d 06:51:29, localpref 100, from 192.0.2.102
                       AS path: 65500 65422 I, validation-state: unverified
                    >  to 198.51.100.9 via et-0/0/49.0
                       to 198.51.100.11 via et-0/0/51.0
                     [BGP/170] 2d 06:51:26, localpref 100, from 192.0.2.101
                       AS path: 65500 65422 I, validation-state: unverified
                    >  to 198.51.100.9 via et-0/0/49.0
                       to 198.51.100.11 via et-0/0/51.0
1:192.0.2.13:0::11::FFFF:FFFF/192 AD/ESI
                    *[EVPN/170] 02:43:29
                       Indirect
1:192.0.2.13:1::11::0/192 AD/EVI
                    *[EVPN/170] 02:43:30
                       Indirect
```

Example 5-46 *EVPN Type-4 routes on leaf2 and leaf3*

```
root@leaf2> show route table bgp.evpn.0 match-prefix 4:*

bgp.evpn.0: 21 destinations, 36 routes (21 active, 0 holddown, 0 hidden)
+ = Active Route, - = Last Active, * = Both


4:192.0.2.12:0::11:192.0.2.12/296 ES
                    *[EVPN/170] 2d 06:56:23
                       Indirect
4:192.0.2.13:0::11:192.0.2.13/296 ES
                    *[BGP/170] 02:44:26, localpref 100, from 192.0.2.101
                       AS path: 65500 65423 I, validation-state: unverified
                    >  to 198.51.100.5 via et-0/0/48.0
                       to 198.51.100.7 via et-0/0/49.0
                     [BGP/170] 02:44:26, localpref 100, from 192.0.2.102
                       AS path: 65500 65423 I, validation-state: unverified
                    >  to 198.51.100.5 via et-0/0/48.0
                       to 198.51.100.7 via et-0/0/49.0
```

```
root@leaf3> show route table bgp.evpn.0 match-prefix 4:*

bgp.evpn.0: 21 destinations, 36 routes (21 active, 0 holddown, 0 hidden)
+ = Active Route, - = Last Active, * = Both


4:192.0.2.12:0::11:192.0.2.12/296 ES
                    *[BGP/170] 2d 06:52:47, localpref 100, from 192.0.2.102
                      AS path: 65500 65422 I, validation-state: unverified
                    >  to 198.51.100.9 via et-0/0/49.0
                       to 198.51.100.11 via et-0/0/51.0
                     [BGP/170] 2d 06:52:44, localpref 100, from 192.0.2.101
                      AS path: 65500 65422 I, validation-state: unverified
                    >  to 198.51.100.9 via et-0/0/49.0
                       to 198.51.100.11 via et-0/0/51.0
4:192.0.2.13:0::11:192.0.2.13/296 ES
                    *[EVPN/170] 02:44:48
                       Indirect
```

Before going into the details of these routes, it is important to consider some problems that arise with such multihoming designs (most of which are related to BUM traffic) and then circle back to how EVPN Type-1 and Type-4 routes solve these problems.

EVPN Type-4 Routes and the Need for a Designated Forwarder

Consider a situation in which an ARP packet must be flooded in the fabric. Assume leaf1 ingress replicates such a packet, which reaches both leaf2 and leaf3, through spine1. If both leaf2 and leaf3 forward this toward host h2, then it receives duplicate copies of this traffic, as shown in Figure 5-29, which is incorrect behavior.

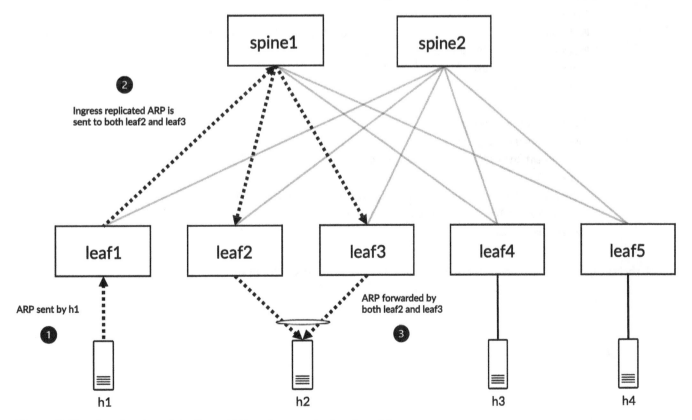

Figure 5-29 *Visualization of duplicate ARP packets received on host h2*

Thus, in a multihomed design like this, it is necessary that only one ESI LAG peer is allowed to forward BUM traffic into the Ethernet Segment. This is achieved by using EVPN Type-4 routes and running an election process locally on each peer to elect a Designated Forwarder. Other peers are selected as *non-Designated Forwarders*, abbreviated henceforth as *nDF* or *non-DF*.

These EVPN Type-4 routes are advertised with a special 6-octet community called *ES-Import*, which allows them to be imported by other ESI LAG peers that are configured for the same Ethernet Segment only. It is simply a condensed form of the Ethernet Segment and stores the first 6 octets of the ESI. Thus, in this way, each ESI LAG peer can build a list of all VTEPs attached to the same Ethernet Segment. The output, shown in Example 5-47, taken from leaf2, confirms that this community is added to the EVPN Type-4 route.

Example 5-47 *ES-Import community in EVPN Type-4 routes*

```
root@leaf2> show route table bgp.evpn.0 match-prefix 4:*192.0.2.12* extensive

bgp.evpn.0: 21 destinations, 36 routes (21 active, 0 holddown, 0 hidden)
4:192.0.2.12:0::111100000000:192.0.2.12/296 ES (1 entry, 1 announced)
TSI:
Page 0 idx 0, (group overlay type External) Type 1 val 0x9fb8a2c (adv_entry)
   Advertised metrics:
     Flags: Nexthop Change
     Nexthop: Self
     AS path: [65422] I
     Communities: encapsulation:vxlan(0x8) es-import-target:0-0-0-11-11-0
   Advertise: 00000003
Path 4:192.0.2.12:0::111100000000:192.0.2.12
Vector len 4.  Val: 0
         *EVPN   Preference: 170
                 Next hop type: Indirect, Next hop index: 0
                 Address: 0x8c06f64
                 Next-hop reference count: 14, key opaque handle: 0x0, non-key opaque handle: 0x0
                 Protocol next hop: 192.0.2.12
                 Indirect next hop: 0x0 - INH Session ID: 0
                 State: <Secondary Active Int Ext>
                 Age: 20:47
                 Validation State: unverified
                 Task: __default_evpn__-evpn
                 Announcement bits (1): 1-BGP_RT_Background
                 AS path: I
                 Communities: encapsulation:vxlan(0x8) es-import-target:0-0-0-11-11-0
                 Primary Routing Table: __default_evpn__.evpn.0
                 Thread: junos-main
```

A packet capture of this route is shown in Figure 5-30 as leaf2 advertises this to spine1.

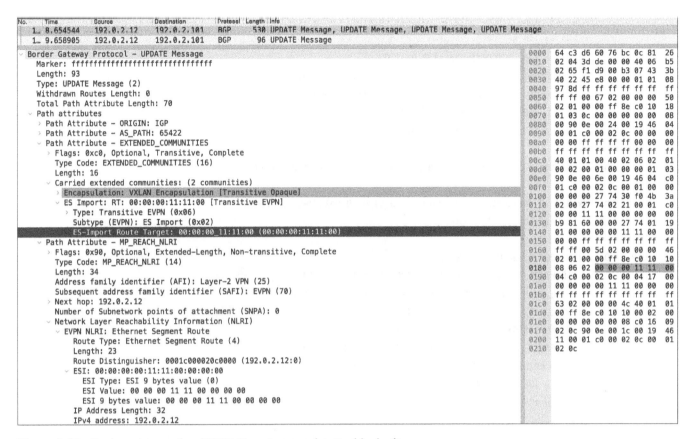

Figure 5-30 *Packet capture of an EVPN Type-4 route advertised by leaf2*

These are imported into a special table called __default_evpn__.evpn.0 via an implicit import policy that is created for the Ethernet Segment. Since this policy is created only on VTEPs that have the same ESI configured, other VTEPs that don't have this ESI simply filter these routes out. This policy is shown in Example 5-48.

Example 5-48 *Implicit policy for filtering EVPN Type-4 routes*

```
root@leaf2> show policy __vrf-import-__default_evpn__-internal__
Policy __vrf-import-__default_evpn__-internal__: [EVPN_ESI/]
    Term unnamed:
        from community __vrf-community-__default_evpn__-import-internal__ [es-import-target:0-0-0-11-11-0 ]
        then accept
    Term unnamed:
        then reject
```

Thus, when this route is received on leaf3, it is pulled into the __default_evpn__.evpn.0 table because it has a matching import policy (since it is configured with the same ESI), and leaf3 can build its ordered list of VTEPs (which now includes leaf2) to run the DF election, as shown in Example 5-49. The same process happens on leaf2 for leaf3's EVPN Type-4 route.

Example 5-49 *Leaf2's EVPN Type-4 route received and imported on leaf3*

```
root@leaf3> show route table bgp.evpn.0 match-prefix 4:*192.0.2.12*

bgp.evpn.0: 21 destinations, 36 routes (21 active, 0 holddown, 0 hidden)
+ = Active Route, - = Last Active, * = Both

4:192.0.2.12:0::111100000000:192.0.2.12/296 ES
                *[BGP/170] 00:48:00, localpref 100, from 192.0.2.102
```

```
                     AS path: 65500 65422 I, validation-state: unverified
                  >  to 198.51.100.9 via et-0/0/49.0
                     to 198.51.100.11 via et-0/0/51.0
                  [BGP/170] 00:43:09, localpref 100, from 192.0.2.101
                     AS path: 65500 65422 I, validation-state: unverified
                  >  to 198.51.100.9 via et-0/0/49.0
                     to 198.51.100.11 via et-0/0/51.0


root@leaf3> show route table __default_evpn__.evpn.0 match-prefix 4:*192.0.2.12*


__default_evpn__.evpn.0: 3 destinations, 4 routes (3 active, 0 holddown, 0 hidden)
+ = Active Route, - = Last Active, * = Both


4:192.0.2.12:0::111100000000:192.0.2.12/296 ES
                  *[BGP/170] 00:48:38, localpref 100, from 192.0.2.102
                     AS path: 65500 65422 I, validation-state: unverified
                  >  to 198.51.100.9 via et-0/0/49.0
                     to 198.51.100.11 via et-0/0/51.0
                  [BGP/170] 00:43:47, localpref 100, from 192.0.2.101
                     AS path: 65500 65422 I, validation-state: unverified
                  >  to 198.51.100.9 via et-0/0/49.0
                     to 198.51.100.11 via et-0/0/51.0
```

The default election process uses a modulo operation to elect the DF for that segment, as defined in RFC 7432, Section 8.5. All discovered VTEPs are organized in an ordered list, starting with the lowest IP address. Each VTEP is then assigned an *ordinal*, starting with 0. Finally, for a VLAN V and for N number of VTEPs (PEs), the VTEP with ordinal i is chosen as the DF for that segment, where i = V mod N. If there is more than one VLAN, then the numerically lowest VLAN value is chosen.

For example, in the reference configuration, on leaf2 and leaf3, the ordered VTEP list will be [192.0.2.12, 192.0.2.13], where IP address 192.0.2.12 (leaf2) is assigned an ordinal of 0, and 192.0.2.13 (leaf3) is assigned an ordinal of 1. Considering V (VLAN) = 100 and N (number of VTEPs) = 2, 100 mod 2 gives us 0 and, thus, leaf2 is elected as the DF for this segment. This can be confirmed as shown in Example 5-50, using the **show evpn instance** [*instance-name*] **extensive** operational mode command. This output confirms the DF for ESI 00:00:00:00:11:11:00:00:00:00 is 192.0.2.12, which is leaf2, and the DF election algorithm that was run is MOD (modulo) based.

Example 5-50   *EVPN instance, on leaf2, showing leaf2 as the elected DF for an ESI*

```
root@leaf2> show evpn instance default-switch extensive
Instance: default-switch
  Route Distinguisher: 192.0.2.12:1
  Encapsulation type: VXLAN
  Duplicate MAC detection threshold: 5
  Duplicate MAC detection window: 180
  MAC database status                    Local   Remote
    MAC advertisements:                    1        3
    MAC+IP advertisements:                 1        3
    Default gateway MAC advertisements:    0        0
  Number of local interfaces: 2 (2 up)
    Interface name  ESI                              Mode          Status    AC-Role
    .local..9       00:00:00:00:00:00:00:00:00:00    single-homed  Up        Root
    ae1.0           00:00:00:00:11:11:00:00:00:00    all-active    Up        Root
```

```
Number of IRB interfaces: 0 (0 up)
Number of protect interfaces: 0
Number of bridge domains: 1
  VLAN  Domain-ID Intfs/up  IRB-intf  Mode          MAC-sync v4-SG-sync v6-SG-sync
  100   10100     1   1               Extended      Enabled  Disabled   Disabled
Number of neighbors: 4
  Address          MAC     MAC+IP    AD      IM     ES Leaf-label Remote-DCI-Peer Flow-label
  192.0.2.11        1        1        0       1      0                            NO
  192.0.2.13        1        1        2       1      0                            NO
  192.0.2.14        1        1        0       1      0                            NO
  192.0.2.15        0        0        0       1      0                            NO
Number of ethernet segments: 1
  ESI: 00:00:00:00:11:11:00:00:00:00
    Status: Resolved by IFL ae1.0
    Local interface: ae1.0, Status: Up/Forwarding
    Number of remote PEs connected: 1
      Remote-PE       MAC-label  Aliasing-label  Mode
      192.0.2.13      10100      0               all-active
    DF Election Algorithm: MOD based
    Designated forwarder: 192.0.2.12
    Backup forwarder: 192.0.2.13
    Last designated forwarder update: May 13 19:07:04
Router-ID: 192.0.2.12
Source VTEP interface IP: 192.0.2.12
SMET Forwarding: Disabled
```

Another way to confirm this is by viewing the extensive output for the interface that belongs to an Ethernet Segment—the interface will be marked with its role for that Ethernet Segment with the state maintained under a flag called *EVPN multihomed status*. Using the **show interface** [*ae-number*] **extensive** operational mode command, Example 5-51 confirms that interface ae1 is forwarding BUM traffic on leaf2 while blocking BUM traffic on leaf3.

Example 5-51 *Forwarding state of interface ae1, for BUM traffic, on leaf2 and leaf3*

```
root@leaf2> show interfaces ae1 extensive
Physical interface: ae1, Enabled, Physical link is Up
  Interface index: 655, SNMP ifIndex: 536, Generation: 150
  Link-level type: Ethernet, MTU: 9200, Speed: 40Gbps, BPDU Error: None, Ethernet-Switching Error: None, MAC-REWRITE
Error: None, Loopback: Disabled, Source filtering: Disabled, Flow control: Disabled, Minimum links needed: 1,
  Minimum bandwidth needed: 1bps
  Device flags   : Present Running
  Interface flags: SNMP-Traps Internal: 0x4000
  Current address: 0c:81:26:d6:83:c0, Hardware address: 0c:81:26:d6:83:c0
  Ethernet segment value: 00:00:00:00:11:11:00:00:00:00, Mode: all-active
  Last flapped   : 2023-05-13 19:07:00 PDT (02:10:08 ago)
  Statistics last cleared: Never
  Traffic statistics:
   Input  bytes  :        184647675           1248 bps
   Output bytes  :        190351558            624 bps
   Input  packets:          1283315              1 pps
   Output packets:          1289252              0 pps
```

```
IPv6 transit statistics:
Input  bytes  :               0
Output bytes  :               0
Input  packets:               0
Output packets:               0
Input errors:
  Errors: 0, Drops: 0, Framing errors: 0, Runts: 0, Giants: 0, Policed discards: 0, Resource errors: 0
Output errors:
  Carrier transitions: 13, Errors: 0, Drops: 0, MTU errors: 0, Resource errors: 0
Egress queues: 10 supported, 5 in use
Queue counters:       Queued packets   Transmitted packets     Dropped packets
0                           7341                  7341                         0
3                              0                     0                         0
4                              0                     0                         0
7                        1281043               1281043                         0
8                            868                   868                         0
Queue number:         Mapped forwarding classes
0                     best-effort
3                     fcoe
4                     no-loss
7                     network-control
8                     mcast


Logical interface ae1.0 (Index 812) (SNMP ifIndex 537) (HW Token 3) (Generation 199)
  Flags: Up SNMP-Traps 0x24024000 Encapsulation: Ethernet-Bridge
  Statistics        Packets       pps       Bytes        bps
  Bundle:
    Input :             0          0           0           0
    Output:             0          0           0           0
  Adaptive Statistics:
    Adaptive Adjusts:       0
    Adaptive Scans  :       0
    Adaptive Updates:       0
  Link:
    et-0/0/50.0
    Input :             0          0           0           0
    Output:           284          0      120107           0
  Aggregate member links: 1
  LACP info:        Role     System           System      Port     Port    Port
                            priority        identifier    priority   number    key
    et-0/0/50.0    Actor       127  00:00:00:00:00:11       127        1       2
    et-0/0/50.0  Partner       127  00:00:00:00:00:22       127        1       2
  LACP Statistics:      LACP Rx     LACP Tx   Unknown Rx   Illegal Rx
    et-0/0/50.0          7721        7758          0           0
  Marker Statistics:  Marker Rx     Resp Tx   Unknown Rx   Illegal Rx
    et-0/0/50.0             0           0          0           0
  Protocol eth-switch, MTU: 9200, Generation: 212, Route table: 9, Mesh Group: __all_ces__, EVPN multi-homed status:
Forwarding, EVPN multi-homed ESI Split Horizon Label: 0, Next-hop: 1720, vpls-status: up
    Local Bias Logical Interface Name: vtep.32769, Index: 826, VXLAN Endpoint Address: 192.0.2.13
    Flags: Is-Primary, 0x4000000
```

```
root@leaf3> show interfaces ae1 extensive
Physical interface: ae1, Enabled, Physical link is Up
  Interface index: 664, SNMP ifIndex: 588, Generation: 155
  Link-level type: Ethernet, MTU: 9200, Speed: 40Gbps, BPDU Error: None, Ethernet-Switching Error: None, MAC-REWRITE
Error: None, Loopback: Disabled, Source filtering: Disabled, Flow control: Disabled, Minimum links needed: 1,
  Minimum bandwidth needed: 1bps
  Device flags   : Present Running
  Interface flags: SNMP-Traps Internal: 0x4000
  Current address: 20:d8:0b:14:b3:c0, Hardware address: 20:d8:0b:14:b3:c0
  Ethernet segment value: 00:00:00:00:11:11:00:00:00:00, Mode: all-active
  Last flapped   : 2023-05-13 19:06:58 PDT (02:11:59 ago)
  Statistics last cleared: Never
  Traffic statistics:
   Input  bytes  :          181814275                  1248 bps
   Output bytes  :          187950642                  1248 bps
   Input  packets:            1267890                     1 pps
   Output packets:            1273878                     1 pps
   IPv6 transit statistics:
   Input  bytes  :                  0
   Output bytes  :                  0
   Input  packets:                  0
   Output packets:                  0
  Input errors:
    Errors: 0, Drops: 0, Framing errors: 0, Runts: 0, Giants: 0, Policed discards: 0, Resource errors: 0
  Output errors:
    Carrier transitions: 11, Errors: 0, Drops: 0, MTU errors: 0, Resource errors: 0
  Egress queues: 10 supported, 5 in use
  Queue counters:       Queued packets  Transmitted packets   Dropped packets
   0                           849                  849                      0
   3                             0                    0                      0
   4                             0                    0                      0
   7                       1273031              1273031                      0
   8                             0                    0                      0
  Queue number:         Mapped forwarding classes
   0                     best-effort
   3                     fcoe
   4                     no-loss
   7                     network-control
   8                     mcast


  Logical interface ae1.0 (Index 821) (SNMP ifIndex 589) (HW Token 8) (Generation 187)
    Flags: Up SNMP-Traps 0x24024000 Encapsulation: Ethernet-Bridge
    Statistics       Packets        pps        Bytes         bps
    Bundle:
      Input :              0          0            0           0
      Output:              0          0            0           0
    Adaptive Statistics:
      Adaptive Adjusts:        0
      Adaptive Scans  :        0
      Adaptive Updates:        0
```

```
Link:
  et-0/0/52.0
    Input :              0            0            0            0
    Output:            289            0       126557            0
Aggregate member links: 1
LACP info:         Role    System              System       Port     Port    Port
                           priority            identifier   priority number  key
  et-0/0/52.0    Actor     127  00:00:00:00:00:11      127        1       2
  et-0/0/52.0  Partner     127  00:00:00:00:00:22      127        2       2
LACP Statistics:       LACP Rx      LACP Tx    Unknown Rx    Illegal Rx
  et-0/0/52.0           7839         7873          0             0
Marker Statistics:   Marker Rx      Resp Tx    Unknown Rx    Illegal Rx
  et-0/0/52.0             0            0            0             0
Protocol eth-switch, MTU: 9200, Generation: 196, Route table: 8, Mesh Group: __all_ces__, EVPN multi-homed status:
Blocking BUM Traffic to ESI, EVPN multi-homed ESI Split Horizon Label: 0, Next-hop: 1756, vpls-status: up
  Local Bias Logical Interface Name: vtep.32769, Index: 830, VXLAN Endpoint Address: 192.0.2.12
    Flags: Is-Primary, 0x4000000
```

Going back to the original problem where both leaf2 and leaf3 received an ingress-replicated ARP request from leaf1, with the DF election complete, leaf2 will forward the ARP request toward host h2 since it is the DF for that Ethernet Segment, while leaf3 will simply discard it, thus solving the problem of duplicate packets being sent to the host, as shown in Figure 5-31.

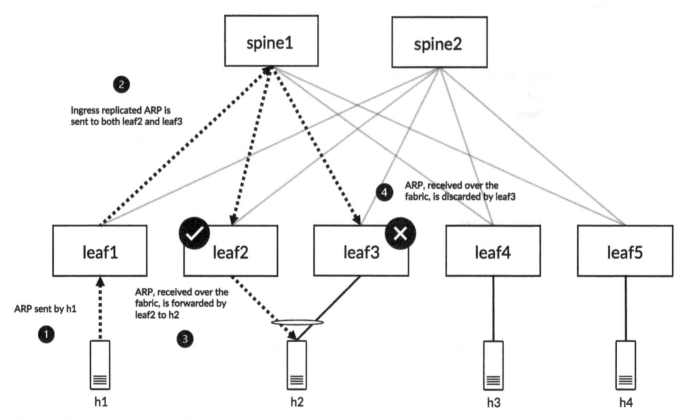

Figure 5-31 *Visualization of BUM traffic, received over the fabric, dropped by nDF leaf3*

Aliasing, Fast Convergence, and Split Horizon with EVPN Type-1 Routes

Now that you understand the use of EVPN Type-4 routes, this section shifts the focus to EVPN Type-1 routes. EVPN Type-1 routes have several important use cases—they are used for aliasing, fast convergence (mass withdrawal), and split horizon.

Consider Figure 5-27 again, where only leaf2 receives traffic from host h2, thus locally learning its address and generating EVPN Type-2 routes for it. Other ESI LAG VTEPs (leaf3, in this case), attached to the same Ethernet Segment, must have a way of letting the rest of the fabric know that they are attached to that segment as well (even though they have not learned any MAC addresses on that segment), which allows traffic to be load-balanced among all the VTEPs. This is called *aliasing* and it is achieved via EVPN Type-1 routes.

EVPN Type-1 routes are of two types: Ethernet Auto-Discovery (EAD) per Ethernet Segment (ES) route and Ethernet Auto-Discovery (EAD) per EVPN Instance (EVI) route. While each route carries the ESI itself, there are differences in the extended communities attached to the route and other properties, so it is important to take a detailed look at these. Figure 5-32 shows an EAD per ES route.

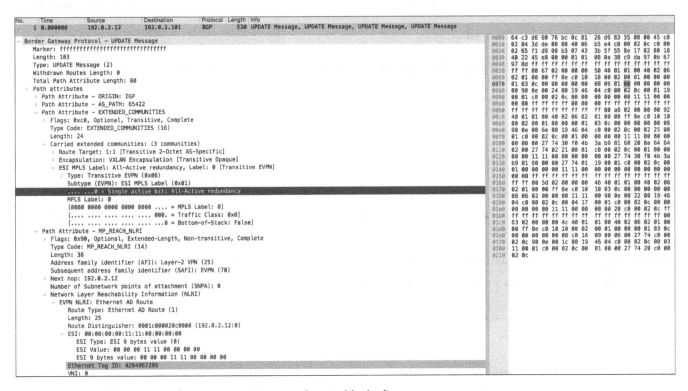

Figure 5-32 *Packet capture of an EAD per ES route advertised by leaf2*

The EAD per ES route sets the Ethernet Tag ID to its maximum value—since it is 4 bytes in length, this is set to the value 4294967295 (all bits are set to 1). This route also carries an extended community called *ESI Label*. This extended community determines the mode of the Ethernet Segment via the least significant bit (LSB)—if the LSB is set to 1, then the mode is Single-Active, and if the LSB is set to 0, then the mode is All-Active (as shown in the packet capture in Figure 5-32). Within this community, an MPLS label (sometimes referred to as the ESI label itself) is also present—in MPLS tunnels, this is used for split horizon, but in non-MPLS IP tunnels (like VXLAN), the MPLS label is set to 0 and a different mechanism is used for split horizon.

Figure 5-33 shows an EAD per EVI route, which has the Ethernet Tag ID set to 0 and simply carries the ESI itself.

A Junos-based VTEP generates both types of EVPN Type-1 routes, and both routes are used, in conjunction, for aliasing: the Type-1 EAD per EVI route is used to build a list of all VTEPs that advertised an EAD per EVI route for the same ESI, while the Type-1 EAD per ES route is used to ensure that only VTEPs that set the Single-Active bit to 0 (implying the Ethernet Segment mode is All-Active) are considered for load-balancing.

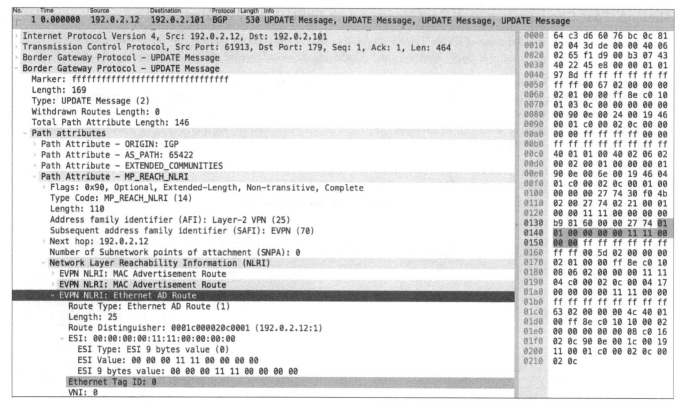

Figure 5-33 *Packet capture of an EAD per EVI route advertised by leaf2*

From the CLI, as shown in Examples 5-52 and 5-53, both leaf2 and leaf3 are advertising an EAD per ES route, as well as an EAD per EVI route for the Ethernet Segment that connects to host h2.

Example 5-52 *EAD per ES route and EAD per EVI route advertised by leaf2*

```
root@leaf2> show route table bgp.evpn.0 match-prefix 1:*192.0.2.12*


bgp.evpn.0: 19 destinations, 32 routes (19 active, 0 holddown, 0 hidden)
+ = Active Route, - = Last Active, * = Both


1:192.0.2.12:0::111100000000::FFFF:FFFF/192 AD/ESI
                    *[EVPN/170] 15:35:02
                        Indirect
1:192.0.2.12:1::111100000000::0/192 AD/EVI
                    *[EVPN/170] 15:35:03
                        Indirect


root@leaf2> show route table bgp.evpn.0 match-prefix 1:*192.0.2.12* extensive


bgp.evpn.0: 19 destinations, 32 routes (19 active, 0 holddown, 0 hidden)
1:192.0.2.12:0::111100000000::FFFF:FFFF/192 AD/ESI (1 entry, 1 announced)
TSI:
Page 0 idx 0, (group overlay type External) Type 1 val 0x9fb8754 (adv_entry)
    Advertised metrics:
        Flags: Nexthop Change
        Nexthop: Self
```

```
        AS path: [65422] I
        Communities: target:1:1 encapsulation:vxlan(0x8) esi-label:0x0:all-active (label 0)
    Advertise: 00000003
Path 1:192.0.2.12:0::111100000000::FFFF:FFFF
Vector len 4.  Val: 0
        *EVPN   Preference: 170
                Next hop type: Indirect, Next hop index: 0
                Address: 0x8c06f64
                Next-hop reference count: 14, key opaque handle: 0x0, non-key opaque handle: 0x0
                Protocol next hop: 192.0.2.12
                Indirect next hop: 0x0 - INH Session ID: 0
                State: <Secondary Active Int Ext>
                Age: 15:35:05
                Validation State: unverified
                Task: __default_evpn__-evpn
                Announcement bits (1): 1-BGP_RT_Background
                AS path: I
                Communities: target:1:1 encapsulation:vxlan(0x8) esi-label:0x0:all-active (label 0)
                Primary Routing Table: __default_evpn__.evpn.0
                Thread: junos-main


1:192.0.2.12:1::111100000000::0/192 AD/EVI (1 entry, 1 announced)
TSI:
Page 0 idx 0, (group overlay type External) Type 1 val 0x9fb894c (adv_entry)
   Advertised metrics:
     Flags: Nexthop Change
     Nexthop: Self
     AS path: [65422] I
     Communities: target:1:1 encapsulation:vxlan(0x8)
    Advertise: 00000003
Path 1:192.0.2.12:1::111100000000::0
Vector len 4.  Val: 0
        *EVPN   Preference: 170
                Next hop type: Indirect, Next hop index: 0
                Address: 0x8c06f64
                Next-hop reference count: 14, key opaque handle: 0x0, non-key opaque handle: 0x0
                Protocol next hop: 192.0.2.12
                Indirect next hop: 0x0 - INH Session ID: 0
                State: <Secondary Active Int Ext>
                Age: 15:35:06
                Validation State: unverified
                Task: default-switch-evpn
                Announcement bits (1): 1-BGP_RT_Background
                AS path: I
                Communities: target:1:1 encapsulation:vxlan(0x8)
                Primary Routing Table: default-switch.evpn.0
                Thread: junos-main
```

Example 5-53 *EAD per ES route and EAD per EVI route advertised by leaf3*

```
root@leaf3> show route table bgp.evpn.0 match-prefix 1:*192.0.2.13*


bgp.evpn.0: 21 destinations, 36 routes (21 active, 0 holddown, 0 hidden)
+ = Active Route, - = Last Active, * = Both


1:192.0.2.13:0::111100000000::FFFF:FFFF/192 AD/ESI
                    *[EVPN/170] 15:37:42
                        Indirect
1:192.0.2.13:1::111100000000::0/192 AD/EVI
                    *[EVPN/170] 15:37:43
                        Indirect


root@leaf3> show route table bgp.evpn.0 match-prefix 1:*192.0.2.13* extensive


bgp.evpn.0: 21 destinations, 36 routes (21 active, 0 holddown, 0 hidden)
1:192.0.2.13:0::111100000000::FFFF:FFFF/192 AD/ESI (1 entry, 1 announced)
TSI:
Page 0 idx 0, (group overlay type External) Type 1 val 0xb66e9a0 (adv_entry)
   Advertised metrics:
     Flags: Nexthop Change
     Nexthop: Self
     AS path: [65423] I
     Communities: target:1:1 encapsulation:vxlan(0x8) esi-label:0x0:all-active (label 0)
   Advertise: 00000003
Path 1:192.0.2.13:0::111100000000::FFFF:FFFF
Vector len 4.  Val: 0
        *EVPN   Preference: 170
                Next hop type: Indirect, Next hop index: 0
                Address: 0x8c06e14
                Next-hop reference count: 14, key opaque handle: 0x0, non-key opaque handle: 0x0
                Protocol next hop: 192.0.2.13
                Indirect next hop: 0x0 - INH Session ID: 0
                State: <Secondary Active Int Ext>
                Age: 15:37:46
                Validation State: unverified
                Task: __default_evpn__-evpn
                Announcement bits (1): 1-BGP_RT_Background
                AS path: I
                Communities: target:1:1 encapsulation:vxlan(0x8) esi-label:0x0:all-active (label 0)
                Primary Routing Table: __default_evpn__.evpn.0
                Thread: junos-main


1:192.0.2.13:1::111100000000::0/192 AD/EVI (1 entry, 1 announced)
TSI:
Page 0 idx 0, (group overlay type External) Type 1 val 0xb66e9bc (adv_entry)
   Advertised metrics:
     Flags: Nexthop Change
```

```
        Nexthop: Self
        AS path: [65423] I
        Communities: target:1:1 encapsulation:vxlan(0x8)
      Advertise: 00000003
Path 1:192.0.2.13:1::111100000000::0
Vector len 4.  Val: 0
        *EVPN   Preference: 170
                Next hop type: Indirect, Next hop index: 0
                Address: 0x8c06e14
                Next-hop reference count: 14, key opaque handle: 0x0, non-key opaque handle: 0x0
                Protocol next hop: 192.0.2.13
                Indirect next hop: 0x0 - INH Session ID: 0
                State: <Secondary Active Int Ext>
                Age: 15:37:47
                Validation State: unverified
                Task: default-switch-evpn
                Announcement bits (1): 1-BGP_RT_Background
                AS path: I
                Communities: target:1:1 encapsulation:vxlan(0x8)
                Primary Routing Table: default-switch.evpn.0
                Thread: junos-main
```

Thus, using these Type-1 routes, all remote leafs can build a list of VTEPs (PEs) attached to a common Ethernet Segment, which allows for load-balancing in the overlay. Example 5-54, taken from leaf1, shows this ESI-to-VTEP mapping for the purposes of aliasing. The output in this example confirms that the ESI resolves to VTEPs 192.0.2.12 (leaf2) and 192.0.2.13 (leaf3).

Example 5-54 *ESI to VTEP mapping on leaf1*

```
root@leaf1> show ethernet-switching vxlan-tunnel-end-point esi
ESI                         RTT              VLNBH INH    ESI-IFL    LOC-IFL   #RVTEPs
00:00:00:00:11:11:00:00:00:00 default-switch   1750  524294  esi.1750             2    Aliasing
    RVTEP-IP        RVTEP-IFL     VENH    MASK-ID   FLAGS     MAC-COUNT
    192.0.2.12      vtep.32771    1749    1         2         1
    192.0.2.13      vtep.32772    1748    0         2         1
```

EVPN Type-1 routes are also used in fast convergence, sometimes referred to as *mass withdrawal*. In the reference topology, there is a single host (h2), multihomed to leaf2 and leaf3, attached to the Ethernet Segment. However, it is possible that there could be hundreds or even thousands of virtualized hosts behind such an Ethernet Segment. If an ESI LAG VTEP loses its local connection to the Ethernet Segment, it must withdraw all addresses that were associated with the interface mapped to the Ethernet Segment, since this VTEP cannot be used to send traffic to that segment anymore. Naturally, sending a BGP EVPN withdraw for every single address can be time consuming (when many addresses need to be withdrawn), leading to slow convergence and, potentially, traffic loss.

There is a simpler solution to this, which is achieved via the Type-1 route, specifically the EAD per ES route. For fast convergence and to quickly signal to other VTEPs (PEs), a VTEP that loses its connection to an Ethernet Segment simply withdraws the associated Type-1 EAD per ES route first before individually withdrawing each of the addresses. This allows the remote VTEPs to update their ESI-to-VTEP mapping (by removing the VTEP that sent the withdraw from the list) and, in turn, their forwarding tables.

Consider a situation in which leaf2's connection to host h2 goes down. This process can be visualized as shown in Figure 5-34.

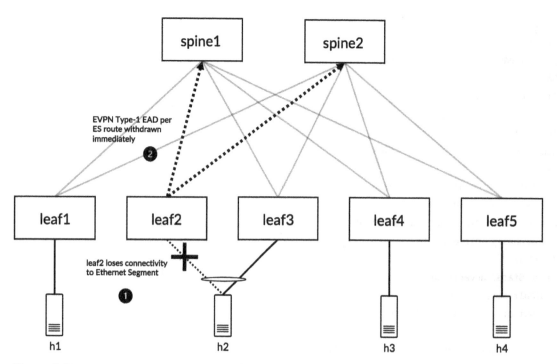

Figure 5-34 *Type-1 EAD per ES route withdrawn when leaf2 loses connectivity to the Ethernet Segment*

A packet capture, taken when leaf2's interface connecting to host h2 goes down, confirms that it sends a withdraw for the Type-1 EAD per ES route first. This is shown in Figure 5-35.

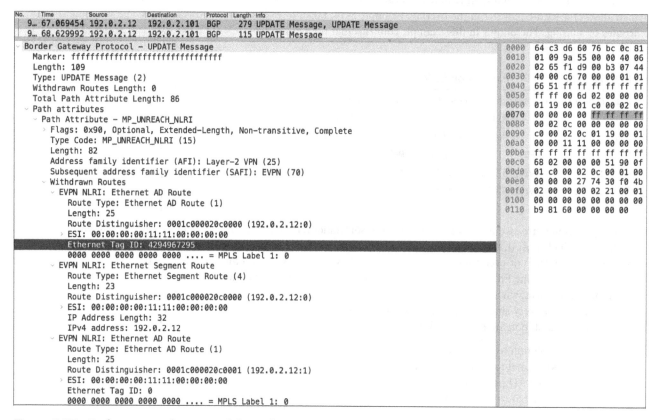

Figure 5-35 *Packet capture showing withdraw of Type-1 EAD per ES route*

On leaf1 (a remote leaf), as an example, host h2's MAC address still points to an egress/exit interface of the ESI, but the ESI-to-VTEP mapping is updated on receipt of the withdraw from leaf2, and leaf3 is the only VTEP mapped to that ESI now, as shown in Example 5-55.

Example 5-55 *ESI-to-VTEP mapping updated on leaf1*

```
root@leaf1> show ethernet-switching table

MAC flags (S - static MAC, D - dynamic MAC, L - locally learned, P - Persistent static
         SE - statistics enabled, NM - non configured MAC, R - remote PE MAC, O - ovsdb MAC)


Ethernet switching table : 4 entries, 4 learned
Routing instance : default-switch
   Vlan          MAC               MAC    GBP   Logical        SVLBNH/     Active
   name          address           flags  tag   interface      VENH Index  source
   v100          f0:4b:3a:b9:80:a7  D            et-0/0/49.0
   v100          f0:4b:3a:b9:80:ab  DR           vtep.32769                 192.0.2.14
   v100          f0:4b:3a:b9:80:bb  DR           vtep.32770                 192.0.2.15
   v100          f0:4b:3a:b9:81:60  DR           esi.1750       1748        00:00:00:00:11:11:00:00:00:00


{master:0}
root@leaf1> show ethernet-switching vxlan-tunnel-end-point esi
ESI                           RTT               VLNBH INH  ESI-IFL   LOC-IFL   #RVTEPs
00:00:00:00:11:11:00:00:00:00 default-switch    1750  524294 esi.1750          1       Aliasing
   RVTEP-IP       RVTEP-IFL      VENH    MASK-ID  FLAGS    MAC-COUNT
   192.0.2.13     vtep.32772     1748    0        2        1
```

EVPN Type-1 routes are also used for split horizon (as defined in RFC 8365). It is possible for a CE, multihomed to two or more PEs (VTEPs), to send broadcast traffic to the nDF for that segment (since this is merely a hashing process, such traffic can get hashed to the nDF). The nDF will flood this locally into other Ethernet Segments, and into the fabric, with this ingress replicated packet eventually reaching the DF for the same segment. Since the DF, for a segment, is allowed to flood traffic into the segment, the packet is sent back to the CE and thus it receives two copies again, as shown in Figure 5-36.

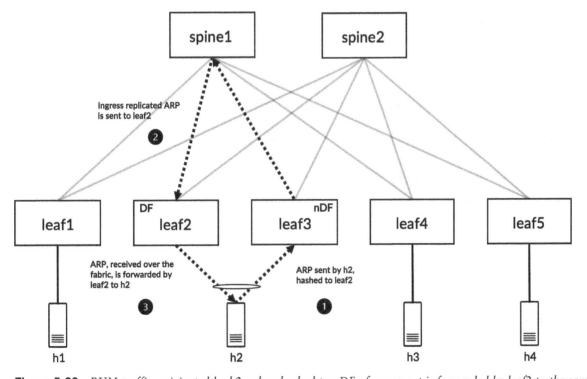

Figure 5-36 *BUM traffic, originated by h2, when hashed to nDF of a segment is forwarded by leaf2 to the same host*

This is obviously a problem, and it is solved by split-horizon filtering. In MPLS, the EAD per ES route carries a valid MPLS label (referred to as the ESI label), and this label is used for building split-horizon rules. However, for VXLAN, this label is not supported and is set to 0. Instead, split-horizon rules are based on tunnel source IP addresses for filtering.

Each ESI peer tracks the VTEP address of every other peer attached to the same Ethernet Segment via EVPN Type-1 routes. When an egress VTEP receives an encapsulated BUM packet from the fabric, the source IP address is matched against a filter, which discards the packet if the source IP address is of one of the ESI LAG peers. Since this rule allows the nDF to forward BUM traffic locally to any directly attached Ethernet Segments, it is also referred to as *Local Bias*. The list of addresses being used for filtering can be viewed in the extensive output of the interface for an Ethernet Segment, as shown in Examples 5-56 and 5-57. These Local Bias filters are built using Type-1 EAD per ES routes specifically.

Example 5-56   *Local Bias on leaf2*

```
root@leaf2> show interfaces ae1 extensive
Physical interface: ae1, Enabled, Physical link is Up
  Interface index: 655, SNMP ifIndex: 536, Generation: 150
  Link-level type: Ethernet, MTU: 9200, Speed: 40Gbps, BPDU Error: None, Ethernet-Switching Error: None, MAC-REWRITE
Error: None, Loopback: Disabled, Source filtering: Disabled, Flow control: Disabled, Minimum links needed: 1,
  Minimum bandwidth needed: 1bps
  Device flags   : Present Running
  Interface flags: SNMP-Traps Internal: 0x4000
  Current address: 0c:81:26:d6:83:c0, Hardware address: 0c:81:26:d6:83:c0
  Ethernet segment value: 00:00:00:00:11:11:00:00:00:00, Mode: all-active
  Last flapped   : 2023-05-14 19:55:42 PDT (00:00:24 ago)
  Statistics last cleared: Never
  Traffic statistics:
   Input  bytes :          195116252                1248 bps
   Output bytes :          201006521                1248 bps
   Input  packets:          1361502                   1 pps
   Output packets:          1367829                   1 pps
   IPv6 transit statistics:
   Input  bytes :                  0
   Output bytes :                  0
   Input  packets:                 0
   Output packets:                 0
  Input errors:
    Errors: 0, Drops: 0, Framing errors: 0, Runts: 0, Giants: 0, Policed discards: 0, Resource errors: 0
  Output errors:
    Carrier transitions: 15, Errors: 0, Drops: 0, MTU errors: 0, Resource errors: 0
  Egress queues: 10 supported, 5 in use
  Queue counters:       Queued packets  Transmitted packets    Dropped packets
   0                         8054              8054                     0
   3                            0                 0                     0
   4                            0                 0                     0
   7                      1358859           1358859                     0
   8                          918               918                     0
  Queue number:         Mapped forwarding classes
   0                     best-effort
   3                     fcoe
   4                     no-loss
   7                     network-control
   8                     mcast
```

```
Logical interface ae1.0 (Index 812) (SNMP ifIndex 537) (HW Token 3) (Generation 199)
  Flags: Up SNMP-Traps 0x24024000 Encapsulation: Ethernet-Bridge
  Statistics       Packets        pps        Bytes        bps
  Bundle:
    Input :            0            0            0            0
    Output:            0            0            0            0
  Adaptive Statistics:
    Adaptive Adjusts:      0
    Adaptive Scans  :      0
    Adaptive Updates:      0
  Link:
    et-0/0/50.0
    Input :            0            0            0            0
    Output:         3009            0      1272782            0
  Aggregate member links: 1
  LACP info:        Role    System             System      Port    Port    Port
                            priority           identifier  priority number  key
    et-0/0/50.0    Actor       127  00:00:00:00:00:11      127       1       2
    et-0/0/50.0    Partner     127  00:00:00:00:00:22      127       1       2
  LACP Statistics:       LACP Rx    LACP Tx    Unknown Rx   Illegal Rx
    et-0/0/50.0          82439      82836          0            0
  Marker Statistics:  Marker Rx    Resp Tx    Unknown Rx   Illegal Rx
    et-0/0/50.0            0          0            0            0
  Protocol eth-switch, MTU: 9200, Generation: 212, Route table: 9, Mesh Group: __all_ces__, EVPN multi-homed status:
Forwarding, EVPN multi-homed ESI Split Horizon Label: 0, Next-hop: 1720, vpls-status: up
  Local Bias Logical Interface Name: vtep.32769, Index: 826, VXLAN Endpoint Address: 192.0.2.13
    Flags: Is-Primary, 0x4000000
```

Example 5-57 *Local Bias on leaf3*

```
root@leaf3> show interfaces ae1 extensive
Physical interface: ae1, Enabled, Physical link is Up
  Interface index: 664, SNMP ifIndex: 588, Generation: 155
  Link-level type: Ethernet, MTU: 9200, Speed: 40Gbps, BPDU Error: None, Ethernet-Switching Error: None, MAC-REWRITE
Error: None, Loopback: Disabled, Source filtering: Disabled, Flow control: Disabled, Minimum links needed: 1,
  Minimum bandwidth needed: 1bps
  Device flags   : Present Running
  Interface flags: SNMP-Traps Internal: 0x4000
  Current address: 20:d8:0b:14:b3:c0, Hardware address: 20:d8:0b:14:b3:c0
  Ethernet segment value: 00:00:00:00:11:11:00:00:00:00, Mode: all-active
  Last flapped   : 2023-05-13 19:06:58 PDT (1d 00:50 ago)
  Statistics last cleared: Never
  Traffic statistics:
   Input  bytes  :        193081618             608 bps
   Output bytes  :        199455834             608 bps
   Input  packets:          1351649               0 pps
   Output packets:          1358032               0 pps
   IPv6 transit statistics:
   Input  bytes  :                0
   Output bytes  :                0
```

```
        Input  packets:                   0
        Output packets:                   0
     Input errors:
        Errors: 0, Drops: 0, Framing errors: 0, Runts: 0, Giants: 0, Policed discards: 0, Resource errors: 0
     Output errors:
        Carrier transitions: 11, Errors: 0, Drops: 0, MTU errors: 0, Resource errors: 0
     Egress queues: 10 supported, 5 in use
     Queue counters:        Queued packets  Transmitted packets    Dropped packets
        0                          935                935                   0
        3                            0                  0                   0
        4                            0                  0                   0
        7                      1357090            1357090                   0
        8                            6                  6                   0
     Queue number:          Mapped forwarding classes
        0                      best-effort
        3                      fcoe
        4                      no-loss
        7                      network-control
        8                      mcast


     Logical interface ae1.0 (Index 821) (SNMP ifIndex 589) (HW Token 8) (Generation 187)
        Flags: Up SNMP-Traps 0x24024000 Encapsulation: Ethernet-Bridge
        Statistics        Packets         pps       Bytes         bps
        Bundle:
           Input :              0           0           0           0
           Output:              0           0           0           0
        Adaptive Statistics:
           Adaptive Adjusts:        0
           Adaptive Scans  :        0
           Adaptive Updates:        0
        Link:
          et-0/0/52.0
           Input :              0           0           0           0
           Output:           3223           0     1411649           0
        Aggregate member links: 1
        LACP info:        Role    System              System      Port      Port    Port
                                  priority          identifier  priority   number    key
           et-0/0/52.0   Actor      127  00:00:00:00:00:11       127         1       2
           et-0/0/52.0 Partner      127  00:00:00:00:00:22       127         2       2
        LACP Statistics:        LACP Rx     LACP Tx   Unknown Rx   Illegal Rx
           et-0/0/52.0            88600       89003            0            0
        Marker Statistics:    Marker Rx     Resp Tx   Unknown Rx   Illegal Rx
           et-0/0/52.0                0           0            0            0
        Protocol eth-switch, MTU: 9200, Generation: 196, Route table: 8, Mesh Group: __all_ces__, EVPN multi-homed status:
     Blocking BUM Traffic to ESI, EVPN multi-homed ESI Split Horizon Label: 0, Next-hop: 1756, vpls-status: up
        Local Bias Logical Interface Name: vtep.32769, Index: 824, VXLAN Endpoint Address: 192.0.2.12
           Flags: Is-Primary, 0x4000000
```

With Local Bias and split-horizon rules applied, leaf2 will discard ARP traffic received over the fabric when it is sent by leaf3, as shown in Figure 5-37.

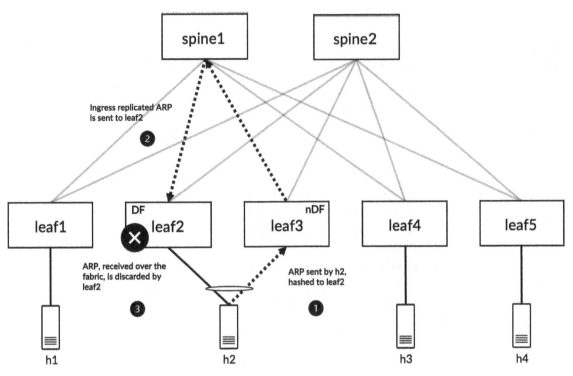

Figure 5-37 *BUM traffic, originated by h2, when hashed to nDF is discarded by DF, leaf2, when received over the fabric*

Core Isolation in an EVPN VXLAN Fabric

With EVPN multihoming, there is a failure condition that must be carefully evaluated. Consider a situation in which an ESI LAG–enabled VTEP loses all its uplinks (links to fabric spines) but does not lose its downlink (link to CE/host), configured with an Ethernet Segment. This means that traffic from the host can be hashed to this VTEP, but since the VTEP has no available uplinks to send the traffic, it gets dropped on this VTEP, leading to traffic loss, as shown in Figure 5-38.

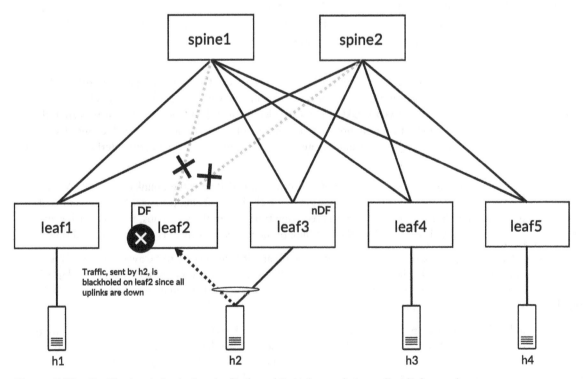

Figure 5-38 *Traffic that is hashed to leaf2, from h2, is dropped since all uplinks are down*

To ensure that this situation does not arise, *Core Isolation* is used, and enabled by default. At its core (pun intended), the feature simply tracks the BGP EVPN neighbors on an ESI LAG–enabled VTEP and, if all neighbors go down, uses LACP to bring down the AE interfaces for the attached Ethernet Segments. This ensures that the CE is forced to hash traffic toward other ESI LAG–enabled VTEPs that still have at least one uplink up and can forward traffic into the fabric.

Let's simulate this behavior by disabling both uplinks on leaf2. Prior to disabling the interface, LACP had successfully negotiated a LAG between leaf2 and host h2, as shown in Example 5-58.

Example 5-58 *LACP state, on the AE interface that is mapped to an Ethernet Segment, while all uplinks are up*

```
root@leaf2> show lacp interfaces ae1 extensive
Aggregated interface: ae1
    LACP state:       Role    Exp  Def  Dist Col  Syn  Aggr  Timeout  Activity
      et-0/0/50       Actor   No   No   Yes  Yes  Yes  Yes   Fast     Active
      et-0/0/50       Partner No   No   Yes  Yes  Yes  Yes   Fast     Active
    LACP protocol:        Receive State  Transmit State       Mux State
      et-0/0/50               Current    Fast periodic Collecting distributing
    LACP info:        Role    System              System       Port    Port   Port
                              priority            identifier   priority number key
      et-0/0/50       Actor       127  00:00:00:00:00:11          127       1    2
      et-0/0/50       Partner     127  00:00:00:00:00:22          127       1    2
```

When the uplinks are disabled, LACP is informed (since all BGP EVPN neighbors go down), and it is moved into a *waiting* state, as shown in Example 5-59.

Example 5-59 *LACP state, on the AE interface that is mapped to an Ethernet Segment, while all uplinks are down*

```
root@leaf2> show lacp interfaces ae1
Aggregated interface: ae1
    LACP state:        Role    Exp  Def  Dist Col  Syn  Aggr  Timeout  Activity
      et-0/0/50 CDN    Actor   No   No   No   No   No   Yes   Fast     Active
      et-0/0/50 CDN    Partner No   No   No   No   Yes  Yes   Fast     Active
    LACP protocol:        Receive State  Transmit State       Mux State
      et-0/0/50               Current    Fast periodic        Waiting
```

At the time of writing, only LACP-enabled interfaces are supported for Core Isolation. However, Juniper Networks is developing a Core Isolation feature that allows the creation of a *network isolation profile* with an action such as link shutdown. This profile can then be attached to any interface, even if LACP is not enabled for it. When Core Isolation is triggered, this network isolation profile will kick in and initiate the configured action. This action is useful on LACP-enabled interfaces as well (by immediately bringing the link down), because normally there can be some delay in bringing the interface down post LACP out-of-sync state.

The other use of this upcoming feature is to delay the bundling of interfaces via LACP after the uplinks and BGP EVPN neighbors come up. This is important because there can be a situation in which the CE-facing ports get bundled via LACP but MAC address state is not synced with this VTEP and it starts receiving traffic from the CE. Thus, to avoid such a situation, a delay parameter is introduced as well, which delays the bundling of interfaces via LACP as per the specified time.

In certain designs, Core Isolation can be more detrimental than it is useful, and it is important to be aware of this. This is typically seen in a collapsed spine design, like that shown in Figure 5-39. Note that the terminology used in a collapsed spine design may vary—the spines may also be called top-of-rack (ToR) leafs, while the ToRs may be called access switches. Functionally, the design is the same in both cases.

In such designs, there is no leaf layer, and the spines are directly connected over a Layer 3 link. Top-of-rack switches are typically multihomed to both spines, with EVPN multihoming. Both the underlay and overlay BGP peering is over this Layer 3 link only. Thus, if the Layer 3 link between the spines goes down (or the BGP EVPN neighbor goes down for whatever reason), then this triggers Core Isolation since this Layer 3 link was the only "uplink."

Collapsed Spine

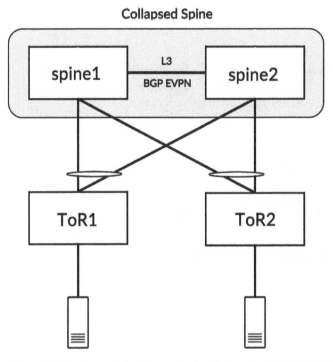

Figure 5-39 *A typical collapsed spine design for EVPN VXLAN*

Assuming this happens on spine1, the LACP-enabled downlinks are brought down, but at the same time, spine2 also loses its only "uplink," which was the Layer 3 connection back to spine1, and it brings down its LACP-enabled downlinks as well, thus completely isolating the CE/host. For these reasons, in a collapsed spine design, the Core Isolation feature must be disabled using the configuration mode command **set protocols evpn no-core-isolation**.

Route Targets in an EVPN VXLAN Fabric

Like MPLS VPNs, a *Route Target* is an 8-byte extended community that is expected to be added to every BGP EVPN route advertised by a VTEP in EVPN VXLAN fabrics. It is easier to think of this as a tag attached to BGP routes. The general format of BGP extended communities is defined in RFC 4360, as shown in Figure 5-40. These were introduced to extend the standard BGP community, defined by RFC 1997, by providing an extended range for value encoding (since standard BGP communities are only 4 bytes long) and to provide structure, using the *Type* and *Sub-type* fields.

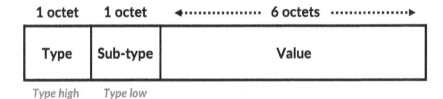

Figure 5-40 *Format of BGP extended communities*

RFC 4360 also defines Route Targets as a well-known BGP extended community, with the Sub-type field set to a value of 0x02. The encoding format of a Route Target is shown in Figure 5-41, where the 6-byte *Value* field is further divided into a 2-byte *Global Administrator* field and a 4-byte *Local Administrator* field.

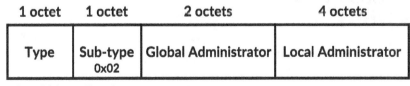

Figure 5-41 *Format of the Route Target BGP extended community*

Route Targets allow for easy definition of import and export policies, controlling how EVPN routes are eventually exported and imported on VTEPs, which, in turn, controls how the fabric itself is built and how hosts can (or cannot) communicate with each other.

When using a Type of 0x00, the Global Administrator field is set to the ASN of the device, while the Local Administrator field is any 4-byte numeric value. However, typically when Route Targets are manually configured, both the Global Administrator and Local Administrator fields are set to any administratively relevant numeric values.

From a configuration perspective, a Route Target is represented as *x:y*, where *x* is the Global Administrator value and *y* is the Local Administrator value. In Junos, the Route Target is defined under the **switch-options** configuration hierarchy for the default EVPN Instance, using the **vrf-target** configuration option. This is a device-wide Route Target, used by all EVPN route types. Example 5-60 demonstrates how this is configured on leaf1 by setting the Route Target to a value of 1:1.

It is mandatory to use the keyword *target* preceding the Route Target itself, in the format of target:*x:y*. This keyword signifies the Sub-type of the BGP extended community, and the keyword *target* indicates that it is a Sub-type of 0x02.

Example 5-60 *Route Target configuration on leaf1*

```
root@leaf1# show switch-options
vtep-source-interface lo0.0;
route-distinguisher 192.0.2.11:1;
vrf-target target:1:1;
```

Configuring a Route Target, as shown in Example 5-60, creates two implicit policies: an export policy that adds this Route Target to EVPN routes as they are advertised by BGP EVPN, and an import policy that accepts any EVPN route with this Route Target. These policies are shown in Example 5-61, taking leaf1 as a reference.

Example 5-61 *Implicit export and import policies created for Route Target*

```
root@leaf1> show policy __vrf-export-default-switch-internal__
Policy __vrf-export-default-switch-internal__: [RESOLVED/]
    Term unnamed:
        then community + __vrf-community-default-switch-common-internal__ [target:1:1 ] accept


root@leaf1> show policy __vrf-import-default-switch-internal__
Policy __vrf-import-default-switch-internal__: [RESOLVED/]
    Term unnamed:
        from community __vrf-community-default-switch-common-internal__ [target:1:1 ]
        then accept
    Term unnamed:
        then reject
```

To confirm that this Route Target is added to EVPN routes advertised by leaf1, an EVPN Type-3 route and an EVPN Type-2 route are examined, as shown in Example 5-62.

Example 5-62 *Route Target attached to EVPN Type-3 and Type-2 routes advertised by leaf1*

```
root@leaf1> show route table bgp.evpn.0 match-prefix 3:*192.0.2.11* extensive

bgp.evpn.0: 15 destinations, 27 routes (15 active, 0 holddown, 0 hidden)
3:192.0.2.11:1::10100::192.0.2.11/248 IM (1 entry, 1 announced)
TSI:
Page 0 idx 0, (group overlay type External) Type 1 val 0xae66e38 (adv_entry)
    Advertised metrics:
     Flags: Nexthop Change
```

```
        Nexthop: Self
        AS path: [65421] I
        Communities: target:1:1 encapsulation:vxlan(0x8)
        PMSI: Flags 0x0: Label 631: Type INGRESS-REPLICATION 192.0.2.11
     Advertise: 00000003
Path 3:192.0.2.11:1::10100::192.0.2.11
Vector len 4.  Val: 0
        *EVPN    Preference: 170
                 Next hop type: Indirect, Next hop index: 0
                 Address: 0x8c067f4
                 Next-hop reference count: 8, key opaque handle: 0x0, non-key opaque handle: 0x0
                 Protocol next hop: 192.0.2.11
                 Indirect next hop: 0x0 - INH Session ID: 0
                 State: <Secondary Active Int Ext>
                 Age: 5d 11:14:14
                 Validation State: unverified
                 Task: default-switch-evpn
                 Announcement bits (1): 1-BGP_RT_Background
                 AS path: I
                 Communities: target:1:1 encapsulation:vxlan(0x8)
                 Route Label: 10100
                 PMSI: Flags 0x0: Label 10100: Type INGRESS-REPLICATION 192.0.2.11
                 Primary Routing Table: default-switch.evpn.0
                 Thread: junos-main

root@leaf1> show route table bgp.evpn.0 match-prefix 2:*192.0.2.11* extensive

bgp.evpn.0: 15 destinations, 27 routes (15 active, 0 holddown, 0 hidden)
2:192.0.2.11:1::10100::f0:4b:3a:b9:80:a7/304 MAC/IP (1 entry, 1 announced)
TSI:
Page 0 idx 0, (group overlay type External) Type 1 val 0xae66e70 (adv_entry)
   Advertised metrics:
     Flags: Nexthop Change
     Nexthop: Self
     AS path: [65421] I
     Communities: target:1:1 encapsulation:vxlan(0x8)
   Advertise: 00000003
Path 2:192.0.2.11:1::10100::f0:4b:3a:b9:80:a7
Vector len 4.  Val: 0
        *EVPN    Preference: 170
                 Next hop type: Indirect, Next hop index: 0
                 Address: 0x8c067f4
                 Next-hop reference count: 8, key opaque handle: 0x0, non-key opaque handle: 0x0
                 Protocol next hop: 192.0.2.11
                 Indirect next hop: 0x0 - INH Session ID: 0
                 State: <Secondary Active Int Ext>
                 Age: 5d 11:14:39
                 Validation State: unverified
                 Task: default-switch-evpn
```

```
                Announcement bits (1): 1-BGP_RT_Background
                AS path: I
                Communities: target:1:1 encapsulation:vxlan(0x8)
                Route Label: 10100
                ESI: 00:00:00:00:00:00:00:00:00:00
                Primary Routing Table: default-switch.evpn.0
                Thread: junos-main
```

snip

For more granularity and control, more specific Route Targets can be configured at a per-VNI level, under the **protocols evpn vni-options** configuration hierarchy. This does not impact EVPN Type-1 and Type-4 routes, as these are advertised with no dependency on any VNI and continue to use the globally defined Route Target.

Any VNI that does not have any specific Route Target configuration will continue to use the Route Target defined under the **switch-options** configuration hierarchy. As shown in Example 5-63, leaf1 is configured with a global Route Target of 1:1, along with a VNI-specific Route Target of 100:100 for VNI 10100.

Example 5-63 *More specific Route Target configured for VNI 10100 on leaf2*

```
root@leaf1# show switch-options
vtep-source-interface lo0.0;
route-distinguisher 192.0.2.11:1;
vrf-target target:1:1;


root@leaf1# show protocols evpn
encapsulation vxlan;
vni-options {
    vni 10100 {
        vrf-target target:100:100;
    }
}
extended-vni-list all;
```

This creates additional implicit policies: a new import policy now matches Route Targets 100:100 and 1:1 and accepts them both, while a new export policy overrides the export policy for VNI 10100 and sets the Route Target to 100:100, as shown in Example 5-64.

Example 5-64 *Additional implicit policies created for VNI-specific Route Targets*

```
root@leaf1> show policy __evpn-import-autoderive-default-switch-internal__
Policy __evpn-import-autoderive-default-switch-internal__: [CHANGED/RESOLVED/EVPN_VXLAN_AUTO/]
    Term default-switch-bd-override-10100:
        from community __evpn-community-default-switch-bd-override-10100-export-internal__ [target:100:100 ]
        then accept
    Term unnamed:
        from community __vrf-community-default-switch-common-internal__ [target:1:1 ]
        then accept
    Term unnamed:
        then reject
```

```
root@leaf1> show policy __evpn-export-default-switch-bd-override-10100-internal__
Policy __evpn-export-default-switch-bd-override-10100-internal__:  [CHANGED/RESOLVED/EVPN_VXLAN_AUTO/]
    Term unnamed:
        then community + __evpn-community-default-switch-bd-override-10100-export-internal__ [target:100:100 ] accept
```

With these changes in place, the EVPN Type-1 route is still advertised with a Route Target of 1:1, while the EVPN Type-2 route is advertised with a Route Target of 100:100, using the more specific Route Target from the VNI level, as shown in Example 5-65.

Example 5-65 *Route Targets added to Type-1 and Type-2 routes advertised by leaf2*

```
root@leaf2> show route table bgp.evpn.0 match-prefix 1:*192.0.2.12* extensive

bgp.evpn.0: 21 destinations, 36 routes (21 active, 0 holddown, 0 hidden)
1:192.0.2.12:0::111100000000::FFFF:FFFF/192 AD/ESI (1 entry, 1 announced)
TSI:
Page 0 idx 0, (group overlay type External) Type 1 val 0x9fb94e4 (adv_entry)
   Advertised metrics:
     Flags: Nexthop Change
     Nexthop: Self
     AS path: [65422] I
     Communities: target:1:1 encapsulation:vxlan(0x8) esi-label:0x0:all-active (label 0)
   Advertise: 00000003
Path 1:192.0.2.12:0::111100000000::FFFF:FFFF
Vector len 4.  Val: 0
        *EVPN    Preference: 170
                 Next hop type: Indirect, Next hop index: 0
                 Address: 0x8c06f64
                 Next-hop reference count: 14, key opaque handle: 0x0, non-key opaque handle: 0x0
                 Protocol next hop: 192.0.2.12
                 Indirect next hop: 0x0 - INH Session ID: 0
                 State: <Secondary Active Int Ext>
                 Age: 16:30:33
                 Validation State: unverified
                 Task: __default_evpn__-evpn
                 Announcement bits (1): 1-BGP_RT_Background
                 AS path: I
                 Communities: target:1:1 encapsulation:vxlan(0x8) esi-label:0x0:all-active (label 0)
                 Primary Routing Table: __default_evpn__.evpn.0
                 Thread: junos-main

root@leaf2> show route table bgp.evpn.0 match-prefix 2:*192.0.2.12* extensive

bgp.evpn.0: 19 destinations, 32 routes (19 active, 0 holddown, 0 hidden)
2:192.0.2.12:1::10100::f0:4b:3a:b9:81:60/304 MAC/IP (1 entry, 1 announced)
TSI:
Page 0 idx 0, (group overlay type External) Type 1 val 0x9fb9420 (adv_entry)
   Advertised metrics:
     Flags: Nexthop Change
     Nexthop: Self
     AS path: [65422] I
```

```
        Communities: target:100:100 encapsulation:vxlan(0x8)
    Advertise: 00000003
Path 2:192.0.2.12:1::10100::f0:4b:3a:b9:81:60
Vector len 4.  Val: 0
        *EVPN   Preference: 170
                Next hop type: Indirect, Next hop index: 0
                Address: 0x8c06f64
                Next-hop reference count: 14, key opaque handle: 0x0, non-key opaque handle: 0x0
                Protocol next hop: 192.0.2.12
                Indirect next hop: 0x0 - INH Session ID: 0
                State: <Secondary Active Int Ext>
                Age: 17:36
                Validation State: unverified
                Task: default-switch-evpn
                Announcement bits (1): 1-BGP_RT_Background
                AS path: I
                Communities: target:100:100 encapsulation:vxlan(0x8)
                Route Label: 10100
                ESI: 00:00:00:00:11:11:00:00:00:00
                Primary Routing Table: default-switch.evpn.0
                Thread: junos-main
```

As the number of VNIs scale up, it is quite an administrative and operational overhead to manually configure VNI-specific Route Targets. Instead, Junos allows automatic derivation of Route Targets, as defined in RFC 8365. Using leaf2 as an example again, the configuration shown in Example 5-66 demonstrates auto-derived Route Targets, configured with the **auto** configuration option, under the **switch-options vrf-target** configuration hierarchy.

Example 5-66   *Configuration for auto-derived Route Targets*

```
root@leaf2# show switch-options
vtep-source-interface lo0.0;
route-distinguisher 192.0.2.12:1;
vrf-target {
    target:1:1;
    auto;
}
```

An automatically derived Route Target uses the same format as any other Route Target, and the value is divided into two parts: a 2-byte Global Administrator value and a 4-byte Local Administrator value. The Global Administrator is the ASN, while the Local Administrator has the breakdown shown in Figure 5-42.

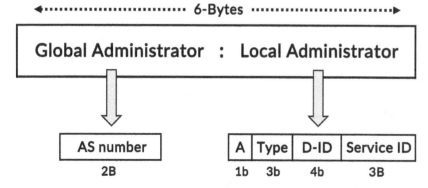

Figure 5-42   *Auto-derived route-target breakdown*

The following list expands on this breakdown:

- The *A* field is a 1-bit field that is simply used to indicate if the Route Target is auto-derived or not, with a value of 0 for auto-derived and 1 for manual.

- The 3-bit *Type* field indicates what is used for the 3-byte service ID—a value of 1 means a VXLAN-based value is used, which is the VNI in this case.

- *D-ID*, which stands for Domain-ID, is a 4-bit field, and is set to 0 by default for nonoverlapping numbering spaces.

- The *Service ID* field is 3 bytes long and holds the VNI itself.

As an example, considering an EVPN Type-2 route advertised by leaf2, the auto-derived Route Target is 65422:268445556, as shown in Example 5-67.

Example 5-67 *Auto-derived Route Target for an EVPN Type-2 route advertised by leaf2*

```
root@leaf2> show route table bgp.evpn.0 match-prefix 2:*192.0.2.12* extensive

bgp.evpn.0: 21 destinations, 36 routes (21 active, 0 holddown, 0 hidden)
2:192.0.2.12:1::10100::f0:4b:3a:b9:81:60/304 MAC/IP (1 entry, 1 announced)
TSI:
Page 0 idx 0, (group overlay type External) Type 1 val 0x9fb9420 (adv_entry)
  Advertised metrics:
    Flags: Nexthop Change
    Nexthop: Self
    AS path: [65422] I
    Communities: target:65422:268445556 encapsulation:vxlan(0x8)
  Advertise: 00000003
Path 2:192.0.2.12:1::10100::f0:4b:3a:b9:81:60
Vector len 4.  Val: 0
        *EVPN    Preference: 170
                 Next hop type: Indirect, Next hop index: 0
                 Address: 0x8c06f64
                 Next-hop reference count: 14, key opaque handle: 0x0, non-key opaque handle: 0x0
                 Protocol next hop: 192.0.2.12
                 Indirect next hop: 0x0 - INH Session ID: 0
                 State: <Secondary Active Int Ext>
                 Age: 28
                 Validation State: unverified
                 Task: default-switch-evpn
                 Announcement bits (1): 1-BGP_RT_Background
                 AS path: I
                 Communities: target:65422:268445556 encapsulation:vxlan(0x8)
                 Route Label: 10100
                 ESI: 00:00:00:00:11:11:00:00:00:00
                 Primary Routing Table: default-switch.evpn.0
                 Thread: junos-main
```

The Global Administrator value is the ASN, which, for leaf2, is 65422. The Local Administrator value looks a little more intimidating, so let's break it down. First, convert the number into hexadecimal, which gives a hexadecimal value of 0x10002774. This is further broken down as shown in Figure 5-43.

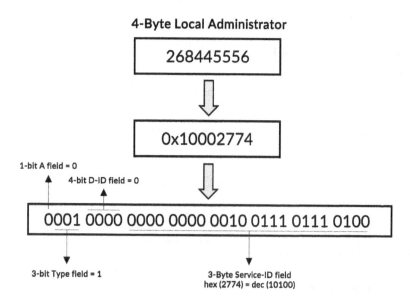

Figure 5-43 *Breakdown of an auto-derived Route Target added to an EVPN Type-2 route advertised by leaf2*

With the BGP ASN scheme that assigns each leaf a unique ASN, auto-derived Route Targets create a bit of a problem: the auto-derived Route Target is different on every leaf since the ASN is unique on each leaf. This implies that none of the leafs will have an implicit policy that matches the Route Target of every other leaf. Because of this, even though a leaf receives an EVPN Type-2 route from another leaf, it is not imported into the default-switch table, since there is no matching Route Target policy, and thus MAC addresses are not installed in the EVPN database or the MAC address table. This is confirmed as shown in Example 5-68.

Example 5-68 *EVPN Type-2 routes, received from leaf4, not imported on leaf1*

```
root@leaf1> show route table bgp.evpn.0 match-prefix 2:*192.0.2.14*

bgp.evpn.0: 19 destinations, 35 routes (19 active, 0 holddown, 0 hidden)
+ = Active Route, - = Last Active, * = Both

2:192.0.2.14:1::10100::f0:4b:3a:b9:80:ab/304 MAC/IP
                  *[BGP/170] 00:00:15, localpref 100, from 192.0.2.102
                    AS path: 65500 65424 I, validation-state: unverified
                    to 198.51.100.1 via et-0/0/48.0, Push 631
                  > to 198.51.100.3 via et-0/0/50.0, Push 631
                  [BGP/170] 00:00:15, localpref 100, from 192.0.2.101
                    AS path: 65500 65424 I, validation-state: unverified
                    to 198.51.100.1 via et-0/0/48.0, Push 631
                  > to 198.51.100.3 via et-0/0/50.0, Push 631
2:192.0.2.14:1::10100::f0:4b:3a:b9:80:ab::10.100.100.3/304 MAC/IP
                  *[BGP/170] 00:00:15, localpref 100, from 192.0.2.102
                    AS path: 65500 65424 I, validation-state: unverified
                    to 198.51.100.1 via et-0/0/48.0, Push 631
                  > to 198.51.100.3 via et-0/0/50.0, Push 631
                  [BGP/170] 00:00:15, localpref 100, from 192.0.2.101
                    AS path: 65500 65424 I, validation-state: unverified
                    to 198.51.100.1 via et-0/0/48.0, Push 631
                  > to 198.51.100.3 via et-0/0/50.0, Push 631
```

```
root@leaf1> show route table default-switch.evpn.0 match-prefix 2.*192.0.2.14*

default-switch.evpn.0: 7 destinations, 11 routes (7 active, 0 holddown, 0 hidden)
```

<no output>

The fix for this is simple: enable the configuration option **import-as** when using auto-derived Route Targets. With this configuration, you can specify all peer ASNs along with a list of VNIs for each peer ASN, and implicit policies are built for these to be accepted. For example, on leaf1, this is configured as shown in Example 5-69. On leaf1, since the peer ASNs are 65422, 65423, 65424, and 65425, each of these are configured using the **import-as** configuration option, with a VNI list that includes the VNI 10100.

Example 5-69 *Auto-derived Route Targets with the import-as option configured on leaf1*

```
root@leaf1# show switch-options
vtep-source-interface lo0.0;
route-distinguisher 192.0.2.11:1;
vrf-target {
    target:1:1;
    auto {
        import-as 65422 {
            vni-list 10100;
        }
        import-as 65423 {
            vni-list 10100;
        }
        import-as 65424 {
            vni-list 10100;
        }
        import-as 65425 {
            vni-list 10100;
        }
    }
}
```

The implicit import policy includes all these auto-derived Route Targets now, as shown in Example 5-70.

Example 5-70 *Implicit policy to accept auto-derived route-targets on leaf1*

```
root@leaf1> show policy __evpn-import-autoderive-default-switch-internal__
Policy __evpn-import-autoderive-default-switch-internal__:  [CHANGED/RESOLVED/EVPN_VXLAN_AUTO/]
    Term 10100:
        from community [ __evpn-community-default-switch-autoderive-10100-internal__
[target:65421:268445556 ] __evpn-community-default-switch-autoderive-10100-65422-internal__
[target:65422:268445556 ] __evpn-community-default-switch-autoderive-10100-65423-internal__
[target:65423:268445556 ] __evpn-community-default-switch-autoderive-10100-65424-internal__
[target:65424:268445556 ] __evpn-community-default-switch-autoderive-10100-65425-internal__
[target:65425:268445556 ] ]
        then accept
    Term unnamed:
        from community __vrf-community-default-switch-common-internal__ [target:1:1 ]
        then accept
    Term unnamed:
        then reject
```

With this configured, EVPN Type-2 routes are successfully imported in the default-switch.evpn.0 table now, as shown in Example 5-71.

Example 5-71 *Successful import of routes received with auto-derived Route Targets on leaf1*

```
root@leaf1> show route table bgp.evpn.0 match-prefix 2:*192.0.2.14*

bgp.evpn.0: 19 destinations, 35 routes (19 active, 0 holddown, 0 hidden)
+ = Active Route, - = Last Active, * = Both


2:192.0.2.14:1::10100::f0:4b:3a:b9:80:ab/304 MAC/IP
                    *[BGP/170] 00:00:13, localpref 100, from 192.0.2.101
                      AS path: 65500 65424 I, validation-state: unverified
                      to 198.51.100.1 via et-0/0/48.0, Push 631
                    > to 198.51.100.3 via et-0/0/50.0, Push 631
                     [BGP/170] 00:00:13, localpref 100, from 192.0.2.102
                      AS path: 65500 65424 I, validation-state: unverified
                      to 198.51.100.1 via et-0/0/48.0, Push 631
                    > to 198.51.100.3 via et-0/0/50.0, Push 631
2:192.0.2.14:1::10100::f0:4b:3a:b9:80:ab::10.100.100.3/304 MAC/IP
                    *[BGP/170] 00:00:13, localpref 100, from 192.0.2.101
                      AS path: 65500 65424 I, validation-state: unverified
                      to 198.51.100.1 via et-0/0/48.0, Push 631
                    > to 198.51.100.3 via et-0/0/50.0, Push 631
                     [BGP/170] 00:00:13, localpref 100, from 192.0.2.102
                      AS path: 65500 65424 I, validation-state: unverified
                      to 198.51.100.1 via et-0/0/48.0, Push 631
                    > to 198.51.100.3 via et-0/0/50.0, Push 631


root@leaf1> show route table default-switch.evpn.0 match-prefix 2:*192.0.2.14*

default-switch.evpn.0: 17 destinations, 31 routes (17 active, 0 holddown, 0 hidden)
+ = Active Route, - = Last Active, * = Both


2:192.0.2.14:1::10100::f0:4b:3a:b9:80:ab/304 MAC/IP
                    *[BGP/170] 00:00:33, localpref 100, from 192.0.2.101
                      AS path: 65500 65424 I, validation-state: unverified
                      to 198.51.100.1 via et-0/0/48.0, Push 631
                    > to 198.51.100.3 via et-0/0/50.0, Push 631
                     [BGP/170] 00:00:33, localpref 100, from 192.0.2.102
                      AS path: 65500 65424 I, validation-state: unverified
                      to 198.51.100.1 via et-0/0/48.0, Push 631
                    > to 198.51.100.3 via et-0/0/50.0, Push 631
2:192.0.2.14:1::10100::f0:4b:3a:b9:80:ab::10.100.100.3/304 MAC/IP
                    *[BGP/170] 00:00:33, localpref 100, from 192.0.2.101
                      AS path: 65500 65424 I, validation-state: unverified
                      to 198.51.100.1 via et-0/0/48.0, Push 631
                    > to 198.51.100.3 via et-0/0/50.0, Push 631
                     [BGP/170] 00:00:33, localpref 100, from 192.0.2.102
```

```
    AS path: 65500 65424 I, validation-state: unverified
       to 198.51.100.1 via et-0/0/48.0, Push 631
  >    to 198.51.100.3 via et-0/0/50.0, Push 631
```

Note If both per-VNI Route Targets and auto-derived Route Targets are configured, the per-VNI Route Targets take precedence, since they are more specific.

MAC Mobility

As the name implies, MAC mobility is the movement of MAC addresses across the network infrastructure. A common example of this is VMware VMotion of virtualized applications, which involves live migration of a virtual machine from one location to another. A VTEP in an EVPN VXLAN fabric must have the functionality to be able to detect such a move and update the rest of the fabric about the new location of this endpoint, identified by a MAC address, in this case.

A new, 8-byte extended community, called *MAC Mobility*, was defined by IANA for this. The community is constructed as shown in Figure 5-44.

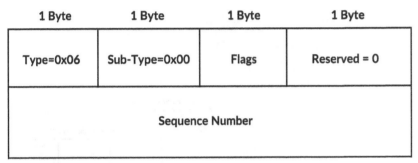

Figure 5-44 *MAC Mobility extended community*

Some fundamental rules (from RFC 7432) for this are as follows:

■ When a new MAC address is learned via the data plane and it is the first time it is learned, the MAC address is advertised either with no MAC Mobility community or with the sequence number inside the MAC Mobility community set to 0. If no MAC Mobility community is added, the sequence number is assumed to be 0.

■ If a MAC address is locally learned on a VTEP, for the same Ethernet Segment, that was previously learned via an EVPN Type-2 route with a sequence number of X, then the VTEP advertises this MAC address with a sequence number of $X+1$.

■ If a VTEP receives an EVPN Type-2 route with a sequence number X, which is higher than the current sequence number for the associated MAC address, then it accepts this new remotely learned MAC address update and withdraws its own route.

Let's simulate some of these situations in the reference topology, shown in Figure 5-2, to understand how this works. During steady state, leaf1 has advertised host h1's MAC address (assume host h1 is a virtualized host on server s1 connected to leaf1) to the rest of the fabric, and the state on other leafs reflects that. Visually, this can be represented as shown in Figure 5-45, taking leaf1 and leaf5 as an example.

From Figure 5-45, leaf1 has locally learned host h1's MAC address over interface et-0/0/49, while leaf5 has learned this via BGP EVPN, and the egress interface points to leaf1's VTEP address. Consider a situation in which the host, h1, moves from server s1 to server s4 while retaining its MAC address and IP address, which is typical of VMotion. When this happens, leaf5 will locally learn h1's MAC address, which was previously learned via leaf1's VTEP address via the BGP EVPN control plane. It will increment the sequence number by 1 and advertise the MAC address via EVPN Type-2 routes. When this is received on leaf1, it compares the sequence number and realizes that, since the sequence number is higher, the MAC address has moved to leaf5. It then sends a BGP EVPN withdraw for this address, as shown in Figure 5-46.

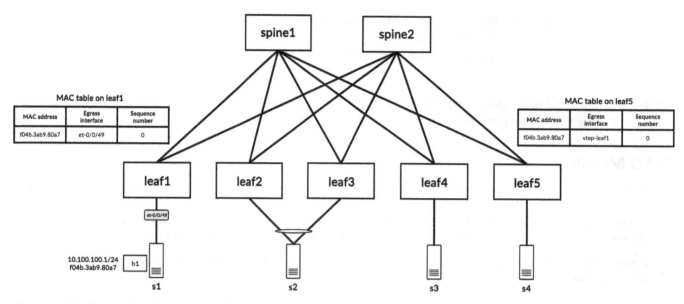

Figure 5-45   *State of host h1's MAC address during steady state, shown on leaf1 and leaf5*

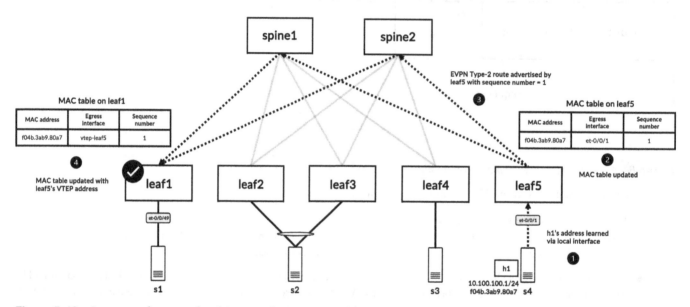

Figure 5-46   *Sequence of events when h1 moves from server s1 to server 4*

This increase in sequence number is confirmed with the packet capture shown in Figure 5-47. This capture was taken on spine1, which shows leaf5 (192.0.2.15) advertised h1's MAC address with a sequence number of 1, in the MAC Mobility extended community.

The EVPN database entry on leaf1, for h1's MAC address, also confirms this MAC mobility event, as shown in Example 5-72. The EVPN database in this example now includes a *Mobility history* for this MAC address, displaying mobility events, which confirms that a remote VTEP, identified by the address 192.0.2.15, advertised this MAC address with a sequence number of 1.

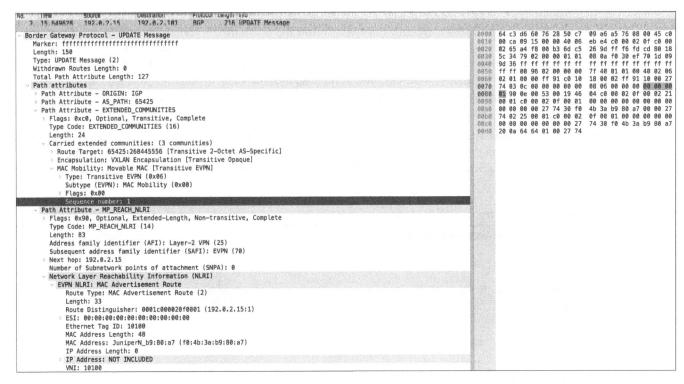

Figure 5-47 *Packet capture of an EVPN Type-2 route with a non-zero sequence number*

Example 5-72 *EVPN database entry for h1's MAC address on leaf1*

```
root@leaf1> show evpn database mac-address f0:4b:3a:b9:80:a7 extensive
Instance: default-switch

VN Identifier: 10100, MAC address: f0:4b:3a:b9:80:a7
  State: 0x0
  Mobility history
    Mobility event time      Type      Source                           Seq num
    May 17 06:53:50.953977   Remote    192.0.2.15                       1
  Source: 192.0.2.15, Rank: 1, Status: Active
    Mobility sequence number: 1 (minimum origin address 192.0.2.15)
    Timestamp: May 17 06:53:50.943730 (0x6464dc6e)
    State: <Remote-To-Local-Adv-Done>
    MAC advertisement route status: Not created (no local state present)
    IP address: 10.100.100.1
    History db:
      Time                      Event
      May 16 03:02:50.800 2023  et-0/0/49.0 : Updating output state (change flags 0x400 <IP-Deleted>)
      May 16 03:08:00.657 2023  et-0/0/49.0 : Updating output state (change flags 0x200 <IP-Added>)
      May 17 06:53:50.943 2023  192.0.2.15 : Remote peer 192.0.2.15 created
      May 17 06:53:50.943 2023  Mobility event for remote source 192.0.2.15 with sequence number 1
      May 17 06:53:50.943 2023  192.0.2.15 : Created
      May 17 06:53:50.943 2023  Updating output state (change flags 0x1 <ESI-Added>)
      May 17 06:53:50.943 2023  Active ESI changing (et-0/0/49.0 -> 192.0.2.15)
      May 17 06:53:51.381 2023  et-0/0/49.0 : 10.100.100.1 Deleting
      May 17 06:53:51.382 2023  et-0/0/49.0 : Deleting
      May 17 06:53:51.382 2023  Updating output state (change flags 0x2 <ESI-Deleted>)
```

There can be situations in which these moves happen many times in a short period, possibly signifying misbehaving applications or some form of loop in the network, typically originating below the ToR leafs. This can cause a lot of churn in the overlay network, and it is quite likely the sequence number increments endlessly. To prevent such situations, a VTEP that detects a MAC address has moved kicks off a timer, with a default value of 180 seconds. If N number of MAC address moves are detected (with N = 5 by default) while this timer is running, then the VTEP declares that this is a duplicate MAC address in the network and stops sending or processing any EVPN Type-2 routes for this MAC address (as per RFC 7432, Section 15.1).

Consider the following situation in the same reference topology, where two hosts (one behind server s1 and another behind server s4) are misconfigured with the same MAC address. As both these hosts are sending traffic into the fabric, there are continuous MAC address moves between leaf1 and leaf5. On leaf5, a duplicate MAC address is detected for this, as shown in Example 5-73.

Example 5-73 *EVPN database entry for h1's MAC address on leaf5*

```
root@leaf5> show evpn database mac-address f0:4b:3a:b9:80:a7 extensive
Instance: default-switch

VN Identifier: 10100, MAC address: f0:4b:3a:b9:80:a7
  State: 0x1 <Duplicate-Detected>
  Mobility history
    Mobility event time      Type    Source                       Seq num
    May 17 06:52:36.308578   Local   et-0/0/1.0                   1
    May 17 06:53:19.922811   Remote  192.0.2.11                   2
    May 17 06:53:30.945333   Local   et-0/0/1.0                   3
    May 17 06:53:34.631544   Remote  192.0.2.11                   4
    May 17 06:53:36.061610   Local   et-0/0/1.0                   5
  Source: et-0/0/1.0, Rank: 1, Status: Active
    Mobility sequence number: 5 (minimum origin address 192.0.2.15)
    Timestamp: May 17 06:53:35.989509 (0x6464dc5f)
    State: <Local-MAC-Only Local-To-Remote-Adv-Allowed>
    MAC advertisement route status: Not created (duplicate MAC suppression)
  Source: 192.0.2.11, Rank: 2, Status: Inactive
    Mobility sequence number: 4 (minimum origin address 192.0.2.11)
    Timestamp: May 17 06:53:34.559278 (0x6464dc5e)
    State: <>
  MAC advertisement route status: Not created (inactive source)
  IP address: 10.100.100.1
  History db:
    Time                       Event
    May 17 06:53:35.989 2023   Duplication detected
    May 17 06:53:35.989 2023   et-0/0/1.0 : Created
    May 17 06:53:35.989 2023   Updating output state (change flags 0x5 <ESI-Added Duplicate-detected>)
    May 17 06:53:35.989 2023   Active ESI changing (192.0.2.11 -> et-0/0/1.0)
    May 17 06:53:35.989 2023   et-0/0/1.0 : Advertisement route cannot be created (duplicate MAC suppression)
    May 17 06:53:35.989 2023   et-0/0/1.0 : Updating output state (change flags 0x20 <ESI-Local-State>)
    May 17 06:53:35.989 2023   et-0/0/1.0 : Advertisement route cannot be created (duplicate MAC suppression)
    May 17 06:53:54.323 2023   et-0/0/1.0 : 10.100.100.1 Deleting
    May 17 06:53:54.323 2023   et-0/0/1.0 : Updating output state (change flags 0x400 <IP-Deleted>)
    May 17 06:53:54.323 2023   et-0/0/1.0 : Advertisement route cannot be created (duplicate MAC suppression)
```

Two important inferences can be made from Example 5-73, as follows:

■ The MAC address state is 0x01, implying it has been marked as a duplicate MAC address and is being suppressed from any advertisement or processing.

■ This device (leaf5) marked this as duplicate because the MAC address moved five times, within 180 seconds, between local interface et-0/0/1 and VTEP address 192.0.2.11 (which is leaf1).

By default, once a duplicate MAC address is detected, and the MAC address is suppressed, there is no automatic recovery. To manually clear this duplicate state, you can use the operational mode command **clear evpn duplicate-mac-suppression mac-address** [*mac-address*]. It is quite possible that the default duplicate MAC detection timers are not appropriate—Junos provides the flexibility to tune these timers to suit different environments and use cases, as shown in Example 5-74. This also allows automatic recovery (after a configurable number of seconds) for MAC addresses that were marked as duplicate.

Example 5-74 *Options to tune MAC address duplicate detection timers*

```
root@leaf1# set protocols evpn duplicate-mac-detection ?
Possible completions:
+ apply-groups          Groups from which to inherit configuration data
+ apply-groups-except   Don't inherit configuration data from these groups
  auto-recovery-time    Automatically unblock duplicate MACs after a time delay (5..360 minutes)
  detection-threshold   Number of moves to trigger duplicate MAC detection (2..20)
  detection-window      Time window for detection of duplicate MACs (5..600 seconds)
```

Loop Detection

Virtualized overlay networks like EVPN VXLAN are inherently loop free. They are built over a Layer 3 underlay, and flooding mechanisms in the overlay ensure that BUM (multi-destination) traffic does not loop, with prevention techniques like split horizon and Designated Forwarder election. However, loops can be created by network topologies connected southbound to the fabric. This includes backdoor links between data centers and switches connected to ToRs that are misconfigured or miscabled. The MAC address duplication detection and protection process (in RFC 7432), which was discussed in the previous section, only limits control plane churn when such duplicate MAC addresses are detected, but the forwarding plane continues to be impacted, leading to a possibly degraded network.

Consider the topologies shown in Figures 5-48 and 5-49, which are examples of network infrastructure connected downstream to an EVPN VXLAN fabric in such a way that it causes a loop in the network.

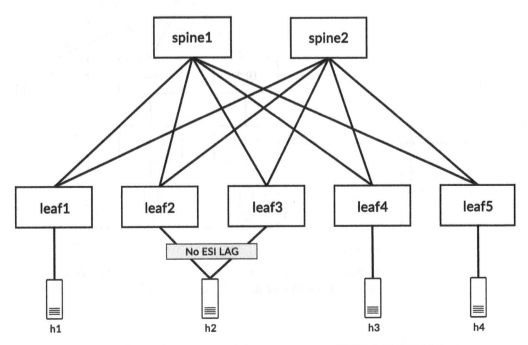

Figure 5-48 *Example topology connected downstream to an EVPN VXLAN fabric that can cause a forwarding loop*

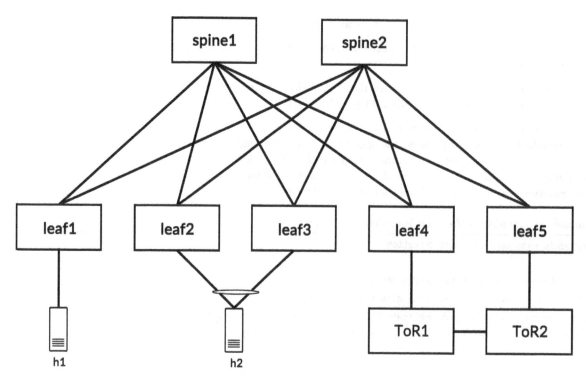

Figure 5-49   *Another example topology connected downstream to an EVPN VXLAN fabric that can cause a forwarding loop*

In the first example, shown in Figure 5-48, host h2 is supposed to be multihomed via ESI LAG, but it was never configured, which creates a Layer 2 loop. In the second example, shown in Figure 5-49, two ToR switches, connected to different leafs, are connected back-to-back as well, leading to a Layer 2 loop again. Another common example where such issues can occur is when two data centers are connected via a backdoor Layer 2 link, as shown in Figure 5-50.

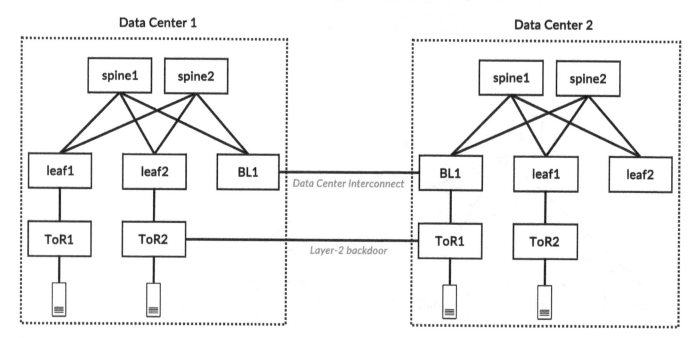

Figure 5-50   *A backdoor link between two data centers causing a loop*

Such loops, originating downstream, not only impact the directly connected switches but also "leaks" into the EVPN VXLAN fabric itself as flooded traffic, and thus it is important to protect the network from such mishaps.

Before discussing different loop detection mechanisms, let's take a look at a loop in action. ESI LAG is not configured for the multihomed host h2 to simulate such a situation, and when the host attempts to send an ARP request in the network (which needs to be flooded), this loops around endlessly. During steady state, there is zero traffic in the network (since this is a controlled lab environment), and when this Layer 2 loop occurs, the packets per second (pps) rate on the VTEP-to-host interfaces, as well as the fabric point-to-point interfaces, goes up substantially. This can be monitored in real time using the **monitor interface traffic** operational mode command, which shows live traffic rates (in pps) per interface, as shown in Example 5-75.

Example 5-75 *Real-time monitoring of traffic rates for all interfaces*

```
root@leaf2> monitor interface traffic
leaf2                        Seconds: 358              Time: 21:39:26


Interface  Link  Input packets    (pps)   Output packets    (pps)
*snip*


et-0/0/49  Up        10901973     (245)        14730919     (1043)
et-0/0/50  Up         2672330     (259)         3126591      (237)


*snip*


root@leaf3> monitor interface traffic
leaf3                        Seconds: 1221             Time: 21:39:20


Interface  Link  Input packets    (pps)   Output packets    (pps)
*snip*


et-0/0/51  Up        10871196     (258)        15653573      (992)
et-0/0/52  Up         2901101     (248)         3309317      (251)


*snip*


root@spine2> monitor interface traffic
spine2                       Seconds: 1246             Time: 21:39:29


Interface  Link  Input packets    (pps)   Output packets    (pps)
*snip*


et-0/0/0   Up        11011336       (6)        13688529      (507)
et-0/0/30  Up        11029563       (6)        13715105      (507)
et-0/0/31  Up        11625450       (7)        13831252      (508)
et-0/0/51  Up        15812743     (969)        12767675      (267)
et-0/0/63  Up        17337795    (1049)        12111627      (246)


*snip*
```

Example 5-75 provides a snippet of real-time traffic rates on leaf2, leaf3, and spine2. This shows a considerable increase in the pps traffic rate on the leaf-spine interfaces, as well as the interfaces connecting down to host h2. Troubleshooting this can be tough—the sudden abnormal increase in traffic rates clearly indicates that something is wrong, but finding the culprit can be tricky. Logs on the devices provide a lot of valuable information, and as shown in Example 5-76, several MAC addresses were marked as duplicate MAC addresses on leaf3.

Example 5-76   *Duplicate MACs reported in log messages on leaf3*

```
root@leaf3> show log messages | grep DUPLICATE
May 18 09:54:25 leaf3 rpd[11612]: EVPN_DUPLICATE_MAC: Duplicate MAC address default-switch::10100::f0:4b:3a:b9:80:a0
detected
May 18 22:09:34 leaf3 rpd[11612]: EVPN_DUPLICATE_MAC: Duplicate MAC address default-switch::10100::f0:4b:3a:b9:80:ab
detected
May 18 22:24:52 leaf3 rpd[11612]: EVPN_DUPLICATE_MAC: Duplicate MAC address default-switch::10100::f0:4b:3a:b9:80:ab
detected
May 18 22:35:51 leaf3 rpd[11612]: EVPN_DUPLICATE_MAC: Duplicate MAC address default-switch::10100::f0:4b:3a:b9:80:a7
detected
```

Additionally, distributed denial-of-service (DDoS) protection policers can also be checked to confirm if excess traffic is possibly leaking to the CPU (like ARP). In our case, the *VXLAN* protocol policer is seeing violations and a large amount of traffic, confirmed with the output from leaf1 shown in Example 5-77.

Example 5-77   *DDoS protection policer on leaf1*

```
root@leaf1> show ddos-protection protocols vxlan statistics
Packet types: 1, Received traffic: 1, Currently violated: 1
Protocol Group: VXLAN

  Packet type: aggregate
    System-wide information:
      Aggregate bandwidth is being violated!
        No. of FPCs currently receiving excess traffic: 1
        No. of FPCs that have received excess traffic:  1
        Violation first detected at: 2023-05-18 21:33:29 PDT
        Violation last seen at:      2023-05-18 22:46:03 PDT
        Duration of violation: 01:12:34 Number of violations: 2
      Received:  4242405         Arrival rate:    501 pps
      Dropped:   309217          Max arrival rate: 60713 pps
    Routing Engine information:
      Aggregate policer is never violated
      Received:  0               Arrival rate:    0 pps
      Dropped:   0               Max arrival rate: 0 pps
        Dropped by individual policers: 0
    FPC slot 0 information:
      Aggregate policer is currently being violated!
        Violation first detected at: 2023-05-18 21:33:29 PDT
        Violation last seen at:      2023-05-18 22:46:03 PDT
        Duration of violation: 01:12:34 Number of violations: 2
      Received:  4242405         Arrival rate:    501 pps
      Dropped:   309217          Max arrival rate: 60713 pps
        Dropped by individual policers: 0
        Dropped by aggregate policer:   309217
        Dropped by flow suppression:    0
      Flow counts:
        Aggregation level   Current    Total detected   State
        Subscriber          0          0                Active
```

Using these clues and any one of the MAC addresses to troubleshoot, the EVPN database, on both leaf2 and leaf3, clearly indicates that the MAC address is moving between interface et-0/0/50 on leaf2 and interface et-0/0/52 on leaf3, as shown in Example 5-78, and the current state of the MAC address is 0x01, implying that it was marked as a duplicate MAC address.

Example 5-78 *EVPN database on leaf2 and leaf3*

```
root@leaf2> show evpn database mac-address f0:4b:3a:b9:80:a0 extensive
Instance: default-switch

VN Identifier: 10100, MAC address: f0:4b:3a:b9:80:a0
  State: 0x1 <Duplicate-Detected>
  Mobility history
    Mobility event time      Type     Source                            Seq num
    May 18 21:33:12.982440   Local    et-0/0/50.0                       2
    May 18 21:33:14.155502   Remote   192.0.2.13                        3
    May 18 21:33:23.575598   Local    et-0/0/50.0                       4
    May 18 21:33:24.752956   Remote   192.0.2.13                        5
    May 18 21:33:25.108577   Local    et-0/0/50.0                       6
  Source: et-0/0/50.0, Rank: 1, Status: Active
    Mobility sequence number: 6 (minimum origin address 192.0.2.12)
    Timestamp: May 18 21:33:25.011214 (0x6466fc15)
    State: <Local-MAC-Only Local-To-Remote-Adv-Allowed>
    MAC advertisement route status: Not created (duplicate MAC suppression)
    IP address: 10.100.100.2
    Flags: <Local-Adv>
  Source: 192.0.2.13, Rank: 2, Status: Inactive
    Mobility sequence number: 5 (minimum origin address 192.0.2.13)
    Timestamp: May 18 21:33:24.409166 (0x6466fc14)
    State: <>
    MAC advertisement route status: Not created (inactive source)
    IP address: 10.100.100.2
    History db:
      Time                     Event
      May 18 21:33:24.764 2023   et-0/0/50.0 : Deleting
      May 18 21:33:24.764 2023   Updating output state (change flags 0x2 <ESI-Deleted>)
      May 18 21:33:24.764 2023   Mobility event for local source et-0/0/50.0 with sequence number 6
      May 18 21:33:24.764 2023   Duplication detected
      May 18 21:33:24.764 2023   et-0/0/50.0 : Created
      May 18 21:33:24.764 2023   Updating output state (change flags 0x5 <ESI-Added Duplicate-detected>)
      May 18 21:33:24.764 2023   Active ESI changing (192.0.2.13 -> et-0/0/50.0)
      May 18 21:33:24.764 2023   et-0/0/50.0 : Advertisement route cannot be created (duplicate MAC suppression)
      May 18 21:33:24.883 2023   et-0/0/50.0 : Updating output state (change flags 0x20 <ESI-Local-State>)
      May 18 21:33:24.883 2023   et-0/0/50.0 : Advertisement route cannot be created (duplicate MAC suppression)

root@leaf3> show evpn database mac-address f0:4b:3a:b9:80:a0 extensive
Instance: default-switch

VN Identifier: 10100, MAC address: f0:4b:3a:b9:80:a0
  State: 0x0
```

```
Mobility history
  Mobility event time      Type     Source                                    Seq num
  May 18 21:29:21.027386   Local    et-0/0/52.0                               1
  May 18 21:33:13.802408   Remote   192.0.2.12                                2
  May 18 21:33:14.158477   Local    et-0/0/52.0                               3
  May 18 21:33:24.397386   Remote   192.0.2.12                                4
  May 18 21:33:24.753697   Local    et-0/0/52.0                               5
Source: et-0/0/52.0, Rank: 1, Status: Active
  Mobility sequence number: 5 (minimum origin address 192.0.2.13)
  Timestamp: May 18 21:33:24.148634 (0x6466fc14)
  State: <Local-MAC-Only Local-To-Remote-Adv-Allowed>
  MAC advertisement route status: Created
  IP address: 10.100.100.2
  Flags: <Local-Adv>
  History db:
    Time                     Event
    May 18 21:33:24.000 2023   Updating output state (change flags 0x2 <ESI-Deleted>)
    May 18 21:33:24.000 2023   Mobility event for local source et-0/0/52.0 with sequence number 5
    May 18 21:33:24.000 2023   et-0/0/52.0 : Created
    May 18 21:33:24.000 2023   Updating output state (change flags 0x1 <ESI-Added>)
    May 18 21:33:24.000 2023   Active ESI changing (192.0.2.12 -> et-0/0/52.0)
    May 18 21:33:24.000 2023   et-0/0/52.0 : Updating output state (change flags 0x20 <ESI-Local-State>)
    May 18 21:33:24.826 2023   192.0.2.12 : 10.100.100.2 Deleting
    May 18 21:33:24.826 2023   192.0.2.12 : Remote peer 192.0.2.12 deleted
    May 18 21:33:24.826 2023   192.0.2.12 : Deleting
    May 18 21:33:24.826 2023   Updating output state (change flags 0x2 <ESI-Deleted>)
```

Even though the MAC address is marked as duplicate on leaf2, and there is no further control plane churn with regard to BGP EVPN, the forwarding plane continues to be impacted as per the traffic rates shown in Example 5-75. Thus, it is important to quickly hunt down the source of the problem and fix it. The fastest way to fix something like this is to cut the loop (by shutting down the interface or interfaces that would break it).

This is where loop protection mechanisms come into play—they protect the fabric from situations like this by taking some action that breaks the loop as soon as it is detected. In Junos, there are two approaches or mechanisms for this:

- Connectivity fault management (CFM)-based loop protection as defined in the Ethernet OAM standard 802.1ag

- Implementation of a loop prevention mechanism as described in IETF draft *draft-snr-bess-evpn-loop-protect*

Connectivity Fault Management

CFM provides a lightweight detection mechanism that uses multicast PDUs called *continuity check messages (CCMs)* for loop detection. These messages act as simple probes and are sent periodically over interfaces enabled for this. If a probe is received on an interface enabled for CFM, then a loop is detected and the configured action is taken (actions available are interface shutdown and laser off). CFM also offers automatic recovery—before bringing the interface back up (after recovery timer expires), a probe is sent out to ensure there is no loop. If a loop is detected again, the interface stays suspended.

It is crucial to understand which interfaces should be enabled for CFM—it is enabled on the VTEP-to-host interfaces, as shown in Figure 5-51 for the reference topology.

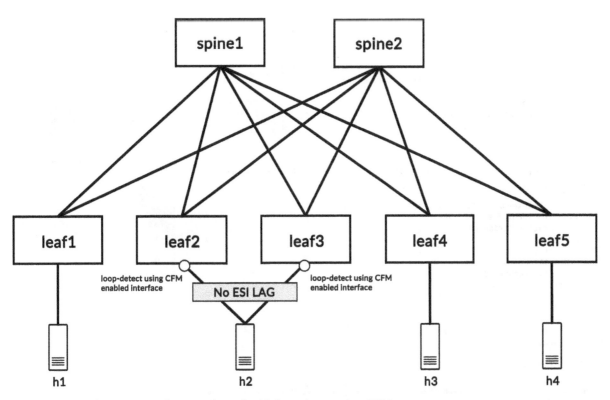

Figure 5-51 *PE-to-CE interfaces configured with loop-detect using CFM*

This is configured under the **protocols loop-detect** configuration hierarchy and must be configured on all the VTEP-to-host interfaces, as shown in Example 5-79.

Example 5-79 *Loop-detect, using CFM, configuration on leaf2 and leaf3*

```
root@leaf2# show protocols loop-detect
enhanced {
    interface et-0/0/50.0 {
        vlan-id 100;
        loop-detect-action interface-down;
        transmit-interval 1s;
    }
}

root@leaf3# show protocols loop-detect
enhanced {
    interface et-0/0/52.0 {
        vlan-id 100;
        loop-detect-action interface-down;
        transmit-interval 1s;
    }
}
```

The packet capture in Figure 5-52 shows a CCM probe that is sent out from a leaf to a host-facing interface.

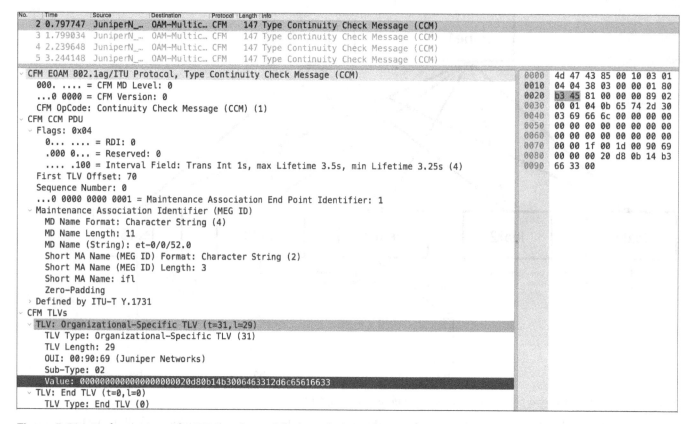

```
No.   Time       Source       Destination    Protocol  Length  Info
  2 0.797747  JuniperN_...  OAM-Multic... CFM       147    Type Continuity Check Message (CCM)
  3 1.799034  JuniperN_...  OAM-Multic... CFM       147    Type Continuity Check Message (CCM)
  4 2.239648  JuniperN_...  OAM-Multic... CFM       147    Type Continuity Check Message (CCM)
  5 3.244148  JuniperN_...  OAM-Multic... CFM       147    Type Continuity Check Message (CCM)

v CFM EOAM 802.1ag/ITU Protocol, Type Continuity Check Message (CCM)         0000  4d 47 43 85 00 10 03 01
    000. .... = CFM MD Level: 0                                              0010  04 04 38 03 00 00 01 80
    ...0 0000 = CFM Version: 0                                               0020  b3 45 81 00 00 00 89 02
    CFM OpCode: Continuity Check Message (CCM) (1)                           0030  00 01 04 0b 65 74 2d 30
v CFM CCM PDU                                                                0040  03 69 66 6c 00 00 00 00
  v Flags: 0x04                                                              0050  00 00 00 00 00 00 00 00
      0... .... = RDI: 0                                                     0060  00 00 00 00 00 00 00 00
      .000 0... = Reserved: 0                                                0070  00 00 1f 00 1d 00 90 69
      .... .100 = Interval Field: Trans Int 1s, max Lifetime 3.5s, min Lifetime 3.25s (4)  0080  00 00 00 20 d8 0b 14 b3
    First TLV Offset: 70                                                     0090  66 33 00
    Sequence Number: 0
    ...0 0000 0000 0001 = Maintenance Association End Point Identifier: 1
  v Maintenance Association Identifier (MEG ID)
      MD Name Format: Character String (4)
      MD Name Length: 11
      MD Name (String): et-0/0/52.0
      Short MA Name (MEG ID) Format: Character String (2)
      Short MA Name (MEG ID) Length: 3
      Short MA Name: ifl
      Zero-Padding
  > Defined by ITU-T Y.1731
v CFM TLVs
  v TLV: Organizational-Specific TLV (t=31,l=29)
      TLV Type: Organizational-Specific TLV (31)
      TLV Length: 29
      OUI: 00:90:69 (Juniper Networks)
      Sub-Type: 02
      Value: 00000000000000000000020d80b14b3006463312d6c65616633
  v TLV: End TLV (t=0,l=0)
      TLV Type: End TLV (0)
```

Figure 5-52 *Packet capture of a CFM probe used for loop detection*

With this configuration in place, a loop is instantly detected and the respective interfaces are brought down, as shown in Example 5-80 on both leaf2 and leaf3. This is confirmed using the **show loop-detect enhanced interface** operational mode command.

Example 5-80 *Loop detected using CFM*

```
root@leaf2> show loop-detect enhanced interface
Interface               :et-0/0/50.0
Vlan-id                 :100
ESI                     :00:00:00:00:00:00:00:00:00:00
Current status          :Loop-detected
        Remote Host     :leaf3
        Remote Chassis  :20:d8:0b:14:b3:00
        Remote Interface :et-0/0/52.0
        Remote ESI      :00:00:00:00:00:00:00:00:00:00
Last loop-detect time   :Thu May 18 23:15:03 2023
Receive statistics      :59
Action configured       :Interface-down
Action count            :2
Transmit Interval       :1s
Revert Interval         :0s


root@leaf3> show loop-detect enhanced interface
Interface               :et-0/0/52.0
Vlan-id                 :100
ESI                     :00:00:00:00:00:00:00:00:00:00
```

```
Current status         :Loop-detected
        Remote Host      :leaf2
        Remote Chassis   :0c:81:26:d6:83:00
        Remote Interface :et-0/0/50.0
        Remote ESI       :00:00:00:00:00:00:00:00:00:00
Last loop-detect time    :Thu May 18 23:15:04 2023
Receive statistics       :45
Action configured        :Interface-down
Action count             :2
Transmit Interval        :1s
Revert Interval          :0s
```

Loop Prevention Mechanism Using IETF Draft draft-snr-bess-evpn-loop-protect

The second approach is a loop protection mechanism that is described in the *draft-snr-bess-evpn-loop-protect* IETF draft. This draft simply extends the current MAC address duplicate detection process to include an action that can be taken when a duplicate MAC address is detected. This is a far simpler approach, with no additional overhead, because it is rooted in EVPN as a protocol itself, and no additional packets need to be sent out for this. The actions shown in Example 5-81 are available to be configured.

Example 5-81   *Configurable actions with EVPN duplicate MAC detection*

```
root@leaf2# set protocols evpn duplicate-mac-detection action ?
Possible completions:
  block            Drop packet with duplicate MAC as source or destination
  shutdown         Shutdown the port to prevent loop
```

With the action configured as *block*, the leaf that detects the duplicate MAC address creates a discard route for that MAC address, thus dropping any packets sourced or destined for it. In the L2ALD view, the B flag is set against the MAC address, meaning it is blocked with a discard route, shown in Example 5-82.

Example 5-82   *B flag set for a duplicate MAC address in the MAC table*

```
root@leaf3> show ethernet-switching table


MAC flags (S - static MAC, D - dynamic MAC, L - locally learned, P - Persistent static
          SE - statistics enabled, NM - non configured MAC, R - remote PE MAC, O - ovsdb MAC,
          B - Blocked MAC)



Ethernet switching table : 4 entries, 3 learned
Routing instance : default-switch
   Vlan        MAC              MAC    GBP   Logical       SVLBNH/     Active
   name        address          flags  tag   interface     VENH Index  source
   v100        f0:4b:3a:b9:80:a0  S,B         et-0/0/52.0
   v100        f0:4b:3a:b9:80:a7  DR          vtep.32770                192.0.2.11
   v100        f0:4b:3a:b9:80:ab  DR          vtep.32769                192.0.2.14
   v100        f0:4b:3a:b9:80:bb  DR          vtep.32771                192.0.2.15


root@leaf3> show route forwarding-table destination f0:4b:3a:b9:80:a0
Routing table: default-switch.evpn-vxlan
Bridging domain: v100.evpn-vxlan
```

```
VPLS:
Enabled protocols: Bridging, ACKed by all peers, EVPN VXLAN,
Destination       Type RtRef Next hop        Type Index   NhRef Netif
f0:4b:3a:b9:80:a0/48 user    0                dscd 1729    2
```

Bidirectional Forwarding Detection in an EVPN VXLAN Fabric

Before this chapter is closed out, it is important to address the necessity of BFD in EVPN VXLAN fabrics and how to configure and validate it.

Bidirectional Forwarding Detection is a lightweight UDP-based protocol used for detection of network failure that allows the network to converge faster by not relying on upper-layer protocol timers for convergence (which can be much slower). BFD uses a simple *hello* mechanism to detect such network failures, independently validating links and protocol connectivity between network devices.

Consider BGP configured for the underlay and overlay in a 3-stage Clos fabric—the protocol relies on keepalives exchanged to keep a session up, with a hold time timer of 90 seconds and a keepalive timer of 30 seconds, in the case of the reference topology in Figure 5-2. This indicates that within a span of 90 seconds, no keepalive packet from the neighbor must be processed to declare the neighbor down and start the teardown. These timers can be changed to be much shorter, but this creates a heavier, and possibly detrimental, load on the Routing Engine (CPU).

Another problem that exists is specific to the overlay: because the peering is between the loopbacks of the leafs and the spines, while a physical link going down between a leaf and a spine can immediately notify BGP and tear down the underlay BGP peering (because the BGP peering for the underlay uses the point-to-point interfaces themselves), it does not bring the overlay BGP peering down. As an example, let's administratively disable the interface between leaf1 and spine2 and confirm, as shown in Example 5-83, that despite the interface being shut down and the underlay BGP peering going down, the overlay BGP peering continues to be in an Established state and will only go down once the 90-second hold time timer expires.

Example 5-83   *BGP overlay session between leaf1 and spine2 in an Established state despite physical interface being shut down*

```
root@leaf1# set interfaces et-0/0/50 disable

root@leaf1# commit
configuration check succeeds
commit complete

root@leaf1> show bgp summary
Threading mode: BGP I/O
Default eBGP mode: advertise - accept, receive - accept
Groups: 2 Peers: 4 Down peers: 1
Table          Tot Paths  Act Paths Suppressed    History Damp State    Pending
inet.0
                       5          5          0          0          0          0
bgp.evpn.0
                      36         18          0          0          0          0
Peer                     AS      InPkt     OutPkt     OutQ    Flaps Last Up/Dwn State|#Active/Received/Accepted/Damped...
192.0.2.101           65500       3511       2876        0        0   21:45:53 Establ
  bgp.evpn.0: 16/18/18/0
  default-switch.evpn.0: 14/16/16/0
  __default_evpn__.evpn.0: 0/0/0/0
192.0.2.102           65500        807        635        0        2    4:47:39 Establ
  bgp.evpn.0: 2/18/18/0
  default-switch.evpn.0: 2/16/16/0
```

```
__default_evpn__.evpn.0: 0/0/0/0
198.51.100.1          65500      3655      3694      0      4  1d 3:57:46 Establ
  inet.0: 5/5/5/0
198.51.100.3          65500       636       638      0      7         16 Idle
```

While the general recommendation is to configure BFD for the overlay for reasons discussed previously, it is equally important to have BFD configured for the underlay as well. In today's market of high-speed optics, it is quite possible to experience unidirectional loss over these optics. BFD can help detect such situations and bring the upper-layer protocol down, thus redirecting traffic through other functional interfaces and paths.

BFD is typically configured by attaching it to an upper-layer protocol that is notified when a BFD session goes down. For the reference topology in Figure 5-2, BFD is configured for BGP since both the underlay and overlay use BGP. An example of how to do this is shown in Example 5-84, with a configuration snippet from leaf1. BFD is configured under a BGP group using the **bfd-liveness-detection** configuration hierarchy.

Example 5-84   *BFD configuration on leaf1 for the underlay and overlay*

```
root@leaf1# show protocols bgp group underlay
type external;
family inet {
    unicast;
}
export allow-loopback;
peer-as 65500;
multipath;
bfd-liveness-detection {
    minimum-interval 333;
    multiplier 3;
}
neighbor 198.51.100.1;
neighbor 198.51.100.3;


root@leaf1# show protocols bgp group overlay
type external;
multihop;
local-address 192.0.2.11;
family evpn {
    signaling;
}
peer-as 65500;
multipath;
bfd-liveness-detection {
    minimum-interval 333;
    multiplier 3;
}
neighbor 192.0.2.101;
neighbor 192.0.2.102;
```

BFD is configured for BGP with a minimum interval of 333ms and a multiplier of 3. This means that the BFD control packet (think of it as a simple hello message) is sent every 333ms, and if no BFD control packet is received within 999ms (minimum interval times multiplier), then the BFD session is declared dead. Such subsecond BFD detection, at scale, is achieved by offloading the processing of BFD packets to the hardware. This is also called *hardware-assisted inline BFD*. Depending on the platform, this may or may not be enabled by default. For example, on the Juniper QFX5120s, the default mode is *Centralized BFD*, meaning all BFD packet processing is handled by the Routing Engine (CPU). To enable inline BFD, the configuration shown in Example 5-85 is required, under the **routing-options** configuration hierarchy.

Example 5-85   *Configuration to enable inline BFD on a QFX5120*

```
root@leaf1# show routing-options
router-id 192.0.2.11;
autonomous-system 65421;
ppm {
    inline-processing-enable;
}
forwarding-table {
    export ECMP;
}
```

For other platforms, publicly available Juniper documentation can confirm the default BFD mode.

The same BFD configuration is done on the other leafs and spines, at the end of which two single-hop BFD sessions for the underlay and two multi-hop BFD sessions for the overlay are present on each leaf, as confirmed in Example 5-86 on leaf1.

Example 5-86   *BFD sessions on leaf1 for the underlay and overlay*

```
root@leaf1> show bfd session
                                           Detect   Transmit
Address              State    Interface    Time     Interval   Multiplier
192.0.2.101          Up                    0.999    0.333      3
192.0.2.102          Up                    0.999    0.333      3
198.51.100.1         Up       et-0/0/48.0  0.999    0.333      3
198.51.100.3         Up       et-0/0/50.0  0.999    0.333      3


4 sessions, 4 clients
Cumulative transmit rate 12.0 pps, cumulative receive rate 12.0 pps


root@leaf1> show bfd session extensive
                                           Detect   Transmit
Address              State    Interface    Time     Interval   Multiplier
192.0.2.101          Up                    0.999    0.333      3
 Client BGP, TX interval 0.333, RX interval 0.333
 Session up time 00:05:00
 Local diagnostic None, remote diagnostic None
 Remote state Up, version 1
 Session type: Multi hop BFD
 Min async interval 0.333, min slow interval 1.000
 Adaptive async TX interval 0.333, RX interval 0.333
 Local min TX interval 0.333, minimum RX interval 0.333, multiplier 3
 Remote min TX interval 0.333, min RX interval 0.333, multiplier 3
 Local discriminator 19, remote discriminator 21
 Echo TX interval 0.000, echo detection interval 0.000
```

```
Echo mode disabled/inactive
Remote is control-plane independent
Multi-hop route table 0, local-address 192.0.2.11
 Session ID: 0
```

			Detect	Transmit	
Address	State	Interface	Time	Interval	Multiplier
192.0.2.102	Up		0.999	0.333	3

```
 Client BGP, TX interval 0.333, RX interval 0.333
 Session up time 00:04:46
 Local diagnostic None, remote diagnostic None
 Remote state Up, version 1
 Session type: Multi hop BFD
 Min async interval 0.333, min slow interval 1.000
 Adaptive async TX interval 0.333, RX interval 0.333
 Local min TX interval 0.333, minimum RX interval 0.333, multiplier 3
 Remote min TX interval 0.333, min RX interval 0.333, multiplier 3
 Local discriminator 20, remote discriminator 22
 Echo TX interval 0.000, echo detection interval 0.000
 Echo mode disabled/inactive
 Remote is control-plane independent
 Multi-hop route table 0, local-address 192.0.2.11
  Session ID: 0
```

			Detect	Transmit	
Address	State	Interface	Time	Interval	Multiplier
198.51.100.1	Up	et-0/0/48.0	0.999	0.333	3

```
 Client BGP, TX interval 0.333, RX interval 0.333
 Session up time 03:12:13, previous down time 00:00:01
 Local diagnostic None, remote diagnostic CtlExpire
 Remote state Up, version 1
 Session type: Single hop BFD
 Min async interval 0.333, min slow interval 1.000
 Adaptive async TX interval 0.333, RX interval 0.333
 Local min TX interval 0.333, minimum RX interval 0.333, multiplier 3
 Remote min TX interval 0.333, min RX interval 0.333, multiplier 3
 Local discriminator 16, remote discriminator 16
 Echo TX interval 0.000, echo detection interval 0.000
 Echo mode disabled/inactive
 Remote is control-plane independent
  Session ID: 0
```

			Detect	Transmit	
Address	State	Interface	Time	Interval	Multiplier
198.51.100.3	Up	et-0/0/50.0	0.999	0.333	3

```
 Client BGP, TX interval 0.333, RX interval 0.333
 Session up time 03:12:14
 Local diagnostic None, remote diagnostic None
```

```
Remote state Up, version 1

Session type: Single hop BFD

Min async interval 0.333, min slow interval 1.000

Adaptive async TX interval 0.333, RX interval 0.333

Local min TX interval 0.333, minimum RX interval 0.333, multiplier 3

Remote min TX interval 0.333, min RX interval 0.333, multiplier 3

Local discriminator 18, remote discriminator 21

Echo TX interval 0.000, echo detection interval 0.000

Echo mode disabled/inactive

Remote is control-plane independent

 Session ID: 0

4 sessions, 4 clients

Cumulative transmit rate 12.0 pps, cumulative receive rate 12.0 pps
```

On the wire, a BFD packet is essentially an IP packet with a UDP header and a small BFD payload. There are minor differences in a single-hop versus a multi-hop BFD session, most notably the UDP destination port. For a single-hop BFD session, a UDP destination port of 3784 is used for BFD control packets (in accordance with RFC 5881), as shown in Figure 5-53.

No.	Time	Source	Destination	Protocol	Length	Info
2	0.098359	192.0.2.11	192.0.2.101	BFD Control	66	Diag: No Diagnostic, State: Up, Flags: 0x08
4	0.257179	198.51.100.0	198.51.100.1	BFD Control	66	Diag: No Diagnostic, State: Up, Flags: 0x08
6	0.408644	192.0.2.11	192.0.2.101	BFD Control	66	Diag: No Diagnostic, State: Up, Flags: 0x08
8	0.569208	198.51.100.0	198.51.100.1	BFD Control	66	Diag: No Diagnostic, State: Up, Flags: 0x08
10	0.680960	192.0.2.11	192.0.2.101	BFD Control	66	Diag: No Diagnostic, State: Up, Flags: 0x08
12	0.867121	198.51.100.0	198.51.100.1	BFD Control	66	Diag: No Diagnostic, State: Up, Flags: 0x08

```
> Frame 4: 66 bytes on wire (528 bits), 66 bytes captured (528 bits)
> Ethernet II, Src: JuniperN_7b:70:75 (40:de:ad:7b:70:75), Dst: JuniperN_60:76:40 (64:c3:d6:60:76:40)
> Internet Protocol Version 4, Src: 198.51.100.0, Dst: 198.51.100.1
v User Datagram Protocol, Src Port: 49152, Dst Port: 3784
    Source Port: 49152
    Destination Port: 3784
    Length: 32
    Checksum: 0x8ed2 [unverified]
    [Checksum Status: Unverified]
    [Stream index: 3]
  > [Timestamps]
    UDP payload (24 bytes)
v BFD Control message
    001. .... = Protocol Version: 1
    ...0 0000 = Diagnostic Code: No Diagnostic (0x00)
    11.. .... = Session State: Up (0x3)
  v Message Flags: 0xc8, Control Plane Independent: Set
    0... .. = Poll: Not set
    .0.. .. = Final: Not set
    ..1. .. = Control Plane Independent: Set
    ...0 .. = Authentication Present: Not set
    .... 0. = Demand: Not set
    .... .0 = Multipoint: Not set
    Detect Time Multiplier: 3 (= 999 ms Detection time)
    Message Length: 24 bytes
    My Discriminator: 0x00000016
    Your Discriminator: 0x0000001a
    Desired Min TX Interval:  333 ms (333000 us)
    Required Min RX Interval:  333 ms (333000 us)
    Required Min Echo Interval:   0 ms (0 us)
```

```
0000  64 c3 d6 60 76 40 40 de
0010  00 34 00 00 00 00 ff 11
0020  64 01 c0 00 0e c8 00 20
0030  00 16 00 00 00 00 1a 00 05
0040  00 00
```

Figure 5-53 *A single-hop BFD session packet capture*

For a multi-hop BFD session, a UDP destination port of 4784 is used (in accordance with RFC 5883), as shown in Figure 5-54.

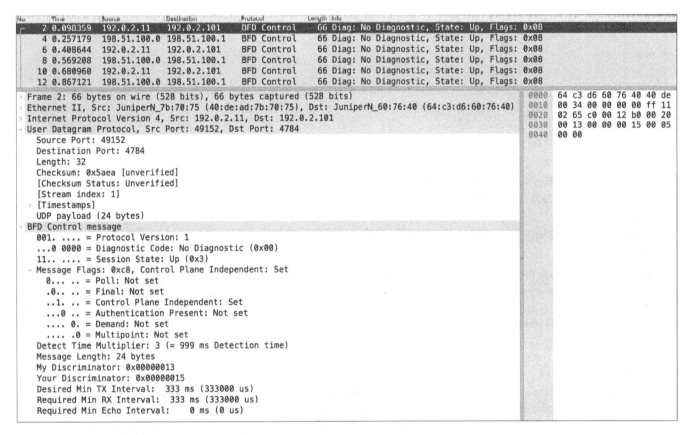

```
No.   Time        Source       Destination    Protocol      Length Info
   2 0.090359   192.0.2.11   192.0.2.101    BFD Control    66 Diag: No Diagnostic, State: Up, Flags: 0x08
   4 0.257179   198.51.100.0 198.51.100.1   BFD Control    66 Diag: No Diagnostic, State: Up, Flags: 0x08
   6 0.408644   192.0.2.11   192.0.2.101    BFD Control    66 Diag: No Diagnostic, State: Up, Flags: 0x08
   8 0.569208   198.51.100.0 198.51.100.1   BFD Control    66 Diag: No Diagnostic, State: Up, Flags: 0x08
  10 0.680960   192.0.2.11   192.0.2.101    BFD Control    66 Diag: No Diagnostic, State: Up, Flags: 0x08
  12 0.867121   198.51.100.0 198.51.100.1   BFD Control    66 Diag: No Diagnostic, State: Up, Flags: 0x08

> Frame 2: 66 bytes on wire (528 bits), 66 bytes captured (528 bits)        0000  64 c3 d6 60 76 40 40 de
> Ethernet II, Src: JuniperN_7b:70:75 (40:de:ad:7b:70:75), Dst: JuniperN_60:76:40 (64:c3:d6:60:76:40)    0010  00 34 00 00 00 00 ff 11
> Internet Protocol Version 4, Src: 192.0.2.11, Dst: 192.0.2.101            0020  02 65 c0 00 12 b0 00 20
v User Datagram Protocol, Src Port: 49152, Dst Port: 4784                   0030  00 13 00 00 00 15 00 05
    Source Port: 49152                                                     0040  00 00
    Destination Port: 4784
    Length: 32
    Checksum: 0x5aea [unverified]
    [Checksum Status: Unverified]
    [Stream index: 1]
  > [Timestamps]
    UDP payload (24 bytes)
v BFD Control message
    001. .... = Protocol Version: 1
    ...0 0000 = Diagnostic Code: No Diagnostic (0x00)
    11.. .... = Session State: Up (0x3)
  v Message Flags: 0xc8, Control Plane Independent: Set
      0... .. = Poll: Not set
      .0.. .. = Final: Not set
      ..1. .. = Control Plane Independent: Set
      ...0 .. = Authentication Present: Not set
      .... 0. = Demand: Not set
      .... .0 = Multipoint: Not set
    Detect Time Multiplier: 3 (= 999 ms Detection time)
    Message Length: 24 bytes
    My Discriminator: 0x00000013
    Your Discriminator: 0x00000015
    Desired Min TX Interval:   333 ms (333000 us)
    Required Min RX Interval:  333 ms (333000 us)
    Required Min Echo Interval:    0 ms (0 us)
```

Figure 5-54 *A multi-hop BFD session packet capture*

With this configuration in place, if the interface between leaf1 and spine2 goes down now, then unlike before, the overlay BGP peering is brought down immediately as well since the BFD session goes down (within a second) and it informs the upper-layer protocol, which is BGP for the overlay in this case. This is shown in Example 5-87.

Example 5-87 *Impact of an interface going down on the BFD session for the overlay*

```
root@leaf1# set interfaces et-0/0/50 disable
root@leaf1# commit
configuration check succeeds
commit complete

root@leaf1> show bfd session
                                       Detect   Transmit
Address          State    Interface    Time     Interval  Multiplier
192.0.2.101      Up                    0.999    0.333     3
192.0.2.102      Down                  0.999    2.000     3
198.51.100.1     Up       et-0/0/48.0  0.999    0.333     3

3 sessions, 3 clients
Cumulative transmit rate 6.5 pps, cumulative receive rate 9.0 pps

root@leaf1> show bgp summary
Threading mode: BGP I/O
Default eBGP mode: advertise - accept, receive - accept
Groups: 2 Peers: 4 Down peers: 2
Table          Tot Paths  Act Paths Suppressed    History Damp State     Pending
```

```
inet.0
                      5          5          0          0          0          0
bgp.evpn.0
                     18         18          0          0          0          0
Peer                AS       InPkt     OutPkt     OutQ    Flaps Last Up/Dwn State|#Active/Received/Accepted/Damped...
192.0.2.101       65500      4151       3389         0        0  1d 1:39:07 Establ
  bgp.evpn.0: 18/18/18/0
  default-switch.evpn.0: 16/16/16/0
  __default_evpn__.evpn.0: 0/0/0/0
192.0.2.102       65500       578        450         0        4             1 Active
198.51.100.1      65500       450        451         0        5  3:24:20 Establ
  inet.0: 5/5/5/0
198.51.100.3      65500       452        452         0        8             2 Idle
```

Thus, with BFD, much faster convergence can be achieved when network failures occur, and possibly even subsecond convergence if the platform supports it. The other advantage of using BFD is that multiple upper-layer protocols (BGP, OSPF, IS-IS, and so on) can register as clients for the same BFD session and can be notified when the session goes down. There's no need to have separate BFD sessions for every upper-layer protocol in your network.

Summary

Although this chapter was long, it was fundamental to the design and deployment of data centers. Through the course of this chapter, a bridged overlay EVPN VXLAN fabric was configured and deployed, which extended a Layer 2 domain over a routed underlay. Understanding how local and remote MAC addresses are learned in such designs is crucial, and this was demonstrated using a combination of commands, traceoptions, and packet walks.

For replication of BUM traffic through the fabric, Junos uses ingress replication. EVPN Type-3 routes are used to build a list of VTEPs (PEs) that are interested in receiving BUM traffic for a virtual network, which allows such traffic to be flooded to these VTEPs. EVPN multihoming is a very common design that allows a host to connect to multiple VTEPs, utilizing EVPN Type-1 and Type-4 routes for different purposes. EVPN Type-1 routes help in aliasing, mass withdrawal, and split horizon, while Type-4 routes ensure only one ESI LAG peer forwards traffic, received over the fabric, into the Ethernet Segment by electing a Designated Forwarder.

Route Targets, added to BGP EVPN routes as extended communities, control the import and export of EVPN routes. For operational simplicity, these Route Targets can be auto-derived on a VTEP. It is common for MAC addresses to move in an EVPN VXLAN fabric (from one VTEP to another)—VTEPs can detect such moves by using the MAC Mobility extended community with the sequence number in it.

Loop prevention in EVPN VXLAN fabrics is a crucial, and often overlooked, design aspect. This can occur in topologies where a loop originates via downstream networks attached to the fabric. When things fail, it is important to fail fast—protocol timers, by default, are slow, and with BFD configured, the network can converge within milliseconds by offloading BFD to the hardware.

## Chapter 6

MAC-VRFs

This chapter introduces the concept of a MAC-VRF. A MAC-VRF, like an IP VRF, is rooted in multitenancy and creates virtual forwarding tables, specifically for MAC addresses in this case. This allows for logical separation of tenants in an EVPN VXLAN fabric, providing better control of Layer 2 segmentation in the overlay.

A MAC-VRF is bound to an EVPN Instance, commonly called *EVI*, that spans multiple PEs (VTEPs). MAC-VRFs are configured on Junos using the *routing instance* construct. Each MAC-VRF has a bridge table (or multiple tables) corresponding to a broadcast domain (or domains) in that MAC-VRF. With MAC-VRFs, flooding of traffic within the fabric is also optimized, with BUM traffic replicated only to the VTEPs that are a part of the same EVPN Instance.

Introducing EVPN Service Types

Several service types are available for EVPN (as described in RFC 7432), which are offered via the MAC-VRF construct on Junos:

- VLAN-Based service type
- VLAN-Aware service type
- VLAN Bundle service type

These service types offer flexibility in design and how a broadcast domain (and corresponding bridge table) is mapped to an EVI. MAC-VRFs enable customer/tenant-specific EVPN Instances to be built, with a combination of the different service types mentioned earlier.

A VLAN-Based service type is an EVPN Instance that includes a single broadcast domain (a single VLAN). Since there is only one VLAN in the EVPN Instance, there is a one-to-one mapping between the VLAN and the MAC-VRF (and the EVI) and the bridge table corresponding to that one VLAN. The Ethernet Tag ID for the appropriate EVPN routes is set to 0 for this service type. Since only a single VLAN exists within a VLAN-Based MAC-VRF, there is one broadcast domain per MAC-VRF. This also means that for every new VLAN that is needed, a new VLAN-Based MAC-VRF must be created, which is an added operational overhead to configure and maintain. Routing instances are also a limited resource, and since MAC-VRFs are configured as a type of routing instance in Junos, this limitation will apply here as well.

Figure 6-1 provides a visual representation of two VLAN-Based MAC-VRFs: macvrf-v100-1, with VLAN 100 and VNI 10100, and macvrf-v200-1, with VLAN 200 and VNI 10200.

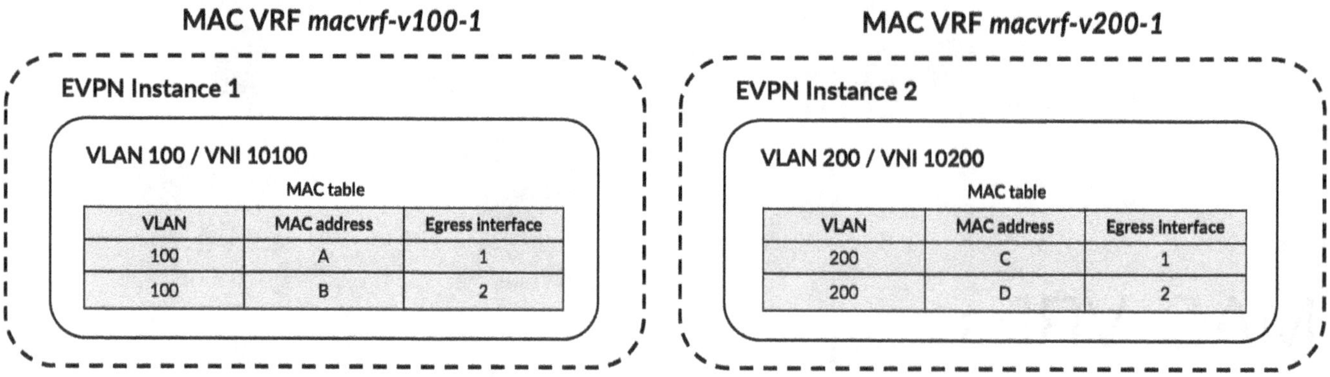

MAC VRF *macvrf-v100-1*

MAC VRF *macvrf-v200-1*

Figure 6-1   *VLAN-Based service type*

In a VLAN-Aware service type, an EVPN Instance can have multiple VLANs (broadcast domains) mapped to it. Each VLAN has its own bridge table, all within the same MAC-VRF. In such a service type, it is important to have a mechanism of identifying the VLAN—the Ethernet Tag ID is used for this purpose, and it is set to the VNI for the appropriate EVPN route types (when no VLAN translation is involved). Even though multiple VLANs exist within the same MAC-VRF, it is important to note that there are multiple broadcast domains within the MAC-VRF (for each VLAN) by generating EVPN Type-3 routes per VNI.

This service type is useful in grouping together several VLANs within the same MAC-VRF that might fall under a common tenant. This is operationally easier since all these VLANs can be grouped under the same MAC-VRF instead of creating a unique VLAN-Based MAC-VRF for every VLAN.

VLAN-Aware MAC-VRFs also have the advantage of generating fewer EVPN infrastructure routes (Type-1/Type-3/Type-4), more specifically, EVPN Type-1 routes.

Figure 6-2 provides a visual representation of a VLAN-Aware MAC-VRF named macvrf-v100-v200 with VLAN 100, VNI 10100 and VLAN 200, VNI 10200.

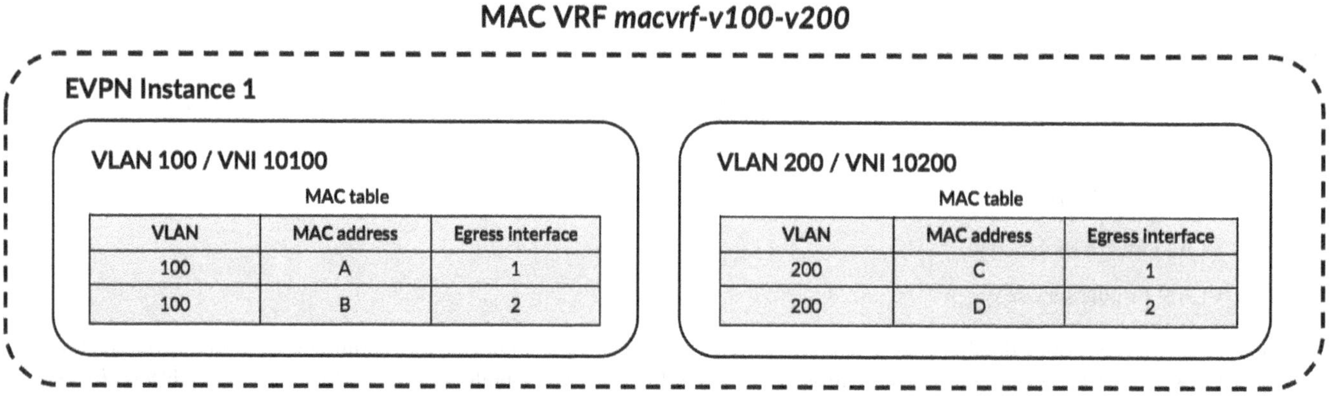

MAC VRF *macvrf-v100-v200*

Figure 6-2   *VLAN-Aware service type*

Finally, for the VLAN Bundle service type, an EVPN Instance can have multiple VLANs (broadcast domains), but they all share the same bridge table, which means that MAC addresses must be unique across all VLANs, and there can be no overlap. This is a many-to-one mapping of VLANs to a MAC-VRF. No VLAN translation (defined later in the "Overlapping VLANs, VLAN Translation, and VLAN Normalization" section) is allowed with this service type, and the Ethernet Tag ID is set to 0. This service type is usually used in Q-in-Q designs and does not support any IRB interfaces on the VTEP when configured (which means only a bridged overlay design is supported when using this service type).

Figure 6-3 provides a visual representation of a VLAN Bundle MAC-VRF named macvrf-v100-v200 with VLANs 100 and 200.

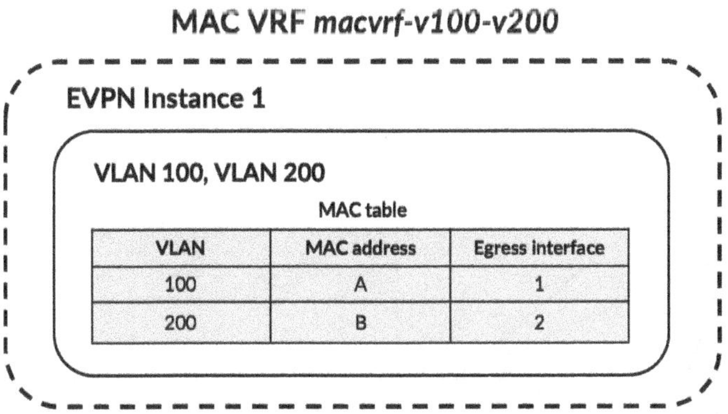

MAC VRF *macvrf-v100-v200*

Figure 6-3 *VLAN Bundle service type*

A high-level summary of the differences between these service types is shown in Figure 6-4.

VLAN-Based	VLAN-Aware	VLAN Bundle
One-to-one mapping of VLAN to MAC-VRF to EVPN Instance	Many-to-one mapping of VLANs to a MAC-VRF and EVPN Instance	Many-to-one mapping of VLANs to a MAC-VRF and EVPN Instance
One broadcast domain per MAC-VRF	Multiple broadcast domains per MAC-VRF (per-VLAN)	Multiple broadcast domains per MAC-VRF (per-VLAN)
One bridge table per MAC-VRF	Multiple bridge tables per MAC-VRF (per-VLAN)	One bridge table per MAC-VRF

Figure 6-4 *High-level differences between MAC-VRF service types*

MAC-VRFs are useful because, outside of just providing a means of multitenancy and logical isolation at Layer 2, they provide granularity and flexibility in design—you can control how VXLAN tunnels are built (since different MAC-VRFs can exist on different switches) and determine exactly which VTEPs the EVPN Instance should extend to. MAC-VRFs also brought in the unification of configuration across different Juniper platforms, making it easier to automate. They are critical for interoperability with other vendors that may be locked into a specific service type only.

While MAC-VRFs appear to be the ideal solution to offering Layer 2 multitenancy in EVPN VXLAN fabrics, it is important to note that there are restrictions to what can be achieved due to various hardware, software (and specific software versions), and protocol limitations across platforms and vendors. The most common limitation is that the same VLAN cannot be used across MAC-VRFs since most hardware and software implementations require a unique bridge domain for lookups. Such a limitation seems counterintuitive to an ideal multitenancy solution. There are ways around this through features such as VLAN translation and VLAN normalization, supported across different Juniper platforms, which are discussed in more detail in later sections of this chapter.

This chapter focuses on how to configure and validate VLAN-Based and VLAN-Aware service types only, as these are the more commonly deployed service types.

VLAN-Based MAC-VRFs

Chapter 5 demonstrated how to deploy a bridged overlay EVPN VXLAN fabric using the default EVPN Instance available on Junos. Using the same topology as a reference (shown again in Figure 6-5), that design is repurposed here to use MAC-VRFs instead of the default EVPN Instance.

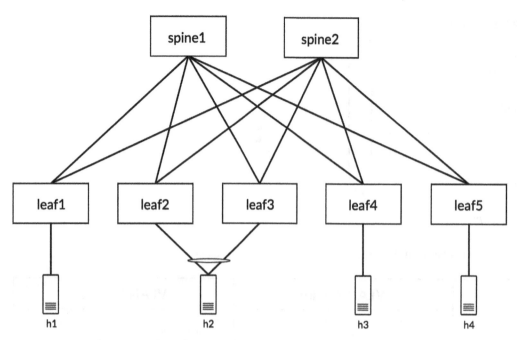

Figure 6-5 *Reference topology for VLAN-Based MAC-VRFs*

To demonstrate how MAC-VRFs allow for multitenancy, and the flexibility it provides, the reference fabric is divided into two EVPN Instances, as shown in Figure 6-6:

- An EVPN Instance that extends between leaf1, leaf2, and leaf3 for hosts h1 and h2, using a VLAN-Based MAC-VRF

- An EVPN Instance that extends between leaf4 and leaf5 for hosts h3 and h4, using another VLAN-Based MAC-VRF

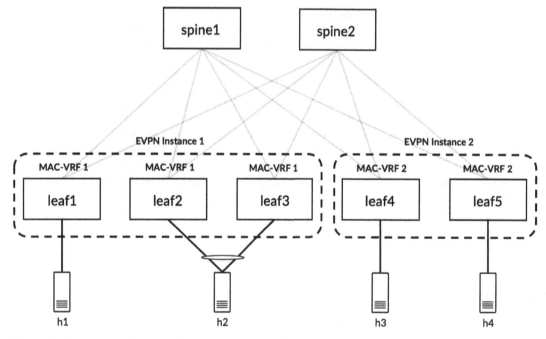

Figure 6-6 *Tenant isolation with MAC-VRFs*

Like other VPNs, controlling how far the EVPN Instance can extend and which VTEPs (PEs) are a part of it is achieved via Route Targets, as discussed at length in Chapter 5, "Bridged Overlay in an EVPN VXLAN Fabric."

By default, an EVPN Instance called default-switch exists in Junos, as shown in Example 6-1, using the **show evpn instance** operational mode command, which displays all configured EVPN Instances.

Example 6-1 *Default EVPN Instance*

```
root@leaf1> show evpn instance
                     Intfs        IRB intfs      MH      MAC addresses
Instance            Total  Up  Total  Up  Nbrs  ESIs   Local  Remote
__default_evpn__                             0
default-switch        2    2    0     0    4     1       1      1
```

MAC-VRFs are configured using the routing instance construct on Junos with an instance-type of mac-vrf. EVPN-specific configuration and all parameters defined via the *switch-options* hierarchy (like the Route Distinguisher, VTEP source, and the Route Target) are now configured within the MAC-VRF routing instance itself, along with the VLANs as well. Layer 2 interfaces from which MAC learning can occur are mapped to this routing instance.

As an example, on leaf1, a VLAN-Based MAC-VRF is configured as shown in Example 6-2. The configuration of a routing instance can be displayed by using the **show routing-instance** [*name*] configuration mode command.

Example 6-2 *VLAN-Based MAC-VRF configuration on leaf1*

```
root@leaf1# show routing-instances macvrf-v100-1
instance-type mac-vrf;
protocols {
    evpn {
        encapsulation vxlan;
        extended-vni-list 10100;
    }
}
vtep-source-interface lo0.0;
service-type vlan-based;
interface et-0/0/49.0;
route-distinguisher 192.0.2.11:100;
vrf-target target:1:1;
vlans {
    v100 {
        vlan-id 100;
        vxlan {
            vni 10100;
        }
    }
}

root@leaf1# show forwarding-options
evpn-vxlan {
    shared-tunnels;
}
```

On platforms such as the Juniper QFX5120s with lower VTEP tunnel scale, it is mandatory to configure **set forwarding-options evpn-vxlan shared-tunnels** for MAC-VRFs. This is confirmed in Example 6-2 by viewing the output of the **show forwarding-options** configuration mode command. This optimization allows the next-hop ID to be shared among different VXLAN tunnels if the remote VTEP is the same across MAC-VRFs (discussed in more detail shortly). When configured for the first time, this requires a system reboot. In the reference topology in Figure 6-5, leaf1, leaf2, and leaf3 are all Juniper QFX5120s and will need this configuration, while leaf4 and leaf5, which are Juniper QFX5130s, do not need this configuration since it is implicitly enabled for this platform.

To complete the configuration, leaf2 and leaf3 are configured in the same way as leaf1, while leaf4 and leaf5 have the configuration shown in Example 6-3, with a unique Route Target within the MAC-VRF.

Example 6-3   *MAC-VRF configuration on leaf4 and leaf5*

```
root@leaf4# show routing-instances macvrf-v100-2
instance-type mac-vrf;
protocols {
    evpn {
        encapsulation vxlan;
        extended-vni-list 10100;
    }
}
vtep-source-interface lo0.0;
service-type vlan-based;
interface et-0/0/4.0;
route-distinguisher 192.0.2.14:100;
vrf-target target:2:2;
vlans {
    v100 {
        vlan-id 100;
        vxlan {
            vni 10100;
        }
    }
}


root@leaf5# show routing-instances macvrf-v100-2
instance-type mac-vrf;
protocols {
    evpn {
        encapsulation vxlan;
        extended-vni-list 10100;
    }
}
vtep-source-interface lo0.0;
service-type vlan-based;
interface et-0/0/1.0;
route-distinguisher 192.0.2.14:100;
vrf-target target:2:2;
vlans {
    v100 {
        vlan-id 100;
        vxlan {
            vni 10100;
        }
    }
}
```

With this configuration in place, the required Layer 2 tenant isolation can be achieved. On leaf1, leaf2, and leaf3, an EVPN Instance called macvrf-v100-1 is created, corresponding to the configured MAC-VRF routing instance. This is shown in Example 6-4.

Example 6-4 *EVPN Instance on leaf1, leaf2, and leaf3 for MAC-VRF*

```
root@leaf1> show evpn instance
                  Intfs       IRB intfs      MH     MAC addresses
Instance          Total  Up  Total  Up  Nbrs  ESIs  Local  Remote
__default_evpn__                          0
macvrf-v100-1       2    2     0    0    2    1      1       2


root@leaf2> show evpn instance
                  Intfs       IRB intfs      MH     MAC addresses
Instance          Total  Up  Total  Up  Nbrs  ESIs  Local  Remote
__default_evpn__                          1
macvrf-v100-1       2    2     0    0    2    1      1       2


root@leaf3> show evpn instance
                  Intfs       IRB intfs      MH     MAC addresses
Instance          Total  Up  Total  Up  Nbrs  ESIs  Local  Remote
__default_evpn__                          1
macvrf-v100-1       2    2     0    0    2    1      1       2
```

While on leaf4 and leaf5, an EVPN Instance called macvrf-v100-2 is created, which again corresponds to the MAC-VRF routing instance configured on these leafs, as shown in Example 6-5.

Example 6-5 *EVPN Instance on leaf4 and leaf5 for MAC-VRF*

```
root@leaf4> show evpn instance
                  Intfs       IRB intfs      MH     MAC addresses
Instance          Total  Up  Total  Up  Nbrs  ESIs  Local  Remote
__default_evpn__                          0
macvrf-v100-2       2    2     0    0    1    0      1       0


root@leaf5> show evpn instance
                  Intfs       IRB intfs      MH     MAC addresses
Instance          Total  Up  Total  Up  Nbrs  ESIs  Local  Remote
__default_evpn__                          0
macvrf-v100-2       2    2     0    0    1    0      0       1
```

The EVPN Instance name itself has no relevance outside of simply being a parameter that an operator or administrator can use to easily identify the EVPN Instance across their fabric. What truly controls which VTEPs (PEs) participate in the same EVPN Instance is the Route Target.

With MAC-VRFs, a new CLI command was introduced that allows a user to specifically look at MAC-VRF–based information only. This is the **show mac-vrf forwarding** [*options*] operational mode command and is used to gather information in relation to MAC-VRF routing instances. This is demonstrated in Example 6-6, which confirms that leaf1 has discovered leaf2 and leaf3 as remote VTEPs, but it remains unaware of leaf4 and leaf5.

Example 6-6   *Remote VTEPs discovered on leaf1*

```
root@leaf1> show mac-vrf forwarding vxlan-tunnel-end-point remote
Logical System Name      Id  SVTEP-IP        IFL  L3-Idx   SVTEP-Mode    ELP-SVTEP-IP
<default>                0   192.0.2.11      lo0.0   0
  RVTEP-IP    IFL-Idx     Interface    NH-Id  RVTEP-Mode  ELP-IP       Flags
  192.0.2.12  835         vtep.32770   1754   RNVE
  192.0.2.13  836         vtep.32771   1758   RNVE
  RVTEP-IP    L2-RTT                   IFL-Idx   Interface   NH-Id  RVTEP-Mode  ELP-IP    Flags
  192.0.2.12  macvrf-v100-1            671088640 vtep-8.32770 1754  RNVE
    VNID       MC-Group-IP
    10100      0.0.0.0
  RVTEP-IP    L2-RTT                   IFL-Idx   Interface   NH-Id  RVTEP-Mode  ELP-IP    Flags
  192.0.2.13  macvrf-v100-1            671088641 vtep-8.32771 1758  RNVE
    VNID       MC-Group-IP
    10100      0.0.0.0
```

Based on the MAC-VRF configuration on different leafs, leaf1 remains unaware of leaf4 and leaf5 because the Route Target, attached as an extended community to the BGP EVPN routes sent by leaf4 and leaf5, is different and there is no import policy that matches this Route Target on leaf1 (and leaf2 and leaf3, for that matter). With an example output of an EVPN Type-3 route received from leaf4 on leaf1, this is confirmed as shown in Example 6-7.

Example 6-7   *Route Target attached to EVPN Type-3 route received from leaf4*

```
root@leaf1> show route table bgp.evpn.0 match-prefix 3:*192.0.2.14*

bgp.evpn.0: 21 destinations, 39 routes (21 active, 0 holddown, 0 hidden)
+ = Active Route, - = Last Active, * = Both


3:192.0.2.14:100::0::192.0.2.14/248 IM
                  *[BGP/170] 01:48:10, localpref 100, from 192.0.2.102
                    AS path: 65500 65424 I, validation-state: unverified
                  >  to 198.51.100.1 via et-0/0/48.0
                     to 198.51.100.3 via et-0/0/50.0
                   [BGP/170] 01:48:10, localpref 100, from 192.0.2.101
                    AS path: 65500 65424 I, validation-state: unverified
                  >  to 198.51.100.1 via et-0/0/48.0
                     to 198.51.100.3 via et-0/0/50.0


root@leaf1> show route table bgp.evpn.0 match-prefix 3:*192.0.2.14* extensive

bgp.evpn.0: 21 destinations, 39 routes (21 active, 0 holddown, 0 hidden)
3:192.0.2.14:100::0::192.0.2.14/248 IM (2 entries, 0 announced)
        *BGP    Preference: 170/-101
                Route Distinguisher: 192.0.2.14:100
                PMSI: Flags 0x0: Label 631: Type INGRESS-REPLICATION 192.0.2.14
                Next hop type: Indirect, Next hop index: 0
                Address: 0x74e5a84
                Next-hop reference count: 2
                Kernel Table Id: 0
```

```
Source: 192.0.2.102
Protocol next hop: 192.0.2.14
Indirect next hop: 0x2 no-forward INH Session ID: 0
State: <Active Ext>
Local AS: 65421 Peer AS: 65500
Age: 1:48:32    Metric2: 0
Validation State: unverified
Task: BGP_65500.192.0.2.102
AS path: 65500 65424 I
Communities: target:2:2 encapsulation:vxlan(0x8)
Accepted
Localpref: 100
Router ID: 192.0.2.102
Thread: junos-main
Indirect next hops: 1
        Protocol next hop: 192.0.2.14 ResolvState: Resolved
        Indirect next hop: 0x2 no-forward INH Session ID: 0
        Indirect path forwarding next hops: 2
                Next hop type: Router
                Next hop: 198.51.100.1 via et-0/0/48.0 weight 0x1
                Session Id: 0
                Next hop: 198.51.100.3 via et-0/0/50.0 weight 0x1
                Session Id: 0
                192.0.2.14/32 Originating RIB: inet.0
                  Node path count: 1
                  Forwarding nexthops: 2
                        Next hop type: Router
                        Next hop: 198.51.100.1 via et-0/0/48.0 weight 0x1
                        Session Id: 0
                        Next hop: 198.51.100.3 via et-0/0/50.0 weight 0x1
                        Session Id: 0
```

The internal import policy, implicitly created for the MAC-VRF, does not match this Route Target since the locally configured Route Target on leaf1 is different, as shown in Example 6-8.

Example 6-8 *Internal import policy created for MAC-VRF*

```
root@leaf1> show policy __vrf-import-macvrf-v100-1-internal__
Policy __vrf-import-macvrf-v100-1-internal__: [RESOLVED/]
    Term unnamed:
        from community __vrf-community-macvrf-v100-1-common-internal__ [target:1:1 ]
        then accept
    Term unnamed:
        then reject
```

Since these routes are not imported into the macvrf-v100-1.evpn.0 table, there is no VTEP discovery, and no MAC addresses are installed for hosts behind those VTEPs, confirmed in Example 6-9.

Example 6-9 *EVPN routes received from leaf4 do not get imported into MAC-VRF EVPN table on leaf1*

```
root@leaf1> show route table bgp.evpn.0 match-prefix *192.0.2.14*

bgp.evpn.0: 19 destinations, 35 routes (19 active, 0 holddown, 0 hidden)
+ = Active Route, - = Last Active, * = Both

2:192.0.2.14:100::0::f0:4b:3a:b9:80:ab/304 MAC/IP
                 *[BGP/170] 00:07:26, localpref 100, from 192.0.2.101
                   AS path: 65500 65424 I, validation-state: unverified
                   to 198.51.100.1 via et-0/0/48.0, Push 631
                 > to 198.51.100.3 via et-0/0/50.0, Push 631
                  [BGP/170] 00:07:26, localpref 100, from 192.0.2.102
                   AS path: 65500 65424 I, validation-state: unverified
                   to 198.51.100.1 via et-0/0/48.0, Push 631
                 > to 198.51.100.3 via et-0/0/50.0, Push 631
2:192.0.2.14:100::0::f0:4b:3a:b9:80:ab::10.100.100.3/304 MAC/IP
                 *[BGP/170] 00:07:26, localpref 100, from 192.0.2.101
                   AS path: 65500 65424 I, validation-state: unverified
                   to 198.51.100.1 via et-0/0/48.0, Push 631
                 > to 198.51.100.3 via et-0/0/50.0, Push 631
                  [BGP/170] 00:07:26, localpref 100, from 192.0.2.102
                   AS path: 65500 65424 I, validation-state: unverified
                   to 198.51.100.1 via et-0/0/48.0, Push 631
                 > to 198.51.100.3 via et-0/0/50.0, Push 631
3:192.0.2.14:100::0::192.0.2.14/248 IM
                 *[BGP/170] 02:20:34, localpref 100, from 192.0.2.102
                   AS path: 65500 65424 I, validation-state: unverified
                 > to 198.51.100.1 via et-0/0/48.0
                   to 198.51.100.3 via et-0/0/50.0
                  [BGP/170] 02:20:34, localpref 100, from 192.0.2.101
                   AS path: 65500 65424 I, validation-state: unverified
                 > to 198.51.100.1 via et-0/0/48.0
                   to 198.51.100.3 via et-0/0/50.0

root@leaf1> show route table macvrf-v100-1.evpn.0 match-prefix *192.0.2.14*

macvrf-v100-1.evpn.0: 13 destinations, 23 routes (13 active, 0 holddown, 0 hidden)

<no output>
```

With this design and configuration in place, hosts h1 and h2 can communicate with each other, while hosts h3 and h4 can communicate with each other. However, these two groups of hosts are logically isolated and have no reachability to one another. Taking host h1 as an example, it can ping h2, while pings to h3 and h4 fail, as shown in Example 6-10.

Example 6-10 *Host h1's reachability to other hosts in the fabric*

```
root@h1> ping 10.100.100.2
PING 10.100.100.2 (10.100.100.2): 56 data bytes
64 bytes from 10.100.100.2: icmp_seq=0 ttl=64 time=1.051 ms
64 bytes from 10.100.100.2: icmp_seq=1 ttl=64 time=0.872 ms
```

```
64 bytes from 10.100.100.2: icmp_seq=2 ttl=64 time=0.845 ms
64 bytes from 10.100.100.2: icmp_seq=3 ttl=64 time=0.889 ms
^C
--- 10.100.100.2 ping statistics ---
4 packets transmitted, 4 packets received, 0% packet loss
round-trip min/avg/max/stddev = 0.845/0.914/1.051/0.080 ms


root@h1> ping 10.100.100.3
PING 10.100.100.3 (10.100.100.3): 56 data bytes
^C
--- 10.100.100.3 ping statistics ---
5 packets transmitted, 0 packets received, 100% packet loss


root@h1> ping 10.100.100.4
PING 10.100.100.4 (10.100.100.4): 56 data bytes
^C
--- 10.100.100.4 ping statistics ---
5 packets transmitted, 0 packets received, 100% packet loss
```

And taking host h4 as a subsequent example, it can ping h3, while pings to h1 and h2 fail, as shown in Example 6-11.

Example 6-11 *Host h3's reachability to other hosts in the fabric*

```
root@h4> ping 10.100.100.3
PING 10.100.100.3 (10.100.100.3): 56 data bytes
64 bytes from 10.100.100.3: icmp_seq=0 ttl=64 time=224.479 ms
64 bytes from 10.100.100.3: icmp_seq=1 ttl=64 time=0.914 ms
64 bytes from 10.100.100.3: icmp_seq=2 ttl=64 time=0.876 ms
64 bytes from 10.100.100.3: icmp_seq=3 ttl=64 time=0.854 ms
64 bytes from 10.100.100.3: icmp_seq=4 ttl=64 time=0.867 ms
^C
--- 10.100.100.3 ping statistics ---
5 packets transmitted, 5 packets received, 0% packet loss
round-trip min/avg/max/stddev = 0.854/45.598/224.479/89.441 ms


root@h4> ping 10.100.100.1
PING 10.100.100.1 (10.100.100.1): 56 data bytes
^C
--- 10.100.100.1 ping statistics ---
5 packets transmitted, 0 packets received, 100% packet loss


root@h4> ping 10.100.100.2
PING 10.100.100.2 (10.100.100.2): 56 data bytes
^C
--- 10.100.100.2 ping statistics ---
5 packets transmitted, 0 packets received, 100% packet loss
```

A packet capture of an EVPN Type-2 route, advertised by leaf1 for host h1's MAC address, shown in Figure 6-7 confirms that the Ethernet Tag ID is set to 0, as expected, when using a VLAN-Based MAC-VRF.

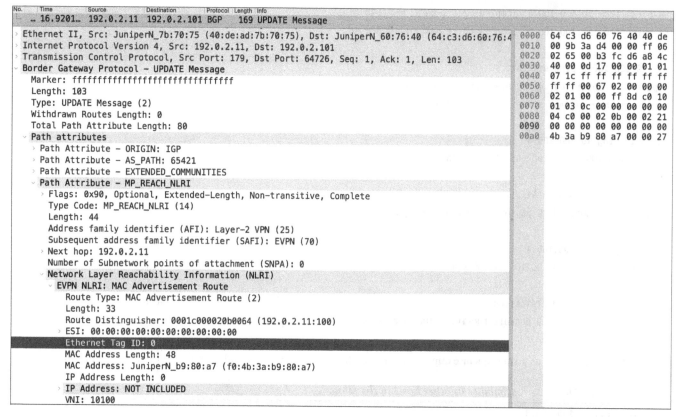

Figure 6-7 *Packet capture of an EVPN Type-2 route with Ethernet Tag ID as 0*

Order of Operations with MAC-VRFs

In the previous section, routes from leaf4 and leaf5 were not imported into the macvrf-v100-1.evpn.0 table because there was no matching import policy. But what is this new route table and how does it relate to everything else?

When a MAC-VRF is configured, an EVPN route table corresponding to the MAC-VRF is also created (similar to how an EVPN table for the *default-switch* instance is created for the default EVPN Instance), with the prefix matching the MAC-VRF name, as shown in Example 6-12.

Example 6-12 *Route table created for MAC-VRF macvrf-v100-1*

```
root@leaf1> show route table ?
Possible completions:
  <table>            Name of routing table
  :vxlan.inet.0
  bgp.evpn.0
  inet.0
  inet6.0
  macvrf-v100-1.evpn.0
```

The order of operations when MAC-VRFs are involved is the following:

1. A locally learned address is installed as an EVPN route in the EVPN table for the MAC-VRF by the RPD daemon (when RPD is informed of the local learn by the L2ALD daemon), which is the macvrf-v100-1.evpn.0 table in Example 6-12.

2. This route is then exported into the BGP table, bgp.evpn.0, to be advertised out to BGP EVPN peers.

3. A BGP EVPN route received from a remote VTEP is received in the bgp.evpn.0 table and, if successfully imported, is pulled into the EVPN route table specific to that MAC-VRF, macvrf-v100-1.evpn.0, and then into the EVPN database. From here, RPD informs L2ALD, and the same sequence of events occurs as described in the previous chapter.

Understanding this order of operations is important because it enables the creation of control points for what is exported from this MAC-VRF and imported into this MAC-VRF. Figure 6-8 depicts this control point and the order of operations for a locally learned address.

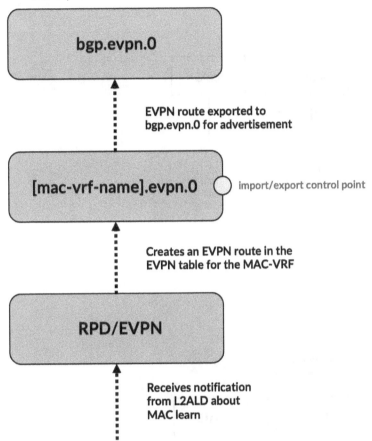

Figure 6-8 *Control point and relationship of different route tables with MAC-VRFs for a locally learned address*

Note A manual export policy, configured with the **vrf-export** configuration option under the MAC-VRF routing instance, overrides the internal export policy that is used to add the Route Target as the route is exported into the bgp.evpn.0 table. Thus, care must be taken to add this Route Target community in a manual export policy explicitly; otherwise, the routes will be exported without any Route Target community added to them.

Shared Tunnels with MAC-VRFs

Returning to the command **set forwarding-options evpn-vxlan shared-tunnels**, shown earlier in Example 6-2, it is important to understand its need (and functional impact) in more detail. To demonstrate this, the MAC-VRF for VLAN 100 from the "VLAN-Based MAC-VRFs" section is extended to leaf4 as well, and an additional MAC-VRF is configured for a new VLAN (200) on leaf1 and leaf4. This change is visually represented in Figure 6-9 and Figure 6-10, which show, respectively, that MAC-VRF 1 extends between leaf1, leaf2, leaf3, and leaf4 and that MAC-VRF 2 extends only between leaf1 and leaf4.

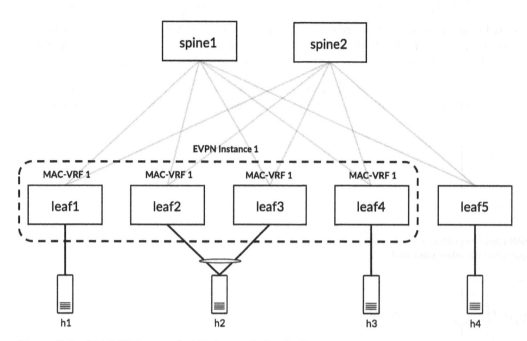

Figure 6-9   *MAC-VRF macvrf-v100-1 extended to leaf4*

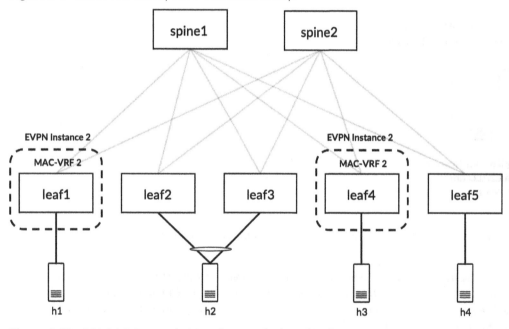

Figure 6-10   *MAC-VRF macvrf-v200-1 between leaf1 and leaf4*

This creates two EVPN Instances, one for each MAC-VRF on both leaf1 and leaf4, confirmed again by using the **show evpn instance** operational mode command, as shown in Example 6-13.

Example 6-13   *EVPN Instances created for MAC-VRFs*

```
root@leaf1> show evpn instance
                Intfs      IRB intfs      MH      MAC addresses
Instance        Total  Up  Total  Up   Nbrs  ESIs   Local  Remote
__default_evpn__                         0
macvrf-v100-1      2   2     0    0     3     1       1       2
macvrf-v200-1      2   2     0    0     1     0       0       0
```

```
root@leaf4> show evpn instance
                        Intfs        IRB intfs         MH    MAC addresses
Instance              Total  Up  Total  Up  Nbrs  ESIs   Local  Remote
__default_evpn__                                    0
macvrf-v100-1            2    2     0    0    3     1      0       3
macvrf-v200-1            2    2     0    0    1     0      0       0
```

Even though there are two MAC-VRFs (and two EVPN Instances in this case), the remote VTEP for both is the same (when viewed individually from the perspective of leaf1 and leaf4). In such cases, instead of assigning unique next-hop IDs for remote VTEPs for each MAC-VRF, the next-hop IDs are simply reused for both MAC-VRFs, thus preserving this resource, which is an important factor when scaling out an EVPN VXLAN fabric. This is achieved via the **set forwarding-options evpn-vxlan shared-tunnels** configuration.

In our case, on leaf1, as shown in Example 6-14, leaf4 (192.0.2.14) was discovered as a remote VTEP for MAC-VRF macvrf-v100-1 and VNI 10100 as well as for MAC-VRF macvrf-v200-1 and VNI 10200. For both, the next-hop ID is the same since the remote VTEP is the same.

Example 6-14 *Shared next-hop IDs on leaf1*

```
root@leaf1> show mac-vrf forwarding vxlan-tunnel-end-point remote
Logical System Name    Id  SVTEP-IP        IFL   L3-Idx  SVTEP-Mode    ELP-SVTEP-IP
<default>              0   192.0.2.11      lo0.0   0
  RVTEP-IP    IFL-Idx    Interface   NH-Id   RVTEP-Mode  ELP-IP      Flags
  192.0.2.12  832        vtep.32771  1747    RNVE
  192.0.2.13  833        vtep.32772  1748    RNVE
  192.0.2.14  831        vtep.32770  1744    RNVE
  RVTEP-IP    L2-RTT              IFL-Idx    Interface      NH-Id  RVTEP-Mode  ELP-IP   Flags
  192.0.2.12  macvrf-v100-1       671088641  vtep-8.32771   1747   RNVE
    VNID      MC-Group-IP
    10100     0.0.0.0
  RVTEP-IP    L2-RTT              IFL-Idx    Interface      NH-Id  RVTEP-Mode  ELP-IP   Flags
  192.0.2.13  macvrf-v100-1       671088642  vtep-8.32772   1748   RNVE
    VNID      MC-Group-IP
    10100     0.0.0.0
  RVTEP-IP    L2-RTT              IFL-Idx    Interface      NH-Id  RVTEP-Mode  ELP-IP   Flags
  192.0.2.14  macvrf-v100-1       671088640  vtep-8.32770   1744   RNVE
    VNID      MC-Group-IP
    10100     0.0.0.0
  RVTEP-IP    L2-RTT              IFL-Idx    Interface      NH-Id  RVTEP-Mode  ELP-IP   Flags
  192.0.2.14  macvrf-v200-1       671088643  vtep-11.32770  1744   RNVE
    VNID      MC-Group-IP
    10200     0.0.0.0
```

Thus, Example 6-14 confirms that the next-hop ID of 1744 is shared across both MAC-VRFs. On leaf4, the configuration option **set forwarding-options evpn-vxlan shared-tunnels** is not needed because the functionality is enabled by default (on the Juniper QFX5130 platform), and the same behavior is observed, as shown in Example 6-15 (next-hop ID of 83020 is shared between MAC-VRFs).

Example 6-15 *Shared next-hop IDs on leaf4*

```
root@leaf4> show mac-vrf forwarding vxlan-tunnel-end-point remote
Logical System Name    Id  SVTEP-IP        IFL   L3-Idx  SVTEP-Mode    ELP-SVTEP-IP
<default>              0   192.0.2.14      lo0.0   0
```

```
RVTEP-IP      IFL-Idx     Interface    NH-Id   RVTEP-Mode  ELP-IP        Flags
192.0.2.11    19305       vtep.32770   83020   RNVE
192.0.2.12    19312       vtep.32771   83050   RNVE
192.0.2.13    19313       vtep.32772   83051   RNVE
RVTEP-IP      L2-RTT                   IFL-Idx     Interface    NH-Id   RVTEP-Mode  ELP-IP        Flags
192.0.2.11    macvrf-v100-1            671088640   vtep-52.32770 83020  RNVE
   VNID       MC-Group-IP
   10100      0.0.0.0
RVTEP-IP      L2-RTT                   IFL-Idx     Interface    NH-Id   RVTEP-Mode  ELP-IP        Flags
192.0.2.12    macvrf-v100-1            671088641   vtep-52.32771 83050  RNVE
   VNID       MC-Group-IP
   10100      0.0.0.0
RVTEP-IP      L2-RTT                   IFL-Idx     Interface    NH-Id   RVTEP-Mode  ELP-IP        Flags
192.0.2.13    macvrf-v100-1            671088642   vtep-52.32772 83051  RNVE
   VNID       MC-Group-IP
   10100      0.0.0.0
RVTEP-IP      L2-RTT                   IFL-Idx     Interface    NH-Id   RVTEP-Mode  ELP-IP        Flags
192.0.2.11    macvrf-v200-1            671088643   vtep-54.32770 83020  RNVE
   VNID       MC-Group-IP
   10200      0.0.0.0
```

VLAN-Aware MAC-VRFs

In this section, the VLAN-Aware service type, offered via MAC-VRFs, is configured and validated. Quite often, servers connected to ToR leafs have multiple virtualized hosts across different VLANs. It is useful to group these VLANs together into the same isolated group for a particular tenant, which is what VLAN-Aware MAC-VRFs help achieve.

Our reference topology is updated to include servers with virtualized hosts now, as shown in Figure 6-11. A VLAN-Aware MAC-VRF for VLAN 100 and VLAN 200 extends between leaf1, leaf2, and leaf3, with servers s1 and s2 each having a virtualized host per VLAN.

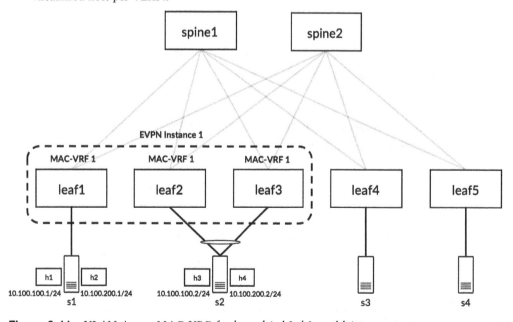

Figure 6-11   *VLAN-Aware MAC-VRF for hosts h1, h2, h3, and h4*

The configuration is similar to that of VLAN-Based MAC-VRFs, but with VLAN-Aware MAC-VRFs, more than one VLAN can be mapped to the same MAC-VRF. Each VLAN has its own bridge table, and is identified by the Ethernet Tag ID, in the VXLAN header, being set to the VNI for that VLAN.

The configuration snippet from leaf1 shown in Example 6-16 is an example of a VLAN-Aware MAC-VRF.

Example 6-16 *VLAN-Aware MAC-VRF on leaf1*

```
root@leaf1# show routing-instances macvrf-v100-v200-1
instance-type mac-vrf;
protocols {
    evpn {
        encapsulation vxlan;
        extended-vni-list all;
    }
}
vtep-source-interface lo0.0;
service-type vlan-aware;
interface et-0/0/49.0;
route-distinguisher 192.0.2.11:12;
vrf-target target:100:200;
vlans {
    v100 {
        vlan-id 100;
        vxlan {
            vni 10100;
        }
    }
    v200 {
        vlan-id 200;

        vxlan {
            vni 10200;
        }
    }
}
```

With similar configuration on leaf2 and leaf3, the EVPN Instance corresponding to these MAC-VRFs now extends between all these leafs. Packet captures of an EVPN Type-3 route and an EVPN Type-2 route confirm that the Ethernet Tag ID is set to the respective VNI in the VXLAN header, as shown in Figure 6-12 and Figure 6-13.

Even though multiple VLANs/VNIs are mapped under a common MAC-VRF and EVPN Instance, there is still a separation of the broadcast domain. Each VLAN has a unique broadcast domain, which is achieved by generating EVPN Type-3 routes per VNI (using the Ethernet Tag ID to match the VNI). With two VLANs (VLAN 100 mapped to VNI 10100, and VLAN 200 mapped to VNI 10200) configured on leaf1, two EVPN Type-3 routes are generated, one for VNI 10100 and another for VNI 10200, as shown in Example 6-17.

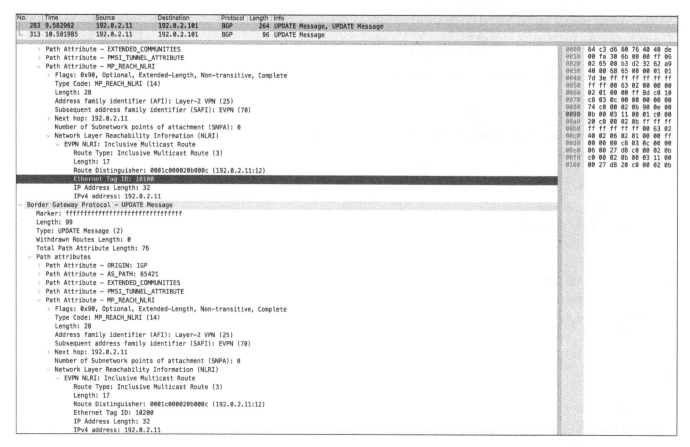

Figure 6-12 *Packet capture of an EVPN Type-3 route for a VLAN-Aware MAC-VRF*

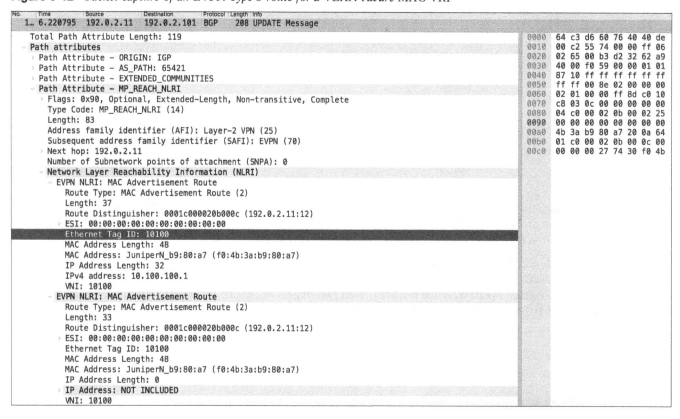

Figure 6-13 *Packet capture of an EVPN Type-2 route for a VLAN-Aware MAC-VRF*

Example 6-17 *EVPN Type-3 routes generated per VNI*

```
root@leaf1> show route table macvrf-v100-v200-1.evpn.0 match-prefix 3:*

macvrf-v100-v200-1.evpn.0: 4 destinations, 4 routes (4 active, 0 holddown, 0 hidden)
+ = Active Route, - = Last Active, * = Both

3:192.0.2.11:12::10100::192.0.2.11/248 IM
                  *[EVPN/170] 03:14:32
                       Indirect
3:192.0.2.11:12::10200::192.0.2.11/248 IM
                  *[EVPN/170] 03:14:32
                       Indirect
```

With these MAC-VRFs created on leaf1, leaf2, and leaf3 now, leaf1 has discovered remote VTEPs leaf2 and leaf3, as shown in Example 6-18. Host h1 can now ping h3, while host h2 can ping h4, as confirmed in Example 6-19.

Example 6-18 *Remote VTEPs discovered on leaf1 with VLAN-Aware MAC-VRF*

```
root@leaf1> show mac-vrf forwarding vxlan-tunnel-end-point remote
Logical System Name     Id  SVTEP-IP        IFL  L3-Idx   SVTEP-Mode     ELP-SVTEP-IP
<default>               0   192.0.2.11      lo0.0  0
  RVTEP-IP    IFL-Idx     Interface    NH-Id   RVTEP-Mode  ELP-IP       Flags
  192.0.2.12  827         vtep.32770   1743    RNVE
  192.0.2.13  830         vtep.32771   1750    RNVE
  RVTEP-IP    L2-RTT               IFL-Idx   Interface      NH-Id  RVTEP-Mode  ELP-IP       Flags
  192.0.2.12  macvrf-v100-v200-1   671088640 vtep-10.32770 1743   RNVE
    VNID      MC-Group-IP
    10200     0.0.0.0
    10100     0.0.0.0
  RVTEP-IP    L2-RTT               IFL-Idx   Interface      NH-Id  RVTEP-Mode  ELP-IP       Flags
  192.0.2.13  macvrf-v100-v200-1   671088641 vtep-10.32771 1750   RNVE
    VNID      MC-Group-IP
    10100     0.0.0.0
    10200     0.0.0.0
```

Example 6-19 *Host reachability with VLAN-Aware MAC-VRFs*

```
root@h1> ping 10.100.100.2
PING 10.100.100.2 (10.100.100.2): 56 data bytes
64 bytes from 10.100.100.2: icmp_seq=0 ttl=64 time=4.219 ms
64 bytes from 10.100.100.2: icmp_seq=1 ttl=64 time=0.977 ms
64 bytes from 10.100.100.2: icmp_seq=2 ttl=64 time=3.680 ms
64 bytes from 10.100.100.2: icmp_seq=3 ttl=64 time=4.244 ms
^C
--- 10.100.100.2 ping statistics ---
4 packets transmitted, 4 packets received, 0% packet loss
round-trip min/avg/max/stddev = 0.977/3.280/4.244/1.349 ms
```

```
root@h2> ping 10.100.200.2
PING 10.100.200.2 (10.100.200.2): 56 data bytes
64 bytes from 10.100.200.2: icmp_seq=0 ttl=64 time=60.069 ms
64 bytes from 10.100.200.2: icmp_seq=1 ttl=64 time=0.947 ms
64 bytes from 10.100.200.2: icmp_seq=2 ttl=64 time=0.880 ms
64 bytes from 10.100.200.2: icmp_seq=3 ttl=64 time=14.688 ms
^C
--- 10.100.200.2 ping statistics ---
4 packets transmitted, 4 packets received, 0% packet loss
round-trip min/avg/max/stddev = 0.880/19.146/60.069/24.287 ms
```

VLAN-Aware MAC-VRFs also provide an operational benefit over VLAN-Based MAC-VRFs: to add a new VLAN, you can simply add it inside the same MAC-VRF, whereas for a VLAN-Based MAC-VRF, a new MAC-VRF must be created since only one VLAN can be mapped to one VLAN-Based MAC-VRF. Because routing instances are a limited resource, this is advantageous.

Additionally, VLAN-Aware MAC-VRFs generate a lower number of EVPN Type-1 (Auto-Discovery) routes—since these routes are generated per EVI (EVPN Instance), several VLANs can be mapped to a common EVPN Instance and only one EVPN Type-1 route is generated for the entire instance (per ESI). Comparing this to a VLAN-Based MAC-VRF, for N number of VLANs, there must be an equal number of MAC-VRFs and EVPN Instances, and thus N number of Type-1 routes are generated.

Overlapping VLANs, VLAN Translation, and VLAN Normalization

To close this chapter out, let's attempt to create another VLAN-Based MAC-VRF on leaf1 that is shared with leaf4 and leaf5, for an overlapping VLAN ID (100), from the perspective of leaf1, and check the configuration before committing it. Configuration of both MAC-VRFs, and a subsequent **commit check** prior to committing the configuration, is shown in Example 6-20.

Example 6-20   *commit check failing with duplicate VLANs across MAC-VRFs*

```
root@leaf1# show routing-instances
macvrf-v100-translate {
    instance-type mac-vrf;
    protocols {
        evpn {
            encapsulation vxlan;
            extended-vni-list 10100;
        }
    }
    vtep-source-interface lo0.0;
    service-type vlan-based;
    interface et-0/0/54.0;
    route-distinguisher 192.0.2.11:100;
    vrf-target target:100:100;
    vlans {
        v100 {
            vlan-id 100;
            vxlan {
                vni 10100;
```

```
            }
        }
    }
}
macvrf-v100-v200-1 {
    instance-type mac-vrf;
    protocols {
        evpn {
            encapsulation vxlan;
            extended-vni-list all;
        }
    }
    vtep-source-interface lo0.0;
    service-type vlan-aware;
    interface et-0/0/49.0;
    route-distinguisher 192.0.2.11:12;
    vrf-target target:100:200;
    vlans {
        v100 {
            vlan-id 100;
            vxlan {
                vni 10100;
            }
        }
        v200 {
            vlan-id 200;
            vxlan {
                vni 10200;
            }
        }
    }
}
root@leaf1# commit check
[edit routing-instances macvrf-v100-translate vlans v100]
  'vxlan'
    warning: requires 'vxlan' license
[edit routing-instances macvrf-v100-v200-1 vlans]
  'v100'
    l2ald: Duplicate vlan-id exists
error: configuration check-out failed
```

The L2ALD daemon throws an error stating that duplicate VLANs exist. MAC-VRFs have a limitation (across vendors and certain platforms) in that the same VLAN cannot be used across different MAC-VRFs. This is challenging, especially in service provider–like environments, in which multiple customers/tenants are onboarded without knowing exactly what VLAN they may be using, which can lead to overlapping VLANs between different customers. This is also commonly encountered when different businesses (and networks) merge, leading to overlapping VLANs between different business functions.

For example, consider the Layer 2 multitenancy requirement shown in Figure 6-14. The example focuses on leaf1, to which two CE devices are connected (to unique MAC-VRFs), both of which require connectivity for the same VLAN. This cannot be achieved even with MAC-VRFs.

Note In the same example shown in Figure 6-14, it is important to note that even if the same VLANs could be reused across MAC-VRFs, the corresponding VNIs must be unique. This is because the VXLAN header includes a single VNI only and, unlike MPLS L3VPNs, there is no way to include a second label (the second label, in the case of MPLS L3VPNs, identifies the VPN or the virtual forwarding table to which the CE is connected).

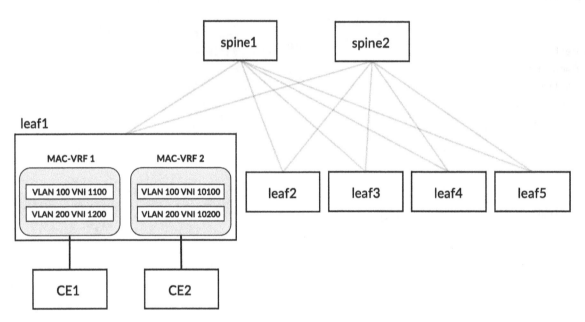

Figure 6-14 *Overlapping VLANs between MAC-VRFs on leaf1*

This limitation exists because the bridge domain (VLAN) must be uniquely identified in a hardware forwarding instance. Higher-end platforms, like the Juniper ACX series, have multiple forwarding instances that allow different MAC-VRFs to be mapped to different forwarding instances, thus overcoming this limitation.

VLAN translation and VLAN normalization can be used to overcome this limitation on the Juniper QFX platforms (which have a single forwarding instance only), and these are explored in the following sections in more detail.

VLAN Translation

On Juniper platforms like the QFX5120s and QFX5130s, to overcome the limitation discussed in the introduction of this section, the VLAN translation feature can be used via the interface-specific **vlan-rewrite** configuration option. This allows a tagged customer VLAN to be swapped to another provider-specific VLAN (sometimes referred to as a *mapped* VLAN) that carries the packet across the EVPN VXLAN fabric to the remote VTEP, where it is swapped back to the customer VLAN again before being sent toward the CE.

The reference topology is updated in Figure 6-15 with a new server (s5) attached to leaf1. This has a virtualized host h6, in VLAN 100, with an IP address of 10.100.100.10/24. Server s3 also has a virtualized host h5 in VLAN 100, with an IP address of 10.100.100.3/24. Visually, MAC-VRF macvrf-v100-v200-1 continues to exist as shown in Figure 6-15.

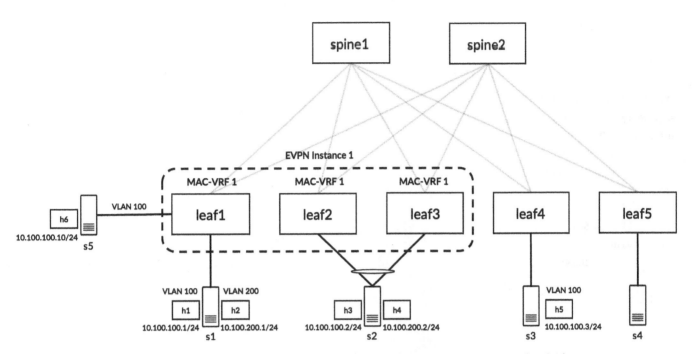

Figure 6-15 *Visual representation of MAC-VRF macvrf-v100-v200-1 with new server s5 connected to leaf1*

At the same time, a new VLAN-Based MAC-VRF macvrf-v100-translate is created on leaf1, leaf4, and leaf5, an example of which is shown in Example 6-21 from leaf1 and leaf4.

Example 6-21 *MAC-VRFs for VLAN translation*

```
root@leaf1# show routing-instances macvrf-v100-translate
instance-type mac-vrf;
protocols {
    evpn {
        encapsulation vxlan;
        extended-vni-list 10500;
    }
}
vtep-source-interface lo0.0;
service-type vlan-based;
interface et-0/0/54.0;
route-distinguisher 192.0.2.11:100;
vrf-target target:100:100;
vlans {
    v500 {
        vlan-id 500;
        vxlan {
            vni 10500;
        }
    }
}

root@leaf4# show routing-instances macvrf-v100-translate
instance-type mac-vrf;
protocols {
    evpn {
```

```
        encapsulation vxlan;
        extended-vni-list 10500;
    }
}
vtep-source-interface lo0.0;
service-type vlan-based;
interface et-0/0/4.0;
route-distinguisher 192.0.2.14:100;
vrf-target target:100:100;
vlans {
    v500 {
        vlan-id 500;
        vxlan {
            vni 10500;
        }
    }
}
```

Visually, this new MAC-VRF macvrf-v100-translate extends between leaf1, leaf4, and leaf5 as shown in Figure 6-16.

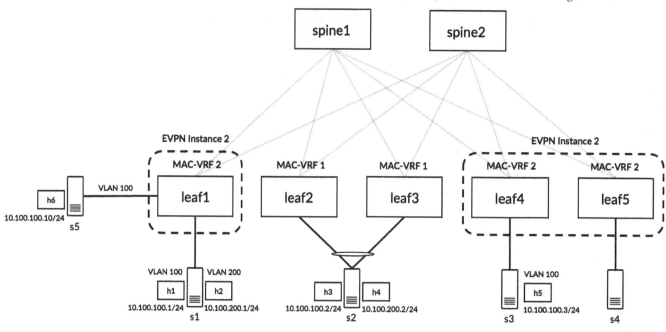

Figure 6-16 *Visual representation of MAC-VRF macvrf-v100-translate with new server s5 connected to leaf1*

It is important to consider how the new MAC-VRF for the overlapping VLAN is configured. The VLAN enabled for EVPN VXLAN is the provider or the mapped VLAN, while on the CE-facing interfaces, VLAN translation is enabled as shown in Example 6-22.

Example 6-22 *Interface configuration for VLAN translation using the **vlan rewrite** command*

```
root@leaf1# show interfaces et-0/0/54
mtu 9200;
unit 0 {
    family ethernet-switching {
        interface-mode trunk;
```

```
    vlan {
        members v500;
    }
    vlan-rewrite {
        translate 100 500;
    }
    }
}
}
```

```
root@leaf4# show interfaces et-0/0/4
speed 40g;
mtu 9200;
unit 0 {
    family ethernet-switching {
        interface-mode trunk;
        vlan {
            members v500;
        }
        vlan-rewrite {
            translate 100 500;
        }
    }
}
```

The interfaces are configured as trunk interfaces, allowing the mapped VLANs over the trunk. The first VLAN in the **vlan-rewrite translate** configuration option is the customer VLAN that is expected to come tagged (with an 802.1Q header), while the second VLAN is the provider/mapped VLAN. Thus, based on the configuration shown in Example 6-22, ingress packets tagged with VLAN 100 are swapped to VLAN 500 before any packet processing happens. This packet makes its way through the EVPN VXLAN fabric using the provider VLAN, and it is swapped back to VLAN 100 before it is sent out of the egress interface on the remote VTEP.

This has crucial implications to MAC learning: MAC learning now happens on the mapped VLAN instead of the customer VLAN. For example, consider host h6 communicating with h5. On leaf1, host h6's MAC address is learned locally on VLAN 500, while host h5 is learned as a remote address, again in VLAN 500, where VLAN 500 is the mapped VLAN. This is shown in Example 6-23, by viewing the MAC address table specific to the MAC-VRF, using the **show mac-vrf forwarding mac-table instance** [*name*] operational mode command.

Example 6-23 *MAC learning on the translated VLAN*

```
root@leaf1> show mac-vrf forwarding mac-table instance macvrf-v100-translate

MAC flags (S - static MAC, D - dynamic MAC, L - locally learned, P - Persistent static
           SE - statistics enabled, NM - non configured MAC, R - remote PE MAC, O - ovsdb MAC,
           B - Blocked MAC)


Ethernet switching table : 2 entries, 2 learned
Routing instance : macvrf-v100-translate


Ethernet switching table : 2 entries, 2 learned
```

```
Routing instance : macvrf-v100-translate
   Vlan              MAC               MAC     GBP    Logical              SVLBNH/      Active
   name              address           flags   tag    interface            VENH Index   source
   v500              00:10:94:00:00:01  D              et-0/0/54.0
   v500              f0:4b:3a:b9:80:ab  DR             vtep-11.32770                     192.0.2.14
```

In the data plane, the VNI, in the VXLAN header, corresponds to the VNI for the mapped VLAN (VLAN 500). The packet capture shown in Figure 6-17 confirms the same.

```
No.    Time       Source         Destination   Protocol  Length  Info
  2 0.007130   10.100.100…   10.100.100…   ICMP      148  Echo (ping) request   id=0x4694, seq=28/7168, ttl=64 (reply in 3)
  3 0.029342   10.100.100…   10.100.100…   ICMP      152  Echo (ping) reply     id=0x4694, seq=28/7168, ttl=64 (request in 2)
 32 1.007917   10.100.100…   10.100.100…   ICMP      148  Echo (ping) request   id=0x4694, seq=29/7424, ttl=64 (reply in 33)
 33 1.046441   10.100.100…   10.100.100…   ICMP      152  Echo (ping) reply     id=0x4694, seq=29/7424, ttl=64 (request in 32)

> Frame 2: 148 bytes on wire (1184 bits), 148 bytes captured (1184 bits)        0000  64 c3 d6 60 76 40 40 de
> Ethernet II, Src: JuniperN_7b:70:75 (40:de:ad:7b:70:75), Dst: JuniperN_60:76:40 (64:c3:d6:60:76:40)   0010  00 86 11 40 00 00 40 11
> Internet Protocol Version 4, Src: 192.0.2.11, Dst: 192.0.2.14                  0020  02 0e 46 1e 12 b5 00 72
> User Datagram Protocol, Src Port: 17950, Dst Port: 4789                        0030  04 00 f0 4b 3a b9 80 ab
v Virtual eXtensible Local Area Network                                         0040  45 00 00 54 76 a2 00 00
  > Flags: 0x0800, VXLAN Network ID (VNI)                                       0050  0a 64 64 03 08 00 77 f0
    Group Policy ID: 0                                                          0060  00 0e 5a c7 08 09 0a 0b
    VXLAN Network Identifier (VNI): 10500                                       0070  14 15 16 17 18 19 1a 1b
    Reserved: 0                                                                 0080  24 25 26 27 28 29 2a 2b
v Ethernet II, Src: Performa_00:00:01 (00:10:94:00:00:01), Dst: JuniperN_b9:80:ab (f0:4b:3a:b9:80:ab)   0090  34 35 36 37
  > Destination: JuniperN_b9:80:ab (f0:4b:3a:b9:80:ab)
  > Source: Performa_00:00:01 (00:10:94:00:00:01)
    Type: IPv4 (0x0800)
v Internet Protocol Version 4, Src: 10.100.100.10, Dst: 10.100.100.3
    0100 .... = Version: 4
    .... 0101 = Header Length: 20 bytes (5)
  > Differentiated Services Field: 0x00 (DSCP: CS0, ECN: Not-ECT)
    Total Length: 84
    Identification: 0x76a2 (30370)
  > 000. .... = Flags: 0x0
    ...0 0000 0000 0000 = Fragment Offset: 0
    Time to Live: 64
    Protocol: ICMP (1)
    Header Checksum: 0x2732 [validation disabled]
    [Header checksum status: Unverified]
    Source Address: 10.100.100.10
    Destination Address: 10.100.100.3
> Internet Control Message Protocol
```

Figure 6-17 *Packet capture of a VXLAN-encapsulated packet post VLAN translation*

In this way, VLAN translation helps facilitate a design in which overlapping VLANs cannot be avoided by translating the customer VLAN into a provider or mapped VLAN. While it does solve the overlapping VLAN problem, VLAN translation is not without its drawbacks. With such a design, it is tedious to track every customer's mapped VLAN, which can be quite an operational overhead. Additionally, it is necessary to be aware of the customer's VLAN—often, this is not the case, and as a service provider, you might not know the customer's VLAN beforehand. In such situations, VLAN normalization can be used to achieve the same goal.

VLAN Normalization

VLAN normalization is a feature available with the service provider (SP) style of configuration for bridges/VLANs in Junos. Service provider style (as opposed to enterprise style, which is how all VLANs have been configured thus far) provides local significance for VLANs, which allows VLANs to be reused across physical interfaces even if they are not in the same broadcast domain.

This configuration is called *service provider style* because it is typically used in SP environments in which VLANs are significant to physical interfaces (instead of having global significance) while allowing different bridging features to be configured per logical interface (configured as a *unit* under a physical interface) for different customer requirements (since multiple customers commonly connect over the same physical interface).

The difference between the two styles is how they are configured using the Junos CLI (and, ultimately, how entries are installed in software/hardware tables): the SP style is more complicated to configure but provides greater flexibility, while the enterprise style is easier to configure but provides less flexibility.

Consider the reference topology that was used for VLAN-Based MAC-VRFs again, as shown in Figure 6-18.

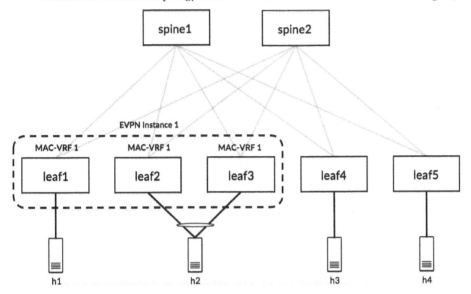

Figure 6-18 *Initial reference topology for VLAN normalization*

An SP-style configuration is used on leaf1 for the MAC-VRF macvrf-v100-1 now. Most notably, the interface facing host h1 is configured with a logical unit (unit 0, in this case) associated to a VLAN for the host, and this logical interface is mapped within the VLAN definition itself. The physical interface, on the other hand, is set to an encapsulation type of *extended-vlan-bridge* with *flexible-vlan-tagging* enabled, meaning that this interface is configured for Layer 2 bridging and can accept untagged, tagged, or double 802.1Q tagged packets. The configuration for the MAC-VRF and the physical interface are shown in Example 6-24.

Example 6-24 *SP-style configuration for a VLAN-Based MAC-VRF on leaf1*

```
root@leaf1# show routing-instances macvrf-v100-1
instance-type mac-vrf;
protocols {
    evpn {
        encapsulation vxlan;
        extended-vni-list 10100;
    }
}
vtep-source-interface lo0.0;
service-type vlan-based;
route-distinguisher 192.0.2.11:100;
vrf-target target:1:1;
vlans {
    v100 {
        vlan-id 100;
        interface et-0/0/49.100;
        vxlan {
            vni 10100;
        }
    }
}

root@leaf1# show interfaces et-0/0/49
flexible-vlan-tagging;
```

```
mtu 9200;
encapsulation extended-vlan-bridge;
unit 100 {
    vlan-id 100;
}
```

With this change to SP-style configuration, host h1 continues to communicate with h2, as shown in Example 6-25. The expectation, however, is that h1 is sending tagged packets to the leaf (with a VLAN ID of 100 in the 802.1Q header).

Example 6-25 *Host h1 to h2 reachability after moving to SP-style configuration on leaf1*

```
root@h1# ping 10.100.100.2
PING 10.100.100.2 (10.100.100.2): 56 data bytes
64 bytes from 10.100.100.2: icmp_seq=0 ttl=64 time=33.686 ms
64 bytes from 10.100.100.2: icmp_seq=1 ttl=64 time=76.188 ms
64 bytes from 10.100.100.2: icmp_seq=2 ttl=64 time=0.860 ms
64 bytes from 10.100.100.2: icmp_seq=3 ttl=64 time=17.142 ms
^C
--- 10.100.100.2 ping statistics ---
4 packets transmitted, 4 packets received, 0% packet loss
round-trip min/avg/max/stddev = 0.860/31.969/76.188/28.044 ms
```

Note   If there is a requirement to support both enterprise-style and SP-style configurations under the same physical interface, then the encapsulation of the physical interface must be set to *flexible-ethernet-services*. Support for these styles of configurations depends on the platform and Junos software version and can be validated using publicly available Juniper documentation.

With a baseline for SP-style configuration established, VLAN normalization can be explored now. For this, consider a new host, h5, connected to leaf1, in the same VLAN (100) as host h1. Host h5, on leaf1, connects into a new MAC-VRF macvrf-v100-2, which extends to leaf4 for connectivity to host h3, as shown in Figure 6-19.

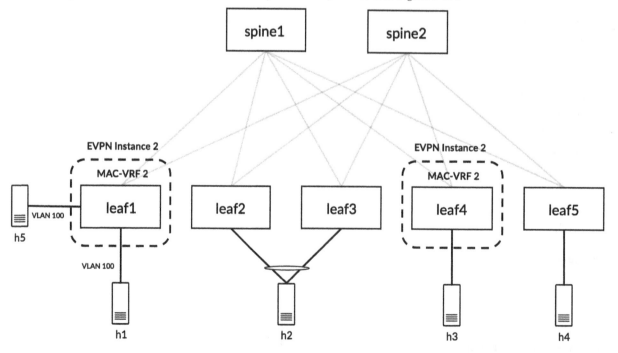

Figure 6-19 *Overlapping VLANs for hosts h1 and h5 across two MAC-VRFs*

The purpose of VLAN normalization is to normalize the VLAN of an ingress packet to that of the bridge domain, which means that the VLAN associated to the bridge domain is swapped with the VLAN of the packet that enters the interface. And when a packet is leaving an interface, it is normalized to the VLAN associated with the egress interface, meaning that the VLAN is again swapped with the VLAN associated to the egress interface.

Overlapping VLAN support for EVPN VXLAN fabrics is enabled with VLAN normalization by setting the VLAN ID to a value of *none*. This means that the VLAN of a packet that enters the interface is *normalized* to a VLAN of none by removing all VLAN tags from the incoming frame. Example 6-26 shows the routing instance configuration for this new MAC-VRF, on both leaf1 and leaf4, as well as the original MAC-VRF for host h1 (modified to VLAN ID of *none*). It is important to note that while the VLAN ID is configured as *none*, the VNI associated to each VLAN within the MAC-VRF must still be unique.

Example 6-26 *MAC-VRFs with VLAN normalization to a VLAN ID of none*

```
root@leaf1# show routing-instances macvrf-v100-1
instance-type mac-vrf;
protocols {
    evpn {
        encapsulation vxlan;
        extended-vni-list 10100;
    }
}
vtep-source-interface lo0.0;
service-type vlan-based;
route-distinguisher 192.0.2.11:100;
vrf-target target:1:1;
vlans {
    v100 {
        vlan-id none;
        interface et-0/0/49.100;
        vxlan {
            vni 10100;
        }
    }
}

root@leaf1# show routing-instances macvrf-v100-2
instance-type mac-vrf;
protocols {
    evpn {
        encapsulation vxlan;
        extended-vni-list 1100;
    }
}
vtep-source-interface lo0.0;
service-type vlan-based;
route-distinguisher 192.0.2.11:1100;
vrf-target target:2:2;
vlans {
    v100-h5 {
        vlan-id none;
        interface et-0/0/54.100;
```

```
            vxlan {
                vni 1100;
            }
        }
    }

root@leaf4# show routing-instances macvrf-v100-2
instance-type mac-vrf;
protocols {
    evpn {
        encapsulation vxlan;
        extended-vni-list 1100;
    }
}
vtep-source-interface lo0.0;
service-type vlan-based;
route-distinguisher 192.0.2.14:100;
vrf-target target:2:2;
vlans {
    v100 {
        vlan-id none;
        interface et-0/0/4.100;
        vxlan {
            vni 1100;
        }
    }
}
```

There are no commit errors when trying to commit this configuration (as opposed to the errors shown in Example 6-20 at the start of this section). With this configuration in place, when a packet comes into interface *et-0/0/54.100* (from host h5) or interface *et-0/0/49.100* (from host h1) on leaf1, the VLAN tag of 100 is stripped at ingress. An inbound *pop* operation for these interfaces confirms this, as shown in Example 6-27. The pop operation, in MPLS networks, refers to the fact that the top MPLS label is removed from the stack. The same terminology is used here again, since functionally, the pop operation does the same thing: instead of an MPLS label, all VLAN tags (802.1Q headers) are removed from the packet, normalizing the VLAN to none.

Example 6-27   *VLAN normalization pop operation on a physical interface*

```
root@leaf1> show interfaces et-0/0/54.100
  Logical interface et-0/0/54.100 (Index 839) (SNMP ifIndex 556)
    Flags: Up SNMP-Traps 0x20004000 VLAN-Tag [ 0x8100.100 ] In(pop) Out(push 0x8100.100)  Encapsulation: Extended-VLAN-
Bridge
    Input packets : 28
    Output packets: 58
    Protocol eth-switch, MTU: 9200
      Flags: Is-Primary, 0x4000000


root@leaf1> show interfaces et-0/0/49.100
  Logical interface et-0/0/49.100 (Index 828) (SNMP ifIndex 552)
```

```
Flags: Up SNMP-Traps 0x20004000 VLAN-Tag [ 0x8100.100 ] In(pop) Out(push 0x8100.100)  Encapsulation: Extended-VLAN-
Bridge
    Input packets : 222
    Output packets: 217
    Protocol eth-switch, MTU: 9200
      Flags: Is-Primary, 0x4000000
```

The unique VNIs corresponding to these overlapping VLANs will carry the packet through the EVPN VXLAN fabric, where the Layer 2 learning and processing will happen against these respective VNIs (and bridge domains corresponding to these VNIs) on the remote leafs. From the PFE, it can be confirmed that the two overlapping VLANs are created as two unique bridge domains, with unique VNIs, as shown in Example 6-28, using the show bridge-domain entry [number] PFE command.

Example 6-28 *Bridge domains for overlapping VLANs with VLAN normalization*

```
FPC0(leaf1 vty)# show bridge-domain
Bridging Domain                    BD-Index RTT-Index  BD-Type   BD-Hw-Token
default+1                                2        8    Regular          3
v100                                     3        9    Regular          4
v100-h5                                  5       11    Regular          6

FPC0(leaf1 vty)# show bridge-domain entry 3
BD Name  : v100
BD Index : 3
 VLAN  : [ 0x8100.4095 ]
 RTB-ID: 9
 Seqno : 0
 BD type          : Regular
 state  flags     : 0x0
 config flags     : 0x40210802
 MAC Limit        : 294912
 IRB IFL index    : 4294967295
 # of IFBDs       : 3 Trunk IFBDs 2
 snoop-enable     : 0
 Input filter index  : 0
 Flood filter index  : 0
 Output filter index : 0
 Generation number   : 4
 BD implicit filters  : None
 VXLAN ID                    : 10100
 VXLAN Mcast group        : 0.0.0.0
 L3 RTT                   : 0
 L3 proto                 : 2
 VxLAN Encap Inner VLAN   : 0
 VxLAN Decap Accept Inner VLAN: 0
 VxLAN Aging Timer        : 300
 VXLAN Source VTEP IP     : 192.0.2.11
 VxLAN Destination UDP Port : 4789
EVPN VxLAN MPLS DCI enabled : 0
 BD nexthop[0]           : 0x0
```

```
BD FTF ptr [0]          : 0x0
BD nexthop[1]           : 0x0
BD FTF ptr [1]          : 0x0
PVLAN Primary BD Id : 0
PVLAN Group Id : 0


FPCO(leaf1 vty)# show bridge-domain entry 5
BD Name  : v100-h5
BD Index : 5
 VLAN   : [ 0x8100.4095 ]
 RTB-ID: 11
 Seqno : 0
 BD type          : Regular
 state  flags     : 0x0
 config flags     : 0x40210802
 MAC Limit        : 294912
 IRB IFL index    : 4294967295
 # of IFBDs       : 2 Trunk IFBDs 1
 snoop-enable     : 0
 Input filter index  : 0
 Flood filter index  : 0
 Output filter index : 0
 Generation number   : 6
 BD implicit filters   : None
 VXLAN ID                    : 1100
 VXLAN Mcast group          : 0.0.0.0
 L3 RTT                     : 0
 L3 proto                   : 2
 VxLAN Encap Inner VLAN     : 0
 VxLAN Decap Accept Inner VLAN: 0
 VxLAN Aging Timer          : 300
 VXLAN Source VTEP IP       : 192.0.2.11
 VxLAN Destination UDP Port : 4789
EVPN VxLAN MPLS DCI enabled : 0
BD nexthop[0]          : 0x0
BD FTF ptr [0]          : 0x0
BD nexthop[1]          : 0x0
BD FTF ptr [1]          : 0x0
PVLAN Primary BD Id : 0
PVLAN Group Id : 0
```

The packet flow for traffic from host h1 to h2 can be visualized as shown in Figure 6-20. The ingress packet from h1 is stripped of all VLAN tags and sent over the fabric with a VNI of 10100. At the egress, on leaf3, the VLAN tag of 100 is added back as the packet is sent out to h2.

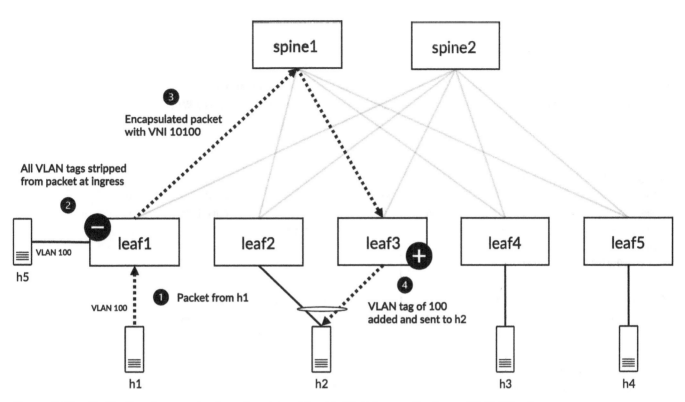

Figure 6-20 *Traffic flow for a packet from host h1 to h2 with VLAN normalization to VLAN ID of none*

The exact same process occurs for traffic from host h5 to h3. However, in this case, a VNI of 1100 is used when the packet is sent over the fabric, as shown in Figure 6-21.

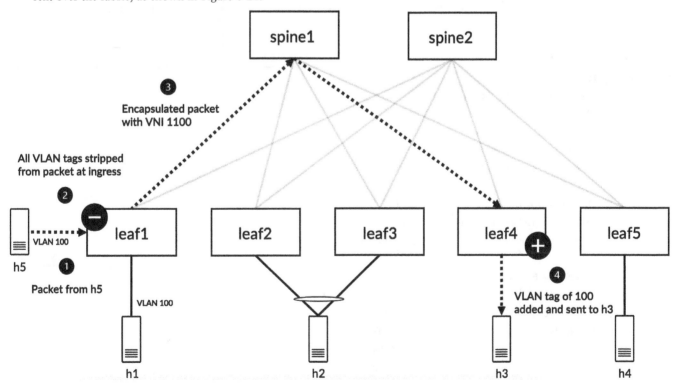

Figure 6-21 *Traffic flow for a packet from host h5 to h3 with VLAN normalization to VLAN ID of none*

The two snippets of output shown in Example 6-29 and Example 6-30 confirm how MAC addresses are learned for these overlapping VLANs, and the reachability of hosts across these two MAC-VRFs.

Example 6-29 *MAC learning with overlapping VLANs across MAC-VRFs*

```
root@leaf1> show mac-vrf forwarding mac-table

MAC flags (S - static MAC, D - dynamic MAC, L - locally learned, P - Persistent static
           SE - statistics enabled, NM - non configured MAC, R - remote PE MAC, O - ovsdb MAC)


Ethernet switching table : 2 entries, 2 learned
Routing instance : macvrf-v100-1
   Vlan             MAC                 MAC    GBP   Logical          SVLBNH/      Active
   name             address             flags  tag   interface        VENH Index   source
   v100             f0:4b:3a:b9:80:a7   D            et-0/0/49.100
   v100             f0:4b:3a:b9:81:65   DR           esi.1754         1755
00:00:00:00:11:11:00:00:00:00


MAC flags (S - static MAC, D - dynamic MAC, L - locally learned, P - Persistent static
           SE - statistics enabled, NM - non configured MAC, R - remote PE MAC, O - ovsdb MAC)


Ethernet switching table : 3 entries, 3 learned
Routing instance : macvrf-v100-2
   Vlan             MAC                 MAC    GBP   Logical          SVLBNH/      Active
   name             address             flags  tag   interface        VENH Index   source
   v100-h5          00:14:94:00:00:02   D            et-0/0/54.100
   v100-h5          f0:4b:3a:b9:80:ab   DR           vtep-11.32774                 192.0.2.14
```

Example 6-30 *Host reachability with overlapping VLANs*

```
root@h2# ping 10.100.100.1
PING 10.100.100.1 (10.100.100.1): 56 data bytes
64 bytes from 10.100.100.1: icmp_seq=0 ttl=64 time=0.946 ms
64 bytes from 10.100.100.1: icmp_seq=1 ttl=64 time=0.875 ms
64 bytes from 10.100.100.1: icmp_seq=2 ttl=64 time=22.784 ms
64 bytes from 10.100.100.1: icmp_seq=3 ttl=64 time=12.793 ms
^C
--- 10.100.100.1 ping statistics ---
4 packets transmitted, 4 packets received, 0% packet loss
round-trip min/avg/max/stddev = 0.875/9.349/22.784/9.148 ms


root@h3# ping 10.100.100.5
PING 10.100.100.5 (10.100.100.5): 56 data bytes
64 bytes from 10.100.100.5: icmp_seq=0 ttl=64 time=0.685 ms
64 bytes from 10.100.100.5: icmp_seq=1 ttl=64 time=0.667 ms
64 bytes from 10.100.100.5: icmp_seq=2 ttl=64 time=10.844 ms
64 bytes from 10.100.100.5: icmp_seq=3 ttl=64 time=0.662 ms
^C
--- 10.100.100.5 ping statistics ---
4 packets transmitted, 4 packets received, 0% packet loss
round-trip min/avg/max/stddev = 0.662/3.215/10.844/4.405 ms
```

Summary

MAC-VRFs provide an important form of network virtualization, multitenancy, and Layer 2 overlay segmentation. With different service types (VLAN-Aware, VLAN-Based, and VLAN Bundle) available, network architects have the flexibility to onboard tenants with different connectivity requirements.

It is mandatory that VLANs are unique across MAC-VRFs, since a forwarding instance cannot have overlapping bridge domains. Higher-end platforms, like the Juniper ACX series, can overcome this limitation by mapping different MAC-VRFs to different forwarding instances, while lower-end platforms, like the Juniper QFX5120s or QFX5130s, can overcome this limitation by using the VLAN translation or VLAN normalization features. This is useful in environments in which multiple tenants share the same VLAN. Even if the VLAN is reused across MAC-VRFs using these features, the VNI, mapped to the VLANs, must be unique.

Centrally Routed Bridging

The previous two chapters described how to extend VLANs (bridge domains) over a routed infrastructure running EVPN VXLAN, using L2VNIs and a bridged overlay design. A logical extension of this design is the requirement to route between VLANs/VNIs. In an EVPN VXLAN fabric, two major design methodologies exist for this: centrally routed bridging (CRB) and edge-routed bridging (ERB). This chapter provides a detailed look at how centrally routed bridging is designed and configured, along with some historical problems with this architecture, how these were solved, and the state of CRB today.

Introducing Integrated Routing and Bridging and CRB Design

Since this is the first chapter in which routing between VLANs/VNIs is being introduced, it is important to understand that at the core of CRB and ERB is *integrated routing and bridging (IRB)*. Traditionally, to route between VLANs, a Layer 3 device (typically a router) was connected to the network, and all routing between VLANs was done by sending traffic upstream to this router, which would route it into the destination VLAN and then send it back down. This is often referred to as a *router-on-a-stick design*. This is visually represented in Figure 7-1, where two hosts, h1 and h2, in VLANs 10 and 20 respectively, are connected to a Layer 2 switch, which connects to a router via a trunk interface, allowing both these VLANs. The physical interface on the router, connecting to the switch, is configured with logical subinterfaces, one for each VLAN. The Layer 2 switch bridges ingress packets from the source VLAN to the router, which routes it from one VLAN to another using the logical subinterfaces and bridges the packet back down to the Layer 2 switch in the destination VLAN.

With Layer 3–capable switches, along with Layer 2 functionality, routed interfaces can be created for corresponding VLANs as well, also called IRB interfaces (or switch virtual interfaces [SVIs] in the case of vendors such as Cisco Systems). With this new IRB construct, both routing and bridging can occur on the same device, without having an additional Layer 3 device dedicated for this. The same concept of IRBs is now extended to VXLAN and VNIs as well. MAC-VRFs, introduced and explored in Chapter 6, provide Layer 2 connectivity for hosts, while IRB interfaces provide Layer 3 connectivity.

Router on a Stick

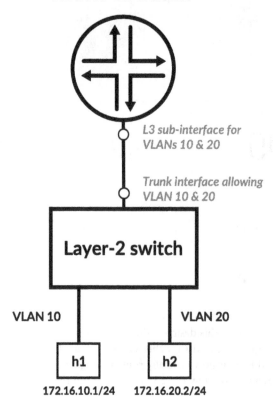

Figure 7-1   *Router-on-a-stick design*

Thus, with IRB interfaces on Layer 3–capable switches, Figure 7-1 can be re-drawn as shown in Figure 7-2, with the routing functionality being moved into the switch itself, visually represented with the router moved inside the switch.

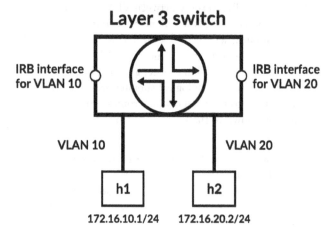

Figure 7-2   *Layer 3–capable switch with IRB interfaces for routing between VLANs*

In a centrally routed bridging architecture, the routing is centralized on a device or a pair of devices (in most cases), which are usually the spines in a 3-stage Clos fabric. This means that with CRB, the IRB interfaces are configured on the spines, as visualized in Figure 7-3.

In an edge-routed bridging architecture, the routing is distributed to the edge of the network (closest to the hosts), which are the leafs in a 3-stage Clos fabric, as visualized in Figure 7-4.

Centralized routing with IRB interfaces on the spines

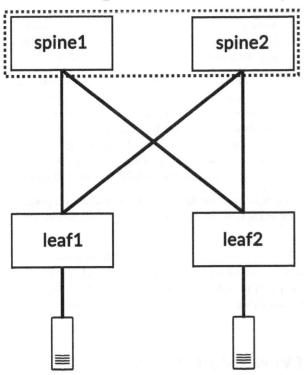

Figure 7-3 *IRB placement in a CRB architecture*

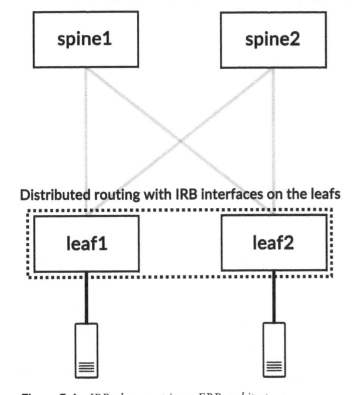

Distributed routing with IRB interfaces on the leafs

Figure 7-4 *IRB placement in an ERB architecture*

A natural consequence of this centralized routing architecture is that even for hosts connected on the same leaf, but on different subnets, traffic needs to be sent upstream to the spines to be routed, and then sent back down, leading to a tromboning traffic pattern. This is highly inefficient and, compounded by the predominance of east-west traffic in modern data centers, is one of the biggest architectural flaws of a CRB design, which is why ERB is generally preferred since routing is done at the edge, closer to source and destination.

The CRB design was, in some cases, a necessity, but in other cases it was purely a design choice, influenced by cost. It was a necessity in some cases because VXLAN routing (or Routing In and Out of Tunnels, often abbreviated to *RIOT*, as it is called in the hardware industry) was not possible on many platforms in the past and only VXLAN bridging was possible. This was because the ASIC pipeline was simply not capable of doing the number of lookups and rewrites needed for RIOT. For example, the Juniper QFX10K can do VXLAN routing, but the QFX5100s (which use Broadcom Trident2) could not.

Add to that equation the cost of these platforms. Positioning Juniper QFX10Ks as all your leafs and spines was costly, since this is a modular chassis–based platform, boasting a much larger feature set and hardware scale, and naturally costlier than the QFX5100, which is a fixed, 1RU device. For all these reasons, it was common to place the QFX5100s at the leaf layer and a pair (or more) of QFX10Ks as the spines, essentially modeling the fabric with L2-only leafs and routing centralized on the spines. With a CRB design, as a network architect, you must also be very conscious about the devices being positioned as the spines—since routing is centralized on the spines, this means that these spines would be holding extremely large ARP and MAC tables. Scale, in this situation, becomes a key factor when choosing the spines, and the QFX10Ks fit the bill very well.

With time, newer ASICs, such as Broadcom's Trident2+ and above, brought in native RIOT (VXLAN routing) support. Vendors also started building custom silicon that could do this, and it made sense to start moving to an ERB design, which clearly had far greater benefits.

So, why learn and understand centrally routed bridging? Even today, many organizations still have CRB deployed and are on a slow path to migrating to ERB. It is important to understand how both CRB and ERB function to safely facilitate such migrations. Of course, from the perspective of simply learning, it is critical to understand the history of a technology, how designs have evolved over time, and, more importantly, what were the driving factors behind these changes. Growth is only growth from the perspective of where we were in the past.

Configuring a Centrally Routed Bridging EVPN VXLAN Fabric

To begin with, this section demonstrates how to configure and deploy a simple two-leaf, two-spine EVPN VXLAN based 3-stage Clos fabric, with routing centralized on the spines, thus creating a CRB fabric. The topology shown in Figure 7-5 is used for this section.

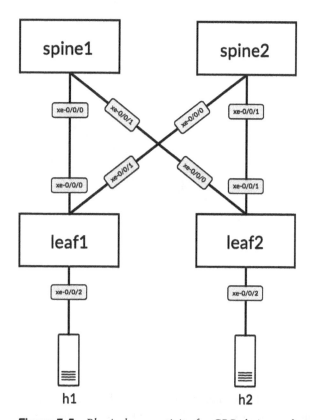

Figure 7-5 *Physical connectivity for CRB design and configuration*

As shown in the previous chapters, in a Clos network, the L2/L3 demarcation is brought down to the leaf layer. This means that the leaf-to-spine interfaces are routed, point-to-point interfaces, constituting a fully Layer 3 underlay, as shown again in Figure 7-6.

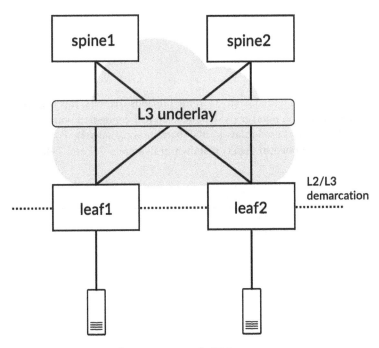

Figure 7-6 *L2/L3 demarcation with CRB*

Let's start by configuring the point-to-point interfaces between the leafs and the spines. These will be /31 IPv4 addresses, from the documentation IPv4 address space 198.51.100.0/24. For the sake of brevity, the configuration from one spine (spine1) and one leaf (leaf1) is shown in Examples 7-1 and 7-2, respectively.

Example 7-1 *Point-to-point interfaces on spine1*

```
admin@spine1# show interfaces xe-0/0/0
unit 0 {
    family inet {
        address 198.51.100.1/31;
    }
}

admin@spine1# show interfaces xe-0/0/1
unit 0 {
    family inet {
        address 198.51.100.5/31;
    }
}
```

Example 7-2 *Point-to-point interfaces on leaf1*

```
admin@leaf1# show interfaces xe-0/0/0
unit 0 {
    family inet {
        address 198.51.100.0/31;
    }
}
```

```
{master:0}[edit]
admin@leaf1# show interfaces xe-0/0/1
unit 0 {
    family inet {
        address 198.51.100.2/31;
    }
}
```

Once these interfaces are configured, BGP for the underlay can be configured next. As in the previous chapters, this is going to be eBGP, with both spines sharing the same BGP autonomous system number (ASN) and each leaf configured with a unique BGP ASN. This ASN scheme, explored in detail in Chapter 3, is used to avoid BGP path hunting natively. For the sake of brevity again, the configuration from one spine (spine1) and one leaf (leaf1) is shown in Examples 7-3 and 7-4, respectively.

Example 7-3   *BGP configuration for the underlay on spine1*

```
admin@spine1# show protocols bgp group underlay
type external;
export allow-loopback;
multipath;
neighbor 198.51.100.0 {
    family inet {
        unicast;
    }
    peer-as 65421;
}
neighbor 198.51.100.4 {
    family inet {
        unicast;
    }
    peer-as 65422;
}

admin@spine1# show policy-options policy-statement allow-loopback
from interface lo0.0;
then accept;
```

Example 7-4   *BGP configuration for the underlay on leaf1*

```
admin@leaf1# show protocols bgp group underlay
type external;
export allow-loopback;
peer-as 65500;
multipath;
neighbor 198.51.100.1 {
    family inet {
        unicast;
    }
}
neighbor 198.51.100.3 {
    family inet {
        unicast;
```

```
        }
}


admin@leaf1# show policy-options policy-statement allow-loopback
from interface lo0.0;
then accept;
```

Once all leafs and spines are configured, BGP should be in an Established state for all neighbors on all devices. This is confirmed on leaf1 and leaf2, shown in Examples 7-5 and 7-6, respectively, using the **show bgp summary group underlay** operational mode command.

Example 7-5   *BGP state for the underlay on leaf1*

```
admin@leaf1> show bgp summary group underlay
Threading mode: BGP I/O
Default eBGP mode: advertise - accept, receive - accept
Groups: 2 Peers: 4 Down peers: 0
Table         Tot Paths  Act Paths Suppressed    History Damp State    Pending
inet.0
                      4          4          0          0          0          0
bgp.evpn.0
                     28         26          0          0          0          0
Peer                     AS      InPkt     OutPkt     OutQ   Flaps Last Up/Dwn State|#Active/Received/Accepted/Damped...
198.51.100.1          65500        135        132        0       0    58:53 Establ
  inet.0: 2/2/2/0
198.51.100.3          65500        135        133        0       0    58:53 Establ
  inet.0: 2/2/2/0
```

Example 7-6   *BGP state for the underlay on leaf2*

```
admin@leaf2> show bgp summary group underlay
Threading mode: BGP I/O
Default eBGP mode: advertise - accept, receive - accept
Groups: 2 Peers: 4 Down peers: 0
Table         Tot Paths  Act Paths Suppressed    History Damp State    Pending
inet.0
                      4          4          0          0          0          0
bgp.evpn.0
                     30         27          0          0          0          0
Peer                     AS      InPkt     OutPkt     OutQ   Flaps Last Up/Dwn State|#Active/Received/Accepted/Damped...
198.51.100.5          65500        141        139        0       0  1:02:12 Establ
  inet.0: 2/2/2/0
198.51.100.7          65500        142        140        0       0  1:02:09 Establ
  inet.0: 2/2/2/0
```

The goal of a VXLAN fabric underlay is to exchange loopback information between all VTEPs in the fabric. In Examples 7-3 and 7-4, the **export** configuration option is used to advertise the loopback addresses into BGP. The result is that leaf1's loopback should have reachability to leaf2's loopback. This is confirmed in Example 7-7, which shows that both leafs have received each other's loopback address, and it is installed in the inet.0 routing table of each leaf.

Example 7-7   *Loopback routes on leaf1 and leaf2*

```
admin@leaf1> show route table inet.0 192.0.2.12/32


inet.0: 12 destinations, 13 routes (12 active, 0 holddown, 0 hidden)
+ = Active Route, - = Last Active, * = Both


192.0.2.12/32      *[BGP/170] 01:09:35, localpref 100, from 198.51.100.1
                      AS path: 65500 65422 I, validation-state: unverified
                       to 198.51.100.1 via xe-0/0/0.0
                    >  to 198.51.100.3 via xe-0/0/1.0
                     [BGP/170] 01:09:35, localpref 100
                      AS path: 65500 65422 I, validation-state: unverified
                    >  to 198.51.100.3 via xe-0/0/1.0


admin@leaf2> show route table inet.0 192.0.2.11/32


inet.0: 12 destinations, 13 routes (12 active, 0 holddown, 0 hidden)
+ = Active Route, - = Last Active, * = Both


192.0.2.11/32      *[BGP/170] 01:09:22, localpref 100, from 198.51.100.5
                      AS path: 65500 65421 I, validation-state: unverified
                       to 198.51.100.5 via xe-0/0/0.0
                    >  to 198.51.100.7 via xe-0/0/1.0
                     [BGP/170] 01:09:22, localpref 100
                      AS path: 65500 65421 I, validation-state: unverified
                    >  to 198.51.100.7 via xe-0/0/1.0
```

Once the respective loopback addresses are in the routing table of each leaf, leaf1 should be able to ping leaf2's loopback (and vice versa), while sourcing its own. This is confirmed in Example 7-8, validating the connectivity necessary for VTEP-to-VTEP reachability in the underlay.

Example 7-8   *Leaf1 pinging leaf2's loopback address successfully*

```
admin@leaf1> ping 192.0.2.12 source 192.0.2.11
PING 192.0.2.12 (192.0.2.12): 56 data bytes
64 bytes from 192.0.2.12: icmp_seq=0 ttl=63 time=120.343 ms
64 bytes from 192.0.2.12: icmp_seq=1 ttl=63 time=145.640 ms
64 bytes from 192.0.2.12: icmp_seq=2 ttl=63 time=211.109 ms
64 bytes from 192.0.2.12: icmp_seq=3 ttl=63 time=165.313 ms
64 bytes from 192.0.2.12: icmp_seq=4 ttl=63 time=206.368 ms
64 bytes from 192.0.2.12: icmp_seq=5 ttl=63 time=116.389 ms
64 bytes from 192.0.2.12: icmp_seq=6 ttl=63 time=114.923 ms
^C
--- 192.0.2.12 ping statistics ---
7 packets transmitted, 7 packets received, 0% packet loss
round-trip min/avg/max/stddev = 114.923/154.298/211.109/38.314 ms
```

BGP for the overlay is configured next. This is, again, an eBGP peering. However, for the overlay, the peering is between the loopbacks of the leafs and the spines, making it a multi-hop peering. As an example, the configuration on spine1 and leaf1 is shown in Examples 7-9 and 7-10, respectively. It is important to note that the spines must not modify the next-hop address of the BGP updates as they are advertised to the leafs, since the VXLAN tunnels are expected to be sourced from, and destined to, these VTEP loopback addresses.

Example 7-9 *BGP overlay configuration on spine1*

```
admin@spine1# show protocols bgp group overlay
type external;
multihop {
    no-nexthop-change;
}
local-address 192.0.2.101;
multipath;
neighbor 192.0.2.11 {
    family evpn {
        signaling;
    }
    peer-as 65421;
}
neighbor 192.0.2.12 {
    family evpn {
        signaling;
    }
    peer-as 65422;
}
```

Example 7-10 *BGP overlay configuration on leaf1*

```
admin@leaf1# show protocols bgp group overlay
type external;
multihop;
local-address 192.0.2.11;
peer-as 65500;
multipath;
neighbor 192.0.2.101 {
    family evpn {
        signaling;
    }
}
neighbor 192.0.2.102 {
    family evpn {
        signaling;
    }
}
```

Once all devices are configured in a similar fashion, BGP EVPN peering should be in an Established state between the leafs and the spines. As shown in Examples 7-11 and 7-12, using the **show bgp summary group overlay** operational mode command, each spine has successfully established a BGP EVPN peering with each leaf.

Example 7-11 *BGP EVPN peering on spine1*

```
admin@spine1> show bgp summary group overlay
Threading mode: BGP I/O
Default eBGP mode: advertise - accept, receive - accept
Groups: 2 Peers: 4 Down peers: 0
```

```
Table          Tot Paths  Act Paths Suppressed     History Damp State     Pending
inet.0
                    2         2         0           0       0            0
bgp.evpn.0
                    6         6         0           0       0            0
Peer               AS      InPkt    OutPkt    OutQ   Flaps Last Up/Dwn State|#Active/Received/Accepted/Damped...
192.0.2.11      65421       548       562      0       0   4:06:23 Establ
  bgp.evpn.0: 3/3/3/0
  default-switch.evpn.0: 3/3/3/0
  __default_evpn__.evpn.0: 0/0/0/0
192.0.2.12      65422       549       560      0       0   4:06:21 Establ
  bgp.evpn.0: 3/3/3/0
  default-switch.evpn.0: 3/3/3/0
  __default_evpn__.evpn.0: 0/0/0/0
```

Example 7-12 *BGP EVPN peering on spine2*

```
admin@spine2> show bgp summary group overlay
Threading mode: BGP I/O
Default eBGP mode: advertise - accept, receive - accept
Groups: 2 Peers: 4 Down peers: 0
Table          Tot Paths  Act Paths Suppressed     History Damp State     Pending
inet.0
                    2         2         0           0       0            0
bgp.evpn.0
                    6         6         0           0       0            0
Peer               AS      InPkt    OutPkt    OutQ   Flaps Last Up/Dwn State|#Active/Received/Accepted/Damped...
192.0.2.11      65421       554       566      0       0   4:08:54 Establ
  bgp.evpn.0: 3/3/3/0
  default-switch.evpn.0: 3/3/3/0
  __default_evpn__.evpn.0: 0/0/0/0
192.0.2.12      65422       554       566      0       0   4:08:50 Establ
  bgp.evpn.0: 3/3/3/0
  default-switch.evpn.0: 3/3/3/0
  __default_evpn__.evpn.0: 0/0/0/0
```

In a CRB design, since the leafs are L2-only (from the perspective of VXLAN forwarding and routing), the configuration specific to VXLAN is like what was done in the previous chapters: VLANs, named v100 and v200, are created on leaf1 and leaf2, respectively. These VLANs are mapped to a corresponding VNI. Using the *switch-options* configuration hierarchy, a Route Target of 1:1 is configured, along with the source of the VXLAN tunnel as lo0.0. For VNI 10100, a more specific Route Target of 100:100 is configured, and for VNI 10200, a more specific Route Target of 200:200 is configured. This configuration, for leaf1 and leaf2, is shown in Examples 7-13 and 7-14, respectively.

Example 7-13 *VXLAN configuration on leaf1*

```
admin@leaf1# show protocols evpn
encapsulation vxlan;
vni-options {
    vni 10100 {
        vrf-target target:100:100;
    }
}
```

```
extended-vni-list 10100;


admin@leaf1# show switch-options
vtep-source-interface lo0.0;
route-distinguisher 192.0.2.11:1;
vrf-target target:1:1;


admin@leaf1# show vlans v100
vlan-id 100;
vxlan {
    vni 10100;
}
```

Example 7-14 *VXLAN configuration on leaf2*

```
admin@leaf2# show protocols evpn
encapsulation vxlan;
vni-options {
    vni 10200 {
        vrf-target target:200:200;
    }
}
extended-vni-list 10200;


admin@leaf2# show switch-options
vtep-source-interface lo0.0;
route-distinguisher 192.0.2.12:1;
vrf-target target:1:1;


admin@leaf2# show vlans v200
vlan-id 200;
vxlan {
    vni 10200;
}
```

The configuration on the spines is more involved (outside of what you just saw for the leafs)—because routing is centralized here, corresponding IRB interfaces for VLANs v100 and v200 are created on the spines. The VLAN must be associated to their respective IRB interfaces, creating a binding between the Layer 2 VLAN and its IRB interface.

In a CRB architecture, IRB interfaces can be created in multiple ways. Some of the more common ways of configuring them, among others, are as follows:

■ Configure IRB interfaces with the same physical IP address and a unique MAC address per spine.

■ Configure IRB interfaces with a unique physical IP address, the same virtual gateway IP address, and the same virtual MAC address per spine.

The first option, while slightly simpler in configuration, adds additional complexity in the control plane and during failure scenarios for convergence. Since each spine is configured with a unique MAC address for the IRB interface, this must be synchronized across all spines, which is achieved by adding the *default gateway* extended community in the EVPN Type-2 routes generated for the IRB interfaces. This enables a spine to proxy-route for any other spine acting as a gateway in the fabric. However, when a failure occurs, the EVPN Type-2 route for the IRB interface is withdrawn, meaning that other spines can no longer proxy-route for the gateway that just failed. Any host still sending traffic to the failed gateway's MAC address must now re-ARP for a new gateway, leading to impact in traffic, until ARP is resolved.

Thus, the second option is the recommended way of configuring the IRB interfaces in a CRB architecture, and that is what is explored here in detail. Figure 7-7 provides a visual representation of the configuration for the IRB interfaces for both VLANs v100 and v200. This includes a physical IP address, a virtual gateway IP address, and a virtual MAC address per IRB interface.

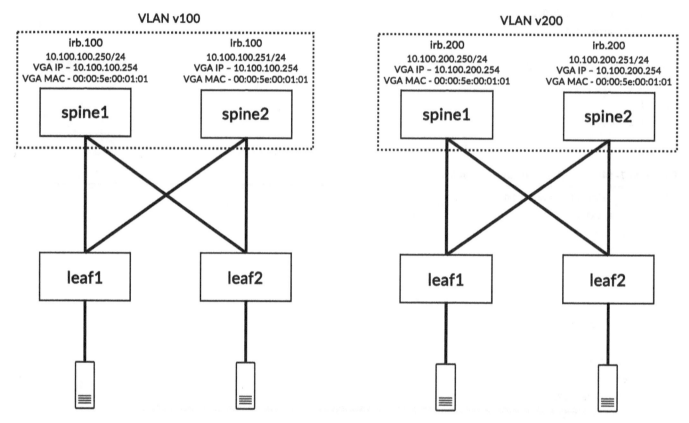

Figure 7-7   *Visualizing the configuration of IRB interfaces for VLANs v100 and v200*

The configuration for the IRB interfaces on the spines is shown in Examples 7-15 and 7-16. The **show interfaces irb.100** and **show interfaces irb.200** configuration mode commands display the IRB interface configuration for VLANs v100 and v200, respectively. It is important to note that the logical unit number for the IRB interface does not need to match the VLAN it is associated to. However, operationally it makes sense to do so, since it is easy to match the VLAN number with the logical unit number of an IRB interface.

Example 7-15   *IRB interfaces configuration on spine1*

```
admin@spine1# show interfaces irb.100
proxy-macip-advertisement;
virtual-gateway-accept-data;
family inet {
    address 10.100.100.250/24 {
        virtual-gateway-address 10.100.100.254;
    }
}

admin@spine1# show interfaces irb.200
proxy-macip-advertisement;
virtual-gateway-accept-data;
family inet {
    address 10.100.200.250/24 {
```

```
        virtual-gateway-address 10.100.200.254;
    }
}


admin@spine1# show vlans v100
vlan-id 100;
l3-interface irb.100;
vxlan {
    vni 10100;
}


admin@spine1# show vlans v200
vlan-id 200;
l3-interface irb.200;
vxlan {
    vni 10200;
}
```

Example 7-16 *IRB interfaces configuration on spine2*

```
admin@spine2# show interfaces irb.100
proxy-macip-advertisement;
virtual-gateway-accept-data;
family inet {
    address 10.100.100.251/24 {
        virtual-gateway-address 10.100.100.254;
    }
}


admin@spine2# show interfaces irb.200
proxy-macip-advertisement;
virtual-gateway-accept-data;
family inet {
    address 10.100.200.251/24 {
        virtual-gateway-address 10.100.200.254;
    }
}


admin@spine2# show vlans v100
vlan-id 100;
l3-interface irb.100;
vxlan {
    vni 10100;
}


admin@spine2# show vlans v200
vlan-id 200;
l3-interface irb.200;
vxlan {
    vni 10200;
}
```

Looking carefully at the IRB interface configurations on the spines in Examples 7-15 and 7-16, note that a virtual MAC address was not configured explicitly. It can be configured using the configuration option set **interfaces irb unit** [*unit-number*] **virtual-gateway-v4-mac** [*mac-address*]. However, when no corresponding virtual MAC address is configured for a virtual gateway address, the MAC address corresponding to group one of the well-known VRRP MAC address range is used. This MAC address range is 00:00:5e:00:01:00 to 00:00:5e:00:01:ff, and group one means the MAC address 00:00:5e:00:01:01 is used as the virtual MAC address. This is in accordance with RFC 9135.

In addition to the virtual gateway address, there are two more configuration options under the IRB interfaces: *proxy-macip-advertisement* and *virtual-gateway-accept-data*. The configuration option *virtual-gateway-accept-data* enables the virtual address to respond to traffic destined to it (such as a host pinging its default gateway, which will be this virtual address). The need for the configuration option *proxy-macip-advertisement* is discussed in detail in an upcoming section, "Historical (and Present Day) Relevance of proxy-macip-advertisement."

For the sake of completeness, the spines are configured as shown in Example 7-17 for EVPN (spine1 used as a reference). This includes configuring a global Route Target of 1:1 and specific Route Targets for VNIs 10100 and 10200, along with the EVPN configuration option *default-gateway no-gateway-community*.

Example 7-17   *EVPN configuration on spine1*

```
admin@spine1# show switch-options
vtep-source-interface lo0.0;
route-distinguisher 192.0.2.101:1;
vrf-target target:1:1;


admin@spine1# show protocols evpn
encapsulation vxlan;
default-gateway no-gateway-community;
vni-options {
    vni 10100 {
        vrf-target target:100:100;
    }
    vni 10200 {
        vrf-target target:200:200;
    }
}
extended-vni-list [ 10100 10200 ];
```

The configuration option *default-gateway no-gateway-community* is configured on the CRB spines because there is no requirement to sync the gateway MAC address between the spines; this is only needed for the first of the two ways of configuring the IRB interfaces (that is, with the same physical IP address and a unique MAC address per spine). By default, the IRB MAC and IP address is advertised by BGP EVPN with the gateway community added. This community, as defined in RFC 7432, is used for aliasing and allows for CRB gateways (the spines, in this case) to sync their unique MAC addresses so that they can proxy-route for each other.

In the case of configuring IRB interfaces with the same virtual gateway address and MAC address, the gateway community is no longer needed since the same virtual gateway IP address and MAC address are defined on all the CRB spines, and there is no need to sync these between them. For this reason, the configuration option *default-gateway no-gateway-community* is used, which omits the gateway community in EVPN Type-2 routes for IRB addresses when advertised via BGP EVPN.

Validating and Understanding EVPN Route Exchange in a CRB Fabric

This section follows some key BGP EVPN routes that are exchanged between the leafs and the spines in a 3-stage Clos fabric with a CRB architecture, and takes a closer look at understanding and validating how these routes are used in building different tables on the VTEPs.

Once the CRB spines are configured with the virtual gateway address, this MAC address is installed in the local EVPN data base and advertised as EVPN Type-2 MAC and MAC+IP routes. This is confirmed on spine1 using the **show evpn database mac-address** [*mac-address*] operational mode command to view the EVPN database, as shown in Example 7-18, and using the **show route table bgp.evpn.0** operational mode command to view the route in the BGP EVPN table, as shown in Example 7-19.

Example 7-18 *EVPN database for the virtual gateway address scoped for VNI 10100 on spine1*

```
admin@spine1> show evpn database mac-address 00:00:5e:00:01:01 extensive l2-domain-id 10100
Instance: default-switch

VN Identifier: 10100, MAC address: 00:00:5e:00:01:01
  State: 0x0
  Source: 05:00:00:ff:dc:00:00:27:74:00, Rank: 1, Status: Active
    Mobility sequence number: 0 (minimum origin address 192.0.2.101)
    Timestamp: Apr 04 11:39:37.489578 (0x642c0c79)
    State: <Local-Virtual-Gateway Local-To-Remote-Adv-Allowed Local-Pinned>
    MAC advertisement route status: Created
    IP address: 10.100.100.254
    Flags: <Local-Adv>
    Local origin: irb.100
    History db:
      Time                      Event
      Apr  4 11:39:37.489 2023   05:00:00:ff:dc:00:00:27:74:00 : Created
      Apr  4 11:39:37.489 2023   Updating output state (change flags 0x1 <ESI-Added>)
      Apr  4 11:39:37.489 2023   Active ESI changing (not assigned -> 05:00:00:ff:dc:00:00:27:74:00)
```

Example 7-19 *EVPN Type-2 route for the virtual gateway address scoped for VNI 10100 on spine1*

```
admin@spine1> show route table bgp.evpn.0 evpn-mac-address 00:00:5e:00:01:01 evpn-ethernet-tag-id 10100

bgp.evpn.0: 18 destinations, 18 routes (18 active, 0 holddown, 0 hidden)
+ = Active Route, - = Last Active, * = Both

2:192.0.2.101:1::10100::00:00:5e:00:01:01/304 MAC/IP
                  *[EVPN/170] 00:50:20
                       Indirect
2:192.0.2.101:1::10100::00:00:5e:00:01:01::10.100.100.254/304 MAC/IP
                  *[EVPN/170] 00:50:20
                       Indirect
```

Let's look at a detailed view of these EVPN Type-2 routes. The keyword **extensive** added at the end of the command gives us detailed information about a route, as shown in Example 7-20.

Example 7-20 *Detailed output for EVPN Type-2 route for the virtual gateway address scoped for VNI 10100 on spine1*

```
admin@spine1> show route table bgp.evpn.0 evpn-mac-address 00:00:5e:00:01:01 evpn-ethernet-tag-id 10100 extensive

bgp.evpn.0: 18 destinations, 18 routes (18 active, 0 holddown, 0 hidden)
2:192.0.2.101:1::10100::00:00:5e:00:01:01/304 MAC/IP (1 entry, 1 announced)
TSI:
Page 0 idx 0, (group overlay type External) Type 1 val 0xeaacdd8 (adv_entry)
  Advertised metrics:
```

```
       Flags: Nexthop Change
       Nexthop: Self
       AS path: [65500] I
       Communities: target:100:100 encapsulation:vxlan(0x8) mac-mobility:0x1:sticky (sequence 0)
     Advertise: 00000003
Path 2:192.0.2.101:1::10100::00:00:5e:00:01:01
Vector len 4.  Val: 0
       *EVPN    Preference: 170
                Next hop type: Indirect, Next hop index: 0
                Address: 0xd32dd28
                Next-hop reference count: 26
                Protocol next hop: 192.0.2.101
                Indirect next hop: 0x0 - INH Session ID: 0
                State: <Secondary Active Int Ext>
                Age: 1:07:03
                Validation State: unverified
                Task: default-switch-evpn
                Announcement bits (1): 1-BGP_RT_Background
                AS path: I
                Communities: target:100:100 encapsulation:vxlan(0x8) mac-mobility:0x1:sticky (sequence 0)
                Route Label: 10100
                ESI: 05:00:00:ff:dc:00:00:27:74:00
                Primary Routing Table: default-switch.evpn.0
                Thread: junos-main


2:192.0.2.101:1::10100::00:00:5e:00:01:01::10.100.100.254/304 MAC/IP (1 entry, 1 announced)
TSI:
Page 0 idx 0, (group overlay type External) Type 1 val 0xeaacda0 (adv_entry)
   Advertised metrics:
     Flags: Nexthop Change
     Nexthop: Self
     AS path: [65500] I
     Communities: target:100:100 encapsulation:vxlan(0x8) mac-mobility:0x1:sticky (sequence 0)
     Advertise: 00000003
Path 2:192.0.2.101:1::10100::00:00:5e:00:01:01::10.100.100.254
Vector len 4.  Val: 0
       *EVPN    Preference: 170
                Next hop type: Indirect, Next hop index: 0
                Address: 0xd32dd28
                Next-hop reference count: 26
                Protocol next hop: 192.0.2.101
                Indirect next hop: 0x0 - INH Session ID: 0
                State: <Secondary Active Int Ext>
                Age: 1:07:03
                Validation State: unverified
                Task: default-switch-evpn
                Announcement bits (1): 1-BGP_RT_Background
                AS path: I
                Communities: target:100:100 encapsulation:vxlan(0x8) mac-mobility:0x1:sticky (sequence 0)
```

```
Route Label: 10100
ESI: 05:00:00:ff:dc:00:00:27:74:00
Primary Routing Table: default-switch.evpn.0
Thread: junos-main
```

As highlighted in Example 7-20, the EVPN Type-2 route for the virtual gateway address is advertised with an Ethernet Segment Identifier (ESI) attached to it. This is an auto-generated, Type-5 ESI, as described in RFC 7432. The ESI itself can be broken down as follows, adhering to the rules described in RFC 7432:

- **05:** The first octet of the ESI is set to 0x05, indicating that this is a Type-5 ESI.

- **0000ffdc:** These four octets represent the ASN. Since a two-octet ASN is used in our case, the higher order octets are 0x0000, following which the remaining two octets are used for the ASN. The spines are configured for AS 65500, which, in hex, is 0xffdc.

- **00002774:** The next four octets represent the local discriminator value. This is encoded with the VNI. The Type-2 route in question is for VNI 10100, which, in hex, is 0x00002774.

- **00:** The lower order octet is simply set to 0x00.

Attaching this ESI to the route provides the advantages of aliasing, which is commonly seen with EVPN multihoming (ESI LAG), discussed in detail in Chapter 5, "Bridged Overlay in an EVPN VXLAN Fabric." Pulling back the curtain a bit, spine2 is advertising the virtual gateway address with the same ESI (for the same VNI), as shown in Example 7-21.

Example 7-21 *Detailed output for EVPN Type-2 route for the virtual gateway address scoped for VNI 10100 on spine2*

```
admin@spine2> show route table bgp.evpn.0 evpn-mac-address 00:00:5e:00:01:01 evpn-ethernet-tag-id 10100 extensive

bgp.evpn.0: 18 destinations, 18 routes (18 active, 0 holddown, 0 hidden)
2:192.0.2.102:1::10100::00:00:5e:00:01:01/304 MAC/IP (1 entry, 1 announced)
TSI:
Page 0 idx 0, (group overlay type External) Type 1 val 0xeaa7f58 (adv_entry)
   Advertised metrics:
     Flags: Nexthop Change
     Nexthop: Self
     AS path: [65500] I
     Communities: target:100:100 encapsulation:vxlan(0x8) mac-mobility:0x1:sticky (sequence 0)
   Advertise: 00000003
Path 2:192.0.2.102:1::10100::00:00:5e:00:01:01
Vector len 4. Val: 0
        *EVPN   Preference: 170
                Next hop type: Indirect, Next hop index: 0
                Address: 0xd32dd28
                Next-hop reference count: 26
                Protocol next hop: 192.0.2.102
                Indirect next hop: 0x0 - INH Session ID: 0
                State: <Secondary Active Int Ext>
                Age: 2:57:16
                Validation State: unverified
                Task: default-switch-evpn
                Announcement bits (1): 1-BGP_RT_Background
                AS path: I
                Communities: target:100:100 encapsulation:vxlan(0x8) mac-mobility:0x1:sticky (sequence 0)
                Route Label: 10100
```

```
            ESI: 05:00:00:ff:dc:00:00:27:74:00
            Primary Routing Table: default-switch.evpn.0
            Thread: junos-main


2:192.0.2.102:1::10100::00:00:5e:00:01:01::10.100.100.254/304 MAC/IP (1 entry, 1 announced)
TSI:
Page 0 idx 0, (group overlay type External) Type 1 val 0xeaa7874 (adv_entry)
   Advertised metrics:
     Flags: Nexthop Change
     Nexthop: Self
     AS path: [65500] I
     Communities: target:100:100 encapsulation:vxlan(0x8) mac-mobility:0x1:sticky (sequence 0)
     Advertise: 00000003
Path 2:192.0.2.102:1::10100::00:00:5e:00:01:01::10.100.100.254
Vector len 4.  Val: 0
        *EVPN    Preference: 170
                 Next hop type: Indirect, Next hop index: 0
                 Address: 0xd32dd28
                 Next-hop reference count: 26
                 Protocol next hop: 192.0.2.102
                 Indirect next hop: 0x0 - INH Session ID: 0
                 State: <Secondary Active Int Ext>
                 Age: 2:57:16
                 Validation State: unverified
                 Task: default-switch-evpn
                 Announcement bits (1): 1-BGP_RT_Background
                 AS path: I
                 Communities: target:100:100 encapsulation:vxlan(0x8) mac-mobility:0x1:sticky (sequence 0)
                 Route Label: 10100
                 ESI: 05:00:00:ff:dc:00:00:27:74:00
                 Primary Routing Table: default-switch.evpn.0
                 Thread: junos-main
```

On the leafs, this virtual gateway MAC address is installed in the MAC address table with an egress/exit interface pointing to the ESI, instead of just a single VTEP next-hop ID, which is typically seen in EVPN VXLAN fabrics, thus leading to load-balancing in the overlay. This is shown in Example 7-22.

Example 7-22 *Virtual gateway address installed on leaf1*

```
admin@leaf1> show ethernet-switching table 00:00:5e:00:01:01


MAC flags (S - static MAC, D - dynamic MAC, L - locally learned, P - Persistent static
         SE - statistics enabled, NM - non configured MAC, R - remote PE MAC, O - ovsdb MAC)



Ethernet switching table : 4 entries, 4 learned
Routing instance : default-switch
    Vlan            MAC              MAC    Logical              SVLBNH/     Active
    name            address          flags  interface            VENH Index  source
    v100            00:00:5e:00:01:01 DRP   esi.1751                         05:00:00:ff:dc:00:00:27:74:00
```

From the output shown in Example 7-22, it is confirmed that the exit interface for this MAC address is an ESI. Looking closer in the EVPN database, as shown in Example 7-23, this ESI has two remote origins: spine1, identified by the IP address 192.0.2.101, and spine2, identified by the IP address 192.0.2.102.

Example 7-23 *EVPN database for the virtual gateway address on leaf1*

```
admin@leaf1> show evpn database mac-address 00:00:5e:00:01:01 l2-domain-id 10100 extensive
Instance: default-switch

VN Identifier: 10100, MAC address: 00:00:5e:00:01:01
  State: 0x0
  Source: 05:00:00:ff:dc:00:00:27:74:00, Rank: 1, Status: Active
  Remote origin: 192.0.2.101
  Remote state: <Mac-Only-Adv Pinned>
  Remote origin: 192.0.2.102
  Remote state: <Mac-Only-Adv Pinned>
  Mobility sequence number: 0 (minimum origin address 192.0.2.101)
  Timestamp: Apr 04 11:39:43.146756 (0x642c0c7f)
  State: <Remote-To-Local-Adv-Done Remote-Pinned>
  MAC advertisement route status: Not created (no local state present)
  IP address: 10.100.100.254
    Remote origin: 192.0.2.101
    Remote state: <Sent-to-l2ald>
    Remote origin: 192.0.2.102
    Remote state: <Sent-to-l2ald>
  History db:
    Time                    Event
    Apr  4 11:39:37.615 2023   05:00:00:ff:dc:00:00:27:74:00 : Remote peer 192.0.2.101 created
    Apr  4 11:39:37.615 2023   05:00:00:ff:dc:00:00:27:74:00 : Created
    Apr  4 11:39:37.616 2023   Updating output state (change flags 0x1 <ESI-Added>)
    Apr  4 11:39:37.616 2023   Active ESI changing (not assigned -> 05:00:00:ff:dc:00:00:27:74:00)
    Apr  4 11:39:43.146 2023   05:00:00:ff:dc:00:00:27:74:00 : Remote peer 192.0.2.102 created
    Apr  4 11:39:43.147 2023   05:00:00:ff:dc:00:00:27:74:00 : Updating output state (change flags 0x80 <ESI-Peer-
Added>)
```

This ESI provides overlay load-balancing by recursively resolving to all VTEPs advertising the ESI, which in this case are spine1 and spine2. The resolution of ESI to VTEP happens via EVPN Type-1 routes that the VTEPs are expected to originate for the respective ESI.

Spine1 and spine2 are indeed advertising these EVPN Type-1 routes to the leafs, as confirmed in Examples 7-24 and 7-25.

Example 7-24 *EVPN Type-1 routes from the spines on leaf1*

```
admin@leaf1> show route table bgp.evpn.0 match-prefix 1:*050000ffdc0000277400*

bgp.evpn.0: 30 destinations, 33 routes (30 active, 0 holddown, 0 hidden)
+ = Active Route, - = Last Active, * = Both

1:192.0.2.101:0::050000ffdc0000277400::FFFF:FFFF/192 AD/ESI
                   *[BGP/170] 1d 02:06:28, localpref 100, from 192.0.2.101
                     AS path: 65500 I, validation-state: unverified
                   >  to 198.51.100.1 via xe-0/0/0.0
```

```
1:192.0.2.102:0::050000ffdc0000277400::FFFF:FFFF/192 AD/ESI
                    *[BGP/170] 1d 02:06:23, localpref 100, from 192.0.2.102
                       AS path: 65500 I, validation-state: unverified
                    >  to 198.51.100.3 via xe-0/0/1.0
```

Example 7-25   *Detailed output of EVPN Type-1 routes from the spines on leaf1*

```
admin@leaf1> show route table bgp.evpn.0 match-prefix 1:*050000ffdc0000277400* extensive

bgp.evpn.0: 30 destinations, 33 routes (30 active, 0 holddown, 0 hidden)
1:192.0.2.101:0::050000ffdc0000277400::FFFF:FFFF/192 AD/ESI (1 entry, 0 announced)
        *BGP    Preference: 170/-101
                Route Distinguisher: 192.0.2.101:0
                Next hop type: Indirect, Next hop index: 0
                Address: 0xd32e0f4
                Next-hop reference count: 19
                Source: 192.0.2.101
                Protocol next hop: 192.0.2.101
                Indirect next hop: 0x2 no-forward INH Session ID: 0
                State: <Active Ext>
                Local AS: 65421 Peer AS: 65500
                Age: 1d 2:07:18  Metric2: 0
                Validation State: unverified
                Task: BGP_65500.192.0.2.101
                AS path: 65500 I
                Communities: target:1:1 encapsulation:vxlan(0x8) esi-label:0x0:all-active (label 0)
                Import Accepted
                Localpref: 100
                Router ID: 192.0.2.101
                Secondary Tables: default-switch.evpn.0
                Thread: junos-main
                Indirect next hops: 1
                        Protocol next hop: 192.0.2.101
                        Indirect next hop: 0x2 no-forward INH Session ID: 0
                        Indirect path forwarding next hops: 1
                            Next hop type: Router
                            Next hop: 198.51.100.1 via xe-0/0/0.0
                            Session Id: 141
                            192.0.2.101/32 Originating RIB: inet.0
                              Node path count: 1
                              Forwarding nexthops: 1
                                    Next hop type: Router
                                    Next hop: 198.51.100.1 via xe-0/0/0.0
                                    Session Id: 141

1:192.0.2.102:0::050000ffdc0000277400::FFFF:FFFF/192 AD/ESI (1 entry, 0 announced)
        *BGP    Preference: 170/-101
                Route Distinguisher: 192.0.2.102:0
                Next hop type: Indirect, Next hop index: 0
                Address: 0xd32dfb0
                Next-hop reference count: 19
                Source: 192.0.2.102
```

```
        Protocol next hop: 192.0.2.102
        Indirect next hop: 0x2 no-forward INH Session ID: 0
        State: <Active Ext>
        Local AS: 65421 Peer AS: 65500
        Age: 1d 2:07:13  Metric2: 0
        Validation State: unverified
        Task: BGP_65500.192.0.2.102
        AS path: 65500 I
        Communities: target:1:1 encapsulation:vxlan(0x8) esi-label:0x0:all-active (label 0)
        Import Accepted
        Localpref: 100
        Router ID: 192.0.2.102
        Secondary Tables: default-switch.evpn.0
        Thread: junos-main
        Indirect next hops: 1
                Protocol next hop: 192.0.2.102
                Indirect next hop: 0x2 no-forward INH Session ID: 0
                Indirect path forwarding next hops: 1
                        Next hop type: Router
                        Next hop: 198.51.100.3 via xe-0/0/1.0
                        Session Id: 140
                        192.0.2.102/32 Originating RIB: inet.0
                          Node path count: 1
                          Forwarding nexthops: 1
                                Next hop type: Router
                                Next hop: 198.51.100.3 via xe-0/0/1.0
                                Session Id: 140
```

EVPN Type-1 routes use the globally configured Route Target, and thus are sent with a Route Target of 1:1, which was configured under the *switch-options* hierarchy shown earlier in Example 7-17. Because the leafs also have the same Route Target configured under their *switch-options* hierarchy, an implicit internal policy is created to import EVPN routes with this Route Target. Such policies are prefixed and suffixed with two underscores, as shown in Example 7-26.

Example 7-26 *Policy to import EVPN routes with a Route Target of 1:1 on leaf1*

```
admin@leaf1> show policy
Configured policies:
ECMP
__evpn-export-default-switch-bd-override-10100-internal__
__evpn-import-autoderive-default-switch-internal__
__vrf-export-default-switch-internal__
__vrf-import-__default_evpn__-internal__
__vrf-import-default-switch-internal__
allow-loopback

admin@leaf1> show policy __vrf-import-default-switch-internal__
Policy __vrf-import-default-switch-internal__:  [RESOLVED/]
    Term unnamed:
        from community __vrf-community-default-switch-common-internal__ [target:1:1 ]
        then accept
    Term unnamed:
        then reject
```

When successfully imported, the route is pulled into the *default-switch* EVPN table of the leaf, called default-switch.evpn.0, and the ESI can now be resolved into remote VTEPs, as shown in Example 7-27, using the **show ethernet-switching vxlan-tunnel-end-point esi esi-identifier** [*esi-value*] operational mode command. This command displays all VTEPs for which an EVPN Type-1 route was received, and successfully imported, for a particular ESI.

Example 7-27   *ESI resolution to remote VTEPs on leaf1*

```
admin@leaf1> show route table default-switch.evpn.0 match-prefix 1:*050000ffdc0000277400*

default-switch.evpn.0: 17 destinations, 17 routes (17 active, 0 holddown, 0 hidden)
+ = Active Route, - = Last Active, * = Both

1:192.0.2.101:0::050000ffdc0000277400::FFFF:FFFF/192 AD/ESI
                  *[BGP/170] 1d 03:11:08, localpref 100, from 192.0.2.101
                    AS path: 65500 I, validation-state: unverified
                  > to 198.51.100.1 via xe-0/0/0.0
1:192.0.2.102:0::050000ffdc0000277400::FFFF:FFFF/192 AD/ESI
                  *[BGP/170] 1d 03:11:03, localpref 100, from 192.0.2.102
                    AS path: 65500 I, validation-state: unverified
                  > to 198.51.100.3 via xe-0/0/1.0


admin@leaf1> show ethernet-switching vxlan-tunnel-end-point esi esi-identifier 05:00:00:ff:dc:00:00:27:74:00
ESI                           RTT                VLNBH INH   ESI-IFL   LOC-IFL   #RVTEPs
05:00:00:ff:dc:00:00:27:74:00 default-switch     1751  131071 esi.1751           2
    RVTEP-IP              RVTEP-IFL      VENH    MASK-ID  FLAGS       MAC-COUNT
    192.0.2.102           vtep.32770     1754    1        2           1
    192.0.2.101           vtep.32769     1749    0        2           1
```

To add the globally configured Route Target to EVPN Type-1 routes as they are advertised to BGP EVPN peers, an implicit internal export policy is automatically created, as shown in Example 7-28.

Example 7-28   *Policy to export EVPN routes with a Route Target of 1:1 on spine1*

```
admin@spine1> show policy __vrf-export-default-switch-internal__
Policy __vrf-export-default-switch-internal__: [RESOLVED/]
    Term unnamed:
        then community + __vrf-community-default-switch-common-internal__ [target:1:1 ] accept
```

Import of these EVPN Type-1 routes is critical to the functionality of CRB. If there was a mismatch, and the leafs were unable to import the Type-1 route, the virtual gateway address would not be installed in the MAC address table, despite receiving an EVPN Type-2 route for the same. This is because the EVPN Type-2 routes are advertised with an ESI attached to them, and since the ESI cannot be resolved into remote VTEPs, the virtual MAC address cannot be installed in the MAC address table.

Understanding the behavior when things are broken is important, so let's simulate this problem state now. On leaf1, a mismatch in Route Targets is created on purpose, which causes the EVPN Type-1 route for the ESI not to be imported. The incorrect Route Target is shown in Example 7-29.

Example 7-29   *Route Target changed to 1:2 on leaf1 to create a mismatch*

```
admin@leaf1# show switch-options
vtep-source-interface lo0.0;
route-distinguisher 192.0.2.11:1;
vrf-target target:1:2;
```

EVPN Type-1 routes are still being received from the spines, but notice that they are no longer marked as *Import Accepted*, as seen previously during steady state. It just says that it is *Accepted* into BGP RIB-In, which is the bgp.evpn.0 table, as shown in Example 7-30. This means that the route, while present in the bgp.evpn.0 table, is not imported in the default-switch.evpn.0 table, and hence the ESI is not resolved into any VTEP.

Example 7-30 *EVPN Type-1 routes not imported on leaf1*

```
admin@leaf1> show route table bgp.evpn.0 match-prefix 1:*050000ffdc0000277400*

bgp.evpn.0: 30 destinations, 33 routes (30 active, 0 holddown, 0 hidden)
+ = Active Route, - = Last Active, * = Both


1:192.0.2.101:0::050000ffdc0000277400::FFFF:FFFF/192 AD/ESI
                    *[BGP/170] 1d 03:17:38, localpref 100, from 192.0.2.101
                      AS path: 65500 I, validation-state: unverified
                    >  to 198.51.100.1 via xe-0/0/0.0
1:192.0.2.102:0::050000ffdc0000277400::FFFF:FFFF/192 AD/ESI
                    *[BGP/170] 1d 03:17:33, localpref 100, from 192.0.2.102
                      AS path: 65500 I, validation-state: unverified
                    >  to 198.51.100.3 via xe-0/0/1.0


admin@leaf1> show route table bgp.evpn.0 match-prefix 1:*050000ffdc0000277400* extensive

bgp.evpn.0: 30 destinations, 33 routes (30 active, 0 holddown, 0 hidden)
1:192.0.2.101:0::050000ffdc0000277400::FFFF:FFFF/192 AD/ESI (1 entry, 0 announced)
        *BGP    Preference: 170/-101
                Route Distinguisher: 192.0.2.101:0
                Next hop type: Indirect, Next hop index: 0
                Address: 0xd32e0f4
                Next-hop reference count: 17
                Source: 192.0.2.101
                Protocol next hop: 192.0.2.101
                Indirect next hop: 0x2 no-forward INH Session ID: 0
                State: <Active Ext>
                Local AS: 65421 Peer AS: 65500
                Age: 1d 3:20:19  Metric2: 0
                Validation State: unverified
                Task: BGP_65500.192.0.2.101
                AS path: 65500 I
                Communities: target:1:1 encapsulation:vxlan(0x8) esi-label:0x0:all-active (label 0)
                Accepted
                Localpref: 100
                Router ID: 192.0.2.101
                Thread: junos-main
                Indirect next hops: 1
                        Protocol next hop: 192.0.2.101
                        Indirect next hop: 0x2 no-forward INH Session ID: 0
                        Indirect path forwarding next hops: 1
                                Next hop type: Router
                                Next hop: 198.51.100.1 via xe-0/0/0.0
                                Session Id: 141
```

```
                              192.0.2.101/32 Originating RIB: inet.0
                                Node path count: 1
                                Forwarding nexthops: 1
                                        Next hop type: Router
                                        Next hop: 198.51.100.1 via xe-0/0/0.0
                                        Session Id: 141


1:192.0.2.102:0::050000ffdc0000277400::FFFF:FFFF/192 AD/ESI (1 entry, 0 announced)
        *BGP     Preference: 170/-101
                 Route Distinguisher: 192.0.2.102:0
                 Next hop type: Indirect, Next hop index: 0
                 Address: 0xd32dfb0
                 Next-hop reference count: 17
                 Source: 192.0.2.102
                 Protocol next hop: 192.0.2.102
                 Indirect next hop: 0x2 no-forward INH Session ID: 0
                 State: <Active Ext>
                 Local AS: 65421 Peer AS: 65500
                 Age: 1d 3:20:14 Metric2: 0
                 Validation State: unverified
                 Task: BGP_65500.192.0.2.102
                 AS path: 65500 I
                 Communities: target:1:1 encapsulation:vxlan(0x8) esi-label:0x0:all-active (label 0)
                 Accepted
                 Localpref: 100
                 Router ID: 192.0.2.102
                 Thread: junos-main
                 Indirect next hops: 1
                         Protocol next hop: 192.0.2.102
                         Indirect next hop: 0x2 no-forward INH Session ID: 0
                         Indirect path forwarding next hops: 1
                                 Next hop type: Router
                                 Next hop: 198.51.100.3 via xe-0/0/1.0
                                 Session Id: 140
                         192.0.2.102/32 Originating RIB: inet.0
                           Node path count: 1
                           Forwarding nexthops: 1
                                   Next hop type: Router
                                   Next hop: 198.51.100.3 via xe-0/0/1.0
                                   Session Id: 140
```

Since these routes are not imported into the default-switch.evpn.0 table, and the ESI remains unresolved, the virtual gateway address exists in the EVPN database but is not installed in the MAC address table, as shown in Example 7-31.

Example 7-31 *Missing virtual gateway address in the MAC table*

```
admin@leaf1> show evpn database mac-address 00:00:5e:00:01:01 extensive
Instance: default-switch
```

```
VN Identifier: 10100, MAC address: 00:00:5e:00:01:01
  State: 0x0
  Source: 05:00:00:ff:dc:00:00:27:74:00, Rank: 1, Status: Active
    Remote origin: 192.0.2.101
    Remote state: <Mac-Only-Adv Pinned>
    Remote origin: 192.0.2.102
    Remote state: <Mac-Only-Adv Pinned>
    Mobility sequence number: 0 (minimum origin address 192.0.2.101)
    Timestamp: Apr 04 11:39:43.146756 (0x642c0c7f)
    State: <Remote-To-Local-Adv-Done Remote-Pinned>
    MAC advertisement route status: Not created (no local state present)
    IP address: 10.100.100.254
      Remote origin: 192.0.2.101
      Remote state: <Sent-to-l2ald>
      Remote origin: 192.0.2.102
      Remote state: <Sent-to-l2ald>
    History db:
      Time                    Event
      Apr  4 11:39:37.615 2023    05:00:00:ff:dc:00:00:27:74:00 : Remote peer 192.0.2.101 created
      Apr  4 11:39:37.615 2023    05:00:00:ff:dc:00:00:27:74:00 : Created
      Apr  4 11:39:37.616 2023    Updating output state (change flags 0x1 <ESI-Added>)
      Apr  4 11:39:37.616 2023    Active ESI changing (not assigned -> 05:00:00:ff:dc:00:00:27:74:00)
      Apr  4 11:39:43.146 2023    05:00:00:ff:dc:00:00:27:74:00 : Remote peer 192.0.2.102 created
      Apr  4 11:39:43.147 2023    05:00:00:ff:dc:00:00:27:74:00 : Updating output state (change flags 0x80 <ESI-Peer-Added>)


admin@leaf1> show route table default-switch.evpn.0 match-prefix 1:*050000ffdc0000277400*


default-switch.evpn.0: 13 destinations, 13 routes (13 active, 0 holddown, 0 hidden)


<no output>


admin@leaf1> show ethernet-switching vxlan-tunnel-end-point esi


<no output>


admin@leaf1> show ethernet-switching table


MAC flags (S - static MAC, D - dynamic MAC, L - locally learned, P - Persistent static
          SE - statistics enabled, NM - non configured MAC, R - remote PE MAC, O - ovsdb MAC)



Ethernet switching table : 3 entries, 3 learned
Routing instance : default-switch
  Vlan          MAC              MAC    Logical            SVLBNH/     Active
  name          address          flags  interface          VENH Index  source
  v100          02:05:86:71:69:00 DRP   vtep.32770                     192.0.2.102
  v100          02:05:86:71:cd:00 DRP   vtep.32769                     192.0.2.101
  v100          aa:c1:ab:65:28:85  D    xe-0/0/2.0
```

A consequence of this is that any traffic, from the host, that needs to be routed (essentially traffic destined to the virtual gateway MAC address, 00:00:5e:00:01:01) will be unknown unicast flooded using ingress replication, since the MAC address is missing in the MAC address table.

Importance of "Sticky" MACs for Virtual Gateway and IRB Addresses

In the context of BGP EVPN, this section explores the concept of a *sticky* MAC address, and why it is needed. Let's take another look at the EVPN Type-2 routes that the spines advertised to the leafs for the virtual gateway address, as shown in Example 7-32 again.

Example 7-32   *Detailed output for EVPN Type-2 route for the virtual gateway address scoped for VNI 10100 on spine1*

```
admin@spine1> show route table bgp.evpn.0 evpn-mac-address 00:00:5e:00:01:01 evpn-ethernet-tag-id 10100 extensive

bgp.evpn.0: 18 destinations, 18 routes (18 active, 0 holddown, 0 hidden)
2:192.0.2.101:1::10100::00:00:5e:00:01:01/304 MAC/IP (1 entry, 1 announced)
TSI:
Page 0 idx 0, (group overlay type External) Type 1 val 0xeaacdd8 (adv_entry)
   Advertised metrics:
     Flags: Nexthop Change
     Nexthop: Self
     AS path: [65500] I
     Communities: target:100:100 encapsulation:vxlan(0x8) mac-mobility:0x1:sticky (sequence 0)
     Advertise: 00000003
Path 2:192.0.2.101:1::10100::00:00:5e:00:01:01
Vector len 4.  Val: 0
        *EVPN    Preference: 170
                 Next hop type: Indirect, Next hop index: 0
                 Address: 0xd32dd28
                 Next-hop reference count: 26
                 Protocol next hop: 192.0.2.101
                 Indirect next hop: 0x0 - INH Session ID: 0
                 State: <Secondary Active Int Ext>
                 Age: 1:07:03
                 Validation State: unverified
                 Task: default-switch-evpn
                 Announcement bits (1): 1-BGP_RT_Background
                 AS path: I
                 Communities: target:100:100 encapsulation:vxlan(0x8) mac-mobility:0x1:sticky (sequence 0)
                 Route Label: 10100
                 ESI: 05:00:00:ff:dc:00:00:27:74:00
                 Primary Routing Table: default-switch.evpn.0
                 Thread: junos-main

2:192.0.2.101:1::10100::00:00:5e:00:01:01::10.100.100.254/304 MAC/IP (1 entry, 1 announced)
TSI:
Page 0 idx 0, (group overlay type External) Type 1 val 0xeaacda0 (adv_entry)
   Advertised metrics:
     Flags: Nexthop Change
     Nexthop: Self
     AS path: [65500] I
```

```
        Communities: target:100:100 encapsulation:vxlan(0x8) mac-mobility:0x1:sticky (sequence 0)
    Advertise: 00000003
Path 2:192.0.2.101:1::10100::00:00:5e:00:01:01::10.100.100.254
Vector len 4. Val: 0
        *EVPN    Preference: 170
                 Next hop type: Indirect, Next hop index: 0
                 Address: 0xd32dd28
                 Next-hop reference count: 26
                 Protocol next hop: 192.0.2.101
                 Indirect next hop: 0x0 - INH Session ID: 0
                 State: <Secondary Active Int Ext>
                 Age: 1:07:03
                 Validation State: unverified
                 Task: default-switch-evpn
                 Announcement bits (1): 1-BGP_RT_Background
                 AS path: I
                 Communities: target:100:100 encapsulation:vxlan(0x8) mac-mobility:0x1:sticky (sequence 0)
                 Route Label: 10100
                 ESI: 05:00:00:ff:dc:00:00:27:74:00
                 Primary Routing Table: default-switch.evpn.0
                 Thread: junos-main
```

In the MAC Mobility community shown in Example 7-32, the *sticky* bit is set. The lower order bit of the 1-octet *Flags* field in the MAC Mobility community is reserved for marking the address as sticky/static, as per RFC 7432. These addresses are also advertised with a sequence number of 0. The packet capture presented in Figure 7-8 shows this sticky bit in more detail.

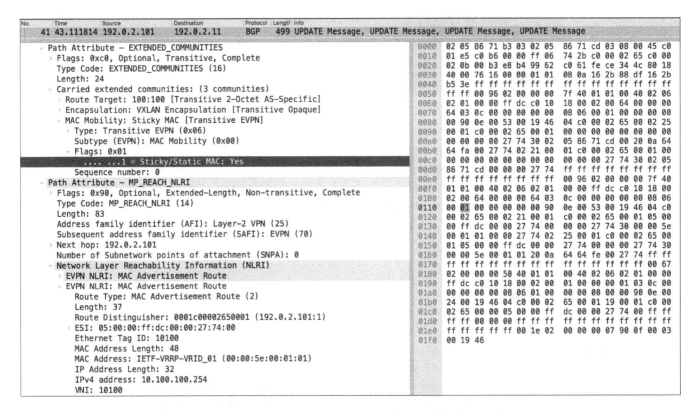

Figure 7-8 *Packet capture showing sticky bit set for virtual gateway address in the advertised EVPN Type-2 route*

This is a security mechanism to prevent rogue users from hijacking gateway addresses and pulling traffic toward themselves. When the CRB spines advertise this virtual gateway address to the leafs, this is dynamically learned via the control plane, on receipt of the EVPN Type-2 route. There is a possibility that a user connected to the leaf can spoof this virtual address, resulting in this user becoming a gateway for the entire data center.

With the sticky bit set, when the leaf receives this update, it installs the MAC address in its table with a *Persistent static* or *P* flag set, and "pins" it to the source that advertised it in the EVPN database, as shown in Example 7-33.

Example 7-33   *Persistent static flag set for the virtual gateway MAC address on leaf1*

```
admin@leaf1> show ethernet-switching table

MAC flags (S - static MAC, D - dynamic MAC, L - locally learned, P - Persistent static
          SE - statistics enabled, NM - non configured MAC, R - remote PE MAC, O - ovsdb MAC)


Ethernet switching table : 4 entries, 4 learned
Routing instance : default-switch
   Vlan            MAC                MAC     Logical           SVLBNH/      Active
   name            address            flags   interface         VENH Index   source
   v100            00:00:5e:00:01:01  DRP     esi.1755                       05:00:00:ff:dc:00:00:27:74:00
   v100            02:05:86:71:69:00  DRP     vtep.32770                     192.0.2.102
   v100            02:05:86:71:cd:00  DRP     vtep.32769                     192.0.2.101
   v100            aa:c1:ab:65:28:85  D       xe-0/0/2.0

admin@leaf1> show evpn database mac-address 00:00:5e:00:01:01 l2-domain-id 10100 extensive
Instance: default-switch


VN Identifier: 10100, MAC address: 00:00:5e:00:01:01
  State: 0x0
  Source: 05:00:00:ff:dc:00:00:27:74:00, Rank: 1, Status: Active
    Remote origin: 192.0.2.101
    Remote state: <Mac-Only-Adv Pinned>
    Remote origin: 192.0.2.102
    Remote state: <Mac-Only-Adv Pinned>
    Mobility sequence number: 0 (minimum origin address 192.0.2.101)
    Timestamp: Apr 10 02:36:38.792914 (0x64337636)
    State: <Remote-To-Local-Adv-Done Remote-Pinned>
    MAC advertisement route status: Not created (no local state present)
    IP address: 10.100.100.254
      Remote origin: 192.0.2.101
      Remote state: <Sent-to-l2ald>
      Remote origin: 192.0.2.102
      Remote state: <Sent-to-l2ald>
    History db:
      Time                      Event
      Apr 10 02:36:38.530 2023  05:00:00:ff:dc:00:00:27:74:00 : Created
      Apr 10 02:36:38.531 2023  Updating output state (change flags 0x1 <ESI-Added>)
      Apr 10 02:36:38.531 2023  Active ESI changing (xe-0/0/2.0 -> 05:00:00:ff:dc:00:00:27:74:00)
      Apr 10 02:36:38.792 2023  05:00:00:ff:dc:00:00:27:74:00 : Remote peer 192.0.2.102 created
      Apr 10 02:36:38.795 2023  Updating output state (change flags 0x1 <ESI-Added>)
      Apr 10 02:36:38.795 2023  05:00:00:ff:dc:00:00:27:74:00 : Updating output state (change flags 0x80 <ESI-Peer-Added>)
```

It is crucial to understand that just ensuring EVPN does not allow such MAC addresses to be learned from anywhere else is insufficient. The reason for this is rooted in how such learning occurs. Taking the example of a typical leaf, such as a Juniper QFX5120, a data plane learn of a MAC address (source MAC address learned from an ARP packet, as an example) first happens in the hardware and Packet Forwarding Engine (PFE) complex. The Layer 2 Address Learning Manager (L2ALM) in the PFE informs the Layer 2 Address Learning Daemon (L2ALD) in the Routing Engine, which then informs the Routing Protocol Daemon (RPD) in the Routing Engine for EVPN.

Thus, there are two learning paths to protect here, which are equally important:

■ EVPN, naturally, to ensure that a rogue user cannot take over this virtual gateway address, which has fabric-wide impact (since if EVPN elects it as the best source for that MAC address, it will advertise it to all its neighbors and, eventually, other leafs will elect it as the best source too); secondly, which is equally important.

■ The leaf, to ensure that it does not accept any data-learn events for a sticky MAC address (that is pinned to a remote source/port) and program it against the incoming interface. This protects all devices connected to the local leaf from potentially using the rogue user as a gateway.

While the first issue is straightforward, the second issue is a little more interesting, so let's simulate that. Consider a situation in which a leaf can incorrectly learn the virtual gateway address via a data plane learn, while EVPN continues to correctly use the virtual MAC address advertised by the spines. The leaf has all the correct entries in the MAC address table during steady state, as shown in Example 7-34.

Example 7-34 *MAC table during steady state on leaf1*

```
admin@leaf1> show ethernet-switching table

MAC flags (S - static MAC, D - dynamic MAC, L - locally learned, P - Persistent static
          SE - statistics enabled, NM - non configured MAC, R - remote PE MAC, O - ovsdb MAC)



Ethernet switching table : 3 entries, 3 learned
Routing instance : default-switch
    Vlan          MAC               MAC    Logical         SVLBNH/      Active
    name          address           flags  interface       VENH Index   source
    v100          00:00:5e:00:01:01 DRP    esi.1753                     05:00:00:ff:dc:00:00:27:74:00
    v100          02:05:86:71:1c:00 DRP    vtep.32771                   192.0.2.102
    v100          02:05:86:71:72:00 DRP    vtep.32769                   192.0.2.101
```

During this time, a rogue user, connected to interface xe-0/0/2 on leaf1, spoofs the virtual gateway MAC address. The leaf incorrectly updates its MAC table and accepts this data plane learn, changing the address from an ESI-based exit interface to the local interface instead. This updated MAC address state is shown in Example 7-35.

Example 7-35 *MAC table incorrectly updated on leaf1*

```
admin@leaf1> show ethernet-switching table

MAC flags (S - static MAC, D - dynamic MAC, L - locally learned, P - Persistent static
          SE - statistics enabled, NM - non configured MAC, R - remote PE MAC, O - ovsdb MAC)



Ethernet switching table : 3 entries, 3 learned
Routing instance : default-switch
    Vlan          MAC               MAC    Logical         SVLBNH/      Active
    name          address           flags  interface       VENH Index   source
    v100          00:00:5e:00:01:01 D      xe-0/0/2.0
    v100          02:05:86:71:1c:00 DRP    vtep.32771                   192.0.2.102
    v100          02:05:86:71:72:00 DRP    vtep.32769                   192.0.2.101
```

The EVPN database, on the other hand, does not select this new source as the active source because the spines sent the virtual gateway address with the sticky bit set, giving them higher priority in the selection criteria, and thus the ESI from the spines (for this virtual address) continues to be the active source, as shown in Example 7-36.

Example 7-36 *EVPN database on leaf1 with ESI as active source*

```
admin@leaf1> show evpn database mac-address 00:00:5e:00:01:01 extensive l2-domain-id 10100
Instance: default-switch

VN Identifier: 10100, MAC address: 00:00:5e:00:01:01
  State: 0x0
  Mobility history
    Mobility event time    Type    Source                          Seq num
    Apr 09 15:57:03.581204  Local   xe-0/0/2.0                      1
  Source: 05:00:00:ff:dc:00:00:27:74:00, Rank: 1, Status: Active
    Remote origin: 192.0.2.101
    Remote state: <Mac-Only-Adv Pinned>
    Remote origin: 192.0.2.102
    Remote state: <Mac-Only-Adv Pinned>
    Mobility sequence number: 0 (minimum origin address 192.0.2.101)
    Timestamp: Apr 09 02:08:12.106390 (0x64321e0c)
    State: <Remote-To-Local-Adv-Done Remote-Pinned>
    MAC advertisement route status: Not created (no local state present)
    IP address: 10.100.100.254
      Remote origin: 192.0.2.101
      Remote state: <Sent-to-l2ald>
      Remote origin: 192.0.2.102
      Remote state: <Sent-to-l2ald>
  Source: xe-0/0/2.0, Rank: 2, Status: Inactive
    Mobility sequence number: 1 (minimum origin address 192.0.2.11)
    Timestamp: Apr 09 15:57:03.438672 (0x6432e04f)
    State: <Local-MAC-Only Local-To-Remote-Adv-Allowed>
    MAC advertisement route status: Not created (inactive source)
    IP address: 10.100.100.1
    Flags: <Local-Adv>
    IP address: 10.100.100.254
    Flags: <Local-Adv>
    History db:
      Time                    Event
      Apr  9 02:08:11.851 2023  Active ESI changing (xe-0/0/2.0 -> 05:00:00:ff:dc:00:00:27:74:00)
      Apr  9 02:08:12.106 2023  05:00:00:ff:dc:00:00:27:74:00 : Remote peer 192.0.2.102 created
      Apr  9 02:08:12.127 2023  Updating output state (change flags 0x1 <ESI-Added>)
      Apr  9 02:08:12.127 2023  05:00:00:ff:dc:00:00:27:74:00 : Updating output state (change flags 0x80 <ESI-Peer-
Added>)
      Apr  9 02:08:12.347 2023  xe-0/0/2.0 : 10.100.100.254 Deleting
      Apr  9 02:08:12.347 2023  xe-0/0/2.0 : Deleting
      Apr  9 02:08:12.347 2023  Updating output state (change flags 0x2 <ESI-Deleted>)
      Apr  9 15:57:03.438 2023  Mobility event for local source xe-0/0/2.0 with sequence number 1
      Apr  9 15:57:03.438 2023  xe-0/0/2.0 : Created
      Apr  9 15:57:03.438 2023  Updating output state (change flags 0x1 <ESI-Added>)
```

Because this new learn was never made the active source, leaf1 does not advertise this change to other leafs. From the perspective of EVPN on leaf1, nothing really changed.

This is why this issue is not as easily visible: it does not have fabric-wide impact, and only affects the leaf where the rogue device is connected. Other hosts connected to this leaf will start using this rogue user as the gateway now, but hosts behind other leafs remain unimpacted. This issue was simulated by bypassing certain checks in code, purely for educational purposes, and does not exist in publicly available Junos software.

Historical (and Present Day) Relevance of proxy-macip-advertisement

From the earlier section "Configuring a Centrally Routed Bridging EVPN VXLAN Fabric," the spines have the configuration for the IRB interfaces (example from spine1) shown in Example 7-37.

Example 7-37 *Configuration of IRB interfaces on spine1*

```
admin@spine1# show interfaces irb
unit 100 {
    proxy-macip-advertisement;
    virtual-gateway-accept-data;
    family inet {
        address 10.100.100.250/24 {
            virtual-gateway-address 10.100.100.254;
        }
    }
}
unit 200 {
    proxy-macip-advertisement;
    virtual-gateway-accept-data;
    family inet {
        address 10.100.200.250/24 {
            virtual-gateway-address 10.100.200.254;
        }
    }
}
```

The configuration option *proxy-macip-advertisement* has some interesting history, which is important to understand because its use has changed over time, and the reason it is used today differs from why it was used earlier. Let's go back in time, shall we?

This command was first released in 2015–2016, and its use was to fix a simple problem that most centralized routing solutions have: syncing state between redundant gateways. Back then, there was no ARP suppression, and the L2-only leafs could generate only EVPN Type-2 MAC routes (no EVPN Type-2 MAC+IP routes were generated). The EVPN Type-2 MAC+IP route is significant because it allows Layer 3–capable VXLAN devices to build their ARP tables and prepopulate MAC+IP bindings. Lack thereof means that the ARP cache can only be built using actual inbound ARP packets in the data plane.

Let's consider an example of host h1, connected to leaf1, in a CRB fabric, as shown in Figure 7-9. Once the host comes online, leaf1 learns its MAC address (from a packet like GARP), installs it in the MAC address table against the interface and VLAN on which the learn occurred, and then generates an EVPN Type-2 MAC route that is sent to both spines via BGP EVPN.

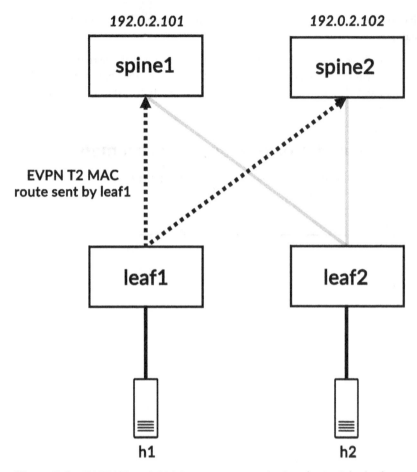

Figure 7-9   *EVPN Type-2 MAC route sent to spine1 and spine2 by leaf1*

The locally learned MAC address in the MAC address table of leaf1 is shown in Example 7-38, while the BGP EVPN advertisement from the leaf to both spines is shown in Example 7-39, using the **show route table bgp.evpn.0 advertising-protocol bgp** [*neighbor-address*] operational mode command.

Example 7-38   *Host h1's MAC address learned on leaf1*

```
admin@leaf1> show ethernet-switching table 08:00:27:29:c8:72

MAC flags (S - static MAC, D - dynamic MAC, L - locally learned, P - Persistent static
          SE - statistics enabled, NM - non configured MAC, R - remote PE MAC, O - ovsdb MAC)


Ethernet switching table : 4 entries, 4 learned
Routing instance : default-switch
    Vlan            MAC              MAC     Logical          Active
    name            address          flags   interface        source
    v100            08:00:27:29:c8:72   D      xe-0/0/2.0
```

Example 7-39   *leaf1 advertising h1's MAC address as an EVPN Type-2 MAC route to both spines*

```
admin@leaf1> show route table bgp.evpn.0 advertising-protocol bgp 192.0.2.101 evpn-mac-address 08:00:27:29:c8:72

bgp.evpn.0: 27 destinations, 29 routes (27 active, 0 holddown, 0 hidden)
```

```
     Prefix     Nexthop         MED     Lclpref    AS path
     2:192.0.2.11:1::10100::08:00:27:29:c8:72/304
*                         Self                                    I


admin@leaf1> show route table bgp.evpn.0 advertising-protocol bgp 192.0.2.102 evpn-mac-address 08:00:27:29:c8:72


bgp.evpn.0: 27 destinations, 29 routes (27 active, 0 holddown, 0 hidden)
     Prefix     Nexthop         MED     Lclpref    AS path
     2:192.0.2.11:1::10100::08:00:27:29:c8:72/304
*                         Self                                    I
```

Both spines install this address in their respective MAC address tables, with leaf1 as the destination VTEP behind which this host resides. Their ARP caches, however, remain empty because there is no information about which IP address is bound to this MAC address (due to the lack of an EVPN Type-2 MAC+IP route). The installation of the host MAC address on both spines is shown in Example 7-40.

Example 7-40 *Host h1's address in the MAC address table of spine1 and spine2*

```
admin@spine1> show ethernet-switching table 08:00:27:29:c8:72


MAC flags (S - static MAC, D - dynamic MAC, L - locally learned, P - Persistent static
          SE - statistics enabled, NM - non configured MAC, R - remote PE MAC, O - ovsdb MAC)



Ethernet switching table : 3 entries, 3 learned
Routing instance : default-switch
    Vlan            MAC              MAC     Logical          Active
    name            address          flags   interface        source
    v100            08:00:27:29:c8:72  D       vtep.32769       192.0.2.11


admin@spine2> show ethernet-switching table 08:00:27:29:c8:72


MAC flags (S - static MAC, D - dynamic MAC, L - locally learned, P - Persistent static
          SE - statistics enabled, NM - non configured MAC, R - remote PE MAC, O - ovsdb MAC)



Ethernet switching table : 3 entries, 3 learned
Routing instance : default-switch
    Vlan            MAC              MAC     Logical          Active
    name            address          flags   interface        source
    v100            08:00:27:29:c8:72  D       vtep.32769       192.0.2.11
```

When host h1 wants to communicate with host h2, it ARPs for its default gateway, which is the virtual IP address, 10.100.100.254, configured on both spines. This ARP packet will be hashed to one of the two available links—toward either spine1 or spine2. If the link toward spine1 is chosen, spine1 will receive this ARP request, as shown in Figure 7-10. Once it is processed, spine1 will respond with an ARP reply. At the same time, it will add this MAC-to-IP binding in its ARP table.

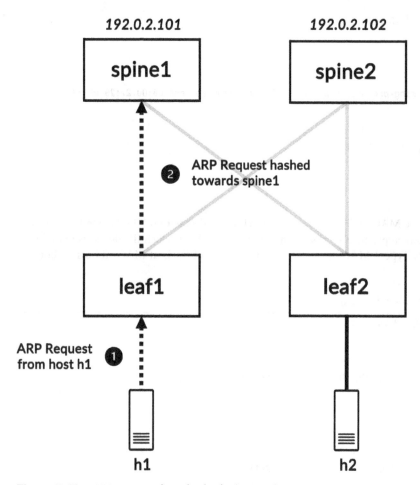

Figure 7-10 *ARP request from h1 hashed toward spine1*

Since spine2 never received this ARP request, it has no knowledge of the MAC-to-IP binding for host h1, and thus its ARP cache does not have this entry, as confirmed in Example 7-41, using the **show arp hostname** [*ip-address*] operational mode command.

Example 7-41 *Missing ARP entry for host h1 on spine2*

```
admin@spine1> show arp hostname 10.100.100.1

MAC Address       Address        Name             Interface             Flags
08:00:27:29:c8:72 10.100.100.1   10.100.100.1     irb.100 [vtep.32769]  none


admin@spine2> show arp hostname 10.100.100.1


<no output>
```

While in this state, it is possible for return traffic from host h2 to get hashed to spine2. Since spine2 does not have an ARP entry for host h1, it must resolve it by generating an ARP request. This causes a small loss in traffic forwarding while the ARP process completes. This problem can be fixed by syncing ARP state between the spines, and this is exactly why the configuration option *proxy-macip-advertisement* was introduced.

Considering the same situation as before, when spine1 receives this ARP request and builds its ARP cache for host h1, with *proxy-macip-advertisement* configured, it generates an EVPN Type-2 MAC+IP route on behalf of the original VTEP behind which the host resides, which is leaf1 in this case. This EVPN Type-2 MAC+IP route is shown in Example 7-42.

Example 7-42   *MAC+IP EVPN Type-2 route for h1 generated by spine1 on behalf of leaf1*

```
admin@spine1> show route table bgp.evpn.0 evpn-mac-address 08:00:27:29:c8:72


bgp.evpn.0: 30 destinations, 42 routes (30 active, 0 holddown, 0 hidden)
+ = Active Route, - = Last Active, * = Both


2:192.0.2.11:1::10100::08:00:27:29:c8:72/304
                  *[BGP/170] 00:09:15, localpref 100, from 192.0.2.11
                     AS path: 65421 I, validation-state: unverified
                   > to 198.51.100.0 via xe-0/0/0.0
2:192.0.2.11:1::10100::08:00:27:29:c8:72::10.100.100.1/304
                  *[EVPN/170] 00:11:28
                     Indirect
```

A detailed view of the route on spine1, using the **extensive** keyword, confirms that the route is generated on behalf of leaf1, as the Route Distinguisher in the route is leaf1's Route Distinguisher (192.0.2.11:1), and the protocol next hop is leaf1's loopback address (192.0.2.11), as shown in Example 7-43.

Example 7-43   *Detailed view of the EVPN Type-2 MAC+IP route for h1 generated by spine1 on behalf of leaf1*

```
admin@spine1> show route table bgp.evpn.0 match-prefix 2*10.100.100.1* extensive


bgp.evpn.0: 30 destinations, 42 routes (30 active, 0 holddown, 0 hidden)
2:192.0.2.11:1::10100::08:00:27:29:c8:72::10.100.100.1/304 (1 entry, 1 announced)
TSI:
Page 0 idx 0, (group overlay type External) Type 1 val 0xa857b44 (adv_entry)
   Advertised metrics:
     Nexthop: 192.0.2.11
     AS path: [65500] I
     Communities: target:1:1 encapsulation0:0:0:0:vxlan
Path 2:192.0.2.11:1::10100::08:00:27:29:c8:72::10.100.100.1 Vector len 4.  Val: 0
        *EVPN    Preference: 170
                 Next hop type: Indirect, Next hop index: 0
                 Address: 0xa88cff0
                 Next-hop reference count: 19
                 Protocol next hop: 192.0.2.11
                 Indirect next hop: 0x0 - INH Session ID: 0x0
                 State: <Secondary Active Int Ext>
                 Age: 12:21
                 Validation State: unverified
                 Task: default-switch-evpn
                 Announcement bits (1): 0-BGP_RT_Background
                 AS path: I
                 Communities: target:1:1 encapsulation0:0:0:0:vxlan
                 Route Label: 10100
                 ESI: 00:00:00:00:00:00:00:00:00:00
                 Primary Routing Table default-switch.evpn.0
```

When spine2 receives this route, it processes it and installs a MAC-to-IP binding in its ARP table for host h1, pointing to leaf1 as the VTEP, as shown in Example 7-44.

Example 7-44   *Host h1's MAC-to-IP binding on spine2*

```
admin@spine2> show route table bgp.evpn.0 evpn-mac-address 08:00:27:29:c8:72

bgp.evpn.0: 30 destinations, 46 routes (30 active, 0 holddown, 2 hidden)
+ = Active Route, - = Last Active, * = Both

2:192.0.2.11:1::10100::08:00:27:29:c8:72/304
                   *[BGP/170] 00:06:41, localpref 100, from 192.0.2.11
                      AS path: 65421 I, validation-state: unverified
                    > to 198.51.100.2 via xe-0/0/0.0
2:192.0.2.11:1::10100::08:00:27:29:c8:72::10.100.100.1/304
                   *[BGP/170] 00:08:55, localpref 100, from 192.0.2.12
                      AS path: 65422 65500 I, validation-state: unverified
                    > to 198.51.100.6 via xe-0/0/1.0

admin@spine2> show arp hostname 10.100.100.1
MAC Address        Address        Name               Interface          Flags
08:00:27:29:c8:72 10.100.100.1    10.100.100.1       irb.100 [vtep.32769]  none
```

With the ARP table now built using the EVPN Type-2 MAC+IP route received from spine1, when traffic hits spine2, it is ready to forward it to host h1 without having to initiate the ARP process. Thus, with the *proxy-macip-advertisement* configuration option, the gateways (spines, in this case) can synchronize MAC-to-IP bindings and build their ARP tables.

With time and new enhancements, these L2-only leafs were able to *snoop* ARP packets inbound and create an ARP entry in the micro-kernel of the PFE. This allowed such leafs to generate EVPN Type-2 MAC+IP routes directly without having the need for a Layer 3–capable device to proxy for them. This rendered the use of the *proxy-macip-advertisement* configuration option obsolete, for this particular use case. Since a L2-only leaf was now capable of generating EVPN Type-2 MAC+IP routes and sending them to the spines, each spine could directly install the MAC-to-IP binding of a host in its ARP table, as shown in Figure 7-11.

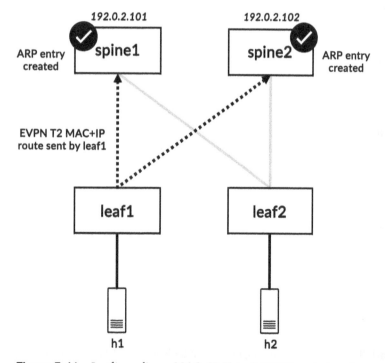

Figure 7-11   *Leaf1 sending a MAC+IP Type-2 EVPN route to spines*

However, there is another use case in which this command is needed, and thus it continues to be a recommended configuration option on CRB-enabled spines. Consider a multihoming scenario in which host h2 is multihomed to leaf2 and leaf3 via EVPN multihoming (ESI LAG), as shown in Figure 7-12.

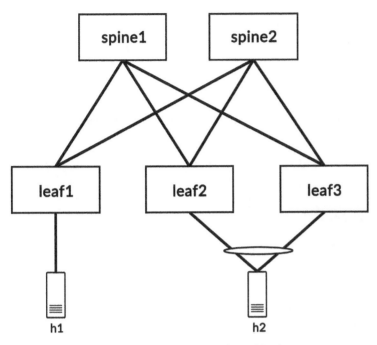

Figure 7-12 *Host h2 multihomed to leaf2 and leaf3 via ESI LAG*

Since these L2-only leafs are snooping ARP packets, they maintain a MAC-to-IP binding in the micro-kernel as well, which has an aging timer associated to it. Once this timer expires, these leafs re-ARP for the destination. This is not a problem in and of itself. The problem is that for re-ARP, the leafs use a source MAC address that belongs to an interface called *pip0*, and this MAC address is unique to every device.

The packet capture presented in Figure 7-13 shows a re-ARP originated from such a L2-only leaf (leaf2, in this case).

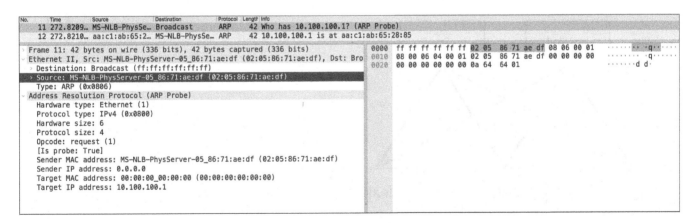

Figure 7-13 *Re-ARP packet (originated from leaf2) showing source MAC address used*

The source MAC address is the MAC address of interface pip0, as shown in Example 7-45.

Example 7-45 *pip0 MAC address on leaf1*

```
admin@leaf2> show interfaces pip0
Physical interface: pip0, Enabled, Physical link is Up
  Interface index: 645, SNMP ifIndex: 507
  Type: Ethernet, Link-level type: Ethernet, MTU: 9192
```

```
Device flags    : Present Running
Interface flags: SNMP-Traps
Link type       : Full-Duplex
Link flags      : None
Current address: 02:05:86:71:ae:df, Hardware address: 02:05:86:71:ae:df
Last flapped    : Never
  Input packets : 0
  Output packets: 0
```

When host h2 responds, the ARP reply is a unicast packet with a destination MAC address of the pip0 interface, as shown in Figure 7-14.

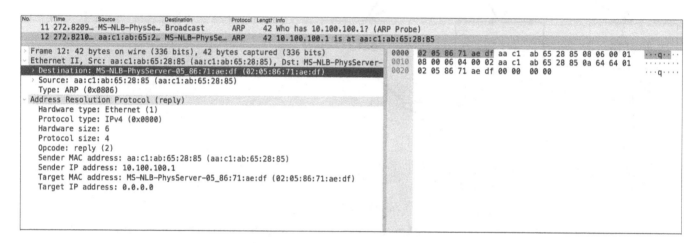

Figure 7-14 *ARP reply from host h2 in response to the re-ARP packet from leaf2*

This ARP reply can get hashed toward leaf2 or leaf3. If it gets hashed toward leaf3, this is a problem—since this pip0 interface MAC address is unique per device, leaf3 does not have this MAC address in its table, which leads to a destination MAC miss for this ARP reply, as shown in Figure 7-15.

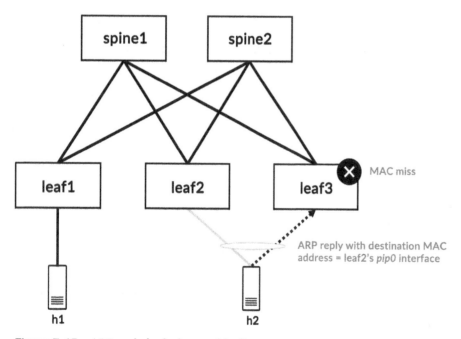

Figure 7-15 *ARP reply hashed toward leaf3*

Since this is a MAC address miss in leaf3's MAC address table, the ARP reply gets unknown unicast flooded in the fabric, using ingress replication, as shown in Figure 7-16. At a small scale, this is irrelevant, but when you consider large-scale data centers with hundreds of thousands of hosts, this is lot of unnecessary flooding of traffic, potentially impacting the network negatively.

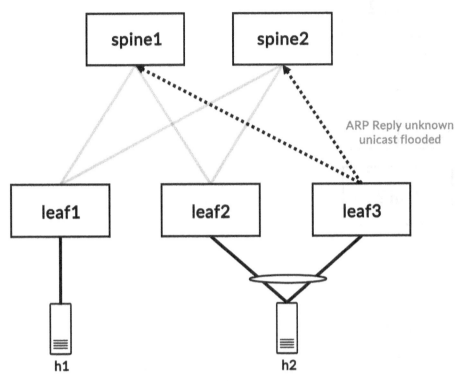

Figure 7-16 *ARP reply unknown unicast flooded by leaf3 in the fabric*

To get past this issue, the *proxy-macip-advertisement* configuration option continues to be a recommendation on CRB spines. With this configuration in place, the spines associate an aging timer against the ARP entries that are installed via EVPN Type-2 MAC+IP routes as well. Once the timer expires, the spines re-ARP for the destination, and when the destination host responds with an ARP reply, the leafs refresh their timer as well, circumventing this problem.

Packet Walk for Hosts in Different Subnets

This section closes out the chapter with a detailed packet walk of what happens when host h1 communicates with host h2. In this section, using important troubleshooting steps (that include debugs, various **show** commands, packet captures, and packet walks), everything that happens from the moment host h1 comes online and communicates with host h2 is broken down.

Let's add more details to our topology and make it an easy reference for this section. Each VTEP is labeled with its router ID, which is also the loopback IP address. Each host is labeled with its IP address and MAC address. The routing is centralized on the spines, with the same virtual addresses configured for VLANs 100 and 200 across both spines. These addresses are the default gateway for the respective hosts. This updated topology is shown in Figure 7-17.

First, Example 7-46 confirms that leaf1 has no knowledge of host h1, and that no MAC address has been learned from the interface xe-0/0/2, to which host h1 is connected. With this confirmation, the rest of this section is divided into exploring the control plane flow and the data plane flow individually.

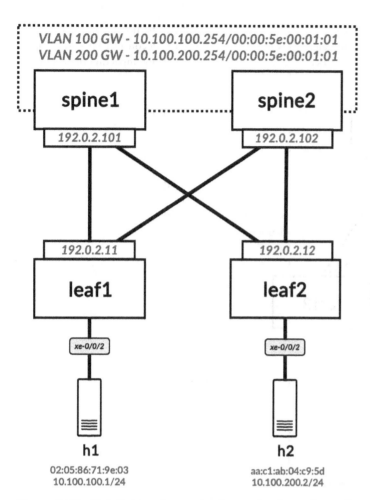

Figure 7-17   *Detailed topology as a reference for the packet walk*

Example 7-46   *MAC table on leaf1 prior to host h1 coming online*

```
admin@leaf1> show ethernet-switching table

MAC flags (S - static MAC, D - dynamic MAC, L - locally learned, P - Persistent static
        SE - statistics enabled, NM - non configured MAC, R - remote PE MAC, O - ovsdb MAC)


Ethernet switching table : 4 entries, 4 learned
Routing instance : default-switch
    Vlan        MAC               MAC     Logical         SVLBNH/       Active
    name        address           flags   interface       VENH Index    source
    v100        00:00:5e:00:01:01 DRP     esi.1753                      05:00:00:ff:dc:00:00:27:74:00
    v100        02:05:86:71:25:00 DRP     vtep.32770                    192.0.2.102
    v100        02:05:86:71:de:00 DRP     vtep.32769                    192.0.2.101
```

Control Plane Flow

When host h1 comes online, it sends a Gratuitous ARP (GARP) to ensure that there is no duplicate IP address in its broadcast domain. On receipt of this GARP, leaf1 learns h1's MAC address dynamically via the data plane. A high-level sequence of the events of how the MAC address is learned is shown in Figure 7-18. This sequence of events was already discussed in detail in Chapter 5.

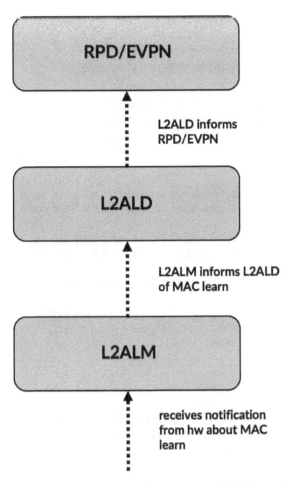

Figure 7-18 *Sequence of events for a MAC learn via data plane*

To dig deeper into how the MAC address is learned via the data plane, the traceoptions shown in Example 7-47 can be enabled.

Example 7-47 *Enabling required traceoptions on leaf1*

```
admin@leaf1# show protocols l2-learning traceoptions
file l2-learn.log size 50m;
level all;
flag all;


admin@leaf1# show protocols evpn traceoptions
file evpn.log size 50m;
flag all;
```

The EVPN traceoptions provides valuable debug information from RPD, while the l2-learning traceoptions provides debug information from L2ALD (in the Routing Engine). Let's look at these traceoptions to get a better understanding.

When a data plane learn occurs, like the one shown Figure 7-18, the hardware layer sends a message to L2ALM (in the PFE), informing it of the learn. L2ALM, in turn, sends this message to L2ALD. From the l2-learning debugs shown in Example 7-48, it can be confirmed that L2ALD receives this update from PFE/L2ALM, adds this new MAC address to its table against the interface and VLAN on which the learn occurred, and then sends this update to RPD.

Example 7-48 *L2ALD debugs via traceoptions on leaf1 for host h1's MAC learn*

```
admin@leaf1> show log l2-learn.log | grep "02:05:86:71:9e:03"
Apr 12 06:31:38.840679 l2ald_mac_ip_msg_handler:3412 rcvd mac+ip entry from pfe: msgin op 1 bd 3 ip_addr 10.100.100.1
mac_addr 02:05:86:71:9e:03 l2 ifl idx 559 ident 0 flags 2
```

```
Apr 12 06:31:38.840721 l2ald_mac_ip_msg_handler:3467 mac 02:05:86:71:9e:03 is not available l2 ifl (559:xe-0/0/2.0).
add mac for mac+ip 10.100.100.1

Apr 12 06:31:38.840748 l2ald_generate_mac_from_mac_ip:3154 [ifl 559 bd 3 vlan 0 mac-address 02:05:86:71:9e:03]

Apr 12 06:31:38.840974 l2ald_mac_msg_handler:1442 From L2ALM [(1) ADD] msgin BD: 3 MAC Address: 02:05:86:71:9e:03

Apr 12 06:31:38.841898 do_mac_process:5871 Processing [mac 02:05:86:71:9e:03(epoch 0 stp 3) bd 3 vlan 0]

Apr 12 06:31:38.842396 l2ald_add_mac_to_global_db:406 Added MAC 02:05:86:71:9e:03 from ifl 0 in global hash table

Apr 12 06:31:38.842490 libl2_add_mac_to_ifd_list:134 Added MAC 02:05:86:71:9e:03 in ifd list for xe-0/0/2

Apr 12 06:31:38.844178 libl2_ifl_access_add_mac_to_bd_info:432 mac 02:05:86:71:9e:03 ADDED to bd_info 0x980ce10, bd vlan is 100

Apr 12 06:31:38.844209 libl2_add_mac_to_ifl_list:285 Added MAC 02:05:86:71:9e:03 in ifl list for le ifl:(xe-0/0/2.0:0x9806008)


Apr 12 06:31:38.851711 l2ald_rpdf_init_dpcpmac:3704 Preparing cmd:MAC IP ROUTE ADD[7] sub_cmd:1 for MAC:02:05:86:71:9e:03
ip address:10.100.100.1 NHID:0 RTRID:0 ifln:xe-0/0/2.0 ifld:559 rtt:5 flags:0x82 ts:0x6436504a bdidgen:0x0000000300000003
vni:10100 rvtep:0.0.0.0 ESI:00:00:00:00:00:00:00:00:00:00

Apr 12 06:31:38.852517 l2ald_rpdf_send_msg_to_peer:3927 MSG sent to RPD msgout op 0 opcode 7 (MAC IP ROUTE ADD) MAC
02:05:86:71:9e:03 ipaddr 10.100.100.1 vlan id 100 rtt id 5 ifl index 559 vni 10100 nh id 0 vtep ipaddr 0.0.0.0  bd id 3
isid 0 flags 0x82 ifl name xe-0/0/2.0, ts 0x6436504a esi 00:00:00:00:00:00:00:00:00:00

Apr 12 06:31:38.852568 l2ald_rpdf_msg_mac_enqueue:6448 Prepare MAC msg to RPD - MAC 02:05:86:71:9e:03 ipaddr 164640a encap
type 0  vtep ipaddr 0  bd id 3 MAC_OP:7

Apr 12 06:31:38.899635 l2ald_rpdf_send_msg_to_peer:3927 MSG sent to RPD msgout op 0 opcode 7 (MAC IP ROUTE ADD) MAC
02:05:86:71:9e:03 ipaddr 10.100.100.1 vlan id 100 rtt id 5 ifl index 559 vni 10100 nh id 0 vtep ipaddr 0.0.0.0  bd id 3
isid 0 flags 0x82 ifl name xe-0/0/2.0, ts 0x6436504a esi 00:00:00:00:00:00:00:00:00:00
```

snip

RPD, on receiving this message from L2ALD, adds this address in its EVPN database, runs through its selection criteria of whether this is the best source or not for that address, and, if marked as best, constructs an EVPN MAC route and a MAC+IP route to be sent via BGP EVPN to applicable peers. This is shown in Example 7-49.

Example 7-49 *RPD debugs via traceoptions on leaf1 for host h1's MAC learn*

```
admin@leaf1> show log evpn.log | grep "02:05:86:71:9e:03"
Apr 12 06:31:38.956242 evpn_mac_msg_receive_from_l2ald:2591 EVPN instance default-switch [VS, Refcount: 5, Intfs: 2 (2
up), IRBs: 0 (0 up), Peers: 2,core-isolation-status-changed 0 Flags: 0x10000181c800] Received MAC+IP add for local MAC
02:05:86:71:9e:03 with L2 domain 10100, timestamp 0x6436504a.954832, interface xe-0/0/2.0, IPv4 address 10.100.100.1

Apr 12 06:31:38.957904 evpn_mirror_mac_update:1297 EVPN instance default-switch [VS, Refcount: 5, Intfs: 2 (2 up),
IRBs: 0 (0 up), Peers: 2,core-isolation-status-changed 0 Flags: 0x10000181c800] Active RE MAC MAC+IP add for local MAC
02:05:86:71:9e:03 with rtt-index 5, VLAN 10100, interface xe-0/0/2.0, flags 0x82, timestamp 0x6436504a, seq num 0,  ESI
00:00:00:00:00:00:00:00:00:00 IPv4 address: 10.100.100.1

Apr 12 06:31:38.958000 evpn_macdb_entry_create:566 EVPN MAC default-switch::10100::02:05:86:71:9e:03 [Flags: 0x0] Created

Apr 12 06:31:38.958082 evpn_intf_add_macdb_esi:1489 EVPN MAC ESI default-switch::10100::02:05:86:71:9e:03::xe-0/0/2.0
[Active: no, Timestamp: 0x0.000000, Flags: 0x0] Added to interface xe-0/0/2.0 list

Apr 12 06:31:38.958144 evpn_macdb_ip_addr_apply_local_state:2149 EVPN MAC IP default-switch::10100::02:05:86:71:9e:03:
:xe-0/0/2.0::10.100.100.1 [ESI flags: 0x40 <Local-To-Remote-Adv-Allowed>, IP flags: 0x0] Applying local state


Apr 12 06:31:38.958810 evpn_macdb_esi_adv_rt_create:3445 EVPN MAC ESI default-switch::10100::02:05:86:71:9e:03::xe-0/0/2.0
[Active: yes, Timestamp: 0x6436504a.954832, Flags: 0x40 <Local-To-Remote-Adv-Allowed>] Creating MAC advertisement route

Apr 12 06:31:38.960588 evpn_adv_MAC_rt:2158 EVPN route (local) [Instance: default-switch, Type: MAC advertisement (2),
ESI: 00:00:00:00:00:00:00:00:00:00, L2domain: 10100 Label 10100] Advertising BMAC 02:05:86:71:9e:03 per instance
default-switch

Apr 12 06:31:38.963874 CHANGE   default-switch     2:192.0.2.11:1::10100::02:05:86:71:9e:03/304 nhid 0 gw zero-len
EVPN    pref 170/0 metric  <Active Int Ext Changed>

Apr 12 06:31:38.963944 ADD      default-switch     2:192.0.2.11:1::10100::02:05:86:71:9e:03/304 nhid 0 gw zero-len
EVPN    pref 170/0 metric  <Active Int Ext Changed>

Apr 12 06:31:38.964037 evpn_adv_rt_add:1547 EVPN instance default-switch [VS, Refcount: 5, Intfs: 2 (2 up), IRBs: 0 (0
up), Peers: 2,core-isolation-status-changed 0 Flags: 0x10000181c800] Added MAC advertisement route (type 2) for 2:192.0.2.
11:1::10100::02:05:86:71:9e:03
```

Apr 12 06:31:38.964095 evpn_macdb_ip_addr_create_output_state:2602 EVPN MAC IP default-switch::10100::02:05:86:71:9e:03:
:xe-0/0/2.0::10.100.100.1 [ESI flags: 0x40 <Local-To-Remote-Adv-Allowed>, IP flags: 0x2 <Local-Adv>] Creating all output
state

Apr 12 06:31:38.965150 evpn_irb_intf_find_by_trans_l2domain:2030 EVPN MAC IP default-switch::10100::02:05:86:71:9e:03:
:xe-0/0/2.0::10.100.100.1 [ESI flags: 0x40 <Local-To-Remote-Adv-Allowed>, IP flags: 0x2 <Local-Adv>] No bd and IRB
interface found by vni 10100

Apr 12 06:31:38.965199 evpn_macdb_ip_addr_create_output_state:2623 EVPN MAC IP default-switch::10100::02:05:86:71:9e:03:
:xe-0/0/2.0::10.100.100.1 [ESI flags: 0x40 <Local-To-Remote-Adv-Allowed>, IP flags: 0x2 <Local-Adv>] IP host route cannot
be created (no IRB interface in L2 domain)

Apr 12 06:31:38.965245 evpn_macdb_ip_addr_adv_rt_create:1709 EVPN MAC IP default-switch::10100::02:05:86:71:9e:03:
:xe-0/0/2.0::10.100.100.1 [ESI flags: 0x40 <Local-To-Remote-Adv-Allowed>, IP flags: 0x2 <Local-Adv>] Creating MAC+IP
advertisement route for locally learnt

Apr 12 06:31:38.965289 evpn_macdb_ip_addr_l3_conext_symmetric_routing_enabled:3351 EVPN MAC IP default-switch::10100::02
:05:86:71:9e:03::xe-0/0/2.0::10.100.100.1 [ESI flags: 0x40 <Local-To-Remote-Adv-Allowed>, IP flags: 0x2 <Local-Adv>] irb
interface not found

Apr 12 06:31:38.965354 evpn_adv_MAC_rt:2140 EVPN route (local) [Instance: default-switch, Type: MAC advertisement (2),
ESI: 00:00:00:00:00:00:00:00:00:00, L2domain: 10100 Label 10100] Advertising MAC 02:05:86:71:9e:03 with IP 10.100.100.1 ND
ext com 0x0 mhapb_val 0x4 per instance default-switch

Apr 12 06:31:38.965476 CHANGE   default-switch   2:192.0.2.11:1::10100::02:05:86:71:9e:03::10.100.100.1/304 nhid 0 gw
zero-len   EVPN   pref 170/0 metric <Active Int Ext Changed>

Apr 12 06:31:38.965528 ADD   default-switch   2:192.0.2.11:1::10100::02:05:86:71:9e:03::10.100.100.1/304 nhid 0 gw
zero-len   EVPN   pref 170/0 metric <Active Int Ext Changed>

Apr 12 06:31:38.965634 evpn_adv_rt_add:1547 EVPN instance default-switch [VS, Refcount: 5, Intfs: 2 (2 up), IRBs: 0 (0
up), Peers: 2,core-isolation-status-changed 0 Flags: 0x10000181c800] Added MAC advertisement route (type 2) for 2:192.0.2.
11:1::10100::02:05:86:71:9e:03::10.100.100.1

Both spine1 and spine2 will receive an EVPN Type-2 MAC route and a MAC+IP route from leaf1. The packet capture shown
in Figure 7-19, from spine1, as an example, shows further details of the BGP EVPN update packet. This includes two EVPN
NLRIs, corresponding to the MAC-only route and the MAC+IP route, advertised with a next-hop address of 192.0.2.11,
which is the loopback address of leaf1. This process is also visualized, as shown in Figure 7-20.

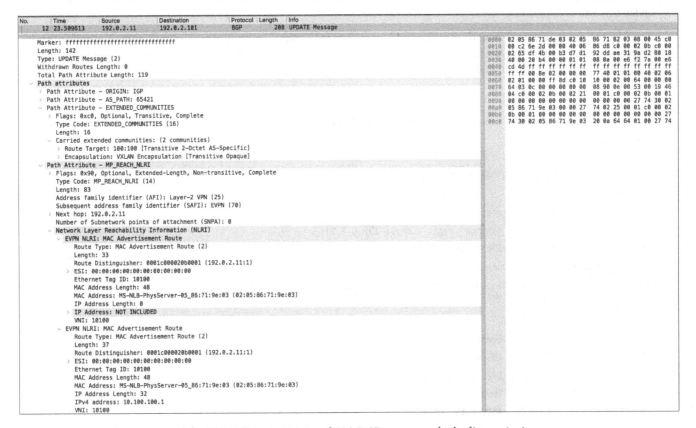

Figure 7-19 *Packet capture of the EVPN Type-2 MAC and MAC+IP route sent by leaf1 to spine1*

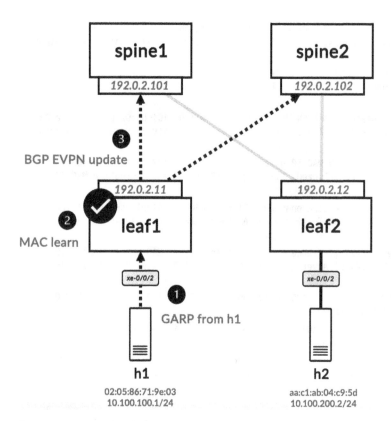

Figure 7-20 *Control-plane visualization for host h1's MAC learn*

When the spines receive this BGP EVPN update, the sequence of events is exactly the opposite. For the sake of brevity, traceoptions are not enabled. Instead, let's use **show** commands this time to look at how these entries are installed on the spines, taking spine1 as an example again. First, RPD/EVPN learns the address from the received BGP EVPN packet and updates its EVPN database.

In the EVPN database, spine1 now has an entry for host h1's MAC address, and it is associated to the IP address that was advertised via the EVPN Type-2 MAC+IP route. This is shown in Example 7-50, using the **show evpn database mac-address** [*mac-address*] **extensive** operational mode command.

Example 7-50 *EVPN database for h1's address on spine1*

```
admin@spine1> show evpn database mac-address 02:05:86:71:9e:03 extensive
Instance: default-switch

VN Identifier: 10100, MAC address: 02:05:86:71:9e:03
  State: 0x0
  Source: 192.0.2.11, Rank: 1, Status: Active
    Mobility sequence number: 0 (minimum origin address 192.0.2.11)
    Timestamp: Apr 12 10:16:39.632709 (0x64368507)
    State: <Remote-To-Local-Adv-Done>
    MAC advertisement route status: Not created (no local state present)
    IP address: 10.100.100.1
    History db:
      Time                    Event
      Apr 12 10:16:39.632 2023    192.0.2.11 : Remote peer 192.0.2.11 created
      Apr 12 10:16:39.632 2023    192.0.2.11 : Created
      Apr 12 10:16:39.634 2023    Updating output state (change flags 0x1 <ESI-Added>)
      Apr 12 10:16:39.634 2023    Active ESI changing (not assigned -> 192.0.2.11)
```

RPD then informs L2ALD of this learn, and L2ALD adds this MAC address to its MAC address table, with an egress/exit interface pointing to the logical VTEP interface for leaf1. At the same time, it sends this update to all applicable BGP EVPN peers, which, in this case, is leaf2. The L2ALD view of the MAC address table is shown in Example 7-51, using the **show ethernet-switching table** [*mac-address*] operational mode command.

Example 7-51 *MAC table on spine1*

```
admin@spine1> show ethernet-switching table 02:05:86:71:9e:03


MAC flags (S - static MAC, D - dynamic MAC, L - locally learned, P - Persistent static
          SE - statistics enabled, NM - non configured MAC, R - remote PE MAC, O - ovsdb MAC)


Ethernet switching table : 2 entries, 2 learned
Routing instance : default-switch
    Vlan              MAC                MAC      Logical              SVLBNH/      Active
    name              address            flags    interface            VENH Index   source
    v100              02:05:86:71:9e:03  DR       vtep.32769                        192.0.2.11


{master:0}
admin@spine1> show interfaces vtep.32769
  Logical interface vtep.32769 (Index 571) (SNMP ifIndex 543)
    Flags: Up SNMP-Traps Encapsulation: ENET2
    VXLAN Endpoint Type: Remote, VXLAN Endpoint Address: 192.0.2.11, L2 Routing Instance: default-switch, L3 Routing
Instance: default
    Input packets : 30
    Output packets: 30
    Protocol eth-switch, MTU: Unlimited
      Flags: Is-Primary, Trunk-Mode
```

Finally, this MAC address information is sent to L2ALM and, in turn, the hardware layer, where it is programmed for hardware forwarding. When this update reaches leaf2 (via BGP EVPN), it drops the update since there is no matching Route Target for import (since leaf2 does not have this VLAN/VNI configured locally). As shown in Example 7-52, the route is only *Accepted* into BGP RIB-In, but not imported into the default-switch.evpn.0 table.

Example 7-52 *BGP and default-switch table on leaf2 showing EVPN Type-2 route for host h1 is not imported*

```
admin@leaf2> show route table bgp.evpn.0 evpn-mac-address 02:05:86:71:9e:03 extensive


bgp.evpn.0: 29 destinations, 32 routes (29 active, 0 holddown, 0 hidden)
2:192.0.2.11:1::10100::02:05:86:71:9e:03/304 MAC/IP (2 entries, 0 announced)
        *BGP    Preference: 170/-101
                Route Distinguisher: 192.0.2.11:1
                Next hop type: Indirect, Next hop index: 0
                Address: 0xd32e088
                Next-hop reference count: 6
                Source: 192.0.2.101
                Protocol next hop: 192.0.2.11
                Indirect next hop: 0x2 no-forward INH Session ID: 0
                State: <Active Ext>
                Local AS: 65422 Peer AS: 65500
                Age: 2:03:28     Metric2: 0
```

```
                    Validation State: unverified
                    Task: BGP_65500.192.0.2.101
                    AS path: 65500 65421 I
                    Communities: target:100:100 encapsulation:vxlan(0x8)
                    Accepted
                    Route Label: 10100
                    ESI: 00:00:00:00:00:00:00:00:00:00
                    Localpref: 100
                    Router ID: 192.0.2.101
                    Thread: junos-main
                    Indirect next hops: 1
                            Protocol next hop: 192.0.2.11
                            Indirect next hop: 0x2 no-forward INH Session ID: 0
                            Indirect path forwarding next hops: 2
                                    Next hop type: Router
                                    Next hop: 198.51.100.5 via xe-0/0/0.0
                                    Session Id: 0
                                    Next hop: 198.51.100.7 via xe-0/0/1.0
                                    Session Id: 0
                                    192.0.2.11/32 Originating RIB: inet.0
                                      Node path count: 1
                                      Forwarding nexthops: 2
                                            Next hop type: Router
                                            Next hop: 198.51.100.5 via xe-0/0/0.0
                                            Session Id: 0
                                            Next hop: 198.51.100.7 via xe-0/0/1.0
                                            Session Id: 0


*snip*


admin@leaf2> show route table default-switch.evpn.0 evpn-mac-address 02:05:86:71:9e:03


default-switch.evpn.0: 16 destinations, 16 routes (16 active, 0 holddown, 0 hidden)


<no output>
```

When host h2 comes online, a similar process happens, and at the end of this process, spine1 and spine2 are aware of where both hosts reside, with their ARP caches populated with information about both hosts. The MAC address table and the ARP cache, for both spines, are shown in Example 7-53.

Example 7-53   *MAC and ARP tables on spine1 and spine2*

```
admin@spine1> show arp
MAC Address        Address          Name            Interface              Flags
02:05:86:71:9e:03  10.100.100.1     10.100.100.1    irb.100 [vtep.32769]   none
aa:c1:ab:04:c9:5d  10.100.200.2     10.100.200.2    irb.200 [vtep.32770]   none
02:05:86:71:82:03  198.51.100.0     198.51.100.0    xe-0/0/0.0             none
02:05:86:71:89:03  198.51.100.4     198.51.100.4    xe-0/0/1.0             none
```

```
admin@spine1> show ethernet-switching table

MAC flags (S - static MAC, D - dynamic MAC, L - locally learned, P - Persistent static
          SE - statistics enabled, NM - non configured MAC, R - remote PE MAC, O - ovsdb MAC)


Ethernet switching table : 2 entries, 2 learned
Routing instance : default-switch
    Vlan            MAC                MAC     Logical             SVLBNH/      Active
    name            address            flags   interface           VENH Index   source
    v100            02:05:86:71:9e:03  DR      vtep.32769                       192.0.2.11
    v200            aa:c1:ab:04:c9:5d  DR      vtep.32770                       192.0.2.12


admin@spine2> show arp
MAC Address        Address        Name            Interface            Flags
02:05:86:71:9e:03  10.100.100.1   10.100.100.1    irb.100 [vtep.32769]  none
aa:c1:ab:04:c9:5d  10.100.200.2   10.100.200.2    irb.200 [vtep.32770]  none
02:05:86:71:82:07  198.51.100.2   198.51.100.2    xe-0/0/0.0           none
02:05:86:71:89:07  198.51.100.6   198.51.100.6    xe-0/0/1.0           none


admin@spine2> show ethernet-switching table

MAC flags (S - static MAC, D - dynamic MAC, L - locally learned, P - Persistent static
          SE - statistics enabled, NM - non configured MAC, R - remote PE MAC, O - ovsdb MAC)


Ethernet switching table : 2 entries, 2 learned
Routing instance : default-switch
    Vlan            MAC                MAC     Logical             SVLBNH/      Active
    name            address            flags   interface           VENH Index   source
    v100            02:05:86:71:9e:03  DR      vtep.32769                       192.0.2.11
    v200            aa:c1:ab:04:c9:5d  DR      vtep.32770                       192.0.2.12
```

When host h1 attempts to communicate with host h2, it will first ARP for its default gateway since it knows that the destination is in a different subnet. This ARP will get hashed to either spine1 or spine2, and assuming this goes to spine1, it will respond with an ARP reply. With the ARP process complete, host h1 now has all the information that is needed to send an IP packet to host h2. The following section explores the data plane flow in a CRB fabric for inter-subnet communication.

Data Plane Flow

To generate test traffic between host h1 and h2, and to validate connectivity between the two hosts, the **ping** tool is used, with host h1 pinging h2. With ARP resolved for the default gateway, h1 generates an ICMP request, which is received by leaf1, as shown in Figure 7-21.

This is just an IP packet, with an ICMP payload, as shown in the packet capture in Figure 7-22. The destination IP address is host h2's IP address, while the destination MAC address in the Ethernet header is the gateway's resolved MAC address, which is the virtual MAC address on the spines, 00:00:5e:00:01:01.

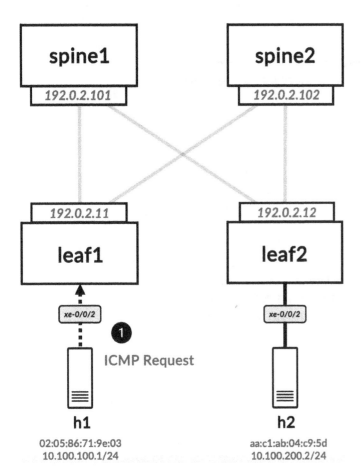

Figure 7-21   *ICMP request from h1 destined for h2*

No.	Time	Source	Destination	Protocol	Length	Info
3	41.043486	10.100.100.1	10.100.200.2	ICMP	98	Echo (ping) request id=0xdf16, seq=0/0, ttl=64 (reply in 4)
4	41.164672	10.100.200.2	10.100.100.1	ICMP	98	Echo (ping) reply id=0xdf16, seq=0/0, ttl=63 (request in 3)

```
> Frame 3: 98 bytes on wire (784 bits), 98 bytes captured (784 bits)
v Ethernet II, Src: MS-NLB-PhysServer-05_86:71:9e:03 (02:05:86:71:9e:03), Dst: IETF-VRRP-VRID_01
  > Destination: IETF-VRRP-VRID_01 (00:00:5e:00:01:01)
  > Source: MS-NLB-PhysServer-05_86:71:9e:03 (02:05:86:71:9e:03)
    Type: IPv4 (0x0800)
v Internet Protocol Version 4, Src: 10.100.100.1, Dst: 10.100.200.2
    0100 .... = Version: 4
    .... 0101 = Header Length: 20 bytes (5)
  > Differentiated Services Field: 0x00 (DSCP: CS0, ECN: Not-ECT)
    Total Length: 84
    Identification: 0x3774 (14196)
  > 000. .... = Flags: 0x0
    ...0 0000 0000 0000 = Fragment Offset: 0
    Time to Live: 64
    Protocol: ICMP (1)
    Header Checksum: 0x026a [validation disabled]
    [Header checksum status: Unverified]
    Source Address: 10.100.100.1
    Destination Address: 10.100.200.2
v Internet Control Message Protocol
    Type: 8 (Echo (ping) request)
    Code: 0
    Checksum: 0x0ba7 [correct]
    [Checksum Status: Good]
    Identifier (BE): 57110 (0xdf16)
    Identifier (LE): 5855 (0x16df)
    Sequence Number (BE): 0 (0x0000)
    Sequence Number (LE): 0 (0x0000)
    [Response frame: 4]
    Timestamp from icmp data: Apr 14, 2023 10:00:50.517892000 IST
    [Timestamp from icmp data (relative): 0.892888000 seconds]
> Data (48 bytes)
```

```
0000  00 00 5e 00 01 01 02 05  86 71 9e 03 08 00 45 00
0010  00 54 37 74 00 00 40 01  02 6a 0a 64 64 01 0a 64
0020  c8 02 08 00 0b a7 df 16  00 00 64 38 d6 fa 00 07
0030  e7 04 08 09 0a 0b 0c 0d  0e 0f 10 11 12 13 14 15
0040  16 17 18 19 1a 1b 1c 1d  1e 1f 20 21 22 23 24 25
0050  26 27 28 29 2a 2b 2c 2d  2e 2f 30 31 32 33 34 35
0060  36 37
```

Figure 7-22   *Packet capture showing ICMP request from h1 destined for h2*

On leaf1, a MAC address table lookup for this MAC address points to an ESI as the egress/exit interface. This ESI provides overlay load-balancing, resolving into two possible VTEPs—spine1 (192.0.2.101) and spine2 (192.0.2.102), as shown in Example 7-54.

Example 7-54 *Ethernet table and ESI resolution to VTEPs on leaf1*

```
admin@leaf1> show ethernet-switching table 00:00:5e:00:01:01


MAC flags (S - static MAC, D - dynamic MAC, L - locally learned, P - Persistent static
          SE - statistics enabled, NM - non configured MAC, R - remote PE MAC, O - ovsdb MAC)



Ethernet switching table : 4 entries, 4 learned
Routing instance : default-switch
   Vlan            MAC               MAC    Logical           SVLBNH/       Active
   name            address           flags  interface         VENH Index    source
   v100            00:00:5e:00:01:01 DRP    esi.1753                        05:00:00:ff:dc:00:00:27:74:00


admin@leaf1> show ethernet-switching vxlan-tunnel-end-point esi esi-identifier 05:00:00:ff:dc:00:00:27:74:00
ESI                            RTT                VLNBH INH    ESI-IFL   LOC-IFL  #RVTEPs
05:00:00:ff:dc:00:00:27:74:00 default-switch      1753  131071 esi.1753           2
   RVTEP-IP        RVTEP-IFL     VENH    MASK-ID  FLAGS    MAC-COUNT
   192.0.2.102     vtep.32770    1754    1        2        1
   192.0.2.101     vtep.32769    1750    0        2        1
```

Assuming the ICMP request is hashed toward spine1, the original packet is encapsulated by leaf1 by adding a VXLAN header, a UDP header, and an outer Ethernet and IP header, totaling a 50-byte increase in the overall packet size. This is visually represented in Figure 7-23.

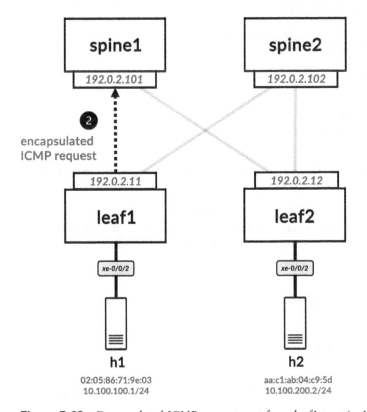

Figure 7-23 *Encapsulated ICMP request sent from leaf1 to spine1*

It is important to look at this encapsulated packet. A packet capture from spine1 shows more details in Figure 7-24.

```
No.    Time        Source         Destination    Protocol Length  Info
    28 61.577473 10.100.100.1 10.100.200.2   ICMP      148 Echo (ping) request  id=0xdf16, seq=0/0, ttl=64 (reply in 29)
    29 61.690060 10.100.200.2 10.100.100.1   ICMP      148 Echo (ping) reply    id=0xdf16, seq=0/0, ttl=63 (request in 28)

> Frame 28: 148 bytes on wire (1184 bits), 148 bytes captured (1184 bits)        0000  02 05 86 71 de 03 02 05  86 71 82 03 08 00 45 00
> Ethernet II, Src: MS-NLB-PhysServer-05_86:71:82:03 (02:05:86:71:82:03), Dst: MS-NLB-PhysServer-  0010  00 86 00 00 00 00 40 11  f5 f6 c0 00 02 0b c0 00
    > Destination: MS-NLB-PhysServer-05_86:71:de:03 (02:05:86:71:de:03)           0020  02 65 26 27 12 b5 00 72  00 00 08 00 00 00 00 27
    > Source: MS-NLB-PhysServer-05_86:71:82:03 (02:05:86:71:82:03)                0030  74 00 00 00 5e 00 01 01  02 05 86 71 9e 03 08 00
      Type: IPv4 (0x0800)                                                        0040  45 00 00 54 37 74 00 00  40 01 02 6a 0a 64 64 01
> Internet Protocol Version 4, Src: 192.0.2.11, Dst: 192.0.2.101                 0050  0a 64 c8 02 08 00 0b a7  df 16 00 00 64 38 d6 fa
      0100 .... = Version: 4                                                     0060  00 07 e7 04 08 09 0a 0b  0c 0d 0e 0f 10 11 12 13
      .... 0101 = Header Length: 20 bytes (5)                                    0070  14 15 16 17 18 19 1a 1b  1c 1d 1e 1f 20 21 22 23
    > Differentiated Services Field: 0x00 (DSCP: CS0, ECN: Not-ECT)              0080  24 25 26 27 28 29 2a 2b  2c 2d 2e 2f 30 31 32 33
      Total Length: 134                                                          0090  34 35 36 37
      Identification: 0x0000 (0)
    > 000. .... = Flags: 0x0
      ...0 0000 0000 0000 = Fragment Offset: 0
      Time to Live: 64
      Protocol: UDP (17)
      Header Checksum: 0xf5f6 [validation disabled]
      [Header checksum status: Unverified]
      Source Address: 192.0.2.11
      Destination Address: 192.0.2.101
> User Datagram Protocol, Src Port: 9767, Dst Port: 4789
      Source Port: 9767
      Destination Port: 4789
      Length: 114
    > Checksum: 0x0000 [zero-value ignored]
      [Stream index: 0]
    > [Timestamps]
      UDP payload (106 bytes)
> Virtual eXtensible Local Area Network
    > Flags: 0x0800, VXLAN Network ID (VNI)
      Group Policy ID: 0
      VXLAN Network Identifier (VNI): 10100
      Reserved: 0
> Ethernet II, Src: MS-NLB-PhysServer-05_86:71:9e:03 (02:05:86:71:9e:03), Dst: IETF-VRRP-VRID_01
> Internet Protocol Version 4, Src: 10.100.100.1, Dst: 10.100.200.2
> Internet Control Message Protocol
```

Figure 7-24 *Packet capture of encapsulated ICMP request sent from leaf1 to spine1*

The outer IP and Ethernet headers are used to carry the packet from VTEP to VTEP—thus, the source IP address, in the outer IP header, is the VTEP address of leaf1 (192.0.2.11), and the destination IP address is the VTEP address of spine1 (192.0.2.101). The source and destination MAC addresses, in the outer Ethernet header, are the addresses of the point-to-point interfaces between leaf1 and spine1, as shown in Example 7-55.

Example 7-55 *MAC addresses of the point-to-point interfaces between leaf1 and spine1*

```
admin@leaf1> show interfaces xe-0/0/0 | grep "Hardware address"
  Current address: 02:05:86:71:82:03, Hardware address: 02:05:86:71:82:03


admin@spine1> show interfaces xe-0/0/0 | grep "Hardware address"
  Current address: 02:05:86:71:de:03, Hardware address: 02:05:86:71:de:03
```

The VXLAN header itself carries the VNI information, which, in this case, is VNI 10100—this is the L2VNI that the packet is bridged in until the gateway, which is spine1, in this case.

Once this packet arrives on spine1, it is decapsulated since the outer IP destination is owned by spine1. A forwarding lookup on spine1 determines where this should be sent. This is done on the inner IP header's destination address, and since the destination is directly attached to spine1 (via irb.200), it is routed from irb.100 to irb.200. This routing lookup for the destination IP address, on spine1, is shown in Example 7-56.

Example 7-56 *Route lookup for the destination, h2, on spine1*

```
admin@spine1> show route table inet.0 10.100.200.2


inet.0: 17 destinations, 17 routes (17 active, 0 holddown, 0 hidden)
+ = Active Route, - = Last Active, * = Both


10.100.200.0/24     *[Direct/0] 1d 23:45:40
                    > via irb.200
```

A directly connected route implies that spine1 can ARP for the destination—from the EVPN Type-2 MAC+IP routes exchanged in the control plane via BGP EVPN, the ARP cache is already built for the destination, host h2. This gives us the IP-to-MAC address binding, and the MAC address, in the MAC address table, determines that the packet should be sent to VTEP leaf2 (192.0.2.12), as shown in Example 7-57.

Example 7-57   *ARP and switching table on spine1 for destination h2*

```
admin@spine1> show arp hostname 10.100.200.2
MAC Address       Address        Name          Interface            Flags
aa:c1:ab:04:c9:5d 10.100.200.2   10.100.200.2  irb.200 [vtep.32770] none


admin@spine1> show ethernet-switching table aa:c1:ab:04:c9:5d


MAC flags (S - static MAC, D - dynamic MAC, L - locally learned, P - Persistent static
          SE - statistics enabled, NM - non configured MAC, R - remote PE MAC, O - ovsdb MAC)



Ethernet switching table : 2 entries, 2 learned
Routing instance : default-switch
    Vlan            MAC            MAC      Logical          SVLBNH/      Active
    name            address        flags    interface        VENH Index   source
    v200            aa:c1:ab:04:c9:5d  DR    vtep.32770                    192.0.2.12
```

The packet is now encapsuled again with the appropriate VXLAN headers and sent toward leaf2, as visualized in Figure 7-25.

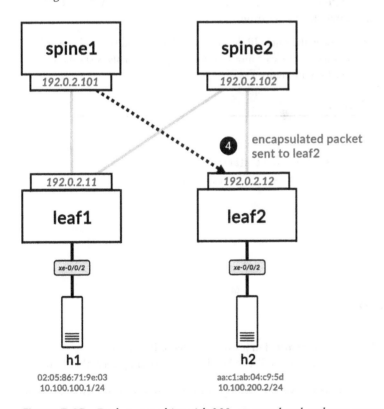

Figure 7-25   *Packet routed into irb.200, encapsulated and sent toward leaf2*

A packet capture on leaf2, shown in Figure 7-26, gives us further details of this encapsulated packet, coming from spine1.

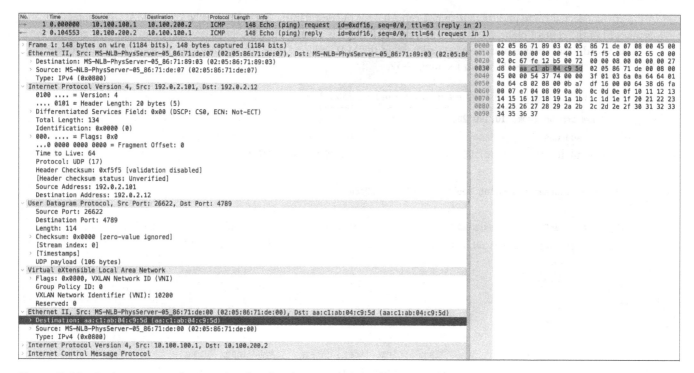

Figure 7-26 *Packet capture of encapsulated packet from spine1 to leaf2*

The inner destination MAC address, as shown in Figure 7-26, is now host h2's MAC address, while the inner source MAC address is of spine1's IRB interface, irb.200. The VNI, in the VXLAN header, has been changed to VNI 10200, which is the L2VNI for host h2. This confirms that the packet was routed into irb.200, and then encapsulated, before being bridged to leaf2. The outer IP and Ethernet headers, like before, simply carry the packet from spine1 to leaf2.

Once the packet arrives on leaf2, it is decapsulated (since leaf2 owns the outer IP destination address) and bridged toward host h2 with a lookup in the MAC address table, which gives us the egress/exit interface for the packet. This is shown in Example 7-58, followed by a visual representation of the packet flow in Figure 7-27.

Example 7-58 *Switching table on leaf2 for MAC address of host h2*

```
admin@leaf2> show ethernet-switching table aa:c1:ab:04:c9:5d


MAC flags (S - static MAC, D - dynamic MAC, L - locally learned, P - Persistent static
          SE - statistics enabled, NM - non configured MAC, R - remote PE MAC, O - ovsdb MAC)



Ethernet switching table : 4 entries, 4 learned
Routing instance : default-switch
    Vlan            MAC               MAC      Logical            SVLBNH/      Active
    name            address           flags    interface          VENH Index   source
    v200            aa:c1:ab:04:c9:5d D        xe-0/0/2.0
```

Host h2 now responds with an ICMP reply, and the packet will be forwarded in a similar fashion, in the reverse direction. This concludes the packet walk for inter-subnet traffic in an EVPN VXLAN fabric, with routing centralized on the spines.

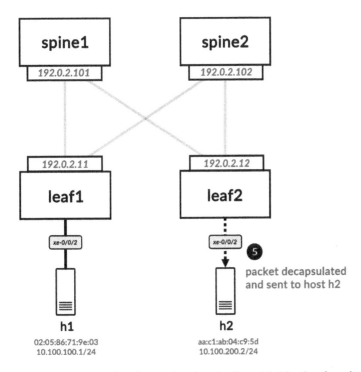

Figure 7-27 *Packet decapsulated on leaf2 and bridged to host h2*

Summary

This chapter covered various details of a centrally routed bridging architecture, including the driving factors behind such a design—these factors have largely been the ability of a device to do RIOT (VXLAN routing) and cost. With newer ASICs that can natively do RIOT, the former factor is mostly a non-issue. However, this architecture is also not well suited for modern data centers, with a predominance of east-west traffic, since such a design can lead to traffic tromboning and inefficient traffic path.

Throughout this chapter, the spines and leafs of a data center were configured to deploy centrally routed bridging in an EVPN VXLAN fabric. This chapter included some history behind a few of these configurations, such as the *proxy-macip-advertisement* configuration option. A trip down memory lane gave some context behind this option, along with an understanding of its relevance in today's data centers implementing a CRB design. A detailed analysis of the EVPN Type-2 routes advertised for the virtual gateway address confirmed that the routes are advertised with an attached ESI. This ESI enables load-balancing in the overlay, by resolving into VTEPs, which have advertised EVPN Type-1 routes for the same ESI.

Finally, this chapter closed out with a packet walk for traffic sent between hosts in different subnets, detailing how EVPN routes are exchanged in the control plane using BGP EVPN. Different tools in the toolset, such as **show** commands and packet captures, helped to confirm how this traffic flows through an EVPN VXLAN fabric in the data plane.

Edge-Routed Bridging

The previous chapter introduced integrated routing and bridging (IRB) as a means of doing both bridging and routing on the same device. Centrally routed bridging, a type of IRB design, models the fabric so that all routing occurs at a central point (usually the spines of a Clos fabric). However, with such a design, traffic tromboning can occur, making it a highly inefficient and impractical design when hosts that are connected to the same leaf, but in different subnets, want to communicate with each other (which is very common in today's large-scale, multitenant data centers).

With advancements in both merchant and custom silicon, cost-effective, feature-rich 1RU devices that can do RIOT (Routing In and Out of Tunnels or, in simpler terms, VXLAN routing) natively are now common. These devices can be used as data center top-of-rack (ToR) leafs, paving the way for routing to be moved to the edge of the network (instead of being centralized on the spines) for efficient routing of inter-subnet traffic. This is called *edge-routed bridging (ERB)* and is the focus of this chapter.

Overview of Different Routing Models with Edge-Routed Bridging

With edge-routed bridging, the routing now occurs on the leafs, which are positioned at the edge of the fabric, as shown in Figure 8-1. This is achieved by moving the IRB interfaces to the leafs and using an anycast distributed gateway model, which means that the same IP address and MAC address for an IRB interface are configured on all leafs.

With edge-routed bridging, there are different deployment options available for routing architecture and design. These are described in RFCs 9135 and 9136, and they are asymmetric IRB and symmetric IRB (covered in this chapter) and a routed overlay with Type-5 routing, along with host-routed bridging (discussed in Chapter 9, "Routed Overlay and Host-Routed Bridging"). These designs are fundamentally different in how they are configured. It is also important to consider how each design impacts the scale, flexibility, and operational ease (and simplicity) of building, maintaining, and troubleshooting a data center fabric.

Asymmetric IRB follows a bridge-route-bridge model. The VLANs, corresponding L2VNIs, and IRB interfaces for all VLANs (that need to be routed) are configured on all leafs in this case. Since all IRB interfaces exist on all leafs, every leaf maintains the ARP and MAC state for all hosts in the fabric, which makes this design difficult to scale for larger data centers. Operationally, this model is easier to troubleshoot and maintain.

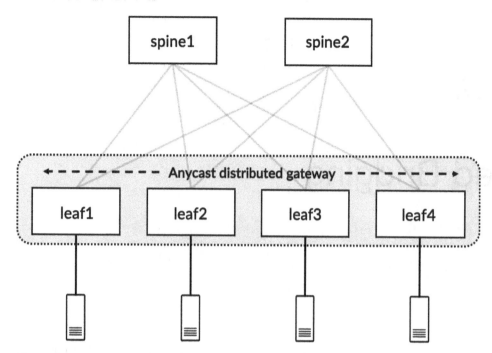

Figure 8-1 *Routing on the leafs in an ERB design*

This model is commonly referred to as *bridge-route-bridge* because a packet is bridged into the ingress leaf on the source VLAN (and L2VNI), routed into the destination VLAN on the ingress leaf itself, and then bridged across the EVPN VXLAN fabric via the L2VNI, corresponding to the destination VLAN, to the egress leaf and, eventually, to the destination. Thus, the ingress leaf does three functions—a MAC lookup, an IP lookup, and then another MAC lookup—while the egress leaf only does a MAC lookup. Visually, using VLAN-Based MAC-VRFs for ease of understanding, this model can be represented as shown in Figure 8-2.

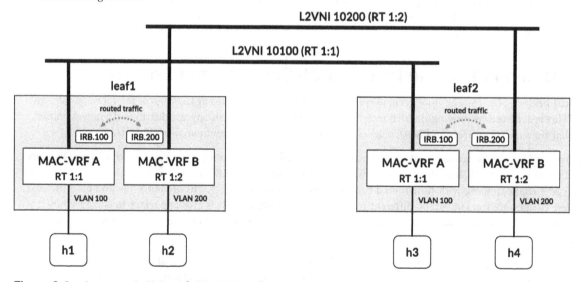

Figure 8-2 *Asymmetric IRB with VLAN-Based MAC-VRFs*

Each leaf has two MAC-VRFs corresponding to their respective VLANs. Any inter-subnet traffic is routed on the ingress leaf between the VLANs, and both VLANs are stretched across the EVPN VXLAN fabric using L2VNIs.

The general flow for inter-subnet traffic for this model is shown in Figure 8-3, using the reference topology from the previous chapters.

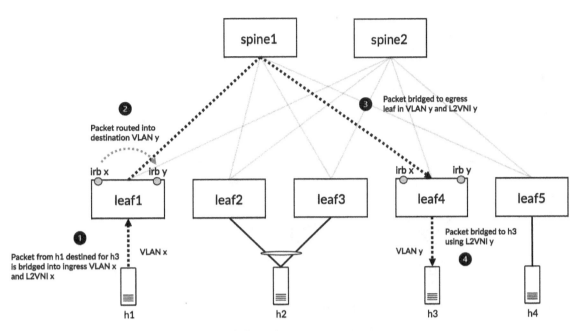

Figure 8-3 *Packet flow for inter-subnet traffic with Asymmetric IRB*

Symmetric IRB, on the other hand, follows a *bridge-route-route-bridge* model. With this model, the VLANs and IRB interfaces only for the necessary VLANs need to exist on the leafs, and a new construct called the *Layer 3 VNI (L3VNI)* is used. This VNI corresponds to an IP VRF that must exist for the tenant on the leafs. Since this methodology of routing does not enforce the creation of all VLANs and IRB interfaces on all leafs, it is far easier to scale to larger data centers. Operationally, this model is more complicated to troubleshoot and maintain.

Visually, using VLAN-Based MAC-VRFs for ease of understanding again, this model can be represented as shown in Figure 8-4. An IP VRF exists per tenant, with the IRB interfaces tied to the IP VRF. In Figure 8-4, leaf1 has both VLANs 100 and 200, while leaf2 only has VLAN 200. An IP VRF called *Tenant1* exists on both leaf1 and leaf2, with the respective IRB interfaces attached to it. Traffic is routed, across the fabric, between VLAN 100 and 200 using the L3VNI 10300 (that is bound to the IP VRF).

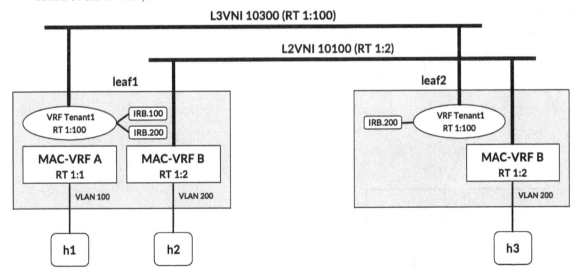

Figure 8-4 *Visual representation of symmetric IRB with IP VRFs and MAC-VRFs*

The general traffic flow for inter-subnet traffic, using symmetric IRB, is shown in Figure 8-5.

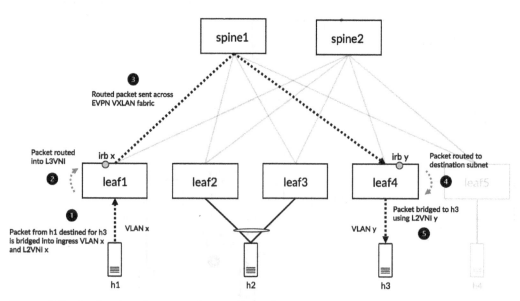

Figure 8-5 *Packet flow for inter-subnet traffic with symmetric IRB*

A routed overlay is not very different from symmetric IRB—both use the same constructs of an IP VRF and a L3VNI corresponding to this IP VRF for routing inter-subnet traffic. A routed overlay is useful for cloud-native architectures and deployments in which many applications (as VMs/containers) exist and there is no Layer 2 requirement. The fabric leafs (VTEPs) connect to the servers via Layer 3, typically running some form of dynamic routing protocol with the servers to exchange host routes. These are then injected into the EVPN VXLAN fabric as Type-5 routes. The general packet flow for inter-subnet traffic continues to be the same, for the most part, as symmetric IRB.

A natural extension of a routed overlay design is *host-routed bridging*. In such a design, the VXLAN tunnel termination is also moved to the hosts, meaning that the leafs (or ToR switches) are simply used for IP forwarding and do not build any VXLAN constructs locally. All VXLAN functionality is moved to the hosts themselves, which typically leverage some form of open-source routing suite/daemon such as Free Range Routing (FRR). This also greatly simplifies multihoming and network reliability to the hosts—hosts can directly uplink to multiple ToR leafs via Layer 3 interfaces, providing native ECMP with no requirement of Ethernet Segment–based DF election and split-horizon rules to prevent loops. Visually, the tunnel termination in such a design can be represented as shown in Figure 8-6.

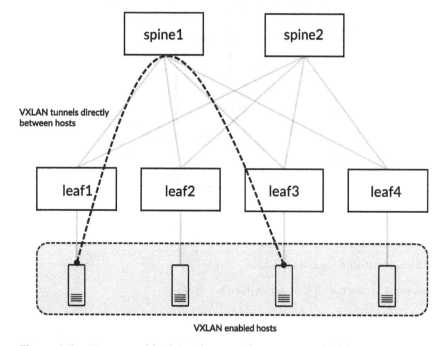

Figure 8-6 *Host-routed bridging design with VXLAN enabled hosts*

There are fundamental differences in how traffic forwarding happens across these routing models, as well as certain control plane and data plane parameters that are different. The remainder of this chapter focuses on how asymmetric and symmetric IRB designs are configured and validated, with detailed packet flows and packet captures that call out the important differences and the reasons for the same. Chapter 9 focuses on routed overlay and host-routed bridging designs. A summary of the high-level differences between these methodologies is tabulated in Figure 8-7.

Asymmetric IRB	Symmetric IRB	Routed Overlay
Useful when all hosts (across VLANs) are attached to all PEs and MAC/IP learning happens everywhere	Useful when hosts and VLANs are scoped to specific leafs and there is no need for all VLANs everywhere	Useful when cloud-native applications are deployed that have no Layer-2 requirements
Operationally easier to deploy and troubleshoot	Operationally more complex to deploy and troubleshoot	Operationally easier to deploy and troubleshoot
Uses a bridge-route-bridge model of forwarding inter-subnet traffic	Uses a bridge-route-route-bridge model of forwarding inter-subnet traffic	Inter-subnet traffic is forwarded using EVPN Type-5 routes only
Uses EVPN Type-2 routes	Uses EVPN Type-2 routes	Uses EVPN Type-5 routes
IP VRF is optional and no L3VNI is used	IP VRF mapped to an L3VNI is mandatory	IP VRF mapped to an L3VNI is mandatory

Figure 8-7 *Differences between asymmetric IRB, symmetric IRB, and a routed overlay design*

Asymmetric IRB

This section takes a detailed look at how to configure and validate an asymmetric IRB routing model in an EVPN VXLAN fabric, with packet walks and packet captures for the control plane and data plane.

Configuring and Validating Asymmetric IRB

Figure 8-8 shows the reference topology used in this section. It identifies the VLAN and IP addressing for the respective hosts, with VLAN-Aware MAC-VRFs configured with VLANs 100, 200, 300, and 400 spread across different leafs.

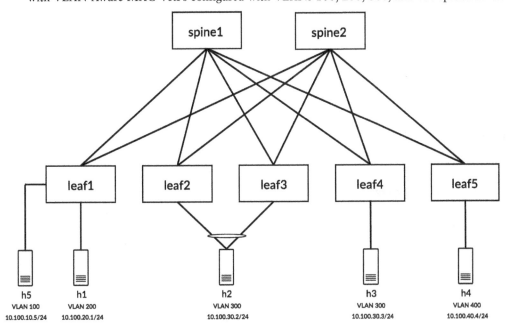

Figure 8-8 *Reference topology for asymmetric IRB*

The core of the fabric remains the same as in the previous chapters. The underlay uses /31 IPv4 addressing on the point-to-point interfaces between the leafs and the spines and uses eBGP for distributing loopback reachability information between the leafs, with each leaf establishing an eBGP peer to both spines. Taking leaf1 and spine1 as an example, this underlay configuration and state is shown in Example 8-1 and Example 8-2. The **show protocols bgp group underlay** operational mode command displays the eBGP configuration for the underlay in both examples, which utilizes an export policy called *allow-loopback* to advertise the loopback address. BGP state is validated using the **show bgp summary group underlay** operational mode command.

Example 8-1   *BGP underlay configuration and state on leaf1*

```
root@leaf1# show protocols bgp group underlay
type external;
family inet {
    unicast;
}
export allow-loopback;
peer-as 65500;
multipath;
bfd-liveness-detection {
    minimum-interval 333;
    multiplier 3;
}
neighbor 198.51.100.1 {
        description "to spine1";
}
neighbor 198.51.100.3 {
        description "to spine2";
}


root@leaf1# show policy-options policy-statement allow-loopback
term 1 {
    from interface lo0.0;
    then accept;
}
term 10 {
    then reject;
}


root@leaf1> show bgp summary group underlay

Threading mode: BGP I/O
Default eBGP mode: advertise - accept, receive - accept
Groups: 2 Peers: 4 Down peers: 0
Table          Tot Paths  Act Paths Suppressed    History Damp State    Pending
inet.0
                     10         10          0          0         0          0
bgp.evpn.0
                    120         60          0          0         0          0
Peer                    AS    InPkt    OutPkt    OutQ   Flaps Last Up/Dwn State|#Active/Received/Accepted/Damped...
198.51.100.1         65500     1539      1551       0       0  11:43:39 Establ
  inet.0: 5/5/5/0
198.51.100.3         65500     1539      1550       0       0  11:43:39 Establ
  inet.0: 5/5/5/0
```

Example 8-2 *BGP underlay configuration on spine1*

```
root@spine1# show protocols bgp group underlay
type external;
family inet {
    unicast;
}
export allow-loopback;
bfd-liveness-detection {
    minimum-interval 333;
    multiplier 3;
}
neighbor 198.51.100.0 {
    description "to leaf1";
    peer-as 65421;
}
neighbor 198.51.100.4 {
    description "to leaf2";
    peer-as 65422;
}
neighbor 198.51.100.8 {
    description "to leaf3";
    peer-as 65423;
}
neighbor 198.51.100.12 {
    description "to leaf4";
    peer-as 65424;
}
neighbor 198.51.100.16 {
    description "to leaf5";
    peer-as 65425;
}


root@spine1# show policy-options policy-statement allow-loopback
term 1 {
    from {
        route-filter 192.0.2.0/24 orlonger;
    }
    then accept;
}
term 2 {
    then reject;
}
```

The overlay also uses eBGP between the leafs and spines. However, this is enabled for the L2VPN EVPN address family. The peering is over loopbacks, making it a multi-hop session. This ensures that when a VTEP advertises a route via BGP EVPN, the next-hop address is set to the loopback address used as the source for the overlay eBGP peering, enabling end-to-end VXLAN tunnels to originate from and terminate to these loopback addresses. The spines are configured to not modify the next-hop address in the BGP updates. BGP configuration and state for the overlay is shown in Example 8-3 and Example 8-4, from leaf1 and spine1, respectively.

Example 8-3 *BGP overlay configuration and state on leaf1*

```
root@leaf1# show protocols bgp group overlay
type external;
multihop;
local-address 192.0.2.11;
family evpn {
    signaling;
}
peer-as 65500;
multipath;
bfd-liveness-detection {
    minimum-interval 333;
    multiplier 3;
}
neighbor 192.0.2.101 {
        description "to spine1";
}
neighbor 192.0.2.102 {
        description "to spine2";
}


root@leaf1> show bgp summary group overlay

Threading mode: BGP I/O
Default eBGP mode: advertise - accept, receive - accept
Groups: 2 Peers: 4 Down peers: 0
Table           Tot Paths  Act Paths Suppressed   History Damp State    Pending
inet.0
                      10         10          0         0         0          0
bgp.evpn.0
                      56         28          0         0         0          0
Peer                    AS    InPkt    OutPkt     OutQ   Flaps Last Up/Dwn State|#Active/Received/Accepted/Damped...
192.0.2.101          65500     4382      4373        0       0 1d 8:59:18 Establ
  bgp.evpn.0: 20/28/28/0
  macvrf-1.evpn.0: 19/26/26/0
  __default_evpn__.evpn.0: 0/0/0/0
192.0.2.102          65500     4382      4372        0       0 1d 8:59:14 Establ
  bgp.evpn.0: 8/28/28/0
  macvrf-1.evpn.0: 7/26/26/0
  __default_evpn__.evpn.0: 0/0/0/0
```

Example 8-4 *BGP overlay configuration on spine1*

```
root@spine1# show protocols bgp group overlay
type external;
multihop {
    no-nexthop-change;
}
```

```
local-address 192.0.2.101;
family evpn {
    signaling;
}
multipath;
bfd-liveness-detection {
    minimum-interval 333;
    multiplier 3;
}
neighbor 192.0.2.11 {
    description "to leaf1";
    peer-as 65421;
}
neighbor 192.0.2.12 {
    description "to leaf2";
    peer-as 65422;
}
neighbor 192.0.2.13 {
    description "to leaf3";
    peer-as 65423;
}
neighbor 192.0.2.14 {
    description "to leaf4";
    peer-as 65424;
}
neighbor 192.0.2.15 {
    description "to leaf5";
    peer-as 65425;
}
```

Each leaf is configured with a VLAN-Aware MAC-VRF that includes all VLANs—this is critical for asymmetric IRB since all routed VLANs must exist on all leafs. As an example, the MAC-VRF configuration on leaf1 is shown in Example 8-5.

Example 8-5 *MAC-VRF configuration on leaf1*

```
root@leaf1# show routing-instances macvrf-1
instance-type mac-vrf;
protocols {
    evpn {
        encapsulation vxlan;
        default-gateway do-not-advertise;
        extended-vni-list all;
    }
}
vtep-source-interface lo0.0;
service-type vlan-aware;
interface et-0/0/49.0;
interface et-0/0/54.0;
route-distinguisher 192.0.2.11:1;
vrf-target target:1:1;
```

```
vlans {
    v100 {
        vlan-id 100;
        l3-interface irb.100;
        vxlan {
            vni 10100;
        }
    }
    v200 {
        vlan-id 200;
        l3-interface irb.200;
        vxlan {
            vni 10200;
        }
    }
    v300 {
        vlan-id 300;
        l3-interface irb.300;
        vxlan {
            vni 10300;
        }
    }
    v400 {
        vlan-id 400;
        l3-interface irb.400;
        vxlan {
            vni 10400;
        }
    }
}


root@leaf1# show interfaces irb
unit 100 {
    family inet {
        mtu 9000;
        address 10.100.10.254/24;
    }
    mac 00:02:00:00:00:11;
}
unit 200 {
    family inet {
        mtu 9000;
        address 10.100.20.254/24;
    }
    mac 00:02:00:00:00:11;
}
unit 300 {
    family inet {
        mtu 9000;
```

```
            address 10.100.30.254/24;
        }
        mac 00:02:00:00:00:11;
    }
    unit 400 {
        family inet {
            mtu 9000;
            address 10.100.40.254/24;
        }
        mac 00:02:00:00:00:11;
    }
}
```

As shown in Example 8-5, each VLAN is associated to its corresponding IRB interface, since routing is moved to the leafs with edge-routed bridging. It is important to note that all leafs are configured with the same IP address and MAC address for the respective IRB interfaces (often referred to as a *distributed anycast gateway*)—this is needed because, typically, when a host moves from behind one leaf to another, it does not change its associated IP address and default gateway. This means that during such a move, the host cache continues to point to the same IP address (and MAC address) of the IRB interface of the original leaf it was connected to, and this must be the same on the leaf it moved to as well; otherwise, traffic can be interrupted or delayed after the host has moved until its cache is cleared or updated.

> **Note** The command **default-gateway do-not-advertise** is configured since each leaf is expected to have the same IRB address configured statically and there is no need to sync this information across leafs. With this configured, the IRB addresses are no longer advertised as EVPN Type-2 routes.

As shown in Example 8-6, taking leaf4 as an example, the same IP address and MAC address (as leaf1) are configured for the respective IRB interfaces, and this is true for all leafs in the reference topology.

Example 8-6 *IRB interfaces configuration on leaf4*

```
root@leaf4# show interfaces irb
unit 100 {
    family inet {
        mtu 9000;
        address 10.100.10.254/24;
    }
    mac 00:02:00:00:00:11;
}
unit 200 {
    family inet {
        mtu 9000;
        address 10.100.20.254/24;
    }
    mac 00:02:00:00:00:11;
}
unit 300 {
    family inet {
        mtu 9000;
        address 10.100.30.254/24;
    }
    mac 00:02:00:00:00:11;
}
```

```
unit 400 {
    family inet {
        mtu 9000;
        address 10.100.40.254/24;
    }
    mac 00:02:00:00:00:11;
}
```

Once the remaining leafs are configured in a similar fashion, host MAC and IP addresses are learned in the fabric, and all hosts can communicate with each other. Taking host h1 as an example, it can communicate with hosts h2, h3, h4, and h5, as shown in Example 8-7.

Example 8-7 *Host h1 reachability to hosts h2, h3, h4, and h5*

```
root@h1> ping 10.100.30.2
PING 10.100.30.2 (10.100.30.2): 56 data bytes
64 bytes from 10.100.30.2: icmp_seq=0 ttl=63 time=11.456 ms
64 bytes from 10.100.30.2: icmp_seq=1 ttl=63 time=5.828 ms
64 bytes from 10.100.30.2: icmp_seq=2 ttl=63 time=0.852 ms
64 bytes from 10.100.30.2: icmp_seq=3 ttl=63 time=0.913 ms
^C
--- 10.100.30.2 ping statistics ---
4 packets transmitted, 4 packets received, 0% packet loss
round-trip min/avg/max/stddev = 0.852/4.762/11.456/4.360 ms


root@h1> ping 10.100.30.3
PING 10.100.30.3 (10.100.30.3): 56 data bytes
64 bytes from 10.100.30.3: icmp_seq=0 ttl=63 time=0.989 ms
64 bytes from 10.100.30.3: icmp_seq=1 ttl=63 time=45.360 ms
64 bytes from 10.100.30.3: icmp_seq=2 ttl=63 time=0.806 ms
64 bytes from 10.100.30.3: icmp_seq=3 ttl=63 time=0.788 ms
^C
--- 10.100.30.3 ping statistics ---
4 packets transmitted, 4 packets received, 0% packet loss
round-trip min/avg/max/stddev = 0.788/9.768/45.360/17.796 ms


root@h1> ping 10.100.40.4
PING 10.100.40.4 (10.100.40.4): 56 data bytes
64 bytes from 10.100.40.4: icmp_seq=0 ttl=63 time=0.971 ms
64 bytes from 10.100.40.4: icmp_seq=1 ttl=63 time=0.865 ms
64 bytes from 10.100.40.4: icmp_seq=2 ttl=63 time=0.874 ms
64 bytes from 10.100.40.4: icmp_seq=3 ttl=63 time=0.941 ms
^C
--- 10.100.40.4 ping statistics ---
4 packets transmitted, 4 packets received, 0% packet loss
round-trip min/avg/max/stddev = 0.865/0.913/0.971/0.045 ms


root@h1> ping 10.100.10.5
PING 10.100.10.5 (10.100.10.5): 56 data bytes
```

```
64 bytes from 10.100.10.5: icmp_seq=0 ttl=63 time=0.797 ms
64 bytes from 10.100.10.5: icmp_seq=1 ttl=63 time=4.675 ms
64 bytes from 10.100.10.5: icmp_seq=2 ttl=63 time=0.668 ms
64 bytes from 10.100.10.5: icmp_seq=3 ttl=63 time=0.641 ms
^C
--- 10.100.10.5 ping statistics ---
4 packets transmitted, 4 packets received, 0% packet loss
round-trip min/avg/max/stddev = 0.641/11.445/43.675/18.608 ms
```

Control Plane and Data Plane with Asymmetric IRB

MAC addresses (and corresponding IP addresses) are learned in the data plane via an ARP/GARP sent by the host, as discussed in the previous chapters. This information is distributed through the fabric via BGP EVPN Type-2 MAC and MAC+IP routes, which allows remote leafs to build their MAC-IP tables, as shown in Figure 8-9.

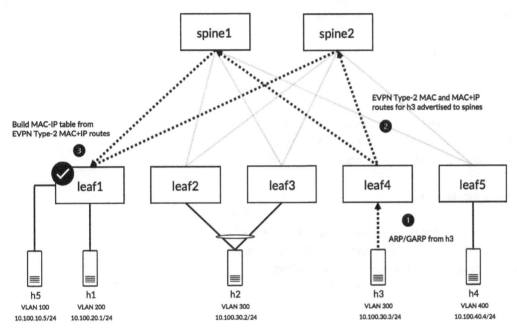

Figure 8-9 *Host h3's address advertised via EVPN Type-2 routes*

Since all leafs have all VLANs and corresponding VNIs configured, each leaf learns the MAC address of all hosts in the fabric in their respective VLANs. For example, on leaf1, MAC addresses for remote hosts h2, h3, and h4 are learned in their respective bridge domains, as shown in Example 8-8, using the **show mac-vrf forwarding mac-table** operational mode command.

Example 8-8 *MAC table on leaf1*

```
root@leaf1> show mac-vrf forwarding mac-table

MAC flags (S - static MAC, D - dynamic MAC, L - locally learned, P - Persistent static
        SE - statistics enabled, NM - non configured MAC, R - remote PE MAC, O - ovsdb MAC)


Ethernet switching table : 5 entries, 5 learned
Routing instance : macvrf-1
    Vlan          MAC            MAC      GBP    Logical          SVLBNH/      Active
    name          address        flags    tag    interface        VENH Index   source
```

v100	00:14:94:00:00:02	D	et-0/0/54.0		
v200	f0:4b:3a:b9:80:a7	D	et-0/0/49.0		
v300	f0:4b:3a:b9:80:ab	DR	vtep-9.32772		192.0.2.14
v300	f0:4b:3a:b9:81:65	DR	esi.1704	1705	
00:00:00:00:11:11:00:00:00:00					
v400	f0:4b:3a:b9:80:bb	DR	vtep-9.32773		192.0.2.15

Through the processing of EVPN Type-2 MAC+IP routes generated by remote leafs, leaf1 also populates its EVPN ARP cache and the MAC-IP table per bridge domain, shown in Example 8-9, using the **show ethernet-switching evpn arp-table** and the **show mac-vrf forwarding mac-ip-table** operational mode commands.

Example 8-9 *MAC-IP table on leaf1*

```
root@leaf1> show ethernet-switching evpn arp-table
```

INET address	MAC address	Logical interface	Routing instance	Bridging domain
10.100.10.5	00:14:94:00:00:02	et-0/0/54.0	macvrf-1	v100
10.100.10.254	00:02:00:00:00:11	irb.100	macvrf-1	v100
10.100.20.254	00:02:00:00:00:11	irb.200	macvrf-1	v200
10.100.20.1	f0:4b:3a:b9:80:a7	et-0/0/49.0	macvrf-1	v200
10.100.30.254	00:02:00:00:00:11	irb.300	macvrf-1	v300
10.100.30.3	f0:4b:3a:b9:80:ab	vtep-9.32772	macvrf-1	v300
10.100.30.2	f0:4b:3a:b9:81:65	esi.1704	macvrf-1	v300
10.100.40.254	00:02:00:00:00:11	irb.400	macvrf-1	v400
10.100.40.4	f0:4b:3a:b9:80:bb	vtep-9.32773	macvrf-1	v400

```
root@leaf1> show mac-vrf forwarding mac-ip-table

MAC IP flags  (S - Static, D - Dynamic, L - Local , R - Remote, Lp - Local Proxy,
               Rp - Remote Proxy, K - Kernel, RT - Dest Route, (N)AD - (Not) Advt to remote,
               RE - Re-ARP/ND, RO - Router, OV - Override, Ur - Unresolved,
               RTS - Dest Route Skipped, RGw - Remote Gateway, GBP - Group Based Policy,
               RTF - Dest Route Forced)
 Routing instance : macvrf-1
 Bridging domain : v100
```

IP address	MAC address	Flags	GBP Tag	Logical Interface	Active source
10.100.10.5	00:14:94:00:00:02	DL,K,RT,AD		et-0/0/54.0	
10.100.10.254	00:02:00:00:00:11	S,K		irb.100	

```
MAC IP flags  (S - Static, D - Dynamic, L - Local , R - Remote, Lp - Local Proxy,
               Rp - Remote Proxy, K - Kernel, RT - Dest Route, (N)AD - (Not) Advt to remote,
               RE - Re-ARP/ND, RO - Router, OV - Override, Ur - Unresolved,
               RTS - Dest Route Skipped, RGw - Remote Gateway, GBP - Group Based Policy,
               RTF - Dest Route Forced)
 Routing instance : macvrf-1
 Bridging domain : v200
```

IP address	MAC address	Flags	GBP Tag	Logical Interface	Active source
10.100.20.254	00:02:00:00:00:11	S,K		irb.200	
10.100.20.1	f0:4b:3a:b9:80:a7	DL,K,RT,AD		et-0/0/49.0	

```
MAC IP flags  (S - Static, D - Dynamic, L - Local , R - Remote, Lp - Local Proxy,
              Rp - Remote Proxy, K - Kernel, RT - Dest Route, (N)AD - (Not) Advt to remote,
              RE - Re-ARP/ND, RO - Router, OV - Override, Ur - Unresolved,
              RTS - Dest Route Skipped, RGw - Remote Gateway, GBP - Group Based Policy,
              RTF - Dest Route Forced)
Routing instance : macvrf-1
Bridging domain : v300
  IP                        MAC               Flags        GBP    Logical       Active
  address                   address                        Tag    Interface     source
  10.100.30.254             00:02:00:00:00:11 S,K                 irb.300
  10.100.30.3               f0:4b:3a:b9:80:ab DR,K,RT             vtep-9.32772  192.0.2.14
  10.100.30.2               f0:4b:3a:b9:81:65 DR,K,RT             esi.1704
00:00:00:00:11:11:00:00:00:00
```

```
MAC IP flags  (S - Static, D - Dynamic, L - Local , R - Remote, Lp - Local Proxy,
              Rp - Remote Proxy, K - Kernel, RT - Dest Route, (N)AD - (Not) Advt to remote,
              RE - Re-ARP/ND, RO - Router, OV - Override, Ur - Unresolved,
              RTS - Dest Route Skipped, RGw - Remote Gateway, GBP - Group Based Policy,
              RTF - Dest Route Forced)
Routing instance : macvrf-1
Bridging domain : v400
  IP                        MAC               Flags        GBP    Logical       Active
  address                   address                        Tag    Interface     source
  10.100.40.254             00:02:00:00:00:11 S,K                 irb.400
  10.100.40.4               f0:4b:3a:b9:80:bb DR,K,RT             vtep-9.32773  192.0.2.15
```

Consider a situation in which host h1 wants to communicate with h3. Since h3 is in a different subnet, h1 attempts to resolve its default gateway first (10.100.20.254), which should exist on its directly attached leaf in a distributed anycast gateway model. This is leaf1, in our case. The ARP process is shown in Figure 8-10.

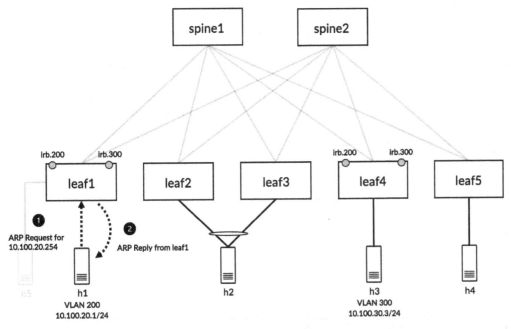

Figure 8-10 *Host h1 resolving its gateway address*

Once the default gateway is resolved and the ARP cache is populated for it on host h1, it can send an IP packet destined for h3. In our case, this is a simple ICMP request generated via the **ping** command on h1. This IP packet from h1, arriving on leaf1, has a source MAC address of h1 and the gateway's MAC address as the destination MAC address, in the Ethernet header. In the IP header, the source IP address is h1's IP address and the destination IP address is h3's IP address, as shown in Figure 8-11.

```
No.   Time        Source        Destination    Protocol  Length  Info
   1 0.000000   10.100.20.1   10.100.30.3    ICMP      102  Echo (ping) request  id=0xb1bb, seq=0/0, ttl=64 (reply in 2)
   2 0.000402   10.100.30.3   10.100.20.1    ICMP      102  Echo (ping) reply    id=0xb1bb, seq=0/0, ttl=63 (request in 1)
   3 0.998499   10.100.20.1   10.100.30.3    ICMP      102  Echo (ping) request  id=0xb1bb, seq=1/256, ttl=64 (reply in 4)
   4 0.998892   10.100.30.3   10.100.20.1    ICMP      102  Echo (ping) reply    id=0xb1bb, seq=1/256, ttl=63 (request in 3)

> Frame 1: 102 bytes on wire (816 bits), 102 bytes captured (816 bits) on interface \\.\pipe\view_capture    0000  00 02 00 00 00 11
v Ethernet II, Src: JuniperN_b9:80:a7 (f0:4b:3a:b9:80:a7), Dst: NetSys_00:00:11 (00:02:00:00:00:11)         0010  00 54 9b 61 00 00
  > Destination: NetSys_00:00:11 (00:02:00:00:00:11)                                                        0020  1e 03 08 00 85 f6
  > Source: JuniperN_b9:80:a7 (f0:4b:3a:b9:80:a7)                                                           0030  91 06 08 09 0a 0b
    Type: IPv4 (0x0800)                                                                                     0040  16 17 18 19 1a 1b
    Frame check sequence: 0xa365e015 [unverified]                                                           0050  26 27 28 29 2a 2b
    [FCS Status: Unverified]                                                                                0060  36 37 a3 65 e0 15
v Internet Protocol Version 4, Src: 10.100.20.1, Dst: 10.100.30.3
    0100 .... = Version: 4
    .... 0101 = Header Length: 20 bytes (5)
  > Differentiated Services Field: 0x00 (DSCP: CS0, ECN: Not-ECT)
    Total Length: 84
    Identification: 0x9b61 (39777)
  > 000. .... = Flags: 0x0
    ...0 0000 0000 0000 = Fragment Offset: 0
    Time to Live: 64
    Protocol: ICMP (1)
    Header Checksum: 0x987c [validation disabled]
    [Header checksum status: Unverified]
    Source Address: 10.100.20.1
    Destination Address: 10.100.30.3
v Internet Control Message Protocol
    Type: 8 (Echo (ping) request)
    Code: 0
    Checksum: 0x85f6 [correct]
    [Checksum Status: Good]
    Identifier (BE): 45499 (0xb1bb)
    Identifier (LE): 48049 (0xbbb1)
    Sequence Number (BE): 0 (0x0000)
    Sequence Number (LE): 0 (0x0000)
    [Response frame: 2]
  > Data (56 bytes)
```

Figure 8-11　*IP packet from h1 destined for h3*

When leaf1 receives this packet, it does a MAC lookup and an IP lookup (since the destination MAC address is owned by leaf1). The IP lookup determines that the destination is attached to leaf1 (because the IRB interface for VLAN 300 is configured on leaf1 as well). This means that leaf1 can directly ARP for the destination. It first checks its MAC-IP table for the destination IP address, and if there is a matching entry, then there is no need to flood an ARP request through the fabric—instead, it can simply use the resolved MAC address that is present in the MAC-IP table. In our case, a matching entry is found in the table, as shown in Example 8-10, using the **show mac-vrf forwarding mac-ip-table** operational mode command.

Example 8-10　*MAC-IP table entry for host h3 on leaf1*

```
root@leaf1> show route table inet.0 10.100.30.3

inet.0: 36 destinations, 40 routes (36 active, 0 holddown, 0 hidden)
@ = Routing Use Only, # = Forwarding Use Only
+ = Active Route, - = Last Active, * = Both

10.100.30.0/24     *[Direct/0] 06:17:09
                    > via irb.300

root@leaf1> show mac-vrf forwarding mac-ip-table | grep 10.100.30.3
  10.100.30.3          f0:4b:3a:b9:80:ab      DR,K,RT            vtep-9.32772       192.0.2.14
```

Since the MAC address for the destination is resolved via the MAC-IP table, leaf1 does another MAC lookup on this MAC address to determine how to forward the packet. The output in Example 8-11 shows the forwarding table entry for this MAC address, using the **show route forwarding-table destination** operational mode command.

Example 8-11 *PFE forwarding result for host h3's MAC address*

```
root@leaf1> show route forwarding-table destination f0:4b:3a:b9:80:ab
Routing table: macvrf-1.evpn-vxlan
Bridging domain: v300.evpn-vxlan
VPLS:
Enabled protocols: Bridging, ACKed by all peers, EVPN VXLAN, mac-vrf,
Destination       Type RtRef Next hop       Type Index    NhRef Netif
f0:4b:3a:b9:80:ab/48 user     0             comp   1706    12
```

This forwarding entry is a composite next-hop ID that provides the necessary instructions to encapsulate the packet with VXLAN headers. As shown in Example 8-12, details of the next-hop ID can be viewed using the **show nhdb id** [*next-hop id*] **extensive** command, executed from the PFE shell. This confirms the encapsulated VXLAN packet uses a source IP address of 0xc000020b (192.0.2.11, which is leaf1's loopback address) and a destination IP address of 0xx000020e (192.0.2.14, which is leaf4's loopback address). The associated bridge domain provides the L2VNI that must be added to the encapsulated packet in the VXLAN header, as shown in Example 8-13, using the **show bridge-domain entry** [*bridge-domain index*], again executed from the PFE shell.

Example 8-12 *Detailed look at next-hop programming on leaf1 for host h3's MAC address*

```
FPC0(leaf1 vty)# show nhdb id 1706 recursive
1706(Compst, BRIDGE, ifl:0:-, pfe-id:0, comp-fn:Vxlan Unicast Encapsulation NH)
    524288(Indirect, IPv4, ifl:827:et-0/0/48.0, pfe-id:0, i-ifl:0:-)
        524286(Unilist, IPv4, ifl:0:-, pfe-id:0)
            1754(Unicast, IPv4, ifl:827:et-0/0/48.0, pfe-id:0)
            1755(Unicast, IPv4, ifl:829:et-0/0/50.0, pfe-id:0)


FPC0(leaf1 vty)# show nhdb id 1706 extensive
  ID     Type      Interface      Next Hop Addr    Protocol     Encap       MTU            Flags PFE internal Flags
  .....  ........  .............  ...............  ..........   ...........  ....  .................... ..................

  1706   Compst    -              -                BRIDGE       -            0   0x0000000000000000  0x0000000000000000


BFD Session Id: 0


Composite NH:
  Function: Vxlan Encap NH with forwarding NH being Unicast
  Hardware Index: 0x0
  Composite flag: 0x0
  Composite pfe flag: 0xe
  Lower-level NH Ids: 524288
  Derived NH Ids:


Vxlan data:
        SIP = 0xc000020b
        DIP = 0xc000020e
        L3RTT = 0
        SVTEP ifl = 831
        proto = 2
        RVTEP ifl = 833
```

```
Dram Bytes : 240
Num of nhs: 1


 Routing-table id: 1
```

Example 8-13 *Bridge domain details for VLAN 300*

```
FPC0(leaf1 vty)# show bridge-domain
Bridging Domain           BD-Index RTT-Index  BD-Type   BD-Hw-Token
default+1                     2         8      Regular        3
v100+100                      3         9      Regular        4
v200+200                      4         9      Regular        5
v300+300                      5         9      Regular        6
v400+400                      6         9      Regular        7


FPC0(leaf1 vty)# show bridge-domain entry 5
BD Name  : v300+300
BD Index : 5
 VLAN   : [ 0x8100.300 0x8100.4095 ]
 RTB-ID: 9
 Seqno : 0
 BD type         : Regular
 state  flags    : 0x0
 config flags    : 0x40210802
 MAC Limit       : 294912
 IRB IFL index   : 835
 # of IFBDs      : 1 Trunk IFBDs 1
 snoop-enable    : 0
 Input filter index  : 0
 Flood filter index  : 0
 Output filter index : 0
 Generation number   : 5
 BD implicit filters  : None
 VXLAN ID                 : 10300
 VXLAN Mcast group        : 0.0.0.0
 L3 RTT                   : 0
 L3 proto                 : 2
 VxLAN Encap Inner VLAN   : 0
 VxLAN Decap Accept Inner VLAN: 0
 VxLAN Aging Timer        : 300
 VXLAN Source VTEP IP     : 192.0.2.11
 VxLAN Destination UDP Port  : 4789
 EVPN VxLAN MPLS DCI enabled : 0
 BD nexthop[0]         : 0x0
 BD FTF ptr [0]        : 0x0
 BD nexthop[1]         : 0x0
 BD FTF ptr [1]        : 0x0
 PVLAN Primary BD Id : 0
 PVLAN Group Id : 0
```

This encapsulated packet is now carried through the fabric, routed toward leaf4, using the outer destination IP header, as show in Figure 8-12.

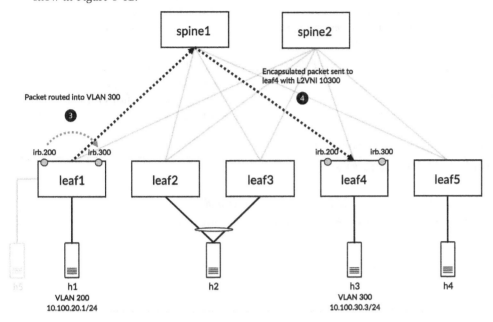

Figure 8-12 *Encapsulated VXLAN packet with L2VNI 10300*

The packet capture shown in Figure 8-13, taken in transit, confirms that the VNI added to the VXLAN header is the L2VNI associated to the bridge domain of the destination (10300, in our case).

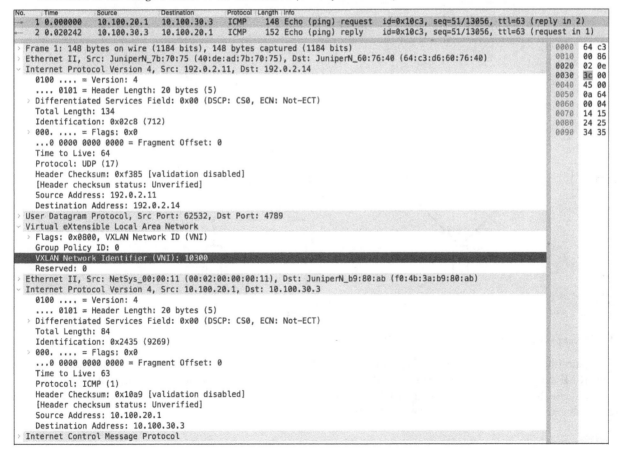

Figure 8-13 *Packet capture of an encapsulated VXLAN paket when h1 communicates with h3*

The inner Ethernet header also confirms that this packet was first routed and then encapsulated—the source address is the IRB's MAC address, and the destination address is h3's MAC address. It is important to note that the TTL is now 63 in the inner IP header (the original IP packet from the host had a TTL of 64)—since the packet is routed, the TTL is decremented by 1. This also means that if the TTL were to be 0 after decrementing it, the packet would be dropped and not forwarded out.

When leaf4 receives this packet, it decapsulates it and does a MAC lookup on the inner Ethernet header, using the L2VNI to determine the bridge domain where this lookup should happen. This returns the egress interface to which host h3 is connected, and the packet is simply bridged down to the host. This is shown in Example 8-14, which confirms the exit interface for this MAC lookup, with a visual representation of the packet path following this in Figure 8-14.

Example 8-14 *MAC table entry for host h3's MAC address on leaf4*

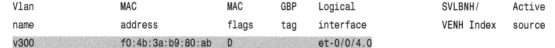

```
root@leaf4> show mac-vrf forwarding mac-table f0:4b:3a:b9:80:ab


MAC flags (S - static MAC, D - dynamic MAC, L - locally learned, P - Persistent static
          SE - statistics enabled, NM - non configured MAC, R - remote PE MAC, O - ovsdb MAC)



Ethernet switching table : 4 entries, 4 learned
Routing instance : macvrf-1
   Vlan          MAC             MAC     GBP   Logical        SVLBNH/     Active
   name          address         flags   tag   interface      VENH Index  source
   v300          f0:4b:3a:b9:80:ab  D            et-0/0/4.0
```

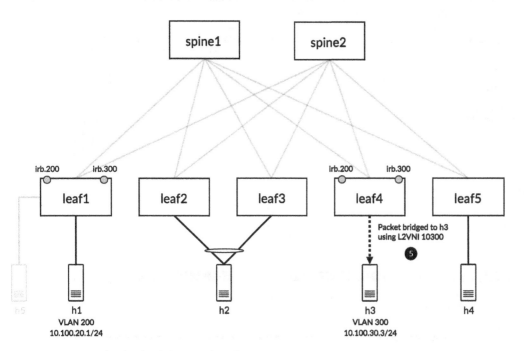

Figure 8-14 *Packet bridged down to host h3 in L2VNI 10300*

The reverse path (the ICMP reply from host h3) goes through similar forwarding decisions; however, it is important to note that for the ICMP reply from host h3 destined to h1, the packet will get routed again on the ingress leaf itself, which will be leaf4 in this case. It is then bridged across the EVPN VXLAN fabric in L2VNI 10200. The visual representation in Figure 8-15 summarizes the packet flow for the ICMP reply from h3.

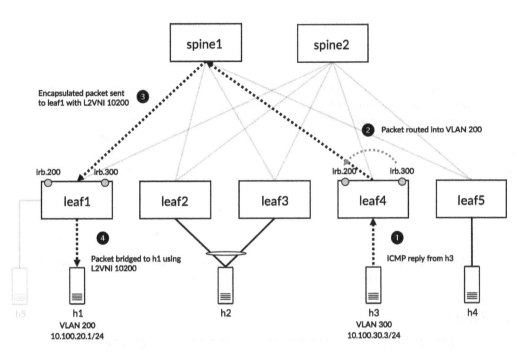

Figure 8-15 *Packet flow for ICMP reply from h3 destined to h1*

A packet capture, taken in transit, confirms that the VNI added to the VXLAN header is the L2VNI 10200, as shown in Figure 8-16.

```
No.   Time       Source        Destination   Protocol  Length Info
   1 0.000000   10.100.20.1   10.100.30.3   ICMP      148 Echo (ping) request  id=0x10c3, seq=51/13056, ttl=63 (reply in 2)
   2 0.020242   10.100.30.3   10.100.20.1   ICMP      152 Echo (ping) reply    id=0x10c3, seq=51/13056, ttl=63 (request in 1)
→  3 0.973972   10.100.20.1   10.100.30.3   ICMP      148 Echo (ping) request  id=0x10c3, seq=52/13312, ttl=63 (reply in 4)
   4 0.974394   10.100.30.3   10.100.20.1   ICMP      152 Echo (ping) reply    id=0x10c3, seq=52/13312, ttl=63 (request in 3)

˅ Internet Protocol Version 4, Src: 192.0.2.14, Dst: 192.0.2.11        0000  40 de ad 7b 70 75 64 c3
    0100 .... = Version: 4                                             0010  08 00 45 00 00 86 00 00
    .... 0101 = Header Length: 20 bytes (5)                            0020  02 0e c0 00 02 0b d0 a4
  › Differentiated Services Field: 0x00 (DSCP: CS0, ECN: Not-ECT)      0030  00 00 00 27 d8 00 f0 4b
    Total Length: 134                                                  0040  00 11 08 00 45 00 00 54
    Identification: 0x0000 (0)                                         0050  0a 64 1e 03 0a 64 14 01
  › 000. .... = Flags: 0x0                                             0060  64 8e 3a fc 00 04 ea d2
    ...0 0000 0000 0000 = Fragment Offset: 0                           0070  10 11 12 13 14 15 16 17
    Time to Live: 63                                                   0080  20 21 22 23 24 25 26 27
    Protocol: UDP (17)                                                 0090  30 31 32 33 34 35 36 37
    Header Checksum: 0xf74d [validation disabled]
    [Header checksum status: Unverified]
    Source Address: 192.0.2.14
    Destination Address: 192.0.2.11
˅ User Datagram Protocol, Src Port: 53412, Dst Port: 4789
    Source Port: 53412
    Destination Port: 4789
    Length: 114
  › Checksum: 0x0000 [zero-value ignored]
    [Stream index: 1]
  › [Timestamps]
    UDP payload (106 bytes)
˅ Virtual eXtensible Local Area Network
  › Flags: 0x0800, VXLAN Network ID (VNI)
    Group Policy ID: 0
    VXLAN Network Identifier (VNI): 10200
    Reserved: 0
˅ Ethernet II, Src: NetSys_00:00:11 (00:02:00:00:00:11), Dst: JuniperN_b9:80:a7 (f0:4b:3a:b9:80:a7)
  › Destination: JuniperN_b9:80:a7 (f0:4b:3a:b9:80:a7)
  › Source: NetSys_00:00:11 (00:02:00:00:00:11)
    Type: IPv4 (0x0800)
› Internet Protocol Version 4, Src: 10.100.30.3, Dst: 10.100.20.1
› Internet Control Message Protocol
```

Figure 8-16 *Packet capture of ICMP reply from h3 destined to h1*

Thus, with asymmetric IRB, every ingress leaf does a MAC lookup, followed by an IP lookup, and then another MAC lookup for the destination, while the egress leaf only does a MAC lookup.

Note   In an asymmetric IRB design, it is quite possible for a VTEP to have VLANs with no physical interface mapped for that VLAN. Typically, EVPN Type-3 routes are not generated unless there is at least one physical interface that is up for that VLAN. This is because there is no sense in sending traffic to a VTEP that does not have any host in that VLAN and has no requirement to receive BUM traffic. Traditionally, IRB interfaces also do not come up unless there is at least one physical interface configured to be in the corresponding VLAN and is up. However, in an EVPN VXLAN deployment, if the VLAN is mapped to an IRB interface, these IRB interfaces are moved to an "up" state and the VTEP generates EVPN Type-3 routes for the corresponding VNI.

Symmetric IRB

This section takes a detailed look at how to configure and validate a symmetric IRB routing model, in an EVPN VXLAN fabric, with packet walks and packet captures for the control plane and data plane.

Configuring and Validating Symmetric IRB

With symmetric IRB, it is not necessary for all routed VLANs (and their respective IRBs) to be configured on all leafs. VLANs can be scoped to leafs that have hosts in that required VLAN only. To route between VLANs, the concept of a *Layer 3 VNI (L3VNI)* is used. This VNI identifies an IP VRF instance that the customer or tenant belongs to.

In the reference topology shown in Figure 8-17, unlike the configuration for asymmetric IRB, only the VLANs that are required per leaf need to be configured.

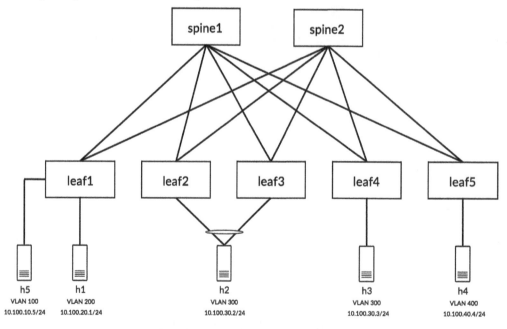

Figure 8-17   *Reference topology for symmetric IRB*

The table shown in Figure 8-18 breaks down what should be configured per leaf, along with the IP VRF and the corresponding L3VNI that will be used for this tenant. This table also serves as an easy reference for the symmetric IRB configuration that follows.

Leaf node	VLANs and L2VNIs	IP VRF	L3VNI
leaf1	100 - 10100 200 - 10200	Tenant1	10500
leaf2	300 - 10300	Tenant1	10500
leaf3	300 - 10300	Tenant1	10500
leaf4	300 - 10300	Tenant1	10500
leaf5	400 - 10400	Tenant1	10500

Figure 8-18 *Reference table showing VLANs, L2VNIs, IP VRF, and L3VNI per leaf for symmetric IRB*

The MAC-VRF configuration is mostly the same as described in the previous section for asymmetric IRB. The VLAN-Aware MAC-VRF configuration for leaf1 is shown in Example 8-15. The big difference is that only the necessary VLANs are configured on the leaf, which, in the case of leaf1, are VLANs 100 and 200.

Example 8-15 *MAC-VRF configuration on leaf1 for symmetric IRB*

```
root@leaf1# show routing-instances macvrf-1
instance-type mac-vrf;
protocols {
    evpn {
        encapsulation vxlan;
        default-gateway do-not-advertise;
        extended-vni-list all;
    }
}
vtep-source-interface lo0.0;
service-type vlan-aware;
interface et-0/0/49.0;
interface et-0/0/54.0;
route-distinguisher 192.0.2.11:1;
vrf-target target:1:1;
vlans {
    v100 {
        vlan-id 100;
        l3-interface irb.100;
        vxlan {
            vni 10100;
        }
    }
    v200 {
        vlan-id 200;
        l3-interface irb.200;
        vxlan {
            vni 10200;
        }
    }
}
```

In addition to the MAC-VRF routing instance, an IP VRF routing instance must be created for the customer. Within this routing instance, symmetric IRB is enabled using the *irb-symmetric-routing* configuration hierarchy and a VNI is associated to it, as shown in Example 8-16. This is the L3VNI. The IP VRF routing instance is also configured with its own Route Target, which facilitates import and export of routes for this VRF. Finally, the IRB interfaces are mapped to this VRF instance, creating a logical separation for the customer.

In addition to this, the *ip-prefix-routes* configuration hierarchy is also configured, which facilitates the advertisement of EVPN Type-5 routes in a symmetric IRB model, which is commonly used to advertise the IRB subnet itself into the fabric to facilitate the discovery of silent hosts, which is discussed in more detail in the section "Silent Hosts in a Symmetric IRB Design."

Example 8-16 *IP VRF configuration on leaf1 for symmetric IRB*

```
root@leaf1# show routing-instances Tenant1
instance-type vrf;
protocols {
    evpn {
        irb-symmetric-routing {
            vni 10500;
        }
        ip-prefix-routes {
            advertise direct-nexthop;
            encapsulation vxlan;
            vni 10500;
        }
    }
}
interface irb.100;
interface irb.200;
route-distinguisher 192.0.2.11:500;
vrf-target target:500:500;
```

Other leafs are configured in the same way, with the configuration of leaf4 shown in Example 8-17. Since leaf4 has a host in VLAN 300 only, this is the only VLAN that needs to be configured in the MAC-VRF. For the IP VRF, it is important that the Route Targets match, since that will control whether or not routes from remote leafs are correctly imported into the VRF. A detailed look at how this functions is discussed in the upcoming section "Control Plane in a Symmetric IRB Design."

Example 8-17 *MAC-VRF and IP VRF configuration on leaf4 for symmetric IRB*

```
root@leaf4# show routing-instances macvrf-1
instance-type mac-vrf;
protocols {
    evpn {
        encapsulation vxlan;
        default-gateway do-not-advertise;
        extended-vni-list all;
    }
}
vtep-source-interface lo0.0;
service-type vlan-aware;
interface et-0/0/4.0;
```

```
route-distinguisher 192.0.2.14:1;
vrf-target target:1:1;
vlans {
    v300 {
        vlan-id 300;
        l3-interface irb.300;
        vxlan {
            vni 10300;
        }
    }
}

root@leaf4# show routing-instances Tenant1
instance-type vrf;
protocols {
    evpn {
        irb-symmetric-routing {
            vni 10500;
        }
        ip-prefix-routes {
            advertise direct-nexthop;
            encapsulation vxlan;
            vni 10500;
        }
    }
}
interface irb.300;
route-distinguisher 192.0.2.14:500;
vrf-target target:500:500;
```

Once all leafs are configured in a similar way, all hosts can communicate with each other. As an example, host h1 can communicate with hosts h2, h3, h4, and h5, as shown in Example 8-18.

Example 8-18 *Host reachability in a symmetric IRB design*

```
root@h1> ping 10.100.30.2
PING 10.100.30.2 (10.100.30.2): 56 data bytes
64 bytes from 10.100.30.2: icmp_seq=0 ttl=62 time=1.026 ms
64 bytes from 10.100.30.2: icmp_seq=1 ttl=62 time=74.986 ms
64 bytes from 10.100.30.2: icmp_seq=2 ttl=62 time=0.881 ms
64 bytes from 10.100.30.2: icmp_seq=3 ttl=62 time=0.927 ms
^C
--- 10.100.30.2 ping statistics ---
4 packets transmitted, 4 packets received, 0% packet loss
round-trip min/avg/max/stddev = 0.881/19.455/74.986/32.061 ms


root@h1> ping 10.100.30.3
PING 10.100.30.3 (10.100.30.3): 56 data bytes
```

```
64 bytes from 10.100.30.3: icmp_seq=0 ttl=62 time=1.024 ms
64 bytes from 10.100.30.3: icmp_seq=1 ttl=62 time=0.870 ms
64 bytes from 10.100.30.3: icmp_seq=2 ttl=62 time=0.879 ms
64 bytes from 10.100.30.3: icmp_seq=3 ttl=62 time=0.937 ms
^C
--- 10.100.30.3 ping statistics ---
4 packets transmitted, 4 packets received, 0% packet loss
round-trip min/avg/max/stddev = 0.870/0.927/1.024/0.061 ms


root@h1> ping 10.100.40.4
PING 10.100.40.4 (10.100.40.4): 56 data bytes
64 bytes from 10.100.40.4: icmp_seq=0 ttl=62 time=90.493 ms
64 bytes from 10.100.40.4: icmp_seq=1 ttl=62 time=0.868 ms
64 bytes from 10.100.40.4: icmp_seq=2 ttl=62 time=0.936 ms
64 bytes from 10.100.40.4: icmp_seq=3 ttl=62 time=0.870 ms
^C
--- 10.100.40.4 ping statistics ---
4 packets transmitted, 4 packets received, 0% packet loss
round-trip min/avg/max/stddev = 0.868/23.292/90.493/38.799 ms


root@h1> ping 10.100.10.5
PING 10.100.10.5 (10.100.10.5): 56 data bytes
64 bytes from 10.100.10.5: icmp_seq=1 ttl=63 time=0.631 ms
64 bytes from 10.100.10.5: icmp_seq=2 ttl=63 time=9.223 ms
64 bytes from 10.100.10.5: icmp_seq=3 ttl=63 time=0.634 ms
64 bytes from 10.100.10.5: icmp_seq=4 ttl=63 time=38.758 ms
^C
--- 10.100.10.5 ping statistics ---
4 packets transmitted, 4 packets received, 0% packet loss
round-trip min/avg/max/stddev = 0.631/12.312/38.758/15.666 ms
```

Control Plane in a Symmetric IRB Design

As described in previous chapters, host addresses are learned when the host sends an ARP/GARP. Considering host h1 as an example, when it sends an ARP/GARP, leaf1 picks up the source MAC address of the packet and installs it against the bridge domain for h1 (which is VLAN 200) within the MAC-VRF table for that VLAN. Additionally, the MAC-IP table is populated from the ARP packet.

With symmetric IRB, when such a learn occurs, the IP address of the host, h1 in this case, is added to the IP VRF table as a host route (a /32 or a /128 route for IPv4 and IPv6, respectively) since the MAC-VRF is aware of the L3 context for this VLAN (via the association of the IRB interface for that VLAN to the IP VRF). The local leaf advertises an EVPN Type-2 MAC and a MAC+IP route for this, along with an EVPN Type-5 subnet route for the IRB subnet. This subnet route is important because it is used to trigger the gleaning process for silent hosts (for discovery of silent hosts). Visually, this can be represented as shown in Figure 8-19 considering leaf1 and leaf4, which provides an overall picture of the control plane with symmetric IRB.

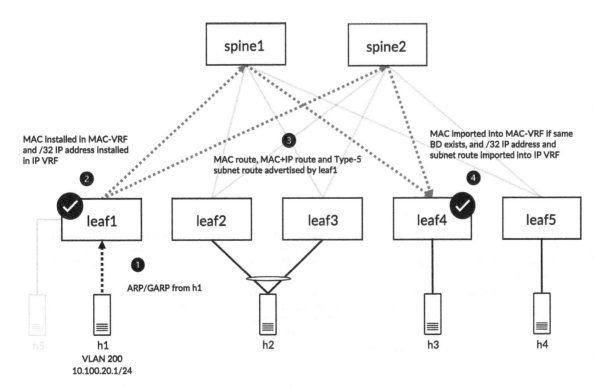

Figure 8-19 *Overall view of the control plane with symmetric IRB*

Since an IP VRF routing instance is created for symmetric IRB, there are additional tables to consider now—the IP VRF routing instance creates a corresponding EVPN table (this table is named [*ip-vrf-name*].evpn.0) and an inet.0 table (since the IPv4 address family is used here). Like with MAC-VRFs, it is crucial to understand the relationship between all these different tables. The flow chart shown in Figure 8-20 describes this, considering a MAC-VRF named macvrf-1 and an IP VRF named Tenant1, when the host address is locally learned on a VTEP, and is advertised into the fabric.

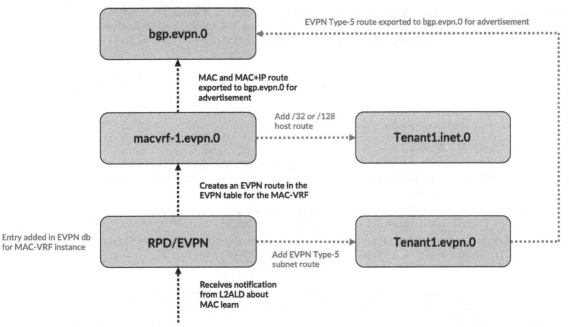

Figure 8-20 *Relationship between different tables in a symmetric IRB design*

With traceoptions enabled within the MAC-VRF, the installation of the host route into the IP VRF for the tenant can be confirmed as shown in Example 8-19.

Example 8-19   *Traceoptions output for host route installation into IP VRF*

```
root@leaf1# show routing-instances macvrf-1 protocols evpn
encapsulation vxlan;
default-gateway do-not-advertise;
extended-vni-list all;
traceoptions {
    file macvrf-evpn.log size 50m;
    flag all;
}


root@leaf1> show log macvrf-evpn.log | grep 10.100.20.1
Jun 19 06:32:53.955829 evpn_mac_msg_receive_from_l2ald:2639 EVPN instance macvrf-1 [MAC-VRF, Refcount: 6, Intfs: 3 (3
up), IRBs: 2 (2 up), Peers: 4,core-isolation-status-changed 0 Flags: 0x801814000,service-type vlan-aware fwding-inst-id
0] Received MAC+IP add for local MAC f0:4b:3a:b9:80:a7 with L2 domain 10200, timestamp Jun 19 06:32:53.955787, interface
et-0/0/49.0, ESI 0, IPv4 address 10.100.20.1

Jun 19 06:32:53.955846 evpn_mirror_mac_update:1310 EVPN instance macvrf-1 [MAC-VRF, Refcount: 6, Intfs: 3 (3 up), IRBs:
2 (2 up), Peers: 4,core-isolation-status-changed 0 Flags: 0x801814000,service-type vlan-aware fwding-inst-id 0] Active RE
MAC MAC+IP add for local MAC f0:4b:3a:b9:80:a7 with rtt-index 9, VLAN 10200, interface et-0/0/49.0, flags 0x82, timestamp
0x64905905, seq num 0,  ESI 00:00:00:00:00:00:00:00:00:00 IPv4 address: 10.100.20.1 gbp-tag 0

Jun 19 06:32:53.955997 evpn_macdb_ip_addr_adv_rt_create:1789 EVPN MAC IP macvrf-1::10200::f0:4b:3a:b9:80:a7:
:et-0/0/49.0::10.100.20.1 [ESI flags: 0x42 <Local-MAC-Only Local-To-Remote-Adv-Allowed>, IP flags: 0x2 <Local-Adv>] Creat-
ing MAC+IP advertisement route for locally learnt

Jun 19 06:32:53.956013 evpn_macdb_ip_addr_l3_context_symmetric_routing_enabled:3466 EVPN MAC IP macvrf-1::10200::f0:4b:3a
:b9:80:a7::et-0/0/49.0::10.100.20.1 [ESI flags: 0x42 <Local-MAC-Only Local-To-Remote-Adv-Allowed>, IP flags: 0x2 <Local-
Adv>] Symmetric Routing Enabled for irb l3 context.

Jun 19 06:32:53.956211 CHANGE    Tenant1          10.100.20.1/32    nhid 0  EVPN    pref 7/0 metric  irb.200 <Active
Int Ext Changed>

Jun 19 06:32:53.956223 ADD       Tenant1          10.100.20.1/32    nhid 0  EVPN    pref 7/0 metric  irb.200 <Active
Int Ext Changed>

Jun 19 06:32:53.956243 evpn_irb_ip_route_add_chg:4052 EVPN MAC IP macvrf-1::10200::f0:4b:3a:b9:80:a7:
:et-0/0/49.0::10.100.20.1 [L3 context: Tenant1/irb.200, ESI flags: 0x42 <Local-MAC-Only Local-To-Remote-Adv-Allowed>, IP
flags: 0x2 <Local-Adv>] Adding IP route 10.100.20.1 in L3 context Tenant1
```

Once EVPN has processed this update, it creates an EVPN Type-2 MAC route and a MAC+IP route and informs BGP to send this out as an update to its BGP EVPN neighbors. This is shown in Example 8-20, with traceoptions enabled for BGP.

Example 8-20   *BGP EVPN updates sent to neighbors after host learn*

```
root@leaf1> show log bgp.log | grep 10.100.20.1
Jun 19 06:32:53.956514 bgp_rt_policy_rt, 7722: flash update group overlay type External nlri:evpn rth(0x9223780
2:192.0.2.11:1::10200::f0:4b:3a:b9:80:a7::10.100.20.1 state:12002)rtt(0x701d000 bgp state:240), rti(0x988ec00 master)
new_rt 0x73cfca0, processed, reach-rto enqueued

Jun 19 06:32:53.957189 BGP SEND       2:192.0.2.11:1::10200::f0:4b:3a:b9:80:a7::10.100.20.1/304 (label field value
0x27d8 [label 637, VNID 10200]) (label2 field value 0x2904 [label 656, VNID 10500]) (esi 00:00:00:00:00:00:00:00:00:00)

Jun 19 06:32:53.957314 BGP SEND       2:192.0.2.11:1::10200::f0:4b:3a:b9:80:a7::10.100.20.1/304 (label field value
0x27d8 [label 637, VNID 10200]) (label2 field value 0x2904 [label 656, VNID 10500]) (esi 00:00:00:00:00:00:00:00:00:00)
```

Along with these EVPN Type-2 routes, the subnet route for the IRB is added to the VRF's inet.0 table as a directly connected route (since the IPv4 address family is being used here) and the VRF's EVPN table as an EVPN Type-5 route, to be advertised out to its BGP EVPN peers. This is needed to trigger the gleaning process for silent hosts, which is covered in detail in the section "Silent Hosts in a Symmetric IRB Design" toward the end of this chapter. The output in Example 8-21 confirms the presence of these routes in the inet.0 and the EVPN table for the VRF (*Tenant1.evpn.0*).

Example 8-21 *Host and subnet routes in IP VRF table*

```
root@leaf1> show route table Tenant1.inet.0

Tenant1.inet.0: 10 destinations, 13 routes (10 active, 0 holddown, 0 hidden)
+ = Active Route, - = Last Active, * = Both

10.100.10.0/24     *[Direct/0] 1d 13:20:43
                    >  via irb.100
10.100.10.254/32   *[Local/0] 1d 13:20:43
                       Local via irb.100
10.100.20.0/24     *[Direct/0] 00:24:13
                    >  via irb.200
10.100.20.1/32     *[EVPN/7] 00:20:21
                    >  via irb.200
10.100.20.254/32   *[Local/0] 00:24:13
                       Local via irb.200
10.100.30.0/24     *[EVPN/170] 1d 13:19:52
                    >  to 198.51.100.1 via et-0/0/48.0
                       to 198.51.100.3 via et-0/0/50.0
                    [EVPN/170] 1d 13:19:39
                    >  to 198.51.100.1 via et-0/0/48.0
                       to 198.51.100.3 via et-0/0/50.0
                    [EVPN/170] 1d 13:19:24
                    >  to 198.51.100.1 via et-0/0/48.0
                       to 198.51.100.3 via et-0/0/50.0
10.100.30.2/32     *[EVPN/7] 1d 13:19:35
                    >  to 198.51.100.1 via et-0/0/48.0
                       to 198.51.100.3 via et-0/0/50.0
                    [EVPN/7] 1d 13:19:35
                    >  to 198.51.100.1 via et-0/0/48.0
                       to 198.51.100.3 via et-0/0/50.0
10.100.30.3/32     *[EVPN/7] 1d 13:13:42
                    >  to 198.51.100.1 via et-0/0/48.0
                       to 198.51.100.3 via et-0/0/50.0
10.100.40.0/24     *[EVPN/170] 1d 13:19:08
                    >  to 198.51.100.1 via et-0/0/48.0
                       to 198.51.100.3 via et-0/0/50.0
10.100.40.4/32     *[EVPN/7] 1d 13:13:56
                    >  to 198.51.100.1 via et-0/0/48.0
                       to 198.51.100.3 via et-0/0/50.0

root@leaf1> show route table Tenant1.evpn.0 match-prefix *192.0.2.11*

Tenant1.evpn.0: 10 destinations, 18 routes (10 active, 0 holddown, 0 hidden)
+ = Active Route, - = Last Active, * = Both

5:192.0.2.11:500::0::10.100.10.0::24/248
                    *[EVPN/170] 1d 13:22:43
                       Fictitious
```

```
5:192.0.2.11:500::0::10.100.20.0::24/248
                    *[EVPN/170] 00:26:13
                        Fictitious
```

> **Note**   It is important to note that the EVPN Type-2 MAC route is sent with the Route Target of the MAC-VRF and a single MPLS label (label1) that corresponds to the L2VNI, whereas the EVPN Type-2 MAC+IP route is sent with two MPLS labels attached to it—the first label (label1) identifies the MAC-VRF for the NLRI being advertised, which corresponds to the L2VNI, and the second label (label2) identifies the IP VRF, which corresponds to the L3VNI. Additionally, Route Targets for both the MAC-VRF and the IP VRF are added to the BGP update as extended communities, along with a new extended community called the *Router MAC community*.

A packet capture, shown in Figure 8-21, confirms that the EVPN Type-2 MAC+IP route is sent with two labels—the first label is 10200, which is the VNI for the L2 domain, and the second label is VNI 10500, which is the VNI configured for the L3 context (Tenant1 routing instance, in our case). The following four extended communities are added to this route:

- A Route Target extended community specific to the MAC-VRF, which is 1:1 in our case.

- Another Route Target extended community specific to the IP VRF, which is 500:500 in our case.

- A tunnel type (encapsulation) extended community, which defines the encapsulation as VXLAN.

- A router-mac extended community, which is set to the MAC address of the advertising VTEP's IRB interface. Usage of this extended community is discussed in more detail in the next section, "Data Plane in a Symmetric IRB Design."

```
No.    | Time      | Source      | Destination  | Protocol | Length | Info
  1... 9.678672     192.0.2.11    192.0.2.101    BGP        247     UPDATE Message, UPDATE Message
  2... 16.973010    192.0.2.11    192.0.2.101    BGP        192     UPDATE Message

> Border Gateway Protocol – UPDATE Message                              0000  64 c3 d6 60 76 40 40 de
    Marker: ffffffffffffffffffffffffffffffff                            0010  00 b2 1c 0f 00 00 40 06
    Length: 126                                                         0020  02 65 e0 47 00 b3 06 dd
    Type: UPDATE Message (2)                                            0030  40 00 6e 98 00 00 01 01
    Withdrawn Routes Length: 0                                          0040  09 b1 ff ff ff ff ff ff
    Total Path Attribute Length: 103                                    0050  ff ff 00 7e 02 00 00 00
  ∨ Path attributes                                                     0060  02 01 00 00 ff 8d c0 10
    > Path Attribute – ORIGIN: IGP                                      0070  01 00 02 01 f4 00 00 01
    > Path Attribute – AS_PATH: 65421                                   0080  08 06 03 40 de ad 7b 70
    ∨ Path Attribute – EXTENDED_COMMUNITIES                             0090  04 c0 00 02 0b 00 02 28
      > Flags: 0xc0, Optional, Transitive, Complete                     00a0  00 00 00 00 00 00 00 00
        Type Code: EXTENDED_COMMUNITIES (16)                            00b0  4b 3a b9 80 a7 20 0a 64
        Length: 32
      ∨ Carried extended communities: (4 communities)
        > Route Target: 1:1 [Transitive 2-Octet AS-Specific]
        > Route Target: 500:500 [Transitive 2-Octet AS-Specific]
        > Encapsulation: VXLAN Encapsulation [Transitive Opaque]
        > EVPN Router's MAC: Router's MAC: 40:de:ad:7b:70:40 [Transitive EVPN]
    ∨ Path Attribute – MP_REACH_NLRI
      > Flags: 0x90, Optional, Extended-Length, Non-transitive, Complete
        Type Code: MP_REACH_NLRI (14)
        Length: 51
        Address family identifier (AFI): Layer-2 VPN (25)
        Subsequent address family identifier (SAFI): EVPN (70)
      > Next hop: 192.0.2.11
        Number of Subnetwork points of attachment (SNPA): 0
      ∨ Network Layer Reachability Information (NLRI)
        ∨ EVPN NLRI: MAC Advertisement Route
            Route Type: MAC Advertisement Route (2)
            Length: 40
            Route Distinguisher: 0001c000020b0001 (192.0.2.11:1)
          > ESI: 00:00:00:00:00:00:00:00:00:00
            Ethernet Tag ID: 10200
            MAC Address Length: 48
            MAC Address: JuniperN_b9:80:a7 (f0:4b:3a:b9:80:a7)
            IP Address Length: 32
            IPv4 address: 10.100.20.1
            VNI: 10200
            VNI: 10500
```

Figure 8-21 *Host h1's address learned and advertised with L3VNI*

The EVPN Type-5 subnet route is advertised with the Route Target for the IP VRF only, since the MAC address is decoupled from such a route and only an IP subnet is being advertised. In addition, the L3VNI is the only label added to this route, as shown in Figure 8-22.

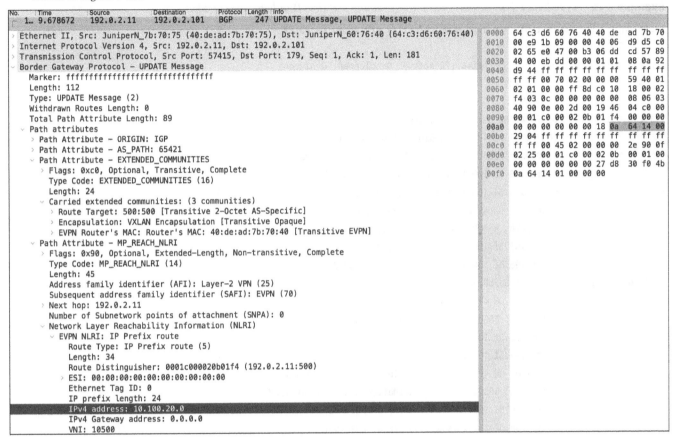

Figure 8-22 *EVPN Type-5 route advertised for the IRB subnet*

The flow chart shown in Figure 8-23 describes how these BGP EVPN updates are processed on a remote leaf that receives them.

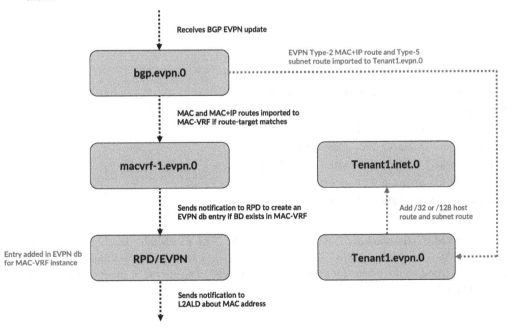

Figure 8-23 *Processing of EVPN Type-2 MAC, MAC+IP, and Type-5 subnet routes with symmetric IRB*

Considering leaf4 as an example, it receives the EVPN Type-2 MAC, MAC+IP route, and the Type-5 subnet route in its *bgp.evpn.0* table. This is confirmed in Example 8-22, by matching host h1's MAC address and IP subnet.

Example 8-22   *Type-2 and Type-5 routes received by remote leaf (leaf4) in bgp.evpn.0 table*

```
root@leaf4> show route table bgp.evpn.0 match-prefix *f0:4b:3a:b9:80:a7*

bgp.evpn.0: 28 destinations, 52 routes (28 active, 0 holddown, 0 hidden)
+ = Active Route, - = Last Active, * = Both


2:192.0.2.11:1::10200::f0:4b:3a:b9:80:a7/304 MAC/IP
                    *[BGP/170] 02:49:25, localpref 100, from 192.0.2.102
                      AS path: 65500 65421 I, validation-state: unverified
                      to 198.51.100.13 via et-0/0/0.0, Push 637
                    > to 198.51.100.15 via et-0/0/2.0, Push 637
                     [BGP/170] 02:49:25, localpref 100, from 192.0.2.101
                      AS path: 65500 65421 I, validation-state: unverified
                      to 198.51.100.13 via et-0/0/0.0, Push 637
                    > to 198.51.100.15 via et-0/0/2.0, Push 637
2:192.0.2.11:1::10200::f0:4b:3a:b9:80:a7::10.100.20.1/304 MAC/IP
                    *[BGP/170] 02:49:25, localpref 100, from 192.0.2.102
                      AS path: 65500 65421 I, validation-state: unverified
                      to 198.51.100.13 via et-0/0/0.0, Push 637
                    > to 198.51.100.15 via et-0/0/2.0, Push 637
                     [BGP/170] 02:49:25, localpref 100, from 192.0.2.101
                      AS path: 65500 65421 I, validation-state: unverified
                      to 198.51.100.13 via et-0/0/0.0, Push 637
                    > to 198.51.100.15 via et-0/0/2.0, Push 637


root@leaf4> show route table bgp.evpn.0 match-prefix *10.100.20.0*

bgp.evpn.0: 28 destinations, 52 routes (28 active, 0 holddown, 0 hidden)
+ = Active Route, - = Last Active, * = Both


5:192.0.2.11:500::0::10.100.20.0::24/248
                    *[BGP/170] 3d 01:32:48, localpref 100, from 192.0.2.102
                      AS path: 65500 65421 I, validation-state: unverified
                      to 198.51.100.13 via et-0/0/0.0, Push 656
                    > to 198.51.100.15 via et-0/0/2.0, Push 656
                     [BGP/170] 3d 01:32:48, localpref 100, from 192.0.2.101
                      AS path: 65500 65421 I, validation-state: unverified
                      to 198.51.100.13 via et-0/0/0.0, Push 656
                    > to 198.51.100.15 via et-0/0/2.0, Push 656
```

Both the EVPN Type-2 MAC and the MAC+IP routes are imported into the MAC-VRF EVPN table *macvrf-1.evpn.0* based on the Route Target matching the MAC-VRF, while the MAC+IP route and the Type-5 subnet route are imported into the IP VRF EVPN table, *Tenant1.evpn.0* based on the Route Target matching the IP VRF. The import of these routes, into the respective tables, is shown in Example 8-23.

Example 0-20 *Type-2 and Type-5 routes inserted into MAC VRF EVPN table*

```
root@leaf4> show route table macvrf-1.evpn.0 match-prefix *f0:4b:3a:b9:80:a7*

macvrf-1.evpn.0: 20 destinations, 37 routes (20 active, 0 holddown, 0 hidden)
+ = Active Route, - = Last Active, * = Both

2:192.0.2.11:1::10200::f0:4b:3a:b9:80:a7/304 MAC/IP
                    *[BGP/170] 02:53:47, localpref 100, from 192.0.2.102
                      AS path: 65500 65421 I, validation-state: unverified
                        to 198.51.100.13 via et-0/0/0.0, Push 637
                    >   to 198.51.100.15 via et-0/0/2.0, Push 637
                     [BGP/170] 02:53:47, localpref 100, from 192.0.2.101
                      AS path: 65500 65421 I, validation-state: unverified
                        to 198.51.100.13 via et-0/0/0.0, Push 637
                    >   to 198.51.100.15 via et-0/0/2.0, Push 637
2:192.0.2.11:1::10200::f0:4b:3a:b9:80:a7::10.100.20.1/304 MAC/IP
                    *[BGP/170] 02:53:47, localpref 100, from 192.0.2.102
                      AS path: 65500 65421 I, validation-state: unverified
                        to 198.51.100.13 via et-0/0/0.0, Push 637
                    >   to 198.51.100.15 via et-0/0/2.0, Push 637
                     [BGP/170] 02:53:47, localpref 100, from 192.0.2.101
                      AS path: 65500 65421 I, validation-state: unverified
                        to 198.51.100.13 via et-0/0/0.0, Push 637
                    >   to 198.51.100.15 via et-0/0/2.0, Push 637

root@leaf4> show route table Tenant1.evpn.0 match-prefix *f0:4b:3a:b9:80:a7*

Tenant1.evpn.0: 10 destinations, 19 routes (10 active, 0 holddown, 0 hidden)
+ = Active Route, - = Last Active, * = Both

2:192.0.2.11:1::10200::f0:4b:3a:b9:80:a7::10.100.20.1/304 MAC/IP
                    *[BGP/170] 02:54:33, localpref 100, from 192.0.2.102
                      AS path: 65500 65421 I, validation-state: unverified
                        to 198.51.100.13 via et-0/0/0.0, Push 637
                    >   to 198.51.100.15 via et-0/0/2.0, Push 637
                     [BGP/170] 02:54:33, localpref 100, from 192.0.2.101
                      AS path: 65500 65421 I, validation-state: unverified
                        to 198.51.100.13 via et-0/0/0.0, Push 637
                    >   to 198.51.100.15 via et-0/0/2.0, Push 637

root@leaf4> show route table Tenant1.evpn.0 match-prefix *10.100.20.0*

Tenant1.evpn.0: 10 destinations, 19 routes (10 active, 0 holddown, 0 hidden)
+ = Active Route, - = Last Active, * = Both

5:192.0.2.11:500::0::10.100.20.0::24/248
                    *[BGP/170] 3d 01:37:50, localpref 100, from 192.0.2.102
                      AS path: 65500 65421 I, validation-state: unverified
```

```
            to 198.51.100.13 via et-0/0/0.0, Push 656
     >  to 198.51.100.15 via et-0/0/2.0, Push 656
        [BGP/170] 3d 01:37:50, localpref 100, from 192.0.2.101
          AS path: 65500 65421 I, validation-state: unverified
            to 198.51.100.13 via et-0/0/0.0, Push 656
     >  to 198.51.100.15 via et-0/0/2.0, Push 656
```

Since the bridge domain does not exist on leaf4, there is no requirement to create an entry in the EVPN database for that MAC address, and thus it is not sent to L2ALD for programming in the MAC address table as well. From the Tenant1.evpn.0 table, both the subnet route and the /32 host route are installed in the Tenant1.inet.0 table, the forwarding table in the Routing Engine, and eventually the PFE and the hardware itself. This is shown in Example 8-24.

Example 8-24   *Host and subnet routes in IP VRF table and in PFE on remote leaf, leaf4*

```
root@leaf4> show route table Tenant1.inet.0 match-prefix *10.100.20*

Tenant1.inet.0: 9 destinations, 12 routes (9 active, 0 holddown, 0 hidden)
+ = Active Route, - = Last Active, * = Both

10.100.20.0/24      *[EVPN/170] 3d 01:40:26
                        to 198.51.100.13 via et-0/0/0.0
                     >  to 198.51.100.15 via et-0/0/2.0
10.100.20.1/32      *[EVPN/7] 02:57:17
                        to 198.51.100.13 via et-0/0/0.0
                     >  to 198.51.100.15 via et-0/0/2.0


root@leaf4> show route forwarding-table destination 10.100.20.0/24 table Tenant1
Routing table: Tenant1.inet
Internet:
Destination        Type RtRef Next hop        Type Index    NhRef Netif
10.100.20.0/24     user    0                  comp  53060    1
                                              indr  53058    1
                                              ulst  53045    1
                                              sftw  53044    1 et-0/0/0.0
                         198.51.100.13        ucst   9001    1 et-0/0/0.0
                                              sftw  53043    1 et-0/0/2.0
                         198.51.100.15        ucst   9000    1 et-0/0/2.0


root@leaf4> show route forwarding-table destination 10.100.20.1/32 table Tenant1
Routing table: Tenant1.inet
Internet:
Destination        Type RtRef Next hop        Type Index    NhRef Netif
10.100.20.1/32     user    0                  comp  53060    1
                                              indr  53058    1
                                              ulst  53045    1
                                              sftw  53044    1 et-0/0/0.0
                         198.51.100.13        ucst   9001    1 et-0/0/0.0
                                              sftw  53043    1 et-0/0/2.0
                         198.51.100.15        ucst   9000    1 et-0/0/2.0
```

Data Plane In a Symmetric IRB Design

To understand the flow of data packets with a symmetric IRB design, consider a situation in which host h1 wants to communicate with h3. Since they are in different subnets, h1 will first resolve its gateway (which exists on leaf1) and then send an IP packet destined to h3. This resolution, achieved via the ARP process and the subsequent IP packet, is visually represented in Figure 8-24 and Figure 8-25.

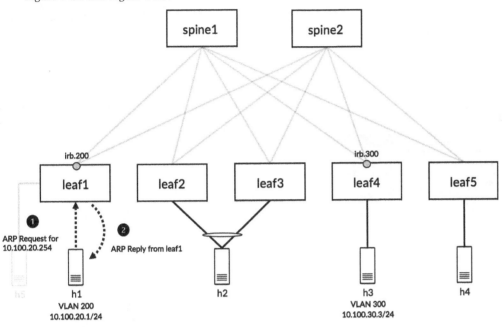

Figure 8-24 *Host h1 resolving its gateway address*

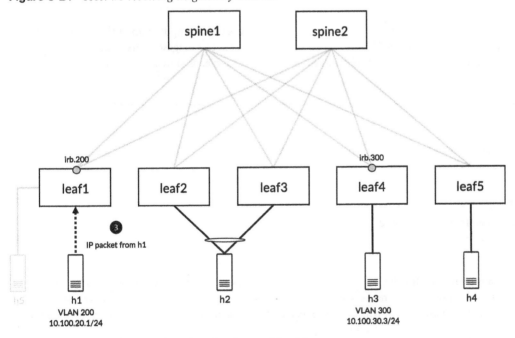

Figure 8-25 *IP packet sent from host h1 destined for h3*

An example IP packet received on leaf1 (from h1 destined for h3) is shown in Figure 8-26. This is an IP packet with an ICMP payload.

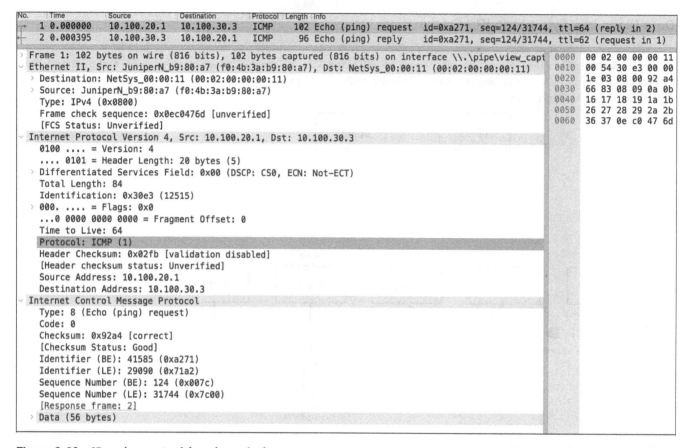

Figure 8-26 *IP packet received from h1 on leaf1*

Since the destination MAC address in the Ethernet header is owned by leaf1, it does a routing lookup in the IP VRF table (as the IRB interface for VLAN 200 is bound to the VRF routing instance Tenant1). The longest prefix match, during this lookup, results in the /32 host route, for host h3, that was installed in the IP VRF table, as shown in Example 8-25.

Example 8-25 *Route lookup for h3's address on leaf1*

```
root@leaf1> show route table Tenant1.inet.0 10.100.30.3


Tenant1.inet.0: 10 destinations, 13 routes (10 active, 0 holddown, 0 hidden)
+ = Active Route, - = Last Active, * = Both


10.100.30.3/32     *[EVPN/7] 6d 12:52:42
                    >  to 198.51.100.1 via et-0/0/48.0
                       to 198.51.100.3 via et-0/0/50.0
```

The forwarding table gives us a next-hop ID for this destination, which is a composite next-hop ID. From the PFE, this next-hop ID can be viewed in detail, and it provides the necessary encapsulation information for the packet to be sent out. It also recursively points to the two underlay ECMP paths, which is the expected behavior for the reference topology, as shown in Example 8-26.

Example 8-26 *PFE entry and next-hop ID details for h3's address on leaf1*

```
root@leaf1> show route forwarding-table destination 10.100.30.3 table Tenant1
Routing table: Tenant1.inet
Internet:
Destination        Type RtRef Next hop         Type Index    NhRef Netif
10.100.30.3/32     user    0                   comp 1749         2
```

```
FPC0(leaf1 vty)# show nhdb id 1749 recursive
1749(Compst, IPv4, ifl:0:-, pfe-id:0, comp-fn:Tunnel)
    524292(Indirect, IPv4, ifl:827:et-0/0/48.0, pfe-id:0, i-ifl:0:-)
        524286(Unilist, IPv4, ifl:0:-, pfe-id:0)
            1754(Unicast, IPv4, ifl:827:et-0/0/48.0, pfe-id:0)
            1755(Unicast, IPv4, ifl:829:et-0/0/50.0, pfe-id:0)


FPC0(leaf1 vty)# show nhdb id 1749 extensive
  ID     Type     Interface      Next Hop Addr     Protocol      Encap     MTU              Flags  PFE internal Flags
  -----  -------  -------------  ---------------    ----------   -----------  ----   -----------------  -----------------
  1749   Compst   -              -                  IPv4            -          0  0x0000000000000000  0x0000000000000000

BFD Session Id: 0

Composite NH:
  Function: Tunnel Function
  Hardware Index: 0x1fff
  Composite flag: 0x0
  Composite pfe flag: 0xe
  Lower-level NH Ids: 524292
  Derived NH Ids:
  Tunnel Data:
      Type       : VXLAN
      Tunnel ID: 806354946
      Encap VRF: 0
      Decap VRF: 11
      MTU      : 0
      Flags    : 0x0
      AnchorId : 0
      Encap Len: 53
      Mode     : Encap-Decap
      Encap    : 0x01 0x0b 0x02 0x00 0xc0 0x00 0x00 0x00
                 0x00 0x00 0x00 0x00 0x00 0x00 0x00 0x00
                 0x00 0x0e 0x02 0x00 0xc0 0x00 0x00 0x00
                 0x00 0x00 0x00 0x00 0x00 0x00 0x00 0x00
                 0x00 0x04 0x29 0x00 0x00 0x04 0x29 0x00
                 0x00 0xb8 0xf0 0x15 0x52 0x5d 0x06 0x40
                 0xde 0xad 0x7b 0x70 0x40
      Data Len : 0

Dram Bytes : 260
Num of nhs: 1
HW NH-ID     : 400011
Module       : 0
DVP GPORT    : 0xb0000013
L3-INTF      : 3
```

```
OL_DMAC        : b8:f0:15:52:5d:6
OL_SMAC        : 40:de:ad:7b:70:40
VFI            : 0x7003
MTU            : 9600
IP profile_id  : 0
VRF            : 4
Ingress_IF     : 4098


Routing-table id: 0
```

With this information, the packet is routed into the L3VNI—this means that the packet is encapsulated with the necessary VXLAN headers, and the VNI in the VXLAN header is the L3VNI. The outer destination IP address carries the packet through the fabric, toward the destination VTEP, which is leaf4 in our case. A visual representation of this is shown in Figure 8-27.

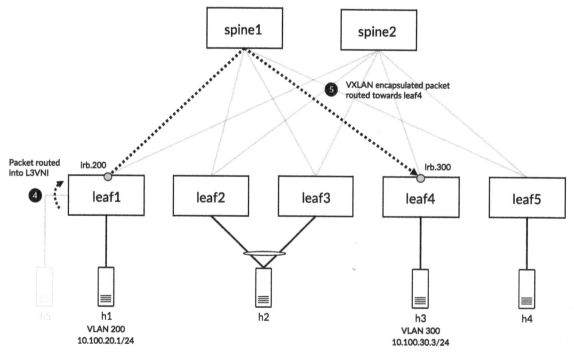

Figure 8-27 *Packed routed into L3VNI and routed toward destination VTEP*

A packet capture, in transit, confirms that the VNI added in the VXLAN header is the L3VNI (the VNI associated with the IP VRF), which is 10500 in our case, as shown in Figure 8-28.

From this packet capture, it is also important to carefully consider the destination MAC address in the inner Ethernet header—this header is constructed by the ingress leaf (leaf1, in our case) and it uses the router MAC extended community in the EVPN Type-2 route that was received for the destination to populate the destination MAC address.

Example 8-27 shows the EVPN Type-2 route again, which was received on leaf1 and imported into the IP VRF–specific EVPN table (and eventually the IP VRF–specific inet.0 table) for the destination 10.100.30.3/32. The value in the router-mac extended community is the MAC address of leaf4's IRB interface (separate from the statically configured anycast MAC address). On the other hand, the source MAC address of the packet in Figure 8-28, in the inner Ethernet header, is the ingress leaf's IRB MAC address (thus, leaf1's IRB MAC address, in our case). This is shown in Example 8-27.

```
  11 0.600062  10.100.20.1  10.100.30.3  ICMP   148 Echo (ping) request  id=0xf97b, seq=32/8192, ttl=63 (reply in 12)
  12 0.600456  10.100.30.3  10.100.20.1  ICMP   152 Echo (ping) reply    id=0xf97b, seq=32/8192, ttl=63 (request in 11)
```

```
> Frame 11: 148 bytes on wire (1184 bits), 148 bytes captured (1184 bits)          0000  64 c3 d6 60 76
> Ethernet II, Src: JuniperN_7b:70:75 (40:de:ad:7b:70:75), Dst: JuniperN_60:76:40 (64:c3:d6:60:76:40)   0010  00 86 09 7a 00
∨ Internet Protocol Version 4, Src: 192.0.2.11, Dst: 192.0.2.14                     0020  02 0e f4 44 12
    0100 .... = Version: 4                                                          0030  04 00 b8 f0 15
    .... 0101 = Header Length: 20 bytes (5)                                         0040  45 00 00 54 a0
  > Differentiated Services Field: 0x00 (DSCP: CS0, ECN: Not-ECT)                   0050  0a 64 1e 03 08
    Total Length: 134                                                               0060  00 0e 4e 16 08
    Identification: 0x097a (2426)                                                   0070  14 15 16 17 18
  > 000. .... = Flags: 0x0                                                          0080  24 25 26 27 28
    ...0 0000 0000 0000 = Fragment Offset: 0                                        0090  34 35 36 37
    Time to Live: 64
    Protocol: UDP (17)
    Header Checksum: 0xecd3 [validation disabled]
    [Header checksum status: Unverified]
    Source Address: 192.0.2.11
    Destination Address: 192.0.2.14
> User Datagram Protocol, Src Port: 62532, Dst Port: 4789
∨ Virtual eXtensible Local Area Network
  > Flags: 0x0800, VXLAN Network ID (VNI)
    Group Policy ID: 0
    VXLAN Network Identifier (VNI): 10500
    Reserved: 0
∨ Ethernet II, Src: JuniperN_7b:70:40 (40:de:ad:7b:70:40), Dst: JuniperN_52:5d:06 (b8:f0:15:52:5d:06)
  > Destination: JuniperN_52:5d:06 (b8:f0:15:52:5d:06)
  > Source: JuniperN_7b:70:40 (40:de:ad:7b:70:40)
    Type: IPv4 (0x0800)
> Internet Protocol Version 4, Src: 10.100.20.1, Dst: 10.100.30.3
> Internet Control Message Protocol
```

Figure 8-28 *Packet capture of VXLAN-encapsulated packet with L3VNI*

Example 8-27 *Router MAC attached to EVPN Type-2 route generated by leaf4 received on leaf1*

```
root@leaf1> show route table Tenant1.evpn.0 match-prefix *10.100.30.3* extensive

Tenant1.evpn.0: 10 destinations, 18 routes (10 active, 0 holddown, 0 hidden)
2:192.0.2.14:1::10300::f0:4b:3a:b9:80:ab::10.100.30.3/304 MAC/IP (2 entries, 1 announced)
       *BGP    Preference: 170/-101
               Route Distinguisher: 192.0.2.14:1
               Next hop type: Indirect, Next hop index: 0
               Address: 0x8c06fd4
               Next-hop reference count: 10, key opaque handle: 0x0, non-key opaque handle: 0x0
               Source: 192.0.2.102
               Protocol next hop: 192.0.2.14
               Label operation: Push 643
               Label TTL action: prop-ttl
               Load balance label: Label 643: None;
               Indirect next hop: 0x2 no-forward INH Session ID: 0
               State: <Secondary Active Ext>
               Local AS: 65421 Peer AS: 65500
               Age: 6d 23:17:20      Metric2: 0
               Validation State: unverified
               Task: BGP_65500.192.0.2.102
               Announcement bits (1): 0-Tenant1-EVPN-L3-context
               AS path: 65500 65424 I
               Communities: target:1:1 target:500:500 encapsulation:vxlan(0x8) router-mac:b8:f0:15:52:5d:06
               Import Accepted
```

```
                      Route Label: 10300
                      Route Label: 10500
                      ESI: 00:00:00:00:00:00:00:00:00:00
                      Localpref: 100
                      Router ID: 192.0.2.102
                      Primary Routing Table: bgp.evpn.0
```

snip

```
root@leaf4> show interfaces irb
Physical interface: irb, Enabled, Physical link is Up
  Interface index: 1005, SNMP ifIndex: 506
  Type: Ethernet, Link-level type: Ethernet, MTU: 1514, Speed: 1Gbps, Auto-negotiation: Disabled
  Device flags   : Present Running
  Interface flags: None
  Current address: b8:f0:15:52:5d:06, Hardware address: b8:f0:15:52:5d:06
  Last flapped   : Never
  Input rate     : 0 bps (0 pps)
  Output rate    : 0 bps (0 pps)
```

snip

```
root@leaf1> show interfaces irb
Physical interface: irb, Enabled, Physical link is Up
  Interface index: 640, SNMP ifIndex: 505
  Type: Ethernet, Link-level type: Ethernet, MTU: 1514
  Device flags   : Present Running
  Interface flags: SNMP-Traps
  Link type      : Full-Duplex
  Link flags     : None
  Current address: 40:de:ad:7b:70:40, Hardware address: 40:de:ad:7b:70:40
  Last flapped   : Never
    Input packets : 0
    Output packets: 0
```

snip

When this encapsulated packet is received on leaf4, it decapsulates the outer headers, and since the inner Ethernet header's destination MAC address is owned by itself (belongs to the IRB interface), it does a routing lookup on the destination IP address, using the L3VNI to determine which table is used for the lookup. Since the L3VNI maps to the Tenant1 IP VRF, the corresponding routing table is used for this, which gives a directly attached exit interface. Thus, the packet is routed from the L3VNI into the L2VNI and then bridged down to the host h3.

This lookup result, in the routing table and the forwarding table, is shown in Example 8-28.

Example 8-28 *Route lookup for h3's address and entry in PFE on leaf4*

```
root@leaf4> show route table Tenant1.inet.0 10.100.30.3

Tenant1.inet.0: 9 destinations, 12 routes (9 active, 0 holddown, 0 hidden)
+ = Active Route, - = Last Active, * = Both
```

```
10.100.30.3/32    *[EVPN/7] 6d 23:31:02
                   > via irb.300
```

```
root@leaf4> show route forwarding-table destination 10.100.30.3 table Tenant1 extensive
Routing table: Tenant1.inet [Index: 53]
Internet:


Destination:  10.100.30.3/32
  Route type: destination
  Route reference: 0            Route interface-index: 1040
  Multicast RPF nh index: 0
  P2mpidx: 0

                                Index: 83043    Reference: 1

  Nexthop: f0:4b:3a:b9:80:ab
  Next-hop type: unicast
  Next-hop interface: et-0/0/4.0
```

Visually this can be represented as shown in Figure 8-29. The reply from host h3 to h1 follows a similar data plane path.

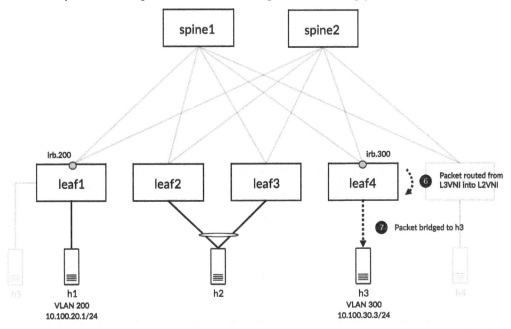

Figure 8-29 *Packet routed from L3VNI to L2VNI on leaf4 and bridged to host h3*

Silent Hosts in a Symmetric IRB Design

Ideally, when a host comes online, it sends out a GARP to ensure it does not have a duplicate IP address (or perhaps an ARP packet to resolve its gateway address), and this causes a data plane learn of the host address on its directly connected leaf. *Silent hosts* are described as end hosts that do not send any traffic once they come online, and thus their directly connected switches (VTEPs/PEs, in this case) are unable to learn their MAC addresses and, in turn, cannot advertise them to the rest of the VTEPs in an EVPN VXLAN fabric. This state can also exist when a host, after sending some initial traffic, goes silent, and eventually ages out of the locally connected VTEP, and thus is purged from the rest of the network as well. Examples of silent hosts can include network printers, IoT devices, and badge readers. Poor implementations of a syslog server can also make it a silent host.

This problem is solved by advertising the IRB subnet routes as EVPN Type-5 routes in the fabric. The subnet route steers traffic toward a VTEP that owns that subnet (via the creation of an IRB interface for that subnet) without a /32 host route and triggers the gleaning process for the destination on the receiving VTEP.

Consider a situation in which host h4 is a silent host and the fabric has no knowledge of where it exists because no traffic was sent from this host and leaf4 never learned its address. Revisiting the IP VRF routing instance configuration, leaf5 is configured to advertise IP prefixes as EVPN Type-5 routes using the *ip-prefix-routes* configuration hierarchy with the L3VNI 10500, as shown in Example 8-29.

Example 8-29 *Configuration to generate and accept EVPN Type-5 routes in an IP VRF on leaf5*

```
root@leaf5# show routing-instances Tenant1
instance-type vrf;
protocols {
    evpn {
        irb-symmetric-routing {
            vni 10500;
        }
        ip-prefix-routes {
            advertise direct-nexthop;
            encapsulation vxlan;
            vni 10500;
        }
    }
}
interface irb.400;
route-distinguisher 192.0.2.15:500;
vrf-target target:500:500;
```

By default, the IRB interface subnets are advertised as EVPN Type-5 routes with the *ip-prefix-routes* configuration hierarchy configured. As shown in Example 8-30, leaf5 is advertising the 10.100.40.0/24 subnet as an EVPN Type-5 route.

Example 8-30 *IRB subnet route inserted into IP VRF table and advertised via bgp.evpn.0 table on leaf5*

```
root@leaf5> show route table Tenant1.evpn.0 match-prefix *10.100.40.0*

Tenant1.evpn.0: 10 destinations, 19 routes (10 active, 0 holddown, 0 hidden)
+ = Active Route, - = Last Active, * = Both

5:192.0.2.15:500::0::10.100.40.0::24/248
                   *[EVPN/170] 1w0d 08:27:13
                         Fictitious


root@leaf5> show route table bgp.evpn.0 match-prefix *10.100.40.0*

bgp.evpn.0: 28 destinations, 52 routes (28 active, 0 holddown, 0 hidden)
+ = Active Route, - = Last Active, * = Both

5:192.0.2.15:500::0::10.100.40.0::24/248
                   *[EVPN/170] 1w0d 08:27:16
                         Fictitious
```

On leaf1 (and other leafs in the topology), this route is received, installed in the IP VRF specific EVPN table, and pulled into the inet.0 table for the IP VRF, as shown in Example 8-31.

Example 8-31 *Leaf5's IRB subnet route received on leaf1 and inserted into IP VRF inet.0 table*

```
root@leaf1> show route table Tenant1.evpn.0 match-prefix *10.100.40.0*


Tenant1.evpn.0: 10 destinations, 18 routes (10 active, 0 holddown, 0 hidden)
+ = Active Route, - = Last Active, * = Both


5:192.0.2.15:500::0::10.100.40.0::24/248
                     *[BGP/170] 1w0d 08:30:04, localpref 100, from 192.0.2.102
                        AS path: 65500 65425 I, validation-state: unverified
                      > to 198.51.100.1 via et-0/0/48.0, Push 656
                        to 198.51.100.3 via et-0/0/50.0, Push 656
                      [BGP/170] 1w0d 08:30:04, localpref 100, from 192.0.2.101
                        AS path: 65500 65425 I, validation-state: unverified
                      > to 198.51.100.1 via et-0/0/48.0, Push 656
                        to 198.51.100.3 via et-0/0/50.0, Push 656


root@leaf1> show route table Tenant1.inet.0 10.100.40.0/24 exact


Tenant1.inet.0: 10 destinations, 13 routes (10 active, 0 holddown, 0 hidden)
+ = Active Route, - = Last Active, * = Both


10.100.40.0/24    *[EVPN/170] 1w0d 08:30:32
                   > to 198.51.100.1 via et-0/0/48.0
                     to 198.51.100.3 via et-0/0/50.0
```

When host h1 sends a packet destined for h4, the longest prefix match in the routing table for the IP VRF is this subnet route (in the absence of the /32 host route for h4). This steers the packet toward leaf5, as shown in Example 8-32, which is followed by a visual representation of this flow in Figure 8-30.

Example 8-32 *Route lookup on leaf1 for IRB subnet route advertised by leaf5*

```
root@leaf1> show route table Tenant1.inet.0 10.100.40.4


Tenant1.inet.0: 9 destinations, 12 routes (9 active, 0 holddown, 0 hidden)
+ = Active Route, - = Last Active, * = Both


10.100.40.0/24    *[EVPN/170] 1w0d 08:38:20
                   > to 198.51.100.1 via et-0/0/48.0
                     to 198.51.100.3 via et-0/0/50.0


root@leaf1> show route forwarding-table destination 10.100.40.4 table Tenant1
Routing table: Tenant1.inet
Internet:
Destination       Type RtRef Next hop       Type Index   NhRef Netif
10.100.40.0/24    user    0                 comp 1798     2
```

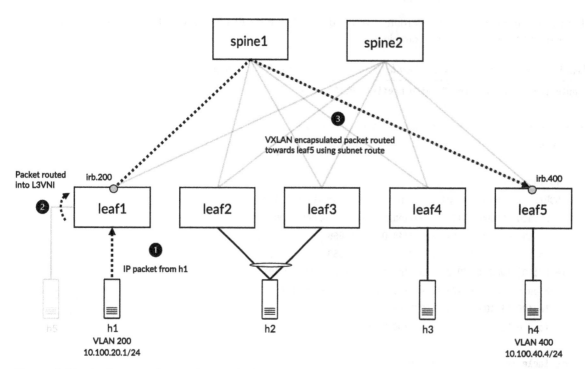

Figure 8-30 *Packet routed toward egress leaf using subnet route*

When leaf5 receives this packet, it decapsulates it and, since the destination MAC address in the inner Ethernet header is owned by itself, does a routing lookup for the destination IP address in the inner IP header. It has no knowledge of h4 at this stage, and thus the routing lookup matches the directly connected IRB interface as the longest prefix, shown in Example 8-33.

Example 8-33 *Directly attached IRB interface on leaf5*

```
root@leaf5> show route table Tenant1.inet.0 10.100.40.4

Tenant1.inet.0: 8 destinations, 11 routes (8 active, 0 holddown, 0 hidden)
+ = Active Route, - = Last Active, * = Both

10.100.40.0/24    *[Direct/0] 1w0d 08:44:48
                   > via irb.400
```

This forces leaf5 to trigger the gleaning process for the destination—it sends an ARP request for 10.100.40.4 (host h4's IP address), which, in turn, forces the silent host, h4, to respond. When h4 responds with an ARP reply, leaf5 learns its address and subsequently advertises it into the EVPN VXLAN fabric, which allows all remote leafs in the fabric to learn the address as well. Since this is a symmetric IRB design, a /32 host route gets installed in the IP VRF table on leaf1, and this route can now be used to send all subsequent traffic from h1 to h4.

A visual representation of this entire process is shown in Figure 8-31.

In this way, advertising a subnet route for the IRB interface facilitates the discovery of silent hosts in the fabric. This does lead to an interesting traffic pattern. Consider a situation in which multiple leafs (leaf4 and leaf5, as an example) advertise the same subnet route. On other remote leafs, this subnet route will have two paths in the overlay via ECMP. If leaf1 receives traffic from a local host destined to a host in this subnet that has not yet been discovered in the fabric (since it is a silent host), traffic will either be sent to leaf4 or leaf5. What happens if the traffic is sent to leaf5, but the host is attached to leaf4?

The ARP process occurs in the same way as shown in Figure 8-31, but it is also sent over the fabric, forcing the host behind leaf4 to respond, and be discovered in the fabric. Eventually, the /32 host route will be installed on the ingress leaf, and traffic will be directed to leaf4. Thus, in such situations, there is a degree of momentary inefficiency that is introduced in the traffic pattern, but it is a small price to pay to allow for the discovery of silent hosts in the fabric.

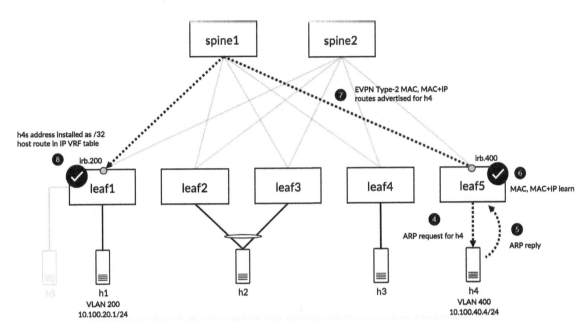

Figure 8-31 *Gleaning process for silent hosts*

Summary

This chapter introduced the asymmetric and symmetric IRB routing models in an EVPN VXLAN fabric and provided a detailed look at the two models. Asymmetric IRB uses a *bridge-route-bridge* model and is simpler from a control plane perspective. Ideally, it is used if all hosts are attached to all VTEPs, meaning that the MAC-IP binding needs to be learned everywhere anyway.

However, if the broadcast domain is not stretched and inter-subnet forwarding is needed, then symmetric IRB makes more sense, which uses a *bridge-route-route-bridge* model, facilitating a design in which VLANs can be scoped to specific VTEPs, and a Layer 3 VNI, associated to an IP VRF, is used to route between VLANs.

Routed Overlay and Host-Routed Bridging

The previous chapter introduced edge-routed bridging, with routing distributed to the leafs using an anycast distributed gateway design. With such a design, different routing models such as asymmetric IRB and symmetric IRB can be implemented, enabling routing between VNIs while still retaining the capability to extend a Layer 2 VLAN over the EVPN VXLAN fabric as needed.

This chapter takes a deeper look at the routed overlay architecture, typically used when there is no need for Layer 2 extension and traffic is routed from the hosts themselves. In addition, this chapter explores the host-routed bridging design where VXLAN functionality is moved to the hosts themselves.

Overview of a Routed Overlay Design

A *routed overlay* is a design that is generally used with cloud-native applications that have no Layer 2 requirements. Instead of moving the L2/L3 demarcation down to the leafs, it is moved all the way down to the hosts themselves, removing all Layer 2 constructs from the fabric, making it a pure IP fabric only, as shown in Figure 9-1. This can be achieved in one of two ways: the leafs and the hosts are connected via point-to-point Layer 3 links and peer with each other over these, or the leafs continue to have a Layer 2 link to the host, along with corresponding IRB interfaces for the respective VLANs, and the hosts peer to these Layer 3 IRB interfaces.

The hosts typically use a routing protocol to peer with the leafs and advertise prefixes upstream, which are injected into the EVPN VXLAN fabric as EVPN Type-5 routes by the leafs for remote learning by other VTEPs in the fabric, as depicted in Figure 9-2. Such a design allows any host to exist anywhere since it can advertise its host-specific /32 or /128 routes to the leafs.

Such an architecture also facilitates designs that require anycast services (very commonly seen in a content delivery network or network infrastructures offering anycast DNS services). In such a design, all servers advertise the same anycast address upstream to their directly connected VTEPs, which is then injected into the EVPN VXLAN fabric as a Type-5 route. Since all VTEPs inject the same /32 or /128 host address, this allows for ECMP in the overlay for these routes. Traffic can then be routed to any of these services. Resilient hashing ensures "stickiness" of a flow toward a particular server, ensuring flows are not remapped with additions/deletions of equal cost paths. This is a very cost-effective solution to a problem that is usually solved by using expensive hardware-based load-balancers to load-balance traffic across servers providing the same service.

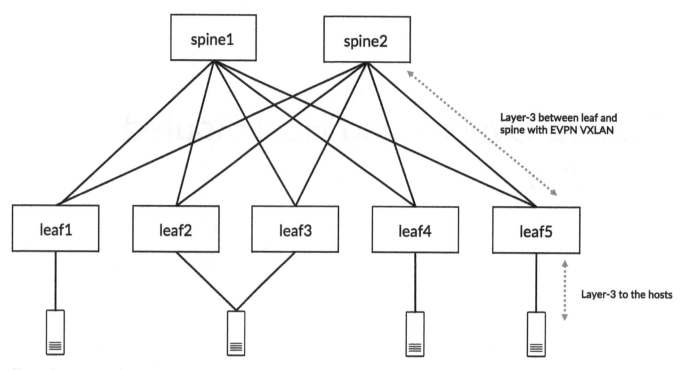

Figure 9-1 *L2/L3 demarcation brought down to the hosts in a routed overlay design*

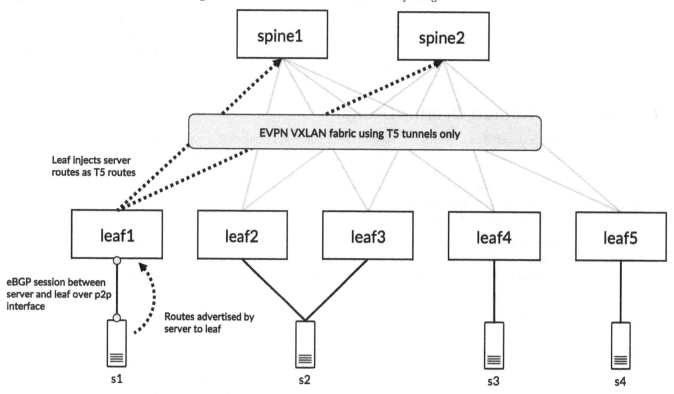

Figure 9-2 *Routed overlay with EVPN VXLAN design overview*

Understanding EVPN Type-5 Routes and Their Use in Data Centers

RFC 9136 (along with RFC 9135) provides details regarding the EVPN Type-5 route and its use cases. EVPN Type-5 routes decouple the MAC address from the IP address and are used to advertise an IP prefix only. The initial use case of EVPN

Type 5 routes, as depicted in Figure 9 3, was to connect data centers (using Data Center Interconnects, explained in Chapter 11) and inject routes from an external domain into an EVPN VXLAN fabric.

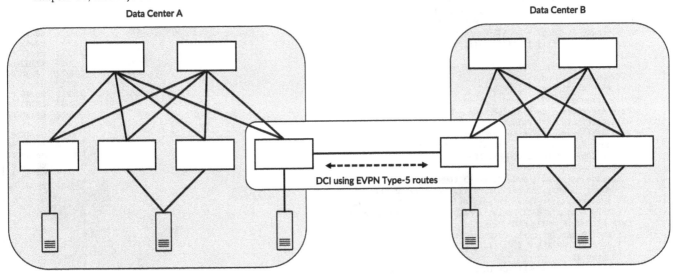

Figure 9-3 *Connecting data centers using EVPN Type-5 routes*

However, over time, the scope of EVPN Type-5 routes has expanded considerably, and it is now commonly used to connect two pods within a data center (a *pod* is a repeatable, modular unit such as a 3-stage Clos fabric connecting to other pods via a superspine layer to build a larger, 5-stage fabric, as described in Chapter 2, "Overview of Data Center Architecture") or even build a single data center purely with Type-5 routing only. This is useful when a bridge domain (VLAN) does not span more than one VTEP—this means that the subnet corresponding to that VLAN exists only behind that one VTEP. Instead of advertising host addresses as EVPN Type-2 routes, the entire subnet can be consolidated and advertised as a single EVPN Type-5 route, while also leaking /32 or /128 host routes as needed. This reduces table explosion due to a large number of EVPN Type-2 routes, while the spines of the fabric continue to be pure IP forwarding devices, with no knowledge of the endpoints and, thus, no requirement to maintain any state for the same.

Other use cases, of EVPN Type-5 routes, also include injecting default routes from an external domain such as a firewall, attached to a leaf, that wants to pull all traffic for inter-subnet routing so that policy is centralized and enforced only via the firewall. This use case is depicted in Figure 9-4.

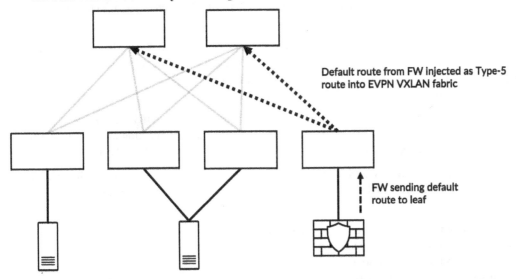

Figure 9-4 *Firewall-originated default route injected into EVPN VXLAN fabric as a Type-5 route*

A packet capture of an EVPN Type-5 route is shown in Figure 9-5 (repeated from Chapter 8, "Edge-Routed Bridging"), with leaf1 originating the IRB subnet as a Type-5 route. It is important to understand how an EVPN Type-5 route differs from an EVPN Type-2 route.

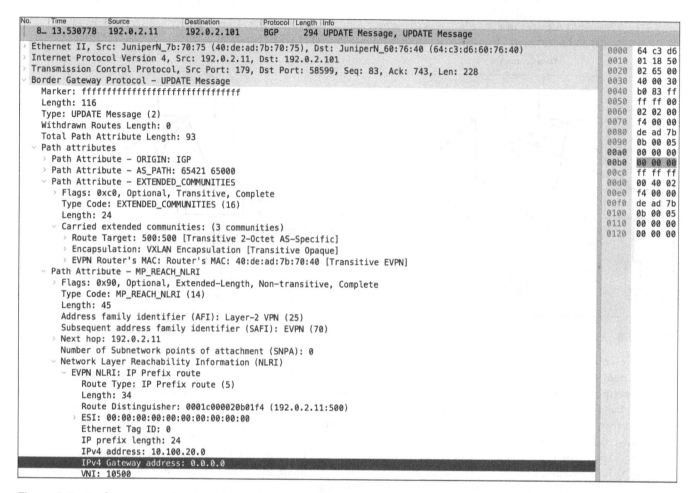

Figure 9-5   *Packet capture of an EVPN Type-5 route*

An EVPN Type-5 route carries only an IP prefix (an IPv4 or IPv6 address with an IP prefix length field) with the VNI set to the L3VNI, corresponding to the IP VRF. Along with the encapsulation type set to VXLAN, this route carries two important extended communities: the Route Target (which is the Route Target of the IP VRF) and the router-mac, which is used when building the inner Ethernet header in the data plane, as discussed in Chapter 8.

Additionally, there is a new field for an EVPN Type-5 route (4 octets for IPv4 and 16 octets for IPv6) called the *Gateway IP address*. This is encoded with the *Overlay Index*. The Overlay Index can be an ESI value or an IP address, and it provides a level of indirection that requires recursive resolution to determine the actual next-hop address for the EVPN Type-5 route. This indirection helps in faster convergence in case of certain failure scenarios.

Consider the topology shown in Figure 9-6. Servers s1 and s2 share a floating virtual IP address vIP3 (since there is no need to reinvent the wheel, this example is a direct interpretation from RFC 9136). The two servers function in an active/standby model, like VRRP, with the active server owning the virtual IP address and servicing a common subnet, SN1.

Without an EVPN Type-5 route, server s1 would have to advertise the subnet SN1 via an EVPN Type-2 route. If server s2 becomes the active peer, this route would be advertised again by s2, and s1 would withdraw it. At large scale, this is highly inefficient.

With EVPN Type-5 routes, using the indirection provided by the gateway IP address, both servers s1 and s2 advertise the subnet SN1 using a Type-5 route with the gateway IP address set to the floating virtual IP address. However, only the active server (s1, in this case) advertises an EVPN Type-2 route for the floating address, thus allowing for recursive resolution to itself for this virtual address. If server s2 becomes the active peer, it simply advertises the EVPN Type-2 route for the floating address, thus changing the recursive resolution to itself for this address.

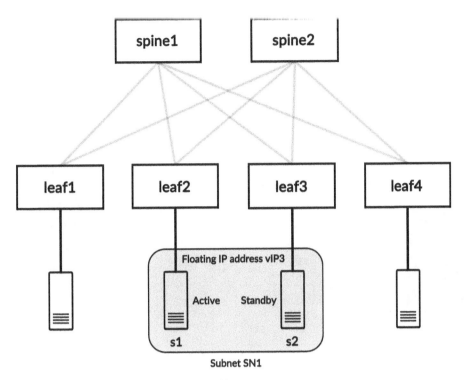

Figure 9-6 *Servers with floating IP address*

Configuring and Validating Routed Overlay

This section updates the reference topology to reflect a routed overlay design, with the server-facing interfaces on the leafs converted to point-to-point interfaces. Since there is no Layer 2 requirement from this fabric, a MAC-VRF is unnecessary. Only the IP VRF construct is retained to provide customer isolation and to inject routes learned from the servers into BGP EVPN as Type-5 routes. Each server has an eBGP peering over the point-to-point interface to its upstream leaf.

With leaf1 as an example, the configuration snippet presented in Example 9-1 demonstrates these changes. Within the IP VRF, a BGP peering is configured for the server, and the point-to-point interface to the server is added in the routing instance itself. An export policy called *s1* is configured to export IPv4 routes received from the server into the EVPN table, and an export policy is configured, under the *protocols bgp* hierarchy, to advertise routes from the inet.0 table (imported from the EVPN table into the inet.0 table) to the server.

Example 9-1 *Routed overlay configuration on leaf1*

```
root@leaf1# show interfaces et-0/0/49
mtu 9200;
unit 0 {
    family inet {
        address 198.51.100.20/31;
    }
}


root@leaf1# show routing-instances Tenant1
instance-type vrf;
protocols {
    bgp {
        group s1 {
            type external;
```

```
                family inet {
                    unicast;
                }
                export export-to-s1;
                peer-as 65000;
                neighbor 198.51.100.21;
            }
        }
        evpn {
            ip-prefix-routes {
                advertise direct-nexthop;
                encapsulation vxlan;
                vni 10500;
                export s1;
            }
        }
    }
    interface et-0/0/49.0;
    route-distinguisher 192.0.2.11:500;
    vrf-target target:500:500;


    root@leaf1# show policy-options policy-statement s1
    term 1 {
        from {
            route-filter 10.100.20.0/24 orlonger;
        }
        then accept;
    }


    {master:0}[edit]
    root@leaf1# show policy-options policy-statement export-to-s1
    term 1 {
        from protocol evpn;
        then accept;
    }
    term 2 {
        then reject;
    }
```

There are multiple policy control points with such a configuration, with their functionalities described as follows:

■ An export policy within the *ip-prefix-routes* hierarchy controls which routes are exported as EVPN Type-5 routes.

■ An export policy within the *protocols bgp* hierarchy controls which routes get exported as IPv4 routes toward the server.

■ An import policy within the *ip-prefix-routes* hierarchy controls the installation of routes from the *vrf-name.evpn.0* table into the *vrf-name.inet.0* table.

■ An import policy for the VRF itself (using the *vrf-import* configuration option) controls what routes get pulled into the *vrf-name.evpn.0* table from the *bgp.evpn.0* table.

Considering an IP VRF named Tenant1, the flow diagram shown in Figure 9-7 provides all available control points for ease of understanding and to be used as an easy reference when deploying such a design.

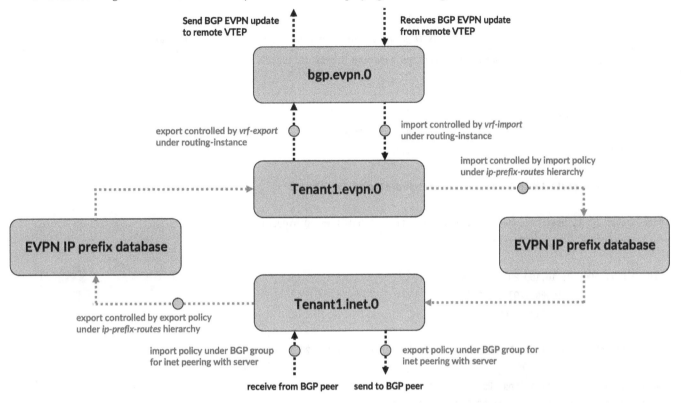

Figure 9-7   *Import and export policy control points with Type-5 routes*

Using Figure 9-7 as a reference, it is important to demonstrate how these routes move between different tables. Considering server s1 and leaf1 as an example, let's follow the prefix 10.100.20.1/32 received from s1. This route is seen in BGP RIB-In, shown in Example 9-2, and inserted into the IP VRF's IPv4 table, Tenant1.inet.0.

Example 9-2   *Host route received from server s1 on leaf1 over eBGP peering*

```
root@leaf1> show route receive-protocol bgp 198.51.100.21 10.100.20.1


inet.0: 31 destinations, 35 routes (31 active, 0 holddown, 0 hidden)


Tenant1.inet.0: 10 destinations, 13 routes (10 active, 0 holddown, 0 hidden)
  Prefix              Nexthop           MED     Lclpref    AS path
* 10.100.20.1/32      198.51.100.21                        65000 I
```

The export policy presented in Example 9-3 controls the export of IPv4 routes into the EVPN table for the IP VRF.

Example 9-3   *Policy to allow export of received IPv4 routes into EVPN IP prefix database on leaf1*

```
root@leaf1# show policy-options policy-statement s1
term 1 {
    from {
        route-filter 10.100.20.0/24 orlonger;
    }
    then accept;
}
```

Since this policy permits any route in the 10.100.20.0/24 subnet (with the same or higher subnet mask), the route 10.100.20.1/32 is exported and installed into the EVPN IP prefix database and eventually into the Tenant1.evpn.0 table, shown in Example 9-4.

Example 9-4 *Host route exported into EVPN IP prefix database and installed in IP VRF EVPN table on leaf1*

```
root@leaf1> show evpn ip-prefix-database direction exported prefix 10.100.20.1
L3 context: Tenant1


IPv4->EVPN Exported Prefixes
Prefix                              EVPN route status
10.100.20.1/32                      Created


root@leaf1> show route table Tenant1.evpn.0 match-prefix 5:*10.100.20.1*


Tenant1.evpn.0: 11 destinations, 20 routes (11 active, 0 holddown, 0 hidden)
+ = Active Route, - = Last Active, * = Both


5:192.0.2.11:500::0::10.100.20.1::32/248
                    *[EVPN/170] 00:20:13
                        Fictitious


root@leaf1> show route table Tenant1.evpn.0 match-prefix 5:*10.100.20.1* extensive


Tenant1.evpn.0: 11 destinations, 20 routes (11 active, 0 holddown, 0 hidden)
5:192.0.2.11:500::0::10.100.20.1::32/248 (1 entry, 1 announced)
        *EVPN    Preference: 170/-101
                 Next hop type: Fictitious, Next hop index: 0
                 Address: 0x8c066a4
                 Next-hop reference count: 4, key opaque handle: 0x0, non-key opaque handle: 0x0
                 Next hop:
                 State: <Active Int Ext>
                 Age: 53
                 Validation State: unverified
                 Task: Tenant1-EVPN-L3-context
                 Announcement bits (1): 1-rt-export
                 AS path: 65000 I
                 Communities: encapsulation:vxlan(0x8) router-mac:40:de:ad:7b:70:40
                 Route Label: 10500
                 Overlay gateway address: 0.0.0.0
                 ESI 00:00:00:00:00:00:00:00:00:00
                 Thread: junos-main
```

From here, the route is inserted into the bgp.evpn.0 table with the appropriate Route Targets—an internal export policy (created with the creation of the IP VRF) adds the Route Target to the route, shown in Example 9-5. This is then sent as a BGP EVPN update to leaf1's neighbors (spine1 and spine2, in this case).

Example 9-5 *Internal policy to export routes from IP VRF EVPN table to bgp.evpn.0 table on leaf1*

```
root@leaf1> show policy __vrf-export-Tenant1-internal__
Policy __vrf-export-Tenant1-internal__:  [RESOLVED/]
    Term unnamed:
        then community + __vrf-community-Tenant1-common-internal__ [target:500:500 ] accept


root@leaf1> show route table bgp.evpn.0 match-prefix 5:*10.100.20.1*


bgp.evpn.0: 11 destinations, 20 routes (11 active, 0 holddown, 0 hidden)
+ = Active Route, - = Last Active, * = Both


5:192.0.2.11:500::0::10.100.20.1::32/248
                    *[EVPN/170] 00:00:14
                        Fictitious


root@leaf1> show route table bgp.evpn.0 match-prefix 5:*10.100.20.1* extensive


bgp.evpn.0: 11 destinations, 20 routes (11 active, 0 holddown, 0 hidden)
5:192.0.2.11:500::0::10.100.20.1::32/248 (1 entry, 1 announced)
TSI:
Page 0 idx 0, (group overlay type External) Type 1 val 0xae428c0 (adv_entry)
   Advertised metrics:
     Flags: Nexthop Change
     Nexthop: Self
     AS path: [65421] 65000 I
     Communities: target:500:500 encapsulation:vxlan(0x8) router-mac:40:de:ad:7b:70:40
     Advertise: 00000003
Path 5:192.0.2.11:500::0::10.100.20.1::32
Vector len 4.  Val: 0
        *EVPN    Preference: 170/-101
                 Next hop type: Fictitious, Next hop index: 0
                 Address: 0x8c066a4
                 Next-hop reference count: 4, key opaque handle: 0x0, non-key opaque handle: 0x0
                 Next hop:
                 State: <Secondary Active Int Ext>
                 Age: 3:15
                 Validation State: unverified
                 Task: Tenant1-EVPN-L3-context
                 Announcement bits (1): 1-BGP_RT_Background
                 AS path: 65000 I
                 Communities: target:500:500 encapsulation:vxlan(0x8) router-mac:40:de:ad:7b:70:40
                 Route Label: 10500
                 Overlay gateway address: 0.0.0.0
                 ESI 00:00:00:00:00:00:00:00:00:00
                 Primary Routing Table: Tenant1.evpn.0
                 Thread: junos-main
```

Junos makes it very easy to determine which table a route originated from—for the 10.100.20.1/32 route shown in Example 9-5, the Primary Routing Table is identified as Tenant1.evpn.0, which means that the route originated from this table. This entire process can be visualized as shown in Figure 9-8.

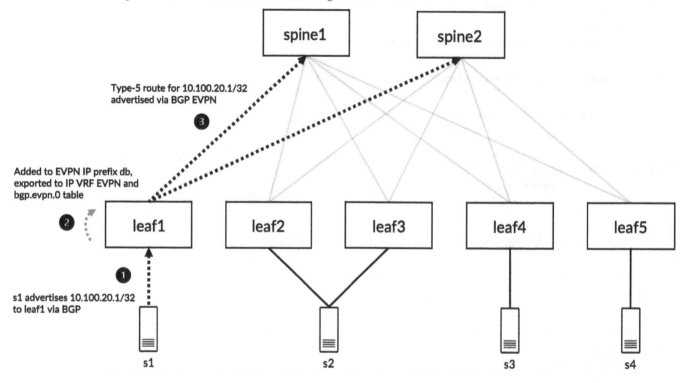

Figure 9-8   *EVPN Type-5 route advertisement process*

This BGP EVPN update is received by all the other VTEPs in the fabric. Considering leaf4 as an example, the route is inserted into the bgp.evpn.0 table first, as shown in Example 9-6.

Example 9-6   *Host route, advertised by leaf1, received in bgp.evpn.0 table on leaf4*

```
root@leaf4> show route table bgp.evpn.0 match-prefix 5:*10.100.20.1*

bgp.evpn.0: 11 destinations, 19 routes (11 active, 0 holddown, 0 hidden)
+ = Active Route, - = Last Active, * = Both

5:192.0.2.11:500::0::10.100.20.1::32/248
                *[BGP/170] 00:10:49, localpref 100, from 192.0.2.101
                   AS path: 65500 65421 65000 I, validation-state: unverified
                >  to 198.51.100.13 via et-0/0/0.0, Push 656
                   to 198.51.100.15 via et-0/0/2.0, Push 656
                 [BGP/170] 00:10:49, localpref 100, from 192.0.2.102
                   AS path: 65500 65421 65000 I, validation-state: unverified
                >  to 198.51.100.13 via et-0/0/0.0, Push 656
                   to 198.51.100.15 via et-0/0/2.0, Push 656
```

An internal policy (again, created with the creation of the IP VRF) imports the route into the Tenant1.evpn.0 table. Thus, it is important to remember that even though no explicit import policy is defined under the routing instance, there is an internal, implicit policy controlling the import. Any explicit import policy overrides this implicit policy, and you should take care to import all required Route Targets. When the route is pulled into Tenant1.evpn.0, the Primary Routing Table again points to the table that originally hosts this route, which is bgp.evpn.0 in this case, shown in Example 9-7.

Example 9-7 *Internal policy to import routes from bgp.evpn.0 table into IP VRF EVPN table*

```
root@leaf4> show policy __vrf-import-Tenant1-internal__
Policy __vrf-import-Tenant1-internal__:  [CHANGED/RESOLVED/]
    Term unnamed:
        from community __vrf-community-Tenant1-common-internal__ [target:500:500 ]
        then accept
    Term unnamed:
        then reject


root@leaf4> show route table Tenant1.evpn.0 match-prefix 5:*10.100.20.1*


Tenant1.evpn.0: 11 destinations, 19 routes (11 active, 0 holddown, 0 hidden)
+ = Active Route, - = Last Active, * = Both


5:192.0.2.11:500::0::10.100.20.1::32/248
                    *[BGP/170] 00:28:53, localpref 100, from 192.0.2.101
                      AS path: 65500 65421 65000 I, validation-state: unverified
                    >  to 198.51.100.13 via et-0/0/0.0, Push 656
                       to 198.51.100.15 via et-0/0/2.0, Push 656
                     [BGP/170] 00:28:53, localpref 100, from 192.0.2.102
                      AS path: 65500 65421 65000 I, validation-state: unverified
                    >  to 198.51.100.13 via et-0/0/0.0, Push 656
                       to 198.51.100.15 via et-0/0/2.0, Push 656


root@leaf4> show route table Tenant1.evpn.0 match-prefix 5:*10.100.20.1* extensive


Tenant1.evpn.0: 11 destinations, 19 routes (11 active, 0 holddown, 0 hidden)
5:192.0.2.11:500::0::10.100.20.1::32/248 (2 entries, 1 announced)
        *BGP    Preference: 170/-101
                Route Distinguisher: 192.0.2.11:500
                Next hop type: Indirect, Next hop index: 0
                Address: 0x55c643d5d59c
                Next-hop reference count: 8, key opaque handle: (nil), non-key opaque handle: (nil)
                Source: 192.0.2.101
                Protocol next hop: 192.0.2.11
                Label operation: Push 656
                Label TTL action: prop-ttl
                Load balance label: Label 656: None;
                Indirect next hop: 0x2 no-forward INH Session ID: 0
                State: <Secondary Active Ext>
                Local AS: 65424 Peer AS: 65500
                Age: 29:22     Metric2: 0
                Validation State: unverified
                Task: BGP_65500.192.0.2.101
                Announcement bits (1): 0-Tenant1-EVPN-L3-context
                AS path: 65500 65421 65000 I
```

```
            Communities: target:500:500 encapsulation:vxlan(0x8) router-mac:40:de:ad:7b:70:40
            Import Accepted
            Route Label: 10500
            Overlay gateway address: 0.0.0.0
            ESI 00:00:00:00:00:00:00:00:00:00
            Localpref: 100
            Router ID: 192.0.2.101
            Primary Routing Table: bgp.evpn.0
            Thread: junos-main
```

snip

Finally, this route is installed in the EVPN IP prefix database and imported into the Tenant1.inet.0 table, from where it is exported by BGP (for the IPv4 family within the IP VRF) and sent as a BGP update to the server connected to leaf4 (s3). This is shown in Example 9-8.

Example 9-8   *Host route imported into EVPN IP prefix database and eventually IP VRF inet.0 table on leaf4*

```
root@leaf4> show evpn ip-prefix-database direction imported prefix 10.100.20.1
L3 context: Tenant1


EVPN->IPv4 Imported Prefixes
Prefix                              Etag
10.100.20.1/32                      0
  Route distinguisher  VNI/Label  Router MAC        Nexthop/Overlay GW/ESI  Route-Status  Reject-Reason
  192.0.2.11:500       10500      40:de:ad:7b:70:40 192.0.2.11              Accepted      n/a


root@leaf4> show route table Tenant1.inet.0 10.100.20.1


Tenant1.inet.0: 12 destinations, 15 routes (12 active, 0 holddown, 0 hidden)
+ = Active Route, - = Last Active, * = Both


10.100.20.1/32      *[EVPN/170] 02:11:50
                        to 198.51.100.13 via et-0/0/0.0
                    >   to 198.51.100.15 via et-0/0/2.0


root@leaf4> show route advertising-protocol bgp 198.51.100.31 10.100.20.1


Tenant1.inet.0: 12 destinations, 15 routes (12 active, 0 holddown, 0 hidden)
  Prefix              Nexthop         MED    Lclpref   AS path
* 10.100.20.1/32      Self                             65500 65421 65000 I
```

This entire receive process can be visualized as shown in Figure 9-9.

From a forwarding plane perspective, consider a situation in which virtualized host h1 on server s1 wants to communicate with another virtualized host h4 on server s4. Host h1 sends an IP packet to leaf1. The destination IP address is h4's address, 10.100.40.4. An IP lookup on leaf1 determines the exit point for this packet—the lookup is done in the Tenant1.inet.0 table since the packet is received on the physical interface mapped to that IP VRF. This forwarding lookup determines that destination can be load-balanced over physical interfaces *et-0/0/48.0* and *et-0/0/50.0* and has a composite next-hop ID of 1781, which provides the necessary information for VXLAN encapsulation, as shown in Example 9-9.

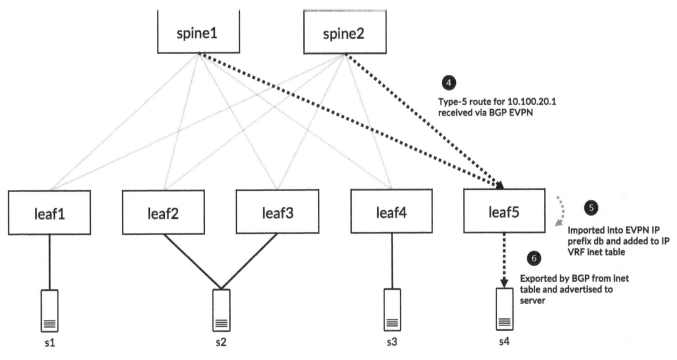

Figure 9-9   *EVPN Type-5 route receive process*

Example 9-9   *Route lookup, on leaf1, for h4's address in IP VRF table*

```
root@leaf1> show route forwarding-table destination 10.100.40.4/32 table Tenant1 extensive
Routing table: Tenant1.inet [Index 5]
Internet:

Destination:  10.100.40.4/32
  Route type: user
  Route reference: 0              Route interface-index: 0
  Multicast RPF nh index: 0
  P2mpidx: 0
  Flags: sent to PFE, VxLAN Local
  Nexthop:
  Next-hop type: composite       Index: 1781     Reference: 3
  Next-hop type: indirect        Index: 524287   Reference: 2
  Next-hop type: unilist         Index: 524286   Reference: 8
  Nexthop: 198.51.100.1
  Next-hop type: unicast         Index: 1780     Reference: 6
  Next-hop interface: et-0/0/48.0   Weight: 0x1
  Nexthop: 198.51.100.3
  Next-hop type: unicast         Index: 1778     Reference: 6
  Next-hop interface: et-0/0/50.0   Weight: 0x1

FPC0(leaf1 vty)# show nhdb id 1781 extensive
  ID    Type    Interface    Next Hop Addr    Protocol    Encap    MTU             Flags  PFE internal Flags
 ----- -------- ------------ ---------------- ---------- ----------- ----  ------------------ -------------------
 1781   Compst  -            -                IPv4        -         0    0x0000000000000000  0x0000000000000000
```

```
BFD Session Id: 0

Composite NH:
  Function: Tunnel Function
  Hardware Index: 0x1fff
  Composite flag: 0x0
  Composite pfe flag: 0xe
  Lower-level NH Ids: 524287
  Derived NH Ids:
  Tunnel Data:
      Type     : VXLAN
      Tunnel ID: 806354944
      Encap VRF: 0
      Decap VRF: 5
      MTU      : 0
      Flags    : 0x0
      AnchorId : 0
      Encap Len: 53
      Mode     : Encap-Decap
      Encap    : 0x01 0x0b 0x02 0x00 0xc0 0x00 0x00 0x00
                 0x00 0x00 0x00 0x00 0x00 0x00 0x00 0x00
                 0x00 0x0f 0x02 0x00 0xc0 0x00 0x00 0x00
                 0x00 0x00 0x00 0x00 0x00 0x00 0x00 0x00
                 0x00 0x04 0x29 0x00 0x00 0x04 0x29 0x00
                 0x00 0x50 0xc7 0x09 0xa6 0xaa 0x04 0x40
                 0xde 0xad 0x7b 0x70 0x40
      Data Len : 0


Dram Bytes : 260
Num of nhs: 1
HW NH-ID      : 400002
Module        : 0
DVP GPORT     : 0xb0000002
L3-INTF       : 1
OL_DMAC       : 50:c7:9:a6:aa:4
OL_SMAC       : 40:de:ad:7b:70:40
VFI           : 0x7001
MTU           : 9600
IP profile_id : 0
VRF           : 4
Ingress_IF    : 4097


  Routing-table id: 0
```

A packet capture, in transit, confirms that the VNI added to the VXLAN header is the L3VNI 10500. Again, the destination MAC address of the inner Ethernet header is the MAC address owned by leaf5's IRB interface (even though there are no IRB interfaces configured, there is a base IRB interface that owns this MAC address)—this is the same logic as seen before with symmetric IRB forwarding. The IRB interface's MAC address is shown in Example 9-10, with the packet itself shown in Figure 9-10 confirming the same.

Example 9-10 *IRB interface MAC address on leaf5, used as router-mac when sending EVPN Type-5 routes*

```
root@leaf5> show interfaces irb
Physical interface: irb, Enabled, Physical link is Up
  Interface index: 1005, SNMP ifIndex: 504
  Type: Ethernet, Link-level type: Ethernet, MTU: 1514, Speed: 1Gbps, Auto-negotiation: Disabled
  Device flags   : Present Running
  Interface flags: None
  Current address: 50:c7:09:a6:aa:04, Hardware address: 50:c7:09:a6:aa:04
  Last flapped   : Never
  Input rate     : 0 bps (0 pps)
  Output rate    : 0 bps (0 pps)
```

```
No.   Time       Source       Destination     Protocol  Length  Info
- 12 0.616084   10.100.20.1  10.100.40.4     ICMP      148 Echo (ping) request  id=0x13e0, seq=106/27136, ttl=63 (reply in 13)
← 13 0.616616   10.100.40.4  10.100.20.1     ICMP      152 Echo (ping) reply    id=0x13e0, seq=106/27136, ttl=63 (request in 12)

> Frame 12: 148 bytes on wire (1184 bits), 148 bytes captured (1184 bits)       0000  d8 b1 22 8a 40 2f 40 de
> Ethernet II, Src: JuniperN_7b:70:7d (40:de:ad:7b:70:7d), Dst: JuniperN_8a:40:2f (d8:b1:22:8a:40:2f)   0010  00 86 2e 4b 00 00 40 11
> Internet Protocol Version 4, Src: 192.0.2.11, Dst: 192.0.2.15                 0020  02 0f 14 d6 12 b5 00 72
> User Datagram Protocol, Src Port: 5334, Dst Port: 4789                         0030  04 00 50 c7 09 a6 aa 04
∨ Virtual eXtensible Local Area Network                                         0040  45 00 00 54 00 ac 00 00
  > Flags: 0x0800, VXLAN Network ID (VNI)                                       0050  0a 64 28 04 08 00 bc 64
    Group Policy ID: 0                                                          0060  00 00 e1 0b 08 09 0a 0b
    VXLAN Network Identifier (VNI): 10500                                       0070  14 15 16 17 18 19 1a 1b
    Reserved: 0                                                                 0080  24 25 26 27 28 29 2a 2b
∨ Ethernet II, Src: JuniperN_7b:70:40 (40:de:ad:7b:70:40), Dst: JuniperN_a6:aa:04 (50:c7:09:a6:aa:04)   0090  34 35 36 37
  > Destination: JuniperN_a6:aa:04 (50:c7:09:a6:aa:04)
  > Source: JuniperN_7b:70:40 (40:de:ad:7b:70:40)
    Type: IPv4 (0x0800)
∨ Internet Protocol Version 4, Src: 10.100.20.1, Dst: 10.100.40.4
    0100 .... = Version: 4
    .... 0101 = Header Length: 20 bytes (5)
  > Differentiated Services Field: 0x00 (DSCP: CS0, ECN: Not-ECT)
    Total Length: 84
    Identification: 0x00ac (172)
  > 000. .... = Flags: 0x0
    ...0 0000 0000 0000 = Fragment Offset: 0
    Time to Live: 63
    Protocol: ICMP (1)
    Header Checksum: 0x2a31 [validation disabled]
    [Header checksum status: Unverified]
    Source Address: 10.100.20.1
    Destination Address: 10.100.40.4
> Internet Control Message Protocol
```

Figure 9-10 *Packet capture of ICMP request from host h1 destined for h4*

When leaf5 receives this packet, it decapsulates it and does an IP lookup for the inner destination IP address (since it owns the inner destination MAC address), with the L3VNI dictating the IP VRF in which the lookup is done. It determines that the packet needs to be sent out its directly attached Layer 3 interface to the server, as shown in Example 9-11. Thus, the server, and the virtualized host h4, now receives this packet and can respond appropriately.

Example 9-11 *Route lookup, on leaf5, for h4's address in IP VRF inet.0 table*

```
root@leaf5> show route 10.100.40.4/32 table Tenant1.inet.0

Tenant1.inet.0: 9 destinations, 12 routes (9 active, 0 holddown, 0 hidden)
+ = Active Route, - = Last Active, * = Both

10.100.40.4/32     *[BGP/170] 4d 01:38:38, localpref 100
                      AS path: 65000 I, validation-state: unverified
                    > to 198.51.100.29 via et-0/0/1.0
```

Host-Routed Bridging

Host-routed bridging is a natural extension of the routed overlay design, with the VXLAN and VTEP functionality being moved down to the host itself, and the leaf or ToR (top-of-rack) device being used for IP forwarding only (like the spines). Thus, with such a design, the VXLAN tunnels are established between the hosts, as shown in Figure 9-11. From the leaf and above, the fabric is a pure IP fabric. For such use cases, the VXLAN data plane is usually offloaded to a smartNIC, installed on the server/host to avoid processing of such packets by the CPU cores and to provide hardware acceleration for VXLAN tunnels.

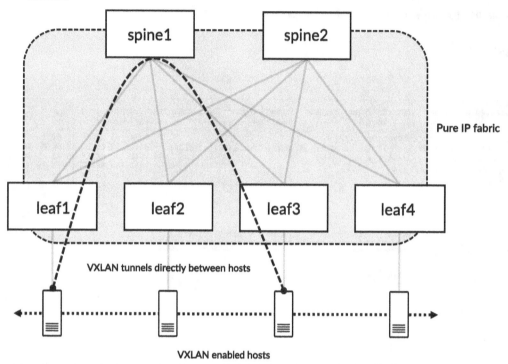

Figure 9-11   *Host-routed bridging with direct VXLAN tunnels between hosts*

Host-routed bridging brings similar advantages as a routed overlay design: multihoming is made much easier and is purely a function of underlay ECMP, eliminating the need for any Designated Forwarder election and split-horizon rules when ESI LAG is used. Such a design also simplifies provisioning in cloud-native environments—lifecycle management can be fully controlled by Kubernetes, with a Container Network Interface (CNI) taking network intent and orchestrating and provisioning the network infrastructure required for the deployment.

To demonstrate host-routed bridging, the reference topology is updated with two hosts, h1 and h2, that are servers implementing a host-routed bridging design, as shown in Figure 9-12. This means that all VTEP functionality is moved down to these hosts, and leaf1, leaf2, and leaf3 (since host h2 is multihomed to both leaf2 and leaf3) are no longer configured as VTEPs. Leafs leaf4 and leaf5 implement a routed overlay design, which means they will still be configured as VTEPs.

Hosts h1 and h2 are servers running Ubuntu 22.04, with Free Range Routing (FRR, an open-source routing suite) installed as the routing suite for BGP and EVPN VXLAN configuration. Each server has a container (container c1 on server h1 and c2 on server h2) in the subnet 10.100.10.0/24 and 10.100.20.0/24, respectively. FRR does not manage interface configuration for the server, and that must be done using Netplan, which is a utility provided for network abstraction in Ubuntu. Netplan is the default utility for interface management on Ubuntu 22.04.

For container networking, a Docker bridge is created on each server: h1 has a bridge named *br-vni10* with an IP address of 10.100.10.254/24, with container c1 attached to it, and h2 has a bridge named *br-vni20* with an IP address of 10.100.20.254/24, with container c2 attached to it. These bridges are default gateways for the containers that attach to them. This is shown in Example 9-12.

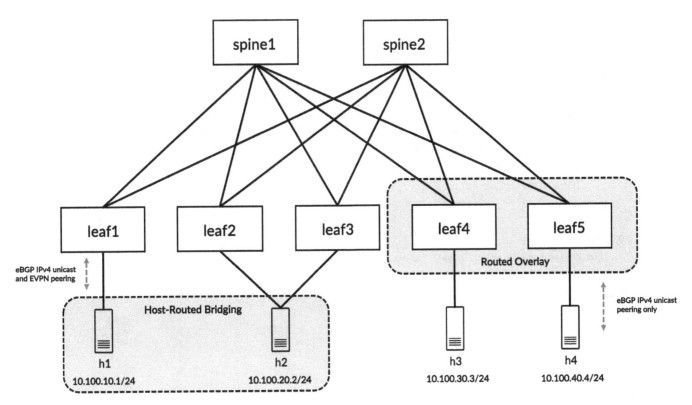

Figure 9-12 *Reference topology for host-routed bridging*

Example 9-12 *Docker bridge on host h1*

```
root@h1:/home/h1# docker network inspect br-vni10
[
    {
        "Name": "br-vni10",
        "Id": "352f0d9cfe5605fabc772b813a7a6eb301c9993cc8c764377111e40768da8da9",
        "Created": "2023-07-17T02:15:47.787864406Z",
        "Scope": "local",
        "Driver": "bridge",
        "EnableIPv6": false,
        "IPAM": {
            "Driver": "default",
            "Options": {},
            "Config": [
                {
                    "Subnet": "10.100.10.0/24",
                    "IPRange": "10.100.10.0/24",
                    "Gateway": "10.100.10.254"
                }
            ]
        },
        "Internal": false,
        "Attachable": false,
        "Ingress": false,
        "ConfigFrom": {
```

```
                "Network": ""
            },
            "ConfigOnly": false,
            "Containers": {
                "76e2179383619ed71c1fa501821b92ed14f05efabe7dd6237d918d337a79c193": {
                    "Name": "c1",
                    "EndpointID": "74be694050e5716df23b8c35d32f17ebc55aca8eeb3ee358707ce95afa8fb8c3",
                    "MacAddress": "02:42:0a:64:0a:01",
                    "IPv4Address": "10.100.10.1/24",
                    "IPv6Address": ""
                }
            },
            "Options": {
                "com.docker.network.bridge.name": "br-vni10"
            },
            "Labels": {}
        }
]


root@h2:/home/h2# docker network inspect br-vni20
[
    {
        "Name": "br-vni20",
        "Id": "6d33b2e55f284dd6410c7ec639c29a09f873dca4d8f06edf3477f2eee3cbe34b",
        "Created": "2023-07-17T08:36:01.116398475Z",
        "Scope": "local",
        "Driver": "bridge",
        "EnableIPv6": false,
        "IPAM": {
            "Driver": "default",
            "Options": {},
            "Config": [
                {
                    "Subnet": "10.100.20.0/24",
                    "IPRange": "10.100.20.0/24",
                    "Gateway": "10.100.20.254"
                }
            ]
        },
        "Internal": false,
        "Attachable": false,
        "Ingress": false,
        "ConfigFrom": {
            "Network": ""
        },
        "ConfigOnly": false,
        "Containers": {
            "59777198ca7a053afc9ab9a9b8ba17b9e6b965b1bce51811dffb74678bb73a14": {
                "Name": "c2",
```

```
        "EndpointID": "0572e01d87cb3o73o0155of0oofafc7af3da137c117a573de5d45c6c33e0f3c1",
        "MacAddress": "02:42:0a:64:14:01",
        "IPv4Address": "10.100.20.1/24",
        "IPv6Address": ""
      }
    },
    "Options": {
        "com.docker.network.bridge.name": "br-vni20"
    },
    "Labels": {}
  }
]
```

Independent of these containers, there is an eBGP peering between server h1 and leaf1 for both the IPv4 underlay (using the point-to-point connection) and the L2VPN EVPN overlay (since this is a host-routed bridging design, the server itself is the VTEP here and has all the necessary VTEP functionality configured), and the same for server h2 to leaf2 and leaf3.

The integrated shell for FRR can be accessed via the command **vtysh**, and that is what is used to configure the server and view various **show** command outputs. The configuration snippet presented in Example 9-13 shows how BGP is configured on server s1. Since this design uses EVPN Type-5 routing, a VRF named *Tenant1* is created on the servers, with the corresponding Docker bridges mapped to this IP VRF. The connected IPv4 routes are inserted into the BGP table by using the **redistribute connected** configuration option within the BGP instance for the IP VRF, and then they are exported into EVPN as Type-5 routes by using the configuration option **advertise ipv4 unicast** under the L2VPN EVPN address family.

Example 9-13 *BGP configuration on host h1 using FRR*

```
root@h1:/home/h1# vtysh

Hello, this is FRRouting (version 9.1-dev-MyOwnFRRVersion-g89bbdb5fd).
Copyright 1996-2005 Kunihiro Ishiguro, et al.


This is a git build of frr-9.1-dev-145-g89bbdb5fd
Associated branch(es):
     local:master
     github/frrouting/frr.git/master


h1# show run
Building configuration...

Current configuration:
!
frr version 9.1-dev-MyOwnFRRVersion
frr defaults traditional
hostname h1
log syslog
service integrated-vtysh-config
!
vrf Tenant1
 vni 10500
exit-vrf
!
```

```
router bgp 65000
 bgp router-id 192.0.2.51
 no bgp ebgp-requires-policy
 no bgp default ipv4-unicast
 neighbor 192.0.2.11 remote-as 65421
 neighbor 192.0.2.11 ebgp-multihop 255
 neighbor 192.0.2.11 update-source lo
 neighbor 192.0.2.11 capability extended-nexthop
 neighbor 198.51.100.101 remote-as 65421
 !
 address-family ipv4 unicast
  network 192.0.2.51/32
  neighbor 198.51.100.101 activate
  neighbor 198.51.100.101 allowas-in origin
 exit-address-family
 !
 address-family l2vpn evpn
  neighbor 192.0.2.11 activate
  neighbor 192.0.2.11 allowas-in origin
  advertise-all-vni
 exit-address-family
exit
!
router bgp 65000 vrf Tenant1
 !
 address-family ipv4 unicast
  redistribute connected
 exit-address-family
 !
 address-family l2vpn evpn
  advertise ipv4 unicast
  rd 192.0.2.51:500
  route-target import 500:500
  route-target export 500:500
 exit-address-family
exit
!
```

On leaf1, the Junos configuration shown in Example 9-14 is used to bring up an eBGP peering to server h1 for both the underlay and overlay. Like the spines, it is important that the leafs are configured to not modify the next-hop address for BGP EVPN updates. This ensures that hosts in a host-routed bridging design can form VXLAN tunnels to each other and not their directly connected leafs.

Example 9-14 *BGP configuration on leaf1*

```
root@leaf1# show protocols bgp group underlay
type external;
family inet {
    unicast;
}
```

```
export allow loopback;
peer-as 65000;
multipath;
neighbor 198.51.100.100 {
    description "to server h1";
}
neighbor 198.51.100.1 {
    description "to spine1";
    peer-as 65500;
    bfd-liveness-detection {
        minimum-interval 333;
        multiplier 3;
    }
}
neighbor 198.51.100.3 {
    description "to spine2";
    peer-as 65500;
    bfd-liveness-detection {
        minimum-interval 333;
        multiplier 3;
    }
}

root@leaf1# show protocols bgp group overlay
type external;
multihop {
    no-nexthop-change;
}
local-address 192.0.2.11;
family evpn {
    signaling;
}
multipath;
neighbor 192.0.2.51 {
    description "overlay peering to server h1";
    peer-as 65000;
}
neighbor 192.0.2.101 {
    description "overlay peering to spine1";
    peer-as 65500;
    bfd-liveness-detection {
        minimum-interval 333;
        multiplier 3;
    }
}
neighbor 192.0.2.102 {
    description "overlay peering to spine2";
    peer-as 65500;
    bfd-liveness-detection {
```

```
        minimum-interval 333;
        multiplier 3;
    }
}
```

With this configuration in place, both servers h1 and h2 have established BGP sessions with their respective leafs (server h2 is connected to both leaf2 and leaf3), as shown in Example 9-15. Again, it is important to note that this is independent of the presence of any containers within these servers.

Example 9-15 *BGP peering on hosts h1 and h2*

```
h1# show bgp summary

IPv4 Unicast Summary (VRF default):
BGP router identifier 192.0.2.51, local AS number 65000 vrf-id 0
BGP table version 145
RIB entries 17, using 3400 bytes of memory
Peers 1, using 725 KiB of memory

Neighbor        V      AS  MsgRcvd  MsgSent  TblVer  InQ OutQ Up/Down State/PfxRcd  PfxSnt Desc
198.51.100.101  4   65421     3603     3354     145    0    0 02:02:42          8       9 N/A

Total number of neighbors 1


L2VPN EVPN Summary (VRF default):
BGP router identifier 192.0.2.51, local AS number 65000 vrf-id 0
BGP table version 0
RIB entries 13, using 2600 bytes of memory
Peers 1, using 725 KiB of memory

Neighbor        V      AS  MsgRcvd  MsgSent  TblVer  InQ OutQ Up/Down State/PfxRcd  PfxSnt Desc
192.0.2.11      4   65421     3607     3347      69    0    0 02:02:40          6       7 N/A

Total number of neighbors 1

h2# show bgp summary

IPv4 Unicast Summary (VRF default):
BGP router identifier 192.0.2.52, local AS number 65000 vrf-id 0
BGP table version 50
RIB entries 17, using 3400 bytes of memory
Peers 2, using 1449 KiB of memory

Neighbor        V      AS  MsgRcvd  MsgSent  TblVer  InQ OutQ Up/Down State/PfxRcd  PfxSnt Desc
198.51.100.103  4   65422     3593     3284      50    0    0 01:27:52          8       9 N/A
198.51.100.105  4   65423     2605     1931      50    0    0 01:27:52          8       9 N/A

Total number of neighbors 2
```

```
L2VPN EVPN Summary (VNI default):
BGP router identifier 192.0.2.52, local AS number 65000 vrf-id 0
BGP table version 0
RIB entries 11, using 2200 bytes of memory
Peers 2, using 1449 KiB of memory

Neighbor        V       AS  MsgRcvd  MsgSent  TblVer  InQ OutQ  Up/Down State/PfxRcd  PfxSnt Desc
192.0.2.12      4    65422     3612     3301      42    0    0 01:27:49           6       7 N/A
192.0.2.13      4    65423     2641     1818      42    0    0 01:27:49           6       7 N/A


Total number of neighbors 2
```

Since bridge *br-vni10* is added to the IP VRF *Tenant1* on server h1, this subnet is added to the BGP RIB and then redistributed into BGP EVPN to be advertised to leaf1. The same logic applies for bridge *br-vni20* on server h2. This is shown in Example 9-16.

Example 9-16 *EVPN Type-5 route for bridge address on hosts h1 and h2*

```
h1# show bgp l2vpn evpn route type prefix self-originate
BGP table version is 29, local router ID is 192.0.2.51
Status codes: s suppressed, d damped, h history, * valid, > best, i - internal
Origin codes: i - IGP, e - EGP, ? - incomplete
EVPN type-1 prefix: [1]:[EthTag]:[ESI]:[IPlen]:[VTEP-IP]:[Frag-id]
EVPN type-2 prefix: [2]:[EthTag]:[MAClen]:[MAC]:[IPlen]:[IP]
EVPN type-3 prefix: [3]:[EthTag]:[IPlen]:[OrigIP]
EVPN type-4 prefix: [4]:[ESI]:[IPlen]:[OrigIP]
EVPN type-5 prefix: [5]:[EthTag]:[IPlen]:[IP]


   Network         Next Hop           Metric LocPrf Weight Path
                   Extended Community
Route Distinguisher: 192.0.2.51:500
 *> [5]:[0]:[24]:[10.100.10.0]
                   192.0.2.51              0           32768 ?
                   ET:8 RT:500:500 Rmac:b6:6f:73:eb:f7:37


Displayed 1 prefixes (1 paths) (of requested type)

h2# show bgp l2vpn evpn route type prefix self-originate
BGP table version is 8, local router ID is 192.0.2.52
Status codes: s suppressed, d damped, h history, * valid, > best, i - internal
Origin codes: i - IGP, e - EGP, ? - incomplete
EVPN type-1 prefix: [1]:[EthTag]:[ESI]:[IPlen]:[VTEP-IP]:[Frag-id]
EVPN type-2 prefix: [2]:[EthTag]:[MAClen]:[MAC]:[IPlen]:[IP]
EVPN type-3 prefix: [3]:[EthTag]:[IPlen]:[OrigIP]
EVPN type-4 prefix: [4]:[ESI]:[IPlen]:[OrigIP]
EVPN type-5 prefix: [5]:[EthTag]:[IPlen]:[IP]


   Network         Next Hop           Metric LocPrf Weight Path
                   Extended Community
```

```
Route Distinguisher: 192.0.2.52:500
 *> [5]:[0]:[24]:[10.100.20.0]
                    192.0.2.52              0         32768 ?
                    ET:8 RT:500:500 Rmac:f6:f8:4f:61:3d:d7
```

When leaf1 receives this EVPN Type-5 route, it advertises it out to its BGP EVPN neighbors (which are the spines), without modifying the next-hop address for the prefix. Thus, when any of the other VTEPs receive this route (leaf4, as an example), the next-hop address is server h1 itself, as shown in Example 9-17. This route is pulled into the VRF's inet.0 table, and a Type-5 tunnel is established to h1.

Example 9-17   *Host h1's subnet as a Type-5 route on leaf4*

```
root@leaf4> show route table bgp.evpn.0 match-prefix 5:*192.0.2.51* extensive

bgp.evpn.0: 7 destinations, 11 routes (7 active, 0 holddown, 0 hidden)
5:192.0.2.51:500::0::10.100.10.0::24/248 (2 entries, 0 announced)
        *BGP    Preference: 170/-101
                Route Distinguisher: 192.0.2.51:500
                Next hop type: Indirect, Next hop index: 0
                Address: 0x55f516b3811c
                Next-hop reference count: 4, key opaque handle: (nil), non-key opaque handle: (nil)
                Source: 192.0.2.101
                Protocol next hop: 192.0.2.51
                Indirect next hop: 0x2 no-forward INH Session ID: 0
                State: <Active Ext>
                Local AS: 65424 Peer AS: 65500
                Age: 11:15     Metric2: 0
                Validation State: unverified
                Task: BGP_65500.192.0.2.101
                AS path: 65500 65421 65000 ?
                Communities: target:500:500 encapsulation:vxlan(0x8) router-mac:b6:6f:73:eb:f7:37
                Import Accepted
                Route Label: 10500
                Overlay gateway address: 0.0.0.0
                ESI 00:00:00:00:00:00:00:00:00:00
                Localpref: 100
                Router ID: 192.0.2.101
                Secondary Tables: Tenant1.evpn.0
                Thread: junos-main

*snip*

root@leaf4> show route table Tenant1.inet.0 10.100.10.0/24 extensive

Tenant1.inet.0: 11 destinations, 11 routes (11 active, 0 holddown, 0 hidden)
10.100.10.0/24 (1 entry, 1 announced)
TSI:
KRT in-kernel 10.100.10.0/24 -> {composite(51060)}
Page 0 idx 0, (group h3 type External) Type 1 val 0x55f51848d3e0 (adv_entry)
    Advertised metrics:
      Nexthop: Self
```

```
        AS path: [65424] 65500 65421 65000 ?
        Communities:
      Advertise: 00000003
Path 10.100.10.0
Vector len 4.  Val: 0
        *EVPN    Preference: 170/-101
                 Next hop type: Indirect, Next hop index: 0
                 Address: 0x55f516b3925c
                 Next-hop reference count: 2, key opaque handle: (nil), non-key opaque handle: (nil)
                 Next hop type: Router, Next hop index: 0
                 Next hop: 198.51.100.13 via et-0/0/0.0, selected
                 Session Id: 0
                 Next hop: 198.51.100.15 via et-0/0/2.0
                 Session Id: 0
                 Protocol next hop: 192.0.2.51
                 Composite next hop: 0x55f516b390c0 51060 INH Session ID: 23
                   VXLAN tunnel rewrite:
                     MTU: 0, Flags: 0x0
                     Encap table ID: 0, Decap table ID: 51
                     Encap VNI: 10500, Decap VNI: 10500
                     Source VTEP: 192.0.2.14, Destination VTEP: 192.0.2.51
                     SMAC: b8:f0:15:52:5d:06, DMAC: b6:6f:73:eb:f7:37
                 Indirect next hop: 0x55f512ca6f88 51057 INH Session ID: 23
                 State: <Active Int Ext>
                 Age: 12:19     Metric2: 0
```

snip

With the previous configuration in place, the servers should have all routes learned via EVPN Type-5 updates and installed in the respective VRF table. Taking server h1 as an example, the remote subnets are installed in the IP VRF Tenant1's table and in the kernel, as shown in Example 9-18. These routes are on the server only—the container simply has a default route that points to the IP address of the bridge it is connected to.

Example 9-18 *IP VRF route table on host h1 and default route in container c1*

```
h1# show ip route vrf Tenant1
Codes: K - kernel route, C - connected, S - static, R - RIP,
       O - OSPF, I - IS-IS, B - BGP, E - EIGRP, N - NHRP,
       T - Table, v - VNC, V - VNC-Direct, A - Babel, F - PBR,
       f - OpenFabric,
       > - selected route, * - FIB route, q - queued, r - rejected, b - backup
       t - trapped, o - offload failure


VRF Tenant1:
C>* 10.100.10.0/24 is directly connected, br-vni10, 18:44:21
B>* 10.100.20.0/24 [20/0] via 192.0.2.52, br500 onlink, weight 1, 14:25:13
B>* 10.100.30.0/24 [20/0] via 192.0.2.14, br500 onlink, weight 1, 00:00:28
B>* 10.100.30.3/32 [20/0] via 192.0.2.14, br500 onlink, weight 1, 00:00:28
B>* 10.100.40.0/24 [20/0] via 192.0.2.15, br500 onlink, weight 1, 17:57:31
B>* 10.100.40.4/32 [20/0] via 192.0.2.15, br500 onlink, weight 1, 17:57:31
```

```
root@h1:/home/h1# ip route show vrf Tenant1
10.100.10.0/24 dev br-vni10 proto kernel scope link src 10.100.10.254
10.100.20.0/24 nhid 254 via 192.0.2.52 dev br500 proto bgp metric 20 onlink
10.100.30.0/24 nhid 30 via 192.0.2.14 dev br500 proto bgp metric 20 onlink
10.100.30.3 nhid 30 via 192.0.2.14 dev br500 proto bgp metric 20 onlink
10.100.40.0/24 nhid 209 via 192.0.2.15 dev br500 proto bgp metric 20 onlink
10.100.40.4 nhid 209 via 192.0.2.15 dev br500 proto bgp metric 20 onlink


root@h1:/home/h1# docker attach c1
root@c1:/# ip route show
default via 10.100.10.254 dev eth0
10.100.10.0/24 dev eth0 proto kernel scope link src 10.100.10.1
```

From a data plane perspective, it is important to understand how the container connects back to the Docker bridge: the Docker bridge connects to the container via a *veth* pair. A visual representation of this connection, focusing just on the server-to-leaf connectivity, is shown in Figure 9-13, along with the container and the Docker bridge on server h1.

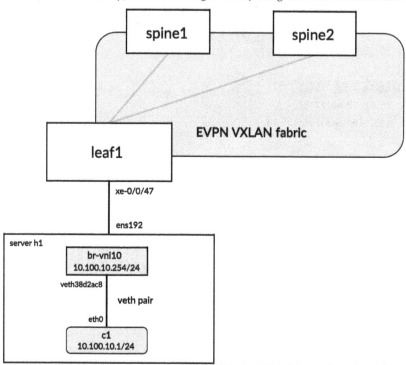

Figure 9-13 *Container c1 internal connection to Docker bridge br-vni10*

This connection can be confirmed by examining the interfaces on the server and the container. On server h1, an interface called *veth38d2ac8* exists, pointing to a remote interface of number 27 (signified by the @ symbol and the number following it). This means that this veth interface connects to a container's interface identified by the number 27. On container c1, this interface number maps to eth0, again pointing to a remote interface number of 28 (which maps to *veth38d2ac8* of the server), as shown in Example 9-19.

Example 9-19 *Interface connection between host h1 and container c1*

```
root@h1:/home/h1# ip addr show veth38d2ac8
28: veth38d2ac8@if27: <BROADCAST,MULTICAST,UP,LOWER_UP> mtu 1500 qdisc noqueue master br-vni10 state UP group default
    link/ether a6:47:a0:fb:82:50 brd ff:ff:ff:ff:ff:ff link-netnsid 0
    inet6 fe80::a447:a0ff:fefb:8250/64 scope link
       valid_lft forever preferred_lft forever
```

```
root@h1:/home/h1# docker attach c1
root@c1:/# ip addr show
1: lo: <LOOPBACK,UP,LOWER_UP> mtu 65536 qdisc noqueue state UNKNOWN group default qlen 1000
    link/loopback 00:00:00:00:00:00 brd 00:00:00:00:00:00
    inet 127.0.0.1/8 scope host lo
       valid_lft forever preferred_lft forever
27: eth0@if28: <BROADCAST,MULTICAST,UP,LOWER_UP> mtu 1500 qdisc noqueue state UP group default
    link/ether 02:42:0a:64:0a:01 brd ff:ff:ff:ff:ff:ff link-netnsid 0
    inet 10.100.10.1/24 brd 10.100.10.255 scope global eth0
       valid_lft forever preferred_lft forever
```

When container c1 wants to reach container c2, it will resolve its default gateway (which is the Docker bridge), which simply forwards it out of the server using the routes learned via BGP EVPN and installed in the IP VRF table. As shown in Example 9-20, with this design and configuration in place, c1 can reach all other hosts (including container c2) in the network.

Example 9-20 *Reachability of container c1 to other hosts in the fabric*

```
root@c1:/# ping 10.100.20.1
PING 10.100.20.1 (10.100.20.1) 56(84) bytes of data.
64 bytes from 10.100.20.1: icmp_seq=1 ttl=62 time=0.912 ms
64 bytes from 10.100.20.1: icmp_seq=2 ttl=62 time=0.922 ms
64 bytes from 10.100.20.1: icmp_seq=3 ttl=62 time=0.860 ms
64 bytes from 10.100.20.1: icmp_seq=4 ttl=62 time=1.00 ms
^C
--- 10.100.20.1 ping statistics ---
4 packets transmitted, 4 received, 0% packet loss, time 3021ms
rtt min/avg/max/mdev = 0.860/0.924/1.004/0.051 ms


root@c1:/# ping 10.100.30.3
PING 10.100.30.3 (10.100.30.3) 56(84) bytes of data.
64 bytes from 10.100.30.3: icmp_seq=1 ttl=62 time=0.913 ms
64 bytes from 10.100.30.3: icmp_seq=2 ttl=62 time=0.888 ms
64 bytes from 10.100.30.3: icmp_seq=3 ttl=62 time=0.920 ms
64 bytes from 10.100.30.3: icmp_seq=4 ttl=62 time=74.3 ms
^C
--- 10.100.30.3 ping statistics ---
4 packets transmitted, 4 received, 0% packet loss, time 3032ms
rtt min/avg/max/mdev = 0.888/19.266/74.343/31.798 ms


root@c1:/# ping 10.100.40.4
PING 10.100.40.4 (10.100.40.4) 56(84) bytes of data.
64 bytes from 10.100.40.4: icmp_seq=1 ttl=62 time=113 ms
64 bytes from 10.100.40.4: icmp_seq=2 ttl=62 time=4.82 ms
64 bytes from 10.100.40.4: icmp_seq=3 ttl=62 time=1.00 ms
64 bytes from 10.100.40.4: icmp_seq=4 ttl=62 time=0.912 ms
^C
--- 10.100.40.4 ping statistics ---
4 packets transmitted, 4 received, 0% packet loss, time 3005ms
rtt min/avg/max/mdev = 0.912/29.991/113.232/48.084 ms
```

Summary

A routed overlay (and host-routed bridging) design is useful when working with cloud-native applications that have no Layer 2 requirements. This design includes moving Layer 3 all the way down to the host, meaning that the host also runs some form of routing protocol (or just static routing) for Layer 3 connectivity to the leaf.

Such a design provides the advantage of eliminating Layer 2 down to the host, allowing for Layer 3 ECMP up to the leafs from the hosts themselves. This is especially advantageous in networks providing anycast DNS services or in a content delivery network in which several content nodes advertise the same anycast IP address to the fabric, facilitating a cleaner approach to integrate into the fabric for such use cases.

DHCP in EVPN VXLAN Fabrics

Dynamic Host Configuration Protocol (DHCP) is a network protocol used for dynamic assignment of IP addresses and other configuration parameters that may be needed for a host or network device to function within a network infrastructure. DHCP is a client/server protocol, wherein a client (a host or a network device, for example) communicates with a DHCP server. The communication itself is connectionless, leveraging UDP as the Layer 4 protocol, with reliability built into the protocol itself.

This chapter explores how DHCP functions in an EVPN VXLAN fabric considering different overlay designs such as bridged overlay and edge-routed bridging.

A DHCP Refresher

IP address and other parameters are allocated using DHCP via a four-step process or packet exchange. This process is often abbreviated to *DORA*, which describes the actual DHCP packets exchanged: DHCP Discover, DHCP Offer, DHCP Request, and DHCP Ack. DHCP Discover and Request packets are usually broadcast packets, setting both the destination IP address to all 255s and the destination MAC address to all Fs. DHCP Offer and Ack packets are unicast packets directed toward the client. The general flow for this DORA process is shown in Figure 10-1.

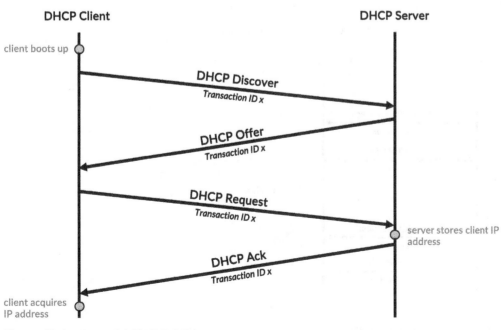

Figure 10-1 *General DHCP DORA process*

Every DHCP packet is identified with a *Transaction ID*, which allows the DHCP server to reliably track the requests as part of a single interaction (or client/server transaction) and eventually store the DHCP state for that client. Thus, for example, all DHCP packets from a specific client (for a particular request) will have the same Transaction ID in the DHCP header (set by the client and honored by the server).

The DHCP packets are described in more detail in the following list:

■ A DHCP Discover is how a client requests an IP address. Since the client does not know where the DHCP server exists, this is a broadcast packet originated by the client. In some designs, this broadcast packet is intercepted by a Layer 3 device (often called a *DHCP relay*) and converted into a unicast packet, directed to the DHCP server. A DHCP Discover can include various parameters that the client expects the DHCP server to provide as well, such as a DNS address, a domain name, and a default gateway.

■ A DHCP Offer is sent by the DHCP server and includes an initial IP address offer to the client. This DHCP Offer identifies the server itself (so that the client has a way to differentiate between servers if multiple servers exist and are responding). Additionally, the DHCP Offer includes the IP address that the server is willing to assign to the client, along with the lease time, subnet mask, and other configuration options. If the broadcast flag is set in the DHCP Discover, then this DHCP Offer is sent as a broadcast; otherwise, it is sent as a unicast packet directed to the client.

■ If the client accepts the server's offer, it responds with a DHCP Request, which is broadcast in nature. This serves as an acknowledgment from the client that it wants to use the IP address and parameters provided by the server in the DHCP Offer. When sending a DHCP Request, the client includes the server's IP address in the packet. This is the server whose offer the client accepted. This is important because if there are multiple DHCP servers, they must be notified whether or not the client accepted their specific DHCP Offer. At this point, the server creates a DHCP binding for the client in its database and sends a DHCP Ack back.

■ A DHCP Ack is an acknowledgment from the server to the client confirming that the DHCP process is over, and the client can now use the IP address to communicate in the network. Typically, if the network stack is written correctly, the client attempts to check that no one else in the network is using this IP address by sending out a Gratuitous ARP (GARP).

Quite often, a DHCP server may not be present in the same Layer 2 domain as the clients. Instead, a dedicated services VLAN or bridge domain might be hosting the DHCP server (and other services). In such cases, naturally, a DHCP Discover from the client will not make it to the DHCP server that is not in its broadcast domain. This problem is solved by using a DHCP relay or a DHCP relay agent.

A *DHCP relay agent* is an intermediate network device that converts DHCP broadcast packets into unicast packets and directs them toward the locally configured DHCP server address. By inserting itself into the packet path of the DHCP packets, the DHCP server responds to the relay agent and not to the client directly. This means that the DHCP Offer and the DHCP Ack are sent to the address of the relay agent and not the address of the client. Thus, the relay agent is expected to receive DHCP packets from the server and forward them toward the client as well.

The general flow of the DORA process with a DHCP relay agent is shown in Figure 10-2.

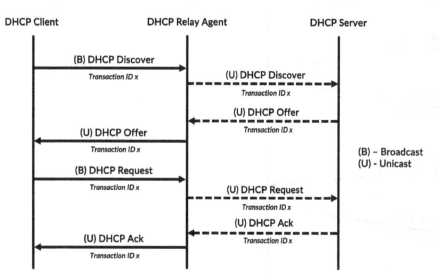

Figure 10-2 *DHCP DORA process with a DHCP relay agent*

While the process demonstrated in Figure 10-1 and Figure 10-2 is specific to IPv4, the DHCP process for IPv6 is largely the same, but with different DHCP messages, and is not explored in detail in this chapter. For DHCPv6, the messages used are DHCP Solicit, DHCP Advertise, DHCP Request, and DHCP Reply, with similar functionality as the DORA process for IPv4. Additionally, instead of broadcast, a well-known multicast destination address (FF02:0:0:0:0:0:1:2) is used for the DHCP Solicit message.

The remainder of this chapter focuses on the finer details of DHCP in the two most widely deployed fabric designs: bridged overlay and edge-routed bridging.

DHCP in a Bridged Overlay Fabric

The reference topology shown in Figure 10-3 is used for this section, with server s3 configured as the DHCP server for the fabric. To narrow down the scope, the DHCP process is considered from the perspective of server s1 booting up for the first time.

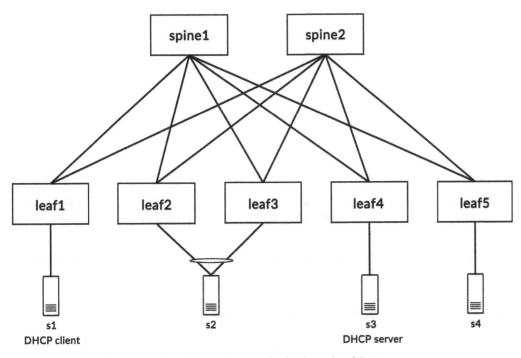

Figure 10-3 *Reference topology for DHCP in a bridged overlay fabric*

All servers in the fabric are in VLAN 100, with an example configuration for interfaces facing servers s1 and s3 shown in Example 10-1. This VLAN is mapped to a VNI of 10100 and extended over the EVPN VXLAN fabric. Thus, any broadcast packet (like a DHCP Discover) will be ingress replicated through the fabric and reach all servers in the same VLAN.

Example 10-1 *VLAN configuration on leaf1 and leaf4*

```
root@leaf1# show interfaces et-0/0/49
description "server s1";
mtu 9200;
unit 0 {
    family ethernet-switching {
        interface-mode access;
        vlan {
            members v100;
        }
    }
}

root@leaf1# show vlans v100
vlan-id 100;
```

```
vxlan {
    vni 10100;
}


root@leaf4# show interfaces et-0/0/8
description "server s3";
mtu 9200;
unit 0 {
    family ethernet-switching {
        interface-mode access;
        vlan {
            members v100;
        }
    }
}


root@leaf4# show vlans v100
vlan-id 100;
vxlan {
    vni 10100;
}
```

When server s1 boots up, since it is configured to acquire an IP address via DHCP, it sends a DHCP Discover for the same. A DHCP Discover is broadcast in nature, with the destination IP address set to all 255s and the destination MAC address set to all Fs.

There are several important fields to consider in the initial DHCP Discover that is sent out. A packet capture of this, originated by server s1, is shown in Figure 10-4.

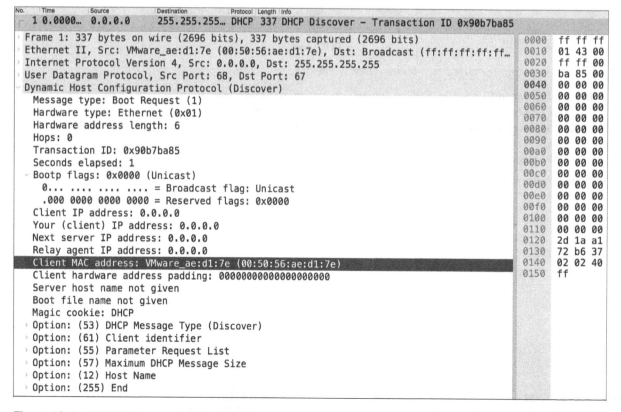

Figure 10-4 *DHCP Discover sent by server s1*

The message type within the DHCP header indicates whether this is a request (from the client) or a reply (from the server). The client (server s1, in this case) identifies itself via the client hardware address or the client MAC address. Based on the network stack implementation on the client, the broadcast flag (in the *Bootp* flags field) is set to 1 or 0—if it is set to 1, it means that the client is not capable of receiving and processing unicast DHCP messages, and this acts as an instruction to the DHCP server to send broadcast packets only (which means that the DHCP Offer and the DHCP Ack will also be broadcast, not unicast).

NOTE The Transaction ID, in Figure 10-4, is 0x90b7ba85 for the DHCP Discover. The same ID will be used for all packets that are a part of this interaction to obtain an IP address.

When leaf1 receives this DHCP Discover, it ingress replicates this to all other VTEPs that have advertised interest in this bridge domain (via EVPN Type-3 routes). To confirm, all other leafs (leaf2, leaf3, leaf4, and leaf5) have indicated interest in this bridge domain and are learned as remote VTEPs for this VNI, as shown in Example 10-2. The bridge domain flood group also confirms all VTEP addresses the packet will be flooded to in the fabric. These commands in Example 10-2, and how to interpret the data presented, are explored in Chapter 5 in the section "Replication of BUM Traffic and EVPN Type-3 Routes."

Example 10-2 *VXLAN flood list on leaf1 for VLAN 100*

```
root@leaf1> show ethernet-switching vxlan-tunnel-end-point remote
Logical System Name     Id  SVTEP-IP        IFL   L3-Idx    SVTEP-Mode    ELP-SVTEP-IP
<default>               0   192.0.2.11      lo0.0  0
  RVTEP-IP      L2-RTT              IFL-Idx   Interface    NH-Id   RVTEP-Mode  ELP-IP        Flags
  192.0.2.12    default-switch      828       vtep.32769   1748    RNVE
    VNID        MC-Group-IP
    10100       0.0.0.0
  RVTEP-IP      L2-RTT              IFL-Idx   Interface    NH-Id   RVTEP-Mode  ELP-IP        Flags
  192.0.2.13    default-switch      832       vtep.32770   1756    RNVE
    VNID        MC-Group-IP
    10100       0.0.0.0
  RVTEP-IP      L2-RTT              IFL-Idx   Interface    NH-Id   RVTEP-Mode  ELP-IP        Flags
  192.0.2.14    default-switch      829       vtep.32771   1749    RNVE
    VNID        MC-Group-IP
    10100       0.0.0.0
  RVTEP-IP      L2-RTT              IFL-Idx   Interface    NH-Id   RVTEP-Mode  ELP-IP        Flags
  192.0.2.15    default-switch      833       vtep.32772   1758    RNVE
    VNID        MC-Group-IP
    10100       0.0.0.0

root@leaf1> show ethernet-switching flood route bd-flood
  Flood route prefix: 0x30005/51
  Flood route type: ALL_FLOOD
  Flood route owner: __all_ces__
  Flood group name: __all_ces__
  Flood group index: 1
  Nexthop type: comp
  Nexthop index: 1744
    Flooding to:
    Name            Type        NhType        Index
    __all_ces__     Group       comp          1743
        Composition: split-horizon
        Flooding to:
        Name            Type        NhType        Index
        et-0/0/49.0     CE          ucst          1740
```

```
Flooding to:
Name              Type         NhType        Index
__ves__           Group        comp          1753
    Composition: flood-to-all
    Flooding to:
    Name          Type         NhType        Index       RVTEP-IP
    vtep.32769    CORE_FACING  venh          1748        192.0.2.12
    vtep.32771    CORE_FACING  venh          1749        192.0.2.14
    vtep.32770    CORE_FACING  venh          1756        192.0.2.13
    vtep.32772    CORE_FACING  venh          1758        192.0.2.15
```

The DHCP Discover is encapsulated with VXLAN headers, and one copy is sent to each of the remote VTEPs as unicast packets. Visually, this can be represented as shown in Figure 10-5.

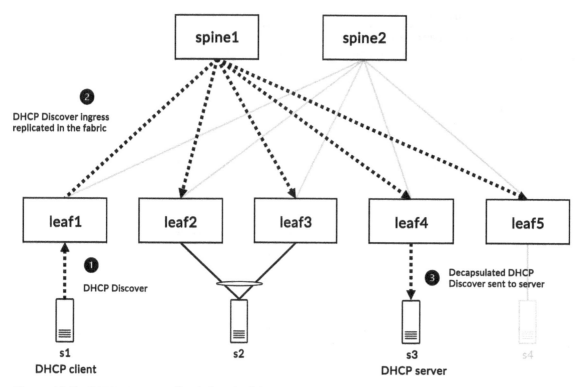

Figure 10-5 *DHCP Discover flooded in the fabric*

At the same time, server s1's MAC address is dynamically learned on leaf1 via the DHCP Discover and then advertised via BGP EVPN to the rest of the fabric, through which leaf4 learns this address as a remote entry and associates it to leaf1's VTEP address, as shown in Example 10-3.

Example 10-3 *MAC address of server s1 learned locally on leaf1 and as a remote address on leaf4*

```
root@leaf1> show ethernet-switching table 00:50:56:ae:d1:7e


MAC flags (S - static MAC, D - dynamic MAC, L - locally learned, P - Persistent static
          SE - statistics enabled, NM - non configured MAC, R - remote PE MAC, O - ovsdb MAC)


Ethernet switching table : 6 entries, 6 learned
Routing instance : default-switch
    Vlan           MAC             MAC      GBP   Logical        SVLBNH/      Active
    name           address         flags    tag   interface      VENH Index   source
    v100           00:50:56:ae:d1:7e  D            et-0/0/49.0
```

```
root@leaf4> show ethernet-switching table 00:50:56:ae:d1:7e


MAC flags (S - static MAC, D - dynamic MAC, L - locally learned, P - Persistent static
          SE - statistics enabled, NM - non configured MAC, R - remote PE MAC, O - ovsdb MAC)


Ethernet switching table : 6 entries, 6 learned
Routing instance : default-switch
   Vlan          MAC                 MAC      Logical                 SVLBNH/        Active
   name          address             flags    interface              VENH Index     source
   v100          00:50:56:ae:d1:7e   DR       vtep-54.32774                         192.0.2.11
```

The packet capture shown in Figure 10-6, captured in transit within the fabric, shows the DHCP Discover ingress replicated in the fabric (notice the Transaction ID, in the DHCP header, is the same as the one in the packet sent by the client shown in Figure 10-4).

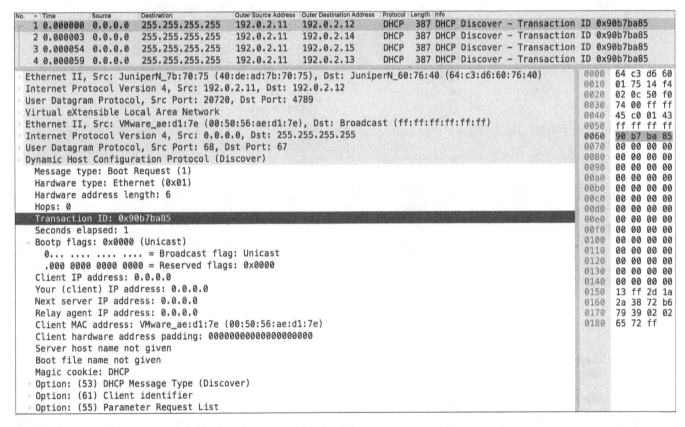

Figure 10-6 *DHCP Discover captured in the EVPN VXLAN fabric*

When the server receives this DHCP Discover, it responds with a DHCP Offer. This offer includes an IP address from the configured pool on the server, along with other requested configuration options that the client might have requested. The server also adds its own IP address within the Server IP address field in the DHCP header.

This DHCP Offer is a unicast packet (since the broadcast flag in the DHCP header was not set in the DHCP Discover) and is directed to the IP address that the server is allocating to the client (10.100.100.50, in this case). In the DHCP header, the *client IP address* is set to the address that the server is offering, along with the subnet mask for that address. Other configuration options that were requested are also added as different DHCP options if the server is configured to provide them.

Since the DHCP Offer is a unicast packet, it is encapsulated with VXLAN headers by leaf4 and directed to leaf1, behind which the client resides. On receipt of this packet, leaf1 decapsulates it and sends the original DHCP Offer to the client, server s1 in this case. This flow is visually represented in Figure 10-7.

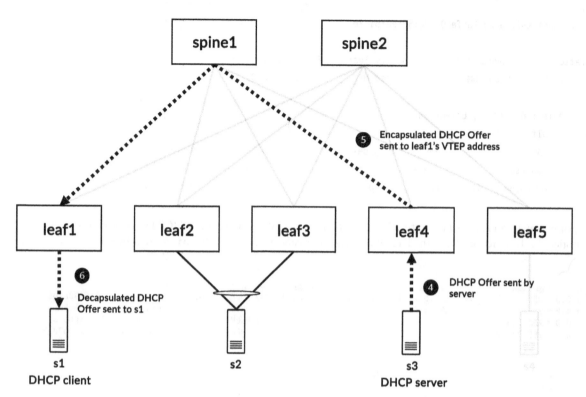

Figure 10-7   *DHCP Offer sent from server to client as a unicast packet*

A packet capture of the DHCP Offer is shown in Figure 10-8.

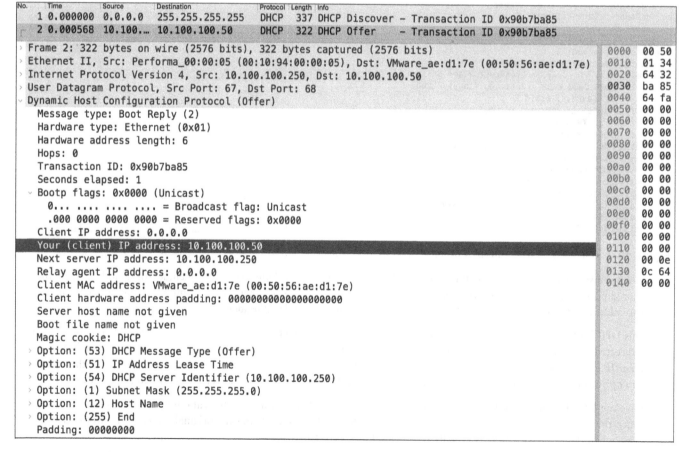

Figure 10-8   *Packet capture of a DHCP Offer sent by server s3*

When the client receives this DHCP Offer, it responds with a DHCP Request (if the client accepts the IP address and the parameters provided by the server). This DHCP Request is broadcast in nature because it tells all other potential servers about the server that the client has chosen to accept the assignment from (by setting this server's IP address in the DHCP Server Identifier field). The DHCP Request also confirms that the IP address the client is requesting is the same that was provided by the server in the DHCP Offer. A packet capture of the DHCP Request for this transaction is shown in Figure 10-9.

```
No.    Time        Source       Destination      Protocol  Length  Info
  1 0.000000  0.0.0.0      255.255.255.255  DHCP      337     DHCP Discover - Transaction ID 0x90b7ba85
  2 0.000568  10.100…      10.100.100.50    DHCP      322     DHCP Offer    - Transaction ID 0x90b7ba85
  3 0.017314  0.0.0.0      255.255.255.255  DHCP      349     DHCP Request  - Transaction ID 0x90b7ba85

∨ Dynamic Host Configuration Protocol (Request)                              0000  ff ff
    Message type: Boot Request (1)                                           0010  01 4f
    Hardware type: Ethernet (0x01)                                           0020  ff ff
    Hardware address length: 6                                               0030  ba 85
    Hops: 0                                                                  0040  00 00
    Transaction ID: 0x90b7ba85                                               0050  00 00
    Seconds elapsed: 1                                                       0060  00 00
  ∨ Bootp flags: 0x0000 (Unicast)                                           0070  00 00
       0... .... .... .... = Broadcast flag: Unicast                         0080  00 00
       .000 0000 0000 0000 = Reserved flags: 0x0000                          0090  00 00
    Client IP address: 0.0.0.0                                               00a0  00 00
    Your (client) IP address: 0.0.0.0                                        00b0  00 00
    Next server IP address: 0.0.0.0                                          00c0  00 00
    Relay agent IP address: 0.0.0.0                                          00d0  00 00
    Client MAC address: VMware_ae:d1:7e (00:50:56:ae:d1:7e)                  00e0  00 00
    Client hardware address padding: 00000000000000000000                    00f0  00 00
    Server host name not given                                               0100  00 00
    Boot file name not given                                                 0110  00 00
    Magic cookie: DHCP                                                       0120  2d 1a
  > Option: (53) DHCP Message Type (Request)                                 0130  72 b6
  > Option: (61) Client identifier                                           0140  02 02
  > Option: (55) Parameter Request List                                      0150  0b 64
  > Option: (57) Maximum DHCP Message Size
  ∨ Option: (54) DHCP Server Identifier (10.100.100.250)
      Length: 4
      DHCP Server Identifier: 10.100.100.250
  ∨ Option: (50) Requested IP Address (10.100.100.50)
      Length: 4
      Requested IP Address: 10.100.100.50
  > Option: (12) Host Name
  > Option: (255) End
```

Figure 10-9 *Packet capture of a DHCP Request sent by client*

When the DHCP server receives this DHCP Request, it creates a binding for the client in its database (storing the IP address that it assigned this client) and responds with a DHCP Ack, which serves as the end of this transaction and confirms to the client that the IP address assigned to it can now be used to communicate in the network.

DHCP in an Edge-Routed Bridging Fabric

In an edge-routed bridging design, explored in detail in Chapter 8, "Edge-Routed Bridging," an anycast distributed gateway is used (see Figure 10-10). This means that for an IRB interface, the same IP address and MAC address are configured across all leafs in the fabric, acting as the gateways for the hosts.

In such designs (where the DHCP server is not in the same bridge domain as the client), a DHCP relay agent is used to package the DHCP broadcast messages and deliver them as unicast packets to the server; the leafs (VTEPs) are configured to be DHCP relay agents, in this case. However, with an anycast distributed gateway model, additional hurdles need to be overcome for this to work.

When a DHCP broadcast packet (such as a DHCP Discover) is relayed to the server, the DHCP relay agent inserts its own IP address as the relay agent address. This address is encoded into the *Relay agent IP address* field in the DHCP header, sometimes called the *giaddr*. By default, this is the address of the ingress Layer 3 interface where the DHCP Discover is received from the client, which, in this case, would be the ingress IRB interface (for the corresponding VLAN).

Typically, a DHCP server uses this address to determine which scope (subnet) the client belongs to and uses that to provide an available IP address. This relay agent address is also used by the server to send a DHCP response—since the communication is unicast, the DHCP server responds to the relay agent (with the relay agent's IP address set as the destination IP address in the IP header). This is problematic since in an anycast distributed gateway design, all leafs have the same address and, thus, it is quite possible that the reply from the DHCP server is consumed by the leaf to which the server is connected (in an asymmetric IRB design) or is sent to the wrong leaf (in a symmetric IRB design). In both cases, the DHCP response will never reach the client.

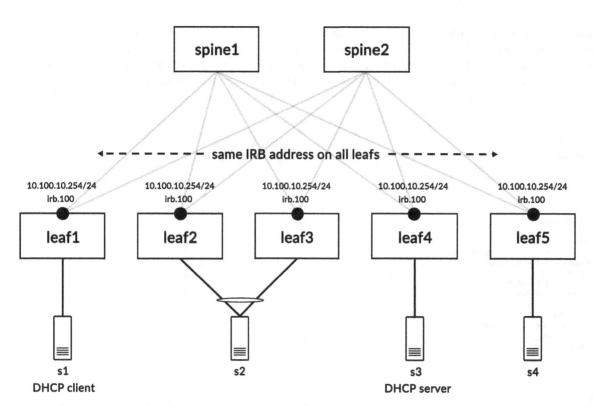

Figure 10-10 *Anycast distributed gateway in an ERB fabric design*

Thus, there are two problems that need to be solved in such data center fabrics:

■ How do you identify the correct relay agent (where the client is connected) to deliver DHCP responses from the server? To solve this, the DHCP relay agent should source the redirected unicast DHCP messages with an IP address that uniquely identifies the agent in the network, and thus, the reply from the server is destined to this address, which is not shared by any other network device in the fabric. For this, the unique loopback address per VTEP is used.

■ How/where do you encode the correct subnet/scope from which the server provides an IP address to the client? This is solved by adding DHCP options (option 82, specifically) when a DHCP packet is relayed to the server by the relay agent.

This problematic traffic flow can be visualized as shown in Figure 10-11.

Thus, in such designs, some additional DHCP configuration is needed to make this work. DHCP has various options (added to the DHCP header itself) that can be used to provide more information to the DHCP server. The server can then be configured to use these options to influence how it responds to DHCP requests.

For example, option 82 (first defined in RFC 3046), also known as the Relay Agent Information option, is added when a relay agent relays a DHCP packet to the server, and it can be used by the server to implement a specific IP address assignment policy. This option was originally used as a security mechanism to provide the location of the client (and can still be used for it), but RFCs such as RFC 3527 and RFC 5107 added additional suboptions to this option: the *Link Selection* and *Server Identifier Override* suboptions, respectively. The Link Selection suboption allows the separation of the giaddr (or the relay address) from the subnet/scope from which an IP address needs to be provided to the client, while the Server Identifier Override suboption enables a client to send all DHCP renewal messages to the relay agent directly (which allows the relay agent to add necessary options before redirecting to the server). These two suboptions are used in ERB designs with an anycast distributed gateway model for successful DHCP functionality.

Considering leaf1, Example 10-4 shows how a DHCP relay agent is configured, sourcing the loopback address, along with the Link Selection and Server Identifier Override suboptions of option 82.

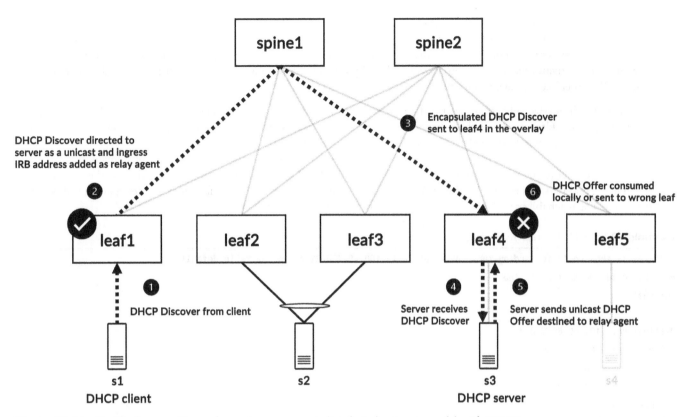

Figure 10-11 *Traffic flow problem when using an anycast distributed gateway model with DHCP*

Example 10-4 *DHCP Relay configuration on leaf1*

```
root@leaf1# show forwarding-options dhcp-relay
server-group {
    server1 {
        10.100.60.250;
    }
}
group relay-group {
    active-server-group server1;
    overrides {
        relay-source lo0.0;
    }
    relay-option-82 {
        server-id-override;
    }
    interface irb.100;
    interface irb.200;
    interface irb.300;
    interface irb.400;
}
```

The *server-group* configuration hierarchy specifies the IP address of the DHCP server (group named *server1* in Example 10-4, with 10.100.60.250 as the IP address of the server). This server-group needs to be activated under the group that manages the DHCP relay agent configuration and any options that need to be added to it. In Example 10-4, a group called *relay-group* is created, which activates the server-group *server1* and enables the Link Selection and Server Identifier Override suboptions. All required IRB interfaces are mapped to this group.

Option 82 (with the two suboptions described previously) solves the second problem. The first problem is solved by using a unique loopback address to source the redirected unicast DHCP messages. To trace the flow of packets, consider a situation in which server s1 (connected to leaf1, in Figure 10-10) comes online in this ERB fabric and attempts to acquire an IP address via DHCP. Server s1 sends a DHCP Discover, which is broadcast in nature. This is flooded in the same domain, but also sent as a unicast packet to the DHCP server s3, with the IP address 10.100.60.250. This address is reachable via the VXLAN fabric on leaf1, and thus it is encapsulated with VXLAN headers and sent to leaf4, where it is decapsulated and handed off to the server. The reachability of the DHCP server, on leaf1, is shown in Example 10-5.

Example 10-5 *DHCP server reachability on leaf1*

```
root@leaf1> show route forwarding-table destination 10.100.60.250/32 extensive table default
Routing table: default.inet [Index 0]
Internet:


Destination:   10.100.60.250/32
  Route type: destination
  Route reference: 0                 Route interface-index: 804
  Multicast RPF nh index: 0
  P2mpidx: 0
  Flags: sent to PFE
  Nexthop: 0:10:94:0:0:5
  Next-hop type: unicast             Index: 1790    Reference: 1


root@leaf1> show ethernet-switching table 0:10:94:0:0:5


MAC flags (S - static MAC, D - dynamic MAC, L - locally learned, P - Persistent static
          SE - statistics enabled, NM - non configured MAC, R - remote PE MAC, O - ovsdb MAC)


Ethernet switching table : 5 entries, 5 learned
Routing instance : macvrf-1
    Vlan         MAC            MAC     GBP   Logical          SVLBNH/     Active
    name         address        flags   tag   interface        VENH Index  source
    v600         00:10:94:00:00:05  DR          vtep-9.32771               192.0.2.14
```

The initial DHCP Discover from the client is shown in Figure 10-12.

When this packet hits leaf1, it is flooded via ingress replication to other VTEPs that have shown interest in this domain (via EVPN Type-3 routes). Since DHCP relay agent configuration also exists on leaf1 (and is applied to the ingress IRB interface where the DHCP Discover is received), the DHCP Discover is packaged as a unicast packet (with a source of 192.0.2.11, which is the loopback address on leaf1) and sent to the DHCP server. Within the DHCP header, option 82 is added, along with the suboptions Link Selection and Server Identifier Override. Both these suboptions are encoded with the IRB interface address, 10.100.10.254. The relay agent address (giaddr) is also set to 192.0.2.11. This unicast DHCP Discover packet is shown in Figure 10-13.

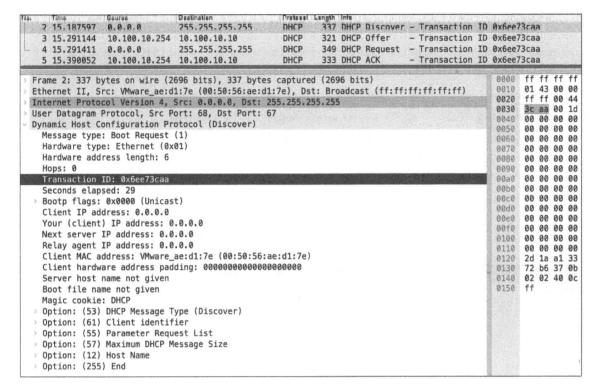

```
No.   Time        Source          Destination          Protocol  Length  Info
  2 15.187597   0.0.0.0         255.255.255.255      DHCP      337     DHCP Discover - Transaction ID 0x6ee73caa
  3 15.291144   10.100.10.254   10.100.10.10         DHCP      321     DHCP Offer    - Transaction ID 0x6ee73caa
  4 15.291411   0.0.0.0         255.255.255.255      DHCP      349     DHCP Request  - Transaction ID 0x6ee73caa
  5 15.390052   10.100.10.254   10.100.10.10         DHCP      333     DHCP ACK      - Transaction ID 0x6ee73caa
```

```
> Frame 2: 337 bytes on wire (2696 bits), 337 bytes captured (2696 bits)          0000  ff ff ff ff
> Ethernet II, Src: VMware_ae:d1:7e (00:50:56:ae:d1:7e), Dst: Broadcast (ff:ff:ff:ff:ff:ff)  0010  01 43 00 00
> Internet Protocol Version 4, Src: 0.0.0.0, Dst: 255.255.255.255                  0020  ff ff 00 44
> User Datagram Protocol, Src Port: 68, Dst Port: 67                               0030  3c aa 00 1d
v Dynamic Host Configuration Protocol (Discover)                                   0040  00 00 00 00
     Message type: Boot Request (1)                                                0050  00 00 00 00
     Hardware type: Ethernet (0x01)                                                0060  00 00 00 00
     Hardware address length: 6                                                    0070  00 00 00 00
     Hops: 0                                                                       0080  00 00 00 00
     Transaction ID: 0x6ee73caa                                                    0090  00 00 00 00
     Seconds elapsed: 29                                                           00a0  00 00 00 00
  >  Bootp flags: 0x0000 (Unicast)                                                 00b0  00 00 00 00
     Client IP address: 0.0.0.0                                                    00c0  00 00 00 00
     Your (client) IP address: 0.0.0.0                                            00d0  00 00 00 00
     Next server IP address: 0.0.0.0                                              00e0  00 00 00 00
     Relay agent IP address: 0.0.0.0                                              00f0  00 00 00 00
     Client MAC address: VMware_ae:d1:7e (00:50:56:ae:d1:7e)                      0100  00 00 00 00
     Client hardware address padding: 00000000000000000000                        0110  00 00 00 00
     Server host name not given                                                    0120  2d 1a a1 33
     Boot file name not given                                                      0130  72 b6 37 0b
     Magic cookie: DHCP                                                            0140  02 02 40 0c
  >  Option: (53) DHCP Message Type (Discover)                                     0150  ff
  >  Option: (61) Client identifier
  >  Option: (55) Parameter Request List
  >  Option: (57) Maximum DHCP Message Size
  >  Option: (12) Host Name
  >  Option: (255) End
```

Figure 10-12 *Packet capture of initial DHCP Discover from client*

```
No.   Time        Source          Destination          Protocol  Length  Info
  5 0.102287    192.0.2.11      10.100.60.250        DHCP      452     DHCP Discover - Transaction ID 0x6ee73caa
```

```
> Ethernet II, Src: JuniperN_7b:70:75 (40:de:ad:7b:70:75), Dst: JuniperN_60:76:40 (64:c3:d6:60:76:40)  0000  64 c3 d6
> Internet Protocol Version 4, Src: 192.0.2.11, Dst: 192.0.2.14                    0010  01 b6 00
> User Datagram Protocol, Src Port: 39215, Dst Port: 4789                          0020  02 0e 99
> Virtual eXtensible Local Area Network                                            0030  68 00 00
> Ethernet II, Src: AristaNe_00:00:01 (00:1c:73:00:00:01), Dst: Performa_00:00:05 (00:10:94:00:00:05)  0040  45 00 01
> Internet Protocol Version 4, Src: 192.0.2.11, Dst: 10.100.60.250                 0050  0a 64 3c
> User Datagram Protocol, Src Port: 67, Dst Port: 67                               0060  6e e7 3c
v Dynamic Host Configuration Protocol (Discover)                                   0070  00 00 00
     Message type: Boot Request (1)                                                0080  00 00 00
     Hardware type: Ethernet (0x01)                                                0090  00 00 00
     Hardware address length: 6                                                    00a0  00 00 00
     Hops: 1                                                                       00b0  00 00 00
     Transaction ID: 0x6ee73caa                                                    00c0  00 00 00
     Seconds elapsed: 29                                                           00d0  00 00 00
  >  Bootp flags: 0x0000 (Unicast)                                                 00e0  00 00 00
     Client IP address: 0.0.0.0                                                    00f0  00 00 00
     Your (client) IP address: 0.0.0.0                                            0100  00 00 00
     Next server IP address: 0.0.0.0                                              0110  00 00 00
     Relay agent IP address: 192.0.2.11                                           0120  00 00 00
     Client MAC address: VMware_ae:d1:7e (00:50:56:ae:d1:7e)                      0130  00 00 00
     Client hardware address padding: 00000000000000000000                        0140  00 00 00
     Server host name not given                                                    0150  13 ff 2d
     Boot file name not given                                                      0160  2a 38 72
     Magic cookie: DHCP                                                            0170  79 39 02
  >  Option: (53) DHCP Message Type (Discover)                                     0180  65 72 52
  >  Option: (61) Client identifier                                                0190  30 3a 76
  >  Option: (55) Parameter Request List                                           01a0  01 00 00
  >  Option: (57) Maximum DHCP Message Size                                        01b0  37 30 3a
  >  Option: (12) Host Name                                                        01c0  64 0a fe
  v  Option: (82) Agent Information Option
        Length: 63
     v  Option 82 Suboption: (1) Agent Circuit ID
           Length: 16
           Agent Circuit ID: 78652d302f302f34372e303a76313030
     v  Option 82 Suboption: (12) Relay Agent Identifier
           Length: 31
           Relay Agent Identifier: 000200000000005830100000034303a64653a61643a37623a37303a34300000
     v  Option 82 Suboption: (5) Link selection (10.100.10.254)
           Length: 4
           Link selection: 10.100.10.254
     >  Option 82 Suboption: (11) Server ID Override (10.100.10.254)
```

Figure 10-13 *Relayed DHCP Discover by leaf1, showing option 82 and its suboptions*

When the DHCP server receives this DHCP Discover, it uses the Link Selection suboption of option 82 to determine which subnet to use to assign an available IP address to this client. Since the server is configured with a scope of 10.100.10.0/24, it uses this subnet and assigns an IP address of 10.100.10.10/24 to this client. This is sent as a unicast DHCP Offer to the DHCP relay agent, which is leaf1 (with IP address of 192.0.2.11), in this case. This unicast DHCP Offer is shown in Figure 10-14.

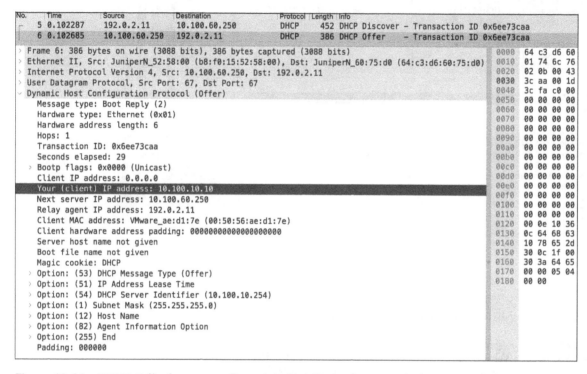

Figure 10-14 *DHCP Offer from server directed to the DHCP relay agent (leaf1)*

The DHCP Request and DHCP Ack follow the same packet forwarding flow as the first two messages and are not shown here for the sake of brevity. As a summary, Figure 10-15 shows the complete DHCP transaction between this client and the server, and how the DHCP relay agent adds additional, necessary information when relaying the packet to the server.

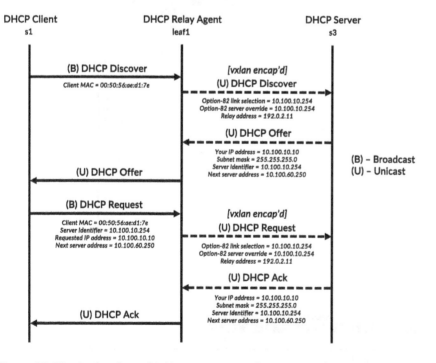

Figure 10-15 *Packet flow of DHCP messages with a DHCP relay agent*

DHCP Server in a Dedicated Services VRF

So far, the DHCP server has been in the same VRF as the clients. However, a common approach to data center network design is to have a dedicated services VRF that houses different services clients across the data center want to access, including a DHCP server. This implies that some form of inter-VRF routing must be enabled for this to work.

The reference topology shown in Figure 10-16 is used to demonstrate such a deployment. A DHCP server, s3, is located behind leaf4 and has an IP address 10.100.60.250/24 in VLAN 600.

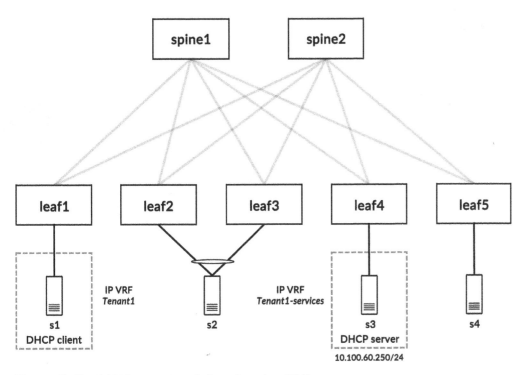

Figure 10-16 *DHCP server in a dedicated services VRF*

There are different approaches to providing connectivity to a common services VRF, where a DHCP server may be located. One way is to have inter-VRF routing natively on each of the VTEPs by manually importing routes into the client VRF from the dedicated services VRF (and vice versa). Since, by design, having a dedicated services VRF is a many-to-one model (many client VRFs access services in the same services VRF), it is easy to extend the same model to an import policy as well, from a configuration point of view. Consider the table shown in Figure 10-17, which lists several client VRFs that need to access a shared services VRF. The import policy on the services VRF simply follows the same many-to-one model and imports the Route Targets of all the client VRFs that need access.

Client VRFs	Client VRFs route-target	Service VRF to be accessed	Service VRF route-target	Import Policy on Client VRFs	Import Policy on Service VRF
Tenant1	500:500	Services-VRF		1000:1000	
Tenant2	600:600	Services-VRF		1000:1000	500:500
Tenant3	700:700	Services-VRF	1000:1000	1000:1000	600:600 700:700
Tenant4	800:800	Services-VRF		1000:1000	800:800
Tenant5	900:900	Services-VRF		1000:1000	900:900

Figure 10-17 *Client and services VRF showing a many-to-one model*

To make matters simple for this example, only one client VRF, Tenant1, is considered. This client VRF has a server, s1, that is configured to acquire an IP address via the DHCP server, s3, which is in the Tenant1-services-vrf VRF. Each VRF is configured as a routing instance on the respective leafs, with a new loopback logical unit configured for this and mapped to the routing instance. This unit of the loopback interface is used to source any DHCP relay requests to the server.

On leaf1, the routing instance for the Tenant1 VRF is configured as shown in Example 10-6, along with the relevant policies and loopback configuration.

Example 10-6   *VRF configuration for client VRF on leaf1*

```
root@leaf1# show routing-instances Tenant1
instance-type vrf;
protocols {
    evpn {
        default-gateway do-not-advertise;
        irb-symmetric-routing {
            vni 10500;
        }
        ip-prefix-routes {
            advertise direct-nexthop;
            encapsulation vxlan;
            vni 10500;
            export export-h1;
        }
    }
}
forwarding-options {
    dhcp-relay {
        server-group {
            server1 {
                10.100.60.250;
            }
        }
        group relay-group {
            active-server-group server1;
            overrides {
                relay-source lo0.1;
            }
            relay-option-82 {
                server-id-override;
            }
            interface irb.100;
            interface irb.200;
            interface irb.300;
            interface irb.400;
        }
    }
}
interface irb.100;
interface irb.200;
interface irb.300;
interface irb.400;
interface lo0.1;
```

```
route-distinguisher 192.0.2.11.500,
vrf-import import-from-service-vrf;
vrf-target target:500:500;


root@leaf1# show interfaces lo0.1
family inet {
    address 192.0.2.111/32;
}


root@leaf1# show policy-options policy-statement export-h1
term 1 {
    from {
        route-filter 10.100.20.0/24 orlonger;
    }
    then accept;
}
term 2 {
    from {
        route-filter 192.0.2.0/24 orlonger;
    }
    then accept;
}
```

There's a lot going on in this client VRF, so let's break it down:

1. The client VRF is configured with symmetric IRB that uses L3VNI 10500. Type-5 routes are exported from this VRF as well, controlled by the policy export-h1. This policy simply matches the subnet for host h1 (10.100.20.0/24 or any subnet mask greater than this) and the loopback subnet.

2. The DHCP relay configuration is moved under this VRF, and the configuration is the same as before, minus one small change: the relay source is now configured to be the loopback that is within this routing instance, which is interface lo0.1 in this case.

3. Routes generated from the services VRF are imported manually by using the import-from-service-vrf policy.

This manual import policy, shown in Example 10-7, matches the Route Target that is expected to be added to the routes generated by the services VRF.

Example 10-7 *Import policy to import routes advertised from services VRF*

```
root@leaf1# show policy-options policy-statement import-from-service-vrf
term service-vrf {
    from community service-vrf;
    then accept;
}
term tenant1-vrf {
    from community tenant1-vrf;
    then accept;
}
root@leaf1# show policy-options community service-vrf
members target:1000:1000;


root@leaf1# show policy-options community tenant1-vrf
members target:500:500;
```

The routing instance created on leaf4 for the services VRF is shown in Example 10-8. The logic used is the same as the client VRF—however, in this case, all other client VRF Route Targets are imported. Since only one client VRF is used here, this may not be as noticeable.

Example 10-8 *VRF configuration for dedicated services VRF on leaf4*

```
root@leaf4# show routing-instances Tenant1-services-vrf
instance-type vrf;
protocols {
    evpn {
        irb-symmetric-routing {
            vni 1000;
        }
        ip-prefix-routes {
            advertise direct-nexthop;
            encapsulation vxlan;
            vni 1000;
            export export-dhcp;
        }
    }
}
interface irb.600;
interface lo0.1;
route-distinguisher 192.0.2.14:1000;
vrf-import import-from-tenant1-vrf;
vrf-target target:1000:1000;


root@leaf4# show policy-options policy-statement export-dhcp
term 1 {
    from {
        route-filter 10.100.60.0/24 orlonger;
    }
    then accept;
}
term 2 {
    from {
        route-filter 192.0.2.0/24 orlonger;
    }
    then accept;
}


root@leaf4# show policy-options policy-statement import-from-tenant1-vrf
term tenant1-vrf {
    from community tenant1-vrf;
    then accept;
}
term default {
    then reject;
}


root@leaf4# show policy-options community tenant1-vrf
members target:500:500;
```

With this configuration in place, leaf1 should receive EVPN Type-5 routes for both the DHCP server subnet and the /32 host address for the server itself. With the manual import configured on leaf1, these are imported into the EVPN table for the client VRF and eventually the inet.0 table as well, providing reachability in the direction of client-to-server VRF, as shown in Example 10-9.

Example 10-9 *EVPN Type-5 routes for DHCP server's IP address and subnet on leaf1*

```
root@leaf1> show route table bgp.evpn.0 match-prefix 5:*10.100.60.*

bgp.evpn.0: 63 destinations, 63 routes (63 active, 0 holddown, 0 hidden)
+ = Active Route, - = Last Active, * = Both

5:192.0.2.14:1000::0::10.100.60.0::24/248
                   *[BGP/170] 2d 18:43:16, localpref 100, from 192.0.2.101
                      AS path: 65500 65424 I, validation-state: unverified
                    > to 198.51.100.1 via et-0/0/48.0, Push 62
5:192.0.2.14:1000::0::10.100.60.250::32/248
                   *[BGP/170] 05:26:40, localpref 100, from 192.0.2.101
                      AS path: 65500 65424 I, validation-state: unverified
                    > to 198.51.100.1 via et-0/0/48.0, Push 62
5:192.0.2.14:1000::0::10.100.60.254::32/248
                   *[BGP/170] 05:26:40, localpref 100, from 192.0.2.101
                      AS path: 65500 65424 I, validation-state: unverified
                    > to 198.51.100.1 via et-0/0/48.0, Push 62


root@leaf1> show route table Tenant1.evpn.0 match-prefix 5:*10.100.60.*

Tenant1.evpn.0: 23 destinations, 23 routes (23 active, 0 holddown, 0 hidden)
+ = Active Route, - = Last Active, * = Both

5:192.0.2.14:1000::0::10.100.60.0::24/248
                   *[BGP/170] 1d 21:49:30, localpref 100, from 192.0.2.101
                      AS path: 65500 65424 I, validation-state: unverified
                    > to 198.51.100.1 via et-0/0/48.0, Push 62
5:192.0.2.14:1000::0::10.100.60.250::32/248
                   *[BGP/170] 05:27:13, localpref 100, from 192.0.2.101
                      AS path: 65500 65424 I, validation-state: unverified
                    > to 198.51.100.1 via et-0/0/48.0, Push 62
5:192.0.2.14:1000::0::10.100.60.254::32/248
                   *[BGP/170] 05:27:13, localpref 100, from 192.0.2.101
                      AS path: 65500 65424 I, validation-state: unverified
                    > to 198.51.100.1 via et-0/0/48.0, Push 62


root@leaf1> show route table Tenant1.inet.0 10.100.60.250

Tenant1.inet.0: 19 destinations, 31 routes (19 active, 0 holddown, 0 hidden)
+ = Active Route, - = Last Active, * = Both

10.100.60.250/32   *[EVPN/7] 1d 21:36:22
                    > to 198.51.100.1 via et-0/0/48.0
                    [EVPN/170] 05:27:34
                    > to 198.51.100.1 via et-0/0/48.0
```

It is important to look at the extensive output for the DHCP server route, as that gives information on how the VXLAN encapsulation will occur and what are the source/destination IP addresses of the outer IP header (the Type-5 tunnel). Example 10-10 confirms that the encapsulation VNI is the L3VNI corresponding to the services VRF (1000), while the expected return traffic should have the L3VNI corresponding to the client VRF (10500).

Example 10-10   *Route-lookup for DHCP server's IP address on leaf1*

```
root@leaf1> show route table Tenant1.inet.0 10.100.60.250 extensive

Tenant1.inet.0: 19 destinations, 31 routes (19 active, 0 holddown, 0 hidden)
10.100.60.250/32 (2 entries, 1 announced)
TSI:
KRT in-kernel 10.100.60.250/32 -> {composite(1665)}
        *EVPN    Preference: 7
                 Next hop type: Indirect, Next hop index: 0
                 Address: 0x8c082a4
                 Next-hop reference count: 9, key opaque handle: 0x0, non-key opaque handle: 0x0
                 Next hop type: Router, Next hop index: 1775
                 Next hop: 198.51.100.1 via et-0/0/48.0, selected
                 Session Id: 0
                 Protocol next hop: 192.0.2.14
                 Composite next hop: 0x74cbfc0 1665 INH Session ID: 0
                   VXLAN tunnel rewrite:
                     MTU: 0, Flags: 0x0
                     Encap table ID: 0, Decap table ID: 11
                     Encap VNI: 1000, Decap VNI: 10500
                     Source VTEP: 192.0.2.11, Destination VTEP: 192.0.2.14
                     SMAC: 40:de:ad:7b:70:40, DMAC: b8:f0:15:52:5d:06
                 Indirect next hop: 0x758a07c 524294 INH Session ID: 0
                 State: <Active Int Ext VxlanLocalRT>
                 Age: 1d 21:38:53        Metric2: 0
*snip*
```

Consider a situation in which server s1 attempts to acquire an IP address from DHCP server s3. To simplify matters, let's assume that s1 already has an IP address and thus is simply requesting for the same address again, which means that the DHCP Discover and the DHCP Offer packets are not exchanged. The client sends a DHCP Request directly, and if the server accepts it, it replies with a DHCP Ack (this is how DHCP makes the process more efficient when a client lease needs to be renewed or the client remembers the previous IP address it was assigned).

Following the same process that was described previously for the DHCP relay in Figure 10-15, the DHCP Request is relayed to the DHCP server as a unicast packet. However, in this case, since the DHCP server is in a different VRF, the VNI (in the VXLAN header) corresponds to the destination L3VNI (1000), as indicated in the packet capture shown in Figure 10-18. It is also important to note that the DHCP packet itself (inner IP packet) is sourced from the loopback in the client VRF, while the outer IP header carries the packet from leaf1 to leaf4 using the loopback addresses that correspond to the end-to-end VXLAN tunnel between the two VTEPs.

When the DHCP server responds with a DHCP Ack, it must respond to the relay agent address, which is leaf1's loopback in the Tenant1 VRF (192.0.2.111). This address is advertised as a Type-5 route by leaf1 and imported into the services VRF on leaf4, as shown in Example 10-11. Thus, unlike the design in which the DHCP server and client are in the same VRF, the response from the server is also encapsulated with VXLAN headers and sent back to the relay agent.

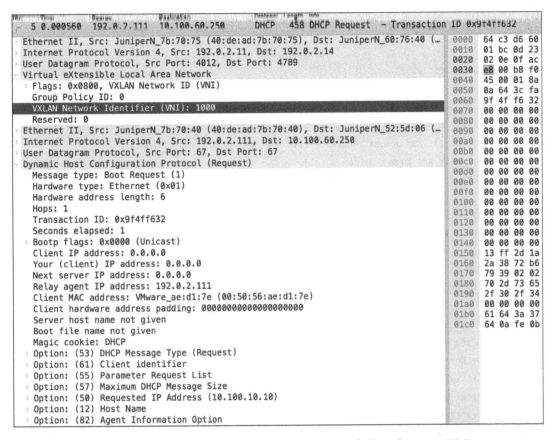

```
  5 0.000560  192.0.2.111  10.100.60.250    DHCP  458 DHCP Request  - Transaction ID 0x9f4ff632
> Ethernet II, Src: JuniperN_7b:70:75 (40:de:ad:7b:70:75), Dst: JuniperN_60:76:40 (…   0000  64 c3 d6 60
> Internet Protocol Version 4, Src: 192.0.2.11, Dst: 192.0.2.14                        0010  01 bc 0d 23
> User Datagram Protocol, Src Port: 4012, Dst Port: 4789                               0020  02 0e 0f ac
∨ Virtual eXtensible Local Area Network                                               0030  e8 00 b8 f0
  > Flags: 0x0800, VXLAN Network ID (VNI)                                             0040  45 00 01 8a
    Group Policy ID: 0                                                                0050  0a 64 3c fa
    VXLAN Network Identifier (VNI): 1000                                              0060  9f 4f f6 32
    Reserved: 0                                                                       0070  00 00 00 00
> Ethernet II, Src: JuniperN_7b:70:40 (40:de:ad:7b:70:40), Dst: JuniperN_52:5d:06 (…  0080  00 00 00 00
> Internet Protocol Version 4, Src: 192.0.2.111, Dst: 10.100.60.250                   0090  00 00 00 00
> User Datagram Protocol, Src Port: 67, Dst Port: 67                                  00a0  00 00 00 00
∨ Dynamic Host Configuration Protocol (Request)                                       00b0  00 00 00 00
    Message type: Boot Request (1)                                                    00c0  00 00 00 00
    Hardware type: Ethernet (0x01)                                                    00d0  00 00 00 00
    Hardware address length: 6                                                        00e0  00 00 00 00
    Hops: 1                                                                           00f0  00 00 00 00
    Transaction ID: 0x9f4ff632                                                        0100  00 00 00 00
    Seconds elapsed: 1                                                                0110  00 00 00 00
  > Bootp flags: 0x0000 (Unicast)                                                     0120  00 00 00 00
    Client IP address: 0.0.0.0                                                        0130  00 00 00 00
    Your (client) IP address: 0.0.0.0                                                 0140  00 00 00 00
    Next server IP address: 0.0.0.0                                                   0150  13 ff 2d 1a
    Relay agent IP address: 192.0.2.111                                               0160  2a 38 72 b6
    Client MAC address: VMware_ae:d1:7e (00:50:56:ae:d1:7e)                           0170  79 39 02 02
    Client hardware address padding: 00000000000000000000                            0180  70 2d 73 65
    Server host name not given                                                        0190  2f 30 2f 34
    Boot file name not given                                                          01a0  00 00 00 00
    Magic cookie: DHCP                                                                01b0  61 64 3a 37
  > Option: (53) DHCP Message Type (Request)                                          01c0  64 0a fe 0b
  > Option: (61) Client identifier
  > Option: (55) Parameter Request List
  > Option: (57) Maximum DHCP Message Size
  > Option: (50) Requested IP Address (10.100.10.10)
  > Option: (12) Host Name
  > Option: (82) Agent Information Option
```

Figure 10-18 *Packet capture of DHCP Request as it is sent to a dedicated services VRF*

Example 10-11 *Route-lookup for relay agent address on leaf4*

```
root@leaf4> show route table bgp.evpn.0 match-prefix *192.0.2.111*

bgp.evpn.0: 63 destinations, 101 routes (63 active, 0 holddown, 0 hidden)
+ = Active Route, - = Last Active, * = Both

5:192.0.2.11:500::0::192.0.2.111::32/248
                  *[BGP/170] 10:01:55, localpref 100, from 192.0.2.101
                    AS path: 65500 65421 I, validation-state: unverified
                  >  to 198.51.100.13 via et-0/0/0.0

root@leaf4> show route table Tenant1-services-vrf.evpn.0 match-prefix *192.0.2.111*

Tenant1-services-vrf.evpn.0: 24 destinations, 38 routes (24 active, 0 holddown, 0 hidden)
+ = Active Route, - = Last Active, * = Both

5:192.0.2.11:500::0::192.0.2.111::32/248
                  *[BGP/170] 10:02:12, localpref 100, from 192.0.2.101
                    AS path: 65500 65421 I, validation-state: unverified
                  >  to 198.51.100.13 via et-0/0/0.0

root@leaf4> show route table Tenant1-services-vrf.inet.0 192.0.2.111 extensive
```

```
Tenant1-services-vrf.inet.0: 17 destinations, 24 routes (17 active, 0 holddown, 0 hidden)
192.0.2.111/32 (1 entry, 1 announced)
TSI:
KRT in-kernel 192.0.2.111/32 -> {composite(51109)}
        *EVPN   Preference: 170/-101
                Next hop type: Indirect, Next hop index: 0
                Address: 0x55cfcc560ddc
                Next-hop reference count: 11, key opaque handle: (nil), non-key opaque handle: (nil)
                Next hop type: Router, Next hop index: 51056
                Next hop: 198.51.100.13 via et-0/0/0.0, selected
                Session Id: 16
                Protocol next hop: 192.0.2.11
                Composite next hop: 0x55cfcc561540 51109 INH Session ID: 73
                  VXLAN tunnel rewrite:
                    MTU: 0, Flags: 0x0
                    Encap table ID: 0, Decap table ID: 56
                    Encap VNI: 10500, Decap VNI: 1000
                    Source VTEP: 192.0.2.14, Destination VTEP: 192.0.2.11
                    SMAC: b8:f0:15:52:5d:06, DMAC: 40:de:ad:7b:70:40
                Indirect next hop: 0x55cfc94a9f08 51106 INH Session ID: 73
                State: <Active Int Ext VxlanLocalRT>
                Age: 10:02:33   Metric2: 0
                Validation State: unverified
                Task: Tenant1-services-vrf-EVPN-L3-context
                Announcement bits (1): 2-KRT
                AS path: 65500 65421 I
                Thread: junos-main
                Composite next hops: 1
                        Protocol next hop: 192.0.2.11
                        Composite next hop: 0x55cfcc561540 51109 INH Session ID: 73
                          VXLAN tunnel rewrite:
                            MTU: 0, Flags: 0x0
                            Encap table ID: 0, Decap table ID: 56
                            Encap VNI: 10500, Decap VNI: 1000
                            Source VTEP: 192.0.2.14, Destination VTEP: 192.0.2.11
                            SMAC: b8:f0:15:52:5d:06, DMAC: 40:de:ad:7b:70:40
*snip*
```

This DHCP Ack, sent by the DHCP server, has a L3VNI of 10500, which matches the destination VRF on leaf1, as shown in the packet capture in Figure 10-19.

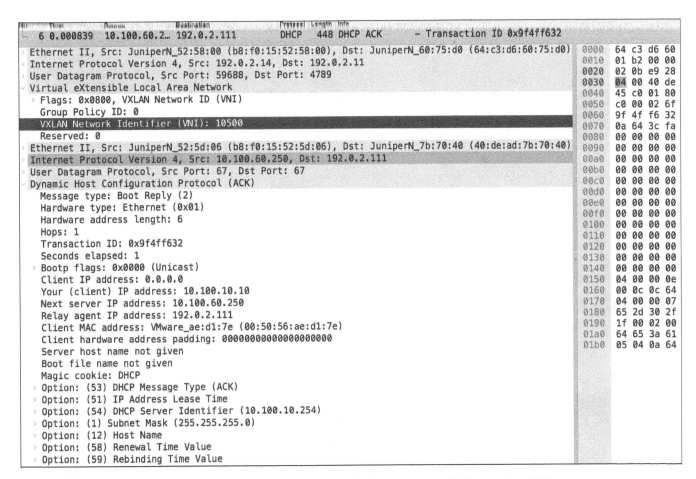

Figure 10-19 *Packet capture of DHCP Ack as it is sent from a dedicated services VRF to a client VRF*

Summary

DHCP is a client/server protocol used for dynamic assignment of IP addresses in a network. With a flat Layer 2 network (with EVPN VXLAN bridged overlay), the broadcast DHCP packets are simply flooded through the fabric to reach the DHCP server, which is in the same bridge domain as the clients.

However, in deployment models such as edge-routed bridging in which the clients and the server are in different VLANs, a DHCP relay agent must be configured for successful DHCP operation. Each leaf is configured as the relay agent, since the leafs are the gateways in the fabric, deployed using an anycast distributed gateway model. With DHCP relay, the leafs can package the DHCP broadcast messages into unicast packets and direct them toward the DHCP server.

Since all leafs share the same address for a particular IRB interface, any redirected DHCP message must be sourced from a unique interface on the leaf (typically the loopback), while also adding DHCP option 82 with the Link Selection suboption. This suboption is used by the DHCP server to determine which pool must be used to provide an available IP address to the client.

This chapter also explored a design where the DHCP server is in a different VRF from the clients, and how a simple import policy model is used to provide connectivity between the client VRF and the services VRF for successful DHCP operation.

Data Center Interconnect

Data Center Interconnect (DCI) is a common term to describe how two or more data centers are connected to each other to allow communication between servers in these different locations. Over time, a DCI has evolved beyond just connecting data centers—it can also be used to connect different pods in the same data center to manage the scale and increasing complexity of a single data center.

This chapter explores different DCI design options, along with their operational implementation in Junos with packet walks and packet captures, demonstrating the flow of traffic between data centers.

Introduction to DCI

It is important to understand when and why a DCI is used. A data center's growth is usually proportional to complexity. As networking expert Russ White often says in many of his online trainings, complexity is a factor of state, volume of that state (scale), and how often that state changes (churn in the network affecting said state). For an EVPN VXLAN–based data center, the state includes underlay/overlay routing adjacencies, routes in the underlay/overlay, tunnel adjacencies, next-hop entries, and so on. Scale becomes a big factor for these parameters, and as these increase, it becomes more complex and operationally challenging to maintain the stability of the network. Thus, it is quite common to see a data center broken into "pods" to build a 5-stage Clos fabric, with each pod connected to the other via a DCI solution, as shown in Figure 11-1.

The DCI, in this case, acts as an interaction surface between pods, which are considered complex systems. These interaction surfaces are abstraction points that can be used to reduce complexity as information is shared between pods—for example, instead of sending all host routes from one pod to another, the gateway (which is where the DCI originates and terminates and is typically the spine of each pod, as in this case) can send an aggregated Type-5 route, thus reducing the state that is passed into the other pod (which is another complex system).

The same logic can be applied to a DCI between two data centers, as depicted in Figure 11-2. It is an abstraction point to exchange state between two or more data centers. This is also ideal for monitoring network parameters such as latency and jitter between these data centers.

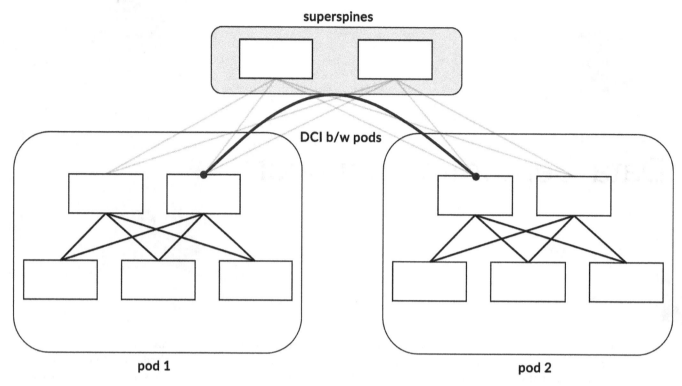

Figure 11-1 *DCI between pods*

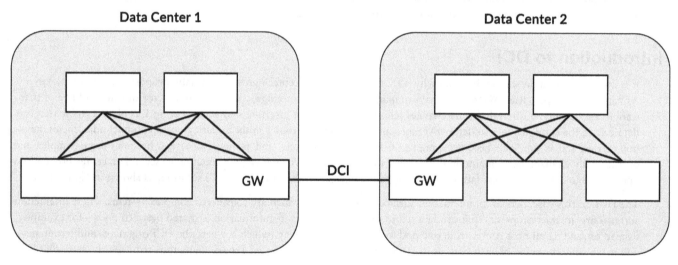

Figure 11-2 *DCI between two data centers*

There are several DCI design options, which vary in complexity and how each impacts the state and scale of said state:

- Over-the-top DCI
- Integrated Interconnect
  - VXLAN-to-VXLAN stitching with an IP transit
  - VXLAN-to-VXLAN stitching with an MPLS transit
  - VXLAN-to-MPLS stitching (IPVPN)
- Hybrid cloud deployment

Over-the-top (OTT) DCI is a simple DCI solution that leaks all state between data centers. There is no logical demarcation between the local DC and its DCI. As the name suggests, this solution provides an "over the top" mechanism of connecting two or more data centers, resulting in a full mesh of VXLAN tunnels between the data centers. While simple in nature, this solution does little to reduce the state and creates additional complexity instead (which is the tradeoff here). Figure 11-3 shows how VXLAN tunnels are built across two data centers with an OTT DCI.

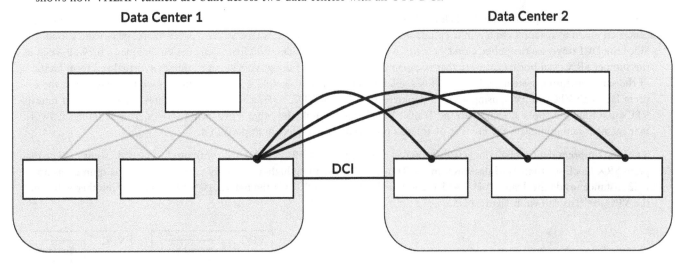

Figure 11-3 *OTT DCI and mesh of VXLAN tunnels across DCs*

In Figure 11-3, to hide unnecessary visual complexity, only one leaf is shown as creating a VXLAN tunnel to every other leaf in DC2. However, this is the case for all leafs—essentially, every leaf will form a VXLAN tunnel with every other leaf in the fabric (both local and remote data center leafs). Thus, such a solution adds considerable overhead in tunnel and next-hop state scale, which are limited resources. Thus, with OTT DCI rooted in simplicity, it is a good choice for connecting two or three data centers, but anything beyond that number may start to hit platform resource limitations.

Integrated Interconnect, also known as *VXLAN stitching* (based on RFC 9014), brings in clear demarcation between a local data center and its DCI. It is called Integrated Interconnect because it couples together two functions—the VXLAN gateway functionality and the WAN edge functionality—thus providing an integrated functionality on a single device. It provides mechanisms to hand off from one domain to another domain (without handing off to a second device), allowing for different transit options between the data centers. *Border gateways* are a key component of such a DCI design. These devices terminate all local data center VXLAN tunnels and originate a new VXLAN tunnel to the remote border gateway (i.e., the border gateway of the other data center). This means that the VXLAN tunnels no longer extend beyond a data center. Figure 11-4 shows a visual representation of how VXLAN tunnels are built in such a design.

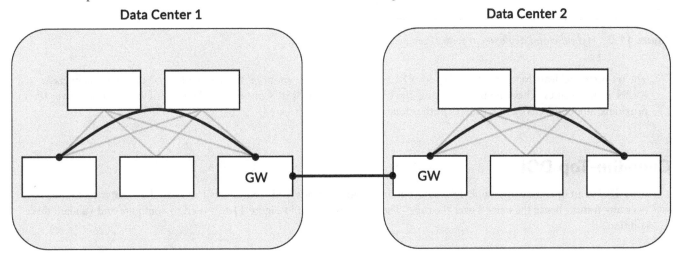

Figure 11-4 *VXLAN stitching between two data centers*

In Figure 11-4, each DC's leaf forms a VXLAN tunnel with its local gateway. This gateway originates a new VXLAN tunnel to the remote gateway, which forms VXLAN tunnels to its local leafs. With this separation of the local DC and its DCI, the growth of one DC does not negatively impact any interconnected DCs since each DC has specific exit points (which are the gateways), and the VXLAN tunnels are built only to these gateways, regardless of how many leafs may exist in the other DCs.

The last DCI design option is a hybrid cloud deployment, in which an on-premises (commonly shortened to "on-prem") data center connects to resources in a public cloud, such as Amazon Web Services (AWS), Microsoft Azure, or Google Cloud. Since the DCI traverses the public cloud, security is an important consideration here. This design includes a firewall, such as the Juniper SRX, as a border gateway that is capable of doing IPsec. Taking AWS as an example, a virtualized form factor of the same operating system (called vSRX) is available in the AWS marketplace as well—this is used to interconnect the on-prem DC with VPCs in AWS, using a vSRX deployed in a Transit VPC. A Transit VPC is commonly used to connect multiple VPCs in a hub-and-spoke design, with the Transit VPC being the hub and other VPCs being spokes. This simplifies network management and minimizes the number of connections needed to connect multiple VPCs.

Since the on-prem data center connects to resources via the Internet, IPsec VPNs are configured to provide security. The on-prem SRX has IPsec tunnels to the vSRX in the Transit VPC (usually a high-availability pair). The vSRX is spun up as an EC2 instance inside the Transit VPC, which connects back to the VPCs via the native AWS VPN client or another vSRX in the VPC itself, as shown in Figure 11-5.

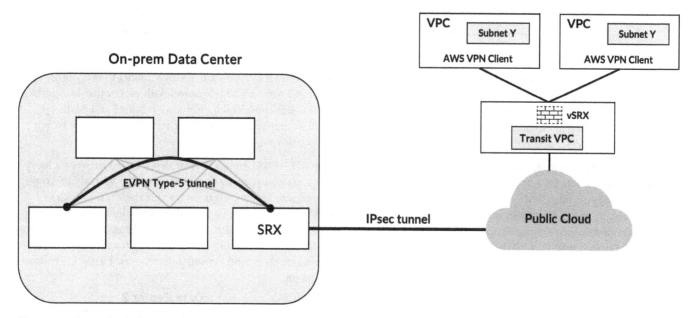

Figure 11-5 *Hybrid cloud deployment with IPsec handoff to public cloud*

The on-prem DC leafs form an EVPN Type-5 VXLAN tunnel with the on-prem SRX and advertise their local subnets as EVPN Type-5 routes. These are then sent over the IPsec tunnel to the vSRX instance in the public cloud (via BGP over IPsec), providing interconnectivity to resources in the cloud.

Over-the-Top DCI

OTT DCI is an operationally simple DCI solution that simply extends VXLAN tunnels from one data center to another over any transit, hence the name "over the top." The topology shown in Figure 11-6 is used to configure and validate this solution.

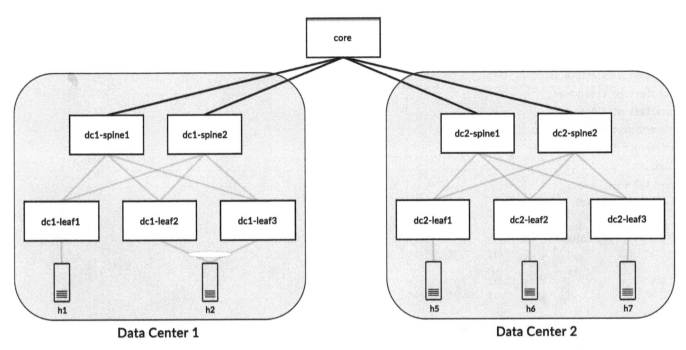

Figure 11-6 *Reference topology for OTT DCI*

While the two DCs are connected via a core device that connects to the spines, the same result can be achieved by connecting the core to border leafs as well. The purpose of the core does not change: it facilitates the control plane exchange of both BGP underlay and BGP EVPN overlay routes between the two DCs and acts as a data plane transit for forwarding traffic between the DCs. The overlay BGP EVPN routes are exchanged via the core without any modification of the next-hop address. In this way, from the perspective of the control plane, the core acts as a route server, meant to forward routes from one eBGP peer to another.

Figure 11-7 shows the addressing and ASN allocation scheme used for the OTT DCI configuration.

Resource	DC1	DC2
Loopbacks	192.0.2.0/24	
Point-to-point L3 interfaces	198.51.100.0/24	
Spine ASNs	65500	65501
Leaf ASNs	65420-65429	65430-65439
VLAN 100	10.100.100.0/24	

Loopback assignment scheme for leafs = 192.0.2.XY where X is DC number and Y is leaf number. For example, dc1-leaf1 will have a loopback address of 192.0.2.11/32.
Loopback assignment scheme for spines = 192.0.2.X0Y where X is DC number and Y is spine number. For example, dc1-spine1 will have a loopback address of 192.0.2.101/32.
Host assignment scheme = 10.100.100.X/24 where X is the host number. For example, h1 will have an address of 10.100.100.1/32.

Figure 11-7 *Addressing and ASN scheme for OTT DCI*

All hosts are in the same subnet (10.100.100.0/24), and each individual data center is configured as an EVPN VXLAN fabric with a bridged overlay design. A single, VLAN-Based MAC-VRF is configured on all leafs, which includes VLAN 100. Let's revisit this configuration to establish a baseline, as shown in Example 11-1, from a leaf in each data center.

Example 11-1 *MAC-VRF configuration on dc1-leaf1 and dc2-leaf1*

```
root@dc1-leaf1# show routing-instances macvrf-v100-1
instance-type mac-vrf;
protocols {
    evpn {
        encapsulation vxlan;
```

```
            extended-vni-list 10100;
        }
    }
    vtep-source-interface lo0.0;
    service-type vlan-based;
    interface et-0/0/49.0;
    route-distinguisher 192.0.2.11:100;
    vrf-target target:1:1;
    vlans {
        v100 {
            vlan-id 100;
            vxlan {
                vni 10100;
            }
        }
    }
}


root@dc2-leaf1# show routing-instances macvrf-v100-1
instance-type mac-vrf;
protocols {
    evpn {
        encapsulation vxlan;
        extended-vni-list 10100;
    }
}
vtep-source-interface lo0.0;
service-type vlan-based;
interface et-0/0/49.0;
route-distinguisher 192.0.2.21:100;
vrf-target target:1:1;
vlans {
    v100 {
        vlan-id 100;
        vxlan {
            vni 10100;
        }
    }
}
```

Each leaf (VTEP) has a BGP IPv4 (inet, in Junos terminology) and EVPN peering with the spines in their respective data centers. The IPv4 peering is used to advertise leaf loopback addresses, while the EVPN peering is used to exchange EVPN routes within the data center. The configuration snippet presented in Example 11-2 shows the BGP configuration from dc1-leaf1, as a reference.

Example 11-2   *BGP configuration from a leaf in DC1*

```
root@dc1-leaf1# show protocols bgp
group underlay {
    type external;
    family inet {
        unicast;
```

```
        }
        export allow-loopback;
        peer-as 65500;
        multipath;
        bfd-liveness-detection {
            minimum-interval 333;
            multiplier 3;
        }
        neighbor 198.51.100.1;
        neighbor 198.51.100.3;
    }
    group overlay {
        type external;
        multihop;
        local-address 192.0.2.11;
        family evpn {
            signaling;
        }
        peer-as 65500;
        multipath;
        bfd-liveness-detection {
            minimum-interval 333;
            multiplier 3;
        }
        neighbor 192.0.2.101;
        neighbor 192.0.2.102;
    }
```

```
root@dc1-leaf1# show policy-options policy-statement allow-loopback
term 1 {
    from interface lo0.0;
    then accept;
}
```

Each spine is connected to the core via a point-to-point Layer 3 interface. The intent is to establish an eBGP IPv4 peering with the core over this point-to-point interface, allowing all underlay routes (specifically, the loopback addresses) to be exchanged between both data centers. The configuration snippet presented in Example 11-3, taken from dc1-spine1 and the core, shows the point-to-point interface between them and the eBGP session for the IPv4 family.

Example 11-3 *Configuration on dc1-spine1 and the core to establish underlay connectivity between them*

```
root@dc1-spine1# show interfaces xe-0/0/5:0
mtu 9200;
unit 0 {
    family inet {
        address 198.51.100.150/31;
    }
}
```

```
root@core# show interfaces xe-0/0/0:0
mtu 9200;
unit 0 {
```

```
        family inet {
            address 198.51.100.151/31;
        }
    }


root@dc1-spine1# show protocols bgp group underlay-dci
type external;
family inet {
    unicast;
}
export dci;
peer-as 65510;
neighbor 198.51.100.151;


root@dc1-spine1# show policy-options policy-statement dci
term 1 {
    from {
        route-filter 192.0.2.0/24 orlonger;
    }
    then accept;
}
term default {
    then reject;
}


root@core# show protocols bgp group underlay-dci
type external;
family inet {
    unicast;
}
export allow-loopback;
neighbor 198.51.100.150 {
    peer-as 65500;
}
neighbor 198.51.100.152 {
    peer-as 65500;
}
neighbor 198.51.100.154 {
    peer-as 65501;
}
neighbor 198.51.100.156 {
    peer-as 65501;
}
```

Once all spines are configured using Example 11-3 as a reference, they should receive the loopback addresses of all devices in the respective remote data center through the core. These routes are further advertised down to the leafs, and thus every leaf has a route to the loopback address of every other leaf across both data centers. Considering dc1-leaf1, the output shown in Example 11-4 confirms the same.

Example 11-4 *Loopback addresses of all leafs in the route table of dc1-leaf1*

```
root@dc1-leaf1> show route table inet.0 match-prefix 192.0.2.*

inet.0: 33 destinations, 43 routes (33 active, 0 holddown, 0 hidden)
@ = Routing Use Only, # = Forwarding Use Only
+ = Active Route, - = Last Active, * = Both


192.0.2.11/32      *[Direct/0] 1d 05:46:41
                    >  via lo0.0
192.0.2.12/32      *[BGP/170] 1d 05:44:47, localpref 100, from 198.51.100.1
                       AS path: 65500 65422 I, validation-state: unverified
                        to 198.51.100.1 via et-0/0/48.0
                    >  to 198.51.100.3 via et-0/0/50.0
                    [BGP/170] 1d 05:44:47, localpref 100
                       AS path: 65500 65422 I, validation-state: unverified
                    >  to 198.51.100.3 via et-0/0/50.0
192.0.2.13/32      *[BGP/170] 1d 05:44:07, localpref 100, from 198.51.100.1
                       AS path: 65500 65423 I, validation-state: unverified
                        to 198.51.100.1 via et-0/0/48.0
                    >  to 198.51.100.3 via et-0/0/50.0
                    [BGP/170] 1d 05:44:07, localpref 100
                       AS path: 65500 65423 I, validation-state: unverified
                    >  to 198.51.100.3 via et-0/0/50.0
192.0.2.21/32      *[BGP/170] 00:07:02, localpref 100, from 198.51.100.3
                       AS path: 65500 65510 65501 65431 I, validation-state: unverified
                    >  to 198.51.100.1 via et-0/0/48.0
                        to 198.51.100.3 via et-0/0/50.0
                    [BGP/170] 00:07:02, localpref 100
                       AS path: 65500 65510 65501 65431 I, validation-state: unverified
                    >  to 198.51.100.1 via et-0/0/48.0
192.0.2.22/32      *[BGP/170] 00:07:02, localpref 100, from 198.51.100.3
                       AS path: 65500 65510 65501 65432 I, validation-state: unverified
                    >  to 198.51.100.1 via et-0/0/48.0
                        to 198.51.100.3 via et-0/0/50.0
                    [BGP/170] 00:07:02, localpref 100
                       AS path: 65500 65510 65501 65432 I, validation-state: unverified
                    >  to 198.51.100.1 via et-0/0/48.0
192.0.2.23/32      *[BGP/170] 00:07:02, localpref 100, from 198.51.100.3
                       AS path: 65500 65510 65501 65433 I, validation-state: unverified
                    >  to 198.51.100.1 via et-0/0/48.0
                        to 198.51.100.3 via et-0/0/50.0
                    [BGP/170] 00:07:02, localpref 100
                       AS path: 65500 65510 65501 65433 I, validation-state: unverified
                    >  to 198.51.100.1 via et-0/0/48.0
192.0.2.101/32     *[BGP/170] 1d 05:45:26, localpref 100
                       AS path: 65500 I, validation-state: unverified
                    >  to 198.51.100.1 via et-0/0/48.0
192.0.2.102/32     *[BGP/170] 1d 05:45:26, localpref 100
                       AS path: 65500 I, validation-state: unverified
```

```
                        >  to 198.51.100.3 via et-0/0/50.0
192.0.2.201/32          *[BGP/170] 00:07:02, localpref 100
                           AS path: 65500 65510 65501 I, validation-state: unverified
                             to 198.51.100.1 via et-0/0/48.0
                        >  to 198.51.100.3 via et-0/0/50.0
                        [BGP/170] 00:07:02, localpref 100
                           AS path: 65500 65510 65501 I, validation-state: unverified
                        >  to 198.51.100.1 via et-0/0/48.0
192.0.2.202/32          *[BGP/170] 00:07:02, localpref 100
                           AS path: 65500 65510 65501 I, validation-state: unverified
                             to 198.51.100.1 via et-0/0/48.0
                        >  to 198.51.100.3 via et-0/0/50.0
                        [BGP/170] 00:07:02, localpref 100
                           AS path: 65500 65510 65501 I, validation-state: unverified
                        >  to 198.51.100.1 via et-0/0/48.0
192.0.2.250/32          *[BGP/170] 00:07:02, localpref 100
                           AS path: 65500 65510 I, validation-state: unverified
                             to 198.51.100.1 via et-0/0/48.0
                        >  to 198.51.100.3 via et-0/0/50.0
                        [BGP/170] 00:07:02, localpref 100
                           AS path: 65500 65510 I, validation-state: unverified
                        >  to 198.51.100.1 via et-0/0/48.0
```

This means that each leaf should be able to communicate with every other leaf's loopback address (across both data centers), while sourcing its own, as shown in Example 11-5, taking dc1-leaf1 as a reference again.

Example 11-5   *Reachability of dc1-leaf1 to loopback addresses of every other leaf*

```
root@dc1-leaf1> ping 192.0.2.12 source 192.0.2.11
PING 192.0.2.12 (192.0.2.12): 56 data bytes
64 bytes from 192.0.2.12: icmp_seq=0 ttl=63 time=10.201 ms
64 bytes from 192.0.2.12: icmp_seq=1 ttl=63 time=6.552 ms
--- 192.0.2.12 ping statistics ---
2 packets transmitted, 2 packets received, 0% packet loss
round-trip min/avg/max/stddev = 6.552/8.377/10.201/1.825 ms


root@dc1-leaf1> ping 192.0.2.13 source 192.0.2.11
PING 192.0.2.13 (192.0.2.13): 56 data bytes
64 bytes from 192.0.2.13: icmp_seq=0 ttl=63 time=9.484 ms
64 bytes from 192.0.2.13: icmp_seq=1 ttl=63 time=5.385 ms
--- 192.0.2.13 ping statistics ---
2 packets transmitted, 2 packets received, 0% packet loss
round-trip min/avg/max/stddev = 5.385/7.434/9.484/2.050 ms


root@dc1-leaf1> ping 192.0.2.21 source 192.0.2.11
PING 192.0.2.21 (192.0.2.21): 56 data bytes
64 bytes from 192.0.2.21: icmp_seq=0 ttl=61 time=10.705 ms
64 bytes from 192.0.2.21: icmp_seq=1 ttl=61 time=7.246 ms
--- 192.0.2.21 ping statistics ---
```

```
2 puukutu tranomittud, 1 packuts received, 0% packet loss
round-trip min/avg/max/stddev = 7.246/8.976/10.705/1.729 ms


root@dc1-leaf1> ping 192.0.2.22 source 192.0.2.11
PING 192.0.2.22 (192.0.2.22): 56 data bytes
64 bytes from 192.0.2.22: icmp_seq=0 ttl=61 time=10.866 ms
64 bytes from 192.0.2.22: icmp_seq=1 ttl=61 time=11.054 ms
--- 192.0.2.22 ping statistics ---
2 packets transmitted, 2 packets received, 0% packet loss
round-trip min/avg/max/stddev = 10.866/10.960/11.054/0.094 ms


root@dc1-leaf1> ping 192.0.2.23 source 192.0.2.11
PING 192.0.2.23 (192.0.2.23): 56 data bytes
64 bytes from 192.0.2.23: icmp_seq=0 ttl=61 time=2.600 ms
64 bytes from 192.0.2.23: icmp_seq=1 ttl=61 time=4.630 ms
--- 192.0.2.23 ping statistics ---
2 packets transmitted, 2 packets received, 0% packet loss
round-trip min/avg/max/stddev = 2.600/3.615/4.630/1.015 ms
```

Once the underlay peering is established, each spine establishes a BGP EVPN peering with the core to exchange EVPN routes. It is important that the core does not modify the next-hop address of the received EVPN routes (as it passes it on), and thus it is configured explicitly to not do so. This makes the core a route server that is simply used to reflect EVPN routes from one data center to the other. The configuration snippet presented in Example 11-6, taken from dc1-spine1 and the core, shows how the BGP EVPN peering is configured, and confirms that the core has successfully established a BGP EVPN peering with all spines.

Example 11-6   *BGP EVPN configuration between dc1-spine1 and the core*

```
root@dc1-spine1# show protocols bgp group overlay-dci
type external;
multihop {
    no-nexthop-change;
}
local-address 192.0.2.101;
family evpn {
    signaling;
}
peer-as 65510;
neighbor 192.0.2.250;


root@core# show protocols bgp group overlay-dci
type external;
multihop {
    no-nexthop-change;
}
local-address 192.0.2.250;
family evpn {
    signaling;
}
neighbor 192.0.2.101 {
```

```
            peer-as 65500;
        }
        neighbor 192.0.2.102 {
            peer-as 65500;
        }
        neighbor 192.0.2.201 {
            peer-as 65501;
        }
        neighbor 192.0.2.202 {
            peer-as 65501;
        }
```

```
root@core> show bgp summary group overlay-dci
Threading mode: BGP I/O
Default eBGP mode: advertise - accept, receive - accept
Groups: 2 Peers: 8 Down peers: 0
Table          Tot Paths  Act Paths Suppressed    History Damp State    Pending
inet.0
                     20         12          0          0         0          0
bgp.evpn.0
                     56         28          0          0         0          0
Peer                   AS    InPkt   OutPkt    OutQ   Flaps Last Up/Dwn
State|#Active/Received/Accepted/Damped...
192.0.2.101         65500     9184     7201       0       0 1d 20:36:04 Establ
  bgp.evpn.0: 17/21/21/0
192.0.2.102         65500     9184     7201       0       0 1d 20:36:00 Establ
  bgp.evpn.0: 4/21/21/0
192.0.2.201         65501     7211     9225       0       0 1d 20:36:04 Establ
  bgp.evpn.0: 3/7/7/0
192.0.2.202         65501     7211     9225       0       0 1d 20:36:03 Establ
  bgp.evpn.0: 4/7/7/0
```

All EVPN routes are now exchanged with no modification to the next-hop address by the spines or the core. This means that when a leaf originates an EVPN route, it continues to be the next-hop address for that route within the local data center as well as the remote data center. Let's follow an EVPN Type-3 route originated by dc1-leaf1 to confirm, as shown in Example 11-7. The route is originated with a next-hop address of 192.0.2.11, which is its local loopback address, as high-lighted in the example.

Example 11-7 *EVPN Type-3 route generated by dc1-leaf1*

```
root@dc1-leaf1> show route table bgp.evpn.0 match-prefix 3:*192.0.2.11* extensive

bgp.evpn.0: 26 destinations, 49 routes (26 active, 0 holddown, 0 hidden)
3:192.0.2.11:100::0::192.0.2.11/248 IM (1 entry, 1 announced)
TSI:
Page 0 idx 0, (group overlay type External) Type 1 val 0xacd7668 (adv_entry)
   Advertised metrics:
     Flags: Nexthop Change
     Nexthop: Self
     AS path: [65421] I
     Communities: target:1:1 encapsulation:vxlan(0x8)
```

```
      PMSI: Flags 0x0: Label 631: Type INGRESS-REPLICATION 192.0.2.11
   Advertise: 00000003
Path 3:192.0.2.11:100::0::192.0.2.11
Vector len 4.  Val: 0
          *EVPN    Preference: 170
                   Next hop type: Indirect, Next hop index: 0
                   Address: 0x8c067f4
                   Next-hop reference count: 8, key opaque handle: 0x0, non-key opaque handle: 0x0
                   Protocol next hop: 192.0.2.11
                   Indirect next hop: 0x0 - INH Session ID: 0
                   State: <Secondary Active Int Ext>
                   Age: 2d 15:30:04
                   Validation State: unverified
                   Task: macvrf-v100-1-evpn
                   Announcement bits (1): 1-BGP_RT_Background
                   AS path: I
                   Communities: target:1:1 encapsulation:vxlan(0x8)
                   Route Label: 10100
                   PMSI: Flags 0x0: Label 10100: Type INGRESS-REPLICATION 192.0.2.11
                   Primary Routing Table: macvrf-v100-1.evpn.0
                   Thread: junos-main
```

This route is sent to the spines, which advertise it back down to other leafs in the local data center, while also advertising it toward the core. To examine this, consider the output in Example 11-8, which shows the EVPN Type-3 route, originated by dc1-leaf1, sent to the core and dc1-leaf2. In both cases, the next-hop continues to be 192.0.2.11, which is dc1-leaf1's loopback address.

Example 11-8 *EVPN Type-3 route, originated by dc1-leaf1, sent to dc1-leaf2 and the core by dc1-spine1*

```
root@dc1-spine1> show route advertising-protocol bgp 192.0.2.250 match-prefix 3:*192.0.2.11* table bgp.evpn.0 extensive

bgp.evpn.0: 23 destinations, 23 routes (23 active, 0 holddown, 0 hidden)
* 3:192.0.2.11:100::0::192.0.2.11/248 IM (1 entry, 1 announced)
 BGP group overlay-dci type External
     Route Distinguisher: 192.0.2.11:100
     Nexthop: 192.0.2.11
     AS path: [65500] 65421 I
     Communities: target:1:1 encapsulation:vxlan(0x8)
     PMSI: Flags 0x0: Label 631: Type INGRESS-REPLICATION 192.0.2.11


root@dc1-spine1> show route advertising-protocol bgp 192.0.2.12 match-prefix 3:*192.0.2.11* table bgp.evpn.0 extensive

bgp.evpn.0: 22 destinations, 22 routes (22 active, 0 holddown, 0 hidden)
* 3:192.0.2.11:100::0::192.0.2.11/248 IM (1 entry, 1 announced)
 BGP group overlay type External
     Route Distinguisher: 192.0.2.11:100
     Nexthop: 192.0.2.11
     AS path: [65500] 65421 I
     Communities: target:1:1 encapsulation:vxlan(0x8)
     PMSI: Flags 0x0: Label 631: Type INGRESS-REPLICATION 192.0.2.11
```

The core will send this route to the remote data center spines, which send it to their local leafs. Thus, on dc2-leaf1, as an example, the same route is received with a next-hop address of 192.0.2.11, which allows it to build a VXLAN tunnel directly to dc1-leaf1, as shown in Example 11-9.

Example 11-9   *EVPN Type-3 route, originated by dc1-leaf1, received on dc2-leaf1*

```
root@dc2-leaf1> show route table bgp.evpn.0 match-prefix 3:*192.0.2.11* extensive


bgp.evpn.0: 26 destinations, 49 routes (26 active, 0 holddown, 0 hidden)
3:192.0.2.11:100::0::192.0.2.11/248 IM (2 entries, 0 announced)
        *BGP    Preference: 170/-101
                Route Distinguisher: 192.0.2.11:100
                PMSI: Flags 0x0: Label 631: Type INGRESS-REPLICATION 192.0.2.11
                Next hop type: Indirect, Next hop index: 0
                Address: 0x8c07354
                Next-hop reference count: 4, key opaque handle: 0x0, non-key opaque handle: 0x0
                Source: 192.0.2.201
                Protocol next hop: 192.0.2.11
                Indirect next hop: 0x2 no-forward INH Session ID: 0
                State: <Active Ext>
                Local AS: 65431 Peer AS: 65501
                Age: 3d 11:23:53        Metric2: 0
                Validation State: unverified
                Task: BGP_65501.192.0.2.201
                AS path: 65501 65510 65500 65421 I
                Communities: target:1:1 encapsulation:vxlan(0x8)
                Import Accepted
                Localpref: 100
                Router ID: 192.0.2.201
                Secondary Tables: macvrf-v100-1.evpn.0
                Thread: junos-main
                Indirect next hops: 1
                        Protocol next hop: 192.0.2.11 ResolvState: Resolved
                        Indirect next hop: 0x2 no-forward INH Session ID: 0
                        Indirect path forwarding next hops: 2
                            Next hop type: Router
                            Next hop: 198.51.100.101 via et-0/0/54.0
                            Session Id: 0
                            Next hop: 198.51.100.103 via et-0/0/50.0
                            Session Id: 0
                            192.0.2.11/32 Originating RIB: inet.0
                              Node path count: 1
                              Forwarding nexthops: 2
                                    Next hop type: Router
                                    Next hop: 198.51.100.101 via et-0/0/54.0
                                    Session Id: 0
                                    Next hop: 198.51.100.103 via et-0/0/50.0
                                    Session Id: 0

*snip*


root@dc2-leaf1> show mac-vrf forwarding vxlan-tunnel-end-point remote ip 192.0.2.11
```

```
MAC flags (S -static MAC, D -dynamic MAC, L -locally learned, C -Control MAC
           SE -Statistics enabled, NM -Non configured MAC, R -Remote PE MAC , P -Pinned MAC)


Logical system    : <default>
Routing instance : macvrf-v100-1
 Bridging domain : v100+100, VLAN : 100
 VXLAN ID : 10100, Multicast Group IP : 0.0.0.0
 Remote VTEP : 192.0.2.11, Nexthop ID : 1694
    MAC             MAC    Logical        Remote VTEP
    address         flags  interface      IP address
    f0:4b:3a:b9:80:a7  DR   vtep-9.32772   192.0.2.11
```

In this way, every leaf forms a VXLAN tunnel with every other leaf across both data centers. All traffic flows over the top, meaning that these VXLAN tunnels exist end to end and everything in between is used for transit only. This can be confirmed by viewing the remote VXLAN peers established on the leafs, as shown in Example 11-10, considering dc1-leaf1 and dc2-leaf2 as references.

Example 11-10 *VXLAN tunnels established on dc1-leaf1 and dc2-leaf1*

```
root@dc1-leaf1> show mac-vrf forwarding vxlan-tunnel-end-point remote
Logical System Name    Id  SVTEP-IP       IFL  L3-Idx  SVTEP-Mode   ELP-SVTEP-IP
<default>              0   192.0.2.11     lo0.0   0
  RVTEP-IP     IFL-Idx    Interface    NH-Id  RVTEP-Mode  ELP-IP      Flags
  192.0.2.12   830        vtep.32770   1752   RNVE
  192.0.2.13   831        vtep.32771   1756   RNVE
  192.0.2.21   833        vtep.32773   1759   RNVE
  192.0.2.22   832        vtep.32772   1758   RNVE
  192.0.2.23   836        vtep.32776   1762   RNVE
  RVTEP-IP     L2-RTT                IFL-Idx   Interface   NH-Id  RVTEP-Mode ELP-IP  Flags
  192.0.2.12   macvrf-v100-1         671088640 vtep-9.32770 1752  RNVE
    VNID       MC-Group-IP
    10100      0.0.0.0
  RVTEP-IP     L2-RTT                IFL-Idx   Interface   NH-Id  RVTEP-Mode ELP-IP  Flags
  192.0.2.13   macvrf-v100-1         671088641 vtep-9.32771 1756  RNVE
    VNID       MC-Group-IP
    10100      0.0.0.0
  RVTEP-IP     L2-RTT                IFL-Idx   Interface   NH-Id  RVTEP-Mode ELP-IP  Flags
  192.0.2.21   macvrf-v100-1         671088643 vtep-9.32773 1759  RNVE
    VNID       MC-Group-IP
    10100      0.0.0.0
  RVTEP-IP     L2-RTT                IFL-Idx   Interface   NH-Id  RVTEP-Mode ELP-IP  Flags
  192.0.2.22   macvrf-v100-1         671088642 vtep-9.32772 1758  RNVE
    VNID       MC-Group-IP
    10100      0.0.0.0
  RVTEP-IP     L2-RTT                IFL-Idx   Interface   NH-Id  RVTEP-Mode ELP-IP  Flags
  192.0.2.23   macvrf-v100-1         671088646 vtep-9.32776 1762  RNVE
    VNID       MC-Group-IP
    10100      0.0.0.0


root@dc2-leaf1> show mac-vrf forwarding vxlan-tunnel-end-point remote
Logical System Name     Id  SVTEP-IP      IFL  L3-Idx  SVTEP-Mode   ELP-SVTEP-IP
```

```
<default>                    0   192.0.2.21     lo0.0    0
RVTEP-IP       IFL-Idx    Interface    NH-Id   RVTEP-Mode  ELP-IP      Flags
192.0.2.11     827        vtep.32772   1694    RNVE
192.0.2.12     826        vtep.32771   1693    RNVE
192.0.2.13     828        vtep.32773   1696    RNVE
192.0.2.22     825        vtep.32770   1690    RNVE
192.0.2.23     831        vtep.32776   1788    RNVE
RVTEP-IP       L2-RTT              IFL-Idx   Interface      NH-Id  RVTEP-Mode ELP-IP      Flags
192.0.2.11     macvrf-v100-1       671088642 vtep-9.32772  1694   RNVE
   VNID        MC-Group-IP
   10100       0.0.0.0
RVTEP-IP       L2-RTT              IFL-Idx   Interface      NH-Id  RVTEP-Mode ELP-IP      Flags
192.0.2.12     macvrf-v100-1       671088641 vtep-9.32771  1693   RNVE
   VNID        MC-Group-IP
   10100       0.0.0.0
RVTEP-IP       L2-RTT              IFL-Idx   Interface      NH-Id  RVTEP-Mode ELP-IP      Flags
192.0.2.13     macvrf-v100-1       671088643 vtep-9.32773  1696   RNVE
   VNID        MC-Group-IP
   10100       0.0.0.0
RVTEP-IP       L2-RTT              IFL-Idx   Interface      NH-Id  RVTEP-Mode ELP-IP      Flags
192.0.2.22     macvrf-v100-1       671088640 vtep-9.32770  1690   RNVE
   VNID        MC-Group-IP
   10100       0.0.0.0
RVTEP-IP       L2-RTT              IFL-Idx   Interface      NH-Id  RVTEP-Mode ELP-IP      Flags
192.0.2.23     macvrf-v100-1       671088646 vtep-9.32776  1788   RNVE
   VNID        MC-Group-IP
   10100       0.0.0.0
```

Visually, this can be represented as shown in Figure 11-8, from the perspective of just one leaf, dc1-leaf1. In the same way, every other leaf will have a tunnel to every other leaf across both data centers.

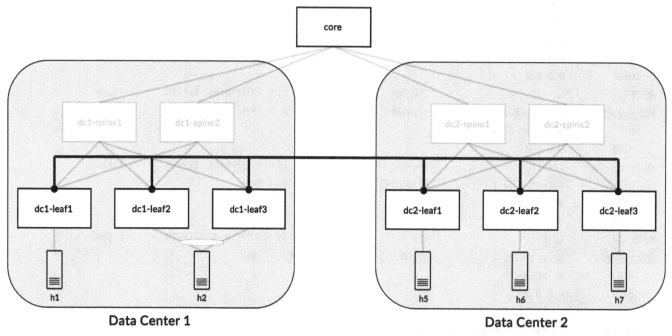

Figure 11-8 *Mesh of VXLAN tunnels from one leaf in DC1*

In the data plane, this is just a VXLAN encapsulated packet that is carried via the underlay transit, from one leaf to another. Let's consider the example of host h1 in DC1 communicating with h5 in DC2. Since both h1 and h5 are in the same subnet, h1 attempts to resolve h5's IP address to its MAC address (via the ARP process). When this ARP request is received on dc1-leaf1, it can use its MAC-IP table to proxy-ARP for host h5, as shown in Example 11-11, and suppress the original ARP request from being flooded in the fabric.

Example 11-11 *MAC-IP table on dc1-leaf1 for host h5's address*

```
root@dc1-leaf1> show mac-vrf forwarding mac-ip-table f0:4b:3a:b9:80:ff


MAC IP flags  (S - Static, D - Dynamic, L - Local , R - Remote, Lp - Local Proxy,
              Rp - Remote Proxy, K - Kernel, RT - Dest Route, (N)AD - (Not) Advt to remote,
              RE - Re-ARP/ND, RO - Router, OV - Override, Ur - Unresolved,
              RTS - Dest Route Skipped, RGw - Remote Gateway, GBP - Group Based Policy,
              RTF - Dest Route Forced)
Routing instance : macvrf-v100-1
Bridging domain : v100
  IP                  MAC               Flags       GBP   Logical      Active
  address             address                       Tag   Interface    source
  10.100.100.5        f0:4b:3a:b9:80:ff DR,K              vtep-9.32773 192.0.2.21
```

With the ARP resolved on host h1, it can generate an IP packet, which is encapsulated by dc1-leaf1 and sent toward dc2-leaf1. Visually, this can be represented as shown in Figure 11-9.

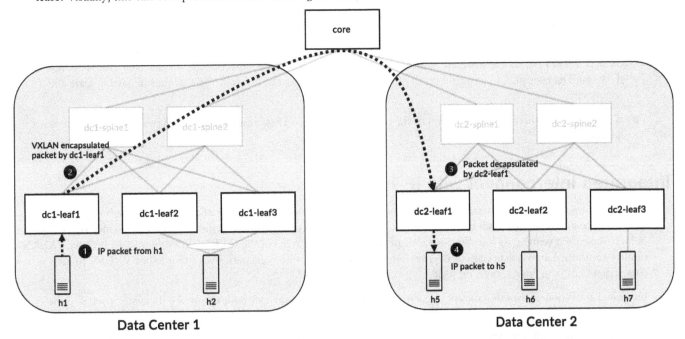

Figure 11-9 *Traffic flow from DC1 to DC2 when hosts in the same subnet communicate with each other*

A packet capture, as shown in Figure 11-10, confirms that the outer IP header has a destination IP address of 192.0.2.21, which belongs to dc2-leaf1. Thus, the transit devices (the spines and the core) simply forward the packet based on this outer IP destination address until it reaches dc2-leaf1, where the packet is decapsulated and sent to the host, h5.

```
No.    Time      Source         Destination      Protocol  Length  Info
→  6 0.339271  10.100.100.1   10.100.100.5     ICMP     148 Echo (ping) request  id=0xf6fd, seq=117/29952, ttl=64 (reply in 7)
←  7 0.339755  10.100.100.5   10.100.100.1     ICMP     152 Echo (ping) reply    id=0xf6fd, seq=117/29952, ttl=64 (request in 6)

> Frame 6: 148 bytes on wire (1184 bits), 148 bytes captured (1184 bits)        0000  64 c3 d6 60 76 40 40
> Ethernet II, Src: JuniperN_7b:70:75 (40:de:ad:7b:70:75), Dst: JuniperN_60:76:40 (64:c3:d6:60:76:40)  0010  00 86 71 34 00 00 40
∨ Internet Protocol Version 4, Src: 192.0.2.11, Dst: 192.0.2.21                  0020  02 15 2e 1d 12 b5 00
    0100 .... = Version: 4                                                       0030  74 00 f0 4b 3a b9 80
    .... 0101 = Header Length: 20 bytes (5)                                      0040  45 00 00 54 18 b6 00
  > Differentiated Services Field: 0x00 (DSCP: CS0, ECN: Not-ECT)                0050  0a 64 64 05 08 00 18
    Total Length: 134                                                            0060  00 0e 2a b7 08 09 0a
    Identification: 0x7134 (28980)                                               0070  14 15 16 17 18 19 1a
  > 000. .... = Flags: 0x0                                                       0080  24 25 26 27 28 29 2a
    ...0 0000 0000 0000 = Fragment Offset: 0                                     0090  34 35 36 37
    Time to Live: 64
    Protocol: UDP (17)
    Header Checksum: 0x8512 [validation disabled]
    [Header checksum status: Unverified]
    Source Address: 192.0.2.11
    Destination Address: 192.0.2.21
> User Datagram Protocol, Src Port: 11805, Dst Port: 4789
∨ Virtual eXtensible Local Area Network
  > Flags: 0x0800, VXLAN Network ID (VNI)
    Group Policy ID: 0
    VXLAN Network Identifier (VNI): 10100
    Reserved: 0
> Ethernet II, Src: JuniperN_b9:80:a7 (f0:4b:3a:b9:80:a7), Dst: JuniperN_b9:80:ff (f0:4b:3a:b9:80:ff)
> Internet Protocol Version 4, Src: 10.100.100.1, Dst: 10.100.100.5
> Internet Control Message Protocol
```

Figure 11-10 *Packet capture of a VXLAN-encapsulated packet sent over an OTT DCI to a remote DC*

An OTT DCI design has drawbacks, which largely revolve around scale due to this full mesh of VXLAN tunnels. The following are some of the important challenges with such a design:

- Data centers are connected as one big fault domain, with a mesh of tunnels across DCs.

- The size of one DC directly impacts any connected DCs: since all tunnels are over the top, and across DCs, it is hard to connect a small DC to a larger (and growing) DC without causing direct impact to the smaller DC. This is because as the larger DC continues to grow, the mesh of tunnels to the smaller DC keeps increasing, thus impacting scale and complexity.

- With OTT DCI, there is no abstraction of the complexity between DCs, and the tunnel and next-hop scale becomes a limiting factor.

Integrated Interconnect with IP Transit

Integrated Interconnect, also referred to as *VXLAN stitching*, is defined in RFC 9014 and provides a one-box (hence the term *integrated*) solution to stitch between multiple domains, while considering the scalability and redundancy requirements of large-scale data centers. As just discussed, one of the biggest drawbacks of the OTT DCI design is scale, because VXLAN tunnels are formed across data centers, over the top of the existing transit/transport. This full mesh of VXLAN tunnels across data centers has large implications on scale.

Integrated Interconnect uses the concept of *gateways (GWs)* that act as the exit points from a data center, rooted in the following logic:

1. GWs terminate all VXLAN tunnels in their respective local data center and originate a new VXLAN tunnel to the remote data center GWs. This is implemented based on a simple routing concept: the next-hop address. VXLAN tunnels are built against the next-hop address advertised in EVPN routes. If this next-hop address were to be changed, the tunnel termination could also be changed, thus controlling where the tunnel terminates.

2. An *Integrated ESI (I-ESI)* is used for redundancy and load-balancing. This I-ESI is not an Ethernet Segment mapped to an actual Aggregated Ethernet or physical interface, as typically used with EVPN multihoming (ESI LAG). This is simply a logical ESI (mapped to a logical or virtual Ethernet Segment) that facilitates multiple GWs to exist via the multihoming logic extended by an Ethernet Segment and ESI.

This logic achieves a demarcation of VXLAN tunnels between data centers. All local leafs form a VXLAN tunnel to the local GWs, and not to other leafs in the remote DC, while the GWs of each DC form VXLAN tunnels with each other. Thus, in this way, a local DC does not get impacted by the growth of a connected DC, because regardless of how many new leafs are added in the remote DC, the local DC leafs will form VXLAN tunnels only to their local GWs (which will only be a few). This can be visualized as shown in Figure 11-11, where a leaf in DC1 forms a VXLAN tunnel to its local GW, this local GW forms a new VXLAN tunnel to the remote GW in DC2, and the GW in DC2 forms a VXLAN tunnel to its local leaf in DC2.

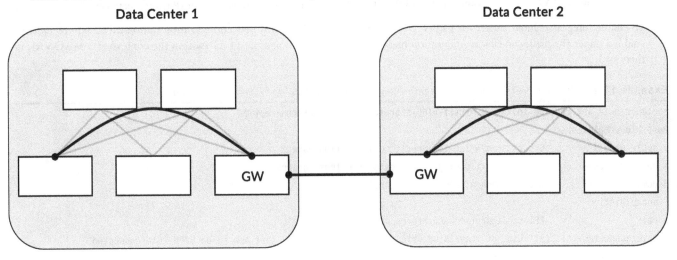

Figure 11-11 *VXLAN tunnels with Integrated Interconnect*

Integrated Interconnect allows for several design options, with different direct transit handoffs:

- Two or more VXLAN domains stitched together via an IP transit
- Two or more VXLAN domains stitched together via an MPLS transit
- A VXLAN domain that hands off to an IPVPN domain

This section explores the first design option, while a subsequent section covers two or more VXLAN domains stitched via an MPLS transit. A VXLAN domain to IPVPN domain design option is not covered in this book. The topology shown in Figure 11-12 is used for the remainder of this section.

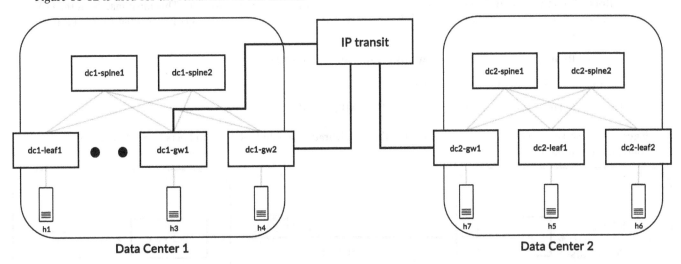

Figure 11-12 *Reference topology for two VXLAN domains stitched via an IP transit*

In this topology, DC1 has two GWs: dc1-gw1 and dc1-gw2. Not shown in the topology are two other leafs in DC1, dc1-leaf2 and dc1-leaf3, which form an ESI LAG pair, connected to host h2. The second DC, DC2, has just one GW, dc2-gw1. All GWs are connected to an IP transit that facilitates the two DCs to be stitched together via Integrated Interconnect.

Stitching Two Bridged Overlay Data Centers via IP Transit

There are several EVPN routes that can be stitched across a transit via Integrated Interconnect. This is enabled using a new configuration option called *interconnect* under the *protocol evpn* top-level configuration hierarchy. However, the placement of this configuration may vary, depending on what type of route needs to be stitched. In this subsection, both data centers have hosts in the same subnet, essentially constituting a bridged overlay fabric. Thus, this subsection focuses on extending a Layer 2 domain (EVPN Type-2 routes with an L2VNI) with Integrated Interconnect via an IP transit between DC1 and DC2.

To enable Integrated Interconnect for EVPN Type-2 routes with L2VNI, this new configuration option called *interconnect* is enabled under the *protocol evpn* configuration hierarchy, as shown in Example 11-12 (within the context of a MAC-VRF, in this case).

Example 11-12 *Interconnect options to configure Integrated Interconnect for Layer 2 extension*

```
root@dc2-gw1# set routing-instances macvrf-v100-1 protocols evpn interconnect ?
Possible completions:
+ apply-groups          Groups from which to inherit configuration data
+ apply-groups-except   Don't inherit configuration data from these groups
> domain-path-id        DCI VRF domain path id configuration
  encapsulation
> esi                   ESI configuration of interconnect
+ interconnected-vni-list  List of translated VNIs (1..16777214) or all, that are to be EVPN interconnected
> irb-symmetric-routing  Enable EVPN T-2 symmetric DCI routing
> route-distinguisher   Route distinguisher for this interconnect
+ vrf-export            Export policy for Interconnect
+ vrf-import            Import policy for Interconnect
> vrf-target            Interconnect target community configuration
```

The following must be mandatorily configured when enabling Integrated Interconnect on a GW:

- An I-ESI that defines the local data centers' Interconnect ESI. This I-ESI must be unique per data center, but it must match on GWs that belong to the same data center.

- A Route Target that controls import and export of routes into the interconnect domain. This must match on the GWs of all data centers being stitched together, but it must be different from the Route Target that is used for the local data center on the GW.

- A unique Route Distinguisher for the GW. This is the Interconnect RD.

- A list of VNIs that are allowed to be stitched.

- The encapsulation for the transit, which can be IP or MPLS, at this time.

Figure 11-13 shows a visual representation of what this configuration would look like, and acts as a reference for the configuration in both DC GWs.

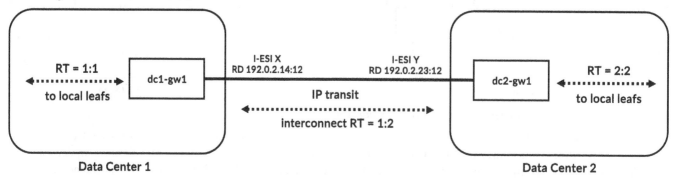

Figure 11-13 *Interconnect details for VXLAN stitching between DC1 and DC2*

Example 11-13 demonstrates how Integrated Interconnect is configured using the details shown in Figure 11-13, considering dc1-gw1 and dc2-gw1 as a reference.

Example 11-13 *Integrated Interconnect configuration on dc1-gw1 and dc2-gw1*

```
root@dc1-gw1# show routing-instances macvrf-v100-1
instance-type mac-vrf;
protocols {
    evpn {
        encapsulation vxlan;
        extended-vni-list 10100;
        interconnect {
            vrf-target target:1:2;
            route-distinguisher 192.0.2.14:12;
            esi {
                00:00:00:00:00:00:00:11:11:11;
                all-active;
            }
            interconnected-vni-list 10100;
        }
    }
}
vtep-source-interface lo0.0;
service-type vlan-based;
interface et-0/0/4.0;
route-distinguisher 192.0.2.14:100;
vrf-target target:1:1;
vlans {
    v100 {
        vlan-id 100;
        vxlan {
            vni 10100;
        }
    }
}

root@dc2-gw1# show routing-instances macvrf-v100-1
instance-type mac-vrf;
protocols {
    evpn {
        encapsulation vxlan;
        extended-vni-list 10100;
        interconnect {
            vrf-target target:1:2;
            route-distinguisher 192.0.2.23:12;
            esi {
                00:00:00:00:00:00:00:22:22:22;
                all-active;
            }
            interconnected-vni-list 10100;
```

```
            }
        }
    }
    vtep-source-interface lo0.0;
    service-type vlan-based;
    interface et-0/0/27.0;
    route-distinguisher 192.0.2.23:100;
    vrf-target target:2:2;
    vlans {
        v100 {
            vlan-id 100;
            vxlan {
                vni 10100;
            }
        }
    }
}
```

Functionally, when a GW receives and imports an EVPN route from a local leaf, it re-originates the route with the following principles:

- The next-hop address for the EVPN route is changed to self.

- The Route Distinguisher is changed to the interconnect Route Distinguisher.

- The Route Target is changed to the interconnect Route Target (all other Route Targets are stripped).

- The configured I-ESI is attached to the route.

Let's consider an example of host h1's MAC address, f0:4b:3a:b9:80:a7, learned on dc1-leaf1. The flow diagram in Figure 11-14 shows the exchange of EVPN routes when Integrated Interconnect is configured with the configuration in Example 11-13.

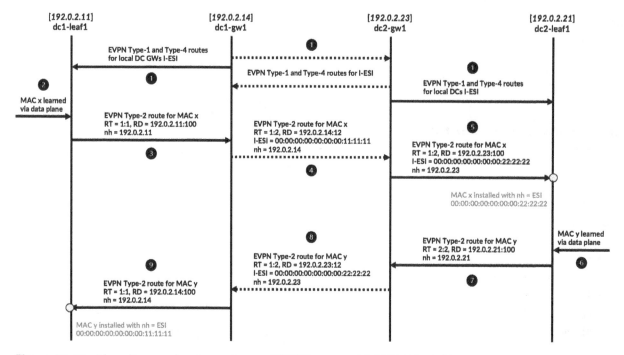

Figure 11-14 *Flow diagram showing exchange of EVPN routes with VXLAN stitching*

For the I-ESI that is used for load-balancing and redundancy across DC GWs, EVPN Type-1 and Type-4 routes are exchanged. As shown in Example 11-14, dc1-gw1 originates EVPN Type-1 and Type-4 routes for its configured I-ESI. This is advertised with the interconnect Route Distinguisher and Route Target toward the remote GW, and with the local DC Route Distinguisher and Route Target toward the local DC leafs. The AD per ESI route is a common EVPN Type-1 route that must be imported both by the local DC and the remote GW, and thus it includes both Route Targets.

Example 11-14 *EVPN Type-1 routes originated by dc1-gw1 for its I-ESI*

```
root@dc1-gw1> show route table bgp.evpn.0 match-prefix 1:*192.0.2.14:*

bgp.evpn.0: 63 destinations, 120 routes (63 active, 0 holddown, 0 hidden)
+ = Active Route, - = Last Active, * = Both

1:192.0.2.14:0::111111::FFFF:FFFF/192 AD/ESI
                   *[EVPN/170] 2d 01:38:11
                       Indirect
1:192.0.2.14:12::111111::0/192 AD/EVI
                   *[EVPN/170] 2d 01:38:12
                       Indirect


*snip*


root@dc1-gw1> show route table bgp.evpn.0 match-prefix 1:*192.0.2.14:* extensive

bgp.evpn.0: 87 destinations, 172 routes (87 active, 0 holddown, 0 hidden)
1:192.0.2.14:0::111111::FFFF:FFFF/192 AD/ESI (1 entry, 1 announced)
TSI:
Page 0 idx 0, (group overlay type External) Type 1 val 0x563393aab988 (adv_entry)
   Advertised metrics:
     Flags: Nexthop Change
     Nexthop: Self
     AS path: [65424] I
     Communities: target:1:1 target:1:2 encapsulation:vxlan(0x8) esi-label:0x0:all-active (label 0)
   Advertise: 00000003
Page 0 idx 1, (group overlay-dci type External) Type 1 val 0x563393aab950 (adv_entry)
   Advertised metrics:
     Flags: Nexthop Change
     Nexthop: Self
     AS path: [65424] I
     Communities: target:1:1 target:1:2 encapsulation:vxlan(0x8) esi-label:0x0:all-active (label 0)
   Advertise: 00000001
Path 1:192.0.2.14:0::111111::FFFF:FFFF
Vector len 4.  Val: 0 1
        *EVPN    Preference: 170
                 Next hop type: Indirect, Next hop index: 0
                 Address: 0x5633923339dc
                 Next-hop reference count: 46
                 Kernel Table Id: 0
                 Protocol next hop: 192.0.2.14
```

```
                    Indirect next hop: (nil) - INH Session ID: 0
                    State: <Secondary Active Int Ext>
                    Age: 2d 1:49:01
                    Validation State: unverified
                    Task: __default_evpn__-evpn
                    Announcement bits (1): 1-BGP_RT_Background
                    AS path: I
                    Communities: target:1:1 target:1:2 encapsulation:vxlan(0x8) esi-label:0x0:all-active (label 0)
                    Primary Routing Table: __default_evpn__.evpn.0
                    Thread: junos-main


1:192.0.2.14:12::111111::0/192 AD/EVI (1 entry, 1 announced)
TSI:
Page 0 idx 0, (group overlay type External) Type 1 val 0x563393aaacd8 (adv_entry)
   Advertised metrics:
     Flags: Nexthop Change
     Nexthop: Self
     AS path: [65424] I
     Communities: target:1:2 encapsulation:vxlan(0x8)
   Advertise: 00000003
Page 0 idx 1, (group overlay-dci type External) Type 1 val 0x563393aa8428 (adv_entry)
   Advertised metrics:
     Flags: Nexthop Change
     Nexthop: Self
     AS path: [65424] I
     Communities: target:1:2 encapsulation:vxlan(0x8)
   Advertise: 00000001
Path 1:192.0.2.14:12::111111::0
Vector len 4.   Val: 0 1
          *EVPN    Preference: 170
                    Next hop type: Indirect, Next hop index: 0
                    Address: 0x5633923339dc
                    Next-hop reference count: 46
                    Kernel Table Id: 0
                    Protocol next hop: 192.0.2.14
                    Indirect next hop: (nil) - INH Session ID: 0
                    State: <Secondary Active Int Ext>
                    Age: 2d 1:49:02
                    Validation State: unverified
                    Task: macvrf-v100-1-evpn
                    Announcement bits (1): 1-BGP_RT_Background
                    AS path: I
                    Communities: target:1:2 encapsulation:vxlan(0x8)
                    Route Label: 10100
                    Primary Routing Table: macvrf-v100-1.evpn.0
                    Thread: junos-main


1:192.0.2.14:100::111111::0/192 AD/EVI (1 entry, 1 announced)
TSI:
```

```
Page 0 idx 0, (group overlay type External) Type 1 val 0x563393aaaf78 (adv_entry)
   Advertised metrics:
     Flags: Nexthop Change
     Nexthop: Self
     AS path: [65424] I
     Communities: target:1:1 encapsulation:vxlan(0x8)
    Advertise: 00000003
Page 0 idx 1, (group overlay-dci type External) Type 1 val 0x563393aa74a0 (adv_entry)
   Advertised metrics:
     Flags: Nexthop Change
     Nexthop: Self
     AS path: [65424] I
     Communities: target:1:1 encapsulation:vxlan(0x8)
    Advertise: 00000001
Path 1:192.0.2.14:100::111111::0
Vector len 4.  Val: 0 1
        *EVPN    Preference: 170
                 Next hop type: Indirect, Next hop index: 0
                 Address: 0x5633923339dc
                 Next-hop reference count: 46
                 Kernel Table Id: 0
                 Protocol next hop: 192.0.2.14
                 Indirect next hop: (nil) - INH Session ID: 0
                 State: <Secondary Active Int Ext>
                 Age: 2d 1:49:02
                 Validation State: unverified
                 Task: macvrf-v100-1-evpn
                 Announcement bits (1): 1-BGP_RT_Background
                 AS path: I
                 Communities: target:1:1 encapsulation:vxlan(0x8)
                 Route Label: 10100
                 Primary Routing Table: macvrf-v100-1.evpn.0
                 Thread: junos-main
```

In the same way, dc2-gw1 also originates EVPN Type-1 routes for its configured I-ESI, and this is sent to the remote GW and the local leafs, respectively, as shown in Example 11-15.

Example 11-15 *EVPN Type-1 routes originated by dc2-gw1 for its I-ESI*

```
root@dc2-gw1> show route table bgp.evpn.0 match-prefix 1:192.0.2.23:* extensive

bgp.evpn.0: 71 destinations, 77 routes (71 active, 0 holddown, 0 hidden)
1:192.0.2.23:0::222222::FFFF:FFFF/192 AD/ESI (1 entry, 1 announced)
TSI:
Page 0 idx 0, (group overlay type External) Type 1 val 0x5589f42e5848 (adv_entry)
   Advertised metrics:
     Flags: Nexthop Change
     Nexthop: Self
     AS path: [65433] I
```

```
         Communities: target:1:2 target:2:2 encapsulation:vxlan(0x8) esi-label:0x0:all-active (label 0)
      Advertise: 00000003
Page 0 idx 1, (group overlay-dci type External) Type 1 val 0x5589f42e5810 (adv_entry)
   Advertised metrics:
      Flags: Nexthop Change
      Nexthop: Self
      AS path: [65433] I
      Communities: target:1:2 target:2:2 encapsulation:vxlan(0x8) esi-label:0x0:all-active (label 0)
      Advertise: 00000001
Path 1:192.0.2.23:0::222222::FFFF:FFFF
Vector len 4.  Val: 0 1
         *EVPN    Preference: 170
                  Next hop type: Indirect, Next hop index: 0
                  Address: 0x5589f2b339dc
                  Next-hop reference count: 34
                  Kernel Table Id: 0
                  Protocol next hop: 192.0.2.23
                  Indirect next hop: (nil) - INH Session ID: 0
                  State: <Secondary Active Int Ext>
                  Age: 2d 2:04:09
                  Validation State: unverified
                  Task: __default_evpn__-evpn
                  Announcement bits (1): 1-BGP_RT_Background
                  AS path: I
                  Communities: target:1:2 target:2:2 encapsulation:vxlan(0x8) esi-label:0x0:all-active (label 0)
                  Primary Routing Table: __default_evpn__.evpn.0
                  Thread: junos-main


1:192.0.2.23:12::222222::0/192 AD/EVI (1 entry, 1 announced)
TSI:
Page 0 idx 0, (group overlay type External) Type 1 val 0x5589f42e4850 (adv_entry)
   Advertised metrics:
      Flags: Nexthop Change
      Nexthop: Self
      AS path: [65433] I
      Communities: target:1:2 encapsulation:vxlan(0x8)
      Advertise: 00000003
Page 0 idx 1, (group overlay-dci type External) Type 1 val 0x5589f42e4818 (adv_entry)
   Advertised metrics:
      Flags: Nexthop Change
      Nexthop: Self
      AS path: [65433] I
      Communities: target:1:2 encapsulation:vxlan(0x8)
      Advertise: 00000001
Path 1:192.0.2.23:12::222222::0
Vector len 4.  Val: 0 1
         *EVPN    Preference: 170
```

```
                Next hop type: Indirect, Next hop index: 0
                Address: 0x5589f2b339dc
                Next-hop reference count: 34
                Kernel Table Id: 0
                Protocol next hop: 192.0.2.23
                Indirect next hop: (nil) - INH Session ID: 0
                State: <Secondary Active Int Ext>
                Age: 2d 2:04:10
                Validation State: unverified
                Task: macvrf-v100-1-evpn
                Announcement bits (1): 1-BGP_RT_Background
                AS path: I
                Communities: target:1:2 encapsulation:vxlan(0x8)
                Route Label: 10100
                Primary Routing Table: macvrf-v100-1.evpn.0
                Thread: junos-main

1:192.0.2.23:100::222222::0/192 AD/EVI (1 entry, 1 announced)
TSI:
Page 0 idx 0, (group overlay type External) Type 1 val 0x5589f42e47e0 (adv_entry)
   Advertised metrics:
     Flags: Nexthop Change
     Nexthop: Self
     AS path: [65433] I
     Communities: target:2:2 encapsulation:vxlan(0x8)
   Advertise: 00000003
Page 0 idx 1, (group overlay-dci type External) Type 1 val 0x5589f42e47a8 (adv_entry)
   Advertised metrics:
     Flags: Nexthop Change
     Nexthop: Self
     AS path: [65433] I
     Communities: target:2:2 encapsulation:vxlan(0x8)
   Advertise: 00000001
Path 1:192.0.2.23:100::222222::0
Vector len 4.  Val: 0 1
        *EVPN    Preference: 170
                Next hop type: Indirect, Next hop index: 0
                Address: 0x5589f2b339dc
                Next-hop reference count: 34
                Kernel Table Id: 0
                Protocol next hop: 192.0.2.23
                Indirect next hop: (nil) - INH Session ID: 0
                State: <Secondary Active Int Ext>
                Age: 2d 2:04:10
                Validation State: unverified
                Task: macvrf-v100-1-evpn
                Announcement bits (1): 1-BGP_RT_Background
                AS path: I
```

```
                    Communities: target:2:2 encapsulation:vxlan(0x8)
                    Route Label: 10100
                    Primary Routing Table: macvrf-v100-1.evpn.0
                    Thread: junos-main
```

These routes are imported into the respective EVPN tables for the MAC-VRFs, and the ESI is resolved to the GW VTEPs. As shown in Example 11-16, dc1-leaf1 imports the EVPN Type-1 routes into its MAC-VRF EVPN table and resolves the I-ESI to 192.0.2.14 and 192.0.2.15, which are the VTEP addresses for dc1-gw1 and dc1-gw2, respectively.

Example 11-16   *EVPN Type-1 routes, originated by dc1-gw1 for its I-ESI, imported by dc1-leaf1*

```
root@dc1-leaf1> show route table macvrf-v100-1.evpn.0 match-prefix 1:192.0.2.14*

macvrf-v100-1.evpn.0: 27 destinations, 51 routes (27 active, 0 holddown, 0 hidden)
+ = Active Route, - = Last Active, * = Both

1:192.0.2.14:0::111111::FFFF:FFFF/192 AD/ESI
                   *[BGP/170] 2d 02:06:36, localpref 100, from 192.0.2.102
                      AS path: 65500 65424 I, validation-state: unverified
                   >  to 198.51.100.1 via et-0/0/48.0
                      to 198.51.100.3 via et-0/0/50.0
                    [BGP/170] 2d 02:06:36, localpref 100, from 192.0.2.101
                      AS path: 65500 65424 I, validation-state: unverified
                   >  to 198.51.100.1 via et-0/0/48.0
                      to 198.51.100.3 via et-0/0/50.0
1:192.0.2.14:100::111111::0/192 AD/EVI
                   *[BGP/170] 2d 02:06:37, localpref 100, from 192.0.2.102
                      AS path: 65500 65424 I, validation-state: unverified
                   >  to 198.51.100.1 via et-0/0/48.0, Push 631
                      to 198.51.100.3 via et-0/0/50.0, Push 631
                    [BGP/170] 2d 02:06:37, localpref 100, from 192.0.2.101
                      AS path: 65500 65424 I, validation-state: unverified
                   >  to 198.51.100.1 via et-0/0/48.0, Push 631
                      to 198.51.100.3 via et-0/0/50.0, Push 631


root@dc1-leaf1> show mac-vrf forwarding vxlan-tunnel-end-point esi esi-identifier 00:00:00:00:00:00:11:11:11
ESI                              RTT               VLNBH INH   ESI-IFL   LOC-IFL   #RVTEPs
00:00:00:00:00:00:11:11:11 macvrf-v100-1          1692  524290 esi.1692           2    Aliasing
    RVTEP-IP          RVTEP-IFL     VENH    MASK-ID  FLAGS     MAC-COUNT
    192.0.2.14        vtep-9.32774  1760    1        2         2
    192.0.2.15        vtep-9.32775  1761    0        2         2
```

When a MAC address is learned on any of the local leafs, it is advertised like any other MAC address (as an EVPN Type-2 route) to other leafs in the fabric, including the local DC GWs. The GWs import this EVPN Type-2 route and re-originate the route into the DCI, with the interconnect Route Distinguisher and Route Target. As shown in Example 11-17, host h1's MAC address is learned locally on dc1-leaf1 over interface et-0/0/49.0 and advertised as an EVPN Type-2 route with the local DC Route Target, which is 1:1.

Example 11-17 EVPN Type-2, originated by dc1-leaf1, for host h1's address

```
root@dc1-leaf1> show mac-vrf forwarding mac-table f0:4b:3a:b9:80:a7

MAC flags (S - static MAC, D - dynamic MAC, L - locally learned, P - Persistent static
          SE - statistics enabled, NM - non configured MAC, R - remote PE MAC, O - ovsdb MAC)


Ethernet switching table : 5 entries, 5 learned
Routing instance : macvrf-v100-1
   Vlan            MAC                MAC      GBP    Logical           SVLBNH/      Active
   name            address            flags    tag    interface         VENH Index   source
   v100            f0:4b:3a:b9:80:a7  D               et-0/0/49.0


root@dc1-leaf1> show route table bgp.evpn.0 match-prefix 2:*192.0.2.11*f0:4b:3a:b9:80:a7*


bgp.evpn.0: 71 destinations, 139 routes (71 active, 0 holddown, 0 hidden)
+ = Active Route, - = Last Active, * = Both


2:192.0.2.11:100::0::f0:4b:3a:b9:80:a7/304 MAC/IP
                   *[EVPN/170] 1w4d 19:52:39
                       Indirect
2:192.0.2.11:100::0::f0:4b:3a:b9:80:a7::10.100.100.1/304 MAC/IP
                   *[EVPN/170] 1w4d 13:51:16
                       Indirect


root@dc1-leaf1> show route table bgp.evpn.0 match-prefix 2:*192.0.2.11*f0:4b:3a:b9:80:a7* extensive


bgp.evpn.0: 71 destinations, 139 routes (71 active, 0 holddown, 0 hidden)
2:192.0.2.11:100::0::f0:4b:3a:b9:80:a7/304 MAC/IP (1 entry, 1 announced)
TSI:
Page 0 idx 0, (group overlay type External) Type 1 val 0xacd7630 (adv_entry)
   Advertised metrics:
     Flags: Nexthop Change
     Nexthop: Self
     AS path: [65421] I
     Communities: target:1:1 encapsulation:vxlan(0x8)
   Advertise: 00000003
Path 2:192.0.2.11:100::0::f0:4b:3a:b9:80:a7
Vector len 4.   Val: 0
        *EVPN   Preference: 170
                Next hop type: Indirect, Next hop index: 0
                Address: 0x8c067f4
                Next-hop reference count: 8, key opaque handle: 0x0, non-key opaque handle: 0x0
                Protocol next hop: 192.0.2.11
                Indirect next hop: 0x0 - INH Session ID: 0
                State: <Secondary Active Int Ext>
                Age: 1w4d 19:52:43
```

```
                  Validation State: unverified
                  Task: macvrf-v100-1-evpn
                  Announcement bits (1): 1-BGP_RT_Background
                  AS path: I
                  Communities: target:1:1 encapsulation:vxlan(0x8)
                  Route Label: 10100
                  ESI: 00:00:00:00:00:00:00:00:00:00
                  Primary Routing Table: macvrf-v100-1.evpn.0
                  Thread: junos-main


*snip*
```

Consider one of the GWs in DC1 (dc1-gw1): it receives and imports this EVPN Type-2 route into the EVPN table for the corresponding MAC-VRF and eventually creates an entry in the EVPN database for this MAC address, as shown in Example 11-18.

Example 11-18   *EVPN Type-2, originated by dc1-leaf1, for host h1's address is imported on dc1-gw1*

```
root@dc1-gw1> show route table macvrf-v100-1.evpn.0 match-prefix 2:*192.0.2.11*f0:4b:3a:b9:80:a7*

macvrf-v100-1.evpn.0: 51 destinations, 105 routes (51 active, 0 holddown, 0 hidden)
+ = Active Route, - = Last Active, * = Both


2:192.0.2.11:100::0::f0:4b:3a:b9:80:a7/304 MAC/IP
                  *[BGP/170] 1w4d 13:53:52, localpref 100, from 192.0.2.101
                     AS path: 65500 65421 I, validation-state: unverified
                   > to 198.51.100.13 via et-0/0/0.0, Push 631
                     to 198.51.100.15 via et-0/0/2.0, Push 631
                   [BGP/170] 1w4d 13:53:52, localpref 100, from 192.0.2.102
                     AS path: 65500 65421 I, validation-state: unverified
                   > to 198.51.100.13 via et-0/0/0.0, Push 631
                     to 198.51.100.15 via et-0/0/2.0, Push 631
2:192.0.2.11:100::0::f0:4b:3a:b9:80:a7::10.100.100.1/304 MAC/IP
                  *[BGP/170] 1w4d 13:53:05, localpref 100, from 192.0.2.101
                     AS path: 65500 65421 I, validation-state: unverified
                   > to 198.51.100.13 via et-0/0/0.0, Push 631
                     to 198.51.100.15 via et-0/0/2.0, Push 631
                   [BGP/170] 1w4d 13:53:05, localpref 100, from 192.0.2.102
                     AS path: 65500 65421 I, validation-state: unverified
                   > to 198.51.100.13 via et-0/0/0.0, Push 631
                     to 198.51.100.15 via et-0/0/2.0, Push 631


root@dc1-gw1> show evpn database mac-address f0:4b:3a:b9:80:a7
Instance: macvrf-v100-1
VLAN  DomainId  MAC address       Active source         Timestamp       IP address
   10100        f0:4b:3a:b9:80:a7 192.0.2.11            Aug 18 10:47:52  10.100.100.1
```

From the EVPN table, a new DCI route is created for this MAC address, as shown in Example 11-19, using the **show evpn database mac-address** [*mac-address*] **extensive** operational mode command. This DCI route is inserted back into the EVPN table for the MAC-VRF and pulled into the *bgp.evpn.0* table to be advertised out to all BGP EVPN neighbors. For this DCI route, the Route Distinguisher is the interconnect Route Distinguisher now.

Example 11-19 *DCI route created on dc1-gw1*

```
root@dc1-gw1> show evpn database mac-address f0:4b:3a:b9:80:a7 extensive
Instance: macvrf-v100-1

VN Identifier: 10100, MAC address: f0:4b:3a:b9:80:a7
  State: 0x0
  Source: 192.0.2.11, Rank: 1, Status: Active
    Mobility sequence number: 0 (minimum origin address 192.0.2.11)
    Timestamp: Aug 18 10:47:52.993632 (0x64dfaec8)
    State: <Remote-To-Local-Adv-Done>
    MAC advertisement route status: Not created (no local state present)
    Interconn advertisement route status: DCI route created
    IP address: 10.100.100.1
      Interconn advertisement route status: DCI route created
    History db: <No entries>


root@dc1-gw1> show route table macvrf-v100-1.evpn.0 match-prefix 2:*192.0.2.14*f0:4b:3a:b9:80:a7*

macvrf-v100-1.evpn.0: 57 destinations, 116 routes (57 active, 0 holddown, 0 hidden)
+ = Active Route, - = Last Active, * = Both

2:192.0.2.14:12::0::f0:4b:3a:b9:80:a7/304 MAC/IP
                  *[EVPN/170] 3d 22:33:54
                      Indirect
2:192.0.2.14:12::0::f0:4b:3a:b9:80:a7::10.100.100.1/304 MAC/IP
                  *[EVPN/170] 3d 22:33:54
                      Indirect


root@dc1-gw1> show route table bgp.evpn.0 match-prefix 2:*192.0.2.14*f0:4b:3a:b9:80:a7*

bgp.evpn.0: 79 destinations, 160 routes (79 active, 0 holddown, 0 hidden)
+ = Active Route, - = Last Active, * = Both

2:192.0.2.14:12::0::f0:4b:3a:b9:80:a7/304 MAC/IP
                  *[EVPN/170] 3d 22:34:16
                      Indirect
2:192.0.2.14:12::0::f0:4b:3a:b9:80:a7::10.100.100.1/304 MAC/IP
                  *[EVPN/170] 3d 22:34:16
                      Indirect
```

When the remote DC GW (dc2-gw1) receives this route, it imports the route (since the interconnect Route Targets match) and then re-originates it into its own local DC with the locally configured I-ESI and the corresponding Route Distinguisher and Route Target for the local DC, as shown in Figure 11-14. This is confirmed in Example 11-20.

Example 11-20   *Remote GW dc2-gw1 re-originating EVPN Type-2 route received from DC1's GWs*

```
root@dc2-gw1> show route table bgp.evpn.0 match-prefix 2:*192.0.2.23*f0:4b:3a:b9:80:a7*

bgp.evpn.0: 87 destinations, 93 routes (87 active, 0 holddown, 0 hidden)
+ = Active Route, - = Last Active, * = Both

2:192.0.2.23:100::0::f0:4b:3a:b9:80:a7/304 MAC/IP
                    *[EVPN/170] 3d 07:43:36
                          Indirect
2:192.0.2.23:100::0::f0:4b:3a:b9:80:a7::10.100.100.1/304 MAC/IP
                    *[EVPN/170] 3d 07:43:36
                          Indirect


root@dc2-gw1> show route table bgp.evpn.0 match-prefix 2:*192.0.2.23*f0:4b:3a:b9:80:a7* extensive

bgp.evpn.0: 87 destinations, 93 routes (87 active, 0 holddown, 0 hidden)
2:192.0.2.23:100::0::f0:4b:3a:b9:80:a7/304 MAC/IP (1 entry, 1 announced)
TSI:
Page 0 idx 0, (group overlay type External) Type 1 val 0x5589f42e4230 (adv_entry)
   Advertised metrics:
     Flags: Nexthop Change
     Nexthop: Self
     AS path: [65433] I
     Communities: target:2:2 encapsulation:vxlan(0x8)
   Advertise: 00000003
Page 0 idx 1, (group overlay-dci type External) Type 1 val 0x5589f42e4150 (adv_entry)
   Advertised metrics:
     Flags: Nexthop Change
     Nexthop: Self
     AS path: [65433] I
     Communities: target:2:2 encapsulation:vxlan(0x8)
   Advertise: 00000001
Path 2:192.0.2.23:100::0::f0:4b:3a:b9:80:a7
Vector len 4.  Val: 0 1
        *EVPN   Preference: 170
                Next hop type: Indirect, Next hop index: 0
                Address: 0x5589f2b339dc
                Next-hop reference count: 46
                Kernel Table Id: 0
                Protocol next hop: 192.0.2.23
                Indirect next hop: (nil) - INH Session ID: 0
                State: <Secondary Active Int Ext>
                Age: 3d 7:43:44
                Validation State: unverified
                Task: macvrf-v100-1-evpn
                Announcement bits (1): 1-BGP_RT_Background
                AS path: I
```

```
Communities: target:2:2 encapsulation:vlan(0x0)
Route Label: 10100
ESI: 00:00:00:00:00:00:00:22:22:22
Primary Routing Table: macvrf-v100-1.evpn.0
Thread: junos-main
```

snip

Eventually, all remote leafs receive this route as well: considering dc2-leaf1 as an example, it imports the route from the BGP EVPN table into the MAC-VRF EVPN table and creates an entry in the EVPN database for this MAC address. From here, an update is sent to L2ALD and L2ALM and the MAC address is installed in hardware, as shown in Example 11-21.

Example 11-21 *DC2 leaf dc2-leaf1 installing host h1's address on receiving an EVPN Type-2 route for it*

```
root@dc2-leaf1> show route table bgp.evpn.0 match-prefix 2:*192.0.2.23*f0:4b:3a:b9:80:a7*

bgp.evpn.0: 87 destinations, 171 routes (87 active, 0 holddown, 0 hidden)
+ = Active Route, - = Last Active, * = Both


2:192.0.2.23:100::0::f0:4b:3a:b9:80:a7/304 MAC/IP
                *[BGP/170] 3d 07:48:20, localpref 100, from 192.0.2.201
                  AS path: 65501 65433 I, validation-state: unverified
                  to 198.51.100.101 via et-0/0/54.0, Push 631
                > to 198.51.100.103 via et-0/0/50.0, Push 631
                 [BGP/170] 3d 07:48:19, localpref 100, from 192.0.2.202
                  AS path: 65501 65433 I, validation-state: unverified
                  to 198.51.100.101 via et-0/0/54.0, Push 631
                > to 198.51.100.103 via et-0/0/50.0, Push 631
2:192.0.2.23:100::0::f0:4b:3a:b9:80:a7::10.100.100.1/304 MAC/IP
                *[BGP/170] 3d 07:48:20, localpref 100, from 192.0.2.201
                  AS path: 65501 65433 I, validation-state: unverified
                  to 198.51.100.101 via et-0/0/54.0, Push 631
                > to 198.51.100.103 via et-0/0/50.0, Push 631
                 [BGP/170] 3d 07:48:19, localpref 100, from 192.0.2.202
                  AS path: 65501 65433 I, validation-state: unverified
                  to 198.51.100.101 via et-0/0/54.0, Push 631
                > to 198.51.100.103 via et-0/0/50.0, Push 631


{master:0}
root@dc2-leaf1> show mac-vrf forwarding mac-table f0:4b:3a:b9:80:a7


MAC flags (S - static MAC, D - dynamic MAC, L - locally learned, P - Persistent static
          SE - statistics enabled, NM - non configured MAC, R - remote PE MAC, O - ovsdb MAC)


Ethernet switching table : 7 entries, 7 learned
Routing instance : macvrf-v100-1
   Vlan         MAC                 MAC      GBP    Logical        SVLBNH/      Active
   name         address             flags    tag    interface      VENH Index   source
   v100         f0:4b:3a:b9:80:a7   DR              esi.1695       1693
00:00:00:00:00:00:00:22:22:22
```

With an understanding of how control plane information propagates between DC GWs and local/remote leafs with Integrated Interconnect configured, let's consider how the packets flow in the data plane, using an example of host h1 communicating with h5. Since host h1 and h5 are in the same subnet, h1 attempts to ARP for h5's IP address directly. With ARP suppression and proxy ARP enabled on dc1-leaf1, it can respond to the incoming ARP request without having to flood it into the fabric, using its MAC-IP table, as visualized in Figure 11-15.

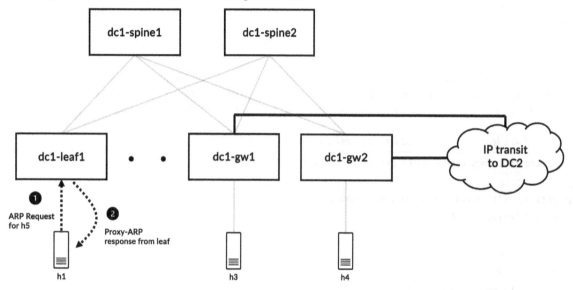

Figure 11-15   *Proxy ARP response from dc1-leaf1 for an ARP request for host h5 (in DC2)*

Host h1 can send an IP packet to h5 once the IP address is resolved via the ARP process. In this case, the IP packet is generated using the **ping** utility on the host (with an ICMP request payload). When dc1-leaf1 receives this packet, it does a lookup in its MAC table and sends the packet to one of the DC GWs since the MAC address is associated to the I-ESI for this DC, and the I-ESI resolves to dc1-gw1 and dc1-gw2, as shown in Example 11-22.

Example 11-22   *MAC lookup for h5's address and resolution of I-ESI into VTEP addresses on dc1-leaf1*

```
root@dc1-leaf1> show mac-vrf forwarding mac-table f0:4b:3a:b9:80:ff


MAC flags (S - static MAC, D - dynamic MAC, L - locally learned, P - Persistent static
          SE - statistics enabled, NM - non configured MAC, R - remote PE MAC, O - ovsdb MAC)


Ethernet switching table : 4 entries, 4 learned
Routing instance : macvrf-v100-1
    Vlan              MAC             MAC    GBP   Logical            SVLBNH/     Active
    name              address         flags  tag   interface          VENH Index  source
    v100              f0:4b:3a:b9:80:ff   DR           esi.1692            1695
00:00:00:00:00:00:00:11:11:11


root@dc1-leaf1> show mac-vrf forwarding vxlan-tunnel-end-point esi esi-identifier 00:00:00:00:00:00:00:11:11:11
ESI                      RTT                    VLNBH INH   ESI-IFL   LOC-IFL   #RVTEPs
00:00:00:00:00:00:00:11:11:11 macvrf-v100-1        1692  524290  esi.1692            2     Aliasing
    RVTEP-IP          RVTEP-IFL      VENH   MASK-ID  FLAGS      MAC-COUNT
    192.0.2.15        vtep-9.32772   1693   1        2          2
    192.0.2.14        vtep-9.32774   1760   0        2          0
```

The packet is encapsulated with VXLAN headers with the L2VNI (10100) and sent to 192.0.2.14 (which is dc1-gw1), since the flow has to be load-balanced to one of the GWs in the overlay. This can be visualized as shown in Figure 11-16.

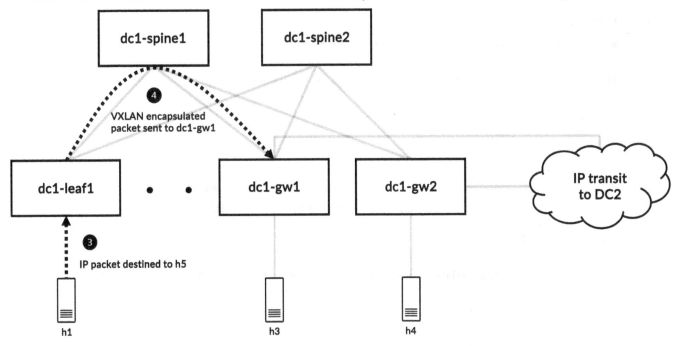

Figure 11-16   *VXLAN-encapsulated packet sent to dc1-gw1 to exit toward DC2*

The packet capture shown in Figure 11-17 confirms that the outer source IP address is 192.0.2.11 (dc1-leaf1) and the outer destination IP address is 192.0.2.14 (dc1-gw1).

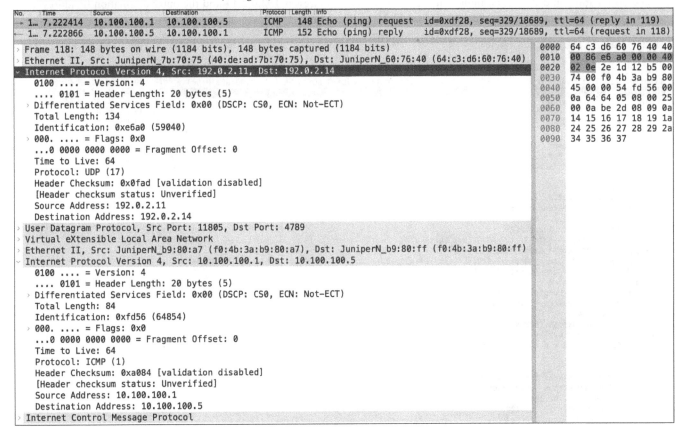

Figure 11-17   *Packet capture of VXLAN-encapsulated packet as it is sent from dc1-leaf1 to dc1-gw1*

When dc1-gw1 receives this packet, it decapsulates the outer header and does a MAC lookup on the inner destination MAC address, which points to the I-ESI of the remote data center, resolving to dc2-gw1, as shown in Example 11-23.

Example 11-23 *MAC lookup for h5's address on dc1-gw1*

```
root@dc1-gw1> show mac-vrf forwarding mac-table f0:4b:3a:b9:80:ff


MAC flags (S - static MAC, D - dynamic MAC, L - locally learned, P - Persistent static
          SE - statistics enabled, NM - non configured MAC, R - remote PE MAC, O - ovsdb MAC,
          B - Blocked MAC)


Ethernet switching table : 5 entries, 5 learned
Routing instance : macvrf-v100-1
  Vlan            MAC               MAC     GBP   Logical            SVLBNH/       Active
  name            address           flags   tag   interface          VENH Index   source
  v100            f0:4b:3a:b9:80:ff DR            esi.83144
00:00:00:00:00:00:00:22:22:22


root@dc1-gw1> show mac-vrf forwarding vxlan-tunnel-end-point esi esi-identifier 00:00:00:00:00:00:22:22:22
ESI                               RTT                    VLNBH INH   ESI-IFL    LOC-IFL  #RVTEPs
00:00:00:00:00:00:22:22:22 macvrf-v100-1               83144 83146  esi.83144           1    Aliasing
    RVTEP-IP        RVTEP-IFL       VENH    MASK-ID  FLAGS       MAC-COUNT
    192.0.2.23      vtep-55.32774  83137   0        18          2
```

This GW will re-encapsulate the packet with VXLAN headers, with the VXLAN tunnel now originating from dc1-gw1 and terminating on dc2-gw2, meaning that the outer source IP address is 192.0.2.14 and the outer destination IP address is 192.0.2.23. The packet capture shown in Figure 11-18 confirms this.

```
No.  Time       Source         Destination     Protocol  Length  Info
- 12 5.010198   10.100.100.1   10.100.100.5    ICMP      148  Echo (ping) request   id=0xdf28, seq=329/18689, ttl=64 (reply in 13)
← 13 5.010574   10.100.100.5   10.100.100.1    ICMP      152  Echo (ping) reply     id=0xdf28, seq=329/18689, ttl=64 (request in 12)

> Frame 12: 148 bytes on wire (1184 bits), 148 bytes captured (1184 bits)              0000  50 c7 09 a6 f0 5e d0
> Ethernet II, Src: JuniperN_0b:3f:15 (d0:dd:49:0b:3f:15), Dst: JuniperN_a6:f0:5e (50:c7:09:a6:f0:5e)   0010  00 86 00 00 00 00 3f
v Internet Protocol Version 4, Src: 192.0.2.14, Dst: 192.0.2.23                        0020  02 17 ce 52 12 b5 00
   0100 .... = Version: 4                                                              0030  74 00 f0 4b 3a b9 80
   .... 0101 = Header Length: 20 bytes (5)                                             0040  45 00 00 54 fd 56 00
 > Differentiated Services Field: 0x00 (DSCP: CS0, ECN: Not-ECT)                       0050  0a 64 64 05 08 00 25
   Total Length: 134                                                                   0060  00 0a be 2d 08 09 0a
   Identification: 0x0000 (0)                                                          0070  14 15 16 17 18 19 1a
 > 000. .... = Flags: 0x0                                                              0080  24 25 26 27 28 29 2a
   ...0 0000 0000 0000 = Fragment Offset: 0                                            0090  34 35 36 37
   Time to Live: 63
   Protocol: UDP (17)
   Header Checksum: 0xf741 [validation disabled]
   [Header checksum status: Unverified]
   Source Address: 192.0.2.14
   Destination Address: 192.0.2.23
> User Datagram Protocol, Src Port: 52818, Dst Port: 4789
> Virtual eXtensible Local Area Network
> Ethernet II, Src: JuniperN_b9:80:a7 (f0:4b:3a:b9:80:a7), Dst: JuniperN_b9:80:ff (f0:4b:3a:b9:80:ff)
v Internet Protocol Version 4, Src: 10.100.100.1, Dst: 10.100.100.5
   0100 .... = Version: 4
   .... 0101 = Header Length: 20 bytes (5)
 > Differentiated Services Field: 0x00 (DSCP: CS0, ECN: Not-ECT)
   Total Length: 84
   Identification: 0xfd56 (64854)
 > 000. .... = Flags: 0x0
   ...0 0000 0000 0000 = Fragment Offset: 0
   Time to Live: 64
   Protocol: ICMP (1)
   Header Checksum: 0xa084 [validation disabled]
   [Header checksum status: Unverified]
   Source Address: 10.100.100.1
   Destination Address: 10.100.100.5
> Internet Control Message Protocol
```

Figure 11-18 *Packet capture of VXLAN-encapsulated packet as it is sent from dc1-gw1 to dc2-gw1*

The IP transit network simply forwards the packet toward dc2-gw1 based on the outer destination IP address. This process can be visualized as shown in Figure 11-19.

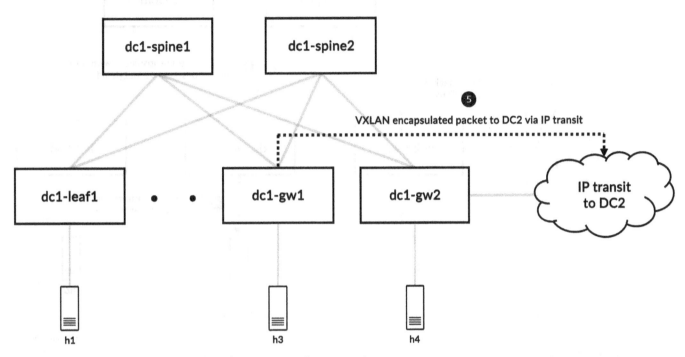

Figure 11-19   *VXLAN-encapsulated packet sent toward DC2 via the IP transit*

When DC2's GW (dc2-gw1) receives this packet, it decapsulates the packet and does a lookup on the destination MAC address in the inner Ethernet header, which results in another re-encapsulation with VXLAN headers, since the destination is behind dc2-leaf1 (192.0.2.21), as shown in Example 11-24.

Example 11-24   *MAC lookup for h5's address on dc2-gw1*

```
root@dc2-gw1> show mac-vrf forwarding mac-table f0:4b:3a:b9:80:ff

MAC flags (S - static MAC, D - dynamic MAC, L - locally learned, P - Persistent static
          SE - statistics enabled, NM - non configured MAC, R - remote PE MAC, O - ovsdb MAC,
          B - Blocked MAC)

Ethernet switching table : 5 entries, 5 learned
Routing instance : macvrf-v100-1
    Vlan            MAC                 MAC     GBP   Logical           SVLBNH/      Active
    name            address             flags   tag   interface         VENH Index   source
    v100            f0:4b:3a:b9:80:ff   DR            vtep-51.32770                  192.0.2.21
```

The re-encapsulated packet is sent toward dc2-leaf1, where it is decapsulated, and the inner IP packet is sent to the host, h5. This process is visualized in Figure 11-20.

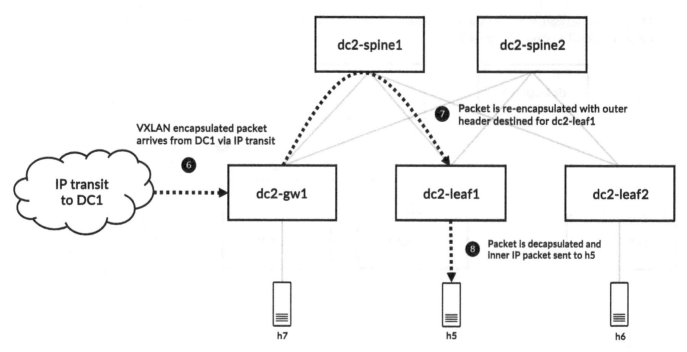

Figure 11-20   *VXLAN-encapsulated packet received from IP transit sent toward dc2-leaf1 and host h5*

The packet capture shown in Figure 11-21 confirms that the outer source IP address is 192.0.2.23 (dc2-gw1) and the outer destination IP address is 192.0.2.21 (dc2-leaf1).

```
No.   Time       Source          Destination     Protocol  Length  Info
► 12  0.686350   10.100.100.1    10.100.100.5    ICMP      152 Echo (ping) request   id=0xdf28, seq=1100/19460, ttl=64 (reply in 13)
◄ 13  0.692354   10.100.100.5    10.100.100.1    ICMP      148 Echo (ping) reply     id=0xdf28, seq=1100/19460, ttl=64 (request in 12)
  23  1.734744   10.100.100.1    10.100.100.5    ICMP      152 Echo (ping) request   id=0xdf28, seq=1101/19716, ttl=64 (reply in 24)
  24  1.735126   10.100.100.5    10.100.100.1    ICMP      148 Echo (ping) reply     id=0xdf28, seq=1101/19716, ttl=64 (request in 23)
  34  2.699882   10.100.100.1    10.100.100.5    ICMP      152 Echo (ping) request   id=0xdf28, seq=1102/19972, ttl=64 (reply in 35)

∨ Internet Protocol Version 4, Src: 192.0.2.23, Dst: 192.0.2.21            0000  c0 bf a7 0d 57 6b 50
    0100 .... = Version: 4                                                  0010  08 00 45 00 00 86 00
    .... 0101 = Header Length: 20 bytes (5)                                 0020  02 17 c0 00 02 15 c4
  › Differentiated Services Field: 0x00 (DSCP: CS0, ECN: Not-ECT)           0030  00 00 00 27 74 00 f0
    Total Length: 134                                                       0040  80 a7 08 00 45 00 00
    Identification: 0x0000 (0)                                              0050  0a 64 64 01 0a 64 64
  › 000. .... = Flags: 0x0                                                  0060  64 ef e6 aa 00 07 17
    ...0 0000 0000 0000 = Fragment Offset: 0                                0070  10 11 12 13 14 15 16
    Time to Live: 64                                                        0080  20 21 22 23 24 25 26
    Protocol: UDP (17)                                                      0090  30 31 32 33 34 35 36
    Header Checksum: 0xf63a [validation disabled]
    [Header checksum status: Unverified]
    Source Address: 192.0.2.23
    Destination Address: 192.0.2.21
› User Datagram Protocol, Src Port: 50330, Dst Port: 4789
› Virtual eXtensible Local Area Network
› Ethernet II, Src: JuniperN_b9:80:a7 (f0:4b:3a:b9:80:a7), Dst: JuniperN_b9:80:ff (f0:4b:3a:b9:80:ff)
∨ Internet Protocol Version 4, Src: 10.100.100.1, Dst: 10.100.100.5
    0100 .... = Version: 4
    .... 0101 = Header Length: 20 bytes (5)
  › Differentiated Services Field: 0x00 (DSCP: CS0, ECN: Not-ECT)
    Total Length: 84
    Identification: 0x63b5 (25525)
  › 000. .... = Flags: 0x0
    ...0 0000 0000 0000 = Fragment Offset: 0
    Time to Live: 64
    Protocol: ICMP (1)
    Header Checksum: 0x3a26 [validation disabled]
    [Header checksum status: Unverified]
    Source Address: 10.100.100.1
    Destination Address: 10.100.100.5
› Internet Control Message Protocol
```

Figure 11-21   *Packet capture of VXLAN-encapsulated packet as it is sent from dc2-gw1 to dc2-leaf1*

When host h5 responds to the ICMP request, the packet path follows a similar pattern, just in reverse. The next section demonstrates how Integrated Interconnect is used to stitch EVPN Type-2 routes with an L3VNI to enable routing between VNIs using a Symmetric IRB model across data centers.

Stitching EVPN Type-2 Symmetric IRB Routes

As a quick refresher, Symmetric IRB uses a *bridge-route-route-bridge* model with the concept of a Layer 3 VNI (L3VNI) that facilitates routing between two L2VNIs in an EVPN VXLAN fabric, as shown in Figure 11-22.

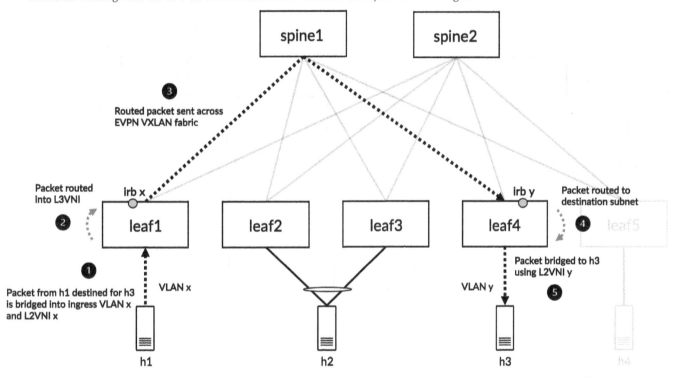

Figure 11-22 *Packet flow with Symmetric IRB*

The intention behind configuring Integrated Interconnect for such a design is the same as before: instead of building VXLAN tunnels across DCs, VXLAN tunnels (for EVPN Type-2 routes with L3VNI) are built to the local DC GWs only, which then re-originate these EVPN Type-2 routes using the interconnect Route Distinguisher, Route Target, and I-ESI. However, this does require all IRBs (and corresponding Layer 2 VLANs) that need to be stitched to be configured on the DC GWs.

The deployment parameters presented in Figure 11-23 are considered to demonstrate how Integrated Interconnect works for a Symmetric IRB model.

Host	Data Center	VLAN and subnet	IP VRF	MAC VRF	L2VNI	L3VNI
h1	DC1	VLAN 10 - 10.100.10.0/24	Tenant1	macvrf-tenant1	10100	5001
h2	DC1	VLAN 20 - 10.100.20.0/24	Tenant1	macvrf-tenant1	10200	5001
h3	DC1	VLAN 30 - 10.100.30.0/24	Tenant1	macvrf-tenant1	10300	5001
h4	DC1	VLAN 40 - 10.100.40.0/24	Tenant1	macvrf-tenant1	10400	5001
h5	DC2	VLAN 50 - 10.100.50.0/24	Tenant1	macvrf-tenant1	10500	5002
h6	DC2	VLAN 60 - 10.100.60.0/24	Tenant1	macvrf-tenant1	10600	5002
h7	DC2	VLAN 70 - 10.100.70.0/24	Tenant1	macvrf-tenant1	10700	5002

Figure 11-23 *Deployment considerations for VXLAN stitching with Symmetric IRB*

As a reference, the topologies shown in Figures 11-24 and 11-25 (separated into two parts, one per DC, for the sake of clarity) will be used for this deployment.

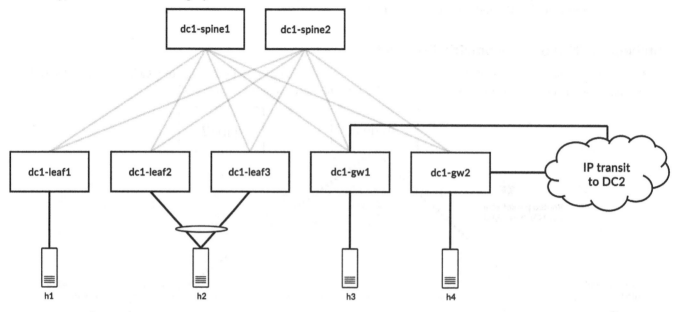

Figure 11-24   *Reference topology showing details of DC1*

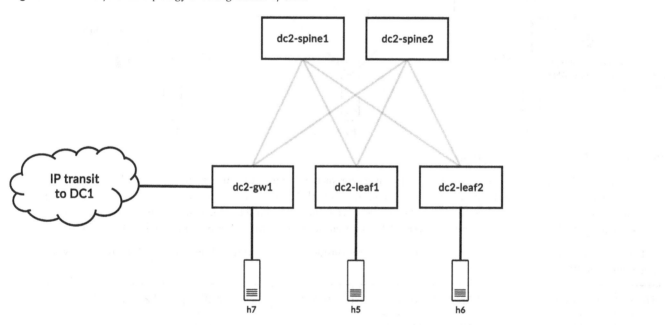

Figure 11-25   *Reference topology showing details of DC2*

Example 11-25 demonstrates Symmetric IRB configuration with an IP VRF and a MAC-VRF, using dc1-leaf1 as a reference.

Example 11-25   *Symmetric IRB configuration on dc1-leaf1*

```
root@dc1-leaf1# show routing-instances Tenant1
instance-type vrf;
protocols {
    evpn {
        irb-symmetric-routing {
            vni 5001;
        }
        ip-prefix-routes {
```

```
            advertise direct-nexthop;
            encapsulation vxlan;
            vni 5001;
        }
    }
}
interface irb.100;
route-distinguisher 192.0.2.11:5001;
vrf-target target:5001:5001;


root@dc1-leaf1# show routing-instances macvrf-tenant1
instance-type mac-vrf;
protocols {
    evpn {
        encapsulation vxlan;
        default-gateway do-not-advertise;
        extended-vni-list 10100;
    }
}
vtep-source-interface lo0.0;
service-type vlan-aware;
interface et-0/0/49.0;
route-distinguisher 192.0.2.11:1;
vrf-target target:1:1;
vlans {
    v100 {
        vlan-id 100;
        l3-interface irb.100;
        vxlan {
            vni 10100;
        }
    }
}
```

With such a design, the data centers being stitched together can be configured with the same L3VNI or different L3VNIs for the IP VRF. Figure 11-26 provides details of how the two DCs are designed. Each data center has a Layer 2 and a Layer 3 Route Target (corresponding to the L2VNI and L3VNI, respectively). The interconnect Route Target includes both the interconnect Route Target for the L2VNI (taken from the MAC-VRF) and the interconnect Route Target for the L3VNI (taken from the IP VRF).

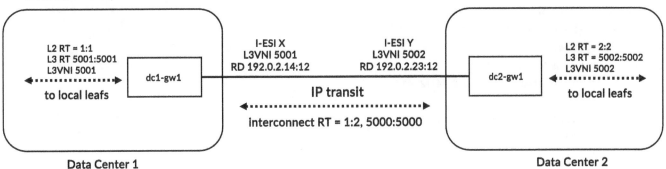

Figure 11-26 *DC1 and DC2 route-target and L2VNI/L3VNI design*

To enable Integrated Interconnect for EVPN Type-2 routes with L3VNI (that facilitates Symmetric IRB), the *interconnect* configuration option must be enabled within the IP VRF as well as the MAC-VRF, with all respective IRBs mapped to the IP VRF (that need to be enabled for Integrated Interconnect). The configuration shown in Example 11-26 demonstrates how Integrated Interconnect for EVPN Type-2 routes with L3VNI is configured on DC1 GW, dc1-gw1.

Example 11-26   *VXLAN stitching configuration for Symmetric IRB on dc1-gw1*

```
root@dc1-gw1# show routing-instances Tenant1
instance-type vrf;
protocols {
    evpn {
        irb-symmetric-routing {
            vni 5001;
        }
        interconnect {
            vrf-target target:5000:5000;
            route-distinguisher 192.0.2.14:5000;
        }
        ip-prefix-routes {
            advertise direct-nexthop;
            encapsulation vxlan;
            vni 5001;
        }
    }
}
interface irb.100;
interface irb.200;
interface irb.300;
interface irb.400;
interface irb.500;
interface irb.600;
interface irb.700;
route-distinguisher 192.0.2.14:5001;
vrf-target target:5001:5001;

root@dc1-gw1# show routing-instances macvrf-tenant1
instance-type mac-vrf;
protocols {
    evpn {
        encapsulation vxlan;
        default-gateway do-not-advertise;
        extended-vni-list all;
        interconnect {
            vrf-target target:1:2;
            route-distinguisher 192.0.2.14:12;
            esi {
                00:00:00:00:00:00:00:11:11:11;
                all-active;
            }
```

```
            interconnected-vni-list all;
        }
    }
}
vtep-source-interface lo0.0;
service-type vlan-aware;
interface et-0/0/4.0;
route-distinguisher 192.0.2.14:1;
vrf-target target:1:1;
vlans {
    v100 {
        vlan-id 100;
        l3-interface irb.100;
        vxlan {
            vni 10100;
        }
    }
    v200 {
        vlan-id 200;
        l3-interface irb.200;
        vxlan {
            vni 10200;
        }
    }
    v300 {
        vlan-id 300;
        l3-interface irb.300;
        vxlan {
            vni 10300;
        }
    }
    v400 {
        vlan-id 400;
        l3-interface irb.400;
        vxlan {
            vni 10400;
        }
    }
    v500 {
        vlan-id 500;
        l3-interface irb.500;
        vxlan {
            vni 10500;
        }
    }
    v600 {
        vlan-id 600;
        l3-interface irb.600;
```

```
            vxlan {
                vni 10600;
            }
        }
        v700 {
            vlan-id 700;
            l3-interface irb.700;
            vxlan {
                vni 10700;
            }
        }
    }
```

The configuration shown in Example 11-27 demonstrates how Integrated Interconnect for EVPN Type-2 routes with L3VNI is configured on DC2 GW, dc2-gw1, with matching interconnect Route Targets for both the IP VRF and the MAC-VRF.

Example 11-27   *VXLAN stitching configuration for Symmetric IRB on dc2-gw1*

```
root@dc2-gw1# show routing-instances Tenant1
instance-type vrf;
protocols {
    evpn {
        irb-symmetric-routing {
            vni 5002;
        }
        interconnect {
            vrf-target target:5000:5000;
            route-distinguisher 192.0.2.23:5000;
        }
        ip-prefix-routes {
            advertise direct-nexthop;
            encapsulation vxlan;
            vni 5002;
        }
    }
}
interface irb.100;
interface irb.200;
interface irb.300;
interface irb.400;
interface irb.500;
interface irb.600;
interface irb.700;
route-distinguisher 192.0.2.23:5002;
vrf-target target:5002:5002;

root@dc2-gw1# show routing-instances macvrf-tenant1
instance-type mac-vrf;
protocols {
    evpn {
```

```
        encapsulation vxlan;
        default-gateway do-not-advertise;
        extended-vni-list all;
        interconnect {
            vrf-target target:1:2;
            route-distinguisher 192.0.2.23:12;
            esi {
                00:00:00:00:00:00:00:22:22:22;
                all-active;
            }
            interconnected-vni-list all;
        }
    }
}
vtep-source-interface lo0.0;
service-type vlan-aware;
interface et-0/0/27.0;
route-distinguisher 192.0.2.23:2;
vrf-target target:2:2;
vlans {
    v100 {
        vlan-id 100;
        l3-interface irb.100;
        vxlan {
            vni 10100;
        }
    }
    v200 {
        vlan-id 200;
        l3-interface irb.200;
        vxlan {
            vni 10200;
        }
    }
    v300 {
        vlan-id 300;
        l3-interface irb.300;
        vxlan {
            vni 10300;
        }
    }
    v400 {
        vlan-id 400;
        l3-interface irb.400;
        vxlan {
            vni 10400;
        }
    }
    v500 {
```

```
            vlan-id 500;
            l3-interface irb.500;
            vxlan {
                vni 10500;
            }
        }
        v600 {
            vlan-id 600;
            l3-interface irb.600;
            vxlan {
                vni 10600;
            }
        }
        v700 {
            vlan-id 700;
            l3-interface irb.700;
            vxlan {
                vni 10700;
            }
        }
    }
}
```

Let's follow the control plane flow for h1's address (10.100.10.1/32) learned on dc1-leaf1 as it is sent toward the local GWs and to the remote DC. When dc1-leaf1 learns h1's address and installs it in the IP VRF table, it is sent to dc1-gw1 with the locally configured Route Targets for the L2VNI and the L3VNI (which are 1:1 and 5001:5001, respectively), as shown in Example 11-28. The router-mac added to this update is dc1-leaf1's router-mac.

Example 11-28 *EVPN Type-2 route originated by dc1-leaf1 for h1's address*

```
root@dc1-leaf1> show route table bgp.evpn.0 match-prefix *2:192.0.2.11:1*10.100.10.1*


bgp.evpn.0: 280 destinations, 556 routes (280 active, 0 holddown, 0 hidden)
+ = Active Route, - = Last Active, * = Both


2:192.0.2.11:1::10100::f0:4b:3a:b9:80:a7::10.100.10.1/304 MAC/IP
                    *[EVPN/170] 1w0d 01:06:31
                        Indirect


{master:0}
root@dc1-leaf1> show route table bgp.evpn.0 match-prefix *2:192.0.2.11:1*10.100.10.1* extensive


bgp.evpn.0: 280 destinations, 556 routes (280 active, 0 holddown, 0 hidden)
2:192.0.2.11:1::10100::f0:4b:3a:b9:80:a7::10.100.10.1/304 MAC/IP (1 entry, 1 announced)
TSI:
Page 0 idx 0, (group overlay type External) Type 1 val 0xaea2894 (adv_entry)
  Advertised metrics:
    Flags: Nexthop Change
    Nexthop: Self
    AS path: [65421] I
```

```
Communities: target:1:1 target:5001:5001 encapsulation.vxlan(0x8) router-mac:40:de:ad:7b:70:40
    Advertise: 00000003
Path 2:192.0.2.11:1::10100::f0:4b:3a:b9:80:a7::10.100.10.1
Vector len 4.  Val: 0
        *EVPN    Preference: 170
                 Next hop type: Indirect, Next hop index: 0
                 Address: 0x8c067f4
                 Next-hop reference count: 9, key opaque handle: 0x0, non-key opaque handle: 0x0
                 Protocol next hop: 192.0.2.11
                 Indirect next hop: 0x0 - INH Session ID: 0
                 State: <Secondary Active Int Ext>
                 Age: 1w0d 1:06:35
                 Validation State: unverified
                 Task: macvrf-tenant1-evpn
                 Announcement bits (1): 1-BGP_RT_Background
                 AS path: I
                 Communities: target:1:1 target:5001:5001 encapsulation:vxlan(0x8) router-mac:40:de:ad:7b:70:40
                 Route Label: 10100
                 Route Label: 5001
                 ESI: 00:00:00:00:00:00:00:00:00:00
                 Primary Routing Table: macvrf-tenant1.evpn.0
                 Thread: junos-main
```

When dc1-gw1 re-originates this route, it uses the interconnect Route Distinguisher from the MAC-VRF, adds the interconnect Route Targets for the L2VNI (from the MAC-VRF) and the L3VNI (from the IP VRF), and adds the I-ESI, as shown in Example 11-29. The GW also sets itself as the protocol next-hop to ensure a new VXLAN tunnel is created to any remote GWs accepting this route.

Example 11-29 *EVPN Type-2 route re-originated by dc1-gw for h1's address*

```
root@dc1-gw1> show route table bgp.evpn.0 match-prefix *2:192.0.2.14:12*10.100.10.1*


bgp.evpn.0: 280 destinations, 480 routes (280 active, 0 holddown, 0 hidden)
+ = Active Route, - = Last Active, * = Both


2:192.0.2.14:12::10100::f0:4b:3a:b9:80:a7::10.100.10.1/304 MAC/IP
                    *[EVPN/170] 1w0d 01:18:36
                        Indirect


root@dc1-gw1> show route table bgp.evpn.0 match-prefix *2:192.0.2.14:12*10.100.10.1* extensive


bgp.evpn.0: 280 destinations, 480 routes (280 active, 0 holddown, 0 hidden)
2:192.0.2.14:12::10100::f0:4b:3a:b9:80:a7::10.100.10.1/304 MAC/IP (1 entry, 1 announced)
TSI:
Page 0 idx 0, (group overlay type External) Type 1 val 0x5628fe93e380 (adv_entry)
    Advertised metrics:
      Flags: Nexthop Change
      Nexthop: Self
      AS path: [65424] I
```

```
      Communities: target:1:2 target:5000:5000 encapsulation:vxlan(0x8) router-mac:b8:f0:15:52:5d:06
   Advertise: 00000003
Page 0 idx 1, (group overlay-dci type External) Type 1 val 0x5628fe940d10 (adv_entry)
   Advertised metrics:
      Flags: Nexthop Change
      Nexthop: Self
      AS path: [65424] I
      Communities: target:1:2 target:5000:5000 encapsulation:vxlan(0x8) router-mac:b8:f0:15:52:5d:06
   Advertise: 00000001
Path 2:192.0.2.14:12::10100::f0:4b:3a:b9:80:a7::10.100.10.1
Vector len 4.  Val: 0 1
         *EVPN    Preference: 170
                  Next hop type: Indirect, Next hop index: 0
                  Address: 0x5628fbd2c21c
                  Next-hop reference count: 99
                  Kernel Table Id: 0
                  Protocol next hop: 192.0.2.14
                  Indirect next hop: (nil) - INH Session ID: 0
                  State: <Secondary Active Int Ext>
                  Age: 1w0d 1:18:40
                  Validation State: unverified
                  Task: macvrf-tenant1-evpn
                  Announcement bits (1): 1-BGP_RT_Background
                  AS path: I
                  Communities: target:1:2 target:5000:5000 encapsulation:vxlan(0x8) router-mac:b8:f0:15:52:5d:06
                  Route Label: 10100
                  Route Label: 5001
                  ESI: 00:00:00:00:00:00:00:11:11:11
                  Primary Routing Table: macvrf-tenant1.evpn.0
                  Thread: junos-main
```

When the remote DC GW (dc2-gw) receives this re-originated EVPN Type-2 route, it has an import policy that matches interconnect Route Target. The route is imported into the MAC-VRF and the IP VRF, and a /32 entry is installed in the IP VRF inet.0 table, as shown in Example 11-30.

Example 11-30 *Host route for h1's address in the IP VRF inet table on dc2-gw1*

```
root@dc2-gw1> show route table Tenant1.inet.0 10.100.10.1

Tenant1.inet.0: 21 destinations, 59 routes (21 active, 0 holddown, 0 hidden)
+ = Active Route, - = Last Active, * = Both

10.100.10.1/32     *[EVPN/7] 6d 21:54:43
                    >  to 198.51.100.155 via et-0/0/24.0
                    [EVPN/7] 6d 21:54:43
                    >  to 198.51.100.155 via et-0/0/24.0
                    [EVPN/170] 6d 21:58:20
                    >  to 198.51.100.155 via et-0/0/24.0
                    [EVPN/170] 6d 21:58:20
                    >  to 198.51.100.155 via et-0/0/24.0
```

At the same time, dc2-gw re-originates this route into its local DC, using the local DC Route Distinguisher, Route Target, and L2VNI/L3VNI, with the I-ESI attached to the route, as shown in Example 11-31. The router-mac added to this route is dc2-gw1's router-mac.

Example 11-31 *EVPN Type-2 route for h1's address re-originated into DC2 by dc2-gw1*

```
root@dc2-gw1> show route table bgp.evpn.0 match-prefix 2:*192.0.2.23:2*10.100.10.1*

bgp.evpn.0: 280 destinations, 286 routes (280 active, 0 holddown, 0 hidden)
+ = Active Route, - = Last Active, * = Both

2:192.0.2.23:2::10100::f0:4b:3a:b9:80:a7::10.100.10.1/304 MAC/IP
                *[EVPN/170] 6d 21:58:52
                    Indirect


root@dc2-gw1> show route table bgp.evpn.0 match-prefix 2:*192.0.2.23:2*10.100.10.1* extensive

bgp.evpn.0: 280 destinations, 286 routes (280 active, 0 holddown, 0 hidden)
2:192.0.2.23:2::10100::f0:4b:3a:b9:80:a7::10.100.10.1/304 MAC/IP (1 entry, 1 announced)
TSI:
Page 0 idx 0, (group overlay type External) Type 1 val 0x55e92dcc5f40 (adv_entry)
   Advertised metrics:
     Flags: Nexthop Change
     Nexthop: Self
     AS path: [65433] I
     Communities: target:2:2 target:5002:5002 encapsulation:vxlan(0x8) router-mac:50:c7:09:a6:f5:04
   Advertise: 00000003
Page 0 idx 1, (group overlay-dci type External) Type 1 val 0x55e92dcc80f0 (adv_entry)
   Advertised metrics:
     Flags: Nexthop Change
     Nexthop: Self
     AS path: [65433] I
     Communities: target:2:2 target:5002:5002 encapsulation:vxlan(0x8) router-mac:50:c7:09:a6:f5:04
   Advertise: 00000001
Path 2:192.0.2.23:2::10100::f0:4b:3a:b9:80:a7::10.100.10.1
Vector len 4.  Val: 0 1
       *EVPN   Preference: 170
               Next hop type: Indirect, Next hop index: 0
               Address: 0x55e92bd2bcdc
               Next-hop reference count: 99
               Kernel Table Id: 0
               Protocol next hop: 192.0.2.23
               Indirect next hop: (nil) - INH Session ID: 0
               State: <Secondary Active Int Ext>
               Age: 6d 21:59:01
               Validation State: unverified
               Task: macvrf-tenant1-evpn
               Announcement bits (1): 1-BGP_RT_Background
               AS path: I
```

```
        Communities: target:2:2 target:5002:5002 encapsulation:vxlan(0x8) router-mac:50:c7:09:a6:f5:04
        Route Label: 10100
        Route Label: 5002
        ESI: 00:00:00:00:00:00:00:22:22:22
        Primary Routing Table: macvrf-tenant1.evpn.0
        Thread: junos-main
```

On receipt of this route, dc2-leaf1, as an example, will import it into its EVPN database and install a /32 host route into the corresponding IP VRF inet.0 table, as shown in Example 11-32.

Example 11-32 *Host h1's address installed in the Tenant1 IP VRF inet table*

```
root@dc2-leaf1> show route table Tenant1.inet.0 10.100.10.1/32


Tenant1.inet.0: 9 destinations, 9 routes (9 active, 0 holddown, 0 hidden)
+ = Active Route, - = Last Active, * = Both


10.100.10.1/32      *[EVPN/7] 1w0d 00:40:59
                     >  to 198.51.100.101 via et-0/0/54.0
                        to 198.51.100.103 via et-0/0/50.0


{master:0}
root@dc2-leaf1> show route table Tenant1.inet.0 10.100.10.1/32 extensive


Tenant1.inet.0: 9 destinations, 9 routes (9 active, 0 holddown, 0 hidden)
10.100.10.1/32 (1 entry, 1 announced)
TSI:
KRT in-kernel 10.100.10.1/32 -> {composite(1693)}
        *EVPN   Preference: 7
                Next hop type: Indirect, Next hop index: 0
                Address: 0x8c07194
                Next-hop reference count: 10, key opaque handle: 0x0, non-key opaque handle: 0x0
                Next hop type: Router, Next hop index: 0
                Next hop: 198.51.100.101 via et-0/0/54.0, selected
                Session Id: 0
                Next hop: 198.51.100.103 via et-0/0/50.0
                Session Id: 0
                Protocol next hop: 192.0.2.23
                Composite next hop: 0x74c9740 1693 INH Session ID: 0
                  VXLAN tunnel rewrite:
                    MTU: 0, Flags: 0x0
                    Encap table ID: 0, Decap table ID: 12
                    Encap VNI: 5002, Decap VNI: 5002
                    Source VTEP: 192.0.2.21, Destination VTEP: 192.0.2.23
                    SMAC: 20:d8:0b:3c:fc:00, DMAC: 50:c7:09:a6:f5:04
                Indirect next hop: 0x7589d4c 524293 INH Session ID: 0
                State: <Active Int Ext VxlanLocalRT>
                Age: 1w0d 0:41:03    Metric2: 0
                Validation State: unverified
```

```
Task: Tenant1-EVPN-L3-context
Announcement bits (1): 1-KRT
AS path: I
Thread: junos-main
Composite next hops: 1
        Protocol next hop: 192.0.2.23 ResolvState: Resolved
        Composite next hop: 0x74c9740 1693 INH Session ID: 0
          VXLAN tunnel rewrite:
            MTU: 0, Flags: 0x0
            Encap table ID: 0, Decap table ID: 12
            Encap VNI: 5002, Decap VNI: 5002
            Source VTEP: 192.0.2.21, Destination VTEP: 192.0.2.23
            SMAC: 20:d8:0b:3c:fc:00, DMAC: 50:c7:09:a6:f5:04
```

snip

In the same way, other host addresses are learned across both DCs, with the GWs stitching Type-2 symmetric routes in this case. In the data plane, the VXLAN tunnels exist between leafs and the local GWs, with the local DC L3VNI being used to transport the packet across. Thus, when host h1 (in DC1) communicates with host h5 (in DC2), the received IP packet is encapsulated by dc1-leaf1 and directed toward dc1-gw1 (or dc1-gw2) with the appropriate VXLAN headers.

The packet capture shown in Figure 11-27 confirms that the outer IP header has a destination of 192.0.2.14 (which is the loopback address of dc1-gw1) and the VNI, in the VXLAN header, is the L3VNI 5001.

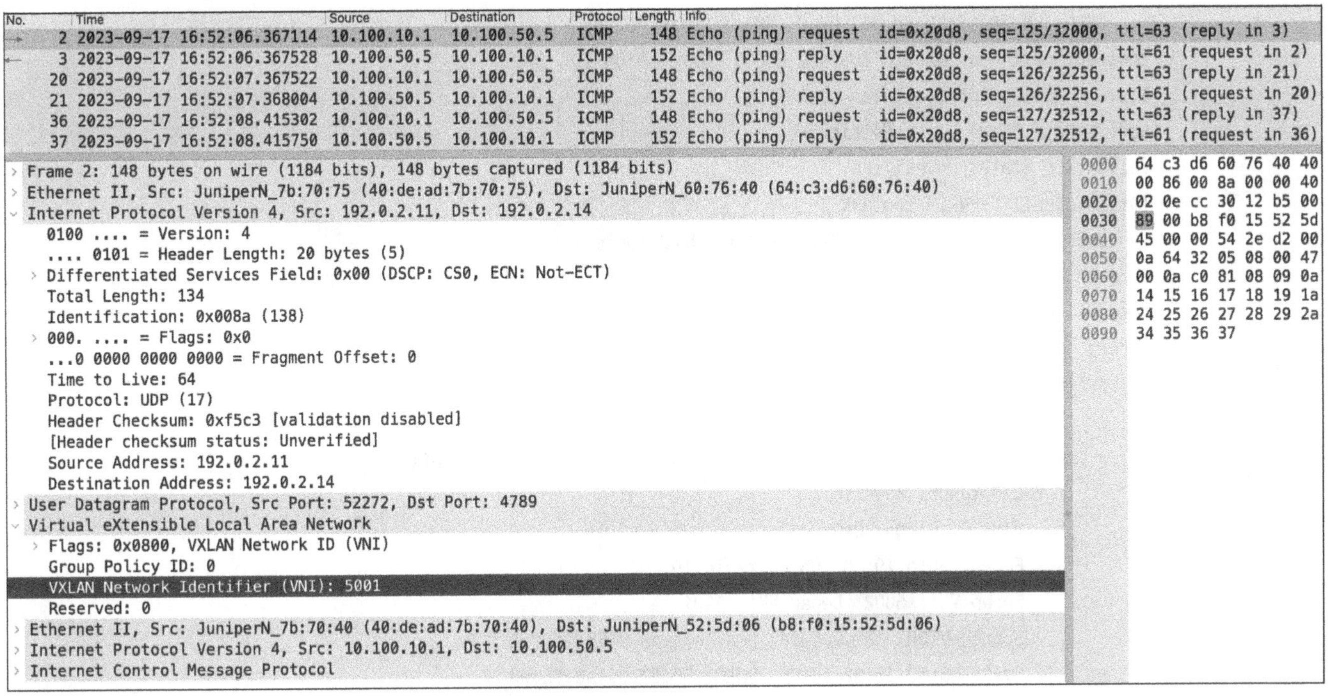

Figure 11-27 *Packet capture of ICMP request, encapsulated by dc1-leaf1, from host h1 to host h5*

When dc1-gw1 receives this packet, it decapsulates the packet and does a lookup on the inner destination IP address (since the inner destination MAC address is owned by it). This results in the packet being re-encapsulated with VXLAN headers, with the outer destination IP address as 192.0.2.23, which is the loopback address of dc2-gw1, along with the outer destination MAC address being the router-mac of this GW as well. The L3VNI, in the VXLAN header, is set to 5002, which is DC2's L3VNI, as confirmed in Example 11-33.

Example 11-33   *Lookup result for host h5's address in the IP VRF inet table of dc1-gw1*

```
root@dc1-gw1> show route table Tenant1.inet.0 10.100.50.5/32 extensive

Tenant1.inet.0: 20 destinations, 41 routes (20 active, 0 holddown, 0 hidden)
10.100.50.5/32 (2 entries, 1 announced)
TSI:
KRT in-kernel 10.100.50.5/32 -> {composite(66013)}
        *EVPN   Preference: 7
                Next hop type: Indirect, Next hop index: 0
                Address: 0x5628fbd46a9c
                Next-hop reference count: 23
                Kernel Table Id: 0
                Next hop type: Router, Next hop index: 66007
                Next hop: 198.51.100.151 via et-0/0/3.0, selected
                Session Id: 3f1
                Protocol next hop: 192.0.2.23
                Composite next hop: 0x5628fbd3dd80 66013 INH Session ID: 1011
                  VXLAN tunnel rewrite:
                    MTU: 0, Flags: 0x0
                    Encap table ID: 0, Decap table ID: 52
                    Encap VNI: 5002, Decap VNI: 5001
                    Source VTEP: 192.0.2.14, Destination VTEP: 192.0.2.23
                    SMAC: b8:f0:15:52:5d:06, DMAC: 50:c7:09:a6:f5:04
                Indirect next hop: 0x5628f80ed488 66012 INH Session ID: 1011
                State: <Active Int Ext VxlanLocalRT>
                Age: 1w0d 1:35:24      Metric2: 0
                Validation State: unverified
                Task: Tenant1-EVPN-L3-context
                Announcement bits (2): 0-KRT 2-Tenant1-EVPN-L3-context
                AS path: I
                Communities: target:1:2 target:5000:5000
                Thread: junos-main
                Composite next hops: 1
                        Protocol next hop: 192.0.2.23 ResolvState: Resolved
                        Composite next hop: 0x5628fbd3dd80 66013 INH Session ID: 1011
                          VXLAN tunnel rewrite:
                            MTU: 0, Flags: 0x0
                            Encap table ID: 0, Decap table ID: 52
                            Encap VNI: 5002, Decap VNI: 5001
                            Source VTEP: 192.0.2.14, Destination VTEP: 192.0.2.23
                            SMAC: b8:f0:15:52:5d:06, DMAC: 50:c7:09:a6:f5:04

*snip*
```

The packet capture shown in Figure 11-28 confirms the same.

```
No.    Time                    Source          Destination     Protocol  Length  Info
  10 2023-09-17 17:09:5… 10.100.10.1    10.100.50.5     ICMP      148  Echo (ping) request  id=0x20d8, seq=1190/42500, ttl=62 (reply in 11)
  11 2023-09-17 17:09:5… 10.100.50.5    10.100.10.1     ICMP      148  Echo (ping) reply    id=0x20d8, seq=1190/42500, ttl=63 (request in 10)

> Frame 10: 148 bytes on wire (1184 bits), 148 bytes captured (1184 bits)       0000  50 c7 09 a6 f0
> Ethernet II, Src: JuniperN_0b:3f:15 (d0:dd:49:0b:3f:15), Dst: JuniperN_a6:f0:5e (50:c7:09:a6:f0:5e)  0010  00 86 00 00 00
v Internet Protocol Version 4, Src: 192.0.2.14, Dst: 192.0.2.23                 0020  02 17 d1 8a 12
    0100 .... = Version: 4                                                      0030  8a 00 50 c7 09
    .... 0101 = Header Length: 20 bytes (5)                                     0040  45 00 00 54 bb
  > Differentiated Services Field: 0x00 (DSCP: CS0, ECN: Not-ECT)               0050  0a 64 32 05 08
    Total Length: 134                                                          0060  00 08 7c cd 08
    Identification: 0x0000 (0)                                                 0070  14 15 16 17 18
  > 000. .... = Flags: 0x0                                                     0080  24 25 26 27 28
    ...0 0000 0000 0000 = Fragment Offset: 0                                   0090  34 35 36 37
    Time to Live: 63
    Protocol: UDP (17)
    Header Checksum: 0xf741 [validation disabled]
    [Header checksum status: Unverified]
    Source Address: 192.0.2.14
    Destination Address: 192.0.2.23
> User Datagram Protocol, Src Port: 53642, Dst Port: 4789
v Virtual eXtensible Local Area Network
  > Flags: 0x0800, VXLAN Network ID (VNI)
    Group Policy ID: 0
    VXLAN Network Identifier (VNI): 5002
    Reserved: 0
> Ethernet II, Src: JuniperN_52:5d:06 (b8:f0:15:52:5d:06), Dst: JuniperN_a6:f5:04 (50:c7:09:a6:f5:04)
> Internet Protocol Version 4, Src: 10.100.10.1, Dst: 10.100.50.5
> Internet Control Message Protocol
```

Figure 11-28 *Packet capture of ICMP request, encapsulated by dc1-gw1, sent toward the DCI*

This packet will get re-encapsulated by dc2-gw1 and sent to dc2-leaf1, eventually reaching the host. When the host responds, dc2-leaf1 will encapsulate the original IP packet and send it toward its local GW, dc2-gw1, as per the lookup shown in Example 11-34. The VNI, in the VXLAN header, is set to DC2's L3VNI, 5002.

Example 11-34 *Lookup result for host h1's address in the IP VRF inet table of dc2-leaf1*

```
root@dc2-leaf1> show route table Tenant1.inet.0 10.100.10.1/32

Tenant1.inet.0: 9 destinations, 9 routes (9 active, 0 holddown, 0 hidden)
+ = Active Route, - = Last Active, * = Both

10.100.10.1/32      *[EVPN/7] 1w0d 20:01:46
                    >  to 198.51.100.101 via et-0/0/54.0
                       to 198.51.100.103 via et-0/0/50.0

{master:0}
root@dc2-leaf1> show route table Tenant1.inet.0 10.100.10.1/32 extensive

Tenant1.inet.0: 9 destinations, 9 routes (9 active, 0 holddown, 0 hidden)
10.100.10.1/32 (1 entry, 1 announced)
TSI:
KRT in-kernel 10.100.10.1/32 -> {composite(1693)}
        *EVPN   Preference: 7
                Next hop type: Indirect, Next hop index: 0
                Address: 0x8c07194
                Next-hop reference count: 10, key opaque handle: 0x0, non-key opaque handle: 0x0
                Next hop type: Router, Next hop index: 0
                Next hop: 198.51.100.101 via et-0/0/54.0, selected
                Session Id: 0
                Next hop: 198.51.100.103 via et-0/0/50.0
```

```
            Session Id: 0
            Protocol next hop: 192.0.2.23
            Composite next hop: 0x74c9740 1693 INH Session ID: 0
              VXLAN tunnel rewrite:
                MTU: 0, Flags: 0x0
                Encap table ID: 0, Decap table ID: 12
                Encap VNI: 5002, Decap VNI: 5002
                Source VTEP: 192.0.2.21, Destination VTEP: 192.0.2.23
                SMAC: 20:d8:0b:3c:fc:00, DMAC: 50:c7:09:a6:f5:04
            Indirect next hop: 0x7589d4c 524293 INH Session ID: 0
            State: <Active Int Ext VxlanLocalRT>
            Age: 1w0d 20:01:48      Metric2: 0
            Validation State: unverified
            Task: Tenant1-EVPN-L3-context
            Announcement bits (1): 1-KRT
            AS path: I
            Thread: junos-main
            Composite next hops: 1
                    Protocol next hop: 192.0.2.23 ResolvState: Resolved
                    Composite next hop: 0x74c9740 1693 INH Session ID: 0
                      VXLAN tunnel rewrite:
                        MTU: 0, Flags: 0x0
                        Encap table ID: 0, Decap table ID: 12
                        Encap VNI: 5002, Decap VNI: 5002
                        Source VTEP: 192.0.2.21, Destination VTEP: 192.0.2.23
                        SMAC: 20:d8:0b:3c:fc:00, DMAC: 50:c7:09:a6:f5:04
```

snip

The packet capture shown in Figure 11-29 confirms the same.

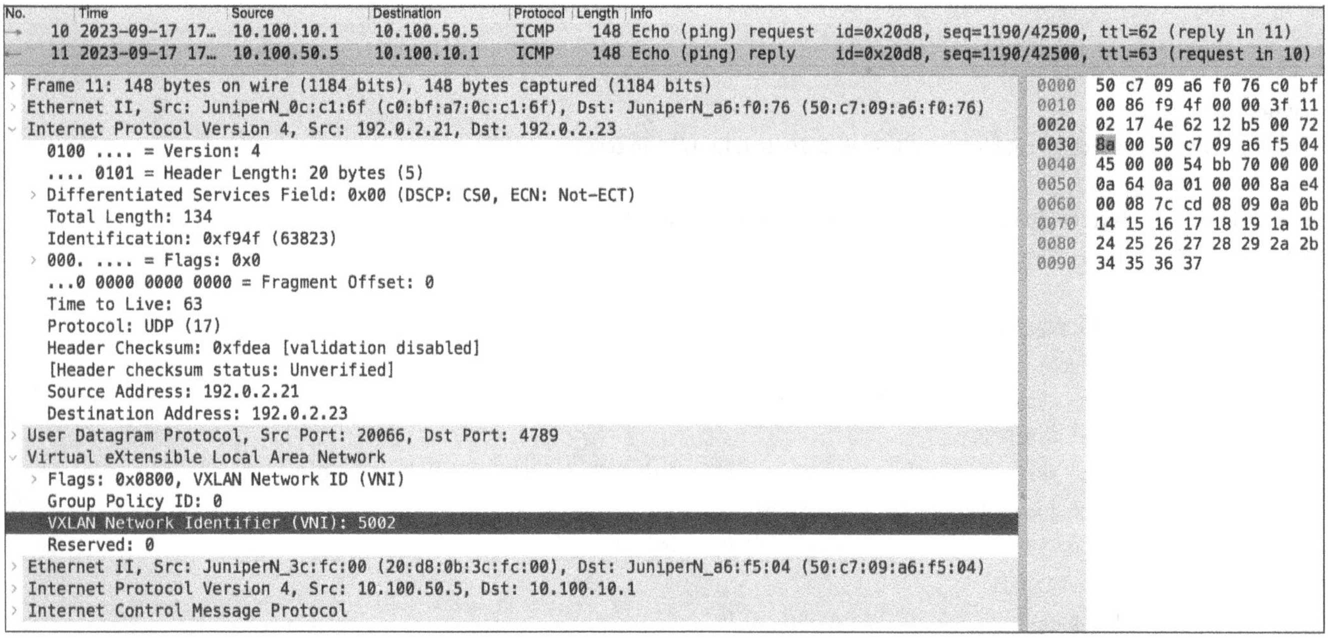

Figure 11-29 *Packet capture of ICMP reply, from host h5 to h1, encapsulated by dc2-leaf1*

A similar process of re-encapsulation will happen as the packet is sent toward host h1. In this way, Integrated Interconnect can be used to integrate multiple DCs with a Symmetric IRB model to route between VNIs.

Stitching EVPN Type-5 Routes

Like everything else discussed so far, the goal of stitching EVPN Type-5 routes is the same: instead of building EVPN Type-5–based VXLAN tunnels across DCs, the idea is to build them against local GWs only and have the GWs re-originate a new tunnel to any remote GWs. The difference with stitching Type-5 routes is that there is no concept of an ESI attached to an EVPN Type-5 route, and thus, when stitching these routes across, the I-ESI is no longer needed. This design is ideal when there is no requirement to extend Layer 2 between DCs, and IP prefix reachability, facilitated by EVPN Type-5 routes, can be leveraged to provide connectivity between DCs.

From a configuration standpoint, this design makes it much simpler. Only the *interconnect* configuration option is needed (with a Route Target and Route Distinguisher) under the *protocol evpn* configuration hierarchy in the IP VRF routing instance. This is shown in Example 11-35, from the perspective of dc1-gw1 and dc2-gw1, where each IP VRF routing instance is configured with an interconnect Route Target of 5000:5000.

Example 11-35 *VXLAN stitching configuration for EVPN Type-5 routes on dc1-gw1 and dc2-gw1*

```
root@dc1-gw1# show routing-instances Tenant1
instance-type vrf;
protocols {
    evpn {
        irb-symmetric-routing {
            vni 5001;
        }
        interconnect {
            vrf-target target:5000:5000;
            route-distinguisher 192.0.2.14:5000;
        }
        ip-prefix-routes {
            advertise direct-nexthop;
            encapsulation vxlan;
            vni 5001;
        }
    }
}
interface irb.300;
route-distinguisher 192.0.2.14:5001;
vrf-target target:5001:5001;


root@dc1-gw1# show routing-instances macvrf-tenant1
instance-type mac-vrf;
protocols {
    evpn {
        encapsulation vxlan;
        default-gateway do-not-advertise;
        extended-vni-list all;
    }
}
```

```
vtep-source-interface lo0.0;
service-type vlan-aware;
interface et-0/0/4.0;
route-distinguisher 192.0.2.14:1;
vrf-target target:1:1;
vlans {
    v300 {
        vlan-id 300;
        l3-interface irb.300;
        vxlan {
            vni 10300;
        }
    }
}

root@dc2-gw1# show routing-instances Tenant1
instance-type vrf;
protocols {
    evpn {
        irb-symmetric-routing {
            vni 5002;
        }
        interconnect {
            vrf-target target:5000:5000;
            route-distinguisher 192.0.2.23:5000;
        }
        ip-prefix-routes {
            advertise direct-nexthop;
            encapsulation vxlan;
            vni 5002;
        }
    }
}
interface irb.700;
route-distinguisher 192.0.2.23:5002;
vrf-target target:5002:5002;

root@dc2-gw1# show routing-instances macvrf-tenant1
instance-type mac-vrf;
protocols {
    evpn {
        encapsulation vxlan;
        default-gateway do-not-advertise;
        extended-vni-list all;
    }
}
vtep-source-interface lo0.0;
service-type vlan-aware;
interface et-0/0/27.0;
```

```
route-distinguisher 192.0.2.23.2,
vrf-target target:2:2;
vlans {
    v700 {
        vlan-id 700;
        l3-interface irb.700;
        vxlan {
            vni 10700;
        }
    }
}
```

By default, this configuration also allows learned /32 host routes to be advertised as EVPN Type-5 routes. If there are no overlapping subnets between any leafs (even within a DC), then there is no requirement to advertise these /32 host routes. This can be controlled by applying an export policy within the *ip-prefix-routes* configuration hierarchy under *protocol evpn* configuration hierarchy for an IP VRF. In this case, the policy (from the perspective of dc1-leaf1) shown in Example 11-36 is used to advertise only /24 subnet routes within a DC and between DCs. The same policy can be applied to all leafs across both DCs.

Example 11-36 *Policy to control routes exported into BGP EVPN as EVPN Type-5 routes*

```
root@dc1-leaf1# show policy-options policy-statement ip-to-evpn
term 1 {
    from {
        route-filter 10.100.0.0/16 upto /24;
    }
    then accept;
}
term default {
    then reject;
}

root@dc1-leaf1# show routing-instances Tenant1
instance-type vrf;
protocols {
    evpn {
        ip-prefix-routes {
            advertise direct-nexthop;
            encapsulation vxlan;
            vni 5001;
            export ip-to-evpn;
        }
    }
}
interface irb.100;
route-distinguisher 192.0.2.11:5001;
vrf-target target:5001:5001;
```

The result is that only routes from IP prefix 10.100.0.0/16 up to a subnet mask of /24 are eligible to be exported as EVPN Type-5 routes. Example 11-37 confirms this, from the perspective of dc1-gw1, using the **show evpn ip-prefix-database direction exported** operational mode command, which shows only IPv4-to-EVPN exported prefixes.

Example 11-37 *EVPN database on dc1-gw1 showing IPv4 routes exported as EVPN Type-5 routes*

```
root@dc1-gw1> show evpn ip-prefix-database direction exported
L3 context: Tenant1

IPv4->EVPN Exported Prefixes
Prefix                          EVPN route status
10.100.10.0/24                  DCI Created
10.100.20.0/24                  DCI Created
10.100.30.0/24                  DC and DCI Created
10.100.50.0/24                  DC Created
10.100.60.0/24                  DC Created
10.100.70.0/24                  DC Created
```

From the perspective of the data plane, this is no different from stitching EVPN Type-2 routes with an L3VNI (for Symmetric IRB), since both use an L3VNI for data plane transport. For example, when host h1, in DC1, communicates with host h5, in DC2, the IP packet from h1 is encapsulated with VXLAN headers and directed to one of its local GWs, dc1-gw1 or dc1-gw2, based on the lookup result shown in Example 11-38.

Example 11-38 *Forwarding lookup result for h5's address on dc1-leaf1*

```
root@dc1-leaf1> show route table Tenant1.inet.0 10.100.50.5

Tenant1.inet.0: 9 destinations, 13 routes (9 active, 0 holddown, 0 hidden)
+ = Active Route, - = Last Active, * = Both

10.100.50.0/24      *[EVPN/170] 01:58:33
                        to 198.51.100.1 via et-0/0/48.0
                    >   to 198.51.100.3 via et-0/0/50.0
                    [EVPN/170] 01:58:33
                        to 198.51.100.1 via et-0/0/48.0
                    >   to 198.51.100.3 via et-0/0/50.0

{master:0}
root@dc1-leaf1> show route table Tenant1.inet.0 10.100.50.5 extensive

Tenant1.inet.0: 9 destinations, 13 routes (9 active, 0 holddown, 0 hidden)
10.100.50.0/24 (2 entries, 1 announced)
TSI:
KRT in-kernel 10.100.50.0/24 -> {composite(1778)}
        *EVPN   Preference: 170/-101
                Next hop type: Indirect, Next hop index: 0
                Address: 0x8c08774
                Next-hop reference count: 8, key opaque handle: 0x0, non-key opaque handle: 0x0
                Next hop type: Router, Next hop index: 0
                Next hop: 198.51.100.1 via et-0/0/48.0 weight 0x1
                Session Id: 0
                Next hop: 198.51.100.3 via et-0/0/50.0 weight 0x1, selected
                Session Id: 0
                Protocol next hop: 192.0.2.14
```

```
Composite next hop: 0xadcfd00 1778 INH Session ID  0
   VXLAN tunnel rewrite:
      MTU: 0, Flags: 0x0
      Encap table ID: 0, Decap table ID: 8
      Encap VNI: 5001, Decap VNI: 5001
      Source VTEP: 192.0.2.11, Destination VTEP: 192.0.2.14
      SMAC: 40:de:ad:7b:70:40, DMAC: b8:f0:15:52:5d:06
Indirect next hop: 0x758a07c 524292 INH Session ID: 0
State: <Active Int Ext>
Age: 1:58:36    Metric2: 0
Validation State: unverified
Task: Tenant1-EVPN-L3-context
Announcement bits (1): 2-KRT
AS path: 65500 65424 65510 65433 65501 65431 I
Thread: junos-main
Composite next hops: 1
        Protocol next hop: 192.0.2.14 ResolvState: Resolved
        Composite next hop: 0xadcfd00 1778 INH Session ID: 0
          VXLAN tunnel rewrite:
            MTU: 0, Flags: 0x0
            Encap table ID: 0, Decap table ID: 8
            Encap VNI: 5001, Decap VNI: 5001
            Source VTEP: 192.0.2.11, Destination VTEP: 192.0.2.14
            SMAC: 40:de:ad:7b:70:40, DMAC: b8:f0:15:52:5d:06
```

snip

The packet capture shown in Figure 11-30 confirms the same.

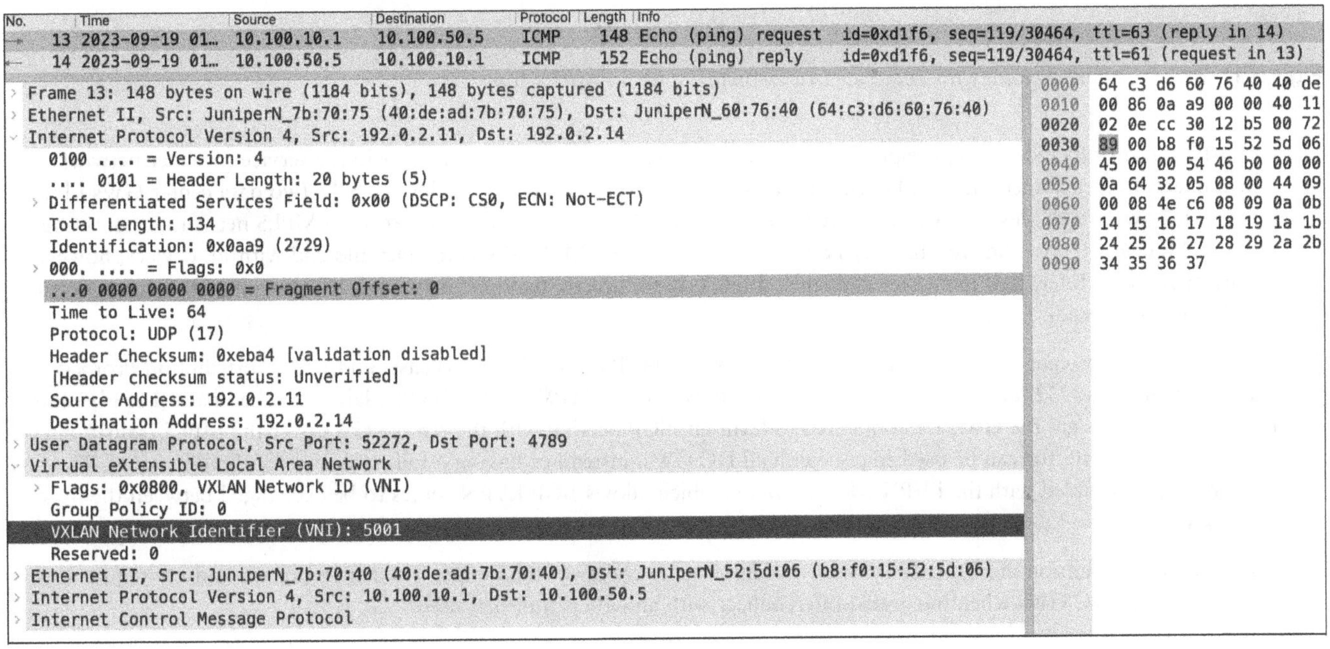

Figure 11-30 *Packet capture of ICMP request, from host h1 to h5, encapsulated by dc1-leaf1*

For the sake of brevity, the remainder of the packet flow and captures is not shown here since it follows the same process as stitching Symmetric IRB routes, which is described in the previous subsection.

Integrated Interconnect with MPLS Transit

This section examines a design in which two (or more) VXLAN domains need to be connected using Integrated Interconnect with an MPLS transit (instead of an IP transit). The function of translating an incoming VXLAN packet into an MPLS packet is integrated into the DC GWs themselves. The GWs in this case are Juniper MX devices, which are more suited for such a design and are typically used for functionality like this, based on the feature set and hardware scale they offer.

The topology shown in Figure 11-31 is used for this section. Two data centers, DC1 and DC2, are connected via an MPLS transit. Each DC has two leafs and one dedicated GW that is used for Integrated Interconnect and translating incoming VXLAN packets into MPLS packets if the traffic is destined for the remote DC, via the MPLS transit. For the sake of transparency and to show end-to-end details of traffic flow in such a design, this section assumes that the MPLS domain is also under the control of the operator as well.

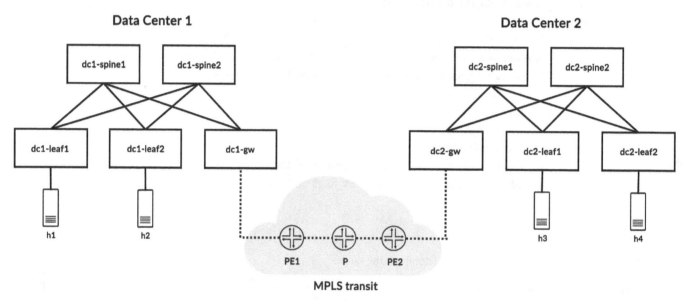

Figure 11-31 *Reference topology for Integrated Interconnect with an MPLS transit*

This MPLS transit includes two provider edge (PE) devices and a P device. A PE device is in the service provider network and connects to a customer edge (CE) device, located in the customer premises. In this case, the two data center GWs (dc1-gw and dc2-gw) are CE devices. A P device is a transit or core device, within the context of an MPLS network, connecting multiple PE devices, providing reachability between them. Typically, MPLS domains start and end with PE devices; however, in this case, where Integrated Interconnect enables a DC GW to directly hand off between VXLAN and MPLS domains, the MPLS domain starts and ends with the DC GWs.

The MPLS transit is enabled with an Interior Gateway Protocol (IGP), OSPF in this case, and Label Distribution Protocol (LDP), which allows /32 loopbacks to be exchanged between the DC GWs and to build a label-switched path (LSP) between them. In such a design, the GWs are configured to form an iBGP peering with the remote GWs over the MPLS transit (alternatively, a route reflector can be used to peer with all DC GWs, instead of having a full mesh style of iBGP peering). This iBGP peering is enabled with the EVPN address family, which allows BGP EVPN routes to be exchanged between the DC GWs.

The visual representation in Figure 11-32 shows a high-level overview of the design. The MPLS domain must extend end to end between the DC GWs when Integrated Interconnect with an MPLS transit is used.

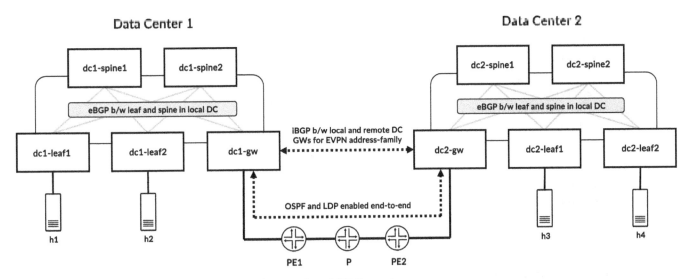

Figure 11-32 *Overall design for VXLAN stitching with an MPLS transit*

The eBGP underlay and overlay configuration for a data center's leaf and spine is shown in Example 11-39, from the perspective of dc1-leaf1 and dc1-spine1. Similar configuration is applied for all the leafs and spines across both data centers.

Example 11-39 *BGP configuration on dc1-leaf1 and dc1-spine1*

```
root@dc1-spine1# show protocols bgp
group underlay {
    type external;
    family inet {
        unicast;
    }
    export export-loopback;
    neighbor 198.51.100.0 {
        description dc1-leaf1;
        peer-as 65421;
    }
    neighbor 198.51.100.4 {
        description dc1-leaf2;
        peer-as 65422;
    }
    neighbor 198.51.100.12 {
        description dc1-gw;
        peer-as 65424;
    }
}
group overlay {
    type external;
    multihop {
        no-nexthop-change;
    }
    local-address 192.0.2.101;
    family evpn {
        signaling;
    }
```

```
        neighbor 192.0.2.11 {
            description dc1-leaf1;
            peer-as 65421;
        }
        neighbor 192.0.2.12 {
            description dc1-leaf2;
            peer-as 65422;
        }
        neighbor 192.0.2.14 {
            description dc1-gw;
            peer-as 65424;
        }
    }


root@dc1-leaf1# show protocols bgp
group underlay {
    type external;
    family inet {
        unicast;
    }
    export export-loopback;
    peer-as 65500;
    neighbor 198.51.100.1 {
        description dc1-spine1;
    }
    neighbor 198.51.100.3 {
        description dc1-spine2;
    }
}
group overlay {
    type external;
    multihop {
        no-nexthop-change;
    }
    local-address 192.0.2.11;
    family evpn {
        signaling;
    }
    peer-as 65500;
    neighbor 192.0.2.101 {
        description dc1-spine1;
    }
    neighbor 192.0.2.102 {
        description dc1-spine2;
    }
}
```

Each leaf has a VLAN-Aware MAC-VRF configured with VLAN 100. Considering dc1-leaf1 as an example, the MAC-VRF configuration is shown in Example 11-40.

Example 11-40 *MAC-VRF configuration on dc1-leaf1*

```
root@dc1-leaf1# show routing-instances macvrf-tenant1
instance-type mac-vrf;
protocols {
    evpn {
        encapsulation vxlan;
        extended-vni-list all;
    }
}
vtep-source-interface lo0.0;
service-type vlan-aware;
interface ge-0/0/2.0;
route-distinguisher 192.0.2.11:1;
vrf-target target:1:1;
vlans {
    v100 {
        vlan-id 100;
        vxlan {
            vni 10100;
        }
    }
}
```

On the DC GWs, Integrated Interconnect is enabled, with configuration from dc1-gw shown in Example 11-41. The encapsulation is configured to be MPLS instead of VXLAN to indicate that the transit for stitching is MPLS. Since this is a Juniper MX device, the configuration is slightly different from the configuration in previous sections, which used Juniper QFX devices as GWs—the instance-type is set to *virtual-switch* and, instead of the *vlans* configuration hierarchy, the *bridge-domains* configuration hierarchy is used to configure VLANs for the MAC-VRF.

Example 11-41 *MAC-VRF configuration on dc1-gw*

```
root@dc1-gw# show routing-instances macvrf-tenant1
instance-type virtual-switch;
protocols {
    evpn {
        encapsulation vxlan;
        extended-vni-list 10100;
        interconnect {
            vrf-target target:1:2;
            route-distinguisher 192.0.2.14:12;
            esi {
                00:00:00:00:00:00:00:00:00:11;
                all-active;
            }
            interconnected-vlan-list 100;
```

```
            encapsulation mpls;
        }
    }
}
vtep-source-interface lo0.0;
bridge-domains {
    v100 {
        domain-type bridge;
        vlan-id 100;
        vxlan {
            vni 10100;
        }
    }
}
route-distinguisher 192.0.2.14:1;
vrf-target target:1:1;
```

As shown in Example 11-42, DC2's GW (dc2-gw) has similar configuration. While the interconnect Route Target is the same, each DC uses a unique I-ESI on its GWs.

Example 11-42 *MAC-VRF configuration on dc2-gw*

```
root@dc2-gw# show routing-instances macvrf-tenant1
instance-type virtual-switch;
protocols {
    evpn {
        encapsulation vxlan;
        extended-vni-list 10100;
        interconnect {
            vrf-target target:1:2;
            route-distinguisher 192.0.2.23:12;
            esi {
                00:00:00:00:00:00:00:00:00:22;
                all-active;
            }
            interconnected-vlan-list 100;
            encapsulation mpls;
        }
    }
}
vtep-source-interface lo0.0;
bridge-domains {
    v100 {
        domain-type bridge;
        vlan-id 100;
        vxlan {
            vni 10100;
        }
    }
}
route-distinguisher 192.0.2.23:1;
vrf-target target:2:2;
```

The GWs also have a BGP group that is used to establish an iBGP peering between the DCs for the DCI. The configuration for this BGP group from both dc1-gw and dc2-gw is shown in Example 11-43. With this configuration in place, both GWs successfully form an iBGP peering with each other.

Example 11-43 *Configuration for iBGP DCI peering on dc1-gw and dc2-gw*

```
root@dc1-gw# show protocols bgp group dci-overlay
type internal;
local-address 192.0.2.14;
family evpn {
    signaling;
}
peer-as 65510;
local-as 65510;
neighbor 192.0.2.23;

admin@dc2-gw# show protocols bgp group dci-overlay
type internal;
local-address 192.0.2.23;
family evpn {
    signaling;
}
peer-as 65510;
local-as 65510;
neighbor 192.0.2.14;

root@dc1-gw> show bgp summary group dci-overlay
Threading mode: BGP I/O
Default eBGP mode: advertise - accept, receive - accept
Groups: 3 Peers: 5 Down peers: 0
Table          Tot Paths  Act Paths Suppressed    History Damp State    Pending
inet.0
                    6          4         0          0        0          0
bgp.evpn.0
                   22         14         0          0        0          0
Peer                 AS      InPkt    OutPkt    OutQ    Flaps Last Up/Dwn
State|#Active/Received/Accepted/Damped...
192.0.2.23        65510       5097      5105       0        1 1d 11:20:26 Establ
  bgp.evpn.0: 10/14/14/0
  macvrf-tenant1.evpn.0: 5/5/5/0
  __default_evpn__.evpn.0: 1/1/1/0

root@dc2-gw> show bgp summary group dci-overlay
Threading mode: BGP I/O
Default eBGP mode: advertise - accept, receive - accept
Groups: 3 Peers: 5 Down peers: 0
Table          Tot Paths  Act Paths Suppressed    History Damp State    Pending
```

```
inet.0
                     6        4        0        0        0        0
bgp.evpn.0
                    22       14        0        0        0        0
Peer                    AS    InPkt    OutPkt   OutQ  Flaps Last Up/Dwn
State|#Active/Received/Accepted/Damped...
192.0.2.14           65510    5113     5102       0      0 1d 11:23:26 Establ
  bgp.evpn.0: 10/14/14/0
  macvrf-tenant1.evpn.0: 5/5/5/0
  __default_evpn__.evpn.0: 1/1/1/0
```

Control Plane Flow

Consider a situation in which host h1's address is learned on dc1-leaf1 and it needs to be advertised across the MPLS transit to DC2. When this MAC address is first learned on dc1-leaf1, all the processes that have been explained for a locally learned MAC address so far remain unchanged—this is a data plane learn and host h1's address is installed in L2ALM, L2ALD, and eventually the EVPN database. From the EVPN database, a BGP EVPN update is generated—this is an EVPN Type-2 MAC and MAC+IP route. Example 11-44 shows the L2ALD view and the EVPN database for h1's MAC address.

Example 11-44 *Host h1's address in L2ALD and EVPN database*

```
root@dc1-leaf1> show mac-vrf forwarding mac-table aa:c1:ab:48:f6:10


MAC flags (S - static MAC, D - dynamic MAC, L - locally learned, P - Persistent static
          SE - statistics enabled, NM - non configured MAC, R - remote PE MAC, O - ovsdb MAC)


Ethernet switching table : 2 entries, 2 learned
Routing instance : macvrf-tenant1
    Vlan              MAC                 MAC    GBP   Logical             SVLBNH/     Active
    name              address             flags  tag   interface           VENH Index  source
    v100              aa:c1:ab:48:f6:10   D            ge-0/0/2.0


root@dc1-leaf1> show evpn database mac-address aa:c1:ab:48:f6:10 extensive
Instance: macvrf-tenant1


VN Identifier: 10100, MAC address: aa:c1:ab:48:f6:10
  State: 0x0
  Source: ge-0/0/2.0, Rank: 1, Status: Active
    Mobility sequence number: 0 (minimum origin address 192.0.2.11)
    Timestamp: Sep 24 16:49:41.063755 (0x651068a5)
    State: <Local-MAC-Only Local-To-Remote-Adv-Allowed>
    MAC advertisement route status: Created
    IP address: 10.100.10.1
    Flags: <Local-Adv>
    History db: <No entries>
```

When dc1-gw receives this EVPN Type-2 route, it imports the route and creates an entry in its EVPN database, eventually installing the address in L2ALD, L2ALM, and the hardware. At the same time, dc1-gw also creates an EVPN Type-2 DCI route for this address with the interconnect Route Distinguisher and attaches the I-ESI to the route. In addition to this, the BGP extended community that specifies the encapsulation as VXLAN is omitted from the route (meaning that traffic for this address does not need to be VXLAN encapsulated over the transit), and the route label attached to this route is an MPLS label (more on this later). This is shown in Example 11-45, with a logical representation of the same shown in Figure 11-33.

Example 11-45 *EVPN Type-2 route generated by dc1-gw for DCI*

```
root@dc1-gw> show route table bgp.evpn.0 match-prefix 2:*192.0.2.14:12*aa:c1:ab:48:f6:10*


bgp.evpn.0: 28 destinations, 32 routes (24 active, 0 holddown, 4 hidden)
+ = Active Route, - = Last Active, * = Both


2:192.0.2.14:12::100::aa:c1:ab:48:f6:10/304 MAC/IP
                   *[EVPN/170] 00:05:48
                        Indirect
2:192.0.2.14:12::100::aa:c1:ab:48:f6:10::10.100.10.1/304 MAC/IP
                   *[EVPN/170] 00:05:48
                        Indirect


admin@dc1-gw> show route table bgp.evpn.0 match-prefix 2:*192.0.2.14:12*aa:c1:ab:48:f6:10* extensive


bgp.evpn.0: 28 destinations, 32 routes (24 active, 0 holddown, 4 hidden)
2:192.0.2.14:12::100::aa:c1:ab:48:f6:10/304 MAC/IP (1 entry, 1 announced)
TSI:
Page 0 idx 0, (group overlay type External) Type 1 val 0xab3e060 (adv_entry)
   Advertised metrics:
     Flags: Nexthop Change
     Nexthop: Self
     AS path: [65424] I
     Communities: target:1:2
   Advertise: 00000003
Page 0 idx 1, (group dci-overlay type Internal) Type 1 val 0x82dd8c8 (adv_entry)
   Advertised metrics:
     Flags: Nexthop Change
     Nexthop: Self
     Localpref: 100
     AS path: [65510] I
     Communities: target:1:2
   Advertise: 00000001
Path 2:192.0.2.14:12::100::aa:c1:ab:48:f6:10
Vector len 4.  Val: 0 1
        *EVPN   Preference: 170
                Next hop type: Indirect, Next hop index: 0
                Address: 0x7b64904
                Next-hop reference count: 22, key opaque handle: 0x0, non-key opaque handle: 0x0
                Protocol next hop: 192.0.2.14
                Indirect next hop: 0x0 - INH Session ID: 0
                State: <Secondary Active Int Ext>
                Age: 6:52
                Validation State: unverified
                Task: macvrf-tenant1-evpn
```

```
Announcement bits (1): 0-BGP_RT_Background
AS path: I
Communities: target:1:2
Route Label: 299872
ESI: 00:00:00:00:00:00:00:00:00:11
Primary Routing Table: macvrf-tenant1.evpn.0
Thread: junos-main
```

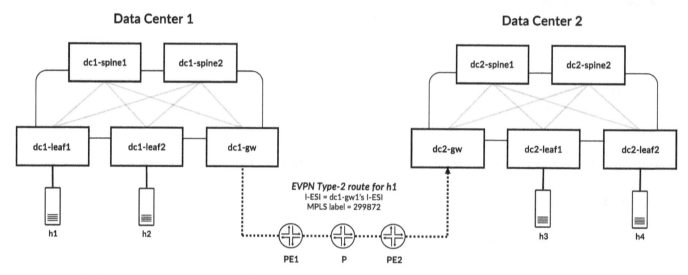

Figure 11-33 *iBGP EVPN route sent from dc1-gw to dc2-gw for host h1's address*

This MPLS label represents the EVPN Instance on dc1-gw and corresponds to the macvrf-tenant1 MAC-VRF, as shown in Example 11-46.

Example 11-46 *MPLS label corresponding to MAC-VRF on dc1-gw*

```
root@dc1-gw> show route table mpls.0 label 299872


mpls.0: 16 destinations, 17 routes (16 active, 0 holddown, 0 hidden)
+ = Active Route, - = Last Active, * = Both


299872              *[EVPN/7] 1d 10:50:52, routing-instance macvrf-tenant1, route-type Ingress-Aliasing
                       to table macvrf-tenant1.evpn-mac.0
                    [EVPN/7] 00:40:51, routing-instance macvrf-tenant1, route-type Ingress-MAC, vlan-id 100
                       to table macvrf-tenant1.evpn-mac.0
```

The packet capture presented in Figure 11-34 shows this BGP EVPN update with the MPLS label, and the I-ESI attached to the route.

The VNI value (which is MPLS Label 1, in this case) does not match the actual label value for the MAC-VRF. This is because the actual label value is encoded into the higher 20 bits of the field. Thus, dec (4797593) gives us a binary of 01001001 00110110 00000001 since this is a 3-octet field. If only the first 20 bits are considered, this gives us a binary of 00000100 10010011 01100000, which is dec (299872).

When dc2-gw receives this route, it imports the route because of the matching interconnect Route Target and installs a corresponding entry in the EVPN database, L2ALD, L2ALM, and the hardware. This entry points to the I-ESI of dc1-gw as the next-hop, as shown in Example 11-47. This resolves to the VTEP address of dc1-gw. Since this is a Juniper MX device, the MAC address table is viewed using the **show bridge mac-table** [*mac-address*] operational mode command.

```
No.    Time        Source         Destination     Protocol  Length  Info
 37 2023-09-24 1.. 192.0.2.14     192.0.2.23      BGP       280 UPDATE Message, UPDATE Message
```

```
> Border Gateway Protocol - UPDATE Message          0000  0c 00 d7 52 00 01 0c 00
  Marker: ffffffffffffffffffffffffffffffff          0010  01 0a 0d a1 00 00 ff 06
  Length: 96                                         0020  02 17 00 b3 ce d9 e1 f0
  Type: UPDATE Message (2)                           0030  40 00 73 5e 00 00 01 01
  Withdrawn Routes Length: 0                         0040  7e 68 ff ff ff ff ff ff
  Total Path Attribute Length: 73                    0050  ff ff 00 76 02 00 00 00
> Path attributes                                    0060  02 03 00 00 ff 90 00 00
  > Path Attribute - ORIGIN: IGP                     0070  04 00 00 00 64 c0 10 10
  > Path Attribute - AS_PATH: empty                  0080  03 0c 00 00 00 00 00 08
  > Path Attribute - LOCAL_PREF: 100                 0090  c0 00 02 0b 00 02 21 00
  > Path Attribute - EXTENDED_COMMUNITIES            00a0  00 00 00 00 00 00 00 00
    > Flags: 0xc0, Optional, Transitive, Complete    00b0  ab 48 f6 10 00 00 27 74
      Type Code: EXTENDED_COMMUNITIES (16)           00c0  ff ff ff ff ff ff ff ff
      Length: 8                                      00d0  01 01 00 40 02 00 40 05
    > Carried extended communities: (1 community)    00e0  00 02 00 01 00 00 00 02
      > Route Target: 1:2 [Transitive 2-Octet AS-Specific]  00f0  c0 00 02 0e 00 02 21 00
  > Path Attribute - MP_REACH_NLRI                   0100  00 00 00 00 00 00 00 00
    > Flags: 0x90, Optional, Extended-Length, Non-transitive, Complete  0110  ab 48 f6 10 00 49 36 01
      Type Code: MP_REACH_NLRI (14)
      Length: 44
      Address family identifier (AFI): Layer-2 VPN (25)
      Subsequent address family identifier (SAFI): EVPN (70)
    > Next hop: 192.0.2.14
      Number of Subnetwork points of attachment (SNPA): 0
    > Network Layer Reachability Information (NLRI)
      > EVPN NLRI: MAC Advertisement Route
          Route Type: MAC Advertisement Route (2)
          Length: 33
          Route Distinguisher: 0001c000020e000c (192.0.2.14:12)
        > ESI: 00:00:00:00:00:00:00:00:00:11
          Ethernet Tag ID: 100
          MAC Address Length: 48
          MAC Address: aa:c1:ab:48:f6:10 (aa:c1:ab:48:f6:10)
          IP Address Length: 0
        > IP Address: NOT INCLUDED
          VNI: 4797953
```

Figure 11-34 *Packet capture of EVPN Type-2 route originated by dc1-gw for DCI*

Example 11-47 *Host h1's address in L2ALD and EVPN database on dc2-gw*

```
root@dc2-gw> show bridge mac-table aa:c1:ab:48:f6:10


MAC flags       (S -static MAC, D -dynamic MAC, L -locally learned, C -Control MAC
   O -OVSDB MAC, SE -Statistics enabled, NM -Non configured MAC, R -Remote PE MAC, P -Pinned MAC)


Routing instance : macvrf-tenant1
 Bridging domain : v100, VLAN : 100
   MAC              MAC      Logical        NH      MAC      active
   address          flags    interface      Index   property source
   aa:c1:ab:48:f6:10 DC      .local..1048584 1048584          00:00:00:00:00:00:00:00:00:11


root@dc2-gw> show evpn database mac-address aa:c1:ab:48:f6:10 extensive
Instance: macvrf-tenant1


VLAN ID: 100, MAC address: aa:c1:ab:48:f6:10
  Nexthop ID: 1048584
  State: 0x0
  Source: 00:00:00:00:00:00:00:00:00:11, Rank: 1, Status: Active
    Remote origin: 192.0.2.14
```

```
Remote state: <Mac-Only-Adv Interconnect-DC>
Mobility sequence number: 0 (minimum origin address 192.0.2.14)
Timestamp: Sep 25 02:37:50.175959 (0x6510f27e)
State: <Remote-To-Local-Adv-Done>
MAC advertisement route status: Not created (no local state present)
Interconn advertisement route status: DC route created
IP address: 10.100.10.1
Flags: <Sent-to-l2ald Interconnect-DC>
  Remote origin: 192.0.2.14
  Remote state: <Interconnect-DC>
  Interconn advertisement route status: DC route created
History db: <No entries>
```

From the EVPN database, dc2-gw originates EVPN Type-2 MAC and MAC+IP routes for host h1's address for its local data center, which are sent to the spines and leafs of DC2 via BGP EVPN. These routes are originated with the Route Distinguisher and I-ESI of dc2-gw, along with the local DC Route Target and encapsulation of VXLAN added as extended communities. This is shown in Example 11-48.

Example 11-48 *Host h1's address re-originated by dc2-gw into local DC as EVPN Type-2 routes*

```
root@dc2-gw> show route table bgp.evpn.0 match-prefix 2:*192.0.2.23:1*aa:c1:ab:48:f6:10*

bgp.evpn.0: 40 destinations, 46 routes (34 active, 0 holddown, 6 hidden)
+ = Active Route, - = Last Active, * = Both

2:192.0.2.23:1::10100::aa:c1:ab:48:f6:10/304 MAC/IP
                    *[EVPN/170] 00:03:52
                        Indirect
2:192.0.2.23:1::10100::aa:c1:ab:48:f6:10::10.100.10.1/304 MAC/IP
                    *[EVPN/170] 00:03:52
                        Indirect


root@dc2-gw> show route table bgp.evpn.0 match-prefix 2:*192.0.2.23:1*aa:c1:ab:48:f6:10* extensive

bgp.evpn.0: 40 destinations, 46 routes (34 active, 0 holddown, 6 hidden)
2:192.0.2.23:1::10100::aa:c1:ab:48:f6:10/304 MAC/IP (1 entry, 1 announced)
TSI:
Page 0 idx 0, (group overlay type External) Type 1 val 0x86334bc (adv_entry)
  Advertised metrics:
    Flags: Nexthop Change
    Nexthop: Self
    AS path: [65433] I
    Communities: target:2:2 encapsulation:vxlan(0x8)
  Advertise: 00000003
Page 0 idx 1, (group dci-overlay type Internal) Type 1 val 0x8633548 (adv_entry)
  Advertised metrics:
    Flags: Nexthop Change
    Nexthop: Self
    Localpref: 100
    AS path: [65510] I
```

```
         Communities: target:2:2 encapsulation:vxlan(0x8)
      Advertise: 00000001
Path 2:192.0.2.23:1::10100::aa:c1:ab:48:f6:10
Vector len 4.  Val: 0 1
        *EVPN    Preference: 170
                 Next hop type: Indirect, Next hop index: 0
                 Address: 0x7b64824
                 Next-hop reference count: 30, key opaque handle: 0x0, non-key opaque handle: 0x0
                 Protocol next hop: 192.0.2.23
                 Indirect next hop: 0x0 - INH Session ID: 0
                 State: <Secondary Active Int Ext>
                 Age: 4:12
                 Validation State: unverified
                 Task: macvrf-tenant1-evpn
                 Announcement bits (1): 0-BGP_RT_Background
                 AS path: I
                 Communities: target:2:2 encapsulation:vxlan(0x8)
                 Route Label: 10100
                 ESI: 00:00:00:00:00:00:00:00:00:22
                 Primary Routing Table: macvrf-tenant1.evpn.0
                 Thread: junos-main


*snip*
```

When other leafs in DC2 receive this route, they import it into their EVPN database and install it in their corresponding L2ALD, L2ALM, and hardware tables. The address is installed with a next-hop of the I-ESI of dc2-gw. Considering dc2-leaf1 as an example, this is shown in Example 11-49.

Example 11-49 *Host h1's address in L2ALD and EVPN database on dc2-leaf1*

```
root@dc2-leaf1> show mac-vrf forwarding mac-table aa:c1:ab:48:f6:10


MAC flags (S - static MAC, D - dynamic MAC, L - locally learned, P - Persistent static
          SE - statistics enabled, NM - non configured MAC, R - remote PE MAC, O - ovsdb MAC)


Ethernet switching table : 4 entries, 4 learned
Routing instance : macvrf-tenant1
    Vlan            MAC              MAC      GBP    Logical              SVLBNH/      Active
    name            address          flags    tag    interface            VENH Index   source
    v100            aa:c1:ab:48:f6:10 DR              esi.603
00:00:00:00:00:00:00:00:00:22


root@dc2-leaf1> show evpn database mac-address aa:c1:ab:48:f6:10 extensive
Instance: macvrf-tenant1


VN Identifier: 10100, MAC address: aa:c1:ab:48:f6:10
  State: 0x0
  Source: 00:00:00:00:00:00:00:00:00:22, Rank: 1, Status: Active
    Remote origin: 192.0.2.23
    Remote state: <Mac-Only-Adv>
```

```
        Mobility sequence number: 0 (minimum origin address 192.0.2.23)
        Timestamp: Sep 25 02:48:50.052132 (0x6510f512)
        State: <Remote-To-Local-Adv-Done>
        MAC advertisement route status: Not created (no local state present)
        IP address: 10.100.10.1
          Remote origin: 192.0.2.23
          Remote state: <Sent-to-l2ald>
        History db: <No entries>
```

```
root@dc2_leaf1> show mac-vrf forwarding vxlan-tunnel-end-point esi
ESI                           RTT                    VLNBH INH   ESI-IFL   LOC-IFL   #RVTEPs
00:00:00:00:00:00:00:00:22 macvrf-tenant1             603   1048574 esi.603           1      Aliasing
    RVTEP-IP          RVTEP-IFL      VENH     MASK-ID   FLAGS      MAC-COUNT
    192.0.2.23        vtep.32770     602      0         2          2
```

With an understanding of the control plane, the following subsection dives into the details of the data plane when using an MPLS transit with Integrated Interconnect.

Data Plane Flow

To demonstrate the data plane flow in such a design, refer to Figure 11-31 and consider host h1 in Data Center 1 communicating with host h3 in Data Center 2. Since both hosts are in the same subnet, when host h1 attempts to communicate with h3 (via the **ping** command issued on h1), it will ARP for the destination directly. With the assumption that addresses of both hosts are learned across the two DCs, h1's local leaf (dc1-leaf1) can proxy-ARP and respond to the ARP request for h3, as shown in Figure 11-35.

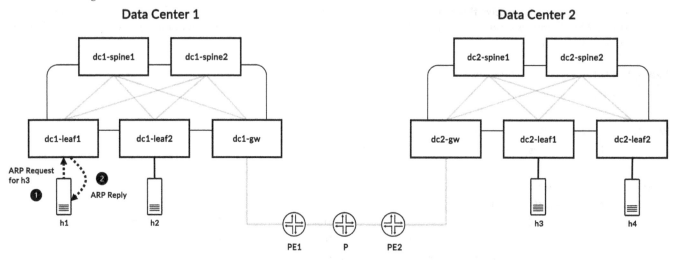

Figure 11-35 *Proxy-ARP reply by dc1-leaf1 to an ARP request destined for host h3*

Once the ARP is resolved on host h1, it can generate an ICMP request for h3. This request, on reaching dc1-leaf1, is encapsulated with VXLAN headers with an outer destination IP address of 192.0.2.14 (which belongs to dc1-gw), as per the lookup shown in Example 11-50.

Example 11-50 *Result of host h3's MAC address lookup on dc1-leaf1*

```
root@dc1-leaf1> show mac-vrf forwarding mac-table aa:c1:ab:c1:23:61

MAC flags (S - static MAC, D - dynamic MAC, L - locally learned, P - Persistent static
```

```
SE - statistics enabled, NM - non configured MAC, R - remote PE MAC, O - ovsdb MAC)

Ethernet switching table : 4 entries, 4 learned
Routing instance : macvrf-tenant1
   Vlan              MAC              MAC     GBP   Logical           SVLBNH/      Active
   name              address          flags   tag   interface         VENH Index   source
   v100              aa:c1:ab:c1:23:61  DR            esi.601
00:00:00:00:00:00:00:00:11


root@dc1-leaf1> show mac-vrf forwarding vxlan-tunnel-end-point esi esi-identifier 00:00:00:00:00:00:00:00:11
ESI                        RTT              VLNBH INH   ESI-IFL   LOC-IFL   #RVTEPs
00:00:00:00:00:00:00:00:11 macvrf-tenant1    601  1048574 esi.601            1      Aliasing
   RVTEP-IP         RVTEP-IFL     VENH    MASK-ID   FLAGS    MAC-COUNT
   192.0.2.14       vtep.32770    600     0         2        2
```

This can be visualized as shown in Figure 11-36.

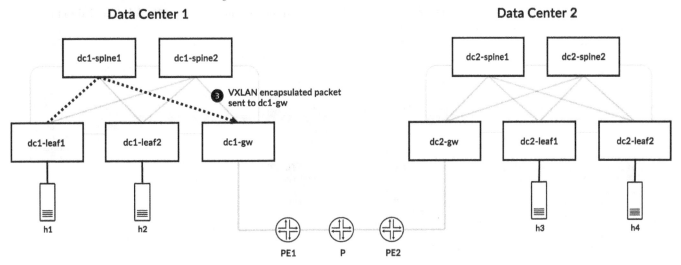

Figure 11-36 *VXLAN-encapsulated packet from dc1-leaf1 to dc1-gw*

When this packet reaches dc1-gw, the MAC address lookup results in an MPLS encapsulation, with two MPLS labels as shown in Example 11-51. The top label (299808) is the transport label that carries the packet across the MPLS transit to dc2-gw, and the bottom label (299904) is the label associated with the MAC-VRF EVPN Instance on dc2-gw.

Example 11-51 *Result of host h3's MAC address lookup on dc1-gw showing MPLS labels to be added*

```
root@dc1-gw> show route forwarding-table destination aa:c1:ab:c1:23:61/48
Routing table: macvrf-tenant1.evpn-vxlan
Bridging domain: v100.evpn-vxlan
VPLS:
Enabled protocols: Bridging, ACKed by all peers, EVPN VXLAN, MPLS DCI Rtt,
Destination      Type RtRef Next hop      Type Index    NhRef Netif
aa:c1:ab:c1:23:61/48 user    0            indr 1048584   4
                          198.51.100.29   Push 299904, Push 299808(top)   610    2 ge-0/0/2.0
```

Visually, this can be represented as shown in Figure 11-37.

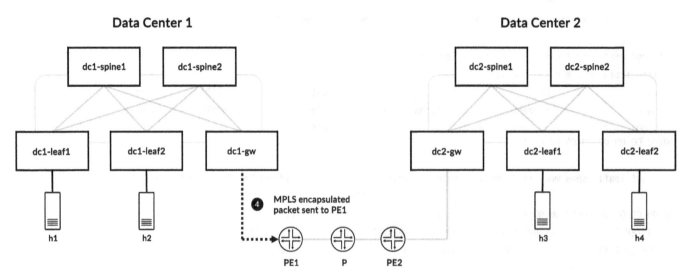

Figure 11-37 *MPLS-encapsulated packet from dc1-gw to PE1*

The packet capture presented in Figure 11-38 confirms the MPLS encapsulation and the two MPLS labels added to the original packet as it is sent from dc1-gw into the MPLS domain.

```
No.   Time              Source            Destination     Protocol Length Info
   1 2023-09-23 0… 10.100.10.1 10.100.10.3 ICMP    124 Echo (ping) request  id=0x000c, seq=341/21761, ttl=64 (reply in 2)
   2 2023-09-23 0… 10.100.10.3 10.100.10.1 ICMP    120 Echo (ping) reply    id=0x000c, seq=341/21761, ttl=64 (request in 1)

> Frame 1: 124 bytes on wire (992 bits), 124 bytes captured (992 bits)            0000  0c 00 d7 52 00
> Ethernet II, Src: 0c:00:02:16:0e:03 (0c:00:02:16:0e:03), Dst: 0c:00:d7:52:00:01 (0c:00:d7:52:00:01)  0010  00 ff 49 38 01
v MultiProtocol Label Switching Header, Label: 299808, Exp: 0, S: 0, TTL: 255     0020  f6 10 81 00 00
     0100 1001 0011 0010 0000 .... .... .... = MPLS Label: 299808 (0x49320)       0030  40 01 fc ff 0a
     .... .... .... .... .... 000. .... .... = MPLS Experimental Bits: 0          0040  00 0c 01 55 9f
     .... .... .... .... .... ...0 .... .... = MPLS Bottom Of Label Stack: 0      0050  00 00 00 00 10
     .... .... .... .... .... .... 1111 1111 = MPLS TTL: 255                      0060  1c 1d 1e 1f 20
v MultiProtocol Label Switching Header, Label: 299904, Exp: 0, S: 1, TTL: 255     0070  2c 2d 2e 2f 30
     0100 1001 0011 1000 0000 .... .... .... = MPLS Label: 299904 (0x49380)
     .... .... .... .... .... 000. .... .... = MPLS Experimental Bits: 0
     .... .... .... .... .... ...1 .... .... = MPLS Bottom Of Label Stack: 1
     .... .... .... .... .... .... 1111 1111 = MPLS TTL: 255
> Ethernet II, Src: aa:c1:ab:48:f6:10 (aa:c1:ab:48:f6:10), Dst: aa:c1:ab:c1:23:61 (aa:c1:ab:c1:23:61)
> 802.1Q Virtual LAN, PRI: 0, DEI: 0, ID: 100
> Internet Protocol Version 4, Src: 10.100.10.1, Dst: 10.100.10.3
> Internet Control Message Protocol
```

Figure 11-38 *Packet capture of MPLS-encapsulated packet from dc1-gw to PE1*

The packet is now label switched through the MPLS transit using the top label. Thus, when PE1 receives it, it has a swap action associated with the label 299808, as shown in Example 11-52.

Example 11-52 *MPLS lookup for label 299808 on PE1*

```
root@pe1> show route table mpls.0 label 299808

mpls.0: 12 destinations, 12 routes (12 active, 0 holddown, 0 hidden)
+ = Active Route, - = Last Active, * = Both

299808             *[LDP/9] 3d 22:39:01, metric 1
                    > to 198.51.100.31 via ge-0/0/1.0, Swap 299792
```

When this reaches the P device, the top label is now 299792, as shown in Figure 11-39.

On the P device, the MPLS lookup of the top label results in another swap action, this time swapping to label 299776. PE2 receives this MPLS packet, and a lookup on this top label results in a behavior called Penultimate Hop Popping (PHP), which simply removes the top label, exposing the inner VPN label. Both these lookups are shown in Example 11-53.

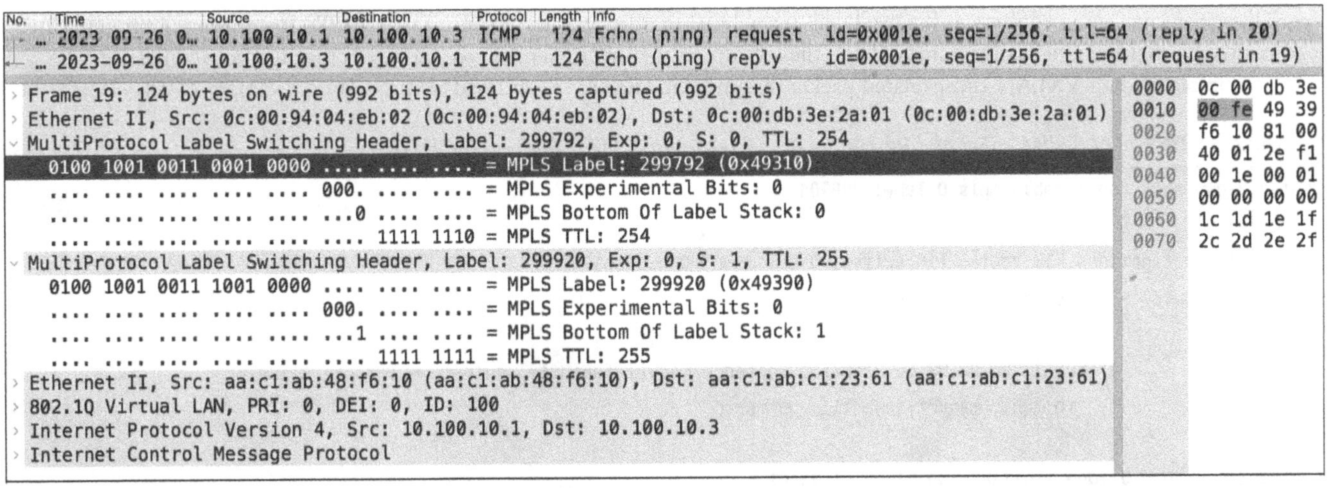

```
No.   Time          Source        Destination   Protocol  Length  Info
 ... 2023 09 26 0... 10.100.10.1  10.100.10.3   ICMP      124  Echo (ping) request   id=0x001e, seq=1/256, ttl=64 (reply in 20)
 ... 2023-09-26 0... 10.100.10.3  10.100.10.1   ICMP      124  Echo (ping) reply     id=0x001e, seq=1/256, ttl=64 (request in 19)
```

```
> Frame 19: 124 bytes on wire (992 bits), 124 bytes captured (992 bits)      0000  0c 00 db 3e
> Ethernet II, Src: 0c:00:94:04:eb:02 (0c:00:94:04:eb:02), Dst: 0c:00:db:3e:2a:01 (0c:00:db:3e:2a:01)  0010  00 fe 49 39
v MultiProtocol Label Switching Header, Label: 299792, Exp: 0, S: 0, TTL: 254  0020  f6 10 81 00
      0100 1001 0011 0001 0000 .... .... .... = MPLS Label: 299792 (0x49310)   0030  40 01 2e f1
      .... .... .... .... .... 000. .... .... = MPLS Experimental Bits: 0      0040  00 1e 00 01
      .... .... .... .... .... ...0 .... .... = MPLS Bottom Of Label Stack: 0  0050  00 00 00 00
      .... .... .... .... .... .... 1111 1110 = MPLS TTL: 254                  0060  1c 1d 1e 1f
v MultiProtocol Label Switching Header, Label: 299920, Exp: 0, S: 1, TTL: 255  0070  2c 2d 2e 2f
      0100 1001 0011 1001 0000 .... .... .... = MPLS Label: 299920 (0x49390)
      .... .... .... .... .... 000. .... .... = MPLS Experimental Bits: 0
      .... .... .... .... .... ...1 .... .... = MPLS Bottom Of Label Stack: 1
      .... .... .... .... .... .... 1111 1111 = MPLS TTL: 255
> Ethernet II, Src: aa:c1:ab:48:f6:10 (aa:c1:ab:48:f6:10), Dst: aa:c1:ab:c1:23:61 (aa:c1:ab:c1:23:61)
> 802.1Q Virtual LAN, PRI: 0, DEI: 0, ID: 100
> Internet Protocol Version 4, Src: 10.100.10.1, Dst: 10.100.10.3
> Internet Control Message Protocol
```

Figure 11-39 *Packet capture of MPLS-encapsulated packet from PE1 to P*

Example 11-53 *MPLS lookup for label 299792 on P device and label 299776 on PE2*

```
root@p> show route table mpls.0 label 299792

mpls.0: 12 destinations, 12 routes (12 active, 0 holddown, 0 hidden)
+ = Active Route, - = Last Active, * = Both

299792             *[LDP/9] 3d 22:51:57, metric 1
                    >  to 198.51.100.33 via ge-0/0/1.0, Swap 299776


admin@pe2> show route table mpls.0 label 299776

mpls.0: 12 destinations, 12 routes (12 active, 0 holddown, 0 hidden)
+ = Active Route, - = Last Active, * = Both

299776             *[LDP/9] 3d 23:01:15, metric 1
                    >  to 198.51.100.35 via ge-0/0/0.0, Pop
299776(S=0)        *[LDP/9] 3d 23:01:15, metric 1
                    >  to 198.51.100.35 via ge-0/0/0.0, Pop
```

Thus, what dc2-gw now receives is an MPLS-encapsulated packet with just one MPLS label, as shown in Figure 11-40.

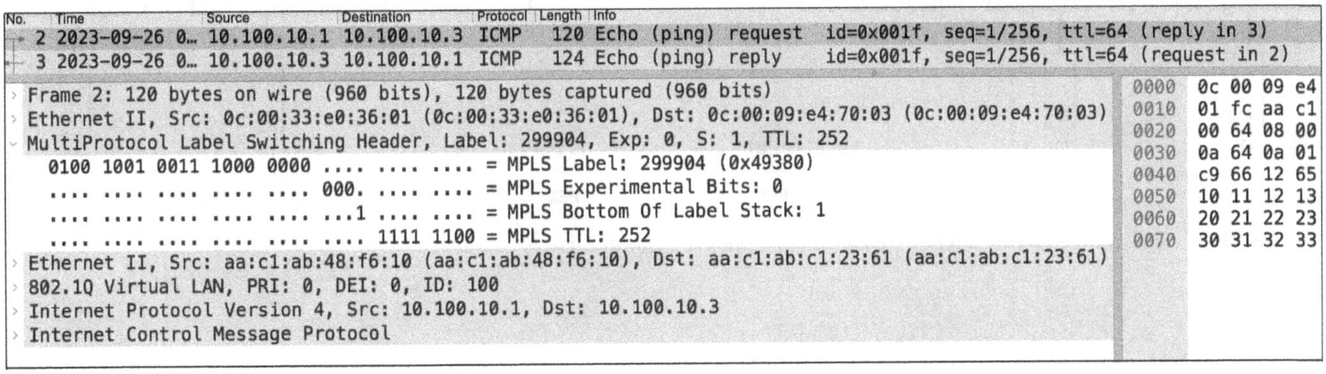

```
No.   Time          Source        Destination   Protocol  Length  Info
 2 2023-09-26 0... 10.100.10.1  10.100.10.3   ICMP      120  Echo (ping) request   id=0x001f, seq=1/256, ttl=64 (reply in 3)
 3 2023-09-26 0... 10.100.10.3  10.100.10.1   ICMP      124  Echo (ping) reply     id=0x001f, seq=1/256, ttl=64 (request in 2)
```

```
> Frame 2: 120 bytes on wire (960 bits), 120 bytes captured (960 bits)        0000  0c 00 09 e4
> Ethernet II, Src: 0c:00:33:e0:36:01 (0c:00:33:e0:36:01), Dst: 0c:00:09:e4:70:03 (0c:00:09:e4:70:03)  0010  01 fc aa c1
v MultiProtocol Label Switching Header, Label: 299904, Exp: 0, S: 1, TTL: 252  0020  00 64 08 00
      0100 1001 0011 1000 0000 .... .... .... = MPLS Label: 299904 (0x49380)   0030  0a 64 0a 01
      .... .... .... .... .... 000. .... .... = MPLS Experimental Bits: 0      0040  c9 66 12 65
      .... .... .... .... .... ...1 .... .... = MPLS Bottom Of Label Stack: 1  0050  10 11 12 13
      .... .... .... .... .... .... 1111 1100 = MPLS TTL: 252                  0060  20 21 22 23
> Ethernet II, Src: aa:c1:ab:48:f6:10 (aa:c1:ab:48:f6:10), Dst: aa:c1:ab:c1:23:61 (aa:c1:ab:c1:23:61)  0070  30 31 32 33
> 802.1Q Virtual LAN, PRI: 0, DEI: 0, ID: 100
> Internet Protocol Version 4, Src: 10.100.10.1, Dst: 10.100.10.3
> Internet Control Message Protocol
```

Figure 11-40 *Packet capture of MPLS-encapsulated packet from PE2 to dc2-gw*

This inner label (now exposed as the top label) is the label that belongs to the MAC-VRF EVPN Instance itself and indicates to dc2-gw that the label can be removed and the lookup on the inner packet must happen in that respective instance. This lookup results in a VXLAN-encapsulated packet that must be directed to dc2-leaf1, as shown in Example 11-54.

Example 11-54 *MPLS VPN label and lookup on inner destination MAC address on dc2-gw*

```
root@dc2-gw> show route table mpls.0 label 299904


mpls.0: 16 destinations, 16 routes (16 active, 0 holddown, 0 hidden)
+ = Active Route, - = Last Active, * = Both


299904            *[EVPN/7] 2d 22:32:52, routing-instance macvrf-tenant1, route-type Ingress-Aliasing
                    to table macvrf-tenant1.evpn-mac.0


root@dc2-gw> show bridge mac-table aa:c1:ab:c1:23:61


MAC flags       (S -static MAC, D -dynamic MAC, L -locally learned, C -Control MAC
    O -OVSDB MAC, SE -Statistics enabled, NM -Non configured MAC, R -Remote PE MAC, P -Pinned MAC)


Routing instance : macvrf-tenant1
 Bridging domain : v100, VLAN : 100
    MAC               MAC      Logical      NH    MAC        active
    address           flags    interface    Index property   source
    aa:c1:ab:c1:23:61 DR       vtep.32769                     192.0.2.21
```

This can be visually represented as shown in Figure 11-41. When this packet arrives at dc2-leaf1, it decapsulates the packet and sends the original IP packet to host h3. Host h3 will respond, and the return path will follow the same process. In this way, Integrated Interconnect can be used to stitch together two or more data centers, deployed with BGP EVPN and VXLAN, with an MPLS transit.

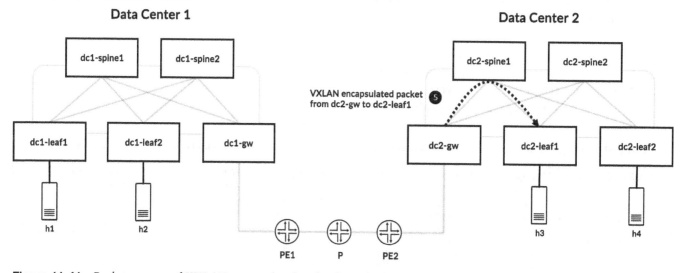

Figure 11-41 *Packet capture of VXLAN-encapsulated packet from dc2-gw to dc2-leaf1*

Summary

This chapter detailed different data center interconnection designs to connect two or more data centers (or pods) together, and the necessity to do this with an understanding of the complexity that is inherent with a data center's growth. This complexity is a function of the state, scale of state, and network churn that impacts this state within a DC. The DCI becomes an abstraction point, which allows reduction in complexity as information is shared between DCs or pods.

This chapter also described why careful evaluation is necessary when choosing between OTT and Integrated Interconnect, as each design has upsides and downsides. While an OTT design is simple to implement and operationalize, it does little to reduce the complexity between DCs. Integrated Interconnect, on the other hand, is more complex to implement and operationalize but it does reduce the complexity shared between DCs and is the recommended design when building large-scale DCs.

Building Data Centers with Juniper Apstra, Part I—Apstra Foundation

As an introduction to Apstra, the goal of this chapter is to focus on the building blocks and how they are used to deploy data center fabrics in Apstra. This chapter includes the following topics:

- Understanding the building blocks of Apstra, such as Logical Devices, Device Profiles, Interface Maps, Rack Types, Templates, and Blueprints

- Manual onboarding of devices and Zero Touch Provisioning

- Creating Rack Types and Templates in Apstra

- Deploying a 3-stage Clos fabric with a bridged overlay design, instantiated as a Blueprint, including assigning resources such as ASN and IP pools, mapping Device Profiles and Interface Maps to generate vendor-specific configuration, and validation of the deployed fabric

- Overall lifecycle of a device in Apstra

This chapter uses Apstra software release 4.2.0. Advanced deployment scenarios such as edge-routed bridging, Data Center Interconnect, 5-stage Clos designs, and policy control for a data center fabric are covered in the subsequent chapter.

Introduction to Juniper Apstra

Juniper Apstra is a multivendor solution for data center automation and insights, catering to various Day-0 (design), Day-1 (build), and Day-2 (operate) activities. It falls under the bracket of *intent-based networks/networking (IBN)*—this is a popular term thrown around in the wild, but Apstra really exemplifies IBN and is essentially an IBN system (IBNS). The general ideology with Apstra is to maintain and validate the network as a whole, and not just individual components of it.

The Apstra network itself is driven by intent—intent provided by the end user but converted into deployable network elements by Apstra. From the perspective of the operator, the intent is captured in the form of various inputs, including the number of racks in a data center, the number of leafs per rack, how many (and what kind of) systems are connected to these leafs, and what kind of redundancy is required per rack. These inputs are then converted into vendor-specific configuration by Apstra (thus providing a level of abstraction) and pushed to the respective fabric devices to bring the intent to life.

In his book *Intent-Based Networking for Dummies*, Jeff Doyle has a great statement about an IBN system: "The system self-operates, self-adjusts, and self-corrects within the parameters of your expressed technical objective." What is the expressed technical objective or expectation? It is simply the intent, provided by the operator.

As an IBN system, Apstra has the following characteristics:

- **Base automation and orchestration:** This includes the conversion of user intent into vendor-specific configuration, eliminating any human error and conforming to reference designs built for different deployment models.

- **A single source of truth:** This is important because you cannot have uniform and nonconflicting intent with multiple sources of truth. Idempotency (consistency in the result of an operation despite running the operation multiple times) can only exist with a single source of truth. In the case of Apstra, a *Blueprint* (discussed in more detail shortly) is instantiated as a graph database, which acts as the single source of truth (SSOT).

- **Closed-loop validation:** This type of validation is continuous verification, in real time, of current network state with intended state, to flag any potential deviation. These deviations are called *anomalies* in Apstra. This eventually leads to self-correction and self-operation.

- **Self-operation:** Only through closed-loop validation can the network self-correct or, at minimum, alert the user that the network is out of compliance and provide possible remediation steps. Apstra provides user-configurable thresholds for many aspects of compliance, tying back to operator intent of the data center fabric.

At a high level, Apstra offers the following key features that make private data center deployments as easy as cloud deployments:

- Multivendor support through abstracted intent converted into vendor-specific configuration.

- Conformance to common data center reference designs, including 3-stage and 5-stage Clos fabrics and collapsed spine designs.

- Operational ability to add custom configurations that are injected and monitored as part of user intent using an Apstra feature called *Configlets*.

- Support for virtual software offerings from vendors for feature and functional testing, and to build virtual fabrics for integration into network continuous integration and continuous delivery (CI/CD) pipelines.

- Telemetry and analytics providing insights, feeding directly into critical Day-2 operational management of the network infrastructure.

- Git-like revision control with the ability to roll back network state through an Apstra feature called *Time Voyager*.

- Granular policy control for data center fabrics.

- Interconnection of two or more data centers using over-the-top (OTT) or Integrated Interconnect models (introduced in Chapter 11, "Data Center Interconnect").

- Apstra *Freeform*, which allows the operator to design their own data center fabrics, if the built-in Apstra reference designs do not meet the design needs.

- Terraform integration for infrastructure-as-code deployment and control, using a Go SDK built for Apstra northbound APIs.

- A graph database of an instantiated fabric, acting as a single source of truth. This graph is queried by Apstra for various reasons, including conformance to user intent. Apstra uses this graph database to eventually create vendor-specific configuration to be pushed to appropriate devices.

NOTE Juniper Apstra is offered as a software-only package and does not ship as a hardware appliance. It can be installed as a VM using various virtualization tools and hypervisors such as VMware ESXi and KVM (Kernel-based Virtual Machine). The installation itself is straightforward, and you can find the installation steps in the *Juniper Apstra User Guide* online. This book does not cover the installation for the sake of brevity.

Building Blocks of Apstra

In an organization, data centers are built uniformly, with the same rack design, the same set of top-of-rack switches and combination of uplinks/downlinks, and the same requirements from services using the network infrastructure. Introducing snowflake requirements in a data center is usually not a good idea—it introduces unique variables that are hard to track as the data center grows and even harder to operationally manage and troubleshoot. Thus, at its core, a data center is built based on reusability and repeatability, with the ability to use the same overall design (scaled up or down) per the organization's network needs.

Apstra is designed based on the same core principle—the general workflow requires that the operator create basic building blocks that can be reused to scale up an existing data center or build additional data centers. To do this, Apstra offers a web-based user interface (UI), accessed over HTTP (not secure) or HTTPS (secure). Figure 12-1 shows your first look at the Apstra UI in software release 4.2.0. It is important to note that there may be differences in the UI across different Apstra software releases.

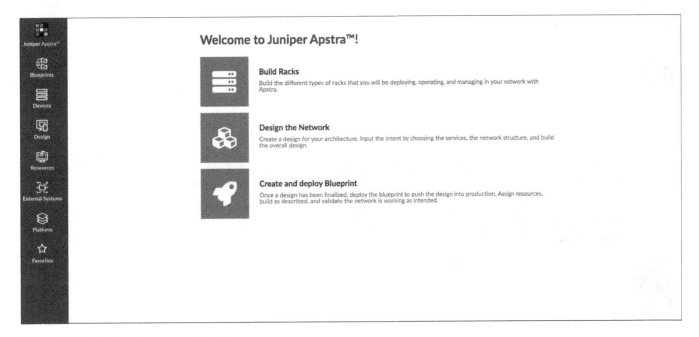

Figure 12-1 *Juniper Apstra user interface*

The following are some terms and constructs that you should be familiar with when working with Apstra:

- **Logical Devices:** In order to facilitate Apstra's multivendor nature, a level of abstraction is necessary. This abstraction allows entire data centers to be *logically* built without even having to map any vendor-specific hardware instances. This enables the operator to design an entire data center fabric without having to choose a specific vendor at the beginning. At the core of this abstraction lie Logical Devices. A *Logical Device* is a logical representation of data center switches, port densities, and their roles in the fabric, defined by the kind of devices it can connect to (such as a leaf, spine, super-spine, or generic devices). For example, a Juniper QFX5120-48Y is a common data center (and campus) leaf that has 48 × 1G/10G /25G downlink ports and 8 × 40G/100G uplink ports. Apstra provides a logical representation of this, abstracting any hardware specifications and simply retaining the port combination.

  These Logical Devices typically follow the naming convention of AOS-*port-combination* in Apstra. Thus, one possible Logical Device that matches the Juniper QFX5120-48Y switch is AOS-48x10+8x100. You can find Logical Devices on the Design tab in the Apstra UI. Many Logical Devices are predefined in Apstra, but there is no limitation in creating user-defined Logical Devices to suit a data center's need. Figure 12-2 shows an example of a Logical Device.

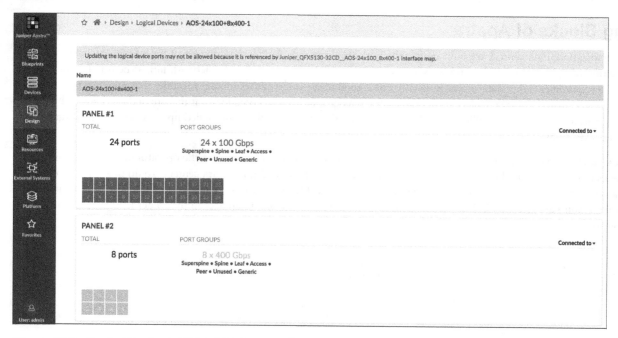

Figure 12-2   *Logical Device AOS-24x100+8x400-1 shown in the Apstra UI*

- **Device Profiles:** These are hardware specifications that describe the type of hardware, the organization and naming of its ports, the kind of CPU and the amount of RAM on the hardware, and the forwarding ASIC in use. The Device Profile is also where port breakouts are configured. Apstra has a list of qualified and supported hardware models available in the *Juniper Apstra User Guide.* You can find Device Profiles on the Devices tab in the Apstra UI.

Figure 12-3 shows an example of a Device Profile (this is just a snippet—a Device Profile contains more information than shown here) for a Juniper QFX5120-48Y switch. Like Logical Devices, you can create additional Device Profiles as needed to match a specific requirement.

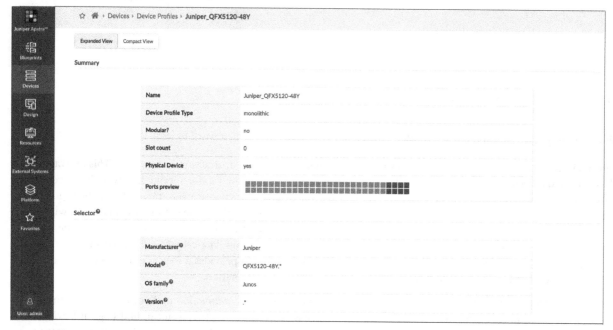

Figure 12-3   *Device Profile for a Juniper QFX5120-48Y shown in the Apstra UI*

- **Interface Maps:** Interface Maps tie together the logical representation of a device (Logical Device) with its hardware representation (Device Profile) to generate an interface schema that matches the actual hardware and operating system, thus facilitating the generation of hardware- and operating system–specific configuration. You can find Interface Maps on the Design tab in the Apstra UI. It is important to note that not all possible port density combinations are predefined in Apstra—with the flexibility that Apstra offers, you can build your own Interface Maps if you need a supported, yet different, port density combination from a specific hardware.

Figure 12-4 shows an Interface Map for a Juniper QFX5220-32C.

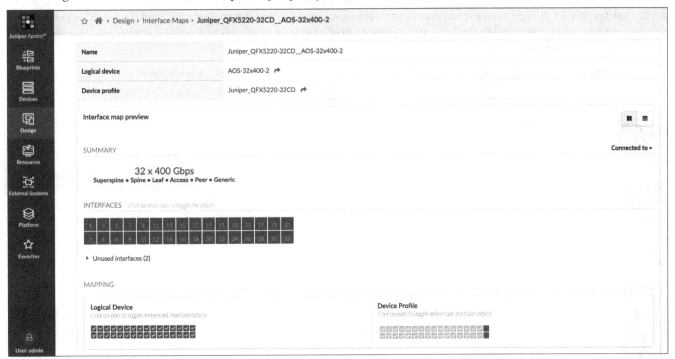

Figure 12-4 *Interface Map for a Juniper QFX5220-32C shown in the Apstra UI*

Visually, the relationship between Logical Devices, Device Profiles, and Interface Maps can be represented as shown in Figure 12-5.

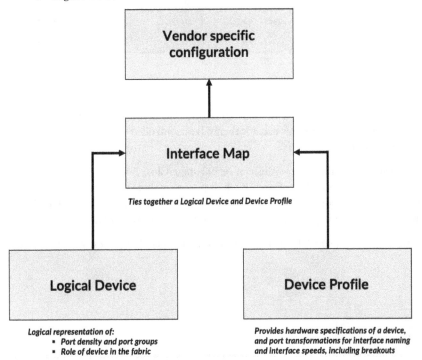

Figure 12-5 *Relationship between Logical Devices, Device Profiles, and Interface Maps*

■ **Rack Types:** Data centers are typically organized as racks that house leafs and servers, physically connected to each other via some form of cable management. Every data center will have a few well-defined types of racks—these could be designed around server-to-leaf redundancy, leaf-to-spine uplinks, port densities, and other parameters. Apstra follows the same methodology when building a data center fabric. In Apstra, *Rack Types* are a logical representation of physical racks that are installed in a data center. Since this is just a logical representation, no hardware specifics are needed when defining a Rack Type: it simply requires you to define the Logical Device for the leafs, the kind (and number) of servers expected to be connected to the leafs, and if some form of redundancy (MLAG or ESI LAG) is required. You can find Rack Types on the Design tab in the Apstra UI.

Figure 12-6 shows the main page for Rack Types in the Apstra UI. Several common Rack Types are predefined in Apstra, with the ability to build user-defined Rack Types as needed.

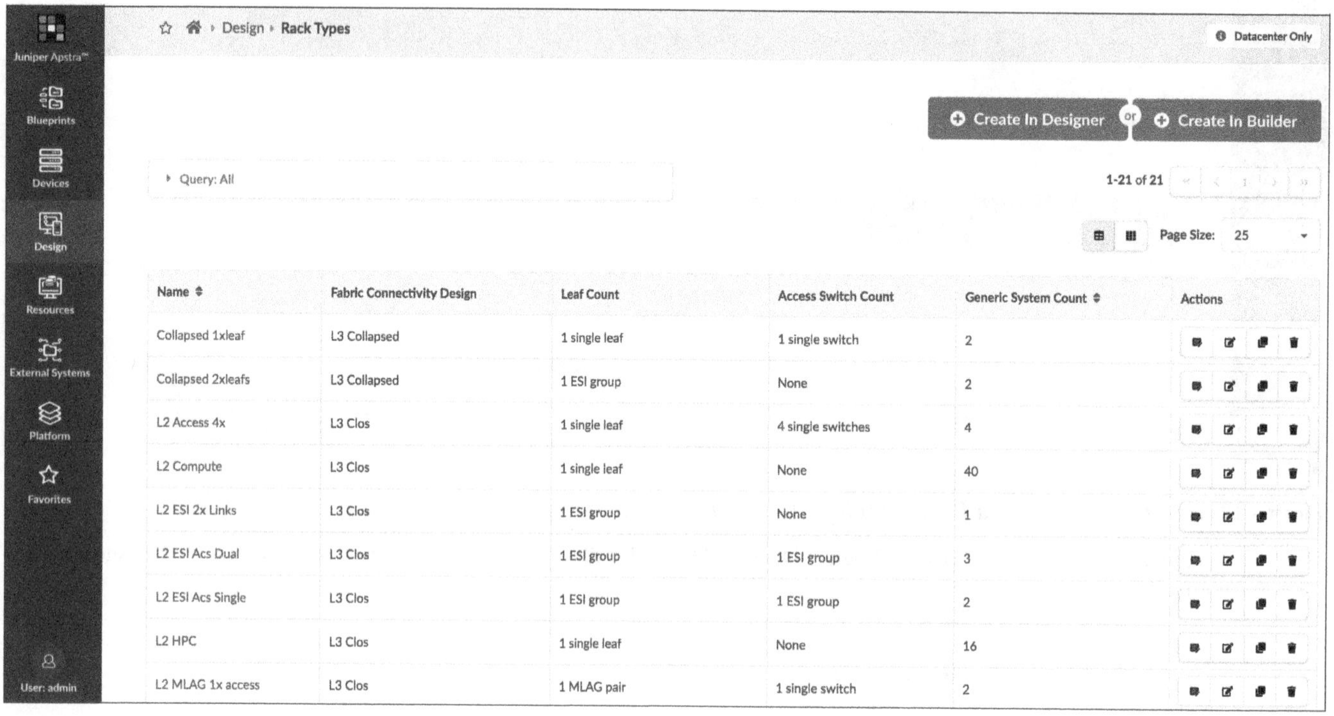

Figure 12-6 *Rack Types shown in the Apstra UI*

Figure 12-7 details some of the intricacies involved in designing a Rack Type in Apstra. Generic Systems, shown in Figure 12-7, are devices attached to an Apstra-controlled fabric but are not themselves controlled by Apstra. This category includes devices such as servers, routers, and firewalls.

■ **Templates:** A *Template* decides the overall schema of a data center—this can be a 3-stage Clos, 5-stage Clos, or a collapsed spine design. Within a Template, Rack Types (and number of each Rack Type) are included to determine what kind of racks will exist in the data center, along with the autonomous system scheme, and if BGP EVPN is used as the overlay control plane protocol for the fabric. You can find Templates on the Design tab in the Apstra UI.

Figure 12-8 shows the main page for Templates in the Apstra UI. There are several predefined Templates, with the ability to build user-defined Templates as needed.

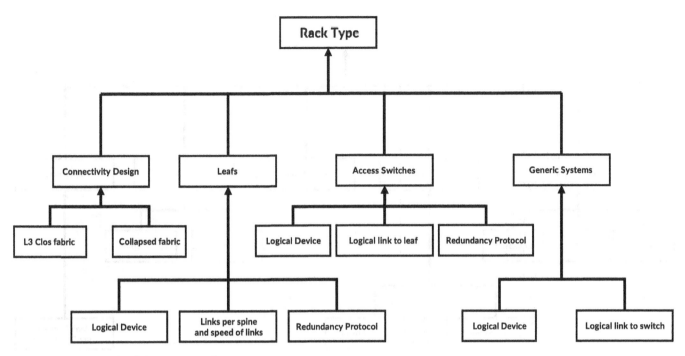

Figure 12-7 *Details of designing Rack Types in Apstra*

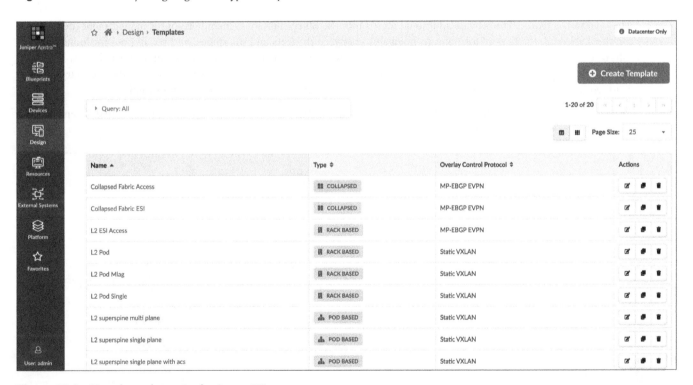

Figure 12-8 *Templates shown in the Apstra UI*

Figure 12-9 details some of the intricacies involved in designing a Template in Apstra.

■ **Blueprints:** A data center fabric in Apstra is an instantiation of a *Blueprint*. A Blueprint can be thought of as a canvas that is populated with everything that is necessary for a data center fabric to function. It takes just one input, which is a Template. Once the initial Blueprint is instantiated, the data center fabric starts to come to life—the Rack Types defined in the Template are expanded as fabric devices, connected to each other, providing a topological view of the fabric to the operator.

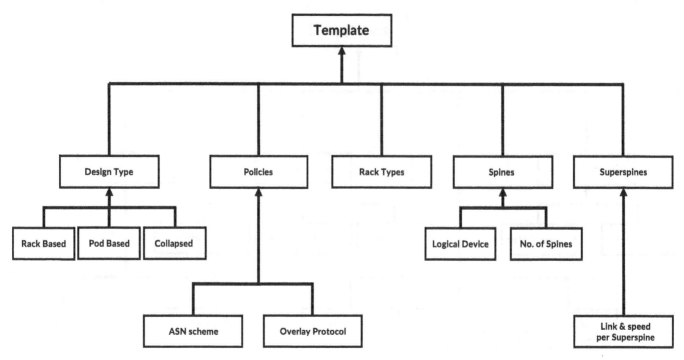

Figure 12-9 *Details of designing a Template in Apstra*

The operator is required to provide additional inputs into the Blueprint—these include resource management (defining the ASN pool, the IP pool for point-to-point links between the leafs and the spines, and the IP pool for loopback interfaces), mapping Interface Maps to devices to build device-specific configuration, and defining Virtual Networks and Routing Zones (VRFs), among other things. The end-to-end deployment of a Blueprint, and all the necessary details required to build it, are covered in subsequent sections, using a bridged overlay fabric as an example.

You can find Blueprints on the tab of the same name in the Apstra UI. Figure 12-10 shows an instantiated Blueprint of a 3-stage Clos fabric, with two spines and five leafs.

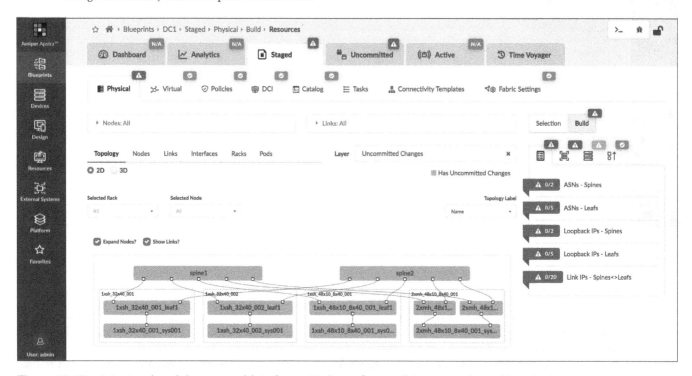

Figure 12-10 *A Juniper-based data center fabric for an AI cluster front end, instantiated as a Blueprint in Apstra*

Figure 12-11 shows the intricacies involved in building a Blueprint. Additional inputs and tasks can be carried out within a Blueprint, but Figure 12-11 depicts the most common ones.

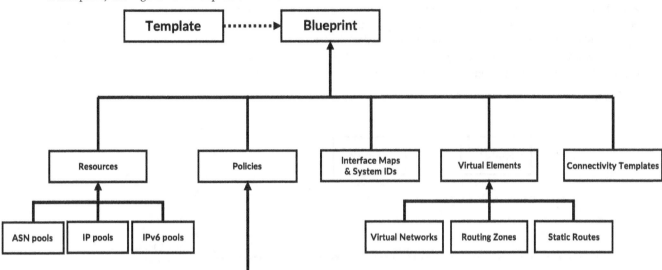

Figure 12-11 *Details of building and deploying a Blueprint in Apstra*

Onboarding Devices in Apstra

Like any other orchestration system, Apstra requires onboarding of devices to manage them for Day-0 through Day-2 operations. To onboard a device in Apstra, a Device Agent needs to be created. A *Device Agent*, as the name suggests, is an agent that is created for a specific device and manages the general lifecycle of that device in Apstra—this includes pushing configuration, telemetry collection, and any communication between Apstra and the device.

Device Agents can be created in two forms:

- **On-box agents:** Agents that are installed on the device itself (if the operating system supports them—for example, Cisco NXOS and Arista EOS).

- **Off-box agents:** Agents that are installed on Apstra (as a Docker container) and communicate with the device via API calls (for Juniper Junos OS, as an example).

Furthermore, there are two ways for the overall onboarding process in Apstra:

- **Zero Touch Provisioning (ZTP):** When a device is in its factory default state, ZTP can be used as an end-to-end process to onboard the device in Apstra. As part of the ZTP process, the device receives an IP address via DHCP, downloads various scripts from a TFTP server to run locally (to bootstrap the device and prepare it for Apstra onboarding), and then is onboarded into Apstra via automated agent creation.

- **Manual creation of Device Agent:** This is used when a device is not in factory default state and the operator is required to manually provide certain details of the device (IP address and login credentials) to onboard into Apstra, with the correct base configuration on the device that supports this onboarding process.

The following subsections cover both these processes.

NOTE   Apstra manages network devices out-of-band only.

Zero Touch Provisioning

Zero Touch Provisioning is the process of remotely provisioning network devices without having to manually provision each device individually. The process typically includes the network device receiving an IP address via DHCP and being redirected to pull additional scripts from a TFTP server (specified in the DHCP Offer) to automatically bootstrap the device and enable it for operation in the network infrastructure. As part of ZTP, the operator can also ensure that any new network device is upgraded to a standardized image for that product type, ensuring image compliance for the network.

Within the context of Apstra, consider the topology in Figure 12-12.

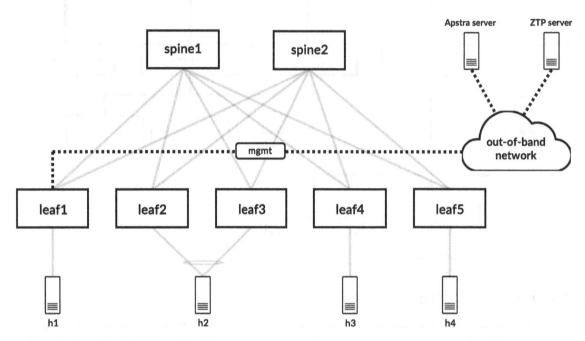

Figure 12-12   *Topology for ZTP with Apstra*

While every device in Figure 12-12 has an out-of-band (OOB) connection via the OOB network, the topology simply focuses on leaf1 and its out-of-band connection for the purposes of demonstrating how ZTP works with Apstra.

Apstra provides a home-grown ZTP server that can be officially downloaded via the Juniper software download page. Both the Apstra server and the ZTP server are connected to this out-of-band network. The ZTP server has the following functions within the overall scope of device onboarding via the ZTP process:

■ Acts as a DHCP server, hosting configured DHCP scopes for the out-of-band management network

■ Hosts various scripts that facilitate onboarding of the device by configuring it appropriately (with base configuration)

■ Talks to Apstra via API calls to create a Device Agent that triggers onboarding of the device in Apstra

With Apstra release 4.2.0 (and the corresponding ZTP server for this release), the ZTP server can also be accessed via a UI over HTTP/HTTPS (previous releases only had CLI access to the ZTP server). As part of the initial setup of the ZTP server, you are required to provide details that enable the ZTP server to talk to Apstra—this includes the IP address of the Apstra server and the credentials required to authenticate to it, as shown in Figure 12-13.

Once the connection between the ZTP server and Apstra is established, Apstra reports the status of various ZTP services under Devices > ZTP Status > Services, as shown in Figure 12-14; all services are being reported as currently up, with a last updated time of validation for each service.

Configure Apstra Server Details

IP Address *

10.92.70.18

Username *

ztp

Password *

••••••••••

Cancel   Save

Figure 12-13 *Apstra details during initial setup of ZTP server*

☆ 🏠 › Devices › ZTP Status › **Services**

▸ Query: All   1-5 of 5

                                                          Page Size: 25   ▾

Service Name ⇕	IP Address ⇕	Service Status ⇕	Last Updated ⇕
tftp	192.168.31.20	Up	2023-10-22, 18:35:16
nginx	192.168.31.21	Up	2023-10-22, 18:35:16
db	192.168.31.17	Up	2023-10-22, 18:35:17
dhcpd		Up	2023-10-22, 18:35:17
status	192.168.31.18	Up	2023-10-22, 18:35:17

Figure 12-14 *ZTP services status on Apstra*

On the ZTP server, these services (DHCP, TFTP, and other services) run as Docker containers, as shown in Example 12-1.

Example 12-1 *ZTP services, run as Docker containers, on the ZTP server*

```
root@apstra-ztp:~# docker ps -a
CONTAINER ID   IMAGE                  COMMAND             CREATED       STATUS       PORTS
NAMES
5f6609074deb   apstra/nginx:4.2.0-34  "sh /init.sh"       7 weeks ago   Up 2 days    0.0.0.0:80->80/tcp, :::80->80/
tcp, 0.0.0.0:443->443/tcp, :::443->443/tcp    nginx
3f0dbe2be17b   apstra/tftp:4.2.0-34   "sh /init.sh"       7 weeks ago   Up 2 days    0.0.0.0:69->69/udp, :::69->69/
udp                                   tftp
1e05ab10a552   apstra/status:4.2.0-34 "sh /init.sh"       7 weeks ago   Up 2 days    8080/tcp
status
cd7aa8ad372b   apstra/dhcpd:4.2.0-34  "sh /init.sh"       7 weeks ago   Up 2 days
dhcpd
12e35bc71b20   mysql:8.0.33           "docker-entrypoint.s…"  7 weeks ago  Up 2 days  3306/tcp, 33060/tcp
```

The DHCP configuration on the ZTP server is maintained under **/containers_data/dhcp/dhcpd.conf**. For the topology in Figure 12-12, leaf1 is expected to receive a specific IP address of 10.92.71.38, with a default gateway of 10.92.71.254. This host-specific scope is configured by matching the Ethernet address of leaf1's management interface (why both vme and em0 addresses are needed will be discussed shortly), as shown in Example 12-2.

Example 12-2   *DHCP configuration file on ZTP server*

```
root@apstra-ztp:~# cat /containers_data/dhcp/dhcpd.conf
group {
    option tftp-server-name "10.92.70.19";
    subnet 10.92.70.0 netmask 255.255.254.0 {
      range 10.92.70.100 10.92.71.253;
      option routers 10.92.71.254;
    }
    host leaf1_vme {
      hardware ethernet 40:de:ad:7b:70:41;
      fixed-address 10.92.71.38;
    }
    host leaf1_em0 {
      hardware ethernet 40:de:ad:7b:75:38;
      fixed-address 10.92.71.38;
    }
}


#ddns-update-style none;
#option domain-search "dc1.yourdatacenter.com";
#option domain-name "dc1.yourdatacenter.com";
#option domain-name-servers 10.1.2.13, 10.1.2.14;


# defaults - do not change unless necessary

default-lease-time 7200;
max-lease-time 9200;
ignore-client-uids true;
authoritative;


option space JUNIPER;
option JUNIPER.config-file-name code 1 = text;
option JUNIPER-encapsulation code 43 = encapsulate JUNIPER;
option user-class-information code 77 = text;


class "juniper" {
    match if (substring(option vendor-class-identifier, 0, 7) = "Juniper") and
            not (suffix(option user-class-information, 4) = "-EVO");
    option JUNIPER.config-file-name "junos_apstra_ztp_bootstrap.sh";
}
class "juniper-evo" {
    match if (substring(option vendor-class-identifier, 0, 7) = "Juniper") and
            (suffix(option user-class-information, 4) = "-EVO");
    option JUNIPER.config-file-name "ztp_py3.py";
}
```

Outside of the DHCP IP address scopes, other options can be configured such as DNS servers, domain names, a TFTP server address (or name), and so on. Additionally, a configuration file is specified that facilitates bootstrapping the device. This DHCP configuration file exists on the ZTP server by default, and typically you only need to adjust the IP address scopes, the DNS server addresses, and the domain name as needed for your environment.

Devices such as the Juniper QFX5120-48Y (leaf1, in this case) have two physical management interfaces: em0 and em1. For such devices, a floating virtual management interface exists, called the *vme* interface (typically used for Virtual Chassis deployments). When leaf1 first boots up and is in factory default state, it sends out DHCP Discover packets via its management interface, in an attempt to acquire an IP address and optionally learn of any TFTP servers and scripts it needs to download and run. On such devices, at first, this is originated from the vme interface, and then it switches over to one of the two physical management interfaces. This is important to note, since DHCP scopes may be set up based on the Ethernet address of an interface, and the vme interface has a unique Ethernet address (when compared to the physical management interfaces, em0 and em1). Because of this, the DHCP scope shown in Example 12-2 has two host-specific scopes: one that matches the Ethernet address of the vme interface, and another that matches the Ethernet address of the em0 interface.

> **NOTE** If a Juniper QFX5120/QFX5130 is not in factory default state and needs to be brought back to this state, you can use the operational mode command **request system zeroize** to achieve this.

The DHCP process itself is no different from a regular DHCP process—the DHCP Discover is responded to with a DHCP Offer by the server, offering the network device an IP address to use. In this case, however, in addition to the offered IP address, a TFTP server address is also provided by adding DHCP option 66 in the DHCP Offer packet. This DHCP Offer packet is shown in Figure 12-15, with DHCP option 66 specifying the TFTP server's IP address in this case, which is 10.92.70.19.

```
No.    Time       Source       Destination      Protocol  Length Info
  987 2023-10-… 0.0.0.0        255.255.255.255 DHCP       344 DHCP Discover - Transaction ID 0x75142217
  989 2023-10-… 10.92.70.19    255.255.255.255 DHCP       356 DHCP Offer    - Transaction ID 0x75142217

> Frame 989: 356 bytes on wire (2848 bits), 356 bytes captured (2848 bits)      0000  ff ff ff
> Ethernet II, Src: RealtekU_dc:ce:30 (52:54:00:dc:ce:30), Dst: Broadcast (ff:ff:ff:ff:ff:ff)  0010  01 56 00
> Internet Protocol Version 4, Src: 10.92.70.19, Dst: 255.255.255.255            0020  ff ff 00
> User Datagram Protocol, Src Port: 67, Dst Port: 68                             0030  22 17 00
v Dynamic Host Configuration Protocol (Offer)                                    0040  46 13 00
    Message type: Boot Reply (2)                                                 0050  00 00 00
    Hardware type: Ethernet (0x01)                                               0060  00 00 00
    Hardware address length: 6                                                   0070  00 00 00
    Hops: 0                                                                      0080  00 00 00
    Transaction ID: 0x75142217                                                   0090  00 00 00
    Seconds elapsed: 0                                                           00a0  00 00 00
  > Bootp flags: 0x8000, Broadcast flag (Broadcast)                              00b0  00 00 00
    Client IP address: 0.0.0.0                                                   00c0  00 00 00
    Your (client) IP address: 10.92.71.38                                        00d0  00 00 00
    Next server IP address: 10.92.70.19                                          00e0  00 00 00
    Relay agent IP address: 0.0.0.0                                              00f0  00 00 00
    Client MAC address: JuniperN_7b:70:41 (40:de:ad:7b:70:41)                    0100  00 00 00
    Client hardware address padding: 00000000000000000000                        0110  00 00 00
    Server host name not given                                                   0120  5c 46 13
    Boot file name not given                                                     0130  04 0a 5c
    Magic cookie: DHCP                                                           0140  31 39 2b
  > Option: (53) DHCP Message Type (Offer)                                       0150  72 61 5f
  > Option: (54) DHCP Server Identifier (10.92.70.19)                            0160  2e 73 68
  > Option: (51) IP Address Lease Time
  > Option: (1) Subnet Mask (255.255.254.0)
  > Option: (3) Router
  v Option: (66) TFTP Server Name
      Length: 11
      TFTP Server Name: 10.92.70.19
  > Option: (43) Vendor-Specific Information
  > Option: (255) End
```

Figure 12-15 *DHCP Offer from ZTP server with option 66 specifying a TFTP server address*

From the same packet capture, the client MAC address is confirmed to be 40:de:ad:7b:70:41, which is the Ethernet address of the vme interface on leaf1, as shown in Example 12-3.

Example 12-3 *Ethernet address of vme interface on leaf1*

```
root@leaf1> show interfaces vme
Physical interface: vme, Enabled, Physical link is Down
  Interface index: 70, SNMP ifIndex: 35
  Type: Mgmt-VLAN, Link-level type: Mgmt-VLAN, MTU: 1514
  Device flags   : Present Running
  Interface flags: Hardware-Down SNMP-Traps
  Link type      : Full-Duplex
  Link flags     : None
  Current address: 40:de:ad:7b:70:41, Hardware address: 40:de:ad:7b:70:41
  Last flapped   : Never
    Input packets : 607
    Output packets: 365
```

The TFTP server, configured as an option in the DHCP configuration file, is the ZTP server's address itself since that acts as the TFTP server also. DHCP option 43, in the DHCP Offer, known as *vendor-specific information*, specifies a list of configuration files that the network device must request, using TFTP, from the TFTP server. This is a hexadecimal value representation of the file name, as shown in Figure 12-16.

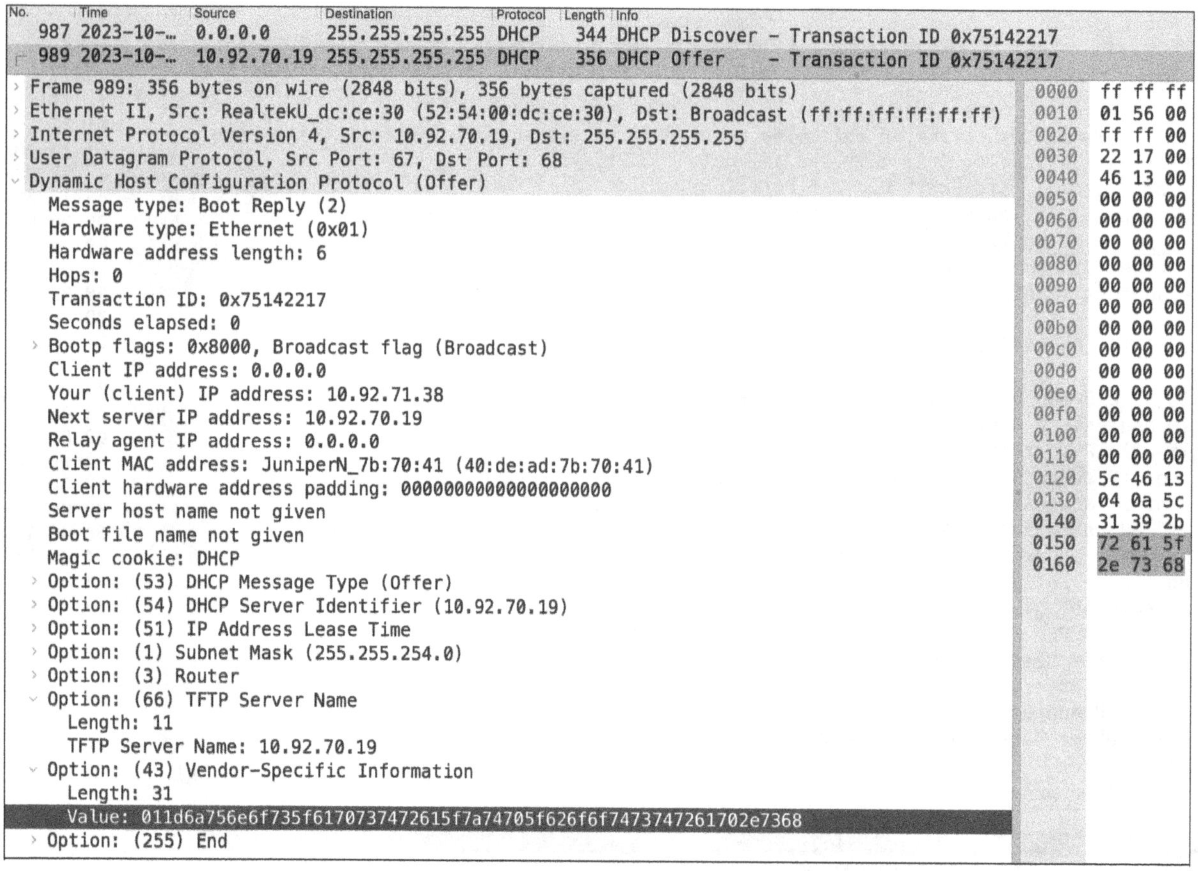

Figure 12-16 *DHCP Offer from ZTP server with option 43 specifying hex representation of a configuration file name*

NOTE   Usage of DHCP option 43 here is different from its use in wireless networking, where it is typically used to provide a wireless access point (AP) with the IP address of the wireless controller for association.

The hexadecimal value in option 43 of the packet in Figure 12-16 matches the file name junos_apstra_ztp_bootstrap.sh, which is what was specified in the DHCP configuration file, highlighted in Example 12-2. Option 43, in this case, is built in the format of an ID, followed by the length of the file name, and then the value of the file name (which is the name of the file itself) in byte array. Thus, this gives us 0x01 as the ID, 0x1d as the length of the file name (29 characters in length), and finally 0x6a756e6f735f6170737472615f7a74705f626f6f7473747261702e7368 as the name of the file in hex.

The network device, leaf1, can now request this file from the TFTP server via TFTP, as shown in Figure 12-17.

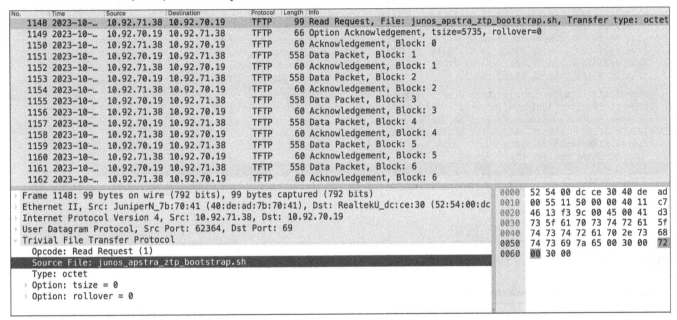

Figure 12-17 *TFTP file transfer of bootstrap file*

NOTE   This bootstrap script is necessary for Junos OS devices (such as Juniper QFX5120, which is the device being used for demonstration purposes here) since the environment must be prepared to run the actual ZTP Python script. On Junos Evolved devices (such as the Juniper QFX5130), this is not needed, and the ZTP Python script is downloaded and executed directly.

Once this script is downloaded, it is executed by the network device. This sets up the environment to run the actual ZTP Python script, which is downloaded next as part of this bootstrap shell script. This is again downloaded via TFTP, as shown in Figure 12-18.

The ZTP Python script establishes communication between the device being provisioned and the ZTP server, to gather various details of the device that are needed to onboard it into Apstra. This includes validating the platform and the version of the operating system running, creating users on the device, and pushing any custom configuration that has been defined by the operator. This is controlled by a JSON file called *ztp.json*, which is in the **/containers_data/tftp** path. This file defines various aspects of the configuration, such as the root password, a username and password for device onboarding, any Junos OS versions against which the device image needs to be compared and upgraded, the path for the image to be used for an upgrade, and various agent parameters needed to create a corresponding Device Agent in Apstra.

A snippet of this file is shown in Example 12-4. This only shows Junos OS-specific parameters; however, the same parameters can be defined for other operating systems as well (such as Junos Evolved, Cisco NXOS, Arista EOS, and SONiC).

No.	Time	Source	Destination	Protocol	Length	Info
1212	2023-10-…	10.92.71.38	10.92.70.19	TFTP	76	Read Request, File: ztp.py, Transfer type: octet, tsize=0,
1213	2023-10-…	10.92.70.19	10.92.71.38	TFTP	68	Option Acknowledgement, tsize=115549, rollover=0
1214	2023-10-…	10.92.71.38	10.92.70.19	TFTP	60	Acknowledgement, Block: 0
1215	2023-10-…	10.92.70.19	10.92.71.38	TFTP	558	Data Packet, Block: 1
1216	2023-10-…	10.92.71.38	10.92.70.19	TFTP	60	Acknowledgement, Block: 1
1217	2023-10-…	10.92.70.19	10.92.71.38	TFTP	558	Data Packet, Block: 2
1218	2023-10-…	10.92.71.38	10.92.70.19	TFTP	60	Acknowledgement, Block: 2
1219	2023-10-…	10.92.70.19	10.92.71.38	TFTP	558	Data Packet, Block: 3
1220	2023-10-…	10.92.71.38	10.92.70.19	TFTP	60	Acknowledgement, Block: 3
1221	2023-10-…	10.92.70.19	10.92.71.38	TFTP	558	Data Packet, Block: 4
1222	2023-10-…	10.92.71.38	10.92.70.19	TFTP	60	Acknowledgement, Block: 4
1223	2023-10-…	10.92.70.19	10.92.71.38	TFTP	558	Data Packet, Block: 5
1224	2023-10-…	10.92.71.38	10.92.70.19	TFTP	60	Acknowledgement, Block: 5
1225	2023-10-…	10.92.70.19	10.92.71.38	TFTP	558	Data Packet, Block: 6
1226	2023-10-…	10.92.71.38	10.92.70.19	TFTP	60	Acknowledgement, Block: 6
1227	2023-10-…	10.92.70.19	10.92.71.38	TFTP	558	Data Packet, Block: 7
1228	2023-10-…	10.92.71.38	10.92.70.19	TFTP	60	Acknowledgement, Block: 7
1229	2023-10-…	10.92.70.19	10.92.71.38	TFTP	558	Data Packet, Block: 8
1230	2023-10-…	10.92.71.38	10.92.70.19	TFTP	60	Acknowledgement, Block: 8

```
> Frame 1212: 76 bytes on wire (608 bits), 76 bytes captured (608 bits)          0000  52 54 00
> Ethernet II, Src: JuniperN_7b:70:41 (40:de:ad:7b:70:41), Dst: RealtekU_dc:ce:30 (52:54:00:dc:ce:30)   0010  00 3e 11
> Internet Protocol Version 4, Src: 10.92.71.38, Dst: 10.92.70.19               0020  46 13 e1
> User Datagram Protocol, Src Port: 57675, Dst Port: 69                         0030  70 79 00
v Trivial File Transfer Protocol                                               0040  00 72 6f
    Opcode: Read Request (1)
    Source File: ztp.py
    Type: octet
  > Option: tsize = 0
  > Option: rollover = 0
```

Figure 12-18 *TFTP file transfer of ZTP Python file*

Example 12-4 *Various parameters defined in ztp.json*

```
root@apstra-ztp:/containers_data/tftp# cat ztp.json
{
  "defaults": {
    "junos-versions": [],
    "junos-image": "",
    "junos-evo-versions": [],
    "junos-evo-image": "",
    "device-root-password": "<password>",
    "device-user": "anindac",
    "device-user-password": "<password>",
    "custom-config": "",
    "management-subnet-prefixlen": "",
    "management-master-ip": "",
    "management-backup-ip": "",
    "management-ip": "",
    "management-gw-ip": "",
    "dual-routing-engine": false,
    "system-agent-params": {
      "agent_type": "onbox",
      "install_requirements": false,
      "force_package_install": false
    }
  },
```

```
"junos": {
  "junos-versions": [],
  "junos-image": "",
  "device-root-password": "<password>",
  "device-user": "anindac",
  "device-user-password": "<password>",
  "custom-config": "junos_custom.sh",
  "management-subnet-prefixlen": "",
  "management-master-ip": "",
  "management-backup-ip": "",
  "management-ip": "",
  "management-gw-ip": "",
  "dual-routing-engine": false,
  "system-agent-params": {
    "agent_type": "offbox",
    "profile": "8ab18d24-dde2-4795-80a7-f093fb4a3e56",
    "install_requirements": true,
    "job_on_create": "install"
  }
}
}
}
```

The script also configures the physical management interfaces (em0 or em1) for DHCP, enabling them to acquire an IP address and switch the device from the virtual management interface to the physical management interface.

NOTE In some devices, this switch to em0 or em1 might not occur through the script since the Auto-Image Upgrade (AIU) process, which is triggered when the device boots up in factory default state, will run internal scripts that automatically configure the virtual and management interfaces for DHCP. In this case, the switch to em0 or em1 will be immediate.

When this part of the ZTP process is complete, the ZTP server creates a Device Agent on Apstra (via API calls to the Apstra server) for this device to be onboarded, using the Device Agent parameters that were defined in the ztp.json file. If this is successful, a Device Agent, corresponding to this IP address, should appear in Apstra.

If needed, you can specify a custom configuration file (the file name is passed as a value to the custom-config field in the ztp. json file) that is used to add any additional, custom configuration required. Example 12-5 shows a sample custom configuration file, which simply sets the hostname of the device.

Example 12-5 *Custom configuration for a Junos OS*

```
root@apstra-ztp:/containers_data/tftp# cat junos_custom.sh
#!/bin/sh

# set hostname
cli -c "configure; \
set system host-name leaf1; \
commit and-quit; "
```

On the ZTP server, the ZTP status for this device should now be marked as Completed, as shown in Figure 12-19.

Figure 12-19 *Device state in ZTP server when the ZTP process has finished successfully*

In Apstra, a Device Agent should have been created, and the same can be confirmed as shown in Figure 12-20. The device must be explicitly acknowledged for further use in any data center fabrics that are built in Apstra.

Figure 12-20 *Device Agent created as part of the ZTP process*

During the ZTP process, the management address acquired via DHCP switches from the virtual vme interface to one of two physical management interfaces (for devices that have two physical management interfaces, such as the QFX5120-48Y). During this process, the IP address acquired by the vme interface is released (by sending a DHCP Release), and the DHCP process is reinitiated from the em0 interface (in this case). This means that the entire DORA process happens again, and em0 now acquires the expected management IP address.

Thus, at the end of the ZTP process, the device has some base configuration (referred to as the *pristine* configuration in Apstra) that was loaded as part of ZTP, and the management IP address should be present on the physical management interface, with reachability back to Apstra via the management (out-of-band) network. Example 12-6 shows this configuration on leaf1.

Example 12-6 *Configuration on leaf1 after the ZTP process is complete*

```
root@leaf1> show configuration
## Last commit: 2023-10-20 14:05:40 UTC by anindac
version 22.4R2.8;
system {
    host-name leaf1;
    root-authentication {
        encrypted-password "$6$iYwtMd3Dt/3kkKXo$8UxeXewN34JUwwy.S8N97xWGO6KTt9iVenVfOfED51JT9nZK8Ix1ZjEwocOmjsStUBDf/
QIrODTtisInWgtqm."; ## SECRET-DATA
    }
    scripts {
        op {
            file ztp.py {
                checksum sha-256 d8f2762ec26e68a0fe9ddd53d2f6636043c517912b208bdf971c7cdc8db94816;
            }
        }
        language python3;
    }
    login {
        user anindac {
            uid 2000;
            class super-user;
            authentication {
                encrypted-password
"$6$ULNv6OoSmHNXXMsB$UhRV5RT/VIA3hb5sM7OxO/Q72DBL2oLCb8xNzVLwFbhpsouJrs/T7unP9cdoNAFEWe4EgYJH58YTK1RlydOD61";
## SECRET-DATA
            }
        }
    }
    services {
        ssh {
            root-login allow;
        }
        extension-service {
            request-response {
                grpc {
                    ssl {
                        port 32767;
                        local-certificate aos_grpc;
                    }
                    routing-instance mgmt_junos;
                }
            }
        }
        netconf {
```

```
                ssh;
            }
        }
        management-instance;
        syslog {
            file interactive-commands {
                interactive-commands any;
            }
            file messages {
                any notice;
                authorization info;
            }
        }
        processes {
            dhcp-service {
                traceoptions {
                    file dhcp_logfile size 10m;
                    level all;
                    flag packet;
                }
            }
        }
        phone-home {
            server https://redirect.juniper.net;
            rfc-compliant;
        }
    }
    interfaces {
        em0 {
            unit 0 {
                family inet {
                    address 10.92.71.38/23;
                }
            }
        }
    }
    routing-instances {
        mgmt_junos {
            routing-options {
                static {
                    route 0.0.0.0/0 next-hop 10.92.71.254;
                }
            }
        }
    }
```

Manual Onboarding

As an alternative to ZTP, devices can be onboarded into Apstra by manually creating Device Agents. For any Device Agent, some minimum configuration is expected to be present on the device (again, referred to as the *pristine* configuration in Apstra) that is being onboarded—this includes authentication into the device (with a username and password that provide full privileges to Apstra) via SSH, NETCONF over SSH access, access to APIs on the device, and configuration necessary to provide reachability back to Apstra. As previously mentioned, you can find Managed Devices on the Devices tab in the Apstra UI, and this is where Device Agents are created and managed, as shown in Figure 12-21.

Figure 12-21 *Managed Devices in the Apstra UI*

To create a Device Agent in Apstra, you must provide some basic input parameters, including the IP address of the device that an agent needs to be created for, the type of operating system (supported platforms include NXOS, Junos, and EOS), and login credentials for the device. Figure 12-22 shows these requirements in the Apstra UI for an off-box agent.

Create Offbox System Agent(s)

Device Addresses (25 max) *

10.92.71.38

Comma-separated list of hostnames, individual IP addresses, and IP address ranges, e.g. '192.168.1.5-192.168.1.10,mydevice.local'

→   10.92.71.38

Operation Mode
◉ FULL CONTROL ○ TELEMETRY ONLY

Platform *

Junos

Username *

anindac

Password *

•••••••••••

Agent Profile

Select...

Create

Figure 12-22 *Creating an off-box agent in the Apstra UI*

Entering the username and password for different agents again and again can get quite repetitive, especially when the same username and password are used either for the same type of network operating system or across an organization for all network devices (or in any other form of grouping). Apstra allows you to create an *Agent Profile*, which groups together an operating system type along with its username and password. Thus, when creating a Device Agent, instead of manually entering the operating system type, username, and password, you can simply choose an Agent Profile, which populates all these fields from the profile.

Agent Profiles are on the Devices tab in the Apstra UI. Figure 12-23 shows the creation of an Agent Profile called *Juniper*, with the operating system set to Junos and a username and password configured.

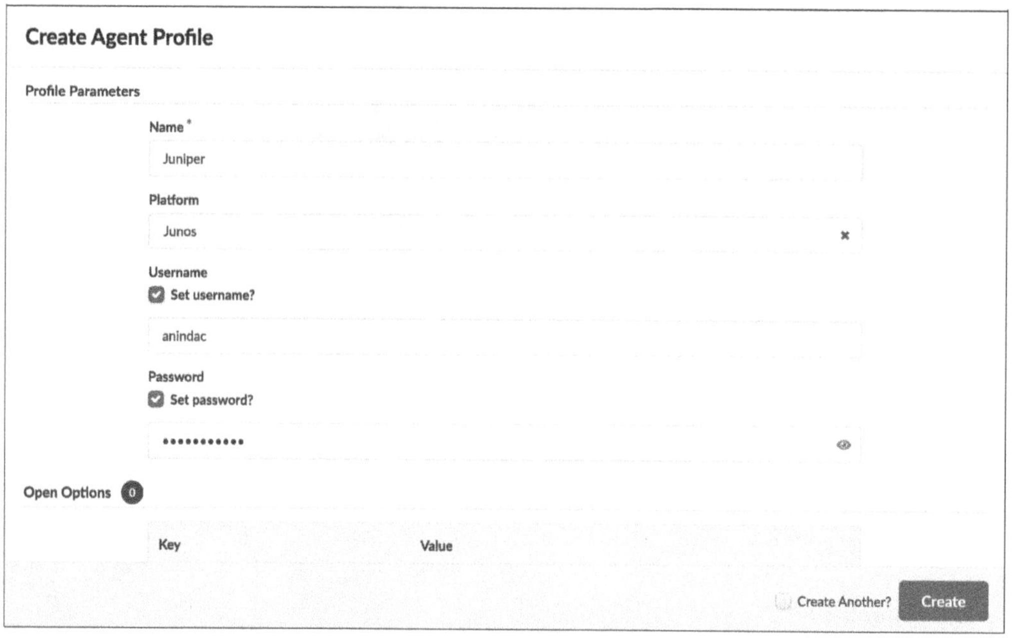

Figure 12-23   *Creating an Agent Profile in the Apstra UI*

Going back to the creation of Device Agents, as shown in Figure 12-24, when an Agent Profile is selected, all other fields are auto-populated using information in the profile. You can override any of these fields if needed during the Device Agent creation.

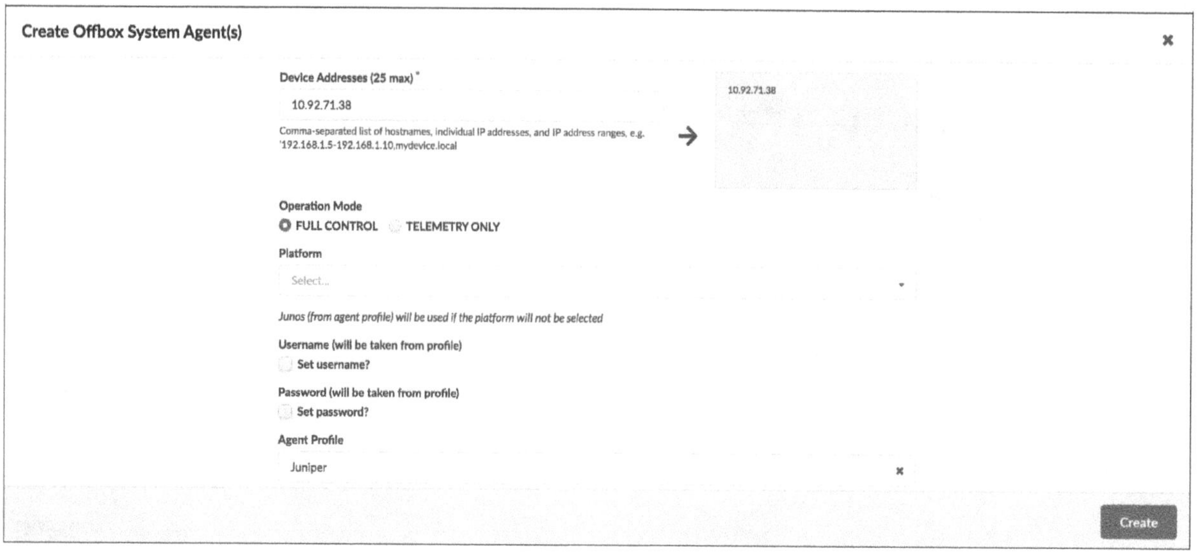

Figure 12-24   *Creating a Device Agent with an Agent Profile in the Apstra UI*

Once the Device Agent is created, the onboarding process of the device begins. By default, as part of the onboarding process, Apstra collects the (previously introduced) pristine configuration from the device—again, this base configuration enables the device to be onboarded, and does not conflict with anything Apstra pushes through the lifecycle of the device, while being managed by Apstra. For example, on the Juniper QFX5120-48Y being onboarded in Figure 12-24, the base configuration shown in Example 12-7 is present.

Example 12-7   *Base configuration on a QFX5120 for Apstra onboarding*

```
root@leaf1# show
version 22.4R2.8;
system {
    host-name leaf1;
    login {
        user anindac {
            uid 2001;
            class super-user;
            authentication {
                encrypted-password
"$6$in.F.sis$lyQUZVGHonkuCW3tIPg5Fp/NJgqyE2ychxb8FBBnOTrXJtgKHcDXwRZrdFXQvkQ5jXpGsO1u59SDWYE87IB/T1"; ## SECRET-DATA
            }
        }
    }
    services {
        ssh;
        netconf {
            ssh;
        }
    }
}
chassis {
    fpc 0 {
        pic 0 {
            port 24 {
                speed 25g;
            }
            port 28 {
                speed 25g;
            }
        }
    }
}
interfaces {
    em0 {
        unit 0 {
            family inet {
                address 10.92.71.38/23;
            }
        }
    }
}
routing-instances {
    mgmt_junos {
        routing-options {
            static {
```

```
        route 0.0.0.0/0 next-hop 10.92.71.254;
      }
    }
  }
}
```

By default, Apstra always collects this configuration when a device is onboarded for the first time, stores it as the pristine configuration in its database, and checks for any configuration present in the device that may conflict with any future configuration pushed by Apstra. Additionally, whenever a device is deleted from Apstra, it first attempts to restore the configuration on the device back to its pristine configuration before deleting it. If you do not require this behavior, you can change it on the Managed Devices page, on the Devices tab. Here, under Advanced Settings, the two options shown in Figure 12-25 are provided, which you can check to disable either or both these features.

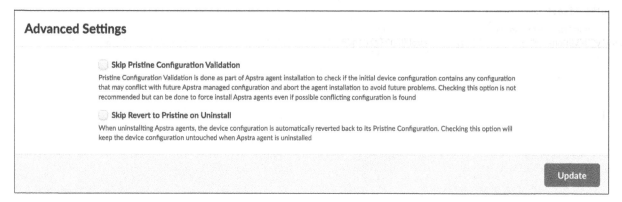

Figure 12-25 *Apstra UI options to disable pristine configuration validation and revert configuration to pristine*

Every device being onboarded is shown as a line item under Managed Devices along with several details about the device, such as the serial number, the operating system version, and the current state of the device in Apstra (which will be discussed shortly), among other things. Each line item is associated with an Actions panel, identified by three dots at the end of every line item.

The onboarding process of a device is logged in Apstra and can be viewed against the line item that is created for the device being onboarded by clicking the Show Log option within the Actions panel, as shown in Figure 12-26.

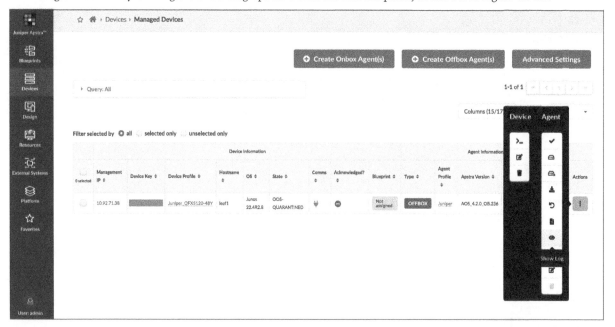

Figure 12-26 *Actions button in the Apstra UI for a device being onboarded*

Figure 12-27 shows a snippet of the onboarding logs for the device being onboarded in Figure 12-24.

Log Preview

```
2023-10-18 08:17:18,382 INFO:10.92.71.38 install
2023-10-18 08:17:18,382 INFO:Ensure stable connection for 60s
2023-10-18 08:17:18,382 INFO:TASK: Check Connectivity
2023-10-18 08:17:18,786 INFO:Successful connection check..
2023-10-18 08:17:48,803 INFO:Successful connection check..
2023-10-18 08:18:18,806 INFO:Successful connection check..
2023-10-18 08:18:18,806 INFO:TASK: Get platform type
2023-10-18 08:18:23,948 INFO:10.92.71.38::junos
2023-10-18 08:18:23,950 INFO:System Agent id:
2023-10-18 08:18:23,951 INFO:TASK: Get device facts
2023-10-18 08:18:23,957 INFO:Command (timeout-120): show chassis hardware | display json
2023-10-18 08:18:23,958 INFO:command (timeout-120): uptime
2023-10-18 08:18:24,785 INFO:Command (timeout-120): show system information | display xml | match Model
2023-10-18 08:18:25,196 INFO:Command (timeout-120): show version | display json
2023-10-18 08:18:26,332 INFO:{'apstra_aos_agent_version': 'absent', 'apstra_aos_operation_mode': 'notInstalled', 'apstra_platform': 'junos', 'apstr
2023-10-18 08:18:26,333 INFO:Intent version = 4.2.0-236
2023-10-18 08:18:26,333 INFO:install_reqs: True, enable_config: True, tls: False, device_encryption: False
2023-10-18 08:18:26,333 INFO:TASK: Collect pristine
2023-10-18 08:18:26,334 INFO:TASK: Configure grpc
2023-10-18 08:18:26,336 INFO:TASK: Validate existing grpc config
2023-10-18 08:18:26,336 INFO:Command (timeout-120): show configuration system services | display json
2023-10-18 08:18:27,169 INFO:Is cert present: False, Is cert valid: False, Is grpc cert configured: False, Is grpc port configured: False, local ce
2023-10-18 08:18:27,169 INFO:TASK: Copy tls certificate to device
2023-10-18 08:18:27,171 INFO:scp local_file: /aos/shared/e9e15b60-tls_certificate remote_file: /var/tmp/aos_grpc_certificate
2023-10-18 08:18:27,171 INFO:sshcmd (timeout=30): file delete /tmp/aos_grpc_certificate | no-more
2023-10-18 08:18:27,586 INFO:Copying to remote: /tmp/aos_grpc_certificate
```

⬇ Download Log File

Figure 12-27 *Logs from device onboarding in Apstra*

When a device is first onboarded in Apstra, it is placed in an *OOS-QUARANTINE* state. During this state, the device only has the pristine configuration in place. To use an onboarded device in an Apstra Blueprint, you must explicitly acknowledge the device—this is a simple security check to ensure no unwanted devices are available to use in a fabric built in Apstra. As shown in Figure 12-28, you click the Acknowledge button for any selected system. This moves the device from an *OOS-QUARANTINED* state to an *OOS-READY* state, indicating that the device is ready to be added in an Apstra Blueprint.

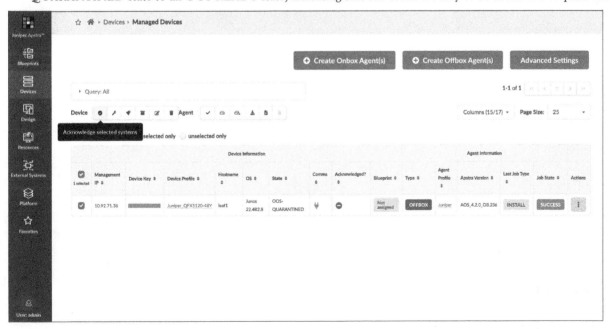

Figure 12-28 *Acknowledging a device in Apstra*

Thus, the onboarding process in Apstra is a multistep, careful process. This is so because Apstra must have full control of a device being onboarded, with knowledge of any configuration being pushed for the device. Without this control, Apstra cannot guarantee that the device will operate correctly within the context and intent of the operator.

When a device is acknowledged in Apstra, some minimal configuration is pushed to the device. This includes enabling all interfaces, setting correct port speeds, and adding LLDP configuration to discover neighbors via LLDP. This configuration (pristine configuration plus all interfaces and LLDP enabled) is called *Discovery-1* configuration.

On leaf1, which was just acknowledged in Figure 12-28, this additional configuration is shown in Example 12-8.

Example 12-8   *Additional configuration added to a QFX5120-48Y once it is acknowledged in Apstra*

```
root@leaf1# show interfaces
xe-0/0/0 {
    unit 0 {
        family inet;
    }
}
xe-0/0/1 {
    unit 0 {
        family inet;
    }
}
xe-0/0/2 {
    unit 0 {
        family inet;
    }
}
xe-0/0/3 {
    unit 0 {
        family inet;
    }
}
xe-0/0/4 {
    unit 0 {
        family inet;
    }
}
xe-0/0/5 {
    unit 0 {
        family inet;
    }
}

*snip*

root@leaf1# show protocols
lldp {
    port-id-subtype interface-name;
    port-description-type interface-description;
    neighbour-port-info-display port-id;
    interface all;
}
```

Creating Rack Types and Templates

Rack Types and Templates, as explained earlier, are base constructs that are needed to build a data center fabric in Apstra. These are logical abstractions, built with modularity and flexibility in mind, focusing on reusability to scale up as needed. Consider the topology shown in Figure 12-29.

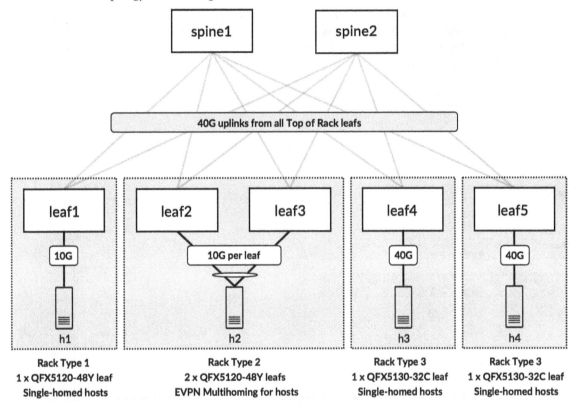

Figure 12-29 *Reference topology to create a Rack Type and Template in Apstra*

This topology is a small representation of a typical data center. The network is cabled in the form of a 3-stage Clos fabric, with each leaf connecting to each spine. The leafs in this design are ToR switches. For the sake of simplicity, only one host is connected per rack, with the details of each rack provided in the following list:

- **Rack Type 1:** This rack has one Juniper QFX5120-48Y as a leaf, utilizing 40G ports for uplinks and 10G ports for downlinks. All hosts are single-homed to this leaf.

- **Rack Type 2:** This rack has two Juniper QFX5120-48Ys as leafs, utilizing 40G ports for uplinks and 10G ports for downlinks. All hosts are multihomed to both leafs using EVPN multihoming (ESI LAG).

- **Rack Type 3:** This rack has one Juniper QFX5130-32C as a leaf, utilizing 40G ports for both uplinks and downlinks. All hosts are single-homed to this leaf. This Rack Type is expected to be used twice, once for leaf4 and then again for leaf5.

In addition to these racks, Juniper QFX5210-64Cs are used for the spines.

NOTE Prior to building Rack Types and Templates, it is important to build or identify the correct Logical Devices, Device Profiles, and Interface Maps, since these effectively influence the kind of physical (or virtual) devices that you are allowed to map to the fabric at a later stage.

Creating Rack Types

This section describes how to create in Apstra the racks defined in Figure 12-29. As previously mentioned, Rack Types are created from the main Design tab. In Apstra 4.2.0, you can create Rack Types using either of two different UI options: designer or builder. This section demonstrates how to use the designer UI to create the three Rack Types in the previous list.

For this demonstration, Rack Type 1 will be named 1xSH_48x10+8x40 and will include one leaf defined as a Logical Device of type AOS-48x10+8x40-1, which will provide 48 × 10G ports that are allowed to connect to access switches, generic systems, and other leaf peers, and 8 × 40G ports that are allowed to connect to spines. This Logical Device is shown in Figure 12-30. This Rack Type will also include one generic system, with a single link to the leaf and no link aggregation (LAG).

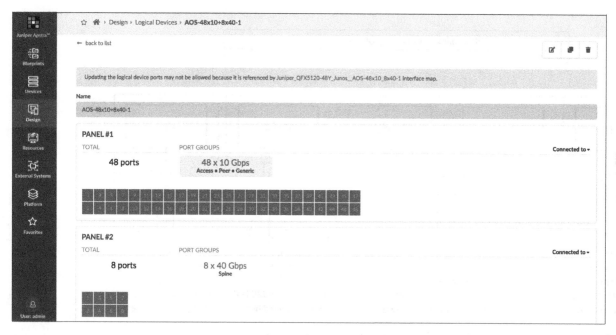

Figure 12-30 *Details of Logical Device AOS-48x10+8x40-1 in Apstra*

When creating a Rack Type, you must select a fabric design type, either L3 Clos (which represents 3-stage and 5-stage Clos fabrics) or a collapsed spine design. In this case, the L3 Clos option is chosen since the overall goal is to build a 3-stage Clos fabric.

The bottom of the designer UI page for Rack Types includes clickable interactive elements that allow the user to create leafs, access switches, and generic systems. For example, Figure 12-31 shows which element to select to create a leaf.

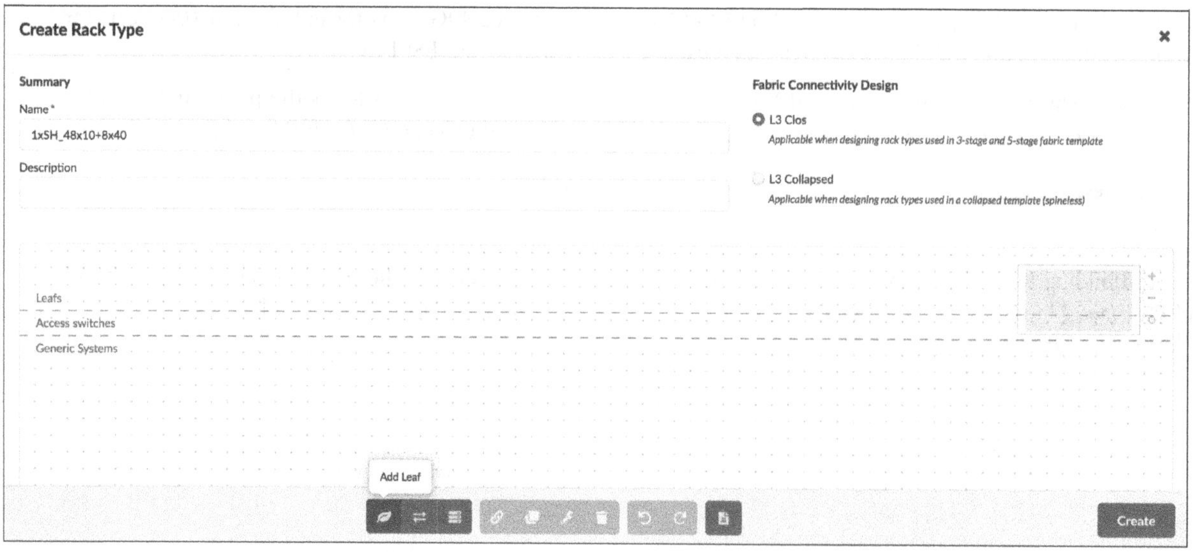

Figure 12-31 *Adding a leaf in the Rack Types designer UI*

When you add a leaf, you must provide the following four mandatory parameters (the fifth parameter is optional). You do so by clicking the gears icon that hovers above any added leaf.

- **Label:** This is simply a name for the leaf in the rack. This is a mandatory parameter.

- **Logical Device:** Since a Rack Type is a logical abstraction of a rack, only a Logical Device must be defined for every leaf in the rack. This is a mandatory parameter.

- **Links per spine:** This determines how many links are connected to each spine, per leaf (and the port speed of each link). This is a mandatory parameter.

- **Redundancy Protocol:** This enables the operator to create a rack with redundancy (by choosing between MLAG or ESI) or no redundancy. This is a mandatory parameter.

- **Tags:** As the name implies, this allows you to attach a tag to the Rack Type, enabling operational changes and queries simply based on the tag itself. This is an optional parameter.

NOTE   Tags, in general, are a very powerful construct in Apstra and can be used in various places, such as Rack Types, and links between a leaf node and a host. These Tags can then be leveraged for different operations, enabling you to identify and take action specific to a Tag. Since Tags are arbitrary in nature, you can name a Tag anything that makes sense within your organization.

Figure 12-32 demonstrates a configured leaf with all necessary parameters filled in as per the specifications of Rack Type 1. It is important to note that in order to configure the number of links per spine, you must first select the port speed by clicking it. Since this leaf has one link per spine, only seven available 40G spine-facing ports remain.

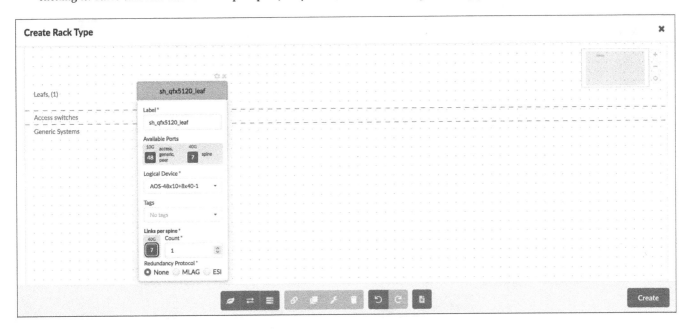

Figure 12-32   *Defining a leaf in the Rack Type designer UI*

In the same fashion, a generic system for the host is created, as shown in Figure 12-33. A generic system is not controlled by Apstra; however, it is still mandatory to provide a Logical Device for the same. This enables Apstra to determine link connectivity of the generic system to the ToR switches.

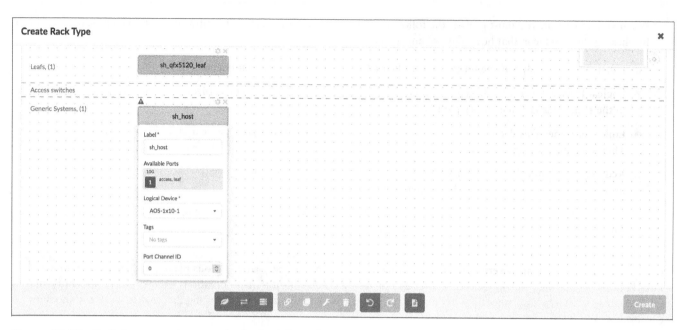

Figure 12-33   *Defining a generic system in the Rack Type designer UI*

A generic system must be linked back to a switch, either an access switch or a leaf. To create a link, two (or more, as applicable) devices must be selected simultaneously, which then enables the *Manage links* interactive element at the bottom, as shown in Figure 12-34 (by selecting both the leaf and the host).

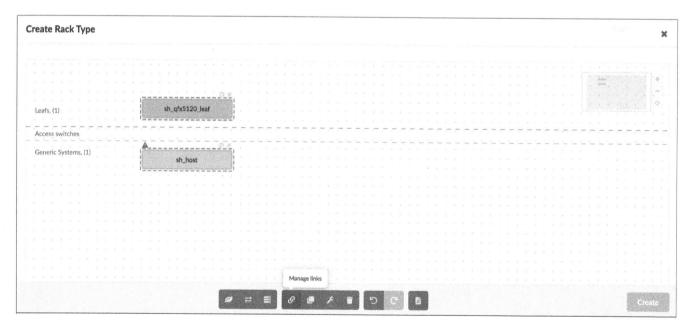

Figure 12-34   *Create a link between supported nodes using the Manage links interactive element in the designer UI*

Using this element creates a link group that connects the two selected devices together. This link group definition includes the number of links (and port speed) in the group, along with link aggregation options. First, the port speed and number of links must be chosen as shown in Figure 12-35.

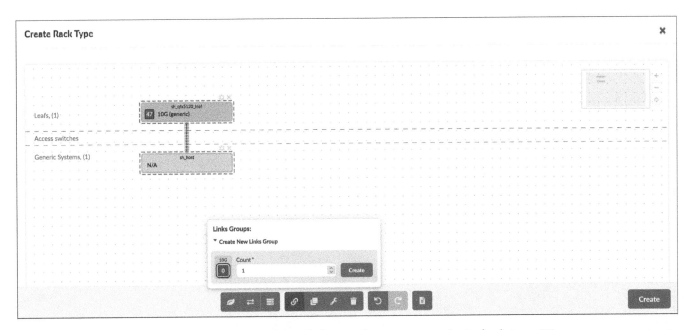

Figure 12-35 *Number of links chosen when creating a link group between two nodes in the designer UI*

Then, an auto-generated Label (which can be modified, if needed) is assigned to this link group, along with the link aggregation mode. In this case, since only a single link is used with no aggregation, the No LAG option is chosen, as shown in Figure 12-36.

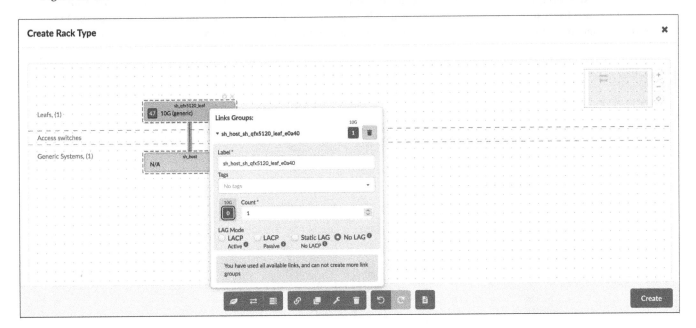

Figure 12-36 *Link group details when connecting two nodes in the designer UI*

For this topology, only a single host is used. However, if needed, you can clone the same generic system (which automatically includes the link group as well) as many times as needed to achieve your desired end goal. You do so by selecting the node (generic system, in this case) and clicking the *Clone selected* interactive element at the bottom of the page, as shown in Figure 12-37.

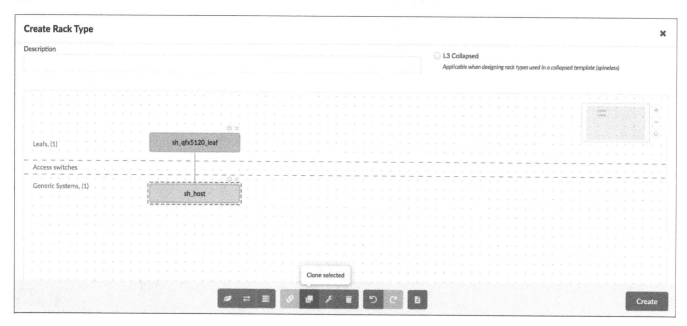

Figure 12-37 *Cloning existing nodes in the designer UI*

This Rack Type can now be saved by clicking the Create button on the bottom right.

Using the same methodology, the second rack in the reference topology shown in Figure 12-29 is created next. Rack Type 2 will be named 2xMH_48x10+8x40 and will include two leafs defined as a Logical Device of type AOS-48x10+8x40-1. This Rack Type also has a single host that is multihomed to both leafs, using EVPN multihoming (ESI LAG). When the ESI option in the Redundancy Protocol section is selected, the UI automatically spawns a second leaf of the same type, as shown in Figure 12-38.

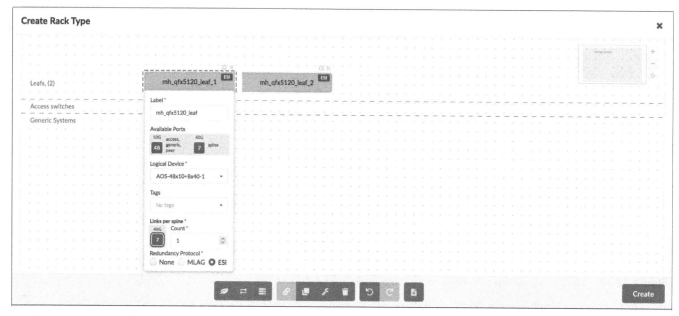

Figure 12-38 *Second leaf of same type created automatically when Redundancy Protocol is set to ESI*

It is possible for a host to be single-homed to a leaf that is also participating in ESI LAG. Apstra gives you the same choice— as shown in Figure 12-39, you can choose which peer switch the host connects to (first peer switch or second peer switch). In this case, however, the host is multihomed and connects to both leafs for EVPN multihoming. This Rack Type can now be created.

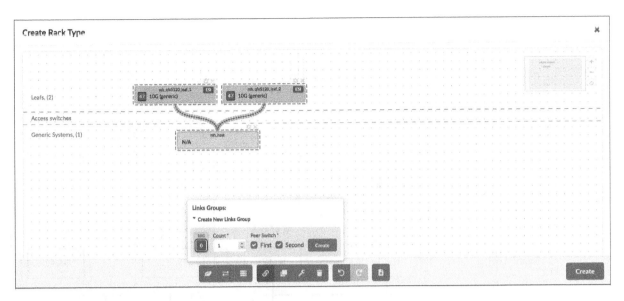

Figure 12-39 *Link group for a multihomed host*

The final rack is Rack Type 3, which has a single leaf, mapped to a Logical Device of type AOS-32x40-4. This Logical Device enables all 32 ports to be 40G ports, and allows them to connect to a spine, leaf, or generic system (among others). There is no EVPN multihoming in this rack, and the host is single-homed to the leaf. This Rack Type will be named 1xSH_32x40 and is shown in Figure 12-40.

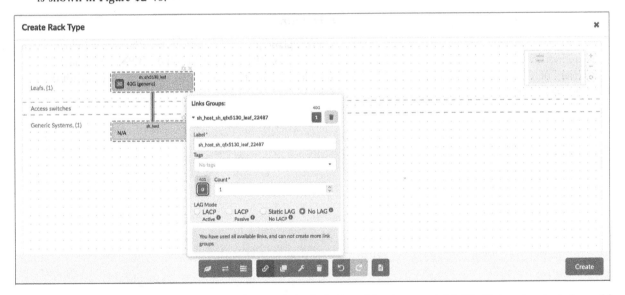

Figure 12-40 *Creation of Rack Type 3 with a single leaf of Logical Device type AOS-32x40-4 and a single-homed host*

Creating Templates

With all Rack Types created, it is time to create a Template. A Template defines the overall schema of a data center fabric and takes in different Rack Types as inputs. To create a Template, go to the main Design tab and choose between a 3-stage Clos fabric (rack based), a 5-stage Clos fabric (pod based), and a collapsed spine fabric.

In addition, you need to select one of the following autonomous system number (ASN) scheme options:

■ **Unique ASN scheme:** Applicable for 3-stage Clos fabrics. Each spine is given a unique ASN (leafs are always given a unique ASN).

■ **Single ASN scheme:** Applicable for 5-stage Clos fabrics. Each spine in a pod is given the same ASN as other spines in the same pod, and all superspines are given another ASN (same on all superspines but unique from other spines in a pod).

These two ASN schemes are visualized in Figure 12-41.

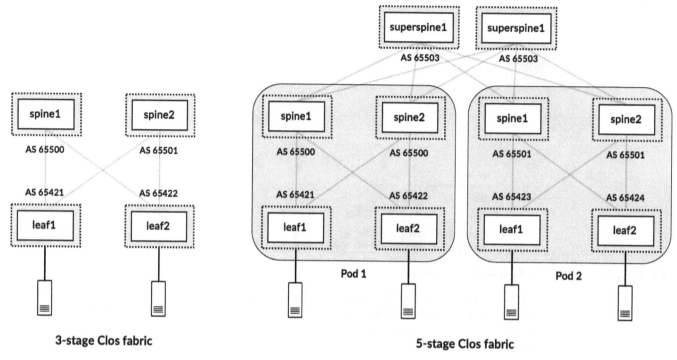

Figure 12-41   *ASN schemes for a 3-stage and a 5-stage Clos fabric in Apstra*

In addition to the ASN scheme, you need to select the overlay control plane protocol—this can be either static (which implies VXLAN peers must be statically defined, and the fabric is created as a pure IP fabric) or MP-BGP EVPN, which facilitates dynamic discovery of VXLAN peers using BGP EVPN. These Template parameters are shown in Figure 12-42, with the Template named DC1-Template and the Rack Based type selected.

Create Template   ✖

Common Parameters

Name *

DC1-Template

Type *
⦿ RACK BASED

Create a 3-stage template based on the type and number of racks you want to connect.

◯ POD BASED

Create a 5-stage template based on the type and number of rack-based templates you want to connect.

◯ COLLAPSED

Policies   *Create a spineless template using L3 Collapsed rack types.*

ASN Allocation Scheme (spine)
⦿ Unique   ◯ Single

Overlay Control Protocol
◯ Static VXLAN ⦿ MP-EBGP EVPN

☐ Create Another?   **Create**

Figure 12-42   *Template parameters defining overall data center schema*

Scrolling down in the Create Template UI, you need to define different Rack Types (along with a count of each Rack Type). All three Rack Types created earlier are attached to this Template, as shown in Figure 12-43, with Rack Type 3 having a count of two. This is a simple example of reusing one construct to scale up a fabric—since the same type of rack is needed for leaf4 and leaf5 in the reference topology shown in Figure 12-29, the Rack Type count can be adjusted to reflect the same.

Figure 12-43 *Rack Types defined during Template creation*

The spines are mapped to a Logical Device of type AOS-64x40-5, which provides 64 × 40G ports on each spine. With all the expected Rack Types added to the Template, you can save it by clicking the Create button on the bottom right. This Template will now be used to instantiate a data center fabric as an Apstra Blueprint in the next section.

Deploying a Bridged Overlay 3-Stage Clos Fabric

A data center fabric is instantiated as a Blueprint in Apstra. A Blueprint takes one primary input, a Template, along with some additional parameters such as the IP version to use between the spines and the leafs, and the spines and the superspines (for 5-stage Clos fabrics)—this can be IPv4, IPv6 (using RFC 5549), or dual-stack.

Figure 12-44 shows how a Blueprint is created, with the previously created Template, DC1-Template. IPv4 is selected as the version for the addressing scheme.

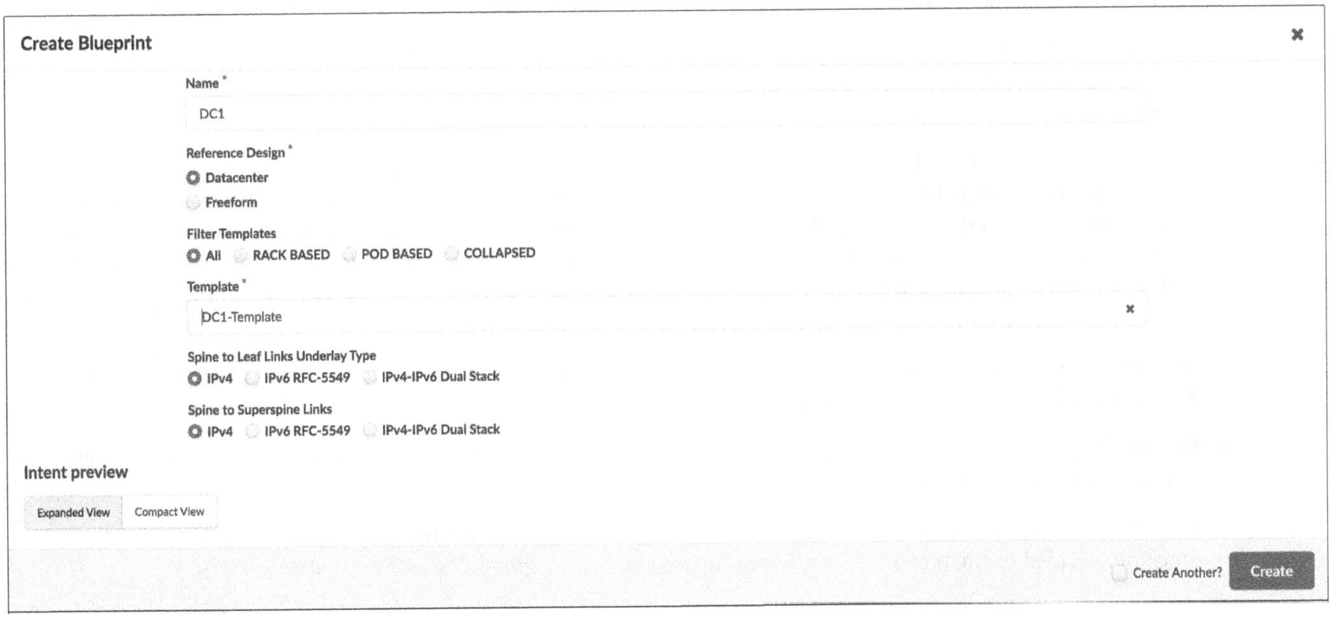

Figure 12-44 *Blueprint creation in Apstra UI*

Scrolling further down in the Create Blueprint UI, a topology preview provides quick confirmation of what the data center will look like, as shown in Figure 12-45. This also breaks down all Rack Types used in the Template, along with the quantity of each Rack Type.

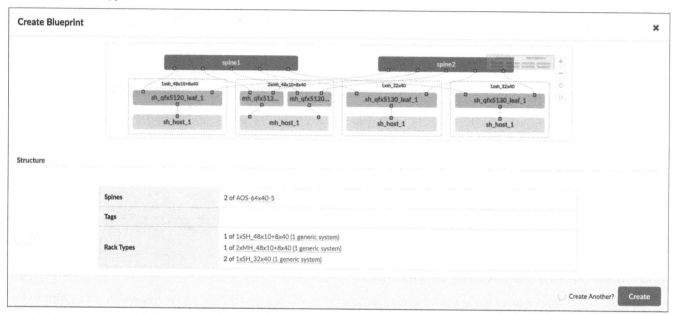

Figure 12-45   *Topology preview during Blueprint creation in Apstra UI*

When a Blueprint is instantiated, it creates a framework for the data center being deployed, based on the Template used. There are several navigation panels inside a Blueprint catering to different aspects of the overall data center, as shown in Figure 12-46:

- **Dashboard:** This shows overall telemetry information for the deployed fabric. Information here is made available only after onboarded devices are mapped to the corresponding fabric nodes in the Blueprint.

- **Analytics:** This provides high-level dashboards for quick viewing of different metrics collected from the deployed Blueprint, including device health, device environmental health, and any traffic hotspots. In addition, any anomalies detected are listed, along with all predefined probes that form the intelligence behind anomaly detection and analysis.

- **Staged:** This is where fabric-specific input is provided (outside of the initial overall fabric schema used from the Template). Apstra follows a Git-like model in which any changes made to the fabric are first staged. The Staged panel includes the following tabs on which attributes of the fabric can be controlled:

  - **Physical:** This tab includes a topology view of the fabric and enables you to assign various resources needed to build the configuration for the fabric, such as ASN pools for the leafs and spines, the IP pool for point-to-point interfaces between the leafs and the spines, the IP pool for loopback address assignment on the leafs and the spines, and any additional IP pools required as part of additional VRF and Virtual Network creation. This is also where you can add additional racks (for 3-stage fabrics), add additional pods (for 5-stage fabrics), and view and edit the auto-generated cabling map (which determines the interfaces connecting two devices in the fabric).

  - **Virtual:** This tab enables you to build virtual services running over the fabric infrastructure in the form of Virtual Networks (which can be VLANs or VXLANs) and VRFs.

  - **Policies:** This tab enables you to create policy-based constraints in the fabric in the form of security policies, interface policies, and routing policies.

  - **DCI:** This tab enables you to build an OTT DCI or a DCI using Integrated Interconnect (also known as VXLAN stitching, detailed in Chapter 11, "Data Center Interconnect") to connect two or more data centers.

- **Catalog:** This tab lists all Logical Devices and Interface Maps used in the fabric. This is also where you can import Configlets for any snowflake configurations that need to be added to a fabric device (or group of devices).

- **Tasks:** This tab lists all tasks executed as part of the overall fabric lifecycle.

- **Connectivity Templates:** This tab enables you to configure Connectivity Templates, which define how to connect to generic systems (hosts inside the fabric) and external generic systems (devices external to the fabric). For example, this is how Layer 2 tagged or untagged connectivity to end hosts is defined.

- **Fabric Settings:** This tab presents the fabric-wide settings that you can modify. These include enabling IPv6 for the fabric, use of MAC-VRFs, redistributing host routes into EVPN on leafs, and many others.

- **Uncommitted:** Since Apstra uses a Git-like commit model, any changes that are staged are naturally uncommitted, until the user manually commits them. These changes can be viewed in the Uncommitted panel, along with any errors associated with them, preventing the configuration build for a device.

- **Active:** Apstra maintains your active intent in the Active panel. Once the first commit is made, the intent is copied and tracked in this panel, along with any subsequent changes and commits.

- **Time Voyager:** This enables you to roll back the fabric state to an older state, based on the commits for the fabric thus far. This closely mimics the Junos configuration process, which also stages configurations before you commit them, with an option to roll back to a previous revision of the configuration. By default, five commit revisions can be stored for Time Voyager.

Figure 12-46 shows an initial look at the Blueprint and the different panels. Details of how to use each of these navigation panels will be explored further as the Blueprint is incrementally built.

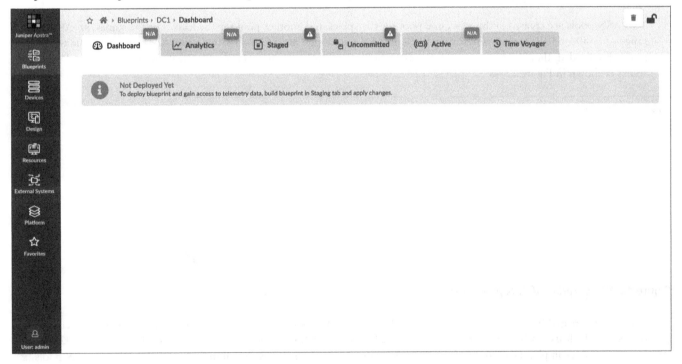

Figure 12-46 *Initial view of a Blueprint*

As part of the fabric deployment, several resources must be added to the Blueprint—these include ASN pools and IP pools for loopback and point-to-point interface address assignment. These resources are created using the Resources tab, as shown in Figure 12-47.

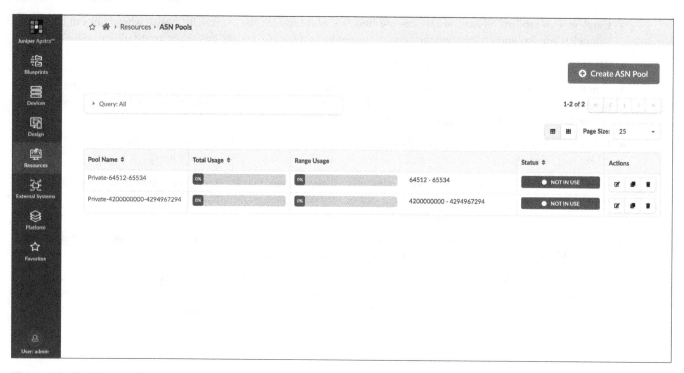

Figure 12-47 *ASN pool creation on the Resources main page in Apstra*

Two ASN pools are created in this case, one pool for the spines and another pool for the leafs. For the spines, an ASN pool range of 65500–65510 is used, and for the leafs, an ASN pool range of 65421–65430 is used. At any point, if additional ranges are needed, they can be created by simply adding a new range. As an example, the creation of the ASN pool for the spines is shown in Figure 12-48.

Figure 12-48 *Creation of ASN pool for spines*

IP pools are created from the same Resources tab, by choosing IP Pools instead. For the point-to-point interfaces between the spines and the leafs, an IPv4 range of 198.51.100.0/24 is used, and for the loopback addresses, an IPv4 range of 192.0.2.0/24 is used. As an example, the creation of the IP pool for loopback addressing is shown in Figure 12-49. Like the ASN pools, if additional pools are needed for IP addressing, they can be created by adding a new range to the respective pool.

Navigate to the Staged panel of the Blueprint, shown in Figure 12-50, to start assigning these resources. The Physical tab provides a topological view of the fabric, with a new (auto-generated) naming convention for the nodes. Apstra assigns each node (including the hosts) a name that is auto-generated based on the name of the Rack Type, the actual number of the Rack Type based on the count, and the number of leafs in that Rack Type. The entire topological view of the fabric is then ordered lexicographically.

Create IP Pool

Name *

loopback

Subnets *

192.0.2.0/24

⊕ Add a subnet

☐ Create Another?   **Create**

Figure 12-49 *Creation of IP pool for loopback IPv4 addressing*

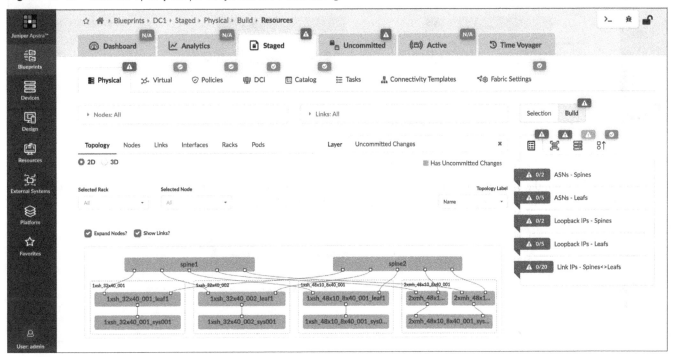

Figure 12-50 *Topological view of a fabric in the Staged panel of a Blueprint in Apstra*

For example, a Rack Type named 1xsh-32x40, with a count of two, is used in this case (with only one leaf in this Rack Type). Thus, as shown in Figure 12-50, Apstra assigns a name of 1xsh-32x40-001-leaf1 to the leaf in the first instance of this Rack Type and a name of 1xsh-32x40-002-leaf1 to the leaf in the second instance of this Rack Type.

On the right side of this page, several resources are listed for assignment, which include the ASNs and the IP pools needed for this fabric to be built. Based on the Template used (and in turn, the Rack Types), Apstra calculates the number of ASNs and IP addresses needed for the fabric. In this case, the following requirements must be met:

■ Two ASNs for the spines

■ Five ASNs for the leafs

■ Two IPv4 addresses for loopbacks on the spines

■ Five IPv4 addresses for loopbacks on the leafs

■ Twenty IPv4 addresses for the point-to-point leaf-spine interfaces

You can start assigning these resources by clicking each and choosing from one of the defined resource pools. For example, Figure 12-51 demonstrates how to assign a resource for the spine ASNs: click the resource to expand it, select the resource pool for assignment (ASN pool spine_asn in this case), and then click the Save button (floppy disk icon) to confirm the selection.

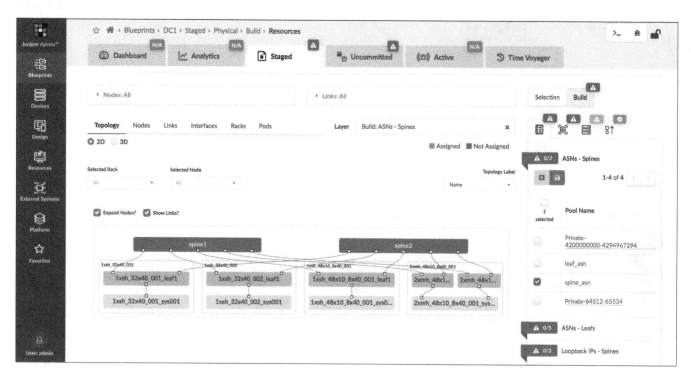

Figure 12-51   *Assignment of an ASN pool for spine ASNs*

In the same fashion, the remaining resources are assigned, and Apstra reports all resource requirements are now met (as indicated by the checkmark for each resource requirement), as shown in Figure 12-52.

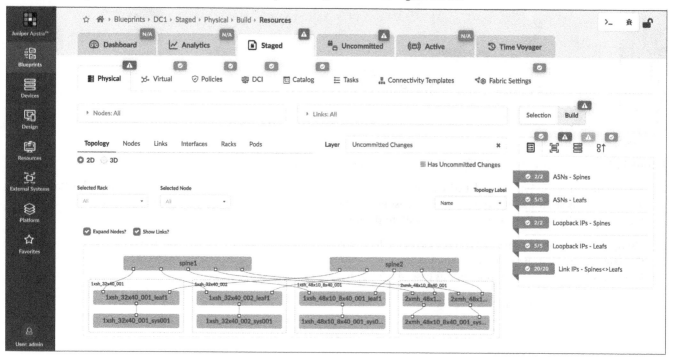

Figure 12-52   *All resources assigned in the Blueprint*

The next step in building the Blueprint is to assign Interface Maps to the fabric nodes, which enables Apstra to build vendor-specific configuration for each of these nodes. This is the last mandatory step that is needed to commit the Blueprint and save the first revision of its state.

Adjacent to resource assignment is the tab to assign Interface Maps, as shown in Figure 12-53 (right side). An Interface Map must be assigned for every Logical Device type that is used in the fabric (assigning Interface Maps for generic systems is optional).

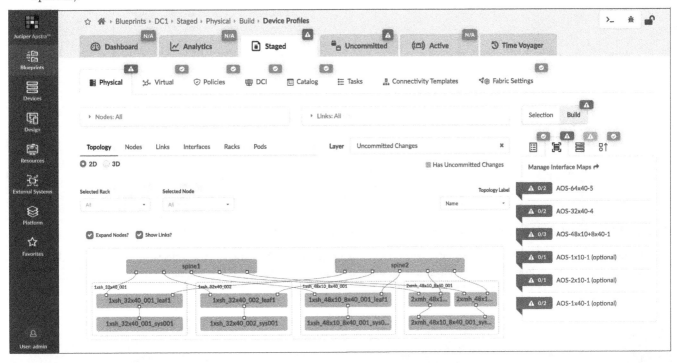

Figure 12-53 *Interface Maps to be assigned for every Logical Device used in the fabric*

Like resource assignment, you can simply click the Logical Device that needs to be mapped to an Interface Map and change or update assignments. For example, three AOS-48x10+8x40-1 Logical Devices are used (corresponding to three leafs in the fabric)—you can choose to individually assign an Interface Map to each Logical Device or, as shown in Figure 12-54, you can select all three Logical Devices and assign the same Interface Map in bulk.

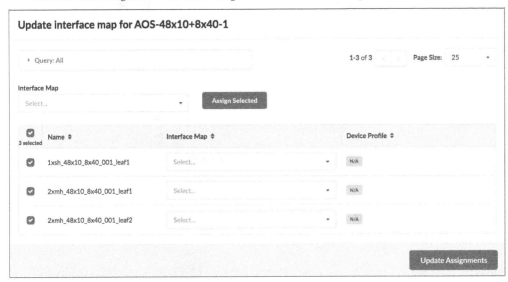

Figure 12-54 *Interface Map assignment in bulk for a Logical Device*

The assignment itself is done by selecting an Interface Map from the drop-down list and clicking the Assign Selected button. All Interface Maps, across vendors, that fit the design are listed, as shown in Figure 12-55, and you can choose which to assign. The Interface Map chosen should now reflect against every instance of the Logical Device, and you can confirm the assignment by clicking the Update Assignments button.

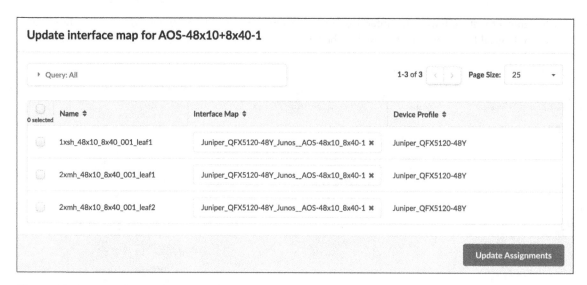

Figure 12-55 *Interface Maps assigned to every instance of Logical Device AOS-48x10+8x40-1*

In the same way, the Interface Map for all Logical Device is updated, and Apstra correctly reflects the same with a checkmark against each, including the main Physical tab, since all requirements for the fabric are now met and it can be committed. This is shown in Figure 12-56.

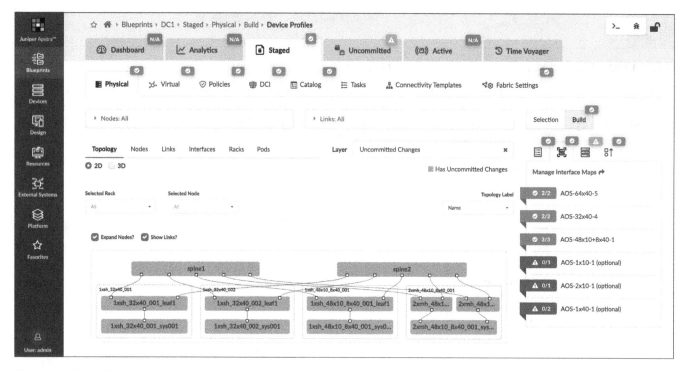

Figure 12-56 *All Interface Maps updated, and all fabric requirements met for initial commit*

To commit changes in a Blueprint, navigate to the Uncommitted panel, shown in Figure 12-57. Here, Apstra provides a list of all changes made, including the ability to view a specific change (by clicking on it) and generate a diff, allowing for easy identification of what has been changed.

Figure 12-57 *Uncommitted panel in Apstra UI from which changes can be committed*

Since, in this case, this is the initial commit of the fabric, all basic fabric building blocks are listed here, including additions of all the Rack Types and all link creations between the leafs and the spines. Once in this panel, a new Commit button is made available, in the top right of the UI, as shown in Figure 12-57. As there are no errors preventing the commit of the Blueprint, the Commit button has an associated checkmark as well.

When committing changes, you can provide an optional commit description that helps tracing through the lifecycle of a Blueprint and the different changes it went through. Figure 12-58 demonstrates this commit process.

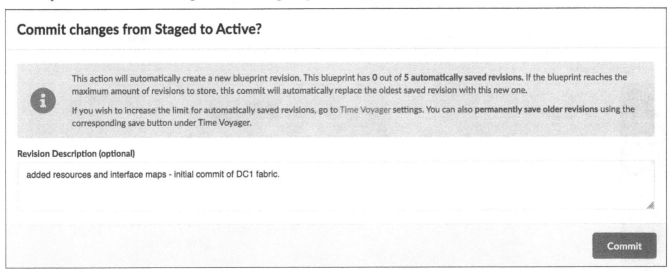

Figure 12-58 *Committing changes in a Blueprint*

With the Interface Maps assigned to fabric nodes, Apstra can generate vendor-specific configuration now. It is important to note that Apstra does this even without any actual devices (physical or virtual) mapped so far. This enables Apstra to stand up an entire fabric *logically*, in preparation for a data center to be deployed. The same logic can be extended into Day-2 operations such as adding another leaf or adding an entirely new rack. These operations can be carried out prior to the actual deployment, with Apstra fully instantiated with relevant vendor- and device-specific configuration already generated.

The assignment of the Interface Maps enables Apstra to build a cabling map for the network topology. Initially, Apstra attempts to infer these connections and assigns interfaces sequentially. However, you can update the cabling map either manually or by using LLDP. For an example of the latter, the auto-generated cabling map displayed in Figure 12-59 does not have accurate interfaces mapped. This can be updated by clicking the button to fetch information from LLDP.

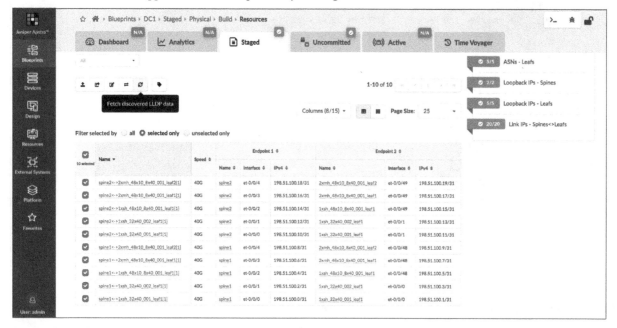

Figure 12-59 *Updating cabling map in Apstra by fetching data from LLDP*

NOTE Fetching data from LLDP only reports accurate topological information (that reflects your real or virtual topology) once System IDs are mapped to fabric nodes, which is described shortly. Alternatively, you can manually update the cabling map as well or import a cabling map in JSON format. This map can then be provided to technicians onsite (exported as an Excel sheet or a JSON file), and it can be leveraged to physically cable up the network.

You can view the rendered configuration by going into a device-specific view in the Physical tab under the Staged panel, clicking a device, and then selecting the Rendered option under Config on the bottom right side of the UI, as shown in Figure 12-60.

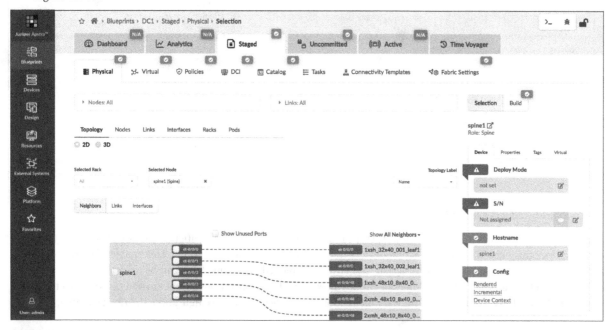

Figure 12-60 *Device-specific view in Apstra*

As an example, for spine1 shown in Figure 12-59, the configuration is already rendered, a snippet of which is shown in Figure 12-61.

spine1 Rendered Config Preview

```
25   interfaces {
26       replace: et-0/0/0 {
27           description "facing_1xsh-32x40-001-leaf1:et-0/0/0";
28           mtu 9216;
29           unit 0 {
30               family inet {
31                   mtu 9170;
32                   address 198.51.100.0/31;
33               }
34           }
35       }
36       replace: et-0/0/1 {
37           description "facing_1xsh-32x40-002-leaf1:et-0/0/0";
38           mtu 9216;
39           unit 0 {
40               family inet {
41                   mtu 9170;
42                   address 198.51.100.2/31;
43               }
44           }
45       }
46       replace: et-0/0/2 {
47           description "facing_1xsh-48x10-8x40-001-leaf1:et-0/0/48";
48           mtu 9216;
49           unit 0 {
50               family inet {
```

Figure 12-61 *Rendered configuration for spine1 in Apstra*

With the initial Blueprint committed, the fabric nodes can be mapped to actual devices now. This process involves mapping System IDs to the respective fabric nodes. The availability of a System ID to be mapped in a Blueprint is determined by the Interface Maps assigned to a fabric node and the state of a managed device—it must be in an *OOS-READY* state, and the Device Profile must be applicable for the Interface Map assigned.

All devices have been onboarded (either via ZTP or manual onboarding) in Apstra and are in an *OOS-READY* state (a device moves from *OOS-QUARANTINED* to *OOS-READY* when it is acknowledged by the operator), as shown in Figure 12-62.

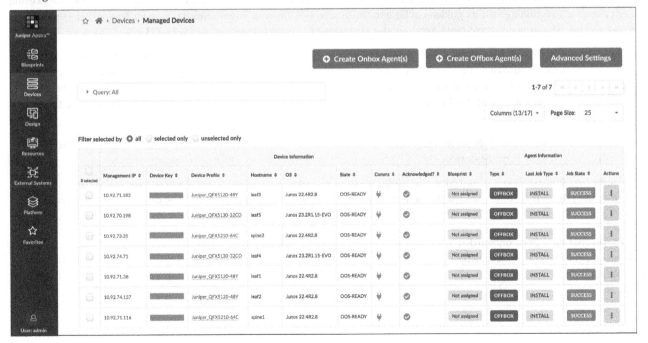

Figure 12-62 *All devices onboarded and acknowledged in Apstra*

The tab to assign System IDs is adjacent to the resource and Interface Maps tab on the right side of the UI (still on the Physical tab of the Staged panel), as shown in Figure 12-63.

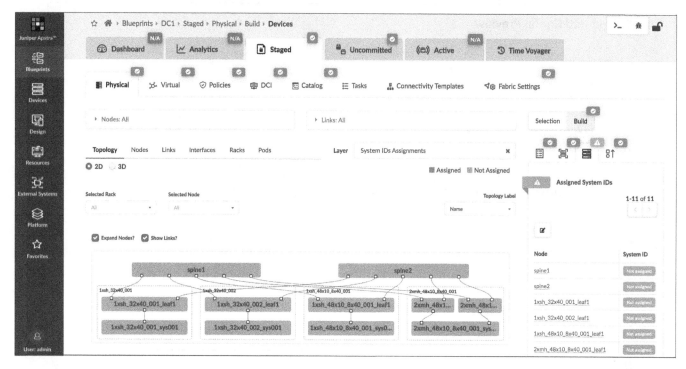

Figure 12-63 *System ID assignment tab in Apstra*

When mapping System IDs to a fabric node, you can assign them to one of the following modes:

- **Deploy:** Apstra deploys the rendered configuration for the device (using a full configuration push). When a device is moved to Deploy mode for the first time, Apstra overwrites the existing device configuration with the pristine configuration plus the rendered configuration in the Blueprint. This means that any additional configuration (apart from the pristine and rendered configuration) that may exist on the device will be discarded. Once this is done, Apstra takes a snapshot of the configuration and stores it as the *golden configuration* for the device, continuously validating the existing device configuration against its golden configuration for any violations in intent (and flagging an anomaly if violations are found). The device is considered Active in the Blueprint and its state is moved to *IS-ACTIVE*.

- **Ready:** Devices are not deployed but are assigned to the Blueprint and the device state is moved to *IS-READY*. In this mode, the device is moved to the *Discovery 2* configuration (using a full configuration push), where the interfaces are configured with their respective descriptions and speeds, and the hostname of the device is updated to match the hostname in the Apstra Blueprint. In this mode, LLDP can be leveraged to determine interconnections between the fabric nodes.

- **Drain:** This mode allows a device to be taken out of service while minimizing impact to traffic flows, by applying policies to drain traffic from the device. This is typically used for device maintenance or decommissioning.

- **Undeploy:** When a device is moved to this mode, all service configuration is removed from it, essentially removing it from the fabric. It is recommended that a device be drained first and then undeployed. The device state is moved back to *IS-READY*.

All devices that have been onboarded are assigned to their respective fabric nodes, placing them in the Ready mode, as shown in Figure 12-64. Apstra pushes Discovery 2 configuration to these devices now, and if needed, LLDP can be used to update the cabling map.

Figure 12-64 *System IDs assigned to respective fabric nodes in Ready mode*

Using LLDP to fetch accurate data on interconnections between fabric nodes, Apstra reports that there are mismatches in the cabling map, as shown in Figure 12-65. You can either choose to update it using the received LLDP information (or update manually) or clear the LLDP state (reverting back to Apstra's initial inferred interconnections by clicking Clear LLDP Data).

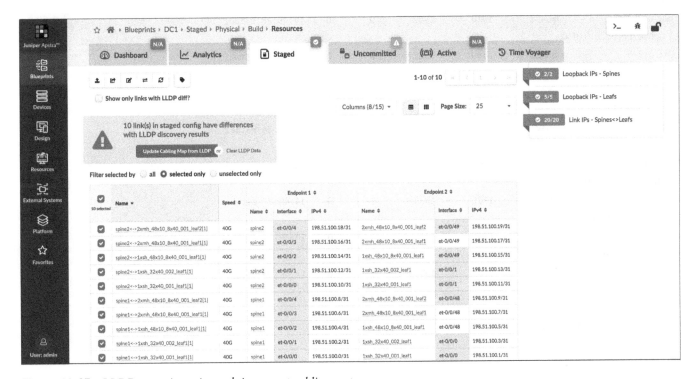

Figure 12-65 *LLDP reporting mismatch in current cabling map*

Once the cable map is confirmed to be correct, the devices can be moved to Deploy mode. Apstra now pushes the service configuration to these devices. Since this is the first time the devices are moved to Deploy mode, a full configuration push occurs—existing configuration is overwritten with the pristine configuration and the Apstra rendered configuration. This includes (among other things):

- Configuring all Layer 3 interfaces with their respective IPv4/IPv6 addresses

- Configuring BGP on the leafs and the spines

- BFD for a routing protocol, if applicable

- Adding the device (that was moved to Deploy mode) to the graph database

Taking spine1 and spine2 as an example, the BGP peering to all leafs, for both the IPv4 and the EVPN family, is in an Established state, as shown in Example 12-9, after moving all devices to Deploy mode.

Example 12-9 *BGP state on spine1 and spine2 after all devices are moved to Deploy mode in Apstra*

```
root@spine1> show bgp summary


Threading mode: BGP I/O
Default eBGP mode: advertise - accept, receive - accept
Groups: 2 Peers: 10 Down peers: 0
Table          Tot Paths  Act Paths Suppressed    History Damp State      Pending
inet.0

                    15        10         0          0       0           0
bgp.evpn.0

                     0         0         0          0       0           0
Peer                     AS    InPkt    OutPkt    OutQ    Flaps Last Up/Dwn State|#Active/Received/Accepted/Damped...
192.0.2.2              65421    1963      1934      0       0    14:50:31 Establ
  bgp.evpn.0: 0/0/0/0
192.0.2.3              65422    1962      1933      0       0    14:50:26 Establ
  bgp.evpn.0: 0/0/0/0
192.0.2.4              65423    1960      1932      0       0    14:49:25 Establ
  bgp.evpn.0: 0/0/0/0
192.0.2.5              65424    1960      1932      0       0    14:49:17 Establ
  bgp.evpn.0: 0/0/0/0
192.0.2.6              65425    1959      1931      0       0    14:49:09 Establ
  bgp.evpn.0: 0/0/0/0
198.51.100.1           65421    1964      1943      0       0    14:50:34 Establ
  inet.0: 2/3/3/0
198.51.100.3           65422    1963      1942      0       0    14:50:34 Establ
  inet.0: 2/3/3/0
198.51.100.5           65423    1961      1938      0       0    14:49:27 Establ
  inet.0: 2/3/3/0
198.51.100.7           65424    1961      1939      0       0    14:49:29 Establ
  inet.0: 2/3/3/0
198.51.100.9           65425    1960      1936      0       0    14:49:20 Establ
  inet.0: 2/3/3/0


root@spine2> show bgp summary


Threading mode: BGP I/O
```

```
Default eBGP mode: advertise - accept, receive - accept
Groups: 2 Peers: 10 Down peers: 0
Table          Tot Paths  Act Paths Suppressed  History Damp State   Pending
inet.0
                  15         10         0          0       0          0
bgp.evpn.0
                   0          0         0          0       0          0
Peer              AS     InPkt    OutPkt   OutQ   Flaps Last Up/Dwn
State|#Active/Received/Accepted/Damped...
192.0.2.2        65421    1967     1939     0      0    14:52:38 Establ
  bgp.evpn.0: 0/0/0/0
192.0.2.3        65422    1967     1939     0      0    14:52:38 Establ
  bgp.evpn.0: 0/0/0/0
192.0.2.4        65423    1964     1936     0      0    14:51:29 Establ
  bgp.evpn.0: 0/0/0/0
192.0.2.5        65424    1964     1936     0      0    14:51:33 Establ
  bgp.evpn.0: 0/0/0/0
192.0.2.6        65425    1964     1936     0      0    14:51:22 Establ
  bgp.evpn.0: 0/0/0/0
198.51.100.11    65421    1968     1947     0      0    14:52:46 Establ
  inet.0: 2/3/3/0
198.51.100.13    65422    1969     1948     0      0    14:52:46 Establ
  inet.0: 2/3/3/0
198.51.100.15    65423    1965     1941     0      0    14:51:38 Establ
  inet.0: 2/3/3/0
198.51.100.17    65424    1965     1942     0      0    14:51:41 Establ
  inet.0: 2/3/3/0
198.51.100.19    65425    1966     1942     0      0    14:51:36 Establ
  inet.0: 2/3/3/0
```

It is important to take a closer look at some of the configurations that Apstra is pushing to the fabric devices. A noteworthy change is how Apstra prevents BGP path hunting. In Apstra, all spines have a unique AS number in a 3-stage Clos fabric, and thus, to prevent BGP path hunting, export routing policies are used on both the leafs and the spines.

Routing policies for the underlay of a 3-stage Clos fabric, deployed by Apstra, do the following:

- On each spine, a unique set of BGP communities is added to routes that are directly attached and exported into BGP.

- On all spines, the same community value (0:15, as an example) is added to all routes advertised to other leafs.

- On each leaf, an export routing policy matches the 0:15 community added by the spines, and rejects any routes with that community, to prevent them from being sent back to the spine layer.

Example 12-10 shows the BGP configuration pushed by Apstra on spine1 (similar configuration is pushed to spine2 as well). Two export policies are applied to the peering for each leaf: SPINE_TO_LEAF_FABRIC_OUT and BGP-AOS-Policy.

Example 12-10 *BGP configuration pushed by Apstra on spine1*

```
root@spine1# show protocols bgp group l3clos-s
type external;
multipath {
    multiple-as;
}
bfd-liveness-detection {
    minimum-interval 1000;
```

```
        multiplier 3;
    }
    neighbor 198.51.100.1 {
        description facing_1xsh-32x40-001-leaf1;
        local-address 198.51.100.0;
        family inet {
            unicast;
        }
        export ( SPINE_TO_LEAF_FABRIC_OUT && BGP-AOS-Policy );
        peer-as 65421;
    }
    neighbor 198.51.100.3 {
        description facing_1xsh-32x40-002-leaf1;
        local-address 198.51.100.2;
        family inet {
            unicast;
        }
        export ( SPINE_TO_LEAF_FABRIC_OUT && BGP-AOS-Policy );
        peer-as 65422;
    }
    neighbor 198.51.100.5 {
        description facing_1xsh-48x10-8x40-001-leaf1;
        local-address 198.51.100.4;
        family inet {
            unicast;
        }
        export ( SPINE_TO_LEAF_FABRIC_OUT && BGP-AOS-Policy );
        peer-as 65423;
    }
    neighbor 198.51.100.7 {
        description facing_2xmh-48x10-8x40-001-leaf1;
        local-address 198.51.100.6;
        family inet {
            unicast;
        }
        export ( SPINE_TO_LEAF_FABRIC_OUT && BGP-AOS-Policy );
        peer-as 65424;
    }
    neighbor 198.51.100.9 {
        description facing_2xmh-48x10-8x40-001-leaf2;
        local-address 198.51.100.8;
        family inet {
            unicast;
        }
        export ( SPINE_TO_LEAF_FABRIC_OUT && BGP-AOS-Policy );
        peer-as 65425;
    }
    vpn-apply-export;
```

Of the two policies, SPINE_TO_LEAF_FABRIC_OUT is of relevance for path hunting. As shown in Example 12-11, this export policy adds a community of 0:15 for all routes advertised by the spines to the leafs.

Example 12-11 *Routing policy on spine1 adding a community for all routes advertised to leafs*

```
root@spine1# show policy-options policy-statement SPINE_TO_LEAF_FABRIC_OUT
term SPINE_TO_LEAF_FABRIC_OUT-10 {
    then {
        community add FROM_SPINE_FABRIC_TIER;
        accept;
    }
}


root@spine1# show policy-options community FROM_SPINE_FABRIC_TIER
members 0:15;
```

To confirm the same, the route shown in Example 12-12 is advertised with this community. This is the loopback address of one of the leafs being advertised by spine1 to another leaf.

Example 12-12 *BGP community added to a route advertised by spine1 to a leaf*

```
root@spine1> show route advertising-protocol bgp 198.51.100.1 192.0.2.3 extensive

inet.0: 21 destinations, 26 routes (21 active, 0 holddown, 0 hidden)
Restart Complete
* 192.0.2.3/32 (1 entry, 1 announced)
 BGP group l3clos-s type External
     AS path: [65500] 65422 I
     Communities: 0:15 4:20007 21001:26000
```

Let's consider the Juniper QFX5120-48Y leaf, which has only a single-homed host (leaf1, in the reference topology). When it receives this route, it has a routing policy that matches this community and rejects it from being advertised back to the spines, as shown in Example 12-13.

Example 12-13 *Routing policy on leaf rejecting routes with the community added by the spines from being exported*

```
root@1xsh-48x10-8x40-001-leaf1# show protocols bgp group l3clos-1
type external;
multipath {
    multiple-as;
}
bfd-liveness-detection {
    minimum-interval 1000;
    multiplier 3;
}
neighbor 198.51.100.4 {
    description facing_spine1;
    local-address 198.51.100.5;
    family inet {
        unicast;
    }
    export ( LEAF_TO_SPINE_FABRIC_OUT && BGP-AOS-Policy );
    peer-as 65500;
}
```

```
neighbor 198.51.100.14 {
    description facing_spine2;
    local-address 198.51.100.15;
    family inet {
        unicast;
    }
    export ( LEAF_TO_SPINE_FABRIC_OUT && BGP-AOS-Policy );
    peer-as 65501;
}
vpn-apply-export;


root@1xsh-48x10-8x40-001-leaf1# show policy-options policy-statement LEAF_TO_SPINE_FABRIC_OUT
term LEAF_TO_SPINE_FABRIC_OUT-10 {
    from {
        protocol bgp;
        community FROM_SPINE_FABRIC_TIER;
    }
    then reject;
}
term LEAF_TO_SPINE_FABRIC_OUT-20 {
    then accept;
}


root@1xsh-48x10-8x40-001-leaf1# show policy-options community FROM_SPINE_FABRIC_TIER
members 0:15;
```

Thus, together, the spine and leaf routing policies prevent BGP path hunting in an Apstra deployed data center fabric. Visually, this can be represented as shown in Figure 12-66.

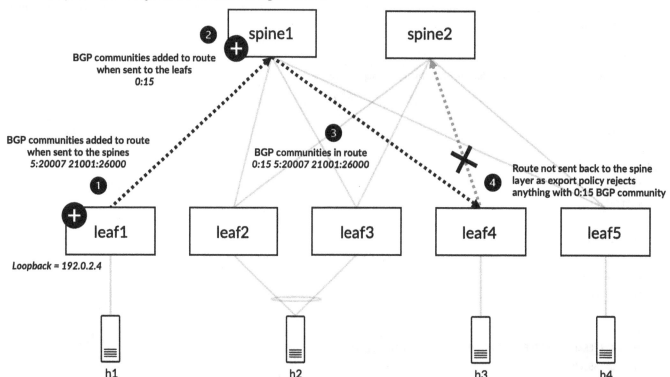

Figure 12-66 *Visual representation of the prevention of BGP path hunting in an Apstra-deployed data center fabric*

With the core infrastructure for the fabric deployed, each leaf can reach the loopback address of every other leaf (while sourcing its own). Taking leaf1 as an example, all loopbacks are in the inet.0 table as /32 routes, as shown in Example 12-14.

Example 12-14   *Routing table for inet.0 on leaf1 displaying all loopback addresses*

```
root@1xsh-48x10-8x40-001-leaf1> show route table inet.0

inet.0: 19 destinations, 33 routes (19 active, 0 holddown, 0 hidden)
Restart Complete
+ = Active Route, - = Last Active, * = Both

192.0.2.0/32        *[BGP/170] 1d 20:10:17, localpref 100
                      AS path: 65500 I, validation-state: unverified
                    >  to 198.51.100.4 via et-0/0/48.0
192.0.2.1/32        *[BGP/170] 1d 20:10:12, localpref 100
                      AS path: 65501 I, validation-state: unverified
                    >  to 198.51.100.14 via et-0/0/50.0
192.0.2.2/32        *[BGP/170] 1d 20:10:12, localpref 100
                      AS path: 65500 65421 I, validation-state: unverified
                    >  to 198.51.100.4 via et-0/0/48.0
                       to 198.51.100.14 via et-0/0/50.0
                     [BGP/170] 1d 20:10:12, localpref 100
                      AS path: 65501 65421 I, validation-state: unverified
                    >  to 198.51.100.14 via et-0/0/50.0
192.0.2.3/32        *[BGP/170] 1d 20:10:12, localpref 100
                      AS path: 65500 65422 I, validation-state: unverified
                    >  to 198.51.100.4 via et-0/0/48.0
                       to 198.51.100.14 via et-0/0/50.0
                     [BGP/170] 1d 20:10:12, localpref 100
                      AS path: 65501 65422 I, validation-state: unverified
                    >  to 198.51.100.14 via et-0/0/50.0
192.0.2.4/32        *[Direct/0] 1d 20:11:45
                    >  via lo0.0
192.0.2.5/32        *[BGP/170] 1d 20:10:12, localpref 100
                      AS path: 65500 65424 I, validation-state: unverified
                    >  to 198.51.100.4 via et-0/0/48.0
                       to 198.51.100.14 via et-0/0/50.0
                     [BGP/170] 1d 20:10:12, localpref 100
                      AS path: 65501 65424 I, validation-state: unverified
                    >  to 198.51.100.14 via et-0/0/50.0
192.0.2.6/32        *[BGP/170] 1d 20:10:10, localpref 100, from 198.51.100.14
                      AS path: 65501 65425 I, validation-state: unverified
                    >  to 198.51.100.4 via et-0/0/48.0
                       to 198.51.100.14 via et-0/0/50.0
                     [BGP/170] 1d 20:10:10, localpref 100
                      AS path: 65500 65425 I, validation-state: unverified
                    >  to 198.51.100.4 via et-0/0/48.0

*snip*
```

With the underlay deployed, VXLAN services can be deployed next. Services, at a high level, are deployed using the Virtual tab under the Staged panel in Apstra, shown in Figure 12-67. This tab enables you to create and edit the following two main constructs (among other things):

■ **Virtual Networks:** A Virtual Network (VN) can be a VLAN or a VXLAN, with different parameters available for assignment for each, such as the VLAN ID or the VNI, the Routing Zone for the VN, any attached DHCP services for the VN, and IPv4/IPv6 connectivity (and subsequently, the IPv4/IPv6 gateway and any corresponding virtual addresses). Apstra also allows you to create an untagged/tagged Connectivity Template during the VN creation process. At the time of VN creation, you must select the leafs in which this VN should be made available.

■ **Routing Zones:** Routing Zones are VRFs, implemented as routing instances of type *vrf*, on Juniper devices. In Apstra, a default Routing Zone exists, which maps to the main routing table. This default Routing Zone cannot be used for VXLAN-based VNs, and thus a user-defined Routing Zone is necessary for such a use case.

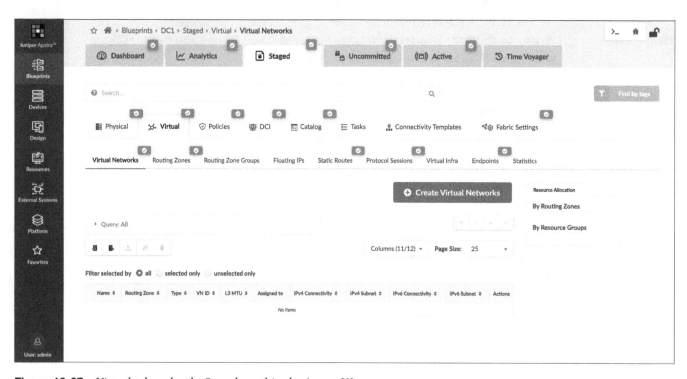

Figure 12-67   *Virtual tab under the Staged panel in the Apstra UI*

To demonstrate a bridged overlay fabric design, a VXLAN-based Virtual Network is created, with IPv4 connectivity disabled (meaning this is a Layer 2 segment only). VXLAN-based VNs cannot exist in the default Routing Zone, and thus a user-defined Routing Zone must be created, and the VN can be mapped to this (or any other user-defined Routing Zone).

As shown in Figure 12-68, a new user-defined Routing Zone called *Tenant1* is created, with a VLAN ID of 500 and a VNI of 10500 (Apstra auto-generates the VLAN ID and VNI if no input is provided). Apstra also auto-generates the import and export Route Targets for this VRF, but, if needed, you can specify additional custom import and export Route Targets as well. For a bridged overlay fabric, the Routing Zone (which corresponds to a Layer 3 VRF) does not have any significance, but it is still needed, with the assumption that Layer 3 services may also be deployed in the future.

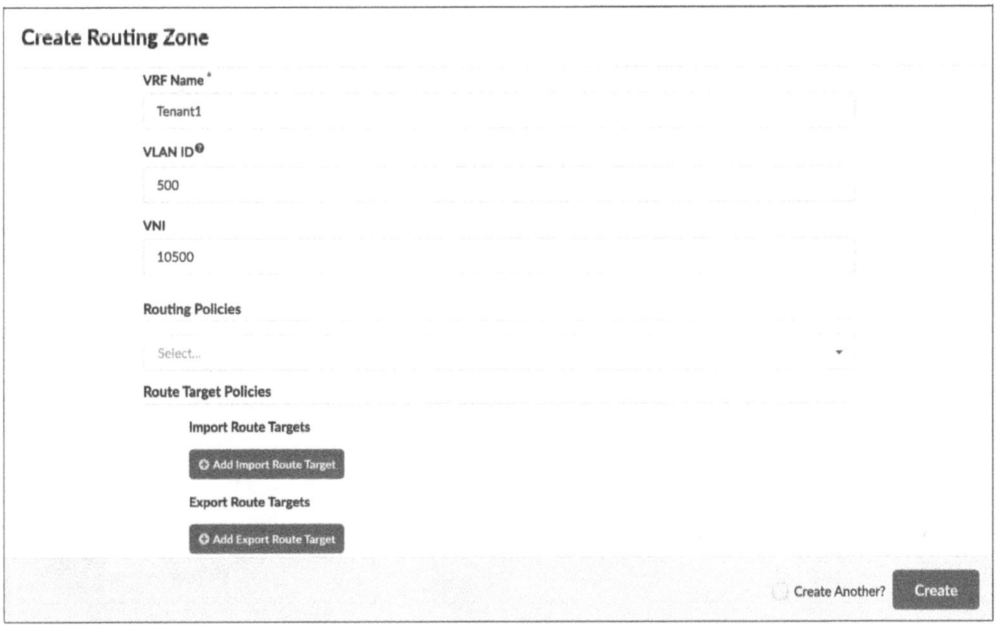

Figure 12-68 *Routing Zone creation in the Apstra UI*

Using this new Routing Zone, a VXLAN-based Virtual Network can be created now. For the bridged overlay use case, a VLAN name of v10, VLAN ID of 10, and VNI of 10010 are used (again, if no input is provided, Apstra auto-generates the VLAN ID and the VNI, giving you the flexibility to be as specific as needed). This is shown in Figure 12-69, with the *Reserve across blueprint* flag set. This ensures that the same VLAN ID is used on all leafs. In addition, an untagged Connectivity Template will also be created as part of this VN creation (since that corresponding flag is set).

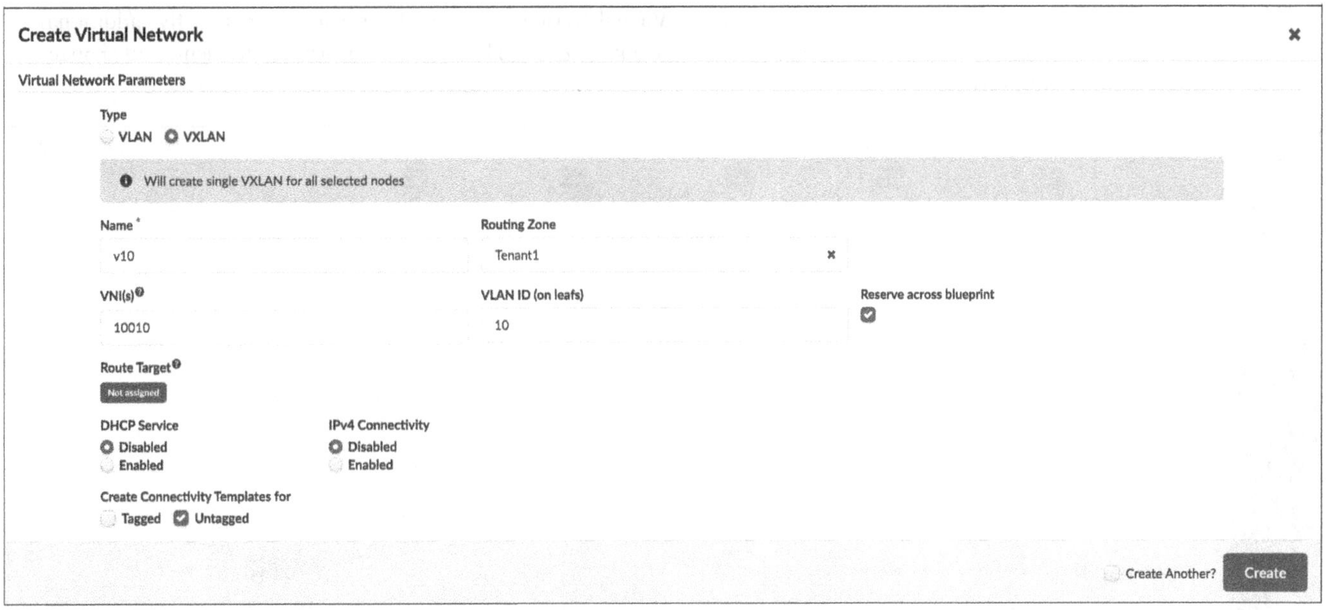

Figure 12-69 *Virtual Network creation for a bridged overlay fabric in the Apstra UI*

Scrolling down in the Create Virtual Network page, you are required to choose to which leafs, and corresponding link labels, this VN is applicable, as shown in Figure 12-70. This allows the assignment of the Connectivity Template to these links. As with Routing Zones, Apstra auto-generates import and export Route Targets for the Layer 2 VNI, but, if needed, you can manually define these as well.

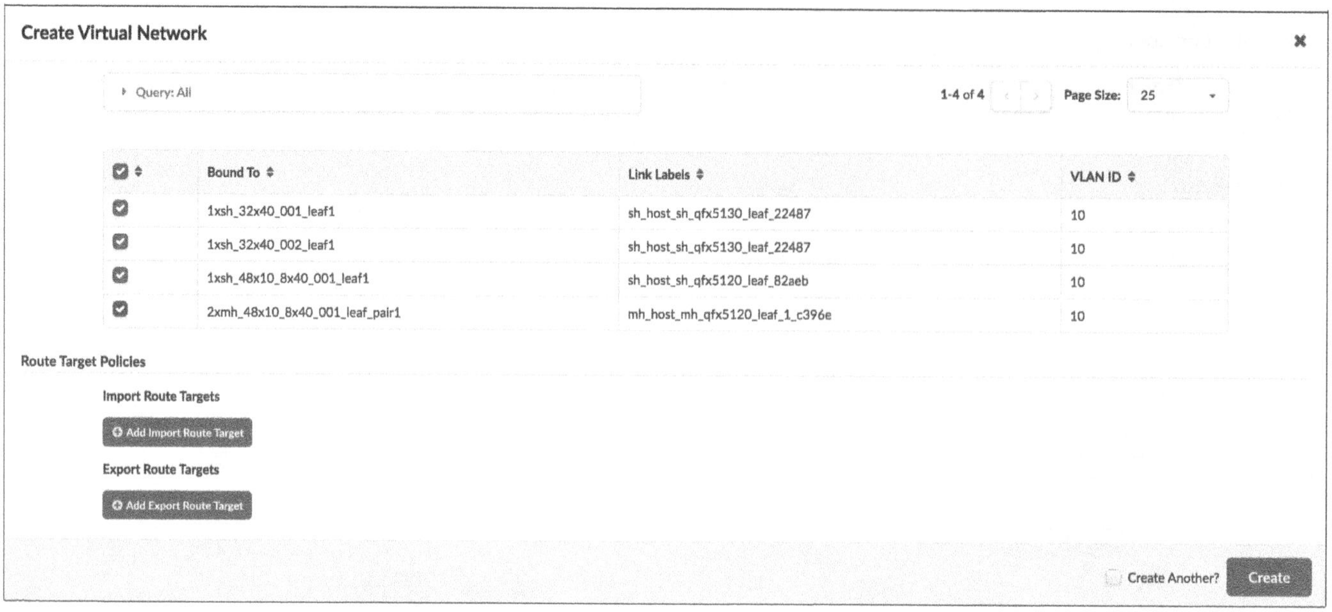

Figure 12-70 *Assignment of a VN to leafs and corresponding link labels*

For every new Routing Zone created, Apstra requires a new loopback address for all applicable leafs when the first Virtual Network is mapped to the Routing Zone. This is a common theme in Apstra: when a new construct is created in the Blueprint and Apstra does not have enough information, it will let you know by creating additional dependencies that must be met. This loopback is mapped to the Layer 3 VRF that is created for the corresponding Routing Zone. This is just a one-time requirement—any additional Virtual Networks mapped to the same Routing Zone do not require new loopback addresses.

As shown in Figure 12-71 (on the right side), when this new Virtual Network is created, Apstra reports that five additional loopback addresses are needed (one per leaf) for the Tenant1 Routing Zone. This is a mandatory requirement, and changes cannot be committed until this is met.

Figure 12-71 *Apstra requirement of additional loopback addresses per Routing Zone*

Taking any leaf into consideration, the incremental changes can be viewed for this deployment of a new Routing Zone and Virtual Network, a snippet of which is shown in Figure 12-72.

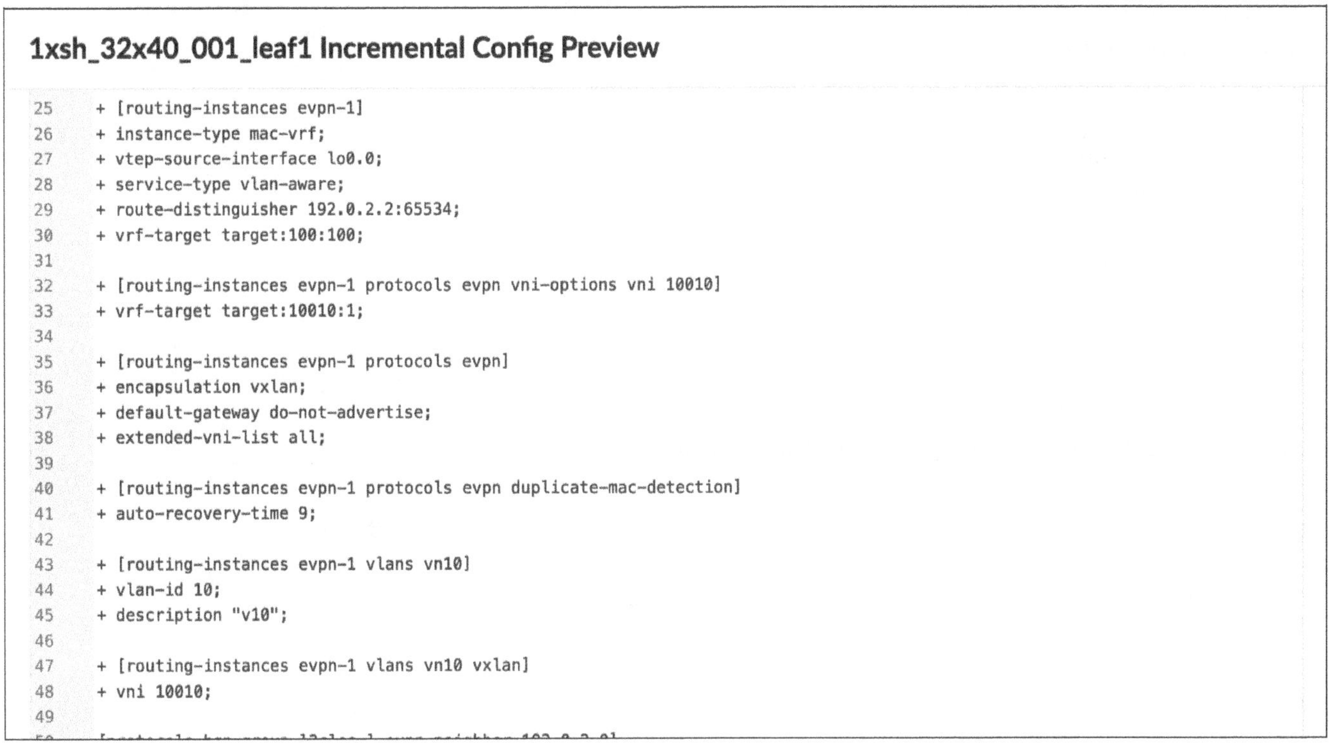

1xsh_32x40_001_leaf1 Incremental Config Preview

```
25   + [routing-instances evpn-1]
26   + instance-type mac-vrf;
27   + vtep-source-interface lo0.0;
28   + service-type vlan-aware;
29   + route-distinguisher 192.0.2.2:65534;
30   + vrf-target target:100:100;
31
32   + [routing-instances evpn-1 protocols evpn vni-options vni 10010]
33   + vrf-target target:10010:1;
34
35   + [routing-instances evpn-1 protocols evpn]
36   + encapsulation vxlan;
37   + default-gateway do-not-advertise;
38   + extended-vni-list all;
39
40   + [routing-instances evpn-1 protocols evpn duplicate-mac-detection]
41   + auto-recovery-time 9;
42
43   + [routing-instances evpn-1 vlans vn10]
44   + vlan-id 10;
45   + description "v10";
46
47   + [routing-instances evpn-1 vlans vn10 vxlan]
48   + vni 10010;
49
```

Figure 12-72 *Incremental configuration shown in the Apstra UI from the addition of a Routing Zone and Virtual Network*

This change translates to the following configurations pushed to the leafs, where this Virtual Network is applicable:

- A MAC-VRF of service-type VLAN-Aware, which includes this newly defined VLAN. As of 4.2.0, Apstra defaults to a single MAC-VRF on Juniper QFX switches, which includes all VLANs that are part of user intent.

- A routing instance of type *vrf*, which is the instantiation of the defined Routing Zone. This Layer 3 routing instance is enabled for EVPN Type-5 routing.

As an example, the configuration of these routing instances is shown in Example 12-15 from one leaf.

Example 12-15 *MAC-VRF and IP VRF routing instances on leaf1*

```
root@1xsh-48x10-8x40-001-leaf1# show routing-instances evpn-1
instance-type mac-vrf;
protocols {
    evpn {
        encapsulation vxlan;
        default-gateway do-not-advertise;
        duplicate-mac-detection {
            auto-recovery-time 9;
        }
        extended-vni-list all;
        vni-options {
            vni 10010 {
                vrf-target target:10010:1;
            }
        }
    }
}
```

```
vtep-source-interface lo0.0;
service-type vlan-aware;
route-distinguisher 192.0.2.4:65534;
vrf-target target:100:100;
vlans {
    vn10 {
        description v10;
        vlan-id 10;
        vxlan {
            vni 10010;
        }
    }
}


root@1xsh-48x10-8x40-001-leaf1# show routing-instances Tenant1
instance-type vrf;
routing-options {
    graceful-restart;
    multipath;
    auto-export;
}
protocols {
    evpn {
        irb-symmetric-routing {
            vni 10500;
        }
        ip-prefix-routes {
            advertise direct-nexthop;
            encapsulation vxlan;
            vni 10500;
            export BGP-AOS-Policy-Tenant1;
        }
    }
}
interface lo0.2;
route-distinguisher 192.0.2.4:500;
vrf-target target:10500:1;
```

Since the flag was checked to automatically create an untagged Connectivity Template for this new Virtual Network, this now exists on the Connectivity Templates tab of the Staged panel, as shown in Figure 12-73.

This Connectivity Template needs to be attached to the links that connect to the generic systems (hosts). The assignment is done by clicking the *assignment* interactive button under the Actions column in Figure 12-73. Figure 12-74 shows the assignment of this Connectivity Template to the link labels (which in turn correspond to the interfaces in the cable map) that connect to the four hosts in this fabric. Apstra also allows bulk assignment if multiple Virtual Networks are created at once.

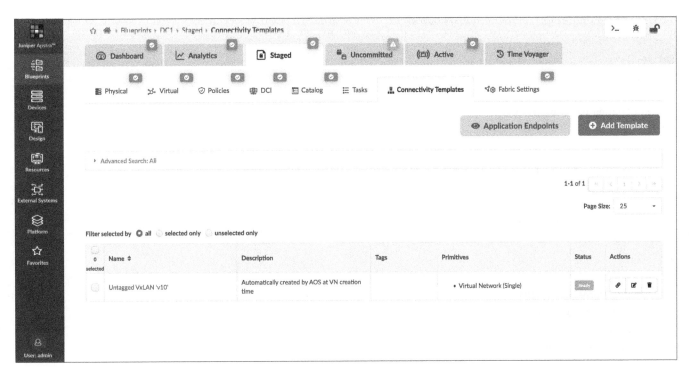

Figure 12-73 *Automatically created Connectivity Template for the new Virtual Network*

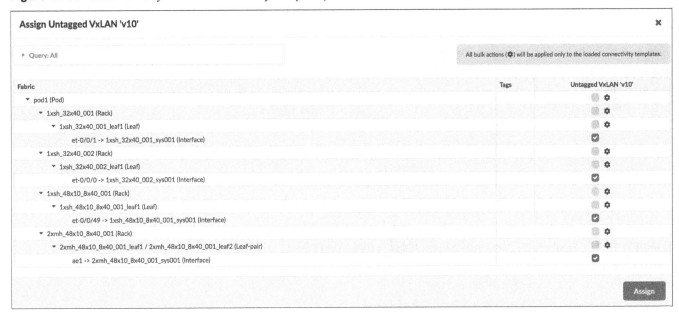

Figure 12-74 *Connectivity Template assignment to links in a fabric*

For leafs that are part of an ESI LAG, this assignment creates an Aggregated Ethernet (AE) interface, and the Ethernet Segment mapping for this LAG. Taking leaf2 as an example, the configuration shown in Example 12-16 is pushed by Apstra for the ESI LAG connecting to host h2.

Example 12-16 *ESI LAG configuration pushed by Apstra on Connectivity Template assignment*

```
root@2xmh-48x10-8x40-001-leaf1# show interfaces et-0/0/50
description to.2xmh-48x10-8x40-001-sys001;
ether-options {
    802.3ad ae1;
}
```

```
root@2xmh-48x10-8x40-001-leaf1# show interfaces ae1
description to.2xmh-48x10-8x40-001-sys001;
native-vlan-id 10;
mtu 9216;
esi {
    00:02:00:00:00:01:00:00:01;
    all-active;
}
aggregated-ether-options {
    lacp {
        active;
        system-id 02:00:00:00:00:01;
    }
}
unit 0 {
    family ethernet-switching {
        interface-mode trunk;
        vlan {
            members vn10;
        }
    }
}


root@2xmh-48x10-8x40-001-leaf1# show chassis
aggregated-devices {
    ethernet {
        device-count 1;
    }
}
```

At this point, all aspects of the fabric are configured and deployed via Apstra, for a bridged overlay fabric. The hosts have connectivity to each other, verified using the **ping** tool on the hosts, as shown in Example 12-17, using host h1 as an example.

Example 12-17   *Host reachability verified using the* **ping** *tool on host h1*

```
root@h1> ping 172.16.10.2
PING 172.16.10.2 (172.16.10.2): 56 data bytes
64 bytes from 172.16.10.2: icmp_seq=0 ttl=64 time=1.017 ms
64 bytes from 172.16.10.2: icmp_seq=1 ttl=64 time=38.126 ms
64 bytes from 172.16.10.2: icmp_seq=2 ttl=64 time=0.903 ms
64 bytes from 172.16.10.2: icmp_seq=3 ttl=64 time=0.955 ms
^C
--- 172.16.10.2 ping statistics ---
4 packets transmitted, 4 packets received, 0% packet loss
round-trip min/avg/max/stddev = 0.903/10.250/38.126/16.094 ms


root@h1> ping 172.16.10.3
PING 172.16.10.3 (172.16.10.3): 56 data bytes
64 bytes from 172.16.10.3: icmp_seq=0 ttl=64 time=13.565 ms
```

```
64 bytes from 172.16.10.3: icmp_seq=1 ttl=64 timo=0.877 ms
64 bytes from 172.16.10.3: icmp_seq=2 ttl=64 time=0.865 ms
64 bytes from 172.16.10.3: icmp_seq=3 ttl=64 time=0.857 ms
^C
--- 172.16.10.3 ping statistics ---
4 packets transmitted, 4 packets received, 0% packet loss
round-trip min/avg/max/stddev = 0.857/4.041/13.565/5.499 ms

root@h1> ping 172.16.10.4
PING 172.16.10.4 (172.16.10.4): 56 data bytes
64 bytes from 172.16.10.4: icmp_seq=0 ttl=64 time=39.141 ms
64 bytes from 172.16.10.4: icmp_seq=1 ttl=64 time=0.914 ms
64 bytes from 172.16.10.4: icmp_seq=2 ttl=64 time=1.221 ms
64 bytes from 172.16.10.4: icmp_seq=3 ttl=64 time=0.880 ms
^C
--- 172.16.10.4 ping statistics ---
4 packets transmitted, 4 packets received, 0% packet loss
round-trip min/avg/max/stddev = 0.880/10.539/39.141/16.514 ms
```

In conclusion, Figure 12-75 shows the Apstra Dashboard for this deployed Blueprint, confirming that the end-state service configuration was deployed to seven devices (two spines and five leafs), and there are no anomalies reported. The user intent fully matches the current state of the network.

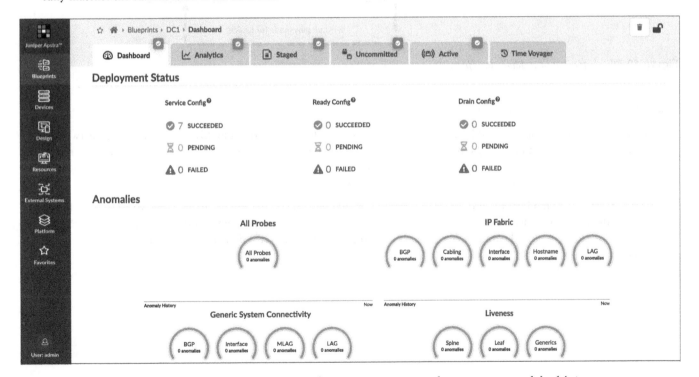

Figure 12-75 *Apstra Dashboard for Blueprint DC1 confirming user intent matches current state of the fabric*

Lifecycle of a Device in Juniper Apstra

As discussed in previous sections, when devices are onboarded in Apstra either via ZTP or manual onboarding, each onboarded device is associated with a state and configuration in Apstra. This state can change based on numerous factors. For instance, when a Device Agent is first created, and it succeeds, the device is in a state of *OOS-QUARANTINED* and it only has the pristine configuration. When a device is acknowledged, it moves from *OOS-QUARANTINED* to *OOS-READY*, and to Discovery-1 configuration, indicating that the device is now ready to be added in a Blueprint.

In closing, it is important to understand the state machine for a device, during its lifecycle in Apstra, which also directly relates to different configuration stages that a device moves between.

Any device in Apstra will be in one of two main states:

- **Out of Service (OOS):** A device that is onboarded in Apstra but not assigned to any Blueprint. There are several minor states associated with this, such as *OOS-QUARANTINED* and *OOS-READY*.

- **In Service (IS):** A device that is assigned to a Blueprint. There are several minor states, such as *IS-READY* and *IS-ACTIVE*, that identify the current state of the device in the Blueprint.

The flow diagram shown in Figure 12-76 provides a high-level state machine for the lifecycle of a device in Apstra.

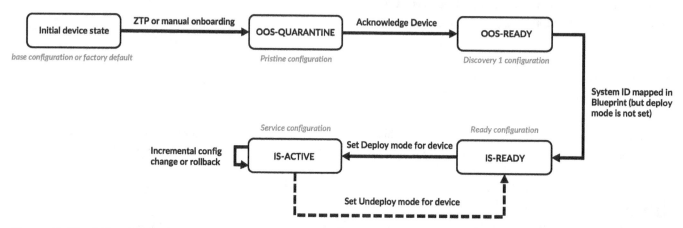

Figure 12-76 *Lifecycle of a device in Apstra*

Summary

This chapter provided foundational knowledge necessary for using Juniper Apstra, a multivendor, intent-based networking system. With an understanding of the basic building blocks of Apstra, such as Logical Devices, Device Profiles, Interface Maps, Rack Types, Templates, and Blueprints, you can quickly stand up a data center fabric, with Apstra converting abstracted user intent into vendor-specific device configuration.

With reusability and modularity built into these blocks as a core function, data centers can easily be scaled up by adding new racks, pods, and hosts. This chapter demonstrated how to use these constructs to build a bridged overlay BGP EVPN–based 3-stage Clos fabric, deployed with a single Virtual Network, extending a Layer 2 domain over the fabric to provide host connectivity.

Building Data Centers with Juniper Apstra, Part II—Advanced Apstra Deployments

Chapter 12 introduced the basic building blocks and foundational constructs needed to build data center fabrics with Juniper Apstra. This was demonstrated by deploying a bridged overlay design in a 3-stage Clos fabric, stretching a single Layer 2 domain over the routed infrastructure to provide end-to-end connectivity for hosts in the same subnet.

In this chapter, the following more advanced and complex deployments are covered:

- An edge-routed bridging fabric with Symmetric IRB for routing between VNIs

- Data Center Interconnects, demonstrating both over-the-top (OTT) and Integrated Interconnect designs

These designs are deployed using the same building blocks that were built and used in Chapter 12, only with additional functionality and Apstra-specific knobs. These building blocks include Logical Devices, Interface Maps, Rack Types, and Templates. Since these designs have been covered in detail in previous chapters, this chapter focuses more on the Apstra-specific nuances to deploy them.

Edge-Routed Bridging with Symmetric IRB

In an edge-routed bridging design, the integrated routing and bridging (IRB) interfaces are positioned at the edge of the fabric (the leafs), using an anycast distributed gateway model, instead of being centralized at the spines, for efficient routing of inter-subnet traffic. In such a design, the same IP address and MAC address are assigned to an IRB interface across all leafs. This also enables VLANs to be scoped to specific leafs instead of being deployed to all leafs, which is necessary for Asymmetric IRB.

From the perspective of Apstra, the same Rack Types from the previous chapter are used for the data center fabric. To re-iterate, these are as follows:

- **Rack Type 1:** This rack has one Juniper QFX5120-48Y as a leaf, utilizing 40G ports for uplinks and 10G ports for downlinks. All hosts are single-homed to this leaf.

- **Rack Type 2:** This rack has two Juniper QFX5120-48Ys as leafs, utilizing 40G ports for uplinks and 10G ports for downlinks. All hosts are multihomed to both leafs using EVPN multihoming (ESI LAG).

- **Rack Type 3:** This rack has one Juniper QFX5130-32C as a leaf, utilizing 40G ports for both uplinks and downlinks. All hosts are single-homed to this leaf. This Rack Type is expected to be used twice, once for leaf4 and then again for leaf5.

This design is shown in Figure 13-1. This is a two-spine, five-leaf, 3-stage Clos fabric, used to demonstrate how an edge-routed bridging design with Symmetric IRB is deployed with Juniper Apstra. In addition, the fabric includes a set of Virtual Networks (VNs), designed to be a part of the same Routing Zone, called *Tenant1*. These Virtual Networks are as follows:

- **v10:** Mapped to VLAN 10 and VNI 10010. This VN is constrained to leaf1, leaf2, and leaf3. The subnet 172.16.10.0/24 with a virtual gateway address of 172.16.10.254 is used for this.

- **v20:** Mapped to VLAN 20 and VNI 10020. This VN is constrained to leaf4. The subnet 172.16.20.0/24 with a virtual gateway address of 172.16.20.254 is used for this.

- **v30:** Mapped to VLAN 30 and VNI 10030. This VN is constrained to leaf5. The subnet 172.16.30.0/24 with a virtual gateway address of 172.16.30.254 is used for this.

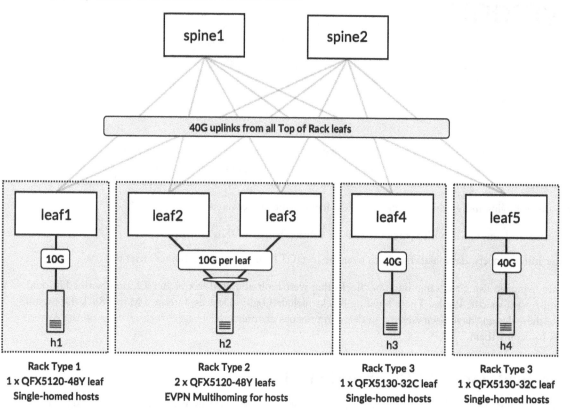

Figure 13-1 *Rack Types design for ERB and Symmetric IRB deployment in Apstra*

The goal of this deployment is to ensure that all hosts have end-to-end connectivity via Symmetric IRB functionality, installing host-specific /32 routes on the leafs and using the L3VNI to route between two different VNIs in the same VRF.

As of Apstra 4.2.0, Apstra offers the choice between an Asymmetric IRB routing model or Symmetric IRB routing model. This is chosen per Routing Zone, with the default being set to Asymmetric IRB. Thus, to enable Symmetric IRB for a specific Routing Zone, it is a simple matter of selecting that mode in the Apstra UI, as shown in Figure 13-2.

NOTE   Changing the mode between Asymmetric and Symmetric (or vice versa) might cause traffic disruption, and thus it is advisable to do this during a maintenance window.

To enable IP routing for a Virtual Network, the IPv4 Connectivity option must be set to Enabled and a subnet must be provided, along with an optional virtual address. For Virtual Network v10, the addressing shown in Figure 13-3 is used.

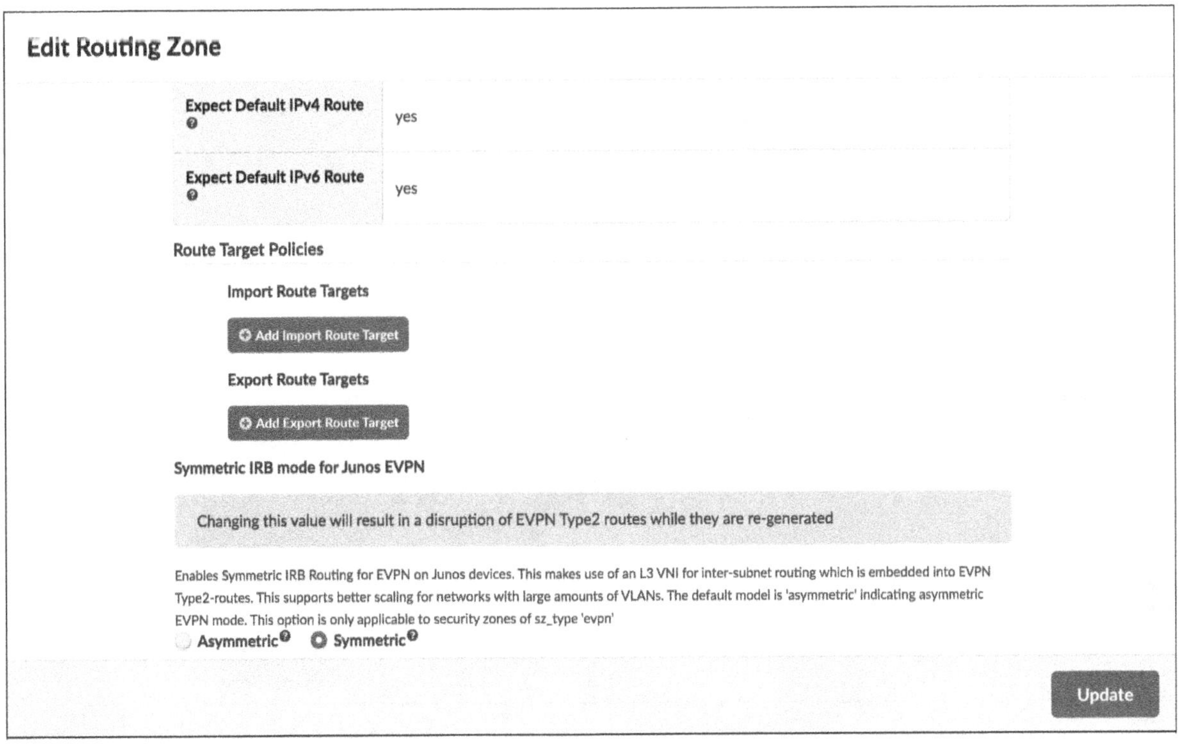

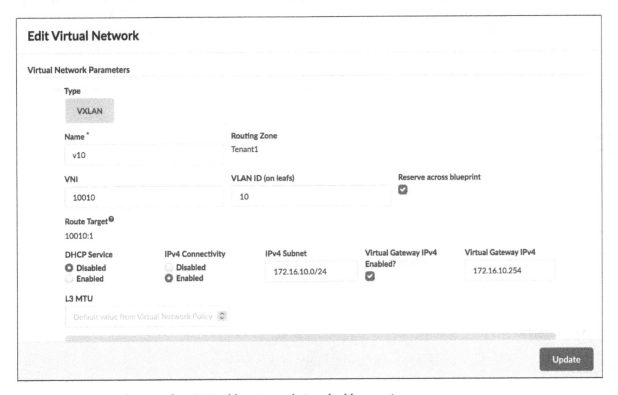

Figure 13-2 *Symmetric IRB mode chosen for Routing Zone Tenant1*

Figure 13-3 *Virtual Network v10 IP addressing and virtual address assignment*

Additionally, the scope of this Virtual Network is limited to leaf1 and to the ESI pair, leaf2 and leaf3. This is achieved by binding the VN only to these leafs in the same VN creation UI, as shown in Figure 13-4.

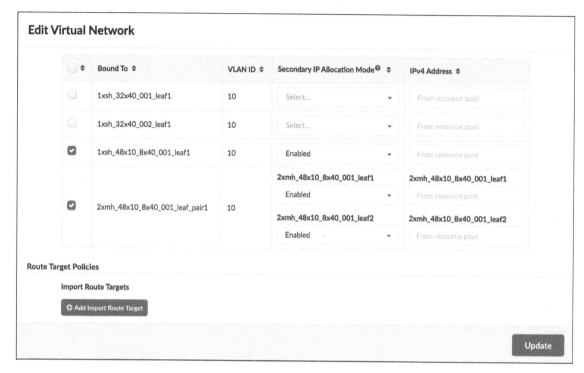

Figure 13-4   *Limiting scope of VN v10 to specific leafs only*

Once this change is committed in Apstra, it configures the corresponding IRB interface on these leafs, with the same IP address and MAC address on all target leafs. This is shown in Example 13-1. In addition, the Layer 2 VLAN is mapped to the IRB interface in the MAC-VRF, and the IRB interface is mapped to the Layer 3 VRF (which is the instantiation of the Routing Zone).

Example 13-1   *Distributed anycast IP address for an IRB interface*

```
root@1xsh-48x10-8x40-001-leaf1# show interfaces irb
unit 10 {
    family inet {
        mtu 9000;
        address 172.16.10.254/24;
    }
    mac 00:1c:73:00:00:01;
}


root@2xmh-48x10-8x40-001-leaf1# show interfaces irb
unit 10 {
    family inet {
        mtu 9000;
        address 172.16.10.254/24;
    }
    mac 00:1c:73:00:00:01;
}


root@2xmh-48x10-8x40-001-leaf2# show interfaces irb
unit 10 {
    family inet {
        mtu 9000;
```

```
            address 172.16.10.254/24;
        }
        mac 00:1c:73:00:00:01;
}


root@1xsh-48x10-8x40-001-leaf1# show routing-instances evpn-1
instance-type mac-vrf;
protocols {
    evpn {
        encapsulation vxlan;
        default-gateway do-not-advertise;
        duplicate-mac-detection {
            auto-recovery-time 9;
        }
        extended-vni-list all;
        vni-options {
            vni 10010 {
                vrf-target target:10010:1;
            }
        }
    }
}
vtep-source-interface lo0.0;
service-type vlan-aware;
interface et-0/0/49.0;
route-distinguisher 192.0.2.4:65534;
vrf-target target:100:100;
vlans {
    vn10 {
        description v10;
        vlan-id 10;
        l3-interface irb.10;
        vxlan {
            vni 10010;
        }
    }
}


root@1xsh-48x10-8x40-001-leaf1# show routing-instances Tenant1
instance-type vrf;
routing-options {
    graceful-restart;
    multipath;
    auto-export;
}
protocols {
    evpn {
        irb-symmetric-routing {
            vni 10500;
```

```
        }
        ip-prefix-routes {
            advertise direct-nexthop;
            encapsulation vxlan;
            vni 10500;
            export BGP-AOS-Policy-Tenant1;
        }
    }
}
interface irb.10;
interface lo0.2;
route-distinguisher 192.0.2.4:500;
vrf-target target:10500:1;
```

Taking a closer look at the Layer 3 VRF routing instance in Example 13-2, Symmetric IRB is enabled using the *irb-symmetric-routing* configuration hierarchy, and the L3VNI, specified in the Apstra UI by the operator, is mapped here.

Example 13-2   *Layer 3 VRF routing-instance enabled for Symmetric IRB*

```
root@1xsh-48x10-8x40-001-leaf1# show routing-instances Tenant1
instance-type vrf;
routing-options {
    graceful-restart;
    multipath;
    auto-export;
}
protocols {
    evpn {
        irb-symmetric-routing {
            vni 10500;
        }
        ip-prefix-routes {
            advertise direct-nexthop;
            encapsulation vxlan;
            vni 10500;
            export BGP-AOS-Policy-Tenant1;
        }
    }
}
interface irb.10;
interface lo0.2;
route-distinguisher 192.0.2.4:500;
vrf-target target:10500:1;
```

In the same way, the Virtual Network v20 is created, as shown in Figure 13-5. This is mapped to leaf4 (from the reference topology in Figure 13-1); however, for the sake of brevity, this assignment is not shown here. During the VN creation, an untagged Connectivity Template is also created, and this is assigned to the host-facing interface on leaf4.

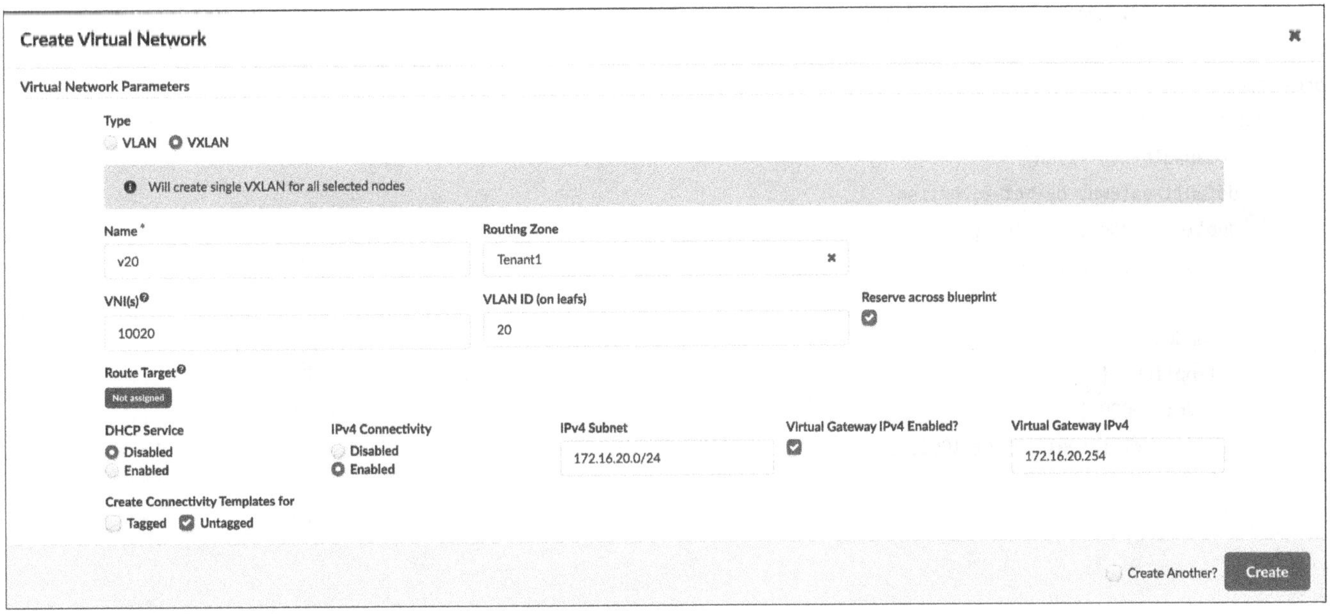

Create Virtual Network   ✖

Virtual Network Parameters

Type
○ VLAN ⦿ VXLAN

ⓘ Will create single VXLAN for all selected nodes

Name*   Routing Zone
v20   Tenant1   ✖

VNI(s)ⓘ   VLAN ID (on leafs)   Reserve across blueprint
10020   20   ☑

Route Targetⓘ
[Not assigned]

DHCP Service   IPv4 Connectivity   IPv4 Subnet   Virtual Gateway IPv4 Enabled?   Virtual Gateway IPv4
⦿ Disabled   ○ Disabled   172.16.20.0/24   ☑   172.16.20.254
○ Enabled   ⦿ Enabled

Create Connectivity Templates for
☐ Tagged ☑ Untagged

                                                           ○ Create Another?   **Create**

Figure 13-5 *Creation of VN v20 in the Apstra UI*

This creates a corresponding IRB interface on leaf4 and configures the host-facing interface to send untagged traffic for this VLAN. Additionally, the Layer 2 VLAN in the MAC-VRF is mapped to this IRB interface, and the IRB interface is mapped to the Layer 3 VRF. This is shown in Example 13-3. Like before, Symmetric IRB is enabled on leaf4 as well by using the *irb-symmetric-routing* configuration hierarchy in the Layer 3 VRF routing instance.

Example 13-3 *Configuration pushed to leaf4 when VN v20 is created in Apstra*

```
root@1xsh-32x40-001-leaf1# show interfaces irb
mtu 9216;
unit 20 {
    family inet {
        mtu 9000;
        address 172.16.20.254/24;
    }
    mac 00:1c:73:00:00:01;
}

root@1xsh-32x40-001-leaf1# show interfaces et-0/0/4
description to.1xsh-32x40-001-sys001;
native-vlan-id 20;
speed 40g;
mtu 9216;
unit 0 {
    family ethernet-switching {
        interface-mode trunk;
        vlan {
            members vn20;
        }
    }
}
```

```
root@1xsh-32x40-001-leaf1# show routing-instances evpn-1
instance-type mac-vrf;
protocols {
    evpn {
        encapsulation vxlan;
        default-gateway do-not-advertise;
        duplicate-mac-detection {
            auto-recovery-time 9;
        }
        extended-vni-list all;
        vni-options {
            vni 10020 {
                vrf-target target:10020:1;
            }
        }
    }
}
vtep-source-interface lo0.0;
service-type vlan-aware;
interface et-0/0/4.0;
route-distinguisher 192.0.2.2:65534;
vrf-target target:100:100;
vlans {
    vn20 {
        description v20;
        vlan-id 20;
        l3-interface irb.20;
        vxlan {
            vni 10020;
        }
    }
}

root@1xsh-32x40-001-leaf1# show routing-instances Tenant1
instance-type vrf;
routing-options {
    graceful-restart;
    multipath;
    auto-export;
}
protocols {
    evpn {
        irb-symmetric-routing {
            vni 10500;
        }
        ip-prefix-routes {
            advertise direct-nexthop;
            encapsulation vxlan;
            vni 10500;
```

```
        export BGP-AOS-Policy-Tenant1;
    }
  }
}
interface irb.20;
interface lo0.2;
route-distinguisher 192.0.2.2:500;
vrf-target target:10500:1;
```

Finally, VN v30 is created, as shown in Figure 13-6. This Virtual Network is mapped to leaf5, along with an untagged Connectivity Template that is assigned to the host-facing interface on leaf5.

Figure 13-6   *Creation of VN v30 in the Apstra UI*

The configuration shown in Example 13-4 is pushed by Apstra to leaf5 when this VN is created.

Example 13-4   *Configuration pushed to leaf5 when VN v30 is created in Apstra*

```
root@1xsh-32x40-002-leaf1# show interfaces irb
mtu 9216;
unit 30 {
    family inet {
        mtu 9000;
        address 172.16.30.254/24;
    }
    mac 00:1c:73:00:00:01;
}

root@1xsh-32x40-002-leaf1# show interfaces et-0/0/1
description to.1xsh-32x40-002-sys001;
native-vlan-id 30;
speed 40g;
mtu 9216;
unit 0 {
```

```
            family ethernet-switching {
                interface-mode trunk;
                vlan {
                    members vn30;
                }
            }
        }

root@1xsh-32x40-002-leaf1# show routing-instances evpn-1
instance-type mac-vrf;
protocols {
    evpn {
        encapsulation vxlan;
        default-gateway do-not-advertise;
        duplicate-mac-detection {
            auto-recovery-time 9;
        }
        extended-vni-list all;
        vni-options {
            vni 10030 {
                vrf-target target:10030:1;
            }
        }
    }
}
vtep-source-interface lo0.0;
service-type vlan-aware;
interface et-0/0/1.0;
route-distinguisher 192.0.2.3:65534;
vrf-target target:100:100;
vlans {
    vn30 {
        description v30;
        vlan-id 30;
        l3-interface irb.30;
        vxlan {
            vni 10030;
        }
    }
}

root@1xsh-32x40-002-leaf1# show routing-instances Tenant1
instance-type vrf;
routing-options {
    graceful-restart;
    multipath;
    auto-export;
}
```

```
protocols {
    evpn {
        irb-symmetric-routing {
            vni 10500;
        }
        ip-prefix-routes {
            advertise direct-nexthop;
            encapsulation vxlan;
            vni 10500;
            export BGP-AOS-Policy-Tenant1;
        }
    }
}
interface irb.30;
interface lo0.2;
route-distinguisher 192.0.2.3:500;
vrf-target target:10500:1;
```

As a quick aside, it is important to understand how DHCP configuration is deployed using Apstra in an edge-routed bridging fabric. Since the IRB interfaces are configured on the leafs themselves, if the DHCP server exists in a different subnet, a DHCP relay must be configured. The DHCP relay configuration enables the leaf to package the incoming broadcast DHCP Discover into a unicast DHCP Discover, destined for the configured relay server address.

DHCP servers are defined per Routing Zone, and then explicitly enabled per Virtual Network by setting the DHCP Service option to Enabled (in Figure 13-6, the DHCP service is set to Disabled). In Figure 13-7, the Routing Zone Tenant1 currently does not have any DHCP servers configured; these can be configured using the Assign DHCP Servers option highlighted on the right side of the UI.

Figure 13-7 *Option to assign DHCP servers to a Routing Zone in the Apstra UI*

This option allows you to configure DHCP servers as IP addresses, as shown in Figure 13-8. If needed, you can configure more than one DHCP server.

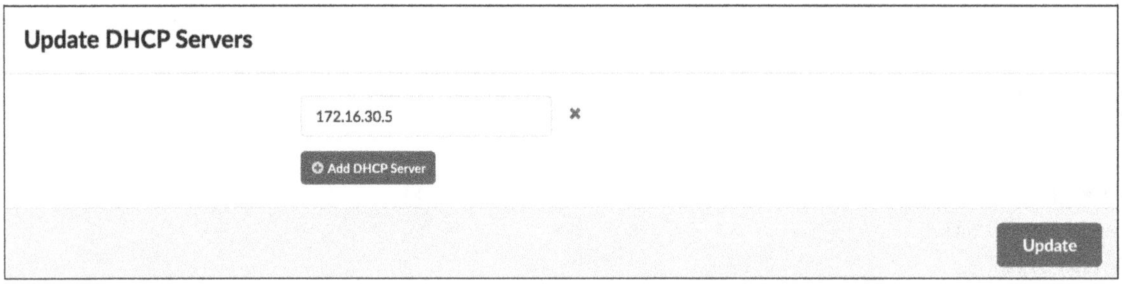

Update DHCP Servers

```
172.16.30.5                    ✖
```

⊕ Add DHCP Server

Update

Figure 13-8 *DHCP server configured in the Tenant1 Routing Zone in Apstra UI*

On the fabric leafs, adding a DHCP server in a Routing Zone and enabling it for a Virtual Network does the following:

■ The *no-dhcp-flood* configuration option is configured under the IRB interface corresponding to the Virtual Network. The default behavior is to both flood a received DHCP Discover and package it into a unicast DHCP Discover, destined for the configured relay address. This option disables flooding of received DHCP Discovers when a relay address is configured. As of Apstra 4.2.0, this is configured on Junos Evolved leafs only (and not Junos OS leafs).

■ A DHCP relay server group is configured with the specified relay address (or addresses) in the Layer 3 VRF routing instance under the *forwarding-options* configuration hierarchy. This server group is then activated as well, using the *active-server-group* configuration option.

■ DHCP option 82 is enabled.

■ Unicast DHCP Discovers destined to the relay address are configured to use the address of the logical unit of the loopback interface, mapped to the Layer 3 VRF routing instance, as the source IP address of the packet, using the *relay-source* configuration option.

This configuration is shown in Example 13-5.

Example 13-5 *Configuration pushed to leaf4 when a DHCP server is configured in Apstra*

```
root@1xsh-32x40-001-leaf1# show interfaces irb
mtu 9216;
unit 20 {
    family inet {
        mtu 9000;
        address 172.16.20.254/24;
    }
    mac 00:1c:73:00:00:01;
    no-dhcp-flood;
}

root@1xsh-32x40-001-leaf1# show routing-instances Tenant1
instance-type vrf;
routing-options {
    graceful-restart;
    multipath;
    auto-export;
}
protocols {
    evpn {
        irb-symmetric-routing {
            vni 10500;
        }
        ip-prefix-routes {
```

```
        advertise direct-nexthop;
        encapsulation vxlan;
        vni 10500;
        export BGP-AOS-Policy-Tenant1;
    }
  }
}
forwarding-options {
    dhcp-relay {
        forward-only;
        server-group {
            Tenant1 {
                172.16.30.5;
            }
        }
        group Tenant1 {
            active-server-group Tenant1;
            relay-option-82 {
                server-id-override;
            }
            interface irb.20 {
                overrides {
                    relay-source lo0.2;
                }
            }
        }
    }
}
interface irb.20;
interface lo0.2;
route-distinguisher 192.0.2.2:500;
vrf-target target:10500:1;
```

With the relevant configuration for all Virtual Networks pushed by Apstra to all leafs now, all hosts can communicate with each other. Taking host h1 communicating with host h4 as an example, this reachability is confirmed using the **ping** tool, as shown in Example 13-6.

Example 13-6 *Host h1 reachability to h4 using the* **ping** *tool*

```
root@h1> ping 172.16.30.4
PING 172.16.30.4 (172.16.30.4): 56 data bytes
64 bytes from 172.16.30.4: icmp_seq=0 ttl=62 time=0.922 ms
64 bytes from 172.16.30.4: icmp_seq=1 ttl=62 time=0.871 ms
64 bytes from 172.16.30.4: icmp_seq=2 ttl=62 time=18.611 ms
64 bytes from 172.16.30.4: icmp_seq=3 ttl=62 time=0.863 ms
^C
--- 172.16.30.4 ping statistics ---
4 packets transmitted, 4 packets received, 0% packet loss
round-trip min/avg/max/stddev = 0.863/5.317/18.611/7.675 ms
```

On leaf1, the route to host h4's IP address confirms that this is routed using the L3VNI, and encapsulated with VXLAN headers, using an outer destination IP address of leaf4's loopback address, as shown in Example 13-7.

Example 13-7   *Route for host h4's address on leaf1 showing VXLAN encapsulation with L3VNI*

```
root@1xsh-48x10-8x40-001-leaf1> show route table Tenant1.inet.0 172.16.30.4/32 extensive

Tenant1.inet.0: 13 destinations, 17 routes (13 active, 0 holddown, 0 hidden)
Restart Complete
172.16.30.4/32 (1 entry, 1 announced)
TSI:
KRT in-kernel 172.16.30.4/32 -> {composite(1765)}
        *EVPN    Preference: 7
                 Next hop type: Indirect, Next hop index: 0
                 Address: 0x7bc9744
                 Next-hop reference count: 6, key opaque handle: 0x0, non-key opaque handle: 0x0
                 Next hop type: Router, Next hop index: 0
                 Next hop: 198.51.100.4 via et-0/0/48.0, selected
                 Session Id: 0
                 Next hop: 198.51.100.14 via et-0/0/50.0
                 Session Id: 0
                 Protocol next hop: 192.0.2.3
                 Composite next hop: 0x98621c0 1765 INH Session ID: 0
                   VXLAN tunnel rewrite:
                     MTU: 0, Flags: 0x0
                     Encap table ID: 0, Decap table ID: 8
                     Encap VNI: 10500, Decap VNI: 10500
                     Source VTEP: 192.0.2.4, Destination VTEP: 192.0.2.3
                     SMAC: 40:de:ad:7b:70:40, DMAC: 50:c7:09:a6:aa:04
                 Indirect next hop: 0x7589bb4 524290 INH Session ID: 0
                 State: <Active Int Ext VxlanLocalRT>
                 Age: 1d 15:45:00        Metric2: 0
                 Validation State: unverified
                 Task: Tenant1-EVPN-L3-context
                 Announcement bits (1): 2-KRT
                 AS path: I
                 Communities: 0:14
                 Thread: junos-main


*snip*
```

The packet capture shown in Figure 13-9 confirms that the L3VNI is used in the VXLAN header when host h1 communicates with h4.

Data Center Interconnect with Juniper Apstra

With an edge-routed bridging–based data center deployed using Apstra in the previous section, the goal of this section is to deploy a second data center and connect the two using over-the-top (OTT) DCI and then an Integrated Interconnect design, demonstrating how each of these designs can be instantiated and deployed by Apstra.

For both these designs, the overall physical interconnection between the two data centers is represented in Figure 13-10. Border leafs from both data centers physically connect to a Juniper MX204, which acts as a DCI router, facilitating the Data Center Interconnect designs. For the sake of brevity, unnecessary elements such as the server leafs are removed from this representation. In DC1, leaf4 and leaf5 are the border leafs, and in DC2, leaf3 is the border leaf.

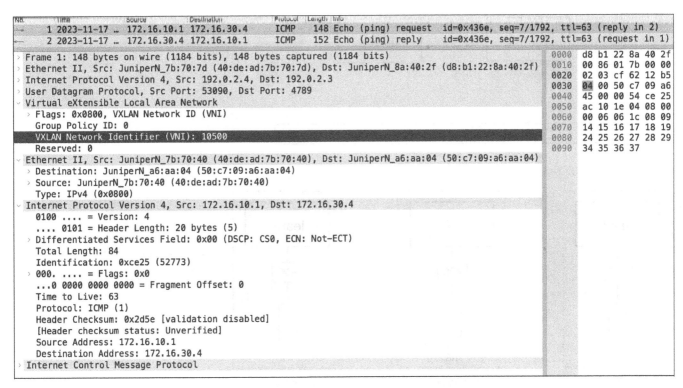

Figure 13-9 *Packet capture of an ICMP request generated by host h1 for h4*

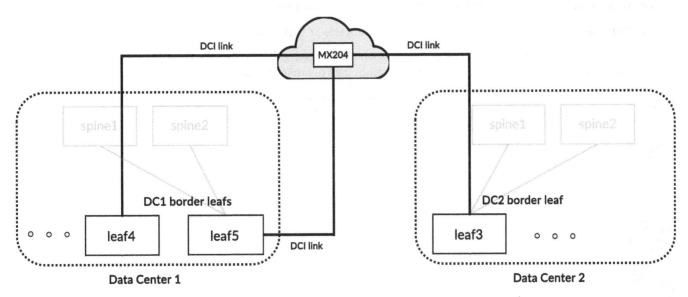

Figure 13-10 *Overall topology for DCI designs, showing how the two data centers are connected*

The second data center is another 3-stage Clos fabric, with two spines and three leafs. Two new Rack Types are built for this, using Figure 13-11 as a reference for overall design of the fabric:

- **Rack Type 1:** This rack has one Juniper QFX5120-48Y as a leaf, utilizing 100G ports for uplinks and 40G ports for downlinks. All hosts are single-homed to this leaf.

- **Rack Type 2:** This rack has one Juniper QFX5130-32C as a leaf, utilizing 100G ports for uplinks and 40G ports for downlinks. All hosts are single-homed to this leaf.

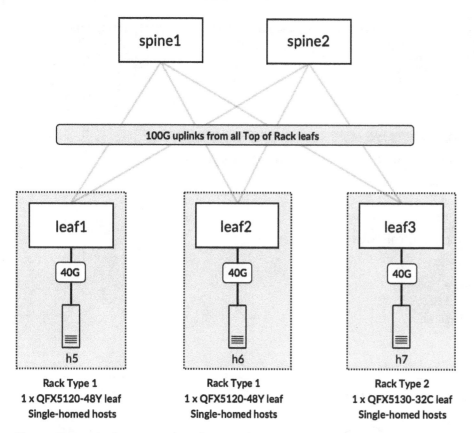

Figure 13-11   *Reference topology for second data center and details of Rack Types to be designed in Apstra*

Using these Rack Types (creation of the Rack Types is not shown here, again, for the sake of brevity), a new Apstra Template is created, as shown in Figure 13-12. This Template is then used to instantiate the fabric as an Apstra Blueprint.

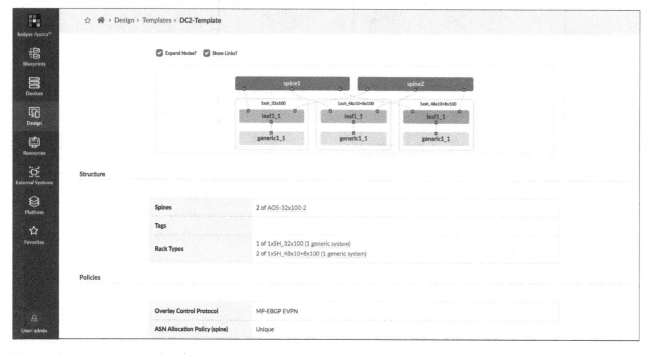

Figure 13-12   *Apstra Template for second data center*

This second data center is configured for Symmetric IRB as well, enabled within a Routing Zone that has the same name and VLAN/VNI as DC1. This means that hosts across both data centers are in the same VRF. This configuration is shown in Figure 13-13.

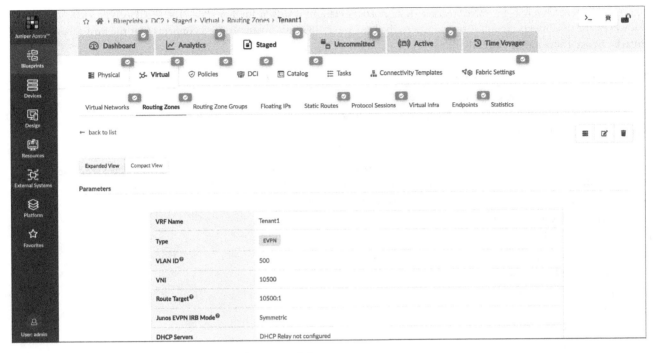

Figure 13-13 *Routing Zone Tenant1 created in second data center*

Additionally, three Virtual Networks are created as follows (with a summary from the Apstra UI shown in Figure 13-14):

- **v10:** Mapped to VLAN 10 and VNI 10010. This VN is constrained to leaf1. The subnet 172.16.10.0/24 with a virtual gateway address of 172.16.10.254 is used for this. This VN is a Layer 2 extended domain between DC1 and DC2.

- **v40:** Mapped to VLAN 40 and VNI 10040. This VN is constrained to leaf2. The subnet 172.16.40.0/24 with a virtual gateway address of 172.16.40.254 is used for this.

- **v50:** Mapped to VLAN 50 and VNI 10050. This VN is constrained to leaf3. The subnet 172.16.50.0/24 with a virtual gateway address of 172.16.50.254 is used for this.

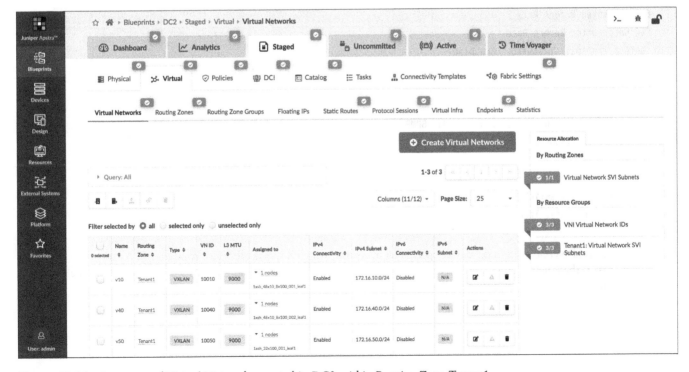

Figure 13-14 *Summary of Virtual Networks created in DC2 within Routing Zone Tenant1*

Based on how the Rack Types were created, all 32 ports of leaf3 (which is a Juniper QFX5130-32CD switch) are 100G ports. However, the design expectation is to connect to the host via a 40G link. Example 13-8 confirms that the host-facing interface is at 100G and is currently down.

Example 13-8 *Host-facing link on leaf3 set to 100G and thus currently down*

```
root@1xsh-32x100-001-leaf1> show interfaces et-0/0/27
Physical interface: et-0/0/27, Enabled, Physical link is Down
  Interface index: 1043, SNMP ifIndex: 535
  Description: to.1xsh-32x100-001-sys001
  Link-level type: Ethernet, MTU: 9216, LAN-PHY mode, Speed: 100Gbps, BPDU Error: None, Loop Detect PDU Error: None,
Ethernet-Switching Error: None, MAC-REWRITE Error: None, Loopback: Disabled, Source filtering: Disabled,
  Flow control: Disabled, Auto-negotiation: Disabled, Media type: Fiber
  Device flags   : Present Running
  Interface flags: Hardware-Down SNMP-Traps
  CoS queues     : 12 supported, 12 maximum usable queues
  Current address: 50:c7:09:a6:f0:6a, Hardware address: 50:c7:09:a6:f0:6a
  Last flapped   : 2023-11-18 10:27:25 UTC (00:52:13 ago)
  Input rate     : 0 bps (0 pps)
  Output rate    : 0 bps (0 pps)
  Active alarms  : LINK
  Active defects : LINK, LOCAL-FAULT
  PCS statistics                      Seconds
   Bit errors                               0
   Errored blocks                           0
  Ethernet FEC Mode  :                   NONE
   FEC Codeword size                        0
   FEC Codeword rate                    0.000
  Ethernet FEC statistics             Errors
   FEC Corrected Errors                     0
   FEC Uncorrected Errors                   0
   FEC Corrected Errors Rate                0
   FEC Uncorrected Errors Rate              0
  Interface transmit statistics: Disabled
  Link Degrade :
   Link Monitoring                  : Disable


  Logical interface et-0/0/27.0 (Index 1038) (SNMP ifIndex 602)
    Flags: Up SNMP-Traps Encapsulation: Ethernet-Bridge DF
    Input packets : 0
    Output packets: 0
    Protocol ethernet-switching, MTU: 9216
      Flags: Is-Primary, Trunk-Mode
```

This status is also confirmed in the device-specific UI in Apstra, which displays all device connections. As shown in Figure 13-15, the intent in Apstra is to set leaf3's link to the host (interface et-0/0/27) as a 100G link, based on the Logical Device used.

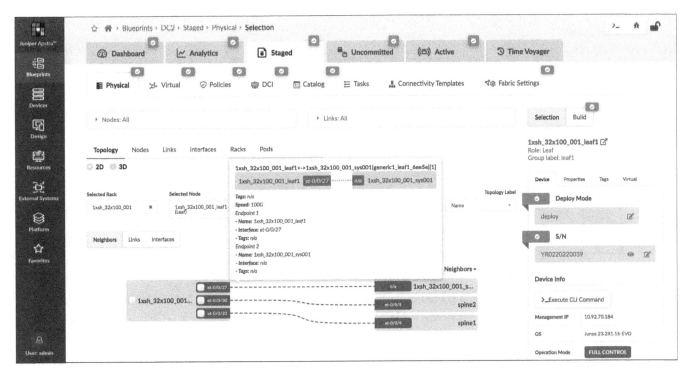

Figure 13-15 *Status of interface et-0/0/27 in Apstra*

Apstra allows you to dynamically adjust link speeds via the UI, for situations like these. Since a Juniper QFX5130-32CD switch supports 40G natively on all ports (without breakout), only the link speed needs to be changed, and that intent must be issued via Apstra, so it is tracked as part of overall fabric intent. This change can be made by checking the checkbox for a particular link, as shown in Figure 13-16. This brings up additional UI options for that interface, one of which is to update the link speed.

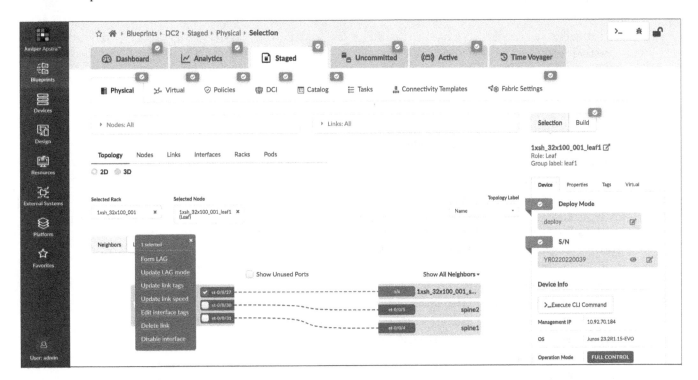

Figure 13-16 *Link-specific options in Apstra UI*

From here, it is simply a matter of choosing the *Update link speed* option and setting the speed to the appropriate value from the Speed drop-down list, as shown in Figure 13-17.

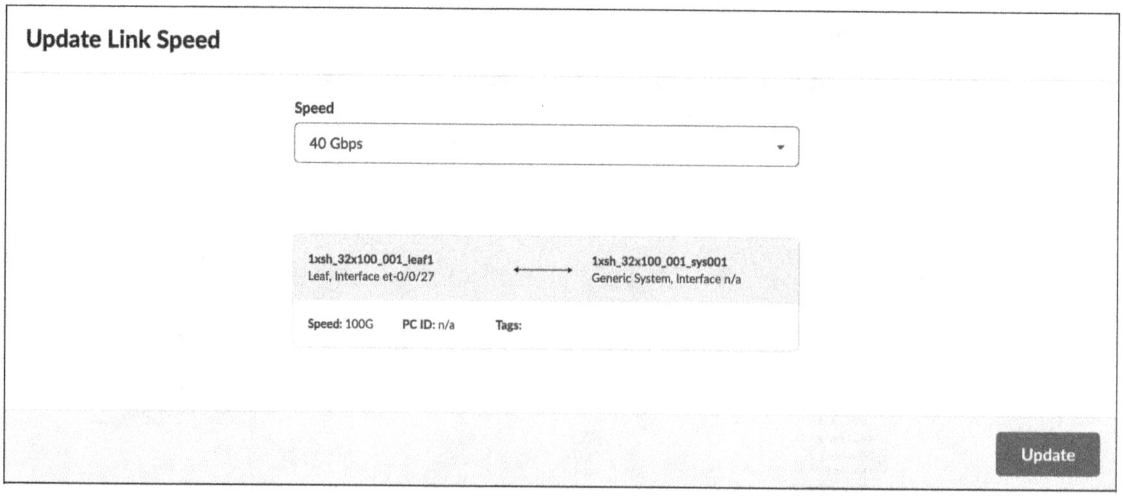

Update Link Speed

Speed

40 Gbps ▾

1xsh_32x100_001_leaf1   1xsh_32x100_001_sys001
Leaf, Interface et-0/0/27   ◄──────►   Generic System, Interface n/a

Speed: 100G   PC ID: n/a   Tags:

Update

Figure 13-17   *Updating link speed of an interface in Apstra UI*

Apstra pushes the change to the intended device, configuring the speed that you specified. This is shown in Example 13-9. With this change, the interface comes up and the leaf has connectivity to the host.

Example 13-9   *Host-facing link on leaf3 adjusted to 40G, bringing the physical connectivity up*

```
root@1xsh-32x100-001-leaf1# show interfaces et-0/0/27
description to.1xsh-32x100-001-sys001;
native-vlan-id 50;
speed 40g;
mtu 9216;
unit 0 {
    family ethernet-switching {
        interface-mode trunk;
        vlan {
            members vn50;
        }
    }
}


root@1xsh-32x100-001-leaf1> show interfaces et-0/0/27
Physical interface: et-0/0/27, Enabled, Physical link is Up
  Interface index: 1036, SNMP ifIndex: 535
  Description: to.1xsh-32x100-001-sys001
  Link-level type: Ethernet, MTU: 9216, LAN-PHY mode, Speed: 40Gbps, BPDU Error: None, Loop Detect PDU Error: None,
Ethernet-Switching Error: None, MAC-REWRITE Error: None, Loopback: Disabled, Source filtering: Disabled,
  Flow control: Disabled, Auto-negotiation: Disabled, Media type: Fiber
  Device flags   : Present Running
  Interface flags: SNMP-Traps
  CoS queues     : 12 supported, 12 maximum usable queues
  Current address: 50:c7:09:a6:f0:6a, Hardware address: 50:c7:09:a6:f0:6a
  Last flapped   : 2023-11-18 11:28:24 UTC (00:12:10 ago)
  Input rate     : 0 bps (0 pps)
  Output rate    : 248 bps (0 pps)
  Active alarms  : None
  Active defects : None
```

```
PCS statistics                  Seconds
  Bit errors                       0
  Errored blocks                   0
Ethernet FEC Mode  :              NONE
  FEC Codeword size                0
  FEC Codeword rate              0.000
Ethernet FEC statistics         Errors
  FEC Corrected Errors             0
  FEC Uncorrected Errors           0
  FEC Corrected Errors Rate        0
  FEC Uncorrected Errors Rate      0
Interface transmit statistics: Disabled
Link Degrade :
  Link Monitoring              :  Disable


Logical interface et-0/0/27.0 (Index 1036) (SNMP ifIndex 602)
  Flags: Up SNMP-Traps Encapsulation: Ethernet-Bridge DF
  Input packets : 0
  Output packets: 0
  Protocol ethernet-switching, MTU: 9216
    Flags: Is-Primary, Trunk-Mode
```

At this point, the second data center is fully deployed, with no anomalies. The service configuration, corresponding to the Virtual Networks and Routing Zones, is pushed to all fabric devices, as shown in the overall Dashboard for this Blueprint in Figure 13-18.

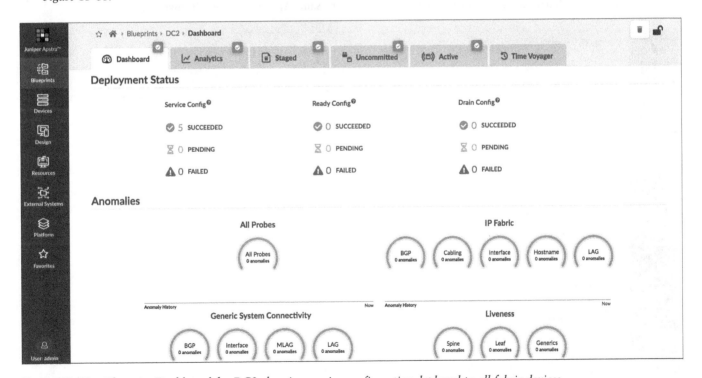

Figure 13-18 *Blueprint Dashboard for DC2 showing service configuration deployed to all fabric devices*

All hosts in this data center can communicate with each other now. This is demonstrated in Example 13-10, from the perspective of host h5. Using the **ping** tool, h5 can successfully communicate with hosts h6 and h7, using a Symmetric IRB model of routing between VNIs.

Example 13-10 *Connectivity between hosts h5, h6, and h7 using the* **ping** *tool*

```
root@h5> ping 172.16.40.6
PING 172.16.40.6 (172.16.40.6): 56 data bytes
64 bytes from 172.16.40.6: icmp_seq=0 ttl=62 time=10.093 ms
64 bytes from 172.16.40.6: icmp_seq=1 ttl=62 time=0.877 ms
64 bytes from 172.16.40.6: icmp_seq=2 ttl=62 time=0.848 ms
64 bytes from 172.16.40.6: icmp_seq=3 ttl=62 time=0.873 ms
^C
--- 172.16.40.6 ping statistics ---
4 packets transmitted, 4 packets received, 0% packet loss
round-trip min/avg/max/stddev = 0.848/3.173/10.093/3.995 ms

{master:0}
root@h5> ping 172.16.50.7
PING 172.16.50.7 (172.16.50.7): 56 data bytes
64 bytes from 172.16.50.7: icmp_seq=0 ttl=62 time=0.903 ms
64 bytes from 172.16.50.7: icmp_seq=1 ttl=62 time=0.869 ms
64 bytes from 172.16.50.7: icmp_seq=2 ttl=62 time=0.890 ms
64 bytes from 172.16.50.7: icmp_seq=3 ttl=62 time=0.899 ms
^C
--- 172.16.50.7 ping statistics ---
4 packets transmitted, 4 packets received, 0% packet loss
round-trip min/avg/max/stddev = 0.869/0.890/0.903/0.013 ms
```

A summary of both data centers, instantiated as Blueprints on the same Apstra instance, is shown in Figure 13-19.

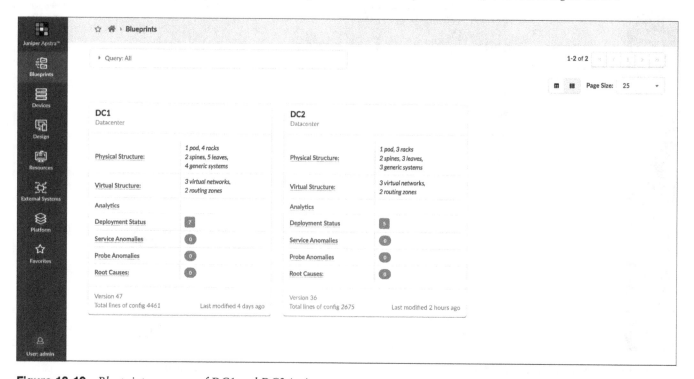

Figure 13-19 *Blueprint summary of DC1 and DC2 in Apstra*

With this baseline of the second data center fully deployed with Apstra, the two DCI options are explored next. As mentioned at the start of this chapter, since these designs have been discussed in detail in Chapter 11, the following subsections are focused on how to deploy these DCI options with Apstra.

Over-the-Top DCI

With an over-the-top (OTT) DCI design, the VTEPs form end-to-end VXLAN tunnels across all participating data centers. This means that the loopback address of the VTEPs must be shared between DCs, enabling reachability between these addresses over the DCI. This is achieved by establishing an IPv4 BGP peering to the DCI router and exchanging these loopback addresses.

In Apstra, an OTT DCI is designed in the following way to connect DC1 and DC2:

- **Add an external generic system:** An external generic system is a device that is external to the fabric, such as an external router, which is not managed by Apstra. This is added to the Blueprint of both data centers, connected to the border leafs of each data center. This external generic system is a logical representation of the DCI router (the Juniper MX204). Although Apstra does not manage this, connecting the system in the Blueprint enables Apstra to build relevant configuration for the border leafs to provide connectivity to the DCI router.

- **Build Connectivity Templates:** Connectivity Templates are leveraged to provide IP connectivity from the border leafs to the DCI router and establish an IPv4 BGP peering between them. Since Apstra does not manage the DCI router, you must complete the corresponding configuration on the DCI router manually. Connectivity Templates are another example of templating in Apstra, rooted in reusability and repeatability; by leveraging the same Connectivity Template for the same kind of use case, you do not have to create it again.

- **Configure OTT DCI parameters:** You must configure the OTT DCI parameters to build end-to-end VXLAN tunnels. This includes providing an IP address for the remote BGP EVPN peer, the remote ASN, and optional parameters such as BGP keepalive and hold-time timers.

Adding an External Generic System

To add an external generic system to the Blueprint, navigate to the Nodes option on the Physical tab, under the Staged panel (this may be different in future Apstra releases; thus, it is important to refer to publicly available Apstra user guides and documentation in case of any deviation). Here, an interactive button with the addition symbol enables you to add external generic systems, as shown in Figure 13-20.

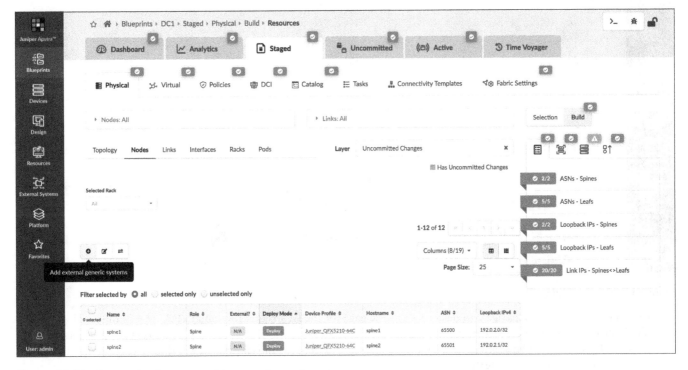

Figure 13-20 *Interactive button to add external generic systems*

An external generic system simply needs a name for representation in the topology view, and an optional Logical Device (if you want the device to conform to a specific port density combination, and to constrain its physical connectivity to specific fabric devices only, such as a leaf or a spine). For this design, the external generic system is named *DCI-router*, with no Logical Device specified, shown in Figure 13-21.

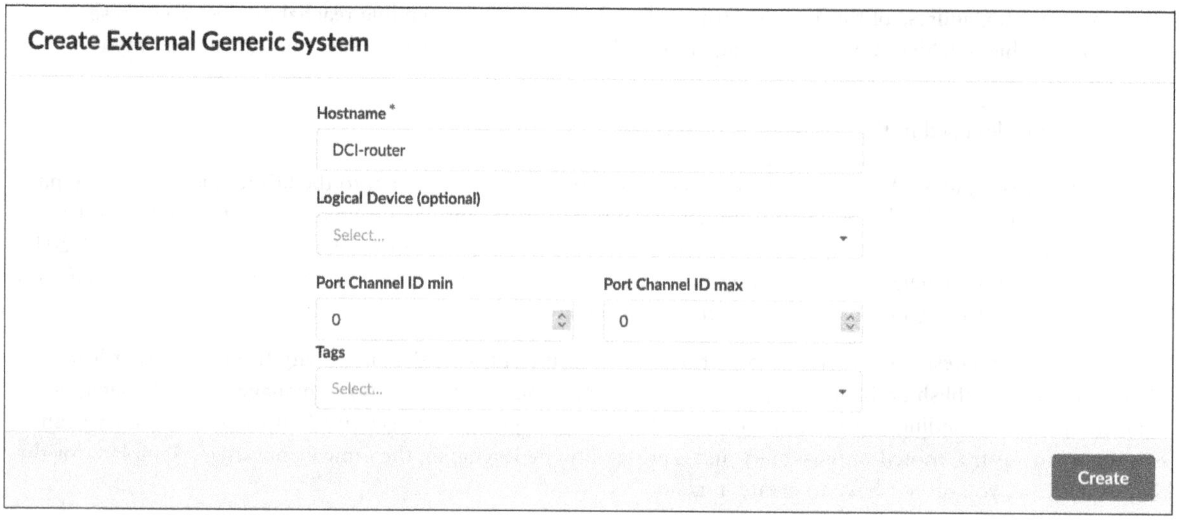

Create External Generic System

Hostname *

DCI-router

Logical Device (optional)

Select...

Port Channel ID min   Port Channel ID max

0   0

Tags

Select...

Create

Figure 13-21 *Adding an external generic system in Apstra*

Navigating back to the topology view of the fabric in the Blueprint, this newly added external generic system now appears in the topology, as shown in Figure 13-22. However, it is not connected to any devices yet. Thus, the next step is to create connections between the border leafs in DC1 and the DCI-router.

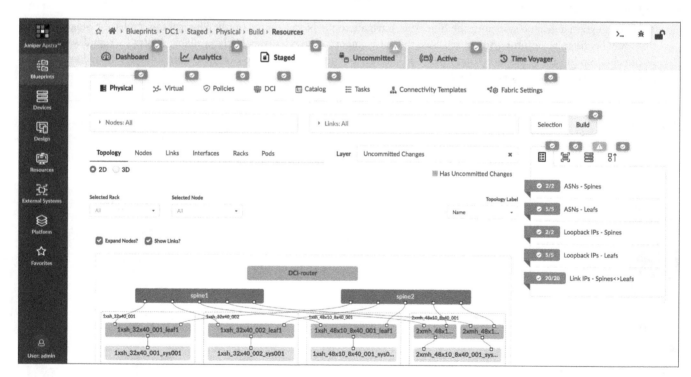

Figure 13-22 *External generic system added to the topology in the Blueprint*

To create the connections, navigate to the device-specific page for the DCI-router (by simply clicking it in the topology view). Check the checkbox by the device name to bring up additional options, one of which is to create links to fabric leafs, as shown in Figure 13-23. (Alternatively, the DCI-router can be connected to the fabric spines, and that is a valid design too.) Click that option to open the Create Links page.

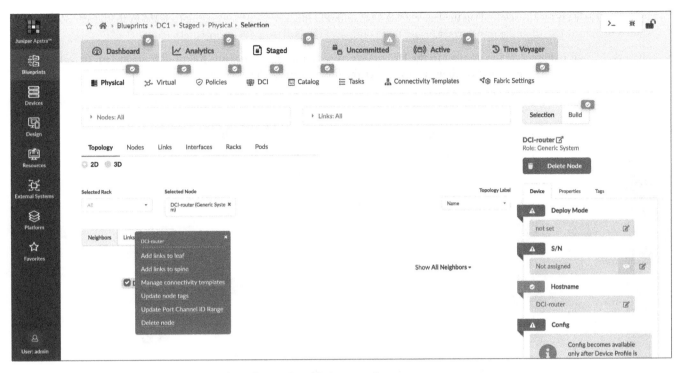

Figure 13-23 *Option to add links to leaf on the newly added external generic system*

To add a new link, follow these steps (in order) on the Create Links page (shown in Figure 13-24):

1. Choose one of the available leafs (or spines, if the link is being added to spines) from the Select Leaf drop-down menu. All ports on that leaf are listed, along with ones already used.

2. Choose one of the unused ports (used ports are marked in the UI).

3. Select the transformation set for that port, which determines the speed of the port (and breakout, if applicable).

4. Click the Add Link option to add the link.

5. Click the Create button to create the chosen link.

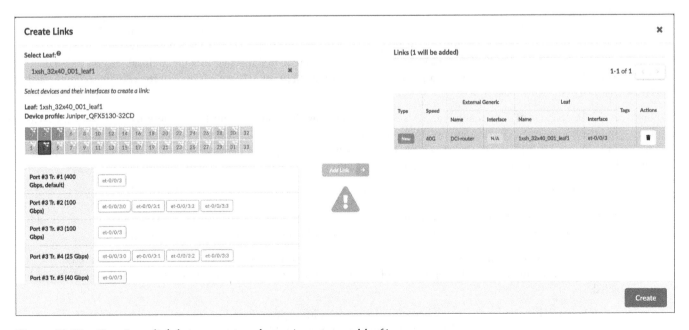

Figure 13-24 *Creating a link between external generic system and leaf4*

In Figure 13-24, port 3 is selected on the leaf named 1xsh_32x40_001_leaf1 (corresponding to leaf4 in the reference topology shown in Figure 13-10) and a transformation set that configures the port as a 40G port is selected.

Since the design requires leaf5 to connect to the DCI-router as well, the same process is followed to connect it to leaf5, at the end of which the DCI-router has two connections, as per the links created. This is confirmed in Figure 13-25.

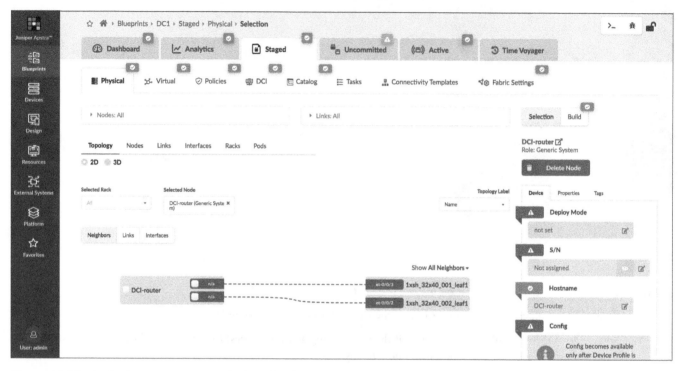

Figure 13-25 *Links from DCI-router to leaf4 and leaf5*

With these links created between the DCI-router and the border leafs, IPv4 connectivity and BGP over IPv4 need to be configured next. The intent for this is provided via Connectivity Templates. Unlike the Connectivity Templates created as part of Virtual Networks, these need to be created manually by the operator.

Creating Connectivity Templates

A *Connectivity Template (CT)* is a construct in Apstra that bundles together common network functions, enabling you to apply it to different application points (such as the physical interface of a fabric device). Connectivity Templates use *primitives* to define the network function itself. Multiple primitives can be tied together in a hierarchical fashion to build the overall network function. For example, a primitive called *Virtual Network (Single)* allows you to create tagged/untagged Layer 2 connectivity for a single VN.

In this case, the design goal is to establish an IPv4 BGP peering using the point-to-point Layer 3 interfaces between the DCI-router and the border leafs. For this purpose, the predefined Connectivity Template called *BGP over L3 connectivity* is used, as shown in Figure 13-26. You can find the Create Connectivity Template page by navigating to the Connectivity Templates tab under the Staged panel and clicking the Add Template button.

This Connectivity Template uses the following primitives tied together (also shown visually in Figure 13-27):

- **IP Link:** This primitive defines various parameters of the link itself, including how the IPv4 and IPv6 addressing should be defined, if the interface should be tagged or untagged, and which Routing Zone the link belongs to.

- **BGP Peering (Generic System):** This primitive defines various parameters for BGP peering, including what kind of interface to peer to and peer from (loopback or physical interface), keepalive and hold-time timers, and if BFD should be enabled.

- **Routing Policy:** This primitive defines what kind of routing policy Apstra should use to track routing intent. This includes whether Apstra expects a default IPv4 route and/or a default IPv6 route and what routes should be imported/exported.

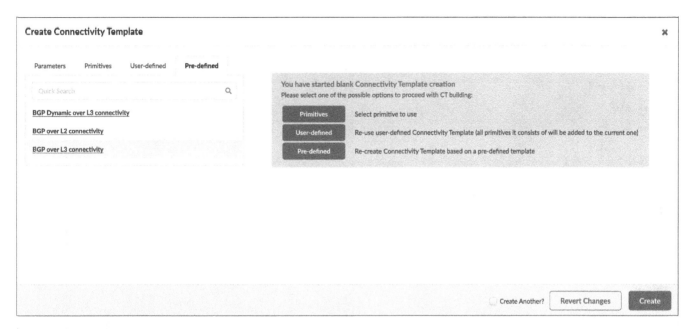

Figure 13-26 *Predefined BGP over L3 connectivity CT*

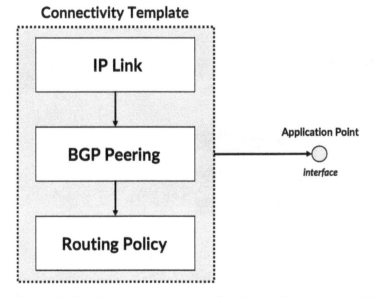

Figure 13-27 *Visual representation of BGP over L3 connectivity CT*

The default Routing Policy cannot be used in this case since it expects default IPv4 and IPv6 routes (if IPv6 is enabled for the fabric) and Apstra will start flagging anomalies for the same when they are not received. The BGP policy for connectivity to the DCI-router only requires the loopback addresses to be advertised, so a new Routing Policy is created (from within Routing Policies on the Policies tab under the Staged panel), as shown in Figure 13-28. The Routing Policy is given a name (*DCI-Routing-Policy*, not shown here for brevity), and you are required to select what kind of routes to export—in this case, only the Loopbacks option is selected, and everything else is unselected (including the IPv4 and IPv6 default routes).

With the DCI-specific Routing Policy created, the Connectivity Template can be created next. For the *IP Link* primitive, the default Routing Zone is used, along with an untagged interface and a numbered IPv4 addressing type, as shown in Figure 13-29.

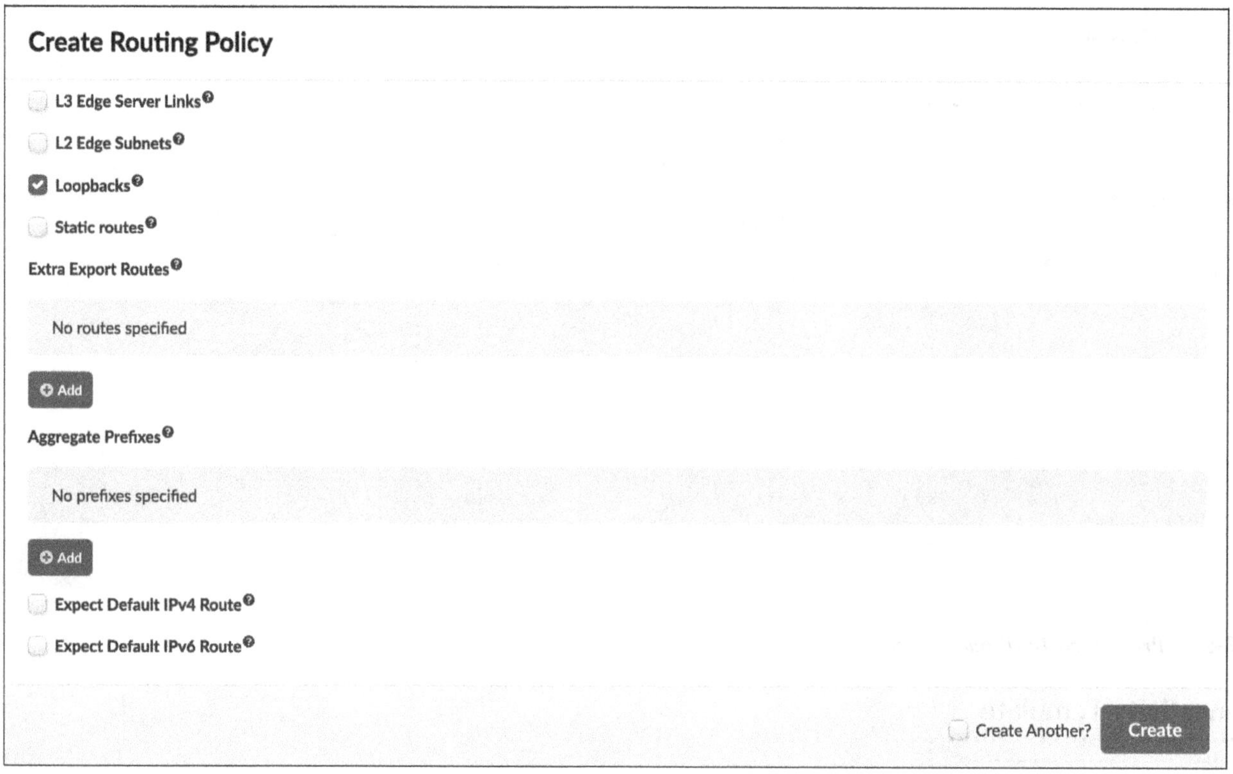

Create Routing Policy

- [ ] L3 Edge Server Links❓
- [ ] L2 Edge Subnets❓
- [✓] Loopbacks❓
- [ ] Static routes❓

Extra Export Routes❓

> No routes specified

⊕ Add

Aggregate Prefixes❓

> No prefixes specified

⊕ Add

- [ ] Expect Default IPv4 Route❓
- [ ] Expect Default IPv6 Route❓

Create Another?   **Create**

Figure 13-28 *Routing Policy creation for connectivity to DCI-router*

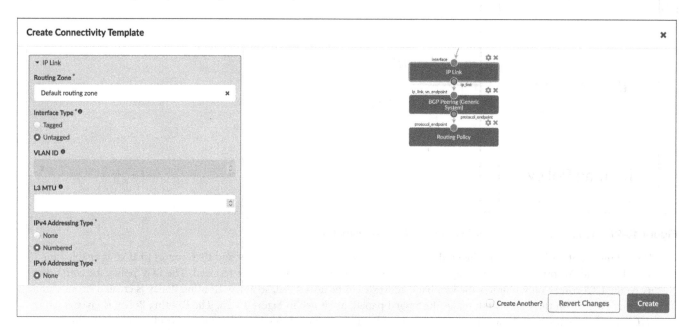

Figure 13-29 *IP Link primitive in Connectivity Template for DCI-router connectivity*

For the *BGP Peering* primitive, a static neighbor ASN is used, which specifies the ASN of DCI-router (meaning that you are required to provide an additional resource for the ASN to be used to peer with the external generic system), and BGP is configured to peer from an IP interface and to a remote IP endpoint or interface. This is shown in Figure 13-30. Other optional parameters such as the hold-time timer and keepalive timer are not changed.

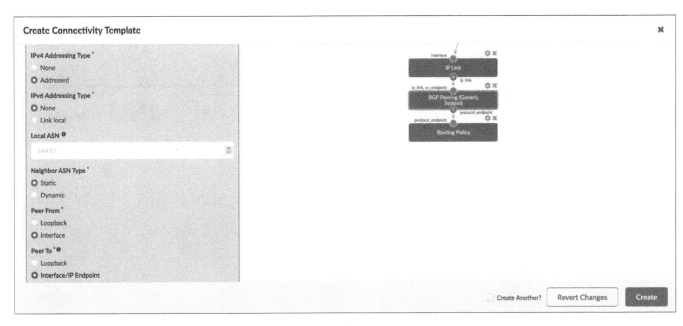

Figure 13-30 *BGP Peering primitive in Connectivity Template for DCI-router connectivity*

Finally, the *Routing Policy* primitive is configured to use the manually created DCI-Routing-Policy, which simply exports the loopback addresses and expects no IPv4 and IPv6 default routes. This is shown in Figure 13-31. With input provided for all mandatory parameters of the primitives used, the Connectivity Template can be created now.

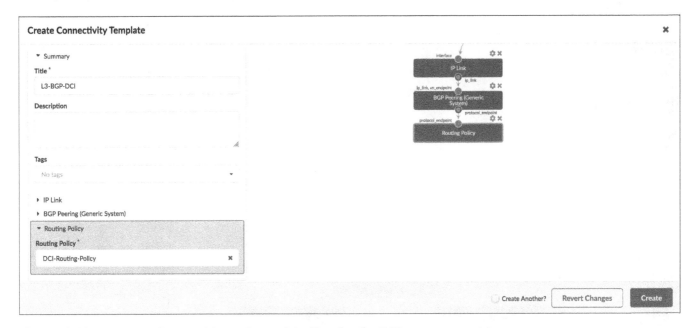

Figure 13-31 *Routing Policy primitive in Connectivity Template for DCI-router connectivity*

Once created, the Connectivity Template (like any other Connectivity Template) needs to be applied to an application point. In this case, the application points are the DCI-router–facing interfaces on DC1's border leafs, as shown in Figure 13-32.

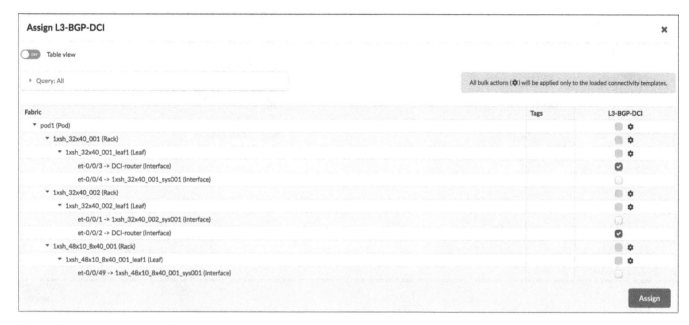

Figure 13-32   *Assignment of Connectivity Template to DCI-router–facing interfaces on DC1's border leafs*

Immediately after this assignment, Apstra reports that it requires an ASN pool for the external generic system, as well as four IP addresses (two /31 IPv4 subnets) to be used for IPv4 connectivity between the external generic system and DC1's border leafs. This is shown in Figure 13-33, where these new requirements are present in the Resources tab on the right side of the UI.

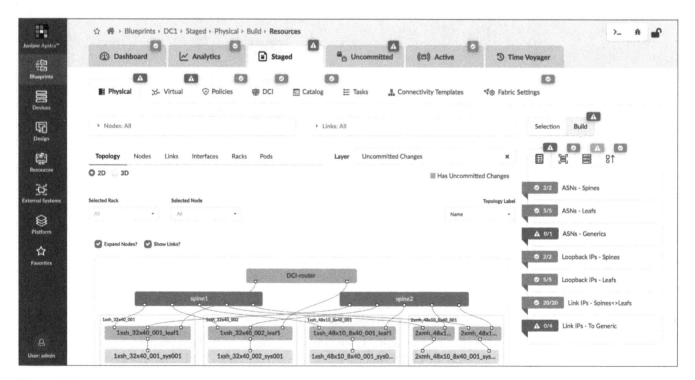

Figure 13-33   *New resource requirements once Connectivity Template is assigned to DC1's border leafs*

Once these resource requirements are met, the operator intent can be committed in Apstra. Taking leaf4 as an example, Apstra pushes the configuration shown in Example 13-11 as part of this intent. A new BGP group called *l3rtr* is created for the DCI-router–facing BGP peering.

Example 13-11 *Configuration pushed by Apstra to leaf4 to provide IPv4 connectivity to DCI-router*

```
root@1xsh-32x40-001-leaf1# show interfaces et-0/0/3
description "VRF default to DCI-router";
speed 40g;
unit 0 {
    family inet {
        address 198.51.100.32/31;
    }
}


root@1xsh-32x40-001-leaf1# show protocols bgp group l3rtr
type external;
multihop {
    ttl 1;
}
family inet {
    unicast {
        loops 2;
    }
}
multipath {
    multiple-as;
}
neighbor 198.51.100.33 {
    description facing_dci-router;
    multihop {
        ttl 2;
    }
    local-address 198.51.100.32;
    hold-time 30;
    import ( RoutesFromExt-default-DCI-Routing-Policy );
    family inet {
        unicast;
    }
    export ( RoutesToExt-default-DCI-Routing-Policy );
    peer-as 65511;
}
vpn-apply-export;
```

The export policy advertises loopback addresses to the DCI-router and strips them of any BGP community before advertisement. This policy is shown in Example 13-12.

Example 13-12 *Export policy configured on leaf4 for connectivity to DCI-router*

```
root@1xsh-32x40-001-leaf1# show policy-options policy-statement RoutesToExt-default-DCI-Routing-Policy
term RoutesToExt-default-DCI-Routing-Policy-10 {
    from {
        family inet;
        route-filter-list RoutesToExt-default-DCI-Routing-Policy;
    }
```

```
    then {
        community delete FABRIC_COMMUNITIES;
        accept;
    }
}
term RoutesToExt-default-DCI-Routing-Policy-30 {
    from family inet;
    then reject;
}
```

```
root@1xsh-32x40-001-leaf1# show policy-options route-filter-list RoutesToExt-default-DCI-Routing-Policy
192.0.2.0/30 upto /32;
192.0.2.4/31 upto /32;
192.0.2.6/32 exact;
```

With corresponding configuration on the Juniper MX204, the BGP peering comes up and is in an Established state for both leaf4 and leaf5. Additionally, the MX204 is receiving all loopback addresses from this data center, as shown in Example 13-13.

Example 13-13 *BGP peering, and routes received on DCI-router*

```
root@DCI-router> show bgp summary
Threading mode: BGP I/O
Default eBGP mode: advertise - accept, receive - accept
Groups: 1 Peers: 2 Down peers: 0
Table          Tot Paths  Act Paths Suppressed    History Damp State    Pending
inet.0
                    14         7         0          0         0          0
Peer                 AS     InPkt    OutPkt    OutQ    Flaps Last Up/Dwn
State|#Active/Received/Accepted/Damped...
198.51.100.32       65421    1205      1201       0        0    2:59:34 Establ
  inet.0: 6/7/6/0
198.51.100.34       65422    1205      1208       0        0    2:59:30 Establ
  inet.0: 1/7/6/0
```

```
root@DCI-router> show route table inet.0 match-prefix *192.0.2*

inet.0: 11 destinations, 18 routes (11 active, 0 holddown, 2 hidden)
+ = Active Route, - = Last Active, * = Both

192.0.2.0/32       *[BGP/170] 00:32:33, localpref 100
                      AS path: 65421 65500 I, validation-state: unverified
                    >  to 198.51.100.32 via et-0/0/3.0
                    [BGP/170] 00:32:33, localpref 100
                      AS path: 65422 65500 I, validation-state: unverified
                    >  to 198.51.100.34 via et-0/0/2.0
192.0.2.1/32       *[BGP/170] 00:32:33, localpref 100
                      AS path: 65421 65501 I, validation-state: unverified
                    >  to 198.51.100.32 via et-0/0/3.0
                    [BGP/170] 00:32:33, localpref 100
                      AS path: 65422 65501 I, validation-state: unverified
                    >  to 198.51.100.34 via et-0/0/2.0
```

```
192.0.2.2/32    *[BGP/170] 02:40:33, localpref 100
                   AS path: 65421 I, validation-state: unverified
                >  to 198.51.100.32 via et-0/0/3.0
192.0.2.3/32    *[BGP/170] 02:40:33, localpref 100
                   AS path: 65422 I, validation-state: unverified
                >  to 198.51.100.34 via et-0/0/2.0
192.0.2.4/32    *[BGP/170] 00:32:33, localpref 100
                   AS path: 65421 65501 65423 I, validation-state: unverified
                >  to 198.51.100.32 via et-0/0/3.0
                 [BGP/170] 00:32:33, localpref 100
                   AS path: 65422 65501 65423 I, validation-state: unverified
                >  to 198.51.100.34 via et-0/0/2.0
192.0.2.5/32    *[BGP/170] 00:32:33, localpref 100
                   AS path: 65421 65501 65424 I, validation-state: unverified
                >  to 198.51.100.32 via et-0/0/3.0
                 [BGP/170] 00:32:33, localpref 100
                   AS path: 65422 65500 65424 I, validation-state: unverified
                >  to 198.51.100.34 via et-0/0/2.0
192.0.2.6/32    *[BGP/170] 00:32:33, localpref 100
                   AS path: 65421 65501 65425 I, validation-state: unverified
                >  to 198.51.100.32 via et-0/0/3.0
                 [BGP/170] 00:32:33, localpref 100
                   AS path: 65422 65500 65425 I, validation-state: unverified
                >  to 198.51.100.34 via et-0/0/2.0
```

For DC2's Blueprint, the same process is followed of adding an external generic system (representing the same DCI-router), adding links to connect to the border leaf, and creating and assigning the predefined *L3 over BGP connectivity* CT. In the Apstra UI, this new external generic system and its connection to the border leaf (leaf3) are shown in Figure 13-34.

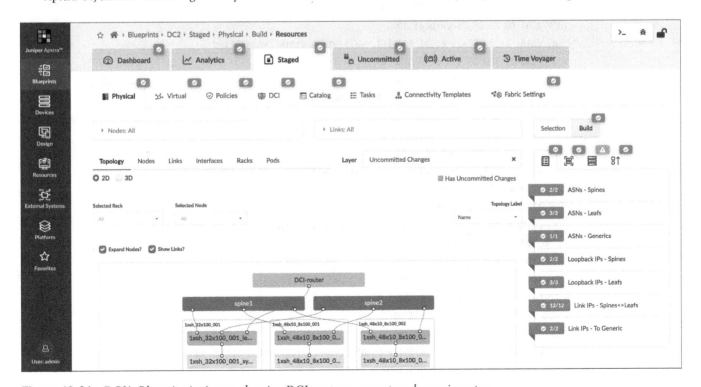

Figure 13-34 *DC2's Blueprint in Apstra showing DCI-router as an external generic system*

Once this change is committed in DC2's Blueprint and the BGP peering to the DCI-router comes up, all leafs across both data centers receive routes for all loopback addresses. This is confirmed in Example 13-14, from the perspective of leaf1 in DC2.

Example 13-14 *IPv4 table on leaf1 in DC2 confirming receipt of all loopback addresses across both data centers*

```
root@1xsh-48x10-8x100-001-leaf1> show route table inet.0 match-prefix *192.0.2*

inet.0: 21 destinations, 37 routes (21 active, 0 holddown, 0 hidden)
Restart Complete
+ = Active Route, - = Last Active, * = Both


192.0.2.0/32        *[BGP/170] 00:22:05, localpref 100
                      AS path: 65502 65426 65511 65421 65500 I, validation-state: unverified
                    >  to 198.51.100.22 via et-0/0/54.0
                       to 198.51.100.28 via et-0/0/50.0
                     [BGP/170] 00:22:05, localpref 100
                      AS path: 65503 65426 65511 65421 65500 I, validation-state: unverified
                    >  to 198.51.100.28 via et-0/0/50.0
192.0.2.1/32        *[BGP/170] 00:22:05, localpref 100
                      AS path: 65502 65426 65511 65421 65501 I, validation-state: unverified
                    >  to 198.51.100.22 via et-0/0/54.0
                       to 198.51.100.28 via et-0/0/50.0
                     [BGP/170] 00:22:05, localpref 100
                      AS path: 65503 65426 65511 65421 65501 I, validation-state: unverified
                    >  to 198.51.100.28 via et-0/0/50.0
192.0.2.2/32        *[BGP/170] 00:22:05, localpref 100
                      AS path: 65502 65426 65511 65421 I, validation-state: unverified
                    >  to 198.51.100.22 via et-0/0/54.0
                       to 198.51.100.28 via et-0/0/50.0
                     [BGP/170] 00:22:05, localpref 100
                      AS path: 65503 65426 65511 65421 I, validation-state: unverified
                    >  to 198.51.100.28 via et-0/0/50.0
192.0.2.3/32        *[BGP/170] 00:22:05, localpref 100
                      AS path: 65502 65426 65511 65422 I, validation-state: unverified
                    >  to 198.51.100.22 via et-0/0/54.0
                       to 198.51.100.28 via et-0/0/50.0
                     [BGP/170] 00:22:05, localpref 100
                      AS path: 65503 65426 65511 65422 I, validation-state: unverified
                    >  to 198.51.100.28 via et-0/0/50.0
192.0.2.4/32        *[BGP/170] 00:22:05, localpref 100
                      AS path: 65502 65426 65511 65421 65501 65423 I, validation-state: unverified
                    >  to 198.51.100.22 via et-0/0/54.0
                       to 198.51.100.28 via et-0/0/50.0
                     [BGP/170] 00:22:05, localpref 100
                      AS path: 65503 65426 65511 65421 65501 65423 I, validation-state: unverified
                    >  to 198.51.100.28 via et-0/0/50.0
192.0.2.5/32        *[BGP/170] 00:22:05, localpref 100
                      AS path: 65502 65426 65511 65421 65501 65424 I, validation-state: unverified
                    >  to 198.51.100.22 via et-0/0/54.0
```

```
                to 198.51.100.28 via et-0/0/50.0
             [BGP/170] 00:22:05, localpref 100
               AS path: 65503 65426 65511 65421 65501 65424 I, validation-state: unverified
             >  to 198.51.100.28 via et-0/0/50.0
192.0.2.6/32   *[BGP/170] 00:22:05, localpref 100
               AS path: 65502 65426 65511 65421 65501 65425 I, validation-state: unverified
             >  to 198.51.100.22 via et-0/0/54.0
                to 198.51.100.28 via et-0/0/50.0
             [BGP/170] 00:22:05, localpref 100
               AS path: 65503 65426 65511 65421 65501 65425 I, validation-state: unverified
             >  to 198.51.100.28 via et-0/0/50.0
```

snip

Since the connectivity to the DCI-router is common to both OTT and Integrated Interconnect DCI designs, this state of the fabric can be permanently saved to roll back to for the next subsection. In Apstra, by default, only five revisions of the fabric are saved in Time Voyager. While this can be increased, there is still a possibility that a certain revision will eventually be overwritten as more changes are saved. Apstra allows you to permanently save up to 25 revisions, circumventing this problem, as shown in Figure 13-35. To do so, navigate to the Time Voyager panel and click the Save button (floppy disk icon) of a commit revision.

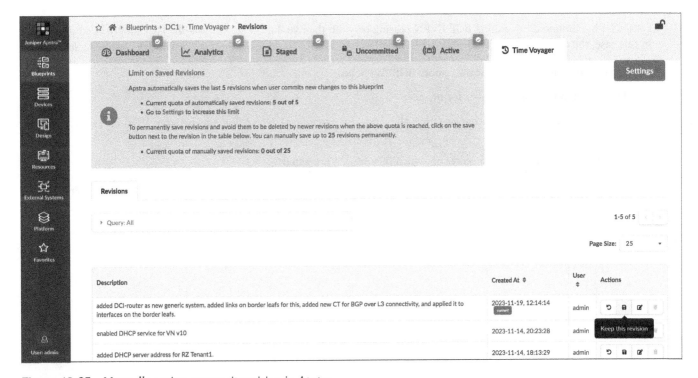

Figure 13-35 *Manually saving a commit revision in Apstra*

With the connection to the DCI-router established, and all loopback addresses exchanged between DC1 and DC2, OTT DCI can be set up now. In Apstra 4.2.0, a new tab called DCI is available under the Staged panel. This is where both OTT and Integrated Interconnect DCI options are available, as shown in Figure 13-36.

Figure 13-36 *OTT DCI in Apstra UI*

Configuring OTT DCI

OTT DCI is configured by creating BGP EVPN peering between the two data centers, using the DCI simply as an underlay. In this case, the peering is between the border leafs of DC1 and DC2. To do this, you must provide the following inputs:

- A name and the IP address for the remote BGP EVPN peer

- The autonomous system number for the peer

- Choice of EVPN routes to exchange, either all routes (for extending Layer 2 domains between DCs) or EVPN Type-5 routes only

- List of nodes in the local data center on which this peering is created

Optionally, you can configure the Time to Live (TTL), keepalive, and hold-time timers. Figure 13-37 shows the initial part of this UI page where the name, IP address, and ASN are configured.

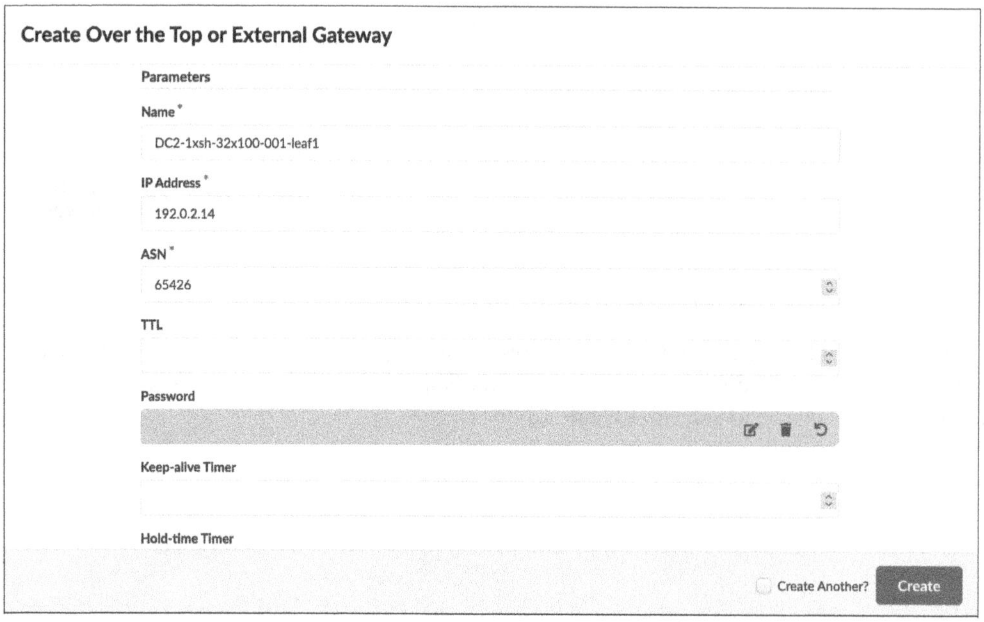

Create Over the Top or External Gateway

Parameters

Name *

    DC2-1xsh-32x100-001-leaf1

IP Address *

    192.0.2.14

ASN *

    65426

TTL

Password

Keep-alive Timer

Hold-time Timer

☐ Create Another?   **Create**

Figure 13-37 *Name, IP address, and ASN input during OTT DCI creation in Apstra*

Scrolling down the same UI page, devices local to the Blueprint must be chosen to determine on which device(s) this peering is configured. In this case, the two border leafs are selected, as shown in Figure 13-38. In addition, all EVPN routes have been selected to be advertised, which enables a Layer 2 domain to extend between the two data centers.

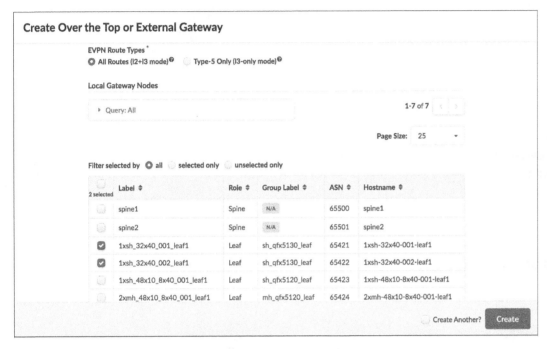

Figure 13-38 *EVPN route type and node selection during OTT DCI creation in Apstra*

In the same way, in the DC2 Blueprint, OTT DCI peers are configured. However, in this case, since DC1 is expected to have two border leafs, both these peers are configured as OTT BGP EVPN peers on DC2, as shown in Figure 13-39.

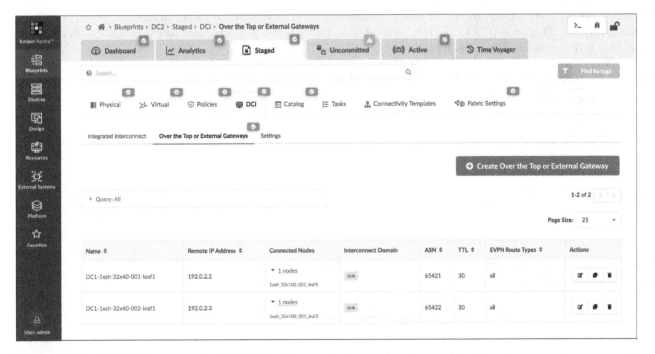

Figure 13-39 *OTT DCI summary in DC2 Blueprint*

With this change committed on both data centers, Apstra pushes the relevant configuration to the nodes that were selected during the OTT DCI creation page. Taking leaf4 as a reference, this configuration is shown in Example 13-15, which includes a new BGP group called *evpn-gw*, configured with the remote IP addresses provided by the operator as neighbors, enabled for the BGP EVPN address family.

Example 13-15 *BGP group for OTT DCI peering*

```
root@1xsh-32x40-001-leaf1# show protocols bgp group evpn-gw
type external;
multihop {
    ttl 30;
    no-nexthop-change;
}
multipath {
    multiple-as;
}
neighbor 192.0.2.14 {
    description facing_dc2-1xsh-32x100-001-leaf1-evpn-gateway;
    local-address 192.0.2.2;
    import ( EVPN_GW_IN );
    family evpn {
        signaling;
    }
    export ( EVPN_GW_OUT && EVPN_EXPORT );
    peer-as 65426;
}
vpn-apply-export;
```

Apstra configures an import policy and an export policy for this BGP group as well. These policies work in conjunction to prevent inefficient routing, path hunting for the overlay, and possible routing loops. These policies are necessary because when there are multiple border leafs between two or more data centers, EVPN routes in the control plane can originate in one data center and then eventually be received back by the same data center.

The import policy accepts EVPN routes and adds a BGP community to these routes, as shown in Example 13-16. Considering host h7's address (172.16.50.7/24), received as an EVPN Type-2 MAC+IP route on DC1's border leaf, this additional BGP community is added to the route.

Example 13-16 *Import policy for OTT DCI BGP peering group*

```
root@1xsh-32x40-001-leaf1# show policy-options policy-statement EVPN_GW_IN
term EVPN_GW_IN-10 {
    from family evpn;
    then {
        community add EVPN_GW_IN;
        accept;
    }
}


root@1xsh-32x40-001-leaf1# show policy-options community EVPN_GW_IN
members [ 3:20001 21000:26000 ];


root@1xsh-32x40-001-leaf1> show route table bgp.evpn.0 match-prefix *172.16.50.7* extensive


bgp.evpn.0: 46 destinations, 72 routes (46 active, 0 holddown, 0 hidden)
Restart Complete
2:192.0.2.14:65534::10050::f0:4b:3a:b9:80:c3::172.16.50.7/304 MAC/IP (1 entry, 1 announced)
TSI:
Page 0 idx 0, (group l3clos-l-evpn type External) Type 1 val 0x55b03882e870 (adv_entry)
```

```
    Advertised metrics:
      Nexthop: 192.0.2.14
      AS path: [65421] 65426 I
      Communities: 3:20001 21000:26000 target:10050:1 target:10500:1 encapsulation:vxlan(0x8) router-mac:50:c7:09:a6:f5:04
    Advertise: 00000003
Path 2:192.0.2.14:65534::10050::f0:4b:3a:b9:80:c3::172.16.50.7
from 192.0.2.14
Vector len 4.  Val: 0
        *BGP    Preference: 170/-101
                Route Distinguisher: 192.0.2.14:65534
                Next hop type: Indirect, Next hop index: 0
                Address: 0x55b037f4285c
                Next-hop reference count: 3
                Kernel Table Id: 0
                Source: 192.0.2.14
                Protocol next hop: 192.0.2.14
                Label operation: Push 628
                Label TTL action: prop-ttl
                Load balance label: Label 628: None;
                Indirect next hop: 0x2 no-forward INH Session ID: 0
                State: <Active Ext>
                Local AS: 65421 Peer AS: 65426
                Age: 3:18:28    Metric2: 0
                Validation State: unverified
                Task: BGP_65426.192.0.2.14
                Announcement bits (1): 1-BGP_RT_Background
                AS path: 65426 I
                Communities: 3:20001 21000:26000 target:10050:1 target:10500:1 encapsulation:vxlan(0x8)
router-mac:50:c7:09:a6:f5:04
                Import Accepted
                Route Label: 10050
                Route Label: 10500
```

The export policy attached to the same BGP group, shown in Example 13-17, rejects any routes with this community.

Example 13-17 *Export policy for OTT DCI BGP peering group*

```
root@1xsh-32x40-001-leaf1# show policy-options policy-statement EVPN_GW_OUT
term EVPN_GW_OUT-10 {
    from {
        family evpn;
        community EVPN_GW_OUT;
    }
    then reject;
}
term EVPN_GW_OUT-20 {
    from family evpn;
    then {
        community delete FABRIC_COMMUNITIES;
        accept;
    }
```

```
    }
```

```
root@1xsh-32x40-001-leaf1# show policy-options community EVPN_GW_OUT
members .+:20001;
```

With the necessary OTT DCI configuration deployed by Apstra, all hosts across both data centers can communicate with each other. In the case of Virtual Network v10, which is extended between both data centers, the traffic for host-to-host communication in this domain uses L2VNI 10010 only. As shown in Example 13-18, host h1 in DC1 is successfully able to communicate with host h5 in DC2, demonstrated using the **ping** tool.

Example 13-18   *Host h1 in DC1 communicating with host h5 in DC2*

```
root@h1> ping 172.16.10.5
PING 172.16.10.5 (172.16.10.5): 56 data bytes
64 bytes from 172.16.10.5: icmp_seq=0 ttl=64 time=0.960 ms
64 bytes from 172.16.10.5: icmp_seq=1 ttl=64 time=0.872 ms
64 bytes from 172.16.10.5: icmp_seq=2 ttl=64 time=6.427 ms
64 bytes from 172.16.10.5: icmp_seq=3 ttl=64 time=0.938 ms
^C
--- 172.16.10.5 ping statistics ---
4 packets transmitted, 4 packets received, 0% packet loss
round-trip min/avg/max/stddev = 0.872/2.299/6.427/2.383 ms
```

A packet capture of the ICMP request originated by host h1, destined for h5, confirms that the VNI in the VXLAN header is L2VNI 10010, as shown in Figure 13-40.

Host h1, again in DC1, can also communicate with host h6 in DC2. This communication is inter-subnet, since h1 is in subnet 172.16.10.0/24 and h6 is in subnet 172.16.40.0/24. Since the Routing Zone is enabled with Symmetric IRB, using the EVPN Type-2 route received for host h6's address, a /32 route is installed on leaf1 in DC1, as shown in Example 13-19.

Example 13-19   *Host h1 in DC1 communicating with host h6 in DC2*

```
root@1xsh-48x10-8x40-001-leaf1> show route table Tenant1.inet.0 172.16.40.6/32

Tenant1.inet.0: 21 destinations, 26 routes (21 active, 0 holddown, 0 hidden)
Restart Complete
@ = Routing Use Only, # = Forwarding Use Only
+ = Active Route, - = Last Active, * = Both

172.16.40.6/32      *[EVPN/7] 12:03:24
                     >  to 198.51.100.4 via et-0/0/48.0
                        to 198.51.100.14 via et-0/0/50.0


root@h1> ping 172.16.40.6
PING 172.16.40.6 (172.16.40.6): 56 data bytes
64 bytes from 172.16.40.6: icmp_seq=0 ttl=62 time=1.055 ms
64 bytes from 172.16.40.6: icmp_seq=1 ttl=62 time=0.849 ms
64 bytes from 172.16.40.6: icmp_seq=2 ttl=62 time=0.903 ms
64 bytes from 172.16.40.6: icmp_seq=3 ttl=62 time=0.871 ms
^C
--- 172.16.40.6 ping statistics ---
4 packets transmitted, 4 packets received, 0% packet loss
round-trip min/avg/max/stddev = 0.849/0.919/1.055/0.081 ms
```

A packet capture of the ICMP request originated by host h1, destined for h6, confirms that L3VNI 10500 is used in the data plane, as shown in Figure 13-41.

```
No.   Time        Source        Destination    Protocol  Length  Info
  1  2023-11-...  172.16.10.1   172.16.10.5    ICMP      148  Echo (ping) request  id=0xea7f, seq=75/19200, ttl=64 (reply in 2)
  2  2023-11-...  172.16.10.5   172.16.10.1    ICMP      152  Echo (ping) reply    id=0xea7f, seq=75/19200, ttl=64 (request in 1)
```

```
> Frame 1: 148 bytes on wire (1184 bits), 148 bytes captured (1184 bits)      0000  64 c3 d6
> Ethernet II, Src: JuniperN_7b:70:75 (40:de:ad:7b:70:75), Dst: JuniperN_60:76:40 (64:c3:d6:60:76:40)  0010  00 86 05
> Internet Protocol Version 4, Src: 192.0.2.4, Dst: 192.0.2.15                 0020  02 0f da
> User Datagram Protocol, Src Port: 55892, Dst Port: 4789                      0030  1a 00 f0
v Virtual eXtensible Local Area Network                                        0040  45 00 00
  > Flags: 0x0800, VXLAN Network ID (VNI)                                      0050  ac 10 0a
    Group Policy ID: 0                                                         0060  00 0e 89
    VXLAN Network Identifier (VNI): 10010                                      0070  14 15 16
    Reserved: 0                                                                0080  24 25 26
> Ethernet II, Src: JuniperN_b9:80:a7 (f0:4b:3a:b9:80:a7), Dst: JuniperN_b9:80:ff (f0:4b:3a:b9:80:ff)  0090  34 35 36
v Internet Protocol Version 4, Src: 172.16.10.1, Dst: 172.16.10.5
    0100 .... = Version: 4
    .... 0101 = Header Length: 20 bytes (5)
  > Differentiated Services Field: 0x00 (DSCP: CS0, ECN: Not-ECT)
    Total Length: 84
    Identification: 0xd5e6 (54758)
  > 000. .... = Flags: 0x0
    ...0 0000 0000 0000 = Fragment Offset: 0
    Time to Live: 64
    Protocol: ICMP (1)
    Header Checksum: 0x389c [validation disabled]
    [Header checksum status: Unverified]
    Source Address: 172.16.10.1
    Destination Address: 172.16.10.5
v Internet Control Message Protocol
    Type: 8 (Echo (ping) request)
    Code: 0
    Checksum: 0x4b7a [correct]
    [Checksum Status: Good]
    Identifier (BE): 60031 (0xea7f)
    Identifier (LE): 32746 (0x7fea)
    Sequence Number (BE): 75 (0x004b)
    Sequence Number (LE): 19200 (0x4b00)
    [Response frame: 2]
    Timestamp from icmp data: Nov 20, 2023 10:31:34.952608000 IST
    [Timestamp from icmp data (relative): 45254.165696000 seconds]
  > Data (48 bytes)
```

Figure 13-40 *Packet capture of an ICMP request originated by host h1 in DC1 destined for h5 in DC2*

```
No.   Time        Source        Destination    Protocol  Length  Info
  1  2023-11-...  172.16.10.1   172.16.40.6    ICMP      148  Echo (ping) request  id=0xed7f, seq=11/2816, ttl=63 (reply in 2)
  2  2023-11-...  172.16.40.6   172.16.10.1    ICMP      152  Echo (ping) reply    id=0xed7f, seq=11/2816, ttl=63 (request in 1)
```

```
> Frame 1: 148 bytes on wire (1184 bits), 148 bytes captured (1184 bits)      0000  64 c3 d6
> Ethernet II, Src: JuniperN_7b:70:75 (40:de:ad:7b:70:75), Dst: JuniperN_60:76:40 (64:c3:d6:60:76:40)  0010  00 86 05
> Internet Protocol Version 4, Src: 192.0.2.4, Dst: 192.0.2.16                 0020  02 10 eb
> User Datagram Protocol, Src Port: 60352, Dst Port: 4789                      0030  04 00 b0
v Virtual eXtensible Local Area Network                                        0040  45 00 00
  > Flags: 0x0800, VXLAN Network ID (VNI)                                      0050  ac 10 28
    Group Policy ID: 0                                                         0060  00 04 83
    VXLAN Network Identifier (VNI): 10500                                      0070  14 15 16
    Reserved: 0                                                                0080  24 25 26
> Ethernet II, Src: JuniperN_7b:70:40 (40:de:ad:7b:70:40), Dst: JuniperN_42:8a:40 (b0:eb:7f:42:8a:40)  0090  34 35 36
v Internet Protocol Version 4, Src: 172.16.10.1, Dst: 172.16.40.6
    0100 .... = Version: 4
    .... 0101 = Header Length: 20 bytes (5)
  > Differentiated Services Field: 0x00 (DSCP: CS0, ECN: Not-ECT)
    Total Length: 84
    Identification: 0xdd14 (56596)
  > 000. .... = Flags: 0x0
    ...0 0000 0000 0000 = Fragment Offset: 0
    Time to Live: 63
    Protocol: ICMP (1)
    Header Checksum: 0x146d [validation disabled]
    [Header checksum status: Unverified]
    Source Address: 172.16.10.1
    Destination Address: 172.16.40.6
v Internet Control Message Protocol
    Type: 8 (Echo (ping) request)
    Code: 0
    Checksum: 0x4e13 [correct]
    [Checksum Status: Good]
    Identifier (BE): 60799 (0xed7f)
    Identifier (LE): 32749 (0x7fed)
    Sequence Number (BE): 11 (0x000b)
    Sequence Number (LE): 2816 (0x0b00)
    [Response frame: 2]
    Timestamp from icmp data: Nov 20, 2023 10:32:38.295825000 IST
    [Timestamp from icmp data (relative): 45254.167555000 seconds]
  > Data (48 bytes)
```

Figure 13-41 *Packet capture of an ICMP request originated by host h1 in DC1 destined for h6 in DC2*

Integrated Interconnect

To begin deploying Integrated Interconnect (also known as VXLAN stitching), the fabric state is first rolled back, using Apstra's Time Voyager functionality, to the revision in which connectivity to the DCI-router was established and no DCI had been configured yet. The fabric state is stable, with no anomalies reported after the rollback, as shown in Figure 13-42.

Figure 13-42   *Stable fabric state across both data centers after Time Voyager rollback*

Integrated Interconnect, like OTT DCI, is configured by navigating to the DCI tab, under the Staged panel of a Blueprint, and clicking the Create Interconnect Domain button, as shown in Figure 13-43.

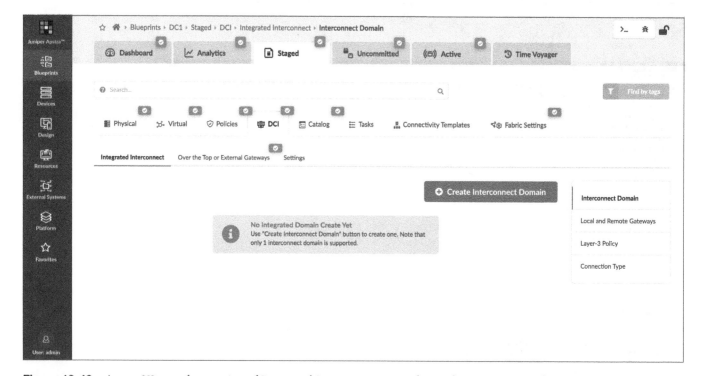

Figure 13-43   *Apstra UI page for creation of Integrated Interconnect to stitch together two or more data centers*

Setting up Integrated Interconnect requires the following steps (which correspond, in order, to the four items on the right side of the Apstra UI in Figure 13-43):

1. Create an interconnect domain, defining the interconnect Route Target and the interconnect ESI. These correspond to the *interconnect* configuration hierarchy in the MAC-VRF configuration.

2. Configure remote BGP EVPN peers (similar to OTT DCI configuration). This requires a name for the peer, the remote IP address, and the remote ASN. In addition, you must select local leafs on which these peers should be configured. Apstra limits the list to show only devices in a leaf role, since configuring Integrated Interconnect requires VTEP functionality, and in Apstra's reference designs, only devices in a leaf role support this.

3. Enable EVPN Type-5 stitching per IP VRF and map a mandatory Routing Policy for this. The Routing Policy determines if loopbacks and static routes should be exported as part of Type-5 stitching, including any manually defined routes for import/export.

4. Choose which Virtual Networks to extend using Integrated Interconnect via Type-2 and/or Type-5 stitching. For VNs being extended with Type-2 stitching, you can define an optional translation VNI. If you choose Type-5, you must also enable Type-5 stitching for the corresponding IP VRF. This step of specifically choosing which VNs to extend provides you the flexibility to select only a subset of VNs if required.

Figure 13-44 provides a visual representation of these steps.

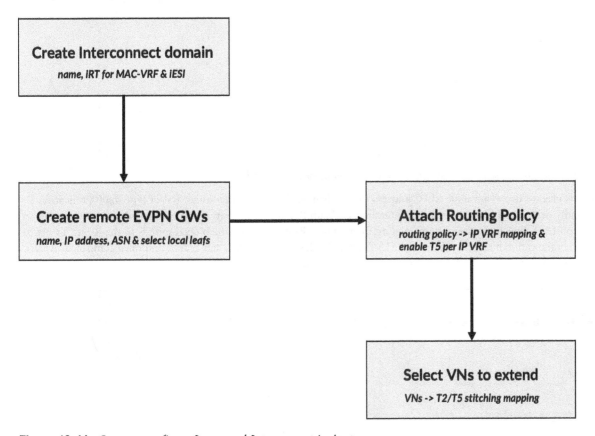

Figure 13-44 *Steps to configure Integrated Interconnect in Apstra*

In this case, the following parameters will be used to deploy Integrated Interconnect between DC1 and DC2:

- An interconnect Route Target of 1:2 will be used for the MAC-VRF on both data centers, along with an auto-generated interconnect ESI on each data center. Apstra enables you to specify the most significant byte (MSB) for auto-generation of interconnect ESIs, to ensure that each data center has a unique interconnect ESI (which is a mandatory requirement). Thus, for DC1 the MSB will be set to a value of 2, and for DC2 the MSB will be set to a value of 4.

- On DC1, a remote EVPN peer of 192.0.2.14 (owned by leaf3 of DC2) will be configured. On DC2, two remote EVPN peers will be configured—one for 192.0.2.2 (owned by leaf4) and the other for 192.0.2.3 (owned by leaf5), as per the reference topology shown in Figure 13-10.

- The existing DCI Routing Policy (used for OTT DCI earlier) will be used and attached to the IP VRF Tenant1. This IP VRF will be enabled for Type-5 stitching, with an interconnect route-target of 5000:5000.

- On both data centers, Virtual Network v10 will be enabled for EVPN Type-2 and Type-5 stitching, while all other VNs (v20 and v30 in DC1, and v40 and v50 in DC2) will be enabled for EVPN Type-5 stitching only.

Interconnect Domain and MSB for Auto-derivation of Interconnect ESI

Before Integrated Interconnect is configured on DC1, the MSB for auto-derivation of the interconnect ESI is set to a value of 2, as shown in Figure 13-45, by navigating to the Settings option in the DCI tab under the Staged panel.

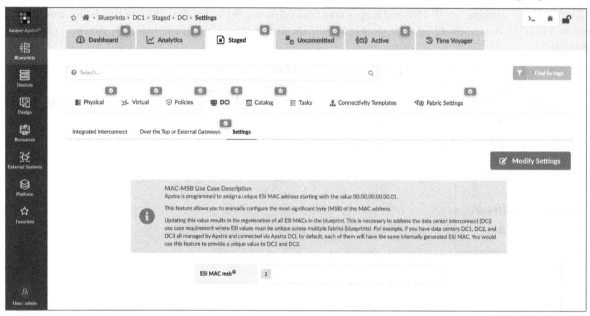

Figure 13-45   *Settings option to configure MSB for auto-derivation of interconnect ESI*

This MSB value is used to derive a unique MAC address that is then used to auto-generate an ESI of type 0x00 (indicating that it is a manually generated ESI) for Integrated Interconnect. With this out of the way, the first step is to define an interconnect domain on DC1, which requires a name and an interconnect Route Target, which corresponds to the Route Target in the *interconnect* configuration hierarchy, under the MAC-VRF. The ESI field is simply left blank, and once confirmed, Apstra auto-generates the MAC address using the MSB value. This interconnect domain is shown in Figure 13-46.

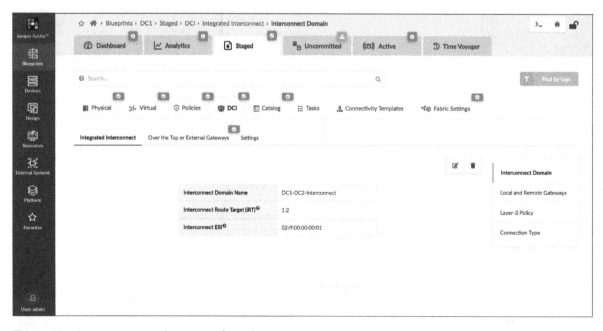

Figure 13-46   *Interconnect domain configured on DC1*

Creating Remote BGP EVPN Peers

Next, remote BGP EVPN peers need to be defined. To do this, navigate to the Local and Remote Gateways option on the right side of the UI and click the Create Remote Interconnect Gateway button, as shown in Figure 13-47. The page for creating the gateway is the same as the page for creating the gateway for OTT DCI, as shown in Figure 13-48, and requires the following:

- A name for the remote BGP EVPN peer

- The IP address and ASN of the remote peer

- Selection of all local leafs on which this peer must be configured

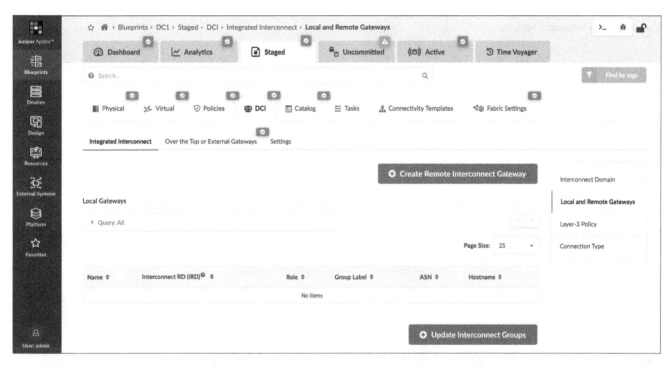

Figure 13-47 *Apstra UI page to create remote BGP EVPN peers for Integrated Interconnect*

Create Remote Interconnect Gateway

Parameters

Name *

> DC2-1xsh-32x100-001-leaf1

IP Address *

> 192.0.2.14

ASN *

> 65426

TTL

Password

Keep-alive Timer

Hold-time Timer

Create Another? Create

Figure 13-48 *Creating remote BGP EVPN peer for Integrated Interconnect*

Optionally, you can configure other BGP parameters such as the TTL, keepalive, and hold-time timers.

Since DC2 has one border leaf, only a single remote BGP EVPN peer needs to be configured on DC1. The initial part of this UI is shown in Figure 13-48, with a name, remote IP address, and remote ASN configured for it. This corresponds to DC2's leaf (hostname 1xsh-32x100-001-leaf1), which has a loopback address of 192.0.2.14 and an ASN of 65426.

Scrolling down the same UI page, the local leafs must be selected on which this remote BGP EVPN peer needs to be configured. In the case of DC1, these leafs are leaf4 and leaf5 (hostnames 1xsh-32x40-001-leaf1 and 1xsh-32x40-001-leaf2), as shown in Figure 13-49. To reiterate, only devices in a leaf role are displayed here since Apstra requires VTEP functionality for this feature.

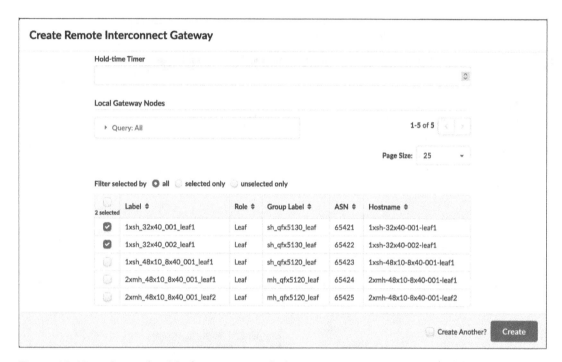

Figure 13-49   *Selecting local leafs on DC1 on which remote BGP EVPN peers are created*

Extending IP VRFs and Virtual Networks

Once the remote BGP EVPN peers are configured, you must choose which IP VRFs (Routing Zones) and Virtual Networks need to be extended between data centers. For any Virtual Network that needs to be configured for Type-5 stitching, its corresponding Routing Zone (IP VRF) must be enabled for Type-5 stitching as well.

In this case, the Routing Zone Tenant1 is enabled for Type-5 stitching, and the Routing Policy DCI-Routing-Policy is associated to it. This is the same policy that was created for the OTT DCI use case, and exports only loopback addresses. This mapping of a policy to the IP VRF and enabling it for Type-5 stitching are shown in Figure 13-50.

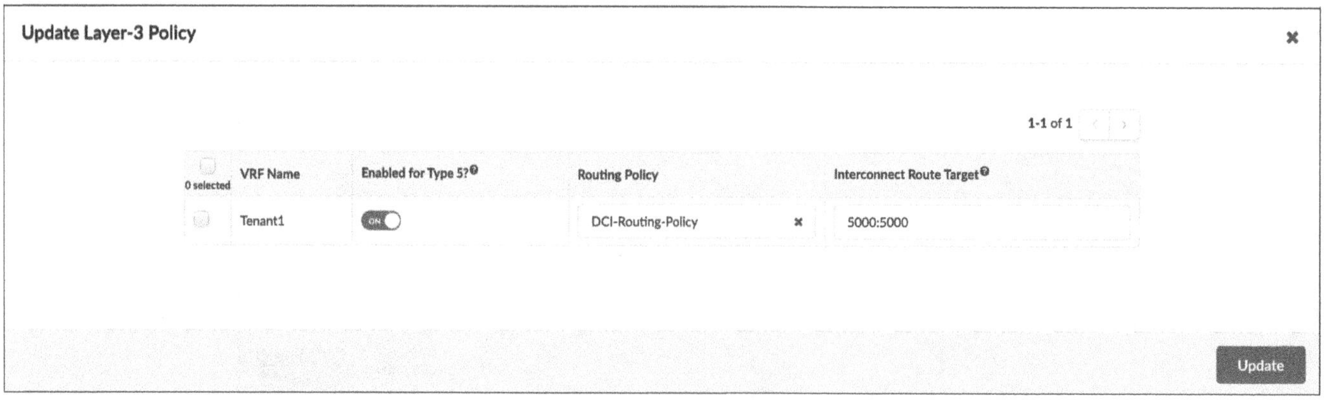

Figure 13-50   *Enabling IP VRF Tenant1 for Type-5 stitching and associating it to a Routing Policy*

NOTE It is important to note that this policy does not control which Virtual Networks' subnets are exported for Type-5 stitching. This policy controls the addition of any loopback or static routes (or any subnets that you manually add) that should be shared between data centers via Type-5 stitching. The subnets, corresponding to Virtual Networks, that require stitching are solely controlled by the Virtual Networks that you enable for Type-5 stitching.

Finally, you must select the Virtual Networks that need to be stitched. To do so, navigate to the Connection Type option on the right side of the UI, on the DCI tab under the Staged panel. Here, a list of all Virtual Networks is provided, and you can select one or more VNs and then click the Edit button, shown in Figure 13-51, to enable Type-2 and/or Type-5 stitching for them, respectively.

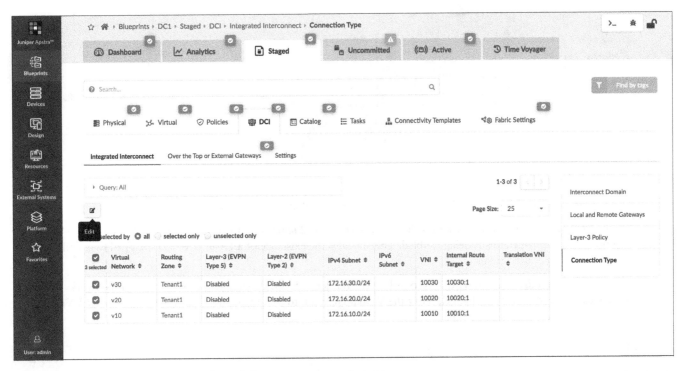

Figure 13-51   *List of Virtual Networks and their current state of stitching*

A list of all Virtual Networks that were selected to be edited is shown, along with sliders for both Type-2 and Type-5 stitching. These sliders are used to enable or disable Type-2 and Type-5 stitching per Virtual Network, as shown in Figure 13-52. In this case, Virtual Networks v20 and v30 are enabled for Type-5 stitching, and Virtual Network v10 is enabled for both Type-2 and Type-5 stitching. For any Virtual Network enabled for Type-2 stitching, you can provide an optional translation VNI.

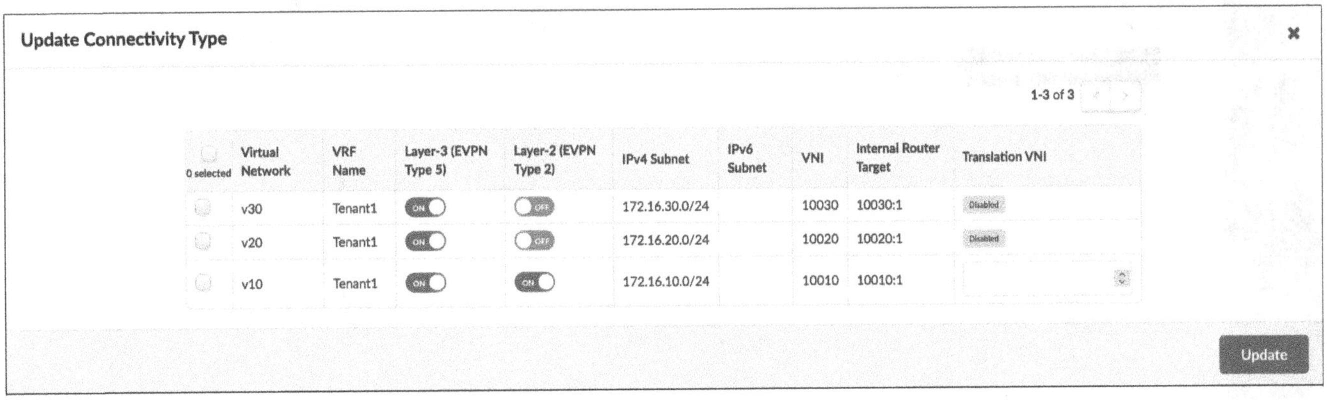

Figure 13-52   *Enabling Virtual Networks for Type-2 and/or Type-5 stitching*

Since the design goal is to enable Virtual Network v10 for Type-2 stitching, this presents a problem, shown in Figure 13-53 (where Virtual Network v10 is being enabled for Type-2 and Type-5 stitching individually). Any Virtual Network enabled for Type-2 stitching must also be mapped to the border leaf on which stitching is being enabled.

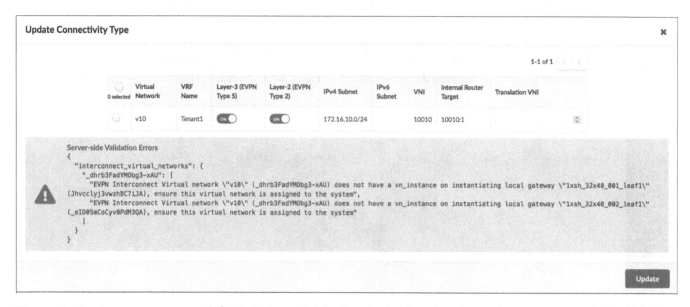

Figure 13-53 *Apstra error presented if VN v10 is enabled for Type-2 stitching when the VN does not exist on the border leafs*

This validation check exists because any VNI that needs to be Type-2 stitched must be configured within the MAC-VRF of the border leafs on which this is being enabled. This includes the existence of a Layer 2 VLAN, mapped to a VNI and a corresponding Layer 3 IRB interface.

To fix this issue, you must add this Virtual Network to the border leafs. To do so, navigate to the Virtual Networks option on the Virtual tab under the Staged panel, select the Virtual Network to be edited, and click the *Assign selected VXLAN networks* button, shown in Figure 13-54.

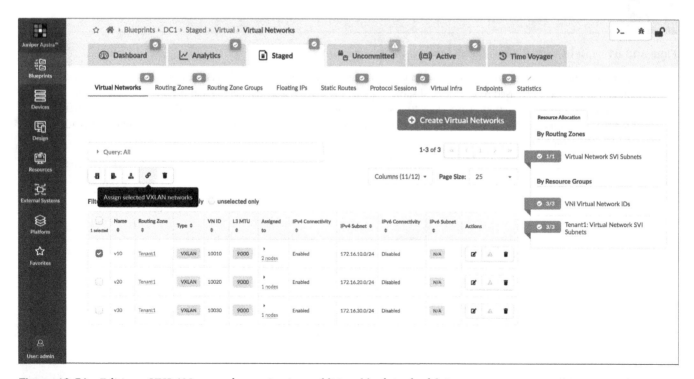

Figure 13-54 *Editing a VXLAN network to assign it to additional leafs in the fabric*

You can now select any additional leafs to which this Virtual Network must be assigned, either individually or in bulk, as shown in Figure 13-55.

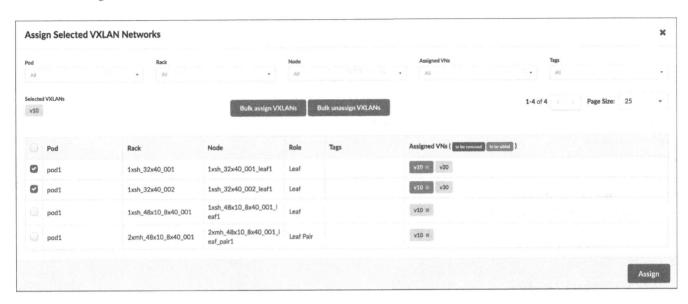

Figure 13-55 *Assigning Virtual Network v10 to additional leafs in bulk*

With this done, Virtual Network v10 is enabled for Type-2 stitching, and these changes can be committed in Apstra, which pushes the rendered incremental configuration to the border leafs.

Considering leaf4 as an example, the IP VRF (named Tenant1) is configured with the new *interconnect* configuration hierarchy and the interconnect Route Target of 5000:5000, as shown in Example 13-20.

Example 13-20 **interconnect** *stanza configured under the IP VRF Tenant1*

```
root@1xsh-32x40-001-leaf1# show routing-instances Tenant1
instance-type vrf;
routing-options {
    graceful-restart;
    multipath;
    auto-export;
}
protocols {
    evpn {
        irb-symmetric-routing {
            vni 10500;
        }
        interconnect {
            vrf-target target:5000:5000;
            route-distinguisher 192.0.2.2:65533;
        }
        ip-prefix-routes {
            advertise direct-nexthop;
            encapsulation vxlan;
            vni 10500;
            export BGP-AOS-Policy-Tenant1;
        }
```

```
        }
    }


*snip*
```

In addition, the MAC-VRF is also configured with an *interconnect* configuration hierarchy, as shown in Example 13-21.

Example 13-21   interconnect *stanza configured under the MAC VRF Tenant1*

```
root@1xsh-32x40-001-leaf1# show routing-instances evpn-1
instance-type mac-vrf;
protocols {
    evpn {
        encapsulation vxlan;
        default-gateway do-not-advertise;
        duplicate-mac-detection {
            auto-recovery-time 9;
        }
        extended-vni-list all;
        interconnect {
            vrf-target target:1:2;
            route-distinguisher 192.0.2.2:65533;
            esi {
                00:02:ff:00:00:00:01:00:00:01;
                all-active;
            }
            interconnected-vni-list 10010;
        }
        vni-options {
            vni 10010 {
                vrf-target target:10010:1;
            }
            vni 10020 {
                vrf-target target:10020:1;
            }
        }
    }
}


*snip*
```

A new BGP group, corresponding to the remote EVPN peers for Integrated Interconnect, is configured with import and export policies that control what routes are exchanged between the two data centers over the DCI, highlighted in Example 13-22.

Example 13-22   *BGP group created for remote EVPN peers*

```
root@1xsh-32x40-001-leaf1# show protocols bgp group evpn-gw
type external;
multihop {
    ttl 30;
    no-nexthop-change;
}
```

```
multipath {
    multiple-as;
}
neighbor 192.0.2.14 {
    description facing_dc2-1xsh-32x100-001-leaf1-evpn-gateway;
    local-address 192.0.2.2;
    import ( EVPN_GW_IN );
    family evpn {
        signaling;
    }
    export ( EVPN_GW_OUT && EVPN_EXPORT );
    peer-as 65426;
}
vpn-apply-export;
```

The export policy does the following (in order):

- Rejects routes from being readvertised that were received over the DCI by validating them against a regex-based BGP community value.

- Permits EVPN routes with a Route Target of 1:2 (corresponding to the interconnect Route Target in the MAC-VRF) and removes all other local fabric communities from the route, before advertising it out via BGP EVPN.

- Permits EVPN routes with a Route Target of 5000:5000 (corresponding to the interconnect Route Target in the IP VRF) and removes all other local fabric communities from the route, before advertising it out via BGP EVPN. The routes are also validated against a route-filter that allows only the subnets corresponding to the Virtual Networks that were enabled by the operator for Type-5 stitching.

- Rejects any other EVPN routes.

This export policy is shown Example 13-23.

Example 13-23 *Export policy for remote BGP EVPN DCI peers*

```
root@1xsh-32x40-001-leaf1# show policy-options policy-statement EVPN_GW_OUT
term EVPN_GW_OUT-10 {
    from {
        family evpn;
        community EVPN_GW_OUT;
    }
    then reject;
}
term EVPN_GW_OUT-20 {
    from {
        family evpn;
        community EVPN_DCI_L2_TARGET;
    }
    then {
        community delete FABRIC_COMMUNITIES;
        accept;
    }
}
term EVPN_GW_OUT-40 {
    from {
```

```
        family evpn;
        community EVPN_DCI_L3_TARGET_Tenant1;
        route-filter-list EVPN_DCI_L3_OUT-Tenant1-DCI-Routing-Policy;
    }
    then {
        community delete FABRIC_COMMUNITIES;
        accept;
    }
}
term EVPN_GW_OUT-50 {
    from family evpn;
    then reject;
}


root@1xsh-32x40-001-leaf1# show policy-options community EVPN_DCI_L2_TARGET
members target:1:2;


root@1xsh-32x40-001-leaf1# show policy-options community EVPN_DCI_L3_TARGET_Tenant1
members target:5000:5000;


root@1xsh-32x40-001-leaf1# show policy-options route-filter-list EVPN_DCI_L3_OUT-Tenant1-DCI-Routing-Policy
172.16.10.0/24 upto /32;
172.16.20.0/24 upto /32;
172.16.30.0/24 upto /32;
192.0.2.7/32 exact;
192.0.2.8/30 upto /32;
```

The import policy does the following (in order):

- Accepts received BGP EVPN routes with a Route Target of 1:2 and adds the BGP no-advertise community to them, ensuring these routes are not advertised to any other BGP peer. This Route Target matches the Layer 2 interconnect Route Target, corresponding to the MAC-VRF.

- Accepts received BGP EVPN routes with a Route Target of 5000:5000 and adds a BGP community that is used to prevent these routes from being advertised back to the originating data center. This Route Target matches the Layer 3 interconnect Route Target, corresponding to the IP VRF.

- Rejects all other routes.

This import policy is shown in Example 13-24.

Example 13-24 *Import policy for remote BGP EVPN DCI peers*

```
root@1xsh-32x40-001-leaf1# show policy-options policy-statement EVPN_GW_IN
term EVPN_GW_IN-10 {
    from {
        family evpn;
        community EVPN_DCI_L2_TARGET;
    }
    then {
        community add EVPN_GW_IN;
        community add NO_ADVERTISE;
```

```
        accept;
    }
}
term EVPN_GW_IN-30 {
    from {
        family evpn;
        community EVPN_DCI_L3_TARGET_Tenant1;
        route-filter-list EVPN_DCI_L3_IN-Tenant1-DCI-Routing-Policy;
    }
    then {
        community add EVPN_GW_IN;
        accept;
    }
}
term EVPN_GW_IN-40 {
    from family evpn;
    then reject;
}
```

Configuring DC2 for Integrated Interconnect

With DC1 configured for Integrated Interconnect and all changes committed in Apstra, DC2 can now be configured in the same way. First, the MSB for the interconnect ESI auto-generation must be unique, and it is set to a numeric value of 4 for DC2, as shown in Figure 13-56.

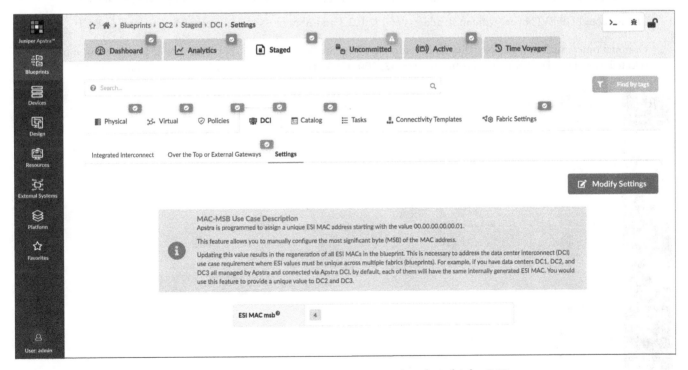

Figure 13-56 *MSB for auto-generation of interconnect ESI set to a numeric value of 4 for DC2*

The interconnect domain, once configured, displays a unique MAC address that will be used for auto-generating the interconnect ESI, as shown in Figure 13-57. The interconnect Route Target matches DC1's interconnect Route Target of 1:2.

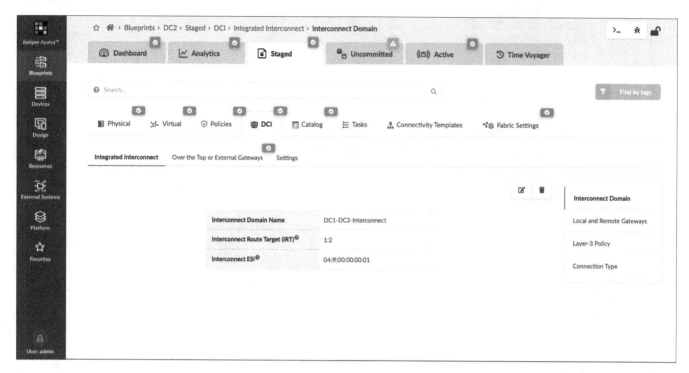

Figure 13-57   *Interconnect domain for DC2*

Next, remote BGP EVPN peers are defined. For DC2, these will be the two border leafs on DC1, configured as follows:

- Remote BGP EVPN peer with an IP address of 192.0.2.2 and ASN of 65421, corresponding to leaf4 in DC1

- Remote BGP EVPN peer with an IP address of 192.0.2.3 and ASN of 65422, corresponding to leaf5 in DC1

Optional timers such as TTL, keepalive, and hold-time timers are not configured. For both remote peers, the local peer is selected as leaf3 in DC2, with the hostname 1xsh-32x100-001-leaf1. A summary of this is shown in Figure 13-58.

Figure 13-58   *Remote BGP EVPN peers configured for Integrated Interconnect in DC2*

Like DCI, the IP VRF Tenant1 is enabled for Type-5 stitching. The Virtual Network v10 is enabled for both Type-2 and Type-5 stitching, while Virtual Networks v40 and v50 are enabled for Type-5 stitching only. A summary of this is shown in Figure 13-59.

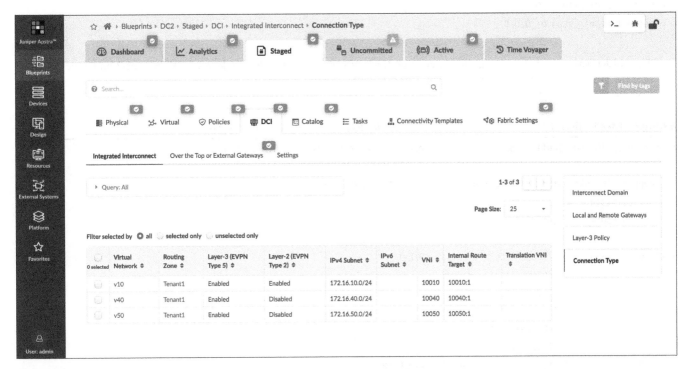

Figure 13-59 *Summary of Virtual Networks enabled for Type-2 and/or Type-5 stitching in DC2*

Validating Integrated Interconnect

With Integrated Interconnect fully configured and committed on DC2 as well, BGP EVPN peers for the DCI are in an Established state, as shown in Example 13-25 from the perspective of leaf3 in DC2.

Example 13-25 *State of BGP EVPN DCI peers from the perspective of leaf3 in DC2*

```
root@1xsh-32x100-001-leaf1> show bgp summary group evpn-gw

Warning: License key missing; requires 'bgp' license

Threading mode: BGP I/O
Default eBGP mode: advertise - accept, receive - accept
Groups: 4 Peers: 7 Down peers: 0
Table          Tot Paths  Act Paths Suppressed    History Damp State    Pending
inet.0
                    23         17         0          0         0           0
bgp.evpn.0
                    58         46         0          0         0           0
Peer                 AS      InPkt     OutPkt    OutQ   Flaps Last Up/Dwn State|#Active/Received/Accepted/Damped...
192.0.2.2         65421      1465       1460       0       0   11:01:29 Establ
  bgp.evpn.0: 18/19/19/0
  Tenant1.evpn.0: 12/12/12/0
  evpn-1.evpn.0: 9/10/10/0
  __default_evpn__.evpn.0: 0/0/0/0
```

```
192.0.2.3              65422      1464      1458     0     0    11:01:25 Establ
  bgp.evpn.0: 18/19/19/0
  Tenant1.evpn.0: 12/12/12/0
  evpn-1.evpn.0: 9/10/10/0
  __default_evpn__.evpn.0: 0/0/0/0
```

The border leafs, enabled for Integrated Interconnect, are now re-originating locally learned EVPN Type-2 and Type-5 routes into the DCI. Taking leaf3 again as an example, this is confirmed in Example 13-26, which shows the routes are originated with the interconnect Route Distinguisher.

Example 13-26   *BGP EVPN routes re-originated by border leaf, leaf3, in DC2, toward DCI*

```
root@1xsh-32x100-001-leaf1> show route table bgp.evpn.0 match-prefix *192.0.2.14:65533*

bgp.evpn.0: 86 destinations, 98 routes (86 active, 0 holddown, 0 hidden)
Restart Complete
+ = Active Route, - = Last Active, * = Both

1:192.0.2.14:65533::04ff00000001000001::0/192 AD/EVI
                *[EVPN/170] 11:14:38
                    Indirect
2:192.0.2.14:65533::10010::00:1c:73:00:00:01/304 MAC/IP
                *[EVPN/170] 11:14:34
                    Indirect
2:192.0.2.14:65533::10010::f0:4b:3a:b9:80:ff/304 MAC/IP
                *[EVPN/170] 11:14:39
                    Indirect
2:192.0.2.14:65533::10010::00:1c:73:00:00:01::172.16.10.254/304 MAC/IP
                *[EVPN/170] 11:14:34
                    Indirect
2:192.0.2.14:65533::10010::f0:4b:3a:b9:80:ff::172.16.10.5/304 MAC/IP
                *[EVPN/170] 11:14:39
                    Indirect
3:192.0.2.14:65533::10010::192.0.2.14/248 IM
                *[EVPN/170] 11:14:39
                    Indirect
5:192.0.2.14:65533::0::172.16.10.0::24/248
                *[EVPN/170] 11:14:40
                    Fictitious
5:192.0.2.14:65533::0::172.16.40.0::24/248
                *[EVPN/170] 11:14:40
                    Fictitious
5:192.0.2.14:65533::0::172.16.50.0::24/248
                *[EVPN/170] 11:14:40
                    Fictitious

*snip*
```

With both data centers deployed with Integrated Interconnect and BGP EVPN routes exchanged over this DCI, host h1 in DC1 can communicate with all hosts across both data centers, as shown in Example 13-27.

Example 13-27 *Host h1's reachability to all hosts across both DCs*

```
root@h1> ping 172.16.10.2
PING 172.16.10.2 (172.16.10.2): 56 data bytes
64 bytes from 172.16.10.2: icmp_seq=0 ttl=64 time=0.948 ms
64 bytes from 172.16.10.2: icmp_seq=1 ttl=64 time=0.872 ms
64 bytes from 172.16.10.2: icmp_seq=2 ttl=64 time=0.869 ms
64 bytes from 172.16.10.2: icmp_seq=3 ttl=64 time=0.925 ms
^C
--- 172.16.10.2 ping statistics ---
4 packets transmitted, 4 packets received, 0% packet loss
round-trip min/avg/max/stddev = 0.869/0.903/0.948/0.034 ms


root@h1> ping 172.16.20.3
PING 172.16.20.3 (172.16.20.3): 56 data bytes
64 bytes from 172.16.20.3: icmp_seq=0 ttl=62 time=0.913 ms
64 bytes from 172.16.20.3: icmp_seq=1 ttl=62 time=85.423 ms
64 bytes from 172.16.20.3: icmp_seq=2 ttl=62 time=12.787 ms
64 bytes from 172.16.20.3: icmp_seq=3 ttl=62 time=0.749 ms
^C
--- 172.16.20.3 ping statistics ---
4 packets transmitted, 4 packets received, 0% packet loss
round-trip min/avg/max/stddev = 0.749/24.968/85.423/35.243 ms


root@h1> ping 172.16.30.4
PING 172.16.30.4 (172.16.30.4): 56 data bytes
64 bytes from 172.16.30.4: icmp_seq=0 ttl=62 time=105.890 ms
64 bytes from 172.16.30.4: icmp_seq=1 ttl=62 time=0.841 ms
64 bytes from 172.16.30.4: icmp_seq=2 ttl=62 time=0.865 ms
64 bytes from 172.16.30.4: icmp_seq=3 ttl=62 time=0.861 ms
^C
--- 172.16.30.4 ping statistics ---
4 packets transmitted, 4 packets received, 0% packet loss
round-trip min/avg/max/stddev = 0.841/27.114/105.890/45.481 ms


root@h1> ping 172.16.10.5
PING 172.16.10.5 (172.16.10.5): 56 data bytes
64 bytes from 172.16.10.5: icmp_seq=0 ttl=64 time=38.961 ms
64 bytes from 172.16.10.5: icmp_seq=1 ttl=64 time=0.902 ms
64 bytes from 172.16.10.5: icmp_seq=2 ttl=64 time=0.868 ms
64 bytes from 172.16.10.5: icmp_seq=3 ttl=64 time=7.211 ms
^C
--- 172.16.10.5 ping statistics ---
4 packets transmitted, 4 packets received, 0% packet loss
round-trip min/avg/max/stddev = 0.868/11.986/38.961/15.787 ms


root@h1> ping 172.16.40.6
PING 172.16.40.6 (172.16.40.6): 56 data bytes
64 bytes from 172.16.40.6: icmp_seq=0 ttl=60 time=50.115 ms
64 bytes from 172.16.40.6: icmp_seq=1 ttl=60 time=0.887 ms
```

```
64 bytes from 172.16.40.6: icmp_seq=2 ttl=60 time=0.911 ms
64 bytes from 172.16.40.6: icmp_seq=3 ttl=60 time=0.931 ms
^C
--- 172.16.40.6 ping statistics ---
4 packets transmitted, 4 packets received, 0% packet loss
round-trip min/avg/max/stddev = 0.887/13.211/50.115/21.307 ms

root@h1> ping 172.16.50.7
PING 172.16.50.7 (172.16.50.7): 56 data bytes
64 bytes from 172.16.50.7: icmp_seq=0 ttl=61 time=0.994 ms
64 bytes from 172.16.50.7: icmp_seq=1 ttl=61 time=0.897 ms
64 bytes from 172.16.50.7: icmp_seq=2 ttl=61 time=85.521 ms
64 bytes from 172.16.50.7: icmp_seq=3 ttl=61 time=0.851 ms
^C
--- 172.16.50.7 ping statistics ---
4 packets transmitted, 4 packets received, 0% packet loss
round-trip min/avg/max/stddev = 0.851/22.066/85.521/36.636 ms
```

Summary

Using the building blocks of Apstra introduced in Chapter 12, this chapter took them a step further and introduced more advanced Apstra deployments. These included edge-routed bridging with a Symmetric IRB model of routing between VNIs and connecting two or more data centers with a DCI using one of two options: OTT DCI or Integrated Interconnect.

Building Virtual Fabrics with vJunos, Containerlab, and Juniper Apstra

Virtual network topologies, also referred to as *digital twins* (depending on the purpose they serve), are becoming increasingly popular, and rightly so. Digital twins can help an organization plan, build, and orchestrate entire networks virtually, prior to deploying in production, which can range from complete brownfield or greenfield deployments to small incremental changes in existing network infrastructure. These virtual network topologies have paved the way for functional and feature testing, demonstrating how a specific deployment would look and feel, and providing familiarity with the protocols in use and the interactions between them.

Digital twins are also often used to stand up complete virtual network infrastructures, mimicking production environments, integrated into CI/CD pipelines. Changes expected to go into production are first tested in the virtual infrastructure, passing through CI/CD pipelines, with pre-change and post-change validation checks at different stages. Based on the result, and operator intent, the change can then be pushed to production.

A virtual network infrastructure also provides a great medium for education—it is a no-risk medium for learning network protocols and understanding their intricacies and complexities, as well as different deployment models, across all networking domains. More importantly, a virtual network infrastructure enables a learner to *learn by breaking*, which arguably is one of the best ways to learn.

This chapter explores how virtual data center fabrics can be deployed using vJunos-switch and Containerlab:

- Juniper Networks has built two new VM-based virtual software offerings, often clumped together and called *vJunos*. Specifically, these are *vJunos-switch*, mimicking the Junos OS, and *vJunosEvolved*, mimicking Junos Evolved. They are free-to-download software images, available in the qcow2 virtual disk format.

- Containerlab is an open-source network emulation tool that offers users the ability to deploy virtual network operating systems as containers, connected via *veth* pairs, to build small, medium, or large-scale network topologies for feature and functional testing. Containerlab supports both native containers and VM-based virtual disk images, which can be packaged inside a Docker container. To deploy a virtual topology, Containerlab requires a topology file, written in a simple, declarative format using YAML. This topology file is essentially a description of the nodes in the network and the interconnections between them. While this chapter uses Containerlab as the chosen emulation tool to deploy virtual network operating systems, alternate tools such as EVE-NG can be used as well.

In addition, this chapter describes how to orchestrate and maintain the entire virtual fabric with Juniper Apstra.

Installing Containerlab and Building the vJunos-switch Image

You can find instructions for installing Containerlab on the Containerlab project's Quick Start page: https://containerlab.dev/quickstart/. Example 14-1 demonstrates how Containerlab can be installed on a bare-metal server running the Ubuntu 22.04 LTS operating system.

Example 14-1   *Containerlab installation on a bare-metal server running Ubuntu 22.04 LTS*

```
root@server1:~# bash -c "$(curl -sL https://get.containerlab.dev)"
Downloading https://github.com/srl-labs/containerlab/releases/download/v0.48.4/containerlab_0.48.4_linux_amd64.deb
Preparing to install containerlab 0.48.4 from package
Selecting previously unselected package containerlab.
(Reading database ... 128537 files and directories currently installed.)
Preparing to unpack .../containerlab_0.48.4_linux_amd64.deb ...
Unpacking containerlab (0.48.4) ...
Setting up containerlab (0.48.4) ...

  ___ __ _  _ ___ _  __ _ __ _ ___ __ _  _   _
 / __/ _ \| \ | |_  _|/ \ |_ _| \ | | ___| _ \ | _ _| |_
| | | | | | \| | | | / _ \ | || \ | | _| | |_) | | |/ _` | '_ \
| |__| |_| | |\  | | |/ ___ \ | || |\  | | |__| _ <| | (_| | |_) |
 _____/|_| \_| |_/_/   \_\___|_| \_|_____|_| \_\_|\__,_|_.__/

      version: 0.48.4
       commit: 6327f9b3
         date: 2023-11-23T12:23:04Z
       source: https://github.com/srl-labs/containerlab
    rel. notes: https://containerlab.dev/rn/0.48/#0484
```

To build VM-based containers (like vJunos-switch), Containerlab uses a fork of the project *vrnetlab*, which was built to run network operating systems inside a Docker container. Maintainers of Containerlab enhanced this project by adding functionality to create a data path between the VMs in a container-native way. Thus, to build the vJunos-switch image for Containerlab, this fork of vrnetlab must be downloaded locally first, as shown in Example 14-2.

Example 14-2   *Cloning fork of vrnetlab locally*

```
root@server1:~# git clone https://github.com/hellt/vrnetlab/
Cloning into 'vrnetlab'...
remote: Enumerating objects: 4139, done.
remote: Counting objects: 100% (1129/1129), done.
remote: Compressing objects: 100% (268/268), done.
remote: Total 4139 (delta 951), reused 934 (delta 861), pack-reused 3010
Receiving objects: 100% (4139/4139), 1.97 MiB | 3.95 MiB/s, done.
Resolving deltas: 100% (2520/2520), done.
```

This directory contains many subdirectories corresponding to different network operating systems (both VM-based and native containers), including one for vJunos-switch, highlighted in Example 14-3.

Example 14-3   *Listing directory of forked vrnetlab project*

```
root@server1:~# cd vrnetlab/
root@server1:~/vrnetlab# ls -l
total 144
-rw-r--r-- 1 root root   94 Nov 23 13:44 CODE_OF_CONDUCT.md
-rw-r--r-- 1 root root  706 Nov 23 13:44 CONTRIBUTING.md
-rw-r--r-- 1 root root 1109 Nov 23 13:44 LICENSE
-rw-r--r-- 1 root root  342 Nov 23 13:44 Makefile
-rw-r--r-- 1 root root 4013 Nov 23 13:44 README.md
drwxr-xr-x 3 root root 4096 Nov 23 13:44 aoscx
```

```
drwxr-xr-x 2 root root 4096 Nov 23 13:44 ci-builder-image
drwxr-xr-x 2 root root 4096 Nov 23 13:44 common
drwxr-xr-x 3 root root 4096 Nov 23 13:44 config-engine-lite
drwxr-xr-x 3 root root 4096 Nov 23 13:44 csr
drwxr-xr-x 3 root root 4096 Nov 23 13:44 ftosv
-rwxr-xr-x 1 root root 5210 Nov 23 13:44 git-lfs-repo.sh
-rw-r--r-- 1 root root 3158 Nov 23 13:44 makefile-install.include
-rw-r--r-- 1 root root  370 Nov 23 13:44 makefile-sanity.include
-rw-r--r-- 1 root root 1898 Nov 23 13:44 makefile.include
drwxr-xr-x 3 root root 4096 Nov 23 13:44 n9kv
drwxr-xr-x 3 root root 4096 Nov 23 13:44 nxos
drwxr-xr-x 3 root root 4096 Nov 23 13:44 ocnos
drwxr-xr-x 3 root root 4096 Nov 23 13:44 openwrt
drwxr-xr-x 3 root root 4096 Nov 23 13:44 pan
drwxr-xr-x 3 root root 4096 Nov 23 13:44 routeros
drwxr-xr-x 3 root root 4096 Nov 23 13:44 sros
drwxr-xr-x 2 root root 4096 Nov 23 13:44 topology-machine
drwxr-xr-x 3 root root 4096 Nov 23 13:44 veos
drwxr-xr-x 3 root root 4096 Nov 23 13:44 vjunosswitch
drwxr-xr-x 3 root root 4096 Nov 23 13:44 vmx
drwxr-xr-x 3 root root 4096 Nov 23 13:44 vqfx
drwxr-xr-x 3 root root 4096 Nov 23 13:44 vr-bgp
drwxr-xr-x 2 root root 4096 Nov 23 13:44 vr-xcon
-rw-r--r-- 1 root root 1135 Nov 23 13:44 vrnetlab.sh
drwxr-xr-x 3 root root 4096 Nov 23 13:44 vrp
drwxr-xr-x 3 root root 4096 Nov 23 13:44 vsr1000
drwxr-xr-x 3 root root 4096 Nov 23 13:44 vsrx
drwxr-xr-x 3 root root 4096 Nov 23 13:44 xrv
drwxr-xr-x 3 root root 4096 Nov 23 13:44 xrv9k
```

The vJunos-switch qcow2 image must be present in this directory. Once it is there, the **make** command can be run to build the corresponding Docker container for it. The *Makefile* and the *Dockerfile* (within the *docker* directory) are used to build this image. A snippet of the image build process is shown in Example 14-4.

Example 14-4 *Building the vJunos-switch docker container*

```
root@server1:~/vrnetlab/vjunosswitch# ls -l
total 1793176
-rw-r--r-- 1 root root        346 Nov 23 13:44 Makefile
-rw-r--r-- 1 root root        513 Nov 23 13:44 README.md
drwxr-xr-x 2 root root       4096 Nov 23 13:44 docker
-rwxr-xr-x 1 root root 1836195840 Nov 23 14:02 vjunos-switch-23.2R1.14.qcow2

root@server1:~/vrnetlab/vjunosswitch# make
for IMAGE in vjunos-switch-23.2R1.14.qcow2; do \
echo "Making $IMAGE"; \
make IMAGE=$IMAGE docker-build; \
done
Making vjunos-switch-23.2R1.14.qcow2
make[1]: Entering directory '/root/vrnetlab/vjunosswitch'
```

```
rm -f docker/*.qcow2* docker/*.tgz* docker/*.vmdk* docker/*.iso
Building docker image using vjunos-switch-23.2R1.14.qcow2 as vrnetlab/vr-vjunosswitch:23.2R1.14
cp ../common/* docker/
make IMAGE=$IMAGE docker-build-image-copy
make[2]: Entering directory '/root/vrnetlab/vjunosswitch'
cp vjunos-switch-23.2R1.14.qcow2* docker/
make[2]: Leaving directory '/root/vrnetlab/vjunosswitch'
(cd docker; docker build --build-arg http_proxy= --build-arg https_proxy= --build-arg IMAGE=vjunos-switch-23.2R1.14.qcow2
-t vrnetlab/vr-vjunosswitch:23.2R1.14 .)
Sending build context to Docker daemon  1.836GB
Step 1/11 : FROM ubuntu:20.04
20.04: Pulling from library/ubuntu
96d54c3075c9: Pull complete
Digest: sha256:ed4a42283d9943135ed87d4ee34e542f7f5ad9ecf2f244870e23122f703f91c2
Status: Downloaded newer image for ubuntu:20.04
 ---> bf40b7bc7a11
Step 2/11 : ENV DEBIAN_FRONTEND=noninteractive
 ---> Running in 7efa4e65d95d
Removing intermediate container 7efa4e65d95d
 ---> 8a3cace494d3
Step 3/11 : RUN apt-get update -qy && apt-get upgrade -qy && apt-get install -y    dosfstools    bridge-utils
iproute2    python3-ipy    socat    qemu-kvm && rm -rf /var/lib/apt/lists/*
 ---> Running in f95d2fbc66e7
Get:1 http://security.ubuntu.com/ubuntu focal-security InRelease [114 kB]
Get:2 http://security.ubuntu.com/ubuntu focal-security/universe amd64 Packages [1130 kB]
Get:3 http://archive.ubuntu.com/ubuntu focal InRelease [265 kB]
Get:4 http://security.ubuntu.com/ubuntu focal-security/multiverse amd64 Packages [29.3 kB]
Get:5 http://security.ubuntu.com/ubuntu focal-security/restricted amd64 Packages [3057 kB]
Get:6 http://security.ubuntu.com/ubuntu focal-security/main amd64 Packages [3221 kB]
Get:7 http://archive.ubuntu.com/ubuntu focal-updates InRelease [114 kB]
Get:8 http://archive.ubuntu.com/ubuntu focal-backports InRelease [108 kB]
Get:9 http://archive.ubuntu.com/ubuntu focal/multiverse amd64 Packages [177 kB]
Get:10 http://archive.ubuntu.com/ubuntu focal/universe amd64 Packages [11.3 MB]
Get:11 http://archive.ubuntu.com/ubuntu focal/restricted amd64 Packages [33.4 kB]
Get:12 http://archive.ubuntu.com/ubuntu focal/main amd64 Packages [1275 kB]
Get:13 http://archive.ubuntu.com/ubuntu focal-updates/restricted amd64 Packages [3206 kB]
Get:14 http://archive.ubuntu.com/ubuntu focal-updates/multiverse amd64 Packages [32.0 kB]
Get:15 http://archive.ubuntu.com/ubuntu focal-updates/universe amd64 Packages [1435 kB]
Get:16 http://archive.ubuntu.com/ubuntu focal-updates/main amd64 Packages [3709 kB]
Get:17 http://archive.ubuntu.com/ubuntu focal-backports/main amd64 Packages [55.2 kB]
Get:18 http://archive.ubuntu.com/ubuntu focal-backports/universe amd64 Packages [28.6 kB]


*snip*


Step 4/11 : ARG IMAGE
 ---> Running in 28c79917e33e
Removing intermediate container 28c79917e33e
 ---> eccff7cf2d79
```

```
Step 5/11 : COPY $TMAGE* /
 ---> 2dcb6e83bceb
Step 6/11 : COPY init.conf /
 ---> 7f3b5c4b63da
Step 7/11 : COPY make-config.sh /
 ---> 20fb09467121
Step 8/11 : COPY *.py /
 ---> 2589c5c03ab6
Step 9/11 : EXPOSE 22 161/udp 830 5000 10000-10099 57400
 ---> Running in 3009ab8211c7
Removing intermediate container 3009ab8211c7
 ---> d5a2b8e876fa
Step 10/11 : HEALTHCHECK CMD ["/healthcheck.py"]
 ---> Running in 853c4490e5c3
Removing intermediate container 853c4490e5c3
 ---> 9faf0a920abb
Step 11/11 : ENTRYPOINT ["/launch.py"]
 ---> Running in f3ae2df082de
Removing intermediate container f3ae2df082de
 ---> 7bd7416a30b8
Successfully built 7bd7416a30b8
Successfully tagged vrnetlab/vr-vjunosswitch:23.2R1.14
make[1]: Leaving directory '/root/vrnetlab/vjunosswitch'
```

Once this process finishes, a new Docker container for vJunos-switch is available and can be verified by using the **docker images** command, as shown in Example 14-5. This container can now be used in a topology file for Containerlab.

Example 14-5 *All available docker containers, confirming presence of new vJunos-switch container*

```
root@server1:~/vrnetlab/vjunosswitch# docker images
REPOSITORY                TAG         IMAGE ID        CREATED           SIZE
vrnetlab/vr-vjunosswitch   23.2R1.14   7bd7416a30b8    About a minute ago  2.24GB
ubuntu                    20.04       bf40b7bc7a11    7 weeks ago       72.8MB
```

Instantiating a Virtual Topology with vJunos-switch and Containerlab

To demonstrate the instantiation of a virtual network topology with Containerlab and vJunos-switch, the topology file shown in Example 14-6 is used.

Example 14-6 *Containerlab topology file*

```
root@server1:/home/anindac/labs/ch14# cat ch14-topology.yml
name: ch14-topology
mgmt:
  bridge: virbr0
  ipv4-subnet: 192.168.122.0/24
topology:
  nodes:
    spine1:
          kind: vr-vjunosswitch
          image: vrnetlab/vr-vjunosswitch:23.2R1.14
```

```
        mgmt-ipv4: 192.168.122.101
        startup-config: spine1.cfg
  spine2:
        kind: vr-vjunosswitch
        image: vrnetlab/vr-vjunosswitch:23.2R1.14
        mgmt-ipv4: 192.168.122.102
        startup-config: spine2.cfg
  leaf1:
        kind: vr-vjunosswitch
        image: vrnetlab/vr-vjunosswitch:23.2R1.14
        mgmt-ipv4: 192.168.122.11
        startup-config: leaf1.cfg
  leaf2:
        kind: vr-vjunosswitch
        image: vrnetlab/vr-vjunosswitch:23.2R1.14
        mgmt-ipv4: 192.168.122.12
        startup-config: leaf2.cfg
  leaf3:
        kind: vr-vjunosswitch
        image: vrnetlab/vr-vjunosswitch:23.2R1.14
        mgmt-ipv4: 192.168.122.13
        startup-config: leaf3.cfg
  h1:
        kind: vr-vjunosswitch
        image: vrnetlab/vr-vjunosswitch:23.2R1.14
        mgmt-ipv4: 192.168.122.51
        startup-config: h1.cfg
  h2:
        kind: linux
        image: aninchat/host:v1
        mgmt-ipv4: 192.168.122.52
        exec:
          - sleep 5
          - sysctl -w net.ipv4.icmp_echo_ignore_broadcasts=0
          - ip route add 172.16.10.0/24 via 172.16.20.254
        binds:
          - hosts/h2_interfaces:/etc/network/interfaces
links:
      - endpoints: ["leaf1:eth1", "spine1:eth1"]
      - endpoints: ["leaf1:eth2", "spine2:eth1"]
      - endpoints: ["leaf2:eth1", "spine1:eth2"]
      - endpoints: ["leaf2:eth2", "spine2:eth2"]
      - endpoints: ["leaf3:eth1", "spine1:eth3"]
      - endpoints: ["leaf3:eth2", "spine2:eth3"]
      - endpoints: ["leaf1:eth3", "h1:eth1"]
      - endpoints: ["leaf2:eth3", "h1:eth2"]
      - endpoints: ["leaf3:eth3", "h2:eth1"]
```

This topology file does the following:

- The network is described under the *topology* key, using two main hierarchical keys: *nodes* and *links*. The *nodes* key describes the nodes in the network, their type, and the image to use. The *links* key describes the interconnections between the previously described nodes.

- This topology file creates five fabric nodes, namely spine1, spine2, leaf1, leaf2, and leaf3. The intention is to have leaf1 and leaf2 as an ESI LAG pair, connecting to host h1 multihomed to both the leafs, and then leaf3 connecting to a single-homed host h2.

- Each node uses a key called *kind* that Containerlab uses to determine the type of node it is (Containerlab uses well-defined naming conventions to determine the type of node). A second key called *image* points to the image to use.

- All nodes are assigned an IPv4 address statically, using the *mgmt-ipv4* key. These addresses are within the custom management subnet, defined with the *mgmt* key at the start of the file.

- All vJunos-switch nodes are passed a startup configuration to boot with, using the *startup-config* key. These configuration files exist in the same directory, and thus an absolute path is not provided.

- Host h2 uses the *binds* key to bind a statically configured interface file, present locally on the server, to the /etc/network/ interfaces file in the container. Also, using the *exec* key, additional commands are passed into the container, once it boots up, for execution.

An example of the startup configuration file used by a vJunos-switch node is shown in Example 14-7. This is essentially additional bootstrap configuration that is necessary for vJunos-switch devices to be onboarded into Apstra.

Example 14-7 *Startup configuration file for a vJunos-switch node*

```
root@server1:/home/anindac/labs/ch14# cat leaf1.cfg
system {
    commit synchronize;
    management-instance;
}
routing-instances {
    mgmt_junos {
        routing-options {
            static {
                route 0.0.0.0/0 next-hop 10.0.0.2;
            }
        }
    }
}
interfaces {
    fxp0 {
        unit 0 {
            family inet {
                address 192.168.122.11/24;
            }
        }
    }
}
```

The network topology can be deployed as shown in Example 14-8. This takes the topology file as an input and instantiates the virtual network, as described by the topology file. Alternatively, if a topology has already been deployed, it can be viewed using the **containerlab inspect -t** [*name of topology file*] command.

Example 14-8   *Deploying a virtual network topology using Containerlab*

```
root@server1:/home/anindac/labs/ch14# containerlab deploy -t ch14-topology.yml
INFO[0000] Containerlab v0.48.3 started
INFO[0000] Parsing & checking topology file: ch14-topology.yml
INFO[0000] Creating lab directory: /home/anindac/labs/ch14/clab-ch14-topology
INFO[0000] Creating container: "h2"
INFO[0000] Creating container: "leaf3"
INFO[0000] Creating container: "leaf2"
INFO[0000] Creating container: "spine2"
INFO[0000] Creating container: "leaf1"
INFO[0000] Creating container: "h1"
INFO[0000] Creating container: "spine1"
INFO[0001] Creating link: leaf2:eth2 <--> spine2:eth2
INFO[0001] Creating link: leaf1:eth2 <--> spine2:eth1
INFO[0001] Creating link: leaf3:eth2 <--> spine2:eth3
INFO[0001] Creating link: leaf1:eth1 <--> spine1:eth1
INFO[0001] Creating link: leaf1:eth3 <--> h1:eth1
INFO[0002] Creating link: leaf3:eth3 <--> h2:eth1
INFO[0002] Creating link: leaf2:eth1 <--> spine1:eth2
INFO[0002] Creating link: leaf2:eth3 <--> h1:eth2
INFO[0002] Creating link: leaf3:eth1 <--> spine1:eth3
INFO[0003] Adding containerlab host entries to /etc/hosts file
INFO[0003] Adding ssh config for containerlab nodes
INFO[0008] Executed command "sleep 5" on the node "h2". stdout:
INFO[0008] Executed command "sysctl -w net.ipv4.icmp_echo_ignore_broadcasts=0" on the node "h2". stdout:
net.ipv4.icmp_echo_ignore_broadcasts = 0
INFO[0008] Executed command "ip route add 172.16.10.0/24 via 172.16.20.254" on the node "h2". stdout:
```

#	Name	Container ID	Image	Kind	State	IPv4 Address	IPv6 Address
1	clab-ch14-topology-h1	00d49972fce5	vrnetlab/vr-vjunosswitch:23.2R1.14	vr-vjunosswitch	running	192.168.122.51/24	N/A
2	clab-ch14-topology-h2	16d2236c0fc6	aninchat/host:v1	linux	running	192.168.122.52/24	N/A
3	clab-ch14-topology-leaf1	4b3fce0ab712	vrnetlab/vr-vjunosswitch:23.2R1.14	vr-vjunosswitch	running	192.168.122.11/24	N/A
4	clab-ch14-topology-leaf2	34bdb5483748	vrnetlab/vr-vjunosswitch:23.2R1.14	vr-vjunosswitch	running	192.168.122.12/24	N/A
5	clab-ch14-topology-leaf3	e7f2c0391211	vrnetlab/vr-vjunosswitch:23.2R1.14	vr-vjunosswitch	running	192.168.122.13/24	N/A
6	clab-ch14-topology-spine1	db5696f4b40d	vrnetlab/vr-vjunosswitch:23.2R1.14	vr-vjunosswitch	running	192.168.122.101/24	N/A
7	clab-ch14-topology-spine2	4aca6a3e0640	vrnetlab/vr-vjunosswitch:23.2R1.14	vr-vjunosswitch	running	192.168.122.102/24	N/A

Visually, this Containerlab deployed network topology can be represented as shown in Figure 14-1.

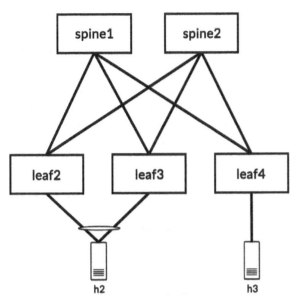

Figure 14-1 *Visual representation of virtual network topology deployed by Containerlab*

Orchestrating a Virtual Fabric with Apstra

With the virtual network topology deployed by Containerlab in the previous subsection, the vJunos-switch fabric nodes can now be onboarded in Apstra.

From Apstra 4.2.0, a predefined Device Profile exists for vJunos-switch, as shown in Figure 14-2. Prior to this release, the Device Profile must be manually created by the operator to successfully onboard these virtual devices.

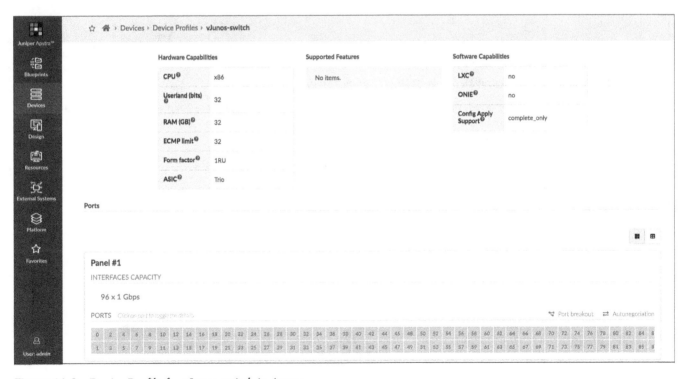

Figure 14-2 *Device Profile for vJunos-switch in Apstra*

However, there are no predefined Logical Devices or Interface Maps that match this Device Profile, and thus this is a good opportunity to demonstrate how you can create these constructs manually.

Logical Devices are created by defining port groups. A port group, as the name suggests, is a grouping of ports with the same speed and the same kind of devices they are allowed to connect to. These could be superspines, spines, leafs, access switches, generic systems, peer switches (for MLAG, as an example), or simply unused. This grouping allows for inherent conformance to operator intent on the role and positioning of a device in a data center fabric.

In the case of vJunos-switch, the Logical Device needs to be a grouping of 96 × 1G ports. Since these devices can be spines or leafs (or superspines, as explored in the next chapter), they are allowed to be connected to superspines, spines, leafs, and generic systems, as shown in Figure 14-3, which also shows a port group of 96 ports is created (not shown is the Logical Device name, *vJunos-LD*). The port group is saved by clicking the Create Port Group button.

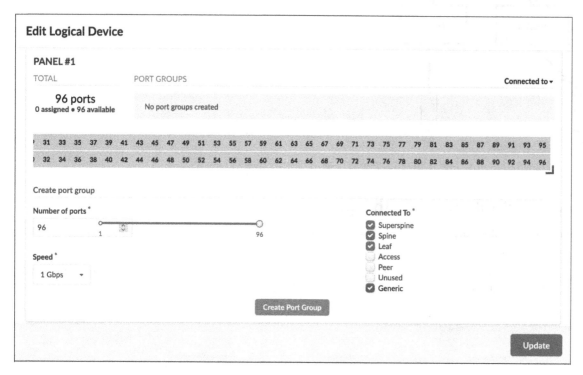

Figure 14-3   *Creating a new Logical Device in Apstra for vJunos-switch*

Once the port group intent is saved, the Logical Device can be created. Next, an Interface Map must be created that ties together the Logical Device and the Device Profile. When creating an Interface Map, you are required to choose a Logical Device and a Device Profile first, as shown in Figure 14-4.

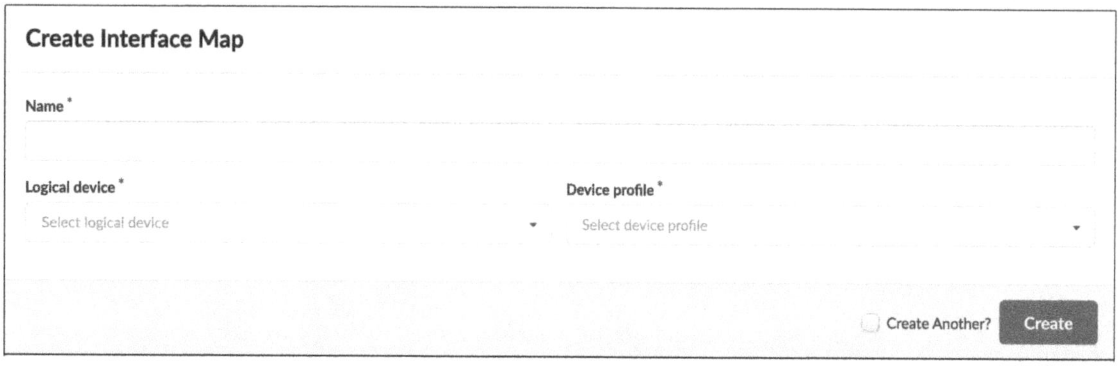

Figure 14-4   *Creating an Interface Map by first choosing a Logical Device and a Device Profile*

Once these are chosen, Apstra displays the port groups for the Logical Device that was selected. You must then map interfaces from the Device Profile to the Logical Device. To do so, expand the Device Profile interfaces by clicking the *Select interfaces* option, and then select all necessary ports (all 96 ports, in this case), as shown in Figure 14-5.

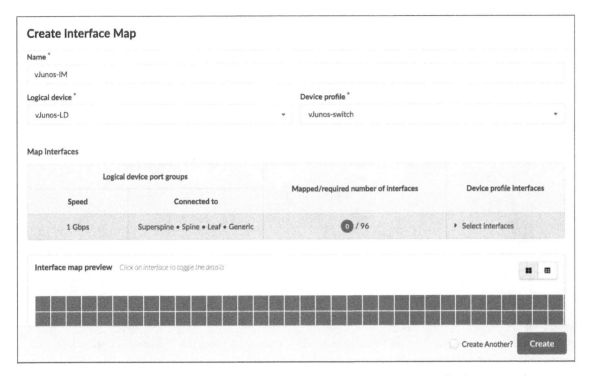

Figure 14-5 *Selecting interfaces after choosing a Logical Device and a Device Profile during Interface Map creation*

With the Logical Device and Interface Map created for a vJunos-switch device, the next task is to create a new Rack Type and Template for the virtual network topology instantiated by Containerlab. In this case, two new Rack Types are created as follows:

■ **Rack Type 1:** This includes two vJunos-switch leafs (Logical Device corresponding to the vJunos-switch Device Profile is selected) as an ESI LAG pair, connecting to a single host, multihomed to both leafs.

■ **Rack Type 2:** This includes a single vJunos-switch leaf connecting to a single host.

For brevity, only the creation of Rack Type 1 is shown in Figure 14-6.

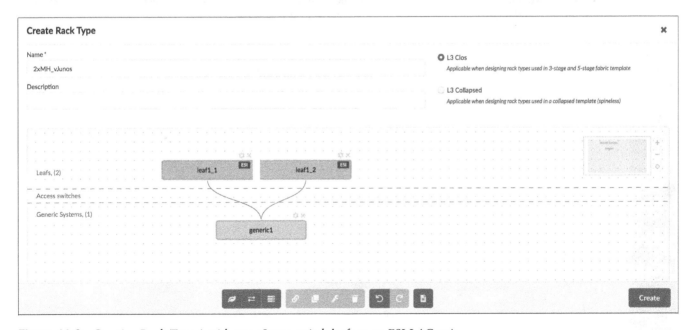

Figure 14-6 *Creating Rack Type 1 with two vJunos-switch leafs as an ESI LAG pair*

Using these Rack Types, a Rack-based Template is created, as shown in Figure 14-7. This Template includes one instance of each Rack Type defined earlier.

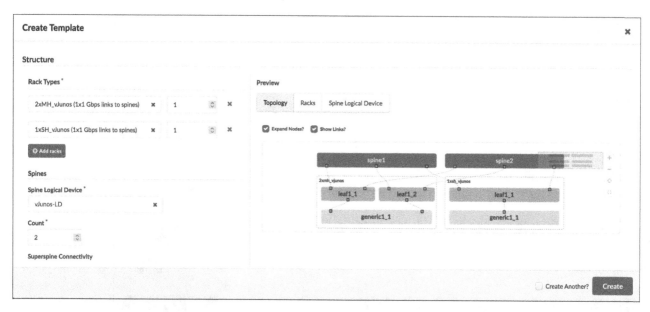

Figure 14-7   *Creating Template using Rack Types previously defined*

Using this Template as an input, a new Blueprint for this virtual fabric is scaffolded. Once the Blueprint is instantiated, like before, the following initial tasks must be done:

- Assign ASN pools for the leafs and spines.

- Assign an IP address pool for the point-to-point interfaces between the leafs and the spines.

- Assign an IP address pool for loopback addresses.

- Assign an Interface Map for the vJunos-switch Logical Device.

- Assign system IDs and set the deploy mode for all fabric devices to Deploy. This is done with the assumption that all virtual devices have been onboarded and acknowledged in Apstra, and their current state is *OOB-READY*.

With all resources added and system IDs mapped correctly, the changes can be committed. The Blueprint for this virtual data center, fully automated and orchestrated by Apstra, is shown in Figure 14-8.

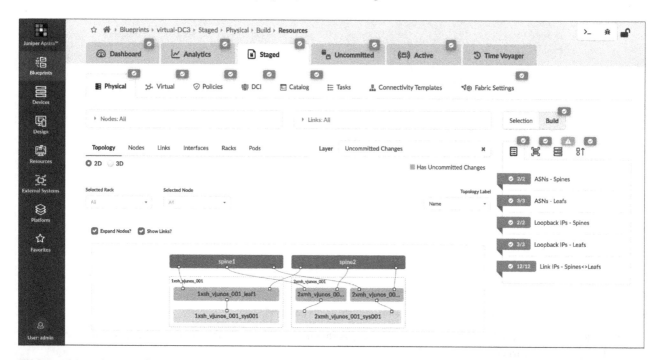

Figure 14-8   *Blueprint for virtual data center fabric with vJunos-switch*

Furthermore, the fabric is stable, with no anomalies reported in the Apstra Dashboard. The service configuration, as part of operator intent, has been pushed to all fabric devices, as shown in Figure 14-9.

Figure 14-9 *Dashboard for Blueprint instantiated for a virtual data center fabric*

From the CLI, it can be confirmed that both spines have established a BGP peering for both the IPv4 and EVPN families to all the leafs, as shown in Example 14-9.

Example 14-9 *BGP state on spine1 and spine2*

```
admin@spine1> show bgp summary

Threading mode: BGP I/O
Default eBGP mode: advertise - accept, receive - accept
Groups: 2 Peers: 6 Down peers: 0
Table          Tot Paths Act Paths Suppressed   History Damp State   Pending
inet.0
                     9         6         0         0        0         0
bgp.evpn.0
                     0         0         0         0        0         0
Peer                   AS    InPkt   OutPkt    OutQ   Flaps Last Up/Dwn State|#Active/Received/Accepted/Damped...
192.0.2.2           65421     353      350       0       0   2:39:21 Establ
  bgp.evpn.0: 0/0/0/0
192.0.2.3           65422     353      350       0       0   2:39:25 Establ
  bgp.evpn.0: 0/0/0/0
192.0.2.4           65423     353      350       0       0   2:39:21 Establ
  bgp.evpn.0: 0/0/0/0
198.51.100.1        65421     355      354       0       0   2:39:29 Establ
  inet.0: 2/3/3/0
```

```
198.51.100.3          65422     355      354      0      0      2:39:28 Establ
   inet.0: 2/3/3/0
198.51.100.5          65423     355      354      0      0      2:39:33 Establ
   inet.0: 2/3/3/0


admin@spine2> show bgp summary

Threading mode: BGP I/O
Default eBGP mode: advertise - accept, receive - accept
Groups: 2 Peers: 6 Down peers: 0
Table          Tot Paths  Act Paths Suppressed   History Damp State    Pending
inet.0
                    9          6          0          0          0          0
bgp.evpn.0
                    0          0          0          0          0          0
Peer                   AS    InPkt    OutPkt    OutQ   Flaps Last Up/Dwn
State|#Active/Received/Accepted/Damped...
192.0.2.2             65421    359      356      0      0      2:41:51 Establ
   bgp.evpn.0: 0/0/0/0
192.0.2.3             65422    359      356      0      0      2:41:42 Establ
   bgp.evpn.0: 0/0/0/0
192.0.2.4             65423    359      356      0      0      2:41:50 Establ
   bgp.evpn.0: 0/0/0/0
198.51.100.7          65421    360      359      0      0      2:41:54 Establ
   inet.0: 2/3/3/0
198.51.100.9          65422    359      358      0      0      2:41:43 Establ
   inet.0: 2/3/3/0
198.51.100.11         65423    360      358      0      0      2:41:52 Establ
   inet.0: 2/3/3/0
```

With the core fabric deployed and validated, virtual services can be deployed over this fabric. In this case, two Virtual Networks named v10 and v20 are created in Apstra, mapped to a Routing Zone called Tenant1. Details of these Virtual Networks are as follows:

- VN v10 uses a VLAN ID of 10, a VNI of 10010, an IPv4 subnet of 172.16.10.0/24, with a default gateway of 172.16.10.254.

- VN v20 uses a VLAN ID of 20, a VNI of 10020, an IPv4 subnet of 172.16.20.0/24, with a default gateway of 172.16.20.254.

Untagged Connectivity Templates are created as part of the Virtual Network creation, and they are assigned to the respective leaf ports, facing the two hosts. A summary of this is shown in Figure 14-10.

With the Virtual Networks and Connectivity Templates mapped and deployed, host h1 can communicate with h2, with a Symmetric IRB model for routing between VNIs, as shown in Example 14-10.

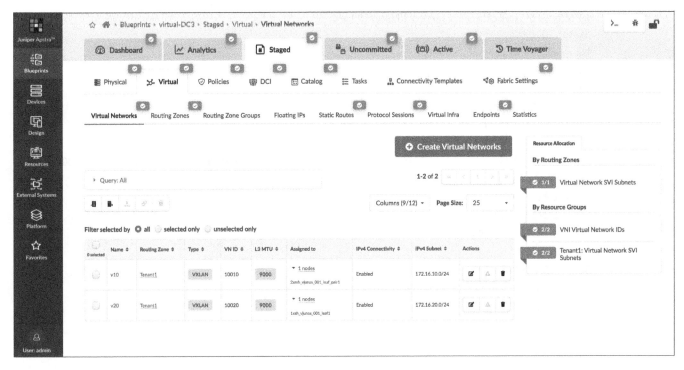

Figure 14-10 *Virtual Networks v10 and v20 created in Apstra*

Example 14-10 *Host h1 communication with h2 with Symmetric IRB model for routing between VNIs*

```
root@h1> ping 172.16.20.2
PING 172.16.20.2 (172.16.20.2): 56 data bytes
64 bytes from 172.16.20.2: icmp_seq=0 ttl=62 time=3.351 ms
64 bytes from 172.16.20.2: icmp_seq=1 ttl=62 time=3.590 ms
64 bytes from 172.16.20.2: icmp_seq=2 ttl=62 time=2.901 ms
64 bytes from 172.16.20.2: icmp_seq=3 ttl=62 time=3.731 ms
^C
--- 172.16.20.2 ping statistics ---
4 packets transmitted, 4 packets received, 0% packet loss
round-trip min/avg/max/stddev = 2.901/3.393/3.731/0.315 ms


admin@2xmh-vjunos-001-leaf1> show route table Tenant1.evpn.0 match-prefix *172.16.20.2/304* extensive

Tenant1.evpn.0: 8 destinations, 14 routes (8 active, 0 holddown, 0 hidden)
Restart Complete
2:192.0.2.2:65534::10020::aa:c1:ab:f1:c9:31::172.16.20.2/304 MAC/IP (2 entries, 1 announced)
        *BGP    Preference: 170/-101
                Route Distinguisher: 192.0.2.2:65534
                Next hop type: Indirect, Next hop index: 0
                Address: 0x77c6f54
                Next-hop reference count: 6
                Kernel Table Id: 0
                Source: 192.0.2.1
                Protocol next hop: 192.0.2.2
                Label operation: Push 626
                Label TTL action: prop-ttl
                Load balance label: Label 626: None;
```

```
Indirect next hop: 0x2 no-forward INH Session ID: 0
State: <Secondary Active Ext>
Local AS: 65422 Peer AS: 65501
Age: 3:42        Metric2: 0
Validation State: unverified
Task: BGP_65501.192.0.2.1
Announcement bits (1): 0-Tenant1-EVPN-L3-context
AS path: 65501 65421 I
Communities: 0:14 target:10020:1 target:10500:1 encapsulation:vxlan(0x8) router-mac:2c:6b:f5:c2:80:f0
Import Accepted
Route Label: 10020
Route Label: 10500
ESI: 00:00:00:00:00:00:00:00:00:00
Localpref: 100
Router ID: 192.0.2.1
Primary Routing Table: bgp.evpn.0
Thread: junos-main
```

snip

Summary

This chapter introduced how virtual data center fabrics can be built using vJunos-switch, a virtual network operating system by Juniper Networks, with a network emulation tool like Containerlab, leveraging Apstra to orchestrate and manage this network.

These virtual topologies are commonly used as digital twins, enabling feature and functional testing prior to deploying in production. They also assist in change control, with virtual networks integrated into CI/CD pipelines, running pre-change and post-change validations.

Large-Scale Fabrics, Inter-VRF Routing, and Security Policies in Apstra

This chapter explores the deployment of 5-stage Clos fabrics, managed and orchestrated by Apstra, demonstrating how large-scale data centers can be built, using the vJunos and Containerlab knowledge acquired from the previous chapter to create a virtual network infrastructure.

Inter-VRF routing is a crucial design aspect of data centers, often centralized on a firewall (or pair of firewalls) connected to data center leafs. This chapter demonstrates the design options for inter-VRF routing in Apstra and takes a deep dive at how it is implemented, while also exploring security policies in Apstra, offering a vendor-agnostic single source of policy control.

Deploying a 5-Stage Clos Fabric

In Apstra, a 5-stage Clos fabric is built by using existing Rack-based Templates, defined with superspine connectivity. Such Templates can be deployed as *pods*, with multiple pods connected via a superspine plane (or planes). Each plane can have multiple superspines for redundancy and load-balancing, and every spine of every pod is connected to every superspine in every plane.

The general workflow to build a 5-stage Clos fabric in Apstra is shown in Figure 15-1.

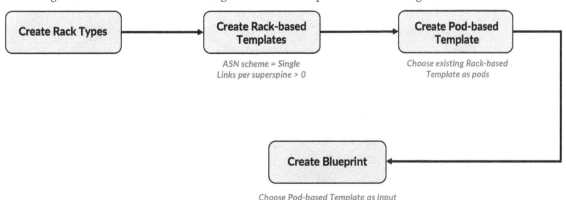

Figure 15-1   *High-level workflow to create a 5-stage Clos fabric in Apstra*

The Rack Types created in the previous chapter will be leveraged again. For the 5-stage Clos fabric, two Rack-based Templates will be created—one for Pod1 and the other for Pod2—with a visual representation of the overall topology for this fabric shown in Figure 15-2.

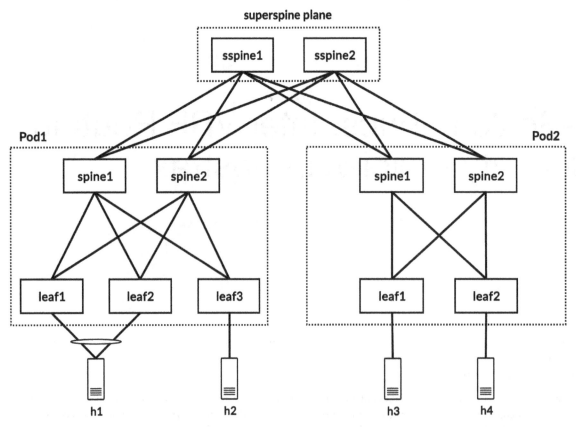

Figure 15-2 *Visual representation of 5-stage Clos fabric to be deployed in Apstra*

When creating a Rack-based Template to be used for a 5-stage Clos fabric, the number of links per superspine must be set to a numerical value greater than zero. Apstra filters available Rack-based Templates (which can be used to build a Pod-based Template) based on this parameter, and thus displays only Templates that satisfy this condition. Figure 15-3 demonstrates how a Rack-based Template for Pod1 is created with the ASN scheme set to Single (not shown here).

Figure 15-3 *Rack-based Template creation for Pod1 for use in a 5-stage Clos Template*

In the same way, another Rack-based Template for Pod2 is created, as shown in Figure 15-4.

Figure 15-4 *Rack-based Template creation for Pod2 for use in a 5-stage Clos Template*

Finally, a Pod-based Template must be created, which includes all necessary Rack-based Templates as pods. In this case, the two previously created Rack-based Templates for Pod1 and Pod2 are added in this Pod-based Template, shown in Figure 15-5. Apstra provides you an option to have multiple planes (planes, as stated earlier, are simply groups of super-spines). For this Template, only a single plane is used, with two superspines, defined by the Per Plane Count.

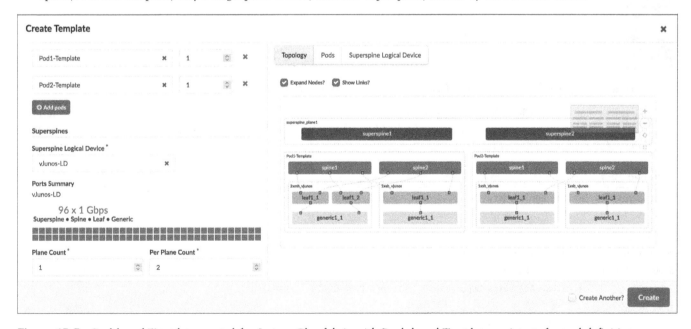

Figure 15-5 *Pod-based Template created for 5-stage Clos fabric with Rack-based Templates as inputs for pod definitions*

This Pod-based Template is used as an input to create a 5-stage Clos fabric, instantiated as a Blueprint, in Apstra. Like other Blueprints, the following initial tasks must be done, including some new resource requirements for the superspines:

- Assign ASN pools for the leafs, spines, and superspines.

- Assign an IP address pool for the point-to-point interfaces between the leafs and the spines.

- Assign an IP address pool for the point-to-point interfaces between the spines and the superspines.

- Assign an IP address pool for loopback addresses.

- Assign Interface Maps for the vJunos-switch Logical Devices.

- Assign system IDs and set the deploy mode for all fabric devices to Deploy. This is done with the assumption that all virtual devices have been onboarded and acknowledged in Apstra, and their current state is *OOB-READY*.

With all these tasks completed and the devices set to Deploy mode, Apstra reports all service configuration has been pushed to the fabric devices, with no anomalies present, as shown in the Blueprint Dashboard in Figure 15-6, after committing the changes.

Figure 15-6 *5-stage Clos fabric instantiated as a Blueprint in Apstra with all resources assigned*

The spines in a 5-stage Clos fabric establish an IPv4 and BGP EVPN peering with all superspines. As shown in Example 15-1, from the perspective of superspine1, it has established both the underlay and overlay BGP peering to all four spines, constituting a full mesh of BGP peering.

Example 15-1 *Superspine plane to spine layer BGP peering*

```
admin@sspine001-1> show bgp summary

Threading mode: BGP I/O
Default eBGP mode: advertise - accept, receive - accept
Groups: 2 Peers: 8 Down peers: 0
Table           Tot Paths  Act Paths Suppressed    History Damp State      Pending
inet.0
                      42         28          0          0          0          0
bgp.evpn.0
                       0          0          0          0          0          0
Peer                     AS      InPkt     OutPkt     OutQ   Flaps Last Up/Dwn
State|#Active/Received/Accepted/Damped...
192.0.2.2             65501       1473       1474        0       0  11:16:54 Establ
  bgp.evpn.0: 0/0/0/0
192.0.2.3             65501       1472       1474        0       0  11:16:50 Establ
  bgp.evpn.0: 0/0/0/0
192.0.2.4             65502       1475       1474        0       0  11:16:57 Establ
  bgp.evpn.0: 0/0/0/0
```

```
192.0.2.5            65502      1476      1474      0      0    11:16:46 Establ
  bgp.evpn.0: 0/0/0/0
198.51.100.0         65501      1476      1479      0      0    11:17:01 Establ
  inet.0: 8/12/12/0
198.51.100.4         65501      1476      1479      0      0    11:16:59 Establ
  inet.0: 8/12/12/0
198.51.100.8         65502      1478      1480      0      0    11:17:02 Establ
  inet.0: 6/9/9/0
198.51.100.12        65502      1478      1479      0      0    11:16:58 Establ
  inet.0: 6/9/9/0
```

With the core fabric deployed, virtual services can now be orchestrated on top of this. For this 5-stage Clos fabric, a Routing Zone called *Tenant1* is created (enabled for Symmetric IRB), and three Virtual Networks are mapped to it. Details of these Virtual Networks are as follows:

- VN v10 uses a VLAN ID of 10 and VNI of 10010. This is mapped to an IPv4 subnet of 172.16.10.0/24, with a default gateway of 172.16.10.254. This VN is assigned to the ESI LAG pair (leaf1 and leaf2) in Pod1, and leaf1 in Pod2.

- VN v20 uses a VLAN ID of 20 and VNI of 10020. This is mapped to an IPv4 subnet of 172.16.20.0/24, with a default gateway of 172.16.20.254. This VN is assigned to leaf3 in Pod1.

- VN v30 uses a VLAN ID of 30 and VNI of 10030. This is mapped to an IPv4 subnet of 172.16.30.0/24, with a default gateway of 172.16.30.254. This VN is assigned to leaf4 in Pod2.

For each of these Virtual Networks, an untagged Connectivity Template is created during the VN creation, and then assigned to the respective host-facing ports on the leafs. A summary of these VNs is shown in Figure 15-7.

Figure 15-7 *Virtual Networks deployed in the 5-stage Clos fabric*

Like the spines in a 3-Stage Clos fabric, the superspines in a 5-stage Clos fabric act as a high-speed, load-balanced transit layer between pods. VXLAN tunnels terminate end-to-end between leafs of different pods, meaning that the loopback addresses must be shared between all pods. This is confirmed in Example 15-2, which shows loopback addresses of all leafs, across both pods, from the perspective of leaf1 in Pod1.

Example 15-2   *Loopback address of all leafs shown from the perspective of leaf1 in Pod1*

```
admin@leaf001-001-1> show route table inet.0 match-prefix *192.0.2*

inet.0: 31 destinations, 57 routes (31 active, 0 holddown, 0 hidden)
Restart Complete
Limit/Threshold: 1048576/1048576 destinations
+ = Active Route, - = Last Active, * = Both


192.0.2.0/32        *[BGP/170] 12:59:44, localpref 100
                      AS path: 65501 65500 I, validation-state: unverified
                    >  to 198.51.100.16 via ge-0/0/0.0
                       to 198.51.100.22 via ge-0/0/1.0
                     [BGP/170] 12:59:44, localpref 100
                      AS path: 65501 65500 I, validation-state: unverified
                    >  to 198.51.100.22 via ge-0/0/1.0
192.0.2.1/32        *[BGP/170] 12:59:44, localpref 100
                      AS path: 65501 65500 I, validation-state: unverified
                    >  to 198.51.100.16 via ge-0/0/0.0
                       to 198.51.100.22 via ge-0/0/1.0
                     [BGP/170] 12:59:44, localpref 100
                      AS path: 65501 65500 I, validation-state: unverified
                    >  to 198.51.100.22 via ge-0/0/1.0
192.0.2.2/32        *[BGP/170] 12:59:48, localpref 100
                      AS path: 65501 I, validation-state: unverified
                    >  to 198.51.100.16 via ge-0/0/0.0
192.0.2.3/32        *[BGP/170] 12:59:44, localpref 100
                      AS path: 65501 I, validation-state: unverified
                    >  to 198.51.100.22 via ge-0/0/1.0
192.0.2.4/32        *[BGP/170] 12:59:44, localpref 100
                      AS path: 65501 65500 65502 I, validation-state: unverified
                    >  to 198.51.100.16 via ge-0/0/0.0
                       to 198.51.100.22 via ge-0/0/1.0
                     [BGP/170] 12:59:44, localpref 100
                      AS path: 65501 65500 65502 I, validation-state: unverified
                    >  to 198.51.100.22 via ge-0/0/1.0
192.0.2.5/32        *[BGP/170] 12:59:44, localpref 100
                      AS path: 65501 65500 65502 I, validation-state: unverified
                    >  to 198.51.100.16 via ge-0/0/0.0
                       to 198.51.100.22 via ge-0/0/1.0
                     [BGP/170] 12:59:44, localpref 100
                      AS path: 65501 65500 65502 I, validation-state: unverified
                    >  to 198.51.100.22 via ge-0/0/1.0
192.0.2.6/32        *[Direct/0] 13:00:05
                    >  via lo0.0
192.0.2.7/32        *[BGP/170] 12:59:44, localpref 100
                      AS path: 65501 65422 I, validation-state: unverified
                    >  to 198.51.100.16 via ge-0/0/0.0
                       to 198.51.100.22 via ge-0/0/1.0
                     [BGP/170] 12:59:44, localpref 100
```

```
                            AS path: 65501 65422 I, validation-state: unverified
                        >  to 198.51.100.22 via ge-0/0/1.0
192.0.2.8/32           *[BGP/170] 12:59:44, localpref 100, from 198.51.100.16
                            AS path: 65501 65423 I, validation-state: unverified
                            to 198.51.100.16 via ge-0/0/0.0
                        >  to 198.51.100.22 via ge-0/0/1.0
                        [BGP/170] 12:59:44, localpref 100
                            AS path: 65501 65423 I, validation-state: unverified
                        >  to 198.51.100.22 via ge-0/0/1.0
192.0.2.9/32           *[BGP/170] 12:59:44, localpref 100, from 198.51.100.16
                            AS path: 65501 65500 65502 65424 I, validation-state: unverified
                            to 198.51.100.16 via ge-0/0/0.0
                        >  to 198.51.100.22 via ge-0/0/1.0
                        [BGP/170] 12:59:44, localpref 100
                            AS path: 65501 65500 65502 65424 I, validation-state: unverified
                        >  to 198.51.100.22 via ge-0/0/1.0
192.0.2.10/32          *[BGP/170] 12:59:44, localpref 100, from 198.51.100.16
                            AS path: 65501 65500 65502 65425 I, validation-state: unverified
                            to 198.51.100.16 via ge-0/0/0.0
                        >  to 198.51.100.22 via ge-0/0/1.0
                        [BGP/170] 12:59:44, localpref 100
                            AS path: 65501 65500 65502 65425 I, validation-state: unverified
                        >  to 198.51.100.22 via ge-0/0/1.0
```

With the Virtual Networks designed and committed in Apstra, all hosts can communicate with each other. Considering host h1, Example 15-3 demonstrates its reachability to hosts h2, h3, and h4 using the **ping** tool.

Example 15-3 *Host h1's reachability to all other hosts across both pods*

```
root@h1> ping 172.16.20.2
PING 172.16.20.2 (172.16.20.2): 56 data bytes
64 bytes from 172.16.20.2: icmp_seq=0 ttl=62 time=3.927 ms
64 bytes from 172.16.20.2: icmp_seq=1 ttl=62 time=3.161 ms
64 bytes from 172.16.20.2: icmp_seq=2 ttl=62 time=4.512 ms
64 bytes from 172.16.20.2: icmp_seq=3 ttl=62 time=3.687 ms
^C
--- 172.16.20.2 ping statistics ---
4 packets transmitted, 4 packets received, 0% packet loss
round-trip min/avg/max/stddev = 3.161/3.822/4.512/0.485 ms


root@h1> ping 172.16.10.3
PING 172.16.10.3 (172.16.10.3): 56 data bytes
64 bytes from 172.16.10.3: icmp_seq=0 ttl=64 time=7.262 ms
64 bytes from 172.16.10.3: icmp_seq=1 ttl=64 time=4.517 ms
64 bytes from 172.16.10.3: icmp_seq=2 ttl=64 time=5.305 ms
64 bytes from 172.16.10.3: icmp_seq=3 ttl=64 time=5.167 ms
^C
--- 172.16.10.3 ping statistics ---
4 packets transmitted, 4 packets received, 0% packet loss
round-trip min/avg/max/stddev = 4.517/5.563/7.262/1.025 ms
```

```
root@h1> ping 172.16.30.4
PING 172.16.30.4 (172.16.30.4): 56 data bytes
64 bytes from 172.16.30.4: icmp_seq=0 ttl=62 time=5.455 ms
64 bytes from 172.16.30.4: icmp_seq=1 ttl=62 time=5.139 ms
64 bytes from 172.16.30.4: icmp_seq=2 ttl=62 time=5.326 ms
64 bytes from 172.16.30.4: icmp_seq=3 ttl=62 time=5.870 ms
^C
--- 172.16.30.4 ping statistics ---
4 packets transmitted, 4 packets received, 0% packet loss
round-trip min/avg/max/stddev = 5.139/5.448/5.870/0.269 ms
```

For any intra-pod communication, traffic does not traverse the superspine plane. Instead, it stays locally within the pod itself. For example, if host h1 wants to communicate with h2, traffic is routed using the Symmetric IRB model, and it does not leave the pod. Example 15-4 shows the BGP EVPN Type-2 MAC+IP route received on leaf1 for host h2's address, with an L3VNI and a Route Target that corresponds to the IP VRF.

Example 15-4   *Host h2's address received as an EVPN Type-2 MAC+IP route with L3VNI*

```
admin@leaf001-001-1> show route table bgp.evpn.0 match-prefix *172.16.20.2* extensive

bgp.evpn.0: 31 destinations, 54 routes (31 active, 0 holddown, 0 hidden)
Restart Complete
2:192.0.2.8:65534::10020::aa:c1:ab:8c:ee:fd::172.16.20.2/304 MAC/IP (2 entries, 0 announced)
        *BGP    Preference: 170/-101
                Route Distinguisher: 192.0.2.8:65534
                Next hop type: Indirect, Next hop index: 0
                Address: 0x77c76c4
                Next-hop reference count: 6
                Kernel Table Id: 0
                Source: 192.0.2.3
                Protocol next hop: 192.0.2.8
                Label operation: Push 626
                Label TTL action: prop-ttl
                Load balance label: Label 626: None;
                Indirect next hop: 0x2 no-forward INH Session ID: 0
                State: <Active Ext>
                Local AS: 65421 Peer AS: 65501
                Age: 1:20:21    Metric2: 0
                Validation State: unverified
                Task: BGP_65501.192.0.2.3
                AS path: 65501 65423 I
                Communities: 0:14 target:10020:1 target:10500:1 encapsulation:vxlan(0x8) router-mac:2c:6b:f5:b5:14:f0
                Import Accepted
                Route Label: 10020
                Route Label: 10500
                ESI: 00:00:00:00:00:00:00:00:00:00
                Localpref: 100
                Router ID: 192.0.2.3
                Secondary Tables: Tenant1.evpn.0
```

snip

Assuming traffic from host h1 is hashed toward leaf2, this intra pod communication can be visualized as shown in Figure 15-8.

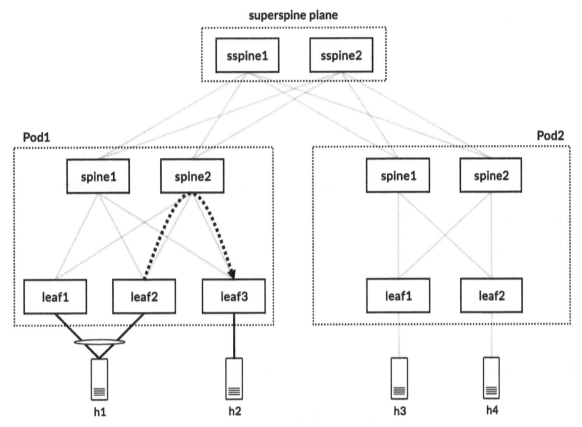

Figure 15-8 *Intra-pod communication in a 5-stage Clos fabric deployed by Apstra*

For inter-pod communication, traffic traverses the superspine plane, directed purely by underlay routing. This is because the next-hop address is not changed at any stage of the fabric, and the originating leaf's next-hop address is retained in the BGP EVPN updates sent through the spine and the superspine layer. For example, consider h4's address, advertised by leaf2 in Pod2 and received by leaf2 in Pod1. The loopback address of leaf2 in Pod2 is the next-hop address in this update, as shown in Example 15-5.

Example 15-5 *Host h4's address, received as an EVPN Type-2 MAC+IP route, with next-hop of Pod2 leaf2's loopback address*

```
admin@leaf002-002-1> show configuration interfaces lo0 unit 0
family inet {
    address 192.0.2.10/32;
}


admin@leaf001-001-2> show route table bgp.evpn.0 match-prefix *172.16.30.4* extensive


bgp.evpn.0: 31 destinations, 54 routes (31 active, 0 holddown, 0 hidden)
Restart Complete
2:192.0.2.10:65534::10030::aa:c1:ab:16:73:60::172.16.30.4/304 MAC/IP (2 entries, 0 announced)
        *BGP    Preference: 170/-101
                Route Distinguisher: 192.0.2.10:65534
                Next hop type: Indirect, Next hop index: 0
                Address: 0x77c7884
                Next-hop reference count: 6
                Kernel Table Id: 0
```

```
Source: 192.0.2.2
Protocol next hop: 192.0.2.10
Label operation: Push 626
Label TTL action: prop-ttl
Load balance label: Label 626: None;
Indirect next hop: 0x2 no-forward INH Session ID: 0
State: <Active Ext>
Local AS: 65422 Peer AS: 65501
Age: 1:37:21        Metric2: 0
Validation State: unverified
Task: BGP_65501.192.0.2.2
AS path: 65501 65500 65502 65425 I
Communities: 0:12 0:14 target:10030:1 target:10500:1 encapsulation:vxlan(0x8) router-mac:2c:6b:f5:6a:ac:f0
Import Accepted
Route Label: 10030
Route Label: 10500
ESI: 00:00:00:00:00:00:00:00:00:00
Localpref: 100
Router ID: 192.0.2.2
```

snip

Visually, the data plane communication for inter-pod traffic is shown in Figure 15-9.

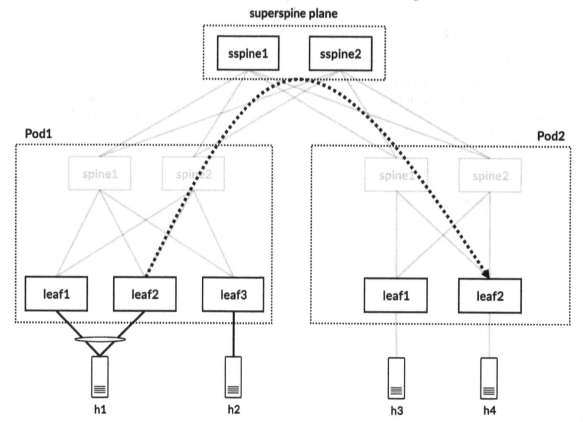

Figure 15-9 *Inter-pod communication in a 5-stage Clos fabric deployed by Apstra*

5-stage Clos fabrics are generally designed for large-scale data centers, providing flexibility to scale out by increasing the number of planes and superspines per plane, as well as the number of spines per pod, as needed.

Inter-VRF Routing in Apstra Deployments

Routing Zones (IP VRFs) offer a mode of segmentation in data center fabrics by building logical routing tables for separation of tenants, grouped together based on operational needs. Often, there are resources in a common VRF that must be accessed by endpoints in all other VRFs, for example, a DHCP server in a services VRF. There may be organizational requirements where endpoints in different VRFs need to communicate with each other as well.

As of Apstra 4.2.0, there are two strategies to facilitate inter-VRF communication:

- Import auto-derived Route Targets of Routing Zones (IP VRFs) that correspond to the IP VRF Route Target (or the L3VNI Route Target) into other Routing Zones, and vice versa.

- Connect an external device (typically a firewall) as an external generic system to a border leaf, directing all inter-VRF traffic to this external device for routing between VRFs.

The topology shown in Figure 15-10 is used for the discussion in this section.

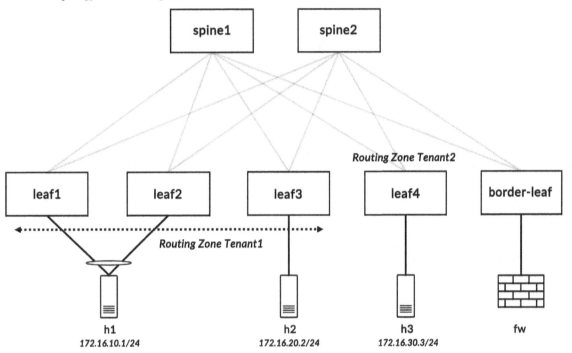

Figure 15-10 *Topology for inter-VRF routing*

In the data center fabric shown in Figure 15-10, two Routing Zones and three Virtual Networks are designed as follows:

- Routing Zone Tenant1 is deployed to leaf1, leaf2, and leaf3. Virtual Network v10 is mapped to this Routing Zone, with a VLAN ID of 10, a VNI of 10010, an IPv4 subnet of 172.16.10.0/24, and a default gateway of 172.16.10.254. This VN is deployed to leaf1 and leaf2, with an untagged Connectivity Template to connect to host h1. A second Virtual Network, v20, is also mapped to this Routing Zone, with a VLAN ID of 20, a VNI of 10020, an IPv4 subnet of 172.16.20.0/24, and a default gateway of 172.16.20.254. This VN is deployed to leaf3, with an untagged Connectivity Template to connect to host h2.

- Routing Zone Tenant2 is deployed to leaf4. Virtual Network v30 is mapped to this Routing Zone, with a VLAN ID of 30, a VNI of 10030, an IPv4 subnet of 172.16.30.0/24, and a default gateway of 172.16.30.254. This VN is deployed to leaf4, with an untagged Connectivity Template to connect to host h3.

In addition, a firewall is connected to a border leaf to demonstrate how an external device can be used for inter-VRF routing as well.

This fabric has been deployed as a Blueprint in Apstra, using vJunos-switch devices, instantiated by Containerlab, as fabric nodes. The topological view of the fabric is shown in Figure 15-11. All initial tasks, such as mapping resources and Interface Maps, have been completed, with all changes committed in Apstra.

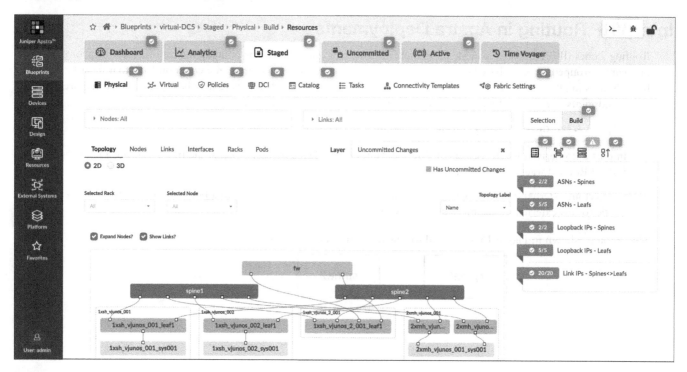

Figure 15-11   *Topological view of fabric deployed in Apstra for inter-VRF routing*

A summary of the Virtual Networks and their corresponding Routing Zones is shown in Figure 15-12.

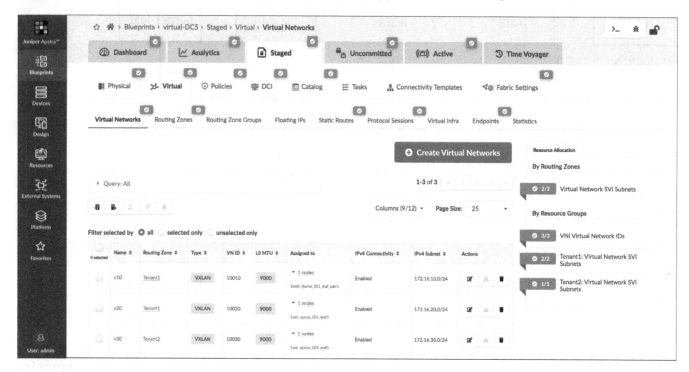

Figure 15-12   *Summary of Virtual Networks and Routing Zones deployed in the fabric*

At this deployment stage of the fabric, hosts h1 and h2 can communicate with each other, but host h3 is isolated completely since it is in a different Routing Zone (IP VRF). This can be confirmed as shown in Example 15-6. When attempting to communicate with host h3, h1 receives an ICMP unreachable back, since the IP VRF on leaf1 (where the packet destined for host h3 is received) does not have a route to the destination IP address, 172.16.30.3.

Example 15-6 *Reachability of hosts in same and different VRFs*

```
root@h1> ping 172.16.20.2
PING 172.16.20.2 (172.16.20.2): 56 data bytes
64 bytes from 172.16.20.2: icmp_seq=0 ttl=62 time=7.747 ms
64 bytes from 172.16.20.2: icmp_seq=1 ttl=62 time=4.348 ms
64 bytes from 172.16.20.2: icmp_seq=2 ttl=62 time=4.109 ms
64 bytes from 172.16.20.2: icmp_seq=3 ttl=62 time=4.675 ms
^C
--- 172.16.20.2 ping statistics ---
4 packets transmitted, 4 packets received, 0% packet loss
round-trip min/avg/max/stddev = 4.109/5.220/7.747/1.473 ms


root@h1> ping 172.16.30.3
PING 172.16.30.3 (172.16.30.3): 56 data bytes
36 bytes from 172.16.10.254: Destination Net Unreachable
Vr HL TOS  Len   ID Flg  off TTL Pro  cks      Src      Dst
 4  5  00 0054 7028   0 0000  40  01 8a5c 172.16.10.1  172.16.30.3

36 bytes from 172.16.10.254: Destination Net Unreachable
Vr HL TOS  Len   ID Flg  off TTL Pro  cks      Src      Dst
 4  5  00 0054 7053   0 0000  40  01 8a31 172.16.10.1  172.16.30.3

^C
--- 172.16.30.3 ping statistics ---
2 packets transmitted, 0 packets received, 100% packet loss


admin@2xmh-vjunos-001-leaf1> show route table Tenant1.inet.0 172.16.30.3

<no output>
```

In Apstra, by default, you cannot manually import the internally auto-derived Route Targets for a Routing Zone into any other Routing Zone. This is controlled by a fabric-wide policy, which you can modify if needed. This policy is called *Validation Policy* and is located on the Fabric Settings tab under the Staged panel, as shown in Figure 15-13.

In this policy, the current setting for allowing internal Route Targets in Route Target policies is set to raise an error in Apstra. This can be changed to one of three options:

- **No Warning:** Apstra will not display any warnings if this is selected.

- **Warning:** Apstra will display a warning, but the change is allowed to be committed.

- **Error:** Apstra will display an error, and the change is not allowed to be committed.

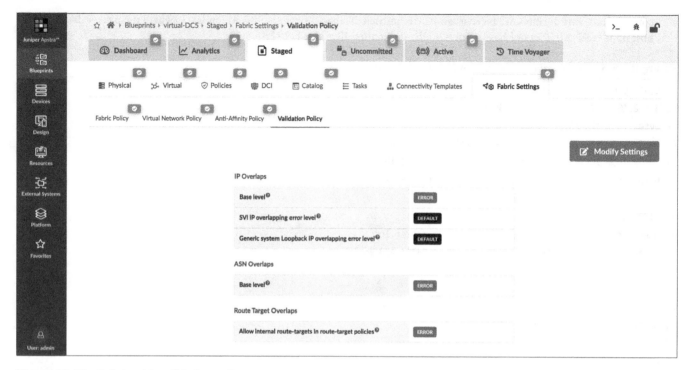

Figure 15-13 *Fabric-wide validation policy*

You can change the policy settings by clicking the Modify Settings button on the right in Figure 15-13. In this case, the setting for allowing internal Route Targets in Route Target policies is changed to No Warning, as shown in Figure 15-14.

Modify Validation Policy Settings

Generic system Loopback IP overlapping error level

NO WARNING   WARNING   ERROR   ○ DEFAULT

Support for uncontrolled generic loopbacks IP overlap errors. This relaxes validation errors and allows IP addresses to be shared between external generic loopbacks and fabric objects both in default and EVPN routing zones. These fabric objects include loopback IPs, physical link IPs, logical link IPs, virtual network subnets and VTEP addresses.

ASN Overlaps

Base level

NO WARNING   WARNING   ○ ERROR

Severity of errors raised on overlap of ASNs

Route Target Overlaps

Allow internal route-targets in route-target policies

○ NO WARNING   WARNING   ERROR

Severity of errors raised on overlap of a user-defined route-target which overlaps with an internal virtual network or routing zone route-target. This can be used for a form of full table inter-vrf route leaking.

Save Changes

Figure 15-14 *Policy change for allowing internal Route Targets in Route Target policies*

Next, manual Route Target imports need to be defined for leaking routes between VRFs. A summary of the Routing Zones and their respective Route Targets is shown in Figure 15-15. Routing Zone Tenant1 has an auto-derived Route Target of 10500:1, and Routing Zone Tenant2 has an auto-derived Route Target of 10600:1. To leak routes between the two IP VRFs, Tenant1 needs to import a Route Target of 10600:1 and Tenant2 needs to import a Route Target of 10500:1.

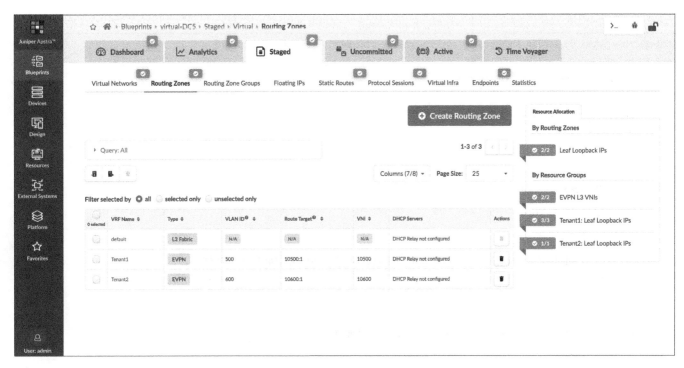

Figure 15-15 *Routing Zones and their Route Targets in Apstra*

This is done by editing the Routing Zone and clicking the Add Import Route Target button, entering a Route Target, and then clicking the Update button on the bottom-right side of the UI, as shown in Figure 15-16.

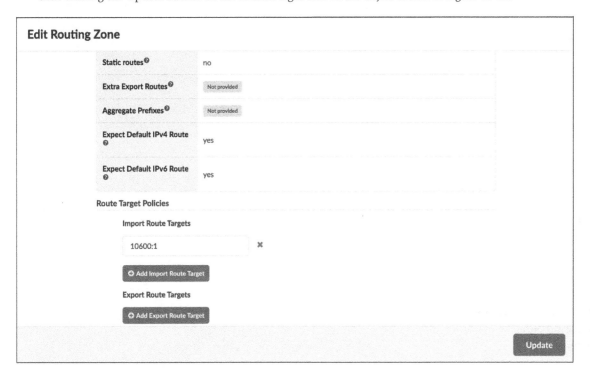

Figure 15-16 *Adding a manual Route Target import value for Routing Zone Tenant1*

This change configures a new community that matches on the newly added Route Target and accepts it to be imported when received in the BGP EVPN table. Taking leaf1 from the reference topology in Figure 15-10 to demonstrate the changes, Example 15-7 shows the addition of this new Route Target, with the import policy used to import routes received from the two spines.

Example 15-7   *EVPN import policy when a new Route Target is added manually in Apstra*

```
admin@2xmh-vjunos-001-leaf1# show policy-options policy-statement EVPN_IMPORT
term EVPN_IMPORT-500 {
    from community VRF_Tenant1_RT_10600_1_IMPORT;
    then {
        community add VRF_Tenant1;
        next term;
    }
}
term EVPN_IMPORT-4095 {
    then accept;
}


admin@2xmh-vjunos-001-leaf1# show policy-options community VRF_Tenant1_RT_10600_1_IMPORT
members target:10600:1;


[edit]
admin@2xmh-vjunos-001-leaf1# show policy-options community VRF_Tenant1
members target:10500:1;


admin@2xmh-vjunos-001-leaf1# show protocols bgp group l3clos-l-evpn
type external;
multihop {
    ttl 1;
    no-nexthop-change;
}
family evpn {
    signaling {
        loops 2;
    }
}
multipath {
    multiple-as;
}
bfd-liveness-detection {
    minimum-interval 3000;
    multiplier 3;
}
neighbor 192.0.2.0 {
    description facing_spine1-evpn-overlay;
    local-address 192.0.2.4;
    import ( EVPN_IMPORT );
    family evpn {
        signaling;
    }
    export ( LEAF_TO_SPINE_EVPN_OUT && EVPN_EXPORT );
    peer-as 65500;
}
neighbor 192.0.2.1 {
    description facing_spine2-evpn-overlay;
```

```
    local-address 192.0.2.4;
    import ( EVPN_IMPORT );
    family evpn {
        signaling;
    }
    export ( LEAF_TO_SPINE_EVPN_OUT && EVPN_EXPORT );
    peer-as 65501;
}
vpn-apply-export;
```

With these changes deployed, the two VRFs can successfully import routes from each other. Consider host h3's IPv4 subnet (172.16.30.0/24) advertised as an EVPN Type-5 route and received on leaf1—this is now imported from the BGP EVPN table into the Tenant1.evpn.0 table and, from there, into the Tenant1.inet.0 table, as shown in Example 15-8.

Example 15-8 *Host h3's address, originated from IP VRF Tenant2, imported into IP VRF Tenant1 on leaf1*

```
admin@2xmh-vjunos-001-leaf1> show route table bgp.evpn.0 match-prefix 5:*172.16.30.0*

bgp.evpn.0: 26 destinations, 44 routes (26 active, 0 holddown, 0 hidden)
Restart Complete
+ = Active Route, - = Last Active, * = Both


5:192.0.2.6:600::0::172.16.30.0::24/248
                    *[BGP/170] 00:12:45, localpref 100, from 192.0.2.0
                      AS path: 65500 65425 I, validation-state: unverified
                    >  to 198.51.100.4 via ge-0/0/0.0, Push 662
                       to 198.51.100.12 via ge-0/0/1.0, Push 662
                     [BGP/170] 00:12:45, localpref 100, from 192.0.2.1
                      AS path: 65501 65425 I, validation-state: unverified
                    >  to 198.51.100.4 via ge-0/0/0.0, Push 662
                       to 198.51.100.12 via ge-0/0/1.0, Push 662


admin@2xmh-vjunos-001-leaf1> show route table Tenant1.evpn.0 match-prefix 5:*172.16.30.0*

Tenant1.evpn.0: 11 destinations, 20 routes (11 active, 0 holddown, 0 hidden)
Restart Complete
+ = Active Route, - = Last Active, * = Both


5:192.0.2.6:600::0::172.16.30.0::24/248
                    *[BGP/170] 00:13:30, localpref 100, from 192.0.2.0
                      AS path: 65500 65425 I, validation-state: unverified
                    >  to 198.51.100.4 via ge-0/0/0.0, Push 662
                       to 198.51.100.12 via ge-0/0/1.0, Push 662
                     [BGP/170] 00:13:30, localpref 100, from 192.0.2.1
                      AS path: 65501 65425 I, validation-state: unverified
                    >  to 198.51.100.4 via ge-0/0/0.0, Push 662
                       to 198.51.100.12 via ge-0/0/1.0, Push 662


admin@2xmh-vjunos-001-leaf1> show route table Tenant1.inet.0 match-prefix 172.16.30.0

Tenant1.inet.0: 11 destinations, 12 routes (11 active, 0 holddown, 0 hidden)
```

```
Restart Complete
@ = Routing Use Only, # = Forwarding Use Only
+ = Active Route, - = Last Active, * = Both


172.16.30.0/24     *[EVPN/170] 00:14:30
                    >  to 198.51.100.4 via ge-0/0/0.0
                       to 198.51.100.12 via ge-0/0/1.0
```

Host h1 can now communicate with h3 as well, demonstrated in Example 15-9 using the **ping** tool.

Example 15-9 *Host h1's reachability to h3, demonstrated using the* **ping** *tool*

```
root@h1> ping 172.16.30.3
PING 172.16.30.3 (172.16.30.3): 56 data bytes
64 bytes from 172.16.30.3: icmp_seq=0 ttl=62 time=5.260 ms
64 bytes from 172.16.30.3: icmp_seq=1 ttl=62 time=3.913 ms
64 bytes from 172.16.30.3: icmp_seq=2 ttl=62 time=3.527 ms
64 bytes from 172.16.30.3: icmp_seq=3 ttl=62 time=4.080 ms
^C
--- 172.16.30.3 ping statistics ---
4 packets transmitted, 4 packets received, 0% packet loss
round-trip min/avg/max/stddev = 3.527/4.195/5.260/0.647 ms
```

An alternate design to importing Route Targets across VRFs is to centralize inter-VRF routing on an external device, typically a firewall. While many-to-one inter-VRF communication is easy to configure and maintain via Route Target imports, many-to-many communication using the same methodology is operationally challenging. In such cases, it is very common to connect a firewall to a border leaf and build per-VRF BGP sessions from the border leaf to the firewall, like a *router-on-a-stick* design. This design pulls all traffic that requires inter-VRF routing toward the firewall, also enabling it to secure this communication via security policies, if needed.

Using the predefined *BGP over L3* Connectivity Template, the border leaf can form an eBGP peering with the firewall. In this case, two templates are defined—one for Routing Zone Tenant1 and another for Routing Zone Tenant2—which enable the border leaf to form a per-VRF eBGP peering to the firewall. From the IP VRF Tenant1, IPv4 subnets 172.16.10.0/24 and 172.16.20.0/24 are imported from EVPN into IPv4 and advertised out to the firewall via the VRF-specific eBGP peering. These routes are then sent back by the firewall to the border leaf, over the IP VRF Tenant2 eBGP peering. The same process (but in reverse) happens for the 172.16.30.0/24 subnet from the IP VRF Tenant2. In this way, routes are leaked between VRFs and sent toward the firewall for inter-VRF routing. This connection scheme is visualized in Figure 15-17, showing how the IP VRF Tenant1's IPv4 subnets are advertised.

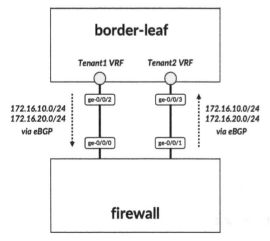

Figure 15-17 *Border leaf to firewall connectivity scheme*

When building Connectivity Templates for this, it is important to place the *IP Link* primitive in the correct Routing Zone. An example of the Connectivity Template built for VRF Tenant1's Layer 3 connection to the firewall is shown in Figure 15-18, with the *IP Link* primitive mapped to the Routing Zone Tenant1.

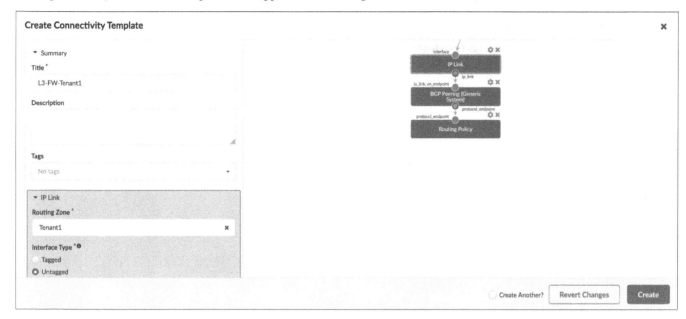

Figure 15-18   *Connectivity Template with IP Link mapped to Tenant1 Routing Zone*

This Connectivity Template is also associated with a custom Routing Policy that determines which routes are allowed to be imported and exported over the BGP peering that will be established to the external generic system. In this case, for the Routing Zone Tenant1, the policy allows the IPv4 subnets 172.16.10.0/24 and 172.16.20.0/24 to be exported and the IPv4 subnet 172.16.30.0/24 to be imported, as shown in Figure 15-19. No other routes are exported or imported.

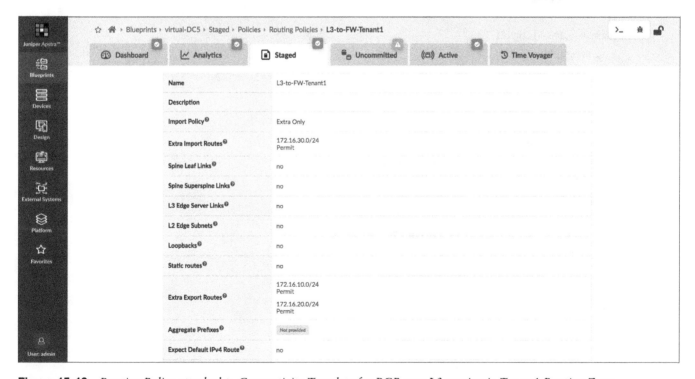

Figure 15-19   *Routing Policy attached to Connectivity Template for BGP over L3 peering in Tenant1 Routing Zone*

With a similar Connectivity Template and Routing Policy deployed for Routing Zone Tenant2 and its Layer 3 connection to the firewall, and all changes committed, Apstra pushes configuration for both VRFs Tenant1 and Tenant2 to the border leaf. These VRFs are created as routing instances, with the appropriate import and export policies applied to the per-VRF BGP peering to the firewall, in accordance with the Routing Policies created in Apstra, as shown in Example 15-10, taking Routing Zone Tenant2 as an example.

Example 15-10   *Configuration for VRF Tenant2 pushed to border leaf by Apstra*

```
admin@1xsh-vjunos-2-001-leaf1# show routing-instances Tenant2
instance-type vrf;
routing-options {
    graceful-restart;
    multipath;
    auto-export;
}
protocols {
    bgp {
        group l3rtr {
            type external;
            multihop {
                ttl 1;
            }
            family inet {
                unicast {
                    loops 2;
                }
            }
            multipath {
                multiple-as;
            }
            neighbor 198.51.100.21 {
                description facing_fw;
                multihop {
                    ttl 2;
                }
                local-address 198.51.100.20;
                hold-time 30;
                import ( RoutesFromExt-Tenant2-L3-to-FW-Tenant2 );
                family inet {
                    unicast;
                }
                export ( RoutesToExt-Tenant2-L3-to-FW-Tenant2 );
                peer-as 65511;
            }
        }
        graceful-restart {
            dont-help-shared-fate-bfd-down;
        }
    }
    evpn {
        irb-symmetric-routing {
            vni 10600;
        }
```

```
        ip-prefix-routes {
            advertise direct-nexthop;
            encapsulation vxlan;
            vni 10600;
            export BGP-AOS-Policy-Tenant2;
        }
    }
}
interface ge-0/0/3.0;
interface lo0.3;
route-distinguisher 192.0.2.3:600;
vrf-target target:10600:1;
```

The import policy attached to the BGP peering imports the 172.16.10.0/24 and 172.16.20.0/24 IPv4 subnets, which are expected to be learned via IP VRF Tenant1's BGP peering to the firewall. This is shown in Example 15-11.

Example 15-11 *Import policy attached to BGP peering to firewall for VRF Tenant2*

```
admin@1xsh-vjunos-2-001-leaf1# show policy-options policy-statement RoutesFromExt-Tenant2-L3-to-FW-Tenant2
term RoutesFromExt-Tenant2-L3-to-FW-Tenant2-10 {
    from {
        family inet;
        route-filter-list RoutesFromExt-Tenant2-L3-to-FW-Tenant2;
    }
    then {
        community add RoutesFromExt-Tenant2-L3-to-FW-Tenant2;
        accept;
    }
}
term RoutesFromExt-Tenant2-L3-to-FW-Tenant2-30 {
    from family inet;
    then reject;
}

admin@1xsh-vjunos-2-001-leaf1# show policy-options route-filter-list RoutesFromExt-Tenant2-L3-to-FW-Tenant2
172.16.10.0/24 exact;
172.16.20.0/24 exact;

admin@1xsh-vjunos-2-001-leaf1# show policy-options community RoutesFromExt-Tenant2-L3-to-FW-Tenant2
members [ 4:20009 21003:26000 ];
```

The export policy allows routes specific to this IP VRF to be exported and advertised toward the firewall. This includes the IPv4 subnet 172.16.20.0/24 corresponding to the Virtual Network v30, as shown in Example 15-12.

Example 15-12 *Export policy attached to BGP peering to firewall for VRF Tenant2*

```
admin@1xsh-vjunos-2-001-leaf1# show policy-options policy-statement RoutesToExt-Tenant2-L3-to-FW-Tenant2
term RoutesToExt-Tenant2-L3-to-FW-Tenant2-10 {
    from {
        family inet;
```

Chapter 15: Large-Scale Fabrics, Inter-VRF Routing, and Security Policies in Apstra

```
        route-filter-list RoutesToExt-Tenant2-L3-to-FW-Tenant2;
    }
    then {
        community delete FABRIC_COMMUNITIES;
        accept;
    }
}
term RoutesToExt-Tenant2-L3-to-FW-Tenant2-30 {
    from family inet;
    then reject;
}


admin@1xsh-vjunos-2-001-leaf1# show policy-options route-filter-list RoutesToExt-Tenant2-L3-to-FW-Tenant2
172.16.30.0/24 exact;


admin@1xsh-vjunos-2-001-leaf1# show policy-options community FABRIC_COMMUNITIES
members [ 0:12 0:13 0:14 0:15 .+:200.. 2....:260.. ];
```

Let's follow the 172.16.30.0/24 IPv4 route to understand how this is exchanged in the control plane for such a design, with the import and export policies shown in Example 15-11 and Example 15-12.

This route is first received by the border leaf as an EVPN Type-5 route, from the BGP EVPN peering to the spines, originated by leaf4. Thus, on the border leaf, it is present in the bgp.evpn.0 table and imported into the Tenant2.evpn.0 table, based on the 10600:1 Route Target attached to the route, as shown in Example 15-13.

Example 15-13 *IPv4 route 172.16.30.0/24 received by border leaf over BGP EVPN as an EVPN Type-5 route*

```
admin@1xsh-vjunos-2-001-leaf1> show route table bgp.evpn.0 match-prefix 5:*192.0.2.6*172.16.30.0*

bgp.evpn.0: 33 destinations, 59 routes (33 active, 0 holddown, 0 hidden)
Restart Complete
+ = Active Route, - = Last Active, * = Both

5:192.0.2.6:600::0::172.16.30.0::24/248
                    *[BGP/170] 1d 15:39:48, localpref 100, from 192.0.2.0
                      AS path: 65500 65425 I, validation-state: unverified
                    >  to 198.51.100.2 via ge-0/0/0.0, Push 662
                       to 198.51.100.10 via ge-0/0/1.0, Push 662
                     [BGP/170] 1d 15:39:48, localpref 100, from 192.0.2.1
                      AS path: 65501 65425 I, validation-state: unverified
                    >  to 198.51.100.2 via ge-0/0/0.0, Push 662
                       to 198.51.100.10 via ge-0/0/1.0, Push 662


admin@1xsh-vjunos-2-001-leaf1> show route table bgp.evpn.0 match-prefix 5:*192.0.2.6*172.16.30.0* extensive

bgp.evpn.0: 33 destinations, 59 routes (33 active, 0 holddown, 0 hidden)
Restart Complete
5:192.0.2.6:600::0::172.16.30.0::24/248 (2 entries, 0 announced)
        *BGP    Preference: 170/-101
                Route Distinguisher: 192.0.2.6:600
```

```
            Next hop type: Indirect, Next hop index: 0
            Address: 0x77c6694
            Next-hop reference count: 8
            Kernel Table Id: 0
            Source: 192.0.2.0
            Protocol next hop: 192.0.2.6
            Label operation: Push 662
            Label TTL action: prop-ttl
            Load balance label: Label 662: None;
            Indirect next hop: 0x2 no-forward INH Session ID: 0
            State: <Active Ext>
            Local AS: 65422 Peer AS: 65500
            Age: 1d 15:39:53    Metric2: 0
            Validation State: unverified
            Task: BGP_65500.192.0.2.0
            AS path: 65500 65425 I
            Communities: 0:14 7:20007 21003:26000 target:10600:1 encapsulation:vxlan(0x8) router-mac:2c:6b:f5:2f:a2:f0
            Import Accepted
            Route Label: 10600


*snip*


admin@1xsh-vjunos-2-001-leaf1> show route table Tenant2.evpn.0 match-prefix 5:*192.0.2.6*172.16.30.0*


Tenant2.evpn.0: 7 destinations, 10 routes (7 active, 0 holddown, 0 hidden)
Restart Complete
+ = Active Route, - = Last Active, * = Both


5:192.0.2.6:600::0::172.16.30.0::24/248
                    *[BGP/170] 13:21:40, localpref 100, from 192.0.2.0
                      AS path: 65500 65425 I, validation-state: unverified
                  >  to 198.51.100.2 via ge-0/0/0.0, Push 662
                     to 198.51.100.10 via ge-0/0/1.0, Push 662
                    [BGP/170] 13:21:40, localpref 100, from 192.0.2.1
                      AS path: 65501 65425 I, validation-state: unverified
                  >  to 198.51.100.2 via ge-0/0/0.0, Push 662
                     to 198.51.100.10 via ge-0/0/1.0, Push 662
```

This EVPN route is then imported in the EVPN IP database as an IPv4 route, and subsequently added into the Tenant2.inet.0 table on the border leaf. This is shown in Example 15-14.

Example 15-14   *IPv4 route creation for EVPN Type-5 route of the 172.16.30.0/24 subnet*

```
admin@1xsh-vjunos-2-001-leaf1> show evpn ip-prefix-database l3-context Tenant2 direction imported prefix
172.16.30.0/24 extensive
L3 context: Tenant2


EVPN->IPv4 Imported Prefixes
```

```
Prefix: 172.16.30.0/24, Ethernet tag: 0
  Change flags: 0x0
  Remote advertisements:
    Route Distinguisher: 192.0.2.6:600
      VNI: 10600
      Router MAC: 2c:6b:f5:2f:a2:f0
      BGP nexthop address: 192.0.2.6
      IP route status: Created
```

The control plane process, thus far, can be visualized as shown in Figure 15-20.

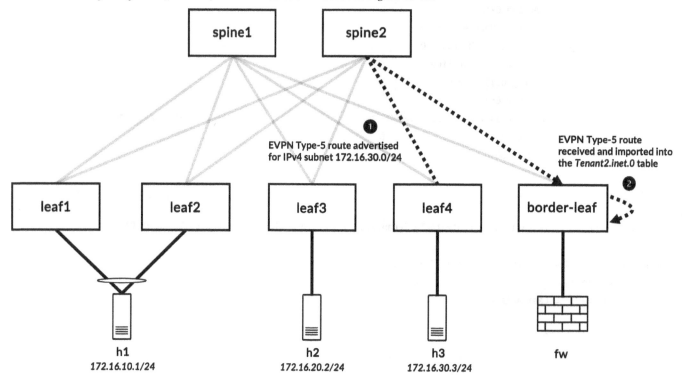

Figure 15-20 *IPv4 subnet 172.16.30.0/24 advertised by leaf4, received by the border leaf, and imported into inet.0 table*

The BGP export policy, applied to the peering with the firewall shown in Example 15-12, controls whether this route is advertised or not. Since the policy permits this within a route-filter, this subnet gets advertised, as shown in Example 15-15.

Example 15-15 *IPv4 route 172.16.30.0/24 advertised to firewall over VRF Tenant2's BGP peering*

```
admin@1xsh-vjunos-2-001-leaf1> show route advertising-protocol bgp 198.51.100.21

Tenant2.inet.0: 8 destinations, 8 routes (8 active, 0 holddown, 0 hidden)
Restart Complete
  Prefix           Nexthop      MED    Lclpref    AS path
* 172.16.30.0/24    Self                           65500 65425 I
```

By default, BGP in Junos does not send routes back to a neighbor that has the same ASN as it was received from. This creates a problem in such designs since the firewall has multiple BGP peerings to the same border leaf, and hence the same ASN. For such cases, this restriction can be eliminated by using the *advertise-peer-as* configuration option, which allows a BGP speaker to advertise routes back to the same ASN it was received from, but to a different BGP neighbor address. Thus, on the firewall, this configuration option must be enabled in the border leaf–facing BGP group, as shown in Example 15-16.

Example 15-16 *Use of knob* advertise peer as *on the firewall*

```
admin@fw# show protocols bgp group dc1
type external;
advertise-peer-as;
family inet {
    unicast;
}
peer-as 65422;
neighbor 198.51.100.20;
neighbor 198.51.100.22;
```

With this option enabled, the firewall can advertise the 172.16.30.0/24 route back to the border leaf, but over the peering to the VRF Tenant1. The border leaf receives this route and exports it from the Tenant1.inet.0 table into the Tenant1.evpn.0 table by creating an EVPN Type-5 route, as shown in Example 15-17.

Example 15-17 *IPv4 route 172.16.30.0/24 received by border leaf in Tenant1 VRF and exported as an EVPN Type-5 route*

```
admin@1xsh-vjunos-2-001-leaf1> show route receive-protocol bgp 198.51.100.23 table Tenant1.inet.0


Tenant1.inet.0: 11 destinations, 15 routes (11 active, 0 holddown, 0 hidden)
Restart Complete
  Prefix          Nexthop         MED    Lclpref    AS path
* 172.16.30.0/24      198.51.100.23                  65511 65422 65500 65425 I


admin@1xsh-vjunos-2-001-leaf1> show evpn ip-prefix-database l3-context Tenant1 direction exported prefix
172.16.30.0/24 extensive
L3 context: Tenant1

IPv4->EVPN Exported Prefixes

Prefix: 172.16.30.0/24
  EVPN route status: Created
  Change flags: 0x0
  Advertisement mode: Direct nexthop
  Encapsulation: VXLAN
  VNI: 10500
  Router MAC: 2c:6b:f5:ad:95:f0


admin@1xsh-vjunos-2-001-leaf1> show route table Tenant1.evpn.0 match-prefix *172.16.30.0*


Tenant1.evpn.0: 12 destinations, 21 routes (12 active, 0 holddown, 0 hidden)
Restart Complete
+ = Active Route, - = Last Active, * = Both


5:192.0.2.3:500::0::172.16.30.0::24/248
                 *[EVPN/170] 13:27:12
                     Fictitious
```

These next steps in the process are visually represented in Figure 15-21.

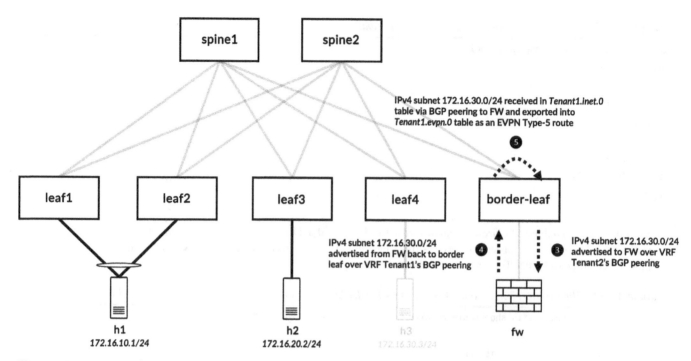

Figure 15-21 *IPv4 subnet 172.16.30.0/24 advertised to FW, received back from the FW, and exported as an EVPN Type-5 route*

From here, the route is pulled into the bgp.evpn.0 table to be advertised to BGP EVPN peers. Eventually, other leafs in the fabric that are configured with the same IP VRF import this route based on the attached Route Target and install it in their VRF-specific inet.0 tables. This is shown in Example 15-18, where the border leaf advertises this route out via BGP EVPN and leaf1 receives it and installs it in its Tenant1.inet.0 table.

Example 15-18 *IPv4 route 172.16.30.0/24 advertised via BGP EVPN, received by leaf1, and imported into the inet.0 table*

```
admin@1xsh-vjunos-2-001-leaf1> show route table bgp.evpn.0 match-prefix 5:*192.0.2.3*172.16.30.0*


bgp.evpn.0: 33 destinations, 59 routes (33 active, 0 holddown, 0 hidden)
Restart Complete
+ = Active Route, - = Last Active, * = Both


5:192.0.2.3:500::0::172.16.30.0::24/248
                    *[EVPN/170] 13:31:03
                         Fictitious


admin@2xmh-vjunos-001-leaf1> show route table bgp.evpn.0 match-prefix 5:*192.0.2.3*172.16.30.0*


bgp.evpn.0: 33 destinations, 58 routes (33 active, 0 holddown, 0 hidden)
Restart Complete
+ = Active Route, - = Last Active, * = Both


5:192.0.2.3:500::0::172.16.30.0::24/248
                    *[BGP/170] 13:31:36, localpref 100, from 192.0.2.0
                      AS path: 65500 65422 65511 65422 65500 65425 I, validation-state: unverified
                       to 198.51.100.4 via ge-0/0/0.0, Push 656
                  >   to 198.51.100.12 via ge-0/0/1.0, Push 656
                     [BGP/170] 13:31:36, localpref 100, from 192.0.2.1
```

```
        AS path: 65501 65422 65511 65422 65500 65425 I, validation state: unverified
            to 198.51.100.4 via ge-0/0/0.0, Push 656
        >   to 198.51.100.12 via ge-0/0/1.0, Push 656
```

```
admin@2xmh-vjunos-001-leaf1> show route table Tenant1.inet.0 172.16.30.0
```

```
Tenant1.inet.0: 11 destinations, 12 routes (11 active, 0 holddown, 0 hidden)
Restart Complete
@ = Routing Use Only, # = Forwarding Use Only
+ = Active Route, - = Last Active, * = Both
```

```
172.16.30.0/24     *[EVPN/170] 13:31:54
                   >  to 198.51.100.4 via ge-0/0/0.0
                      to 198.51.100.12 via ge-0/0/1.0
```

This process can be visualized as shown in Figure 15-22.

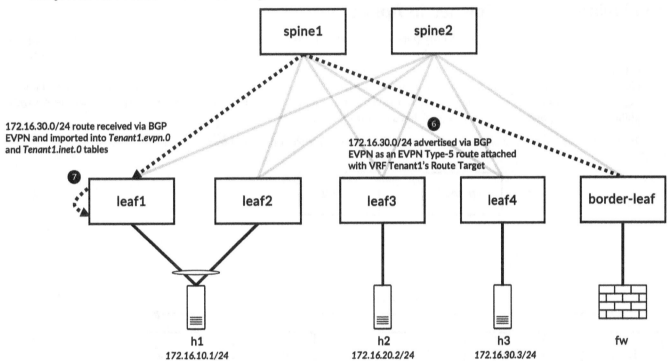

Figure 15-22 *IPv4 subnet 172.16.30.0/24 received by leaf1 via BGP EVPN and imported into Tenant1's EVPN and inet.0 tables*

With these changes pushed by Apstra, and the routes successfully exchanged in the control plane (and installed in the forwarding tables per VRF), inter-VRF communication occurs via the firewall. This is demonstrated in Example 15-19, with host h1 using the **ping** tool to test reachability to host h3, and the **traceroute** tool to confirm the exact path taken.

Example 15-19 *Host h1 to h3 reachability, tested using the* ping *and* traceroute *tools*

```
admin@h1> ping 172.16.30.3
PING 172.16.30.3 (172.16.30.3): 56 data bytes
64 bytes from 172.16.30.3: icmp_seq=0 ttl=59 time=7.582 ms
64 bytes from 172.16.30.3: icmp_seq=1 ttl=59 time=7.415 ms
64 bytes from 172.16.30.3: icmp_seq=2 ttl=59 time=7.376 ms
```

```
64 bytes from 172.16.30.3: icmp_seq=3 ttl=59 time=7.074 ms
^C
--- 172.16.30.3 ping statistics ---
4 packets transmitted, 4 packets received, 0% packet loss
round-trip min/avg/max/stddev = 7.074/7.362/7.582/0.183 ms

admin@h1> traceroute 172.16.30.3
traceroute to 172.16.30.3 (172.16.30.3), 30 hops max, 52 byte packets
 1  172.16.10.254  2.008 ms  1.201 ms  1.362 ms
 2  192.0.2.11  3.010 ms  2.557 ms  4.303 ms
 3  198.51.100.23  3.584 ms  3.702 ms  3.432 ms
 4  198.51.100.20  3.990 ms  4.190 ms  4.335 ms
 5  172.16.30.254  5.969 ms  5.653 ms  7.434 ms
 6  172.16.30.3  6.014 ms  7.560 ms  4.982 ms
```

Deploying Security Policies in Apstra

A data center is only as good as its security policies, ensuring conformance to the organization's security requirements. Apstra provides a single source of policy control that enables organizations to implement consistent security policies, across different operating systems and vendors, for the Apstra-deployed data centers. With Apstra's inherent multivendor capability, these security policies are automatically translated into vendor-specific rules. This section serves as a simple introduction to building security policies to control communication between hosts in a data center fabric deployed by Apstra. It describes Apstra's ability to resolve policy conflicts using predefined operator choices.

To demonstrate the creation and use of security policies, the reference topology shown in Figure 15-23 is used.

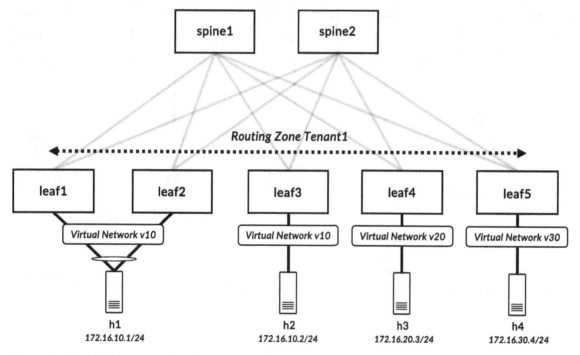

Figure 15-23 *Reference topology for security policies in Apstra*

This is an edge-routed bridging fabric, deployed as an Apstra Blueprint. It has a single Routing Zone called Tenant1, with the following Virtual Networks:

- VN v10, with a VLAN ID of 10, VNI of 10010, an IPv4 subnet of 172.16.10.0/24, and a default gateway of 172.16.10.1. Hosts h1 and h2 belong to this VN.

- VN v20, with a VLAN ID of 20, VNI of 10020, an IPv4 subnet of 172.16.20.0/24, and a default gateway of 172.16.20.1. Host h3 belongs to this VN.

- VN v30, with a VLAN ID of 30, VNI of 10030, an IPv4 subnet of 172.16.30.0/24, and a default gateway of 172.16.30.1. Host h4 belongs to this VN.

To create a security policy in Apstra, navigate to the Policies tab under the Staged panel, which by default displays the Security Policies subtab, as shown in Figure 15-24. Click the Create Security Policy button.

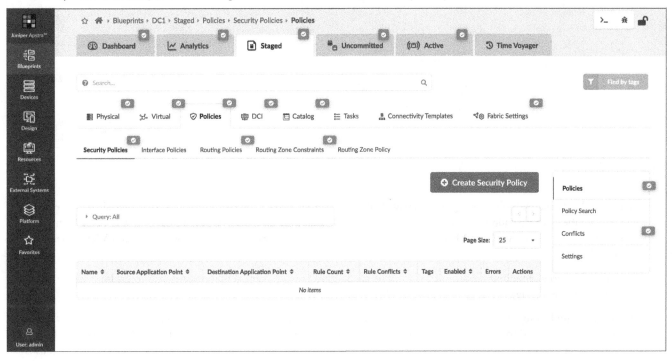

Figure 15-24 *Security Policies subtab in Apstra*

As shown in Figure 15-25, Apstra security policies are bound to source and destination application points, which can be different constructs in Apstra, such as the following:

- Internal/external endpoints

- Internal/external endpoint groups

- Virtual Networks

- Routing Zones

NOTE When building a security policy in Apstra, it is important to remember that the policy applies in the direction of the source application point to the destination application point, and it is not inherently bidirectional.

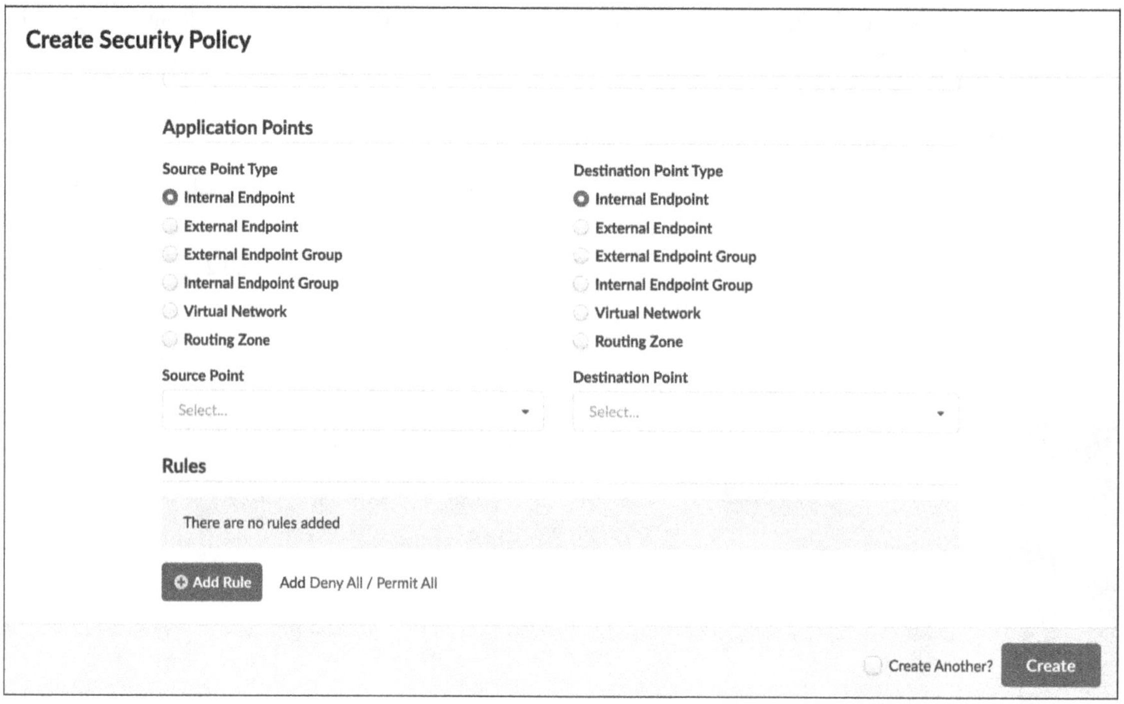

Create Security Policy

Application Points

Source Point Type	Destination Point Type
⦿ Internal Endpoint	⦿ Internal Endpoint
External Endpoint	External Endpoint
External Endpoint Group	External Endpoint Group
Internal Endpoint Group	Internal Endpoint Group
Virtual Network	Virtual Network
Routing Zone	Routing Zone

Source Point

Select... ▾

Destination Point

Select... ▾

Rules

There are no rules added

⊕ Add Rule   Add Deny All / Permit All

◯ Create Another?   **Create**

Figure 15-25 *Security policy creation in Apstra*

Internal and external endpoints are operator-created IPv4/IPv6 subnets, catering to endpoints within the fabric and endpoints outside the fabric. These endpoints typically are used when an organization needs more granular policy control than can be offered by Virtual Networks and Routing Zones, which cover a much broader scope, subnet-wide and VRF-wide, respectively.

Internal and external endpoint groups offer a form of group-based policy control that enables you to group together two or more endpoints in a group and apply a security policy to the entire group.

Each of these application points offers different levels of abstraction and granularity. For example, consider a Virtual Network that is mapped to a /24 IPv4 subnet mask—you can create two internal endpoints of /25 subnet masks each, or four internal endpoints of /26 subnet masks each, and so on, all the way up to 256 internal endpoints of /32 subnet masks each. In the same way, a Virtual Network encompasses the entire IPv4/IPv6 subnet it is configured for, while a Routing Zone encompasses all Virtual Networks mapped to it and, inherently, all IPv4/IPv6 subnets assigned to these Virtual Networks, respectively.

In addition to providing a single source of policy control, Apstra also offers the following within the overall policy infrastructure:

- **Policy search:** This allows you to search through a combination of source and destination application points and determine if it matches any existing security policy in Apstra (and which policy, if any).

- **Conflict resolution:** With large-scale policies, it is common to have conflicts between policies. These conflicts are hard to track manually, and even harder to remediate. Apstra provides automated conflict resolution, with predefined operator parameters that determine how a conflict should be resolved.

To create an internal endpoint, navigate to the Virtual tab under the Staged panel, select the Endpoints subtab, and click the Create Internal Endpoint. As shown in Figure 15-26, you need to give the internal endpoint a name, choose the Virtual Network it belongs to from the drop-down list, and provide an IPv4/IPv6 address for it.

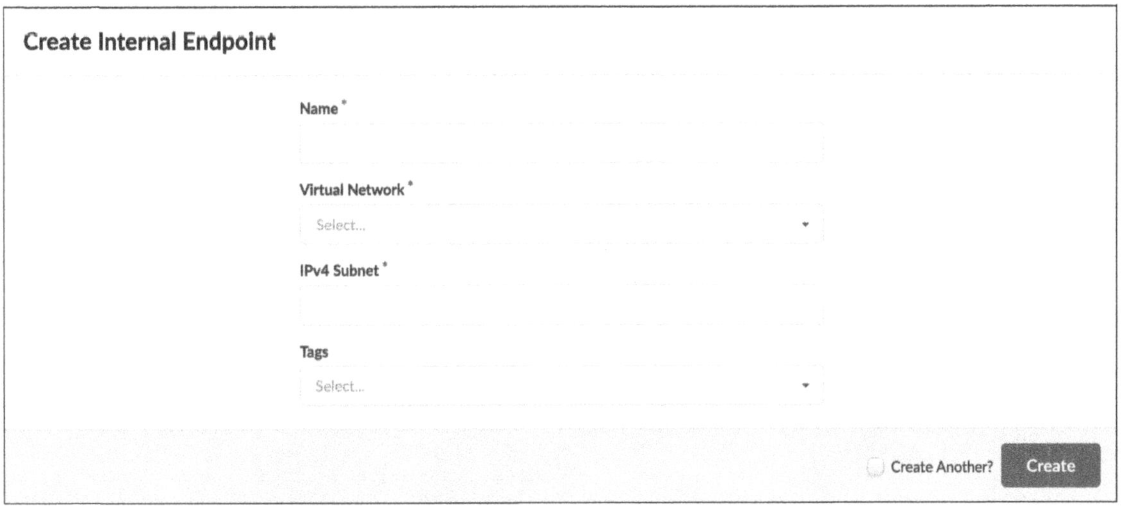

Create Internal Endpoint

Name *

Virtual Network *

Select... ▾

IPv4 Subnet *

Tags

Select... ▾

Create Another?   **Create**

Figure 15-26   *Input requirements to create an internal endpoint in Apstra*

In the case of the reference topology shown in Figure 15-23, all four hosts in the fabric are created as internal endpoints, with a /32 subnet mask for each, as shown in Figure 15-27.

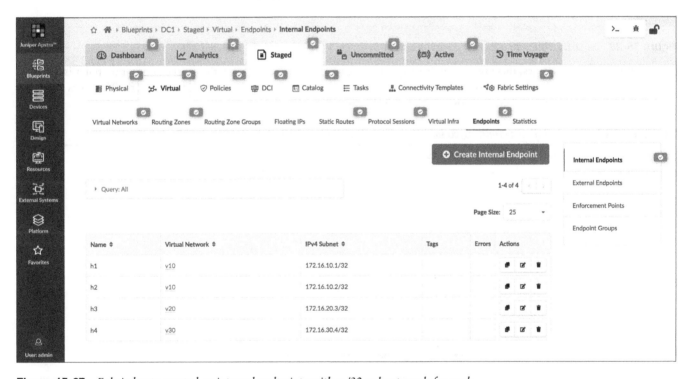

Figure 15-27   *Fabric hosts created as internal endpoints with a /32 subnet mask for each*

Let's assume that based on the organization's security requirements, hosts in Virtual Network v10 can talk to hosts in Virtual Network v20 only and not to any other Virtual Network in the Routing Zone. Two security policies are created for this:

- The first policy uses a source application point of Virtual Network v10 and a destination application point of Virtual Network v20 and permits IP communication between them.

- The second policy uses a source application point of Virtual Network v10 and a destination application point of the Routing Zone Tenant1 and denies all IP communication.

The first policy is shown in Figure 15-28.

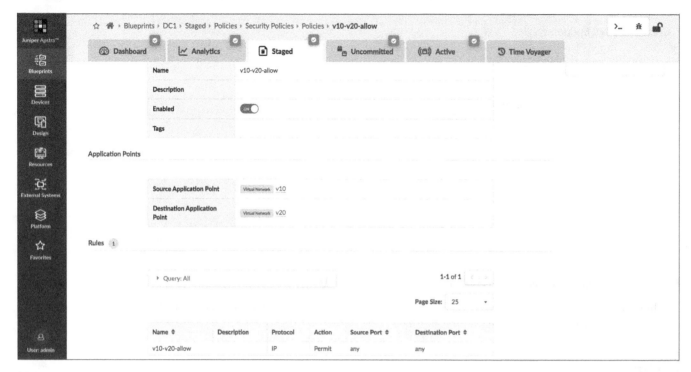

Figure 15-28 *Security policy to allow IP communication between Virtual Networks v10 and v20*

For Juniper QFX switches, these security policies are deployed as firewall filters. Since the source application point is Virtual Network v10, the filter gets applied inbound on the IRB interface for the corresponding Virtual Network. This firewall filter configuration, pushed by Apstra, is shown in Example 15-20.

Example 15-20 *Firewall filter permitting communication between Virtual Networks v10 and v20*

```
root@1xsh-48x10-8x40-001-leaf1# show interfaces irb.10
family inet {
    mtu 9000;
    filter {
        input ACL_VLAN_10_IN;
    }
    address 172.16.10.254/24;
}
mac 00:1c:73:00:00:01;
no-dhcp-flood;


root@1xsh-48x10-8x40-001-leaf1# show firewall family inet filter ACL_VLAN_10_IN
/* Policy: 'v10-policy' */
term ACL_VLAN_10_IN-5 {
    from {
        source-address {
            172.16.10.0/24;
        }
        destination-address {
            172.16.20.0/24;
        }
    }
```

```
        then accept;
    }
/* Trailing default action rule */
term ACL_VLAN_10_IN-10 {
    from {
        source-address {
            172.16.10.0/24;
        }
        destination-address {
            0.0.0.0/0;
        }
    }
    then accept;
}
```

The filter itself uses the IPv4 subnet of Virtual Network v10 as the source and the IPv4 subnet of Virtual Network v20 in a filter term and accepts it. The second policy can now be created as shown in Figure 15-29.

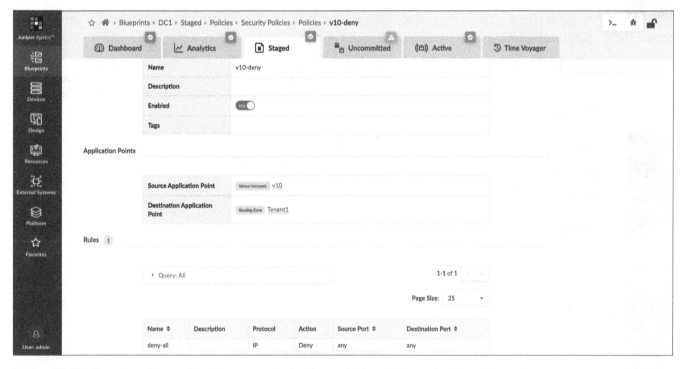

Figure 15-29 *Security policy to deny IP communication between Virtual Network v10 and Tenant1*

Since the destination application point in the second policy is a Routing Zone, Apstra determines all Virtual Networks (and their subnets) mapped to this Routing Zone and uses them as destination addresses in the firewall filter to deny traffic. In this case, the two subnets that are not the same as the source are 172.16.20.0/24 and 172.16.30.0/24. However, this now creates a policy conflict: the first policy permits IP communication from IPv4 subnet 172.16.10.0/24 to 172.16.20.0/24, while the second policy denies IP communication in the same direction.

By default, Apstra resolves conflicts by placing the more specific rule higher in the order, but you can change that setting, as shown in Figure 15-30, which also shows the option to change the default action.

Figure 15-30   *Configurable settings for policy conflict resolution in Apstra*

In this case, since the Virtual Network to Virtual Network policy is more specific than the Virtual Network to a Routing Zone policy, traffic from IPv4 subnet 172.16.10.0/24 to 172.16.20.0/24 is permitted, while traffic to 172.16.30.0/24 is denied. This conflict resolution is shown under the Security Policies tab, with Apstra marking that the conflict was resolved, as shown in Figure 15-31.

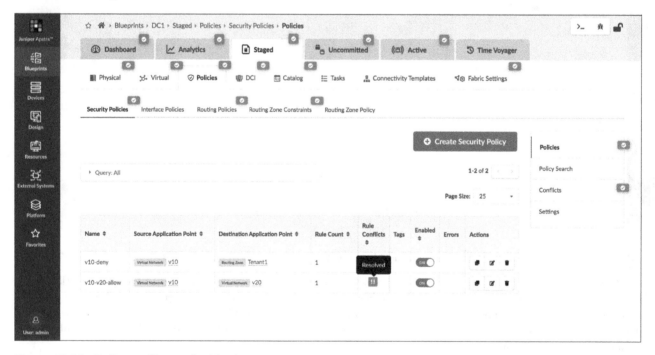

Figure 15-31   *Policy conflict resolved by Apstra*

Example 15-21 shows the configuration on leaf1, with both policies in play and Apstra's conflict resolution. The more specific policy is configured as a term named *ACL_VLAN_10_IN-5* in the firewall filter, which is higher in the order, allowing traffic from IPv4 subnet 172.16.10.0/24 to 172.16.20.0/24 for IP communication.

The term following that, *ACL_VLAN_10_IN-10*, denies IP communication from IPv4 subnet 172.16.10.0/24 to the only other IPv4 subnet in the Routing Zone Tenant1, 172.16.30.0/24.

Example 15-21 *Firewall filter on leaf1 after Apstra's conflict resolution*

```
root@1xsh-48x10-8x40-001-leaf1# show firewall family inet filter ACL_VLAN_10_IN
/* Policy: 'v10-policy' */
term ACL_VLAN_10_IN-5 {
    from {
        source-address {
            172.16.10.0/24;
        }
        destination-address {
            172.16.20.0/24;
        }
    }
    then accept;
}
/* Policy: 'v10-deny' */
term ACL_VLAN_10_IN-10 {
    from {
        source-address {
            172.16.10.0/24;
        }
        destination-address {
            172.16.30.0/24;
        }
    }
    then {
        discard;
    }
}
/* Trailing default action rule */
term ACL_VLAN_10_IN-15 {
    from {
        source-address {
            172.16.10.0/24;
        }
        destination-address {
            0.0.0.0/0;
        }
    }
    then accept;
}
```

At this point, host h1 can communicate with h2 and h3, but cannot communicate with h4, as shown in Example 15-22.

Example 15-22 *Host h1's reachability to hosts h2, h3, and h4 in the fabric*

```
root@h1> ping 172.16.10.2
PING 172.16.10.2 (172.16.10.2): 56 data bytes
64 bytes from 172.16.10.2: icmp_seq=0 ttl=64 time=0.970 ms
64 bytes from 172.16.10.2: icmp_seq=1 ttl=64 time=0.871 ms
64 bytes from 172.16.10.2: icmp_seq=2 ttl=64 time=0.869 ms
```

```
64 bytes from 172.16.10.2: icmp_seq=3 ttl=64 time=0.916 ms
^C
--- 172.16.10.2 ping statistics ---
4 packets transmitted, 4 packets received, 0% packet loss
round-trip min/avg/max/stddev = 0.869/0.906/0.970/0.041 ms

root@h1> ping 172.16.20.3
PING 172.16.20.3 (172.16.20.3): 56 data bytes
64 bytes from 172.16.20.3: icmp_seq=0 ttl=62 time=0.940 ms
64 bytes from 172.16.20.3: icmp_seq=1 ttl=62 time=0.924 ms
64 bytes from 172.16.20.3: icmp_seq=2 ttl=62 time=0.866 ms
64 bytes from 172.16.20.3: icmp_seq=3 ttl=62 time=0.835 ms
^C
--- 172.16.20.3 ping statistics ---
4 packets transmitted, 4 packets received, 0% packet loss
round-trip min/avg/max/stddev = 0.835/0.891/0.940/0.043 ms

root@h1> ping 172.16.30.4
PING 172.16.30.4 (172.16.30.4): 56 data bytes
^C
--- 172.16.30.4 ping statistics ---
5 packets transmitted, 0 packets received, 100% packet loss
```

To further demonstrate how Apstra manages conflict resolution, let's assume another organizational security requirement deems it necessary to block all traffic from Virtual Network v10 to host h3, which has an IPv4 address of 172.16.20.3/24. For this, a new security policy is created with a source application point of Virtual Network v10 and a destination application point of internal endpoint, h3, shown in Figure 15-32.

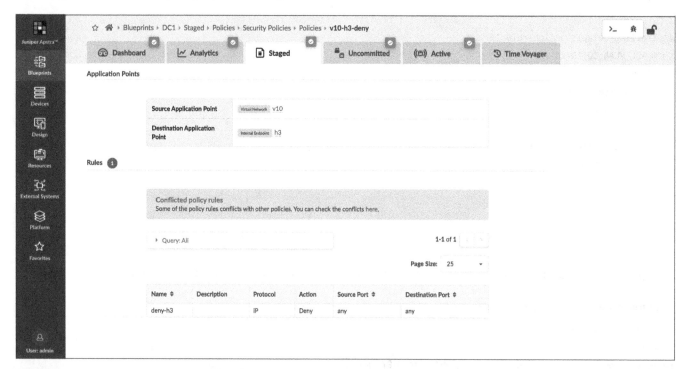

Figure 15-32 *Security policy denying IP communication between Virtual Network v10 and internal endpoint h3*

This reports another conflict in Apstra, since internal endpoint h3 exists in Apstra with an IPv4 address of 172.16.20.3/32, and a previous policy allowed IP communication from Virtual Network v10, mapped to IPv4 subnet 172.16.10.0/24 to Virtual Network v20, mapped to 172.16.20.0/24. This conflict is resolved by placing the more specific policy higher in the order, which, in this case, is the policy to deny IP communication from Virtual Network v10 to internal endpoint h3.

With this new policy configured, and all conflicts resolved, Example 15-23 demonstrates the firewall filter pushed to leaf1.

Example 15-23   *Firewall filter pushed to leaf1 with new security policy*

```
root@1xsh-48x10-8x40-001-leaf1# show firewall family inet filter ACL_VLAN_10_IN
/* Policy: 'v10-h3-deny' */
term ACL_VLAN_10_IN-5 {
    from {
        source-address {
            172.16.10.0/24;
        }
        destination-address {
            172.16.20.3/32;
        }
    }
    then {
        discard;
    }
}
/* Policy: 'v10-policy' */
term ACL_VLAN_10_IN-10 {
    from {
        source-address {
            172.16.10.0/24;
        }
        destination-address {
            172.16.20.0/24;
        }
    }
    then accept;
}
/* Policy: 'v10-deny' */
term ACL_VLAN_10_IN-15 {
    from {
        source-address {
            172.16.10.0/24;
        }
        destination-address {
            172.16.30.0/24;
        }
    }
    then {
        discard;
    }
}
```

```
/* Trailing default action rule */
term ACL_VLAN_10_IN-20 {
    from {
        source-address {
            172.16.10.0/24;
        }
        destination-address {
            0.0.0.0/0;
        }
    }
    then accept;
}
```

You can view all conflicts, and their resolutions, in Apstra by navigating to the Security Policies subtab and clicking Conflicts on the right side of the UI, as shown in Figure 15-33, which displays the existing conflicts and how the conflicting rules were ordered as part of automated resolution.

Figure 15-33   *All conflicts and their resolutions listed in Apstra UI*

Host h1 can only ping h2 now, and no other host in the fabric, as shown in Example 15-24.

Example 15-24   *Host h1 reachability to other hosts in the fabric post new security policy*

```
root@h1> ping 172.16.10.2
PING 172.16.10.2 (172.16.10.2): 56 data bytes
64 bytes from 172.16.10.2: icmp_seq=0 ttl=64 time=0.904 ms
64 bytes from 172.16.10.2: icmp_seq=1 ttl=64 time=0.829 ms
64 bytes from 172.16.10.2: icmp_seq=2 ttl=64 time=35.424 ms
64 bytes from 172.16.10.2: icmp_seq=3 ttl=64 time=0.892 ms
^C
--- 172.16.10.2 ping statistics ---
4 packets transmitted, 4 packets received, 0% packet loss
```

```
round trip min/avg/max/stddev = 0.829/9.512/35.424/14.960 ms


root@h1> ping 172.16.20.3
PING 172.16.20.3 (172.16.20.3): 56 data bytes
^C
--- 172.16.20.3 ping statistics ---
5 packets transmitted, 0 packets received, 100% packet loss


root@h1> ping 172.16.30.4
PING 172.16.30.4 (172.16.30.4): 56 data bytes
^C
--- 172.16.30.4 ping statistics ---
5 packets transmitted, 0 packets received, 100% packet loss
```

Summary

This final chapter of the book demonstrated how to deploy a large-scale data center network using a 5-stage Clos fabric architecture with vJunos-switch and Containerlab, orchestrated and managed by Apstra. It also demonstrated different traffic flows in such designs. In addition, it presented Apstra's deployment options for inter-VRF routing.

Finally, to close, you learned about Apstra's built-in policy infrastructure that offers centralized policy control with varying levels of granularity and abstraction, as needed. This infrastructure comes with features such as conflict resolution and policy search, enabling you to model and validate your intent. This chapter demonstrated how such security policies are built in Apstra and translated into vendor-specific configuration, thus providing a completely vendor-agnostic single source of policy control.

Acronym Legend

A

AE interfaces   Aggregated Ethernet interfaces
API   application programming interface
ARP   Address Resolution Protocol
ASN   autonomous system number

B

BFD   Bidirectional Forwarding Detection
BGP   Border Gateway Protocol
BUM   broadcast, unknown unicast, and multicast

C

CE   customer edge
CI/CD   continuous integration and continuous delivery/deployment
CLI   command line interface
CRB   centrally routed bridging

D

DCD   Device Control Daemon
DDS   Distributed Data Store
DHCP   Dynamic Host Configuration Protocol
DNS   Domain Name System

E

ECMP   equal cost multipath
ERB   edge-routed bridging

ES   Ethernet Segment
ESI   Ethernet Segment Identifier
EVI   EVPN Instance
EVPN   Ethernet VPN (virtual private network)

F

FPC   Flexible PIC Concentrator

G

GARP   Gratuitous ARP
GENEVE   Generic Network Virtualization Encapsulation
GRE   Generic Routing Encapsulation

H

HSRP   Hot Standby Router Protocol
HTTP   Hypertext Transfer Protocol
HTTPS   Hypertext Transfer Protocol Secure

I

IANA   Internet Assigned Numbers Authority
IBN   intent-based networking
IBNS   intent-based networking system
ICMP   Internet Control Message Protocol
IETF   Internet Engineering Task Force
IMET   Inclusive Multicast Ethernet Tag
IPC   inter-process communication
IPv4   Internet Protocol version 4
IPv6   Internet Protocol version 6

IRB   integrated routing and bridging
IS-IS   Intermediate System-to-Intermediate System

J

JSON   JavaScript Object Notation

K

KVM   Kernel-based Virtual Machine

L

L2ALD   Layer 2 Address Learning Daemon
L2VNI   Layer 2 VNI (VXLAN Network Identifier)
L3VNI   Layer 3 VNI (VXLAN Network Identifier)
L3VPN   Layer 3 VPN (virtual private network)
LACP   Link Aggregation Control Protocol
LAG   link aggregation group
LLDP   Link Layer Discovery Protocol
LSP   labeled-switched path

M

MAC   Media Access Control
MGD   Management Daemon
MLAG or MC-LAG   Multi-chassis Link Aggregation Group
MPLS   Multiprotocol Label Switching
MSTP   Multiple Spanning Tree Protocol
MTU   maximum transmission unit

N

NETCONF   Network Configuration Protocol
NLRI   Network Layer Reachability Information
NVGRE   Network Virtualization using Generic Routing Encapsulation
NVO   Network Virtualization Overlay

O

OSPF   Open Shortest Path First

P

PE   provider edge
PFE   Packet Forwarding Engine
PIC   Physical Interface Card
PIM   Protocol Independent Multicast

R

RE   Routing Engine
RIB   routing information base
RP   rendezvous point
RPD   Routing Protocol Daemon
RPF   reverse path forwarding
RSTP   Rapid Spanning Tree Protocol

S

SSH   Secure Shell or Secure Socket Shell
STP   Spanning Tree Protocol
SVI   Switch Virtual Interface

T

TCP   Transmission Control Protocol
TFTP   Trivial File Transfer Protocol
ToR   top of rack
TRILL   Transparent Interconnection of Lots of Links
TTL   Time to Live

U

UDP   User Datagram Protocol
UI   user interface

V

VLAN   virtual LAN (local area network)
VM   virtual machine
VNI   VXLAN Network Identifier
vPC   Virtual Port Channel
VPC   virtual private cloud
VPLS   Virtual Private LAN Service

VPWS   Virtual Private Wire Service
VRF   Virtual Routing and Forwarding
VRRP   Virtual Router Redundancy Protocol
VSS   Virtual Switching System
VSTP   Virtual Spanning Tree Protocol
VTEP   VXLAN Tunnel Endpoint
VXLAN   Virtual Extensible LAN (local area network)

W

WAN   wide area network

X

XML   Extensible Markup Language

Z

ZTP   Zero Touch Provisioning

Quick Reference Guide

Asymmetric IRB in EVPN VXLAN

Asymmetric IRB Design Using VLAN-Based MAC-VRFs

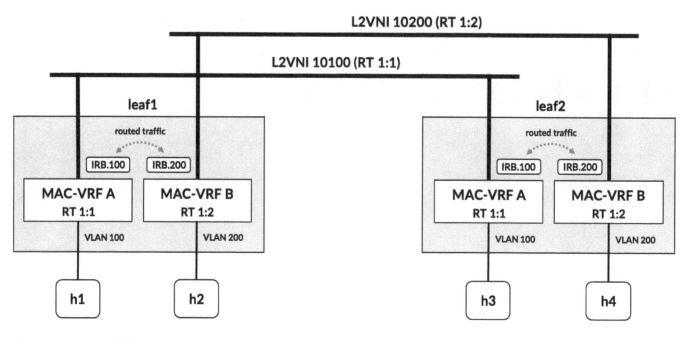

Asymmetric IRB Packet Walk

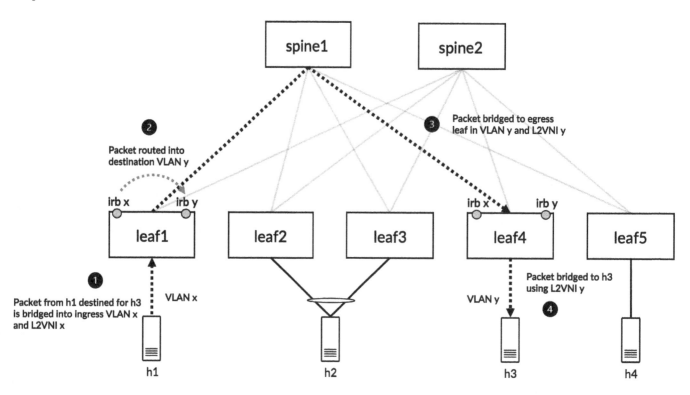

Symmetric IRB in EVPN VXLAN

Symmetric IRB Design Using VLAN-Based MAC-VRFs

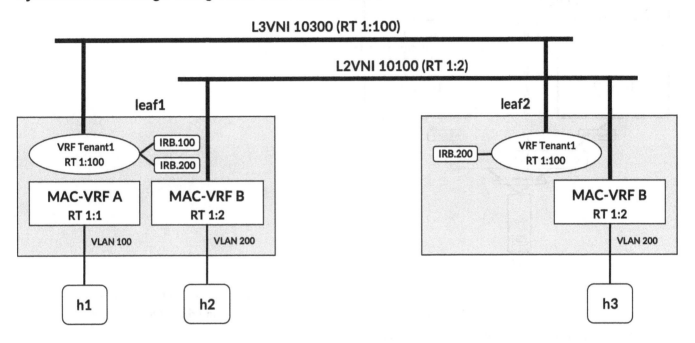

Symmetric IRB Packet Walk

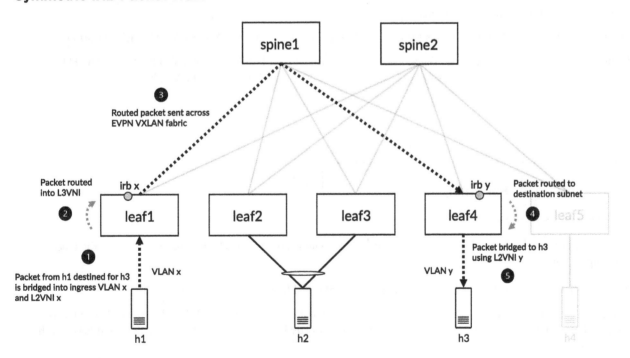

EVPN Multihoming (ESI LAG)

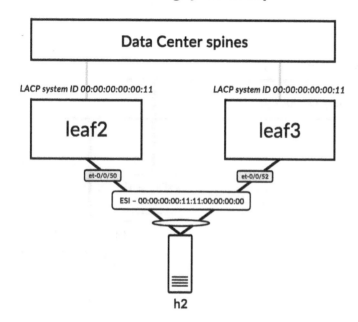

- EVPN multihoming is standards-based (RFC 7432). It enables a CE to connect to multiple PEs (VTEPs, within the context of a data center). This is configured as an Ethernet Segment, identified by an Ethernet Segment Identifier (ESI).

- It is not limited to only two PEs, unlike MC-LAG.

- No requirement of links b/w PEs for ESI LAG (such as ICCP and ICL for MC-LAG).

- Relies on EVPN Type-1 and Type-4 routes.

- The ESI is added to EVPN Type-2 routes (for MAC addresses learned over ESI LAG) for MAC synchronization.

- Remote VTEPs install addresses from Type-2 routes against an ESI next-hop instead of a VTEP address. The ESI recursively resolves to VTEP addresses using Type-1 and Type-4 routes advertised by the VTEPs.

ESI ENCODING

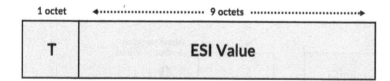

To represent an Ethernet Segment, the ESI is encoded as a 10-byte non-zero integer. The first octet determines the type, with the following six types:

- A Type of 0x00 indicates that the ESI value is manually configured by the operator.

- A Type of 0x01 indicates that the ESI value is auto-generated and derived from the CE LACP system MAC address (high-order 6 octets) and port key (next 2 octets) with the last octet being set to 0x00 when LACP is used between the PE and the CE.

- A Type of 0x02 indicates that the ESI value is auto-generated by listening to STP BPDUs on the Ethernet Segment and using the root bridge MAC address to encode the high-order 6 octets and the root priority to encode the next 2 octets, with the last octet being set to 0x00.

- **A Type of** 0x03 indicates that the ESI value is auto-generated or manually configured and uses the MAC address of the system to encode the high-order 6 octets with a local discriminator being used for the remaining 3 octets.

- **A Type of** 0x04 indicates that the ESI value is auto-generated and uses the router-ID of the system to encode the high-order 4 octets, with a local discriminator being used for the next 4 octets. The last octet is set to 0x00.

- **A Type of** 0x05 indicates that the ESI value is auto-generated and uses the Autonomous System (AS) of the system for the high-order 4 octets. If a 2-octet AS is used, then the high-order 2 octets are set to 0x0000. A local discriminator is used for the next 4 octets, with the last octet being set to 0x00.

DHCP in EVPN VXLAN Fabrics

DHCP Refresher

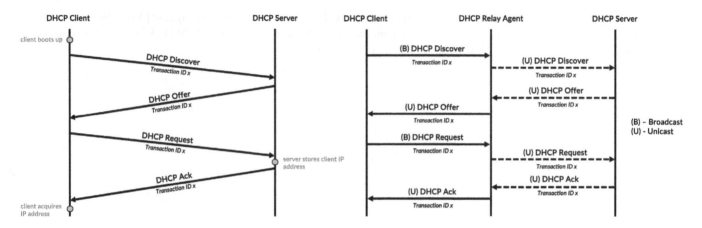

The Problem

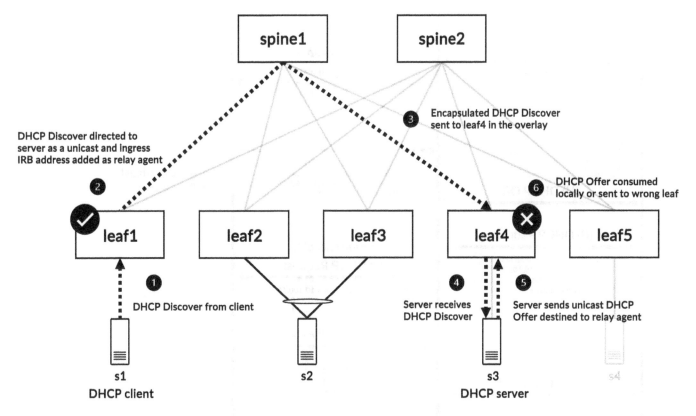

With an ERB design in EVPN VXLAN fabrics, a DHCP broadcast is relayed as a unicast packet by using the Ingress IRB interface as the relay IP address (and the source IP address in the IP header).

Because the IRB address is the same across all leafs in an ERB fabric, the response from the DHCP server can get lost, breaking the DHCP process.

The Solution

Source DHCP relay messages using a unique loopback and add the following option 82 suboptions: link selection and server override.

The link selection suboption provides a subnet from which an IP address can be provided by the server, while the server override suboption enables a client to send renewal messages to the relay agent instead of the DHCP server directly.

With the relay address being set to a leaf's unique loopback, the DHCP response is directed to the correct leaf.

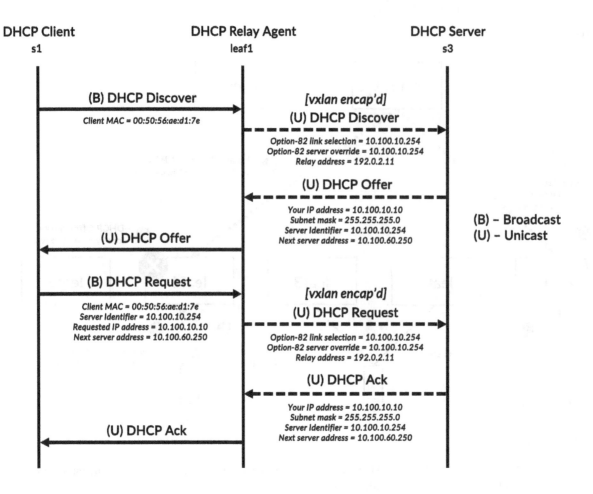

Data Center Interconnect

Over-the-Top DCI Design

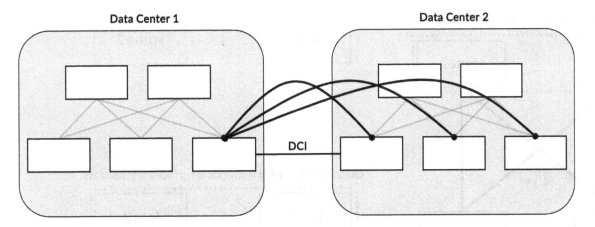

- No demarcation between local DC and DCI

- Provides an "over-the-top" mechanism of connecting two or more data centers with a full mesh of VXLAN tunnels

- Operationally simpler to implement at the cost of high VXLAN tunnel and next-hop state

Integrated Interconnect DCI Design (RFC 9014)

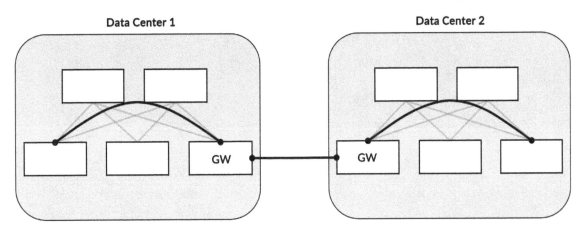

- Clear demarcation between the local DC and the DCI with integrated functionality on one device, facilitating multiple handoff options including IP and MPLS

- Each GW re-originates routes into DCI by using an interconnect ESI (I-ESI) for load-balancing, interconnect RD, and interconnect RT

- The interconnect RT between connected DCs must match while the I-ESI for each DC must be unique

- Operationally complex but reduces VXLAN state across DCs

CRB vs. ERB in the Data Center

Centrally Routed Bridging

Centralized routing with IRB interfaces on the spines

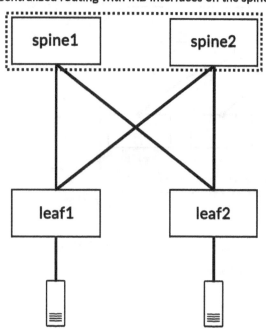

Edge-Routed Bridging

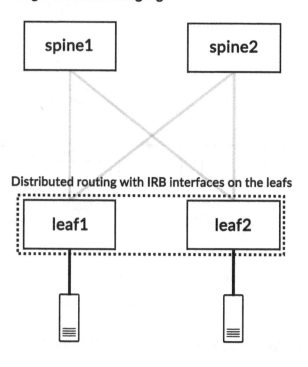

Distributed routing with IRB interfaces on the leafs

Centrally Routed Bridging	Edge-Routed Bridging
VXLAN routing centralized on the spines	VXLAN routing distributed to the leafs
IRB interfaces configured with a virtual IP address and virtual MAC address, which match on all gateways	IRB interfaces configured on all leafs with the same IP address and MAC address
Uses a virtual ESI, in Junos implementation, to achieve overlay load-balancing for gateway MAC address by attaching the ESI to EVPN Type-2 routes advertised for the gateway address	Uses a distributed gateway model enabling all leafs to be gateways for directly attached hosts
Inefficient routing due to a tromboning traffic pattern	More efficient in traffic forwarding as each leaf can route locally

EVPN Route Types 1–5

EVPN Type-1 Route

- Ethernet Auto-discovery (EAD) route, generated per Ethernet Segment (ES) and per EVPN Instance (EVI).

- Used for aliasing, mass withdrawal (for fast convergence), and split-horizon using local bias.

- EAD per EVI route is used to build a list of all VTEPs attached to a specific Ethernet Segment, while EAD per ES is used to filter the list for VTEPs with only all-active Ethernet Segments for load balancing.

- EAD per ES route is also used for mass withdrawal. When a VTEP, say V_1, loses its Ethernet Segment, it can withdraw EAD per ES route, automatically indicating to remote VTEPs to purge V_1 from its list of available VTEPs to load-balance traffic for that Ethernet Segment.

EVPN Type-2 Route

- A MAC/IP route that is used to advertise a MAC address via BGP EVPN, along with an optional IP address.

- Remote VTEPs use this to build an association between the MAC address and the advertising VTEP and install an entry in the MAC address table for forwarding.

- This route enables a VTEP to build a corresponding entry in its ARP cache as well when advertised with an IP address, facilitating features such as ARP suppression and proxy ARP to reduce flooding of broadcast packets in the fabric.

EVPN Type-3 Route

- Inclusive Multicast Ethernet Tag (IMET) route, used to indicate interest in receiving multi-destination (BUM) traffic for a specific VNI.

- Remote VTEPs use this route to build a flood list of all VTEPs traffic can be ingress-replicated to, when flooding BUM traffic into the fabric.

- This route also facilitates remote VTEP discovery.

EVPN Type-4 Route

- Ethernet Segment route used for designated forwarder election, per Ethernet Segment, among all VTEPs attached to the segment.

- A designated forwarder for an Ethernet Segment is allowed to forward multi-destination traffic (BUM) received from the fabric into the Ethernet Segment.

EVPN Type-5 Route

- An IP prefix route used to decouple the MAC address from an IP address, advertising only an IP address via BGP EVPN.

- Use cases include data center interconnects, where each data center has unique subnets, thus exchanging only IP prefix information between data centers with Type-5 routes.

- Also used in routed overlay designs, commonly deployed with cloud-native server architectures where there is no requirement for Layer 2 extension between VTEPs.

Index

C

F

G

H

O

P

Q-R

S

T